BUILT IN BOSTON

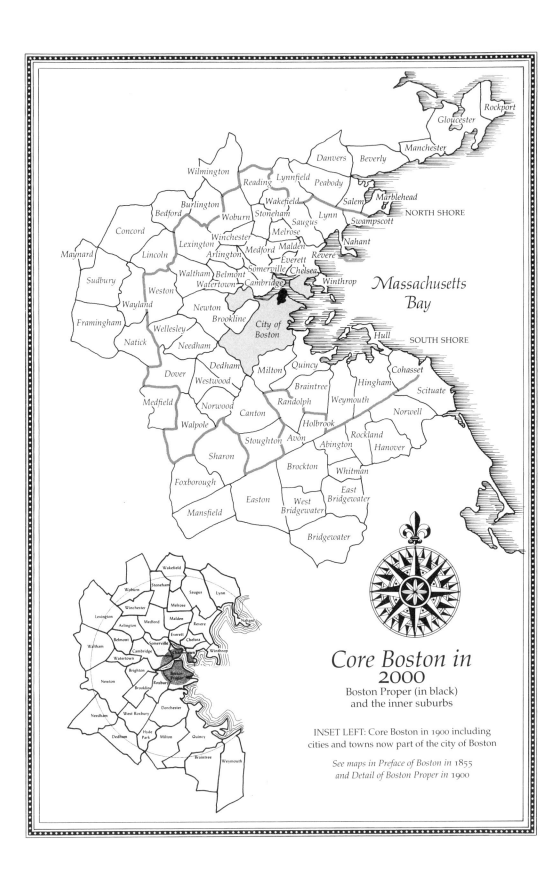

NORTH SHORE

Massachusetts Bay

SOUTH SHORE

Core Boston in
2000
Boston Proper (in black)
and the inner suburbs

INSET LEFT: Core Boston in 1900 including
cities and towns now part of the city of Boston

*See maps in Preface of Boston in 1855
and Detail of Boston Proper in 1900*

DOUGLASS SHAND-TUCCI

Built in Boston

CITY AND SUBURB

1800–2000

Revised and Expanded Edition

FOREWORD BY WALTER MUIR WHITEHILL

UNIVERSITY OF MASSACHUSETTS PRESS
AMHERST

Copyright © 1978, 1988, 1999 by Douglass Shand-Tucci
All rights reserved
Printed in the United States of America
LC 88-14151
ISBN 1-55849-201-1

Library of Congress Cataloging-in-Publication Data

Shand-Tucci, Douglass
    Built in Boston: city and suburb, 1800-2000 /
Douglass Shand-Tucci ; foreword by Walter Muir
Whitehill. — Rev. and expanded. ed.
        p.   cm.
    Includes bibliographic references and index.
    ISBN 1-55849-201-1
    1. Architecture—Massachusetts—Boston. 2.
Architecture, Modern—19th century—
Massachusetts—Boston. 3. Architecture, Modern—
20th century—Massachusetts—Boston. 4. Boston
(Mass.)—Buildings, structures, etc. 5. Architecture—
Massachusetts—Boston Metropolitan Area. 6.
Architecture, Modern—19th century—
Massachusetts—Boston Metropolitan Area. 7.
Architecture, Modern—20th century—
Massachusetts—Boston Metropolitan Area.
I. Title.
NA735.B7S53   1999
720'.9744'61—DC21   99-16750
                                      CIP

British Library Cataloguing in Publication data are
available.

The quotation on pages 57 and 60 is from Bainbridge
Bunting, *Houses of Boston's Back Bay*, The Belknap
Press of Harvard University Press, © 1967 by the
President and Fellows of Harvard College. The
clerihew on page 183 is from *About Boston: Sight,
Sound, Flavor and Inflection* by David McCord, © 1948
reprinted by permission of Little, Brown and
Company. The drawing on page 244 by Frank Lloyd
Wright, © 1999 by the Frank Lloyd Wright
Foundation, Scottsboro, Arizona, reproduced by
permission.

MAP 1, the frontispiece, was prepared from one
entitled "The Four Bostons" which appeared in the
tercentenary history, *Fifty Years of Boston* (1930). The
inset map was prepared from one that appeared in
Sam Bass Warner Jr., *Streetcar Suburbs: The Process of
Growth in Boston* (Cambridge: Harvard University
Press, 1962).

To one only will I tell it.

Buildings are based on beliefs—that is the material
you need to know, to know how to express it. This is the
most important thing.

—Louis Kahn

Two alternatives present themselves to the
contemporary architect. One is complicity with the
processes of manufacturing and consuming culture,
the reduction of architecture to the realms of trends
and fashions in a pseudo-liberal accommodation of
popular or kitsch images. The other is the recognition
that architecture is most itself when it can demonstrate
its autonomy, its difference, even its *opposition* to other
systems of communication that surround it.

—Rodolfo Machado

CONTENTS

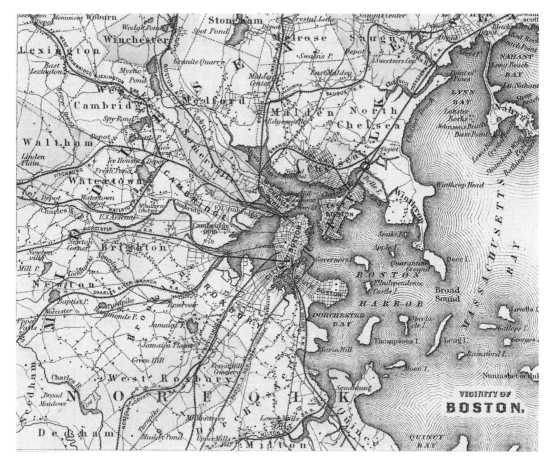

Boston in 1855. Many of today's inner suburbs were then Boston's outer suburbs — the cities of Roxbury and Cambridge, for example, and the towns of Dorchester and Brookline and West Roxbury — places in which wealthy Bostonians maintained country estates before streetcar lines led to the development of those cities and towns.

Preface to the
Revised and Expanded Edition, 2000

Good Design: 1) Fulfills its function. 2) Respects its
materials. 3) Is suited to its method of construction.
4) Combines these in Imaginative Expression.
> — derived from a sign on a curator's wall at
> New York's Museum of Modern Art, 1940.

Two men in a huddle, rather stiffly posed, inspecting a large roll of plans:
"Architectural historian Douglass Shand-Tucci and Daniel J. Coolidge of Shepley,
Bulfinch, Richardson and Abbott, Architects, directing the restoration of the
Research Library's art and architecture."

So the caption of this 1992 photograph reads. Actually, it was more like hoping against
hope we'd be able to outsmart the politicians one more time — library trustee Bill Bulger
always excepted — in what often seemed less a restoration of the Boston Public Library
than an ongoing battle with the philistines. By which I don't just mean politicians, either.
Donors, too, can pose problems. Dan and I used to joke ruefully all the time about the
Time-Warner Reading Room and the Fleet Bank Staircase and what was for sale (a lot) and
what was not (very little).

It was a battle that was lost in the end, as we knew it would be; though, of course, the
lavish library publication our picture adorned was in no danger of foreseeing such truths.
A much bigger truth it did insist on was how urgently Boston's greatest public building of
the nineteenth century required the restoration board president Kevin Moloney promised,
when he launched it in 1984, would be "a triumph of Boston's architectural history."

Thanks largely to Dan, it was that, and for me, far more. Following as it did my work on
the design of the western towers of the Cathedral of St. John the Divine in New York
under John Doran (whose own master, day in and day out, in the late 1920s and 1930s was
Ralph Adams Cram himself), the decade-long Boston Public Library restoration became
for me a formative life experience. And if I had to define what above all I took away from
it — Dan Coolidge having been very much a Modernist as well as a restoration architect
— it would be threefold. First, the sentiments of the MOMA curator's credo (reproduced
above exactly as reported in the *New York Times* by Patricia Leigh Brown, except that I
have substituted "construction" for "production"). Second, an insurance policy against
Post-Modernism. Only once, when my old friend William Buckingham designed a truly
decadent visitors center for Boston Common, each of the four sides of which showed a
different stylistic profile, did I succumb, though I blush today to admit it. Third, the

abiding ambition of this architectural historian to form a partnership with an architect also eager for Modernism (not Post-Modernism) to make its peace with History (not Historicism).

Blah, Blah, Blah and Shand-Tucci, Architecture and Architectural History? I'm afraid it's not very likely, though at least one other time I got a glimmer of how it might work, when I learned enough in the early 1990s from the (then aspiring) architect Fred Atherton on one field trip after another in aid of my study of the work of Ralph Adams Cram, which I dedicated to Fred, to keep the dream alive. (I recall how it went, so to speak, both ways with Fred, in one of whose first designs I effected what he called a "sea change," but who returned the favor more often than not. I remember, for example, his once explaining to me, not entirely to my pleasure at the time, that I had misjudged the quality of some stone detail because the problem was that the stone had been laid the wrong way for carving. I had never thought of that. Historians aren't taught such things!)

Now I do not wish to be misunderstood. I am decidedly not an architect manqué, despite my need of frequent doses of (corrective?) hands-on architectural practice. I am supremely happy to be a historian and critic. But architectural practice does greatly impact my scholarship. And I can only say that it is certainly true that I discern a deep internal resonance throughout the "many mansions" of architecture, a resonance I feel more than ever since becoming architectural critic of the *Boston Phoenix*, for which in 1999 I began to write a biweekly column. For example, if there is something to be gained by the architect (often also a teacher) and the architectural historian (often also a critic), each of the other, whether in my dreamed-of partnership or in the overall universe of discourse of architecture itself, it is something very much akin to what Jorge Silvetti brings to the fore in an essay of 1982, "Representation and Creativity in Architecture: The Pregnant Moment." It is worth quoting from at some length:

> Architects do not build buildings. Architects draw. . . . The task of the architect, as designer and conceiver of a building, ends when the drawing is finished (or by extension, the model, the final presentation . . . .). . . . Creativity in architecture occurs only at the moment of representation, that moment full of partialities, delirium, and concealments—that artistic moment. It is by the movements of the hand guided by the eyes that look into the vastness of the mind that architecture is produced. We imagine (the first representation occurring within the mind itself) and we draw (the second representation, a physical manifestation, which is extracted from the mind).
>
> Finally, the building appears: the world of illusion, of deceit and utopia contained in the representations of the mind and of the hand suddenly comes to an end. . . . Or is this indeed the case? . . . The only way [for the beholder] to decode the building, to understand it, is to represent—a representation that may or may not coincide with that of the architect, and that somehow puts everybody into the process of creation again.

Everybody: critics, the beholder generally, and, eventually, the architectural historian. It is, as it were, a continuum of creativity. And, for me, this is true as well of restoration.

Few people understand how creative restoration can be. Not in the way that having an idea and then developing and shaping it into intellectual and literary form on the proverbial blank yellow pad of paper is. Nor in the way an architect (who expresses ideas visually, not verbally) is creative in starting to cut and bend and shape into a model, of filling a sketchbook with developing forms, one after the other. That is primary creation — *de novo*, in the old phrase (to think out anew or afresh) — the way a composer works in creating out of nothing, really, an original piece of music.

The creativity of restoration is precisely not to think up something out of nothing, but

The program for Harvard's 1930 Bauhaus exhibition, the first in the world. The oppressive conservatism of so many Bostonians in the 1920s and 1930s obscures the fact that Modernism in America was born in Boston. Ada Louise Huxtable would call the Gropius House in Lincoln, built seven years after the exhibition, "the architectural shot heard 'round the world."

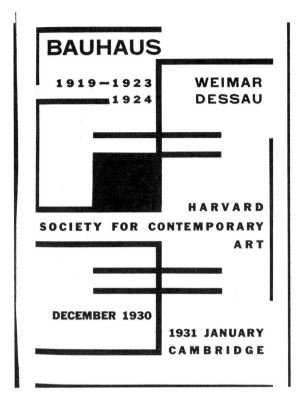

rather, to think it up through the mind of someone else — the (usually long-dead) primary creator — of a work already built. And it is the very limitations themselves that spark the creative impulse of the restorer, who is, as it were, more Yo-Yo Ma than Bach.

Leonard Bernstein, describing how he approached conducting *other* composers' work, caught the essence of the matter of an architect restoring the work of a master architect of past times:

> Perhaps the fact of being myself a composer . . . gives me the advantageous opportunity to identify more closely with the Mozarts, Beethovens, Mahlers and Stravinskys of this world, so that I can at certain points (usually of intense solitary study) feel that I have *become* whoever is my alter ego that day or week. At least I can occasionally reach one or the other on our private "Hot Line," and with luck be given the solution to a problematic passage.

In Chapter 13, in my discussion of how Coolidge and I dealt with the lack of the murals McKim had always wanted in Bates Hall at the library, I explore an architectural example of such a "difficult passage," as well as how much it is a part of the essence, the challenge, of the thing to (at one and the same time) keep that "hot line" open but never grow over-dependent on it. To do otherwise is to lose one's footing in one's own time, for which and for future time — not for time past (however glorious) and people (including Charles McKim) long dead —any architectural project, restoration or otherwise, is mounted in the first place.

All this is as true of architectural history written as of architectural design drawn, even when, as is the case with *Built in Boston*, the reviser (the restorer — to pertinence!) and the original creator (author, shaper, designer) are one and the same. This book has been

Something of the majesty of Edwin Lutyens's imperial New Delhi attaches to the great stair that ascends along the south flank of Boston City Hall. Kallmann and McKinnell's landmark rivals Aalto's and Saarinen's work at M.I.T,, Gropius's own house, Le Corbusier's Carpenter Center, and Kahn's Exeter Library as the masterworks of the Modern Movement in Boston's orbit.

enlarged fully a third in this edition; in many ways it is a new work. On the other hand, only the original introduction to the first edition, so full of names and events long past much caring about now, has been dropped. Otherwise, all ten of the original chapters remain entirely unchanged here — even at the risk of perpetuating several glaring misjudgments.

Youthful misjudgments, I suppose I can call them. And it is certainly true that I believe I've both sharpened and broadened my aesthetic in middle age: among architects I like now the work of Eero Saarinen, Louis Kahn, I. M. Pei, Rafael Moneo, and Tadao Ando, more than all but a very few things by Lutyens or Cram. I prefer early music today to Mahler or the Beatles, baseball to hockey, and modern-language High Mass at the free-standing altar under Cram's severe baldachino at the Cowley Fathers to the antiquarian, overdone, flower-bedecked ceremonial of the Church of the Advent. Indeed, I hardly know a more glorious architectural experience than the weekly Taizé liturgy at Trinity Church, Copley Square, its chancel glittering with hundreds of votive candles in relentlessly straight lines — unless it is the way the Hancock Tower next door holds the last of the setting sun in the equally straight (and for nearly sixty stories) angled incision that gives so sharp an elegance to the façade that faces Trinity. So perhaps my misjudgments of two decades ago — the worst being my abuse of Cram's Boston University and Post Office Square Courthouse and of the Perry office's Jordan Marsh Building — do not foreshadow similar missteps in this edition!

People change. And so does architecture! And linear time always is a delusion. Indeed, so much is this the case that if one is not to lose one's footing in one's own time it is

Surely Boston's first landmark of the twenty-first century, and a most vital and energizing one, Schwartz/Silver's addition to the New England Aquarium on Boston's waterfront.

probably more true to say that the "hot line" has really to run as much into the future as into the past. True in 1978 when I wrote this book, it is still true today.

The first edition of *Built in Boston*, so ably labored over in 1978 by my original editors at Little, Brown — Robin Bledsoe and the late Betsy Pitha — was controversial in its inclusion of movie palaces and apartment houses and gas stations, even three-deckers. Similarly, the University of Massachusetts Press edition of 1988, the result of the determination of Bruce Wilcox, the press's director, to rescue the book before Little, Brown let it (as was planned) go out of print, included the first and still the most extensive exploration of the Arts and Crafts style in Boston's architecture. Commonplace now, such vectors were revolutionary then.

More than twenty years later the situation is very different but the task is the same. In 1978, it was Victorian houses and Deco shopfronts, to say nothing of Cram neo-Gothic and Coolidge neo-Georgian, that needed to be protected (from arrogant late-Modernists). Today it is the Modernist masters like Pei and Sert and Kallmann and McKinnell and Paul Rudolph that need to be better understood — and protected from a different enemy — the preservationist zealots and conservative architectural contextualists whose stultifying repression of Boston's architecture we all need to be wary of, even in what I hope is the twilight of these pernicious ideas.

Change, the happy law of life, is, of course, what the hot line is about in either direction. And how much even Boston changes is often brought home to me by the *New York Times*, which I read daily along with the *Boston Globe*, not least because one can never trust the hometown spin ("piety of place" Vincent Scully once famously called it). Accordingly, I was interested to read R. W. Apple, Jr., in the *New York Times* on 29 January 1999 declare:

Boston is the most historic city in America, a repository of our national past, yet it has an extraordinary capacity to reinvent itself.

The Pilgrims landed nearby. Boston became the cradle of liberty, but later it became a byword for blue-nosed narrow-mindedness. ("Banned in Boston" they used to say when they wanted to tout a naughty book or a risqué play.)

It has traded and manufactured. Nowadays it manages money, and capitalizes on the science and technology developed in its laboratories. It has boomed and busted. . . . The one constant has been ideas: Boston ideas have washed across the nation and the world for two centuries.

The theme of "Boston ideas" is one we will pick up and run quite a way with in the four new chapters of this edition. Just now, though, it is the more basic theme of just plain changefulness I want to address here in order to illustrate how Boston itself changes and how that as much as how architecture has changed and how much I have changed in twenty years, has, in turn, now changed this book.

Here, too, my constant reading of the *New York Times* brings this vector most forcefully home to me: consider the lead story by Holland Carter in the Fine Arts section on August 7, 1998. It was headed "In Boston, All Roads Lead to Museums." It was the list in a boxed side bar of "Boston area" museums that caught my eye.

As I perused it I realized that only three of the ten museums listed were located in what I call core Boston; seven were outside it — four in once-outer (now inner) suburbs (Wellesley, Lincoln, Salem, and Brocton), and three in outlying areas, which have become Boston's outer suburbs in recent decades, and not without chaffing, as Carter seems to know when (anticipating protest?) he notes pointedly that Springfield's museums (pace, Springfieldonians!) are "solidly in the Hub's cultural sphere." What a change since 1978, when the frontispiece (retained here now as mapping in 2000 core Boston) included then the most outlying suburbs, and yet went no farther west that Framingham, north only to Rockport, and no farther south than Scituate. Indeed, the truth is it was outdated even then (being the Boston Metropolitan District of 1930), as was pointed out to me in 1978 by no less than my old mentor, Walter Muir Whitehill, whose foreword to the original edition, included here still, I cherish. Did I mean to rule "Mr. Boston" himself out of Boston? So Whitehill asked, wickedly, for he lived in North Andover — beyond my map.

He'd be pleased his "neighborhood" is in now. Boston's boundaries, he used to say, were just short of Yale and Newport/Providence (where New York began) to the south; while to the west the two cities met at Tanglewood (though on Boston's turf). To the north no boundary, he felt, was discernible (certainly coastal Maine was Boston in the summer). Whitehill was, of course, ahead of his time in disregarding all those antique city and town boundaries and describing instead the social and cultural reality—indeed, the Boston media market of today, the sixth largest in America, with 2.2 million families.

There are two ways, of course, of looking at all this. It is certainly true that, in one sense, to fly into Dulles International Airport is to arrive in Chantily, Virginia. Most of us, however, think we're arriving in Washington, D. C. The point, of course, is to come to terms with the twenty-first-century truth of the matter. We are talking not mayors, but ideas — the "Boston idea," as Sean O'Connell calls it in his *Imagining Boston*, a superb book, in which he dedicates a chapter to "three territories which define the outer edge of the Boston idea: north to New Hampshire, south to Cape Cod, and west to Amherst, the Connecticut Valley and the Berkshires."

O'Connell, of course, focuses on literature. But architecture is no different. Whether one considers the Cape Cod house, of which Boston architect Royal Barry Wills was the great master; the creation by the Boston Manufacturing Company of America's first industrial center in Lowell and Lawrence, the mill architecture of which is so notable; or the work of the Saarinens for the Boston Symphony at Tanglewood; Boston (or Greater Boston, as most call it) has expanded tremendously over the last two centuries, and especially in the twentieth century. Significantly, the title of Robert Frost's *North of Boston*, published first in 1913, was once explained by Frost as having "found a name for itself in the real estate advertising of the *Boston Globe*." Now at the end of the century, the *Globe* itself is "north of Boston," where the leading daily newspaper in Boston's southern New Hampshire suburbs is the *Boston Globe's* New Hampshire edition.

About all of this, of course, New Englanders particularly are apt to be conflicted. At the same time cities in places like western Massachusetts and southern New Hampshire chafe at being called satellite cities in the Boston media market, nearly every tourist guide to the area goes to the opposite extreme, insisting that, actually, Boston is only Beacon Hill, downtown, Back Bay and bits of Cambridge (around Harvard), East Boston (the airport), and Charlestown (around the Bunker Hill Monument). That's it! Then there is the view that, while it does enlarge on the tourist guide's definition of Boston, does so only by a very little, adding to core Boston only suburbs caught in the nineteenth-century annexionist movement, excluding those who escaped.

Annexed to what? You may well ask! Something called "the City of Boston," a good enough idea, but one never really achieved in any credible way (ditto Boston's "Metropolitan District"), and now only a tiny, rather embarrassing rump of a "city" of a huge metropolis, a rump that along with God knows how many other suburban cities and towns (the City of Chelsea, the City of Cambridge, the Town of Framingham, and so on — has anyone ever counted them all?) has no significance at all, really, beyond politics, and the lawyers and bureaucrats who thrive so often on the archaic.

They, and the politicians who hire them, are the only people who ever talk about "the City of This" or "Town of That."

According to this point of view all those State Street businessmen who live in Brookline, and all those Back Bay doctors who live in Lincoln are not, like Walter Whitehill in North Andover, Bostonians. They, of course, in turn, like their cousins on Beacon Hill and in Cambridge, are quite sure they are the Bostonians, and scoff huffily at such pretensions by residents of Dorchester and Roslindale.

This is, after all, the home of the New England town meeting and the People's Republic of Cambridge. And so on. But change Boston has, just as architecture has, as I have, and as this book now has.

Would I, pre–Dan Coolidge, have cited the MOMA credo as my own in the first edition of *Built in Boston*? I doubt it. Nor, after all, did I include North Andover. Yet as this book goes to press in 2000 the executive director of the Rhode Island Economic Policy Council is quoted in *Boston Magazine* print as saying: "Boston doesn't grasp that Rhode Island is part of the Boston Metro area, and Rhode Islanders do not grasp, by and large, that Rhode Island is part of Boston Metro." Already my definition here of Boston would seem to be on the conservative side.

Pace, Providence. The next edition of *Built in Boston* will probably be subtitled "City, Suburbs and Satellite Cities," or perhaps just — Boston, Inc.

P. D. S-T.

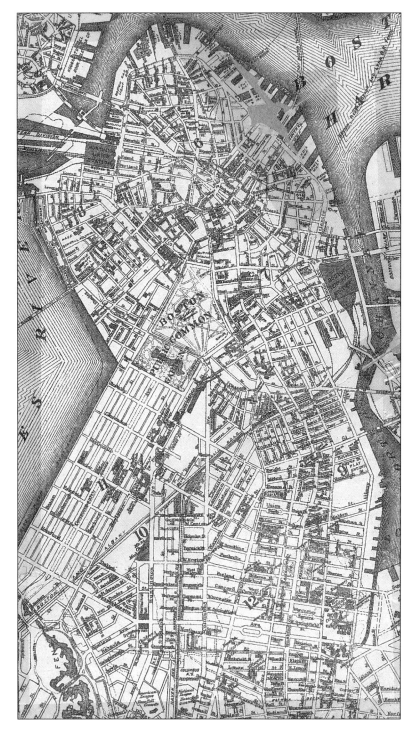

Detail of Boston Proper in 1900. At the top, the North End and
Waterfront; to the right, the Financial District; Downtown to the right of
the Common; Beacon Hill to the left; Back Bay below the Common to the
left; the South End to the right; the Fenway at bottom left.

PREFACE TO THE
FIRST PAPERBACK EDITION, 1988

THE LATE SIR JOHN BETJEMAN, whose passion for Victorian and Edwardian architecture was a light in the darkness for many of my generation, once kindly invited me to stay to luncheon after a marvelous morning's talk at his London house, to which I had been asked through the good offices of my kinsman Bruce Shand. Struck by how remarkably alike were our responses to everything from the rigors of boarding school to the intricacies of High Church Anglican ceremonial, I was not surprised that this was even more the case with architecture. I remember particularly one remark of the Queen's Poet Laureate, his eyes twinkling: "I do love architecture," he said, "don't you? It never answers back."

How very true, and thank goodness for it. I think of my own architectural "first loves" — the Radcliffe Camera at Oxford, King's College Chapel at Cambridge, the Abbey Room of the Boston Public Library, all pictured on my desk as I write; the nave of St. John the Divine in New York, the Viceroy's House at Delhi (photographs of which hang on the wall facing me in my study); Palace Square in Leningrad, the Royal Pavilion in Brighton, London's House of Lords and St. Cyprian's, Clarence Gate, and St. Paul's and Westminster cathedrals; the M.I.T. Chapel; the steep Baroque vistas of Prague and of Rome; so much of Venice; at least a half dozen English country houses; seemingly *all* of Paris and Oxford; and yes, Beacon Hill and Harvard Yard and Lowell House and the exquisite small church of All Saints in Peterborough, New Hampshire. One may stand in such places as these, even if only in memory or imagination, pouring out one's heart in the most extraordinary way toward something that — in just the same key — will always give back more than one could have imagined. Only music, perhaps (certainly not poetry, which so often has a mind of its own), seems to me to yield so immediately and profoundly to such outpouring in so personally and intensely fulfilling a way as does architecture.

That is why, ten years ago, I wrote *Built in Boston* — with this difference: that I felt then incredibly frustrated because so many of the buildings that moved me seemed to move no one else. Despite the books that had got me going, so to speak, as an undergraduate in the late 1960s — Walter Muir Whitehill's *Topographical History of Boston, Houses of Boston's Back Bay* by Bainbridge Bunting, the early *Survey of Cambridge Architecture* volumes, and Sam Bass Warner's *Streetcar Suburbs* — few people at that time were really very interested in the Harvard Houses or the architecture of the streetcar suburbs or apartment houses, or even in the work of Ralph Adams Cram. And almost no one had yet been intrigued by movie palaces or by three-deckers or by Colonial Revival suburban houses.

There were some kindred spirits: John Coolidge at Harvard, Walter Whitehill, Frank Moloney at the Boston Public Library, Robert Bell Rettig, Margaret Henderson Floyd, William Morgan at Princeton, Wheaton Holden, and George R. Ursul. But not many. And how could it have been otherwise, given the sorry state of so much American cultural and art history then? Truly, it is no exaggeration to say that *Built in Boston* was born of my outrage that the architectural history not just of Boston but of America had been so distorted and misrepresented by art historians who in my youth were writing not history but polemics.

This was an easy distinction for me to make in 1978, fresh as I was from the rigors of Elliott Perkins's Harvard History Department (where the name of Samuel Eliot Morison could still be invoked without risk). For the History Department was a very different place from the Fogg Museum and the Fine Arts Department, where it seemed to me that even the most distinguished art historians might know much more than I of art but assuredly knew much less of how to write history. Having as a young scholar foraged so often in one index after another, but quite in vain, for architects and artists whose work excited my interest and who I was sure were not insignificant, I had begun to wonder (for all my youthful confidence) if the fault could be mine after all and their work really unimportant. In his 1973 Leslie Stephen lecture at Cambridge, however, Quentin Bell said what only a major figure could get away with saying, and it became my battle cry. Writing of what he called the "grotesque travesty of history" that so riddled art history in those days, he boldly declared:

> It is not right and proper when we allow our value judgments to lead us into a falsification of history, that is to say when the historian allows his own personal predilections to determine which facts should and which facts should not be recorded. . . . The student [for example] who relies upon Professor Janson's large and handsome history of art, published in 1962, or an Upjohn, Wingert and Mahler's *History of World Art* (1957) . . . will not discover that the Pre-Raphaelites ever existed. There is . . . a kind of semi-mythology masquerading as history which is confidently imparted to students . . . and then, as any examiner knows to his cost, is regurgitated in the form of almost pure misinformation.

At first I went at the problem of trying to arouse interest in the art and architecture I liked — which I learned was rather patronizingly put down as "historicist" by the then still triumphant "modernist" establishment — by writing what I'm afraid were really my own polemics. In my two earliest books, *The Second Settlement* and *Church Building in Boston*, each privately printed for limited circulation and more enthusiastic than critical, I had begun to argue the case for historicist architects, and in two later (and better) books, *All Saints' Ashmont: A Centennial History* and *Ralph Adams Cram: American Medievalist*, to focus on the work of Cram and Bertram Grosvenor Goodhue, whose historicism (or eclecticism, or whatever one cares to call it) yielded one brilliant synthesis after another. The Cram book in particular cheered me because it was published by the Boston Public Library to mark the first retrospective exhibition anywhere of Cram and Goodhue's work. This exhibition began in Boston in December of 1975 and then went on to open in New York the following May. As the opening speakers included Ada

Louise Huxtable, John Coolidge, Kenneth Conant, Walter Whitehill and Henry-Russell Hitchcock, I think it fair to say that though it was a small show and necessarily limited in scope, the Cram exhibition helped to do for the study of the Gothic Revival in this country what was done for the study of the Classical Revival, also in 1975–1976, through the marvelous Beaux-Arts exhibition mounted by the Museum of Modern Art in New York. Indeed, its sponsorship of such a show in the first place constituted a historic revolution. Suddenly, my enthusiasms were not just respectable; they were becoming fashionable.

Notwithstanding this, I no more desired to go on writing historicist polemics than I wanted to continue reading modernist polemics; I wished instead to avoid the critical limbo that sort of thing thrives in and to write not polemics but history — the sort of history that would restore the balance the modernist zealots had disrupted and that would put architectural history back together again by placing modernism *and* historicism *in context*. This interested me all the more because I had begun to conclude that the late nineteenth- and early twentieth-century historicists who had taken so different a road from Louis Sullivan's and Frank Lloyd Wright's had nevertheless begun at the same place — with that fecund progenitor (as it turns out) of both schools, Henry Hobson Richardson. Moreover, at about the same time my own scholarly enthusiasms were usefully broadened by a visit to Chicago, where I had been invited by the Illinois chapter of the Society of Architectural Historians to lecture on Cram at the Art Institute of Chicago. I went really to see the work of the Boston historicists Cram and Shepley, Rutan and Coolidge in Chicago. What struck me, however, were Louis Sullivan's magnificent Stock Exchange Trading Floor and a long evening's talk with Leland Roth, who helped me see that McKim, Mead and White and Cram, Goodhue and Ferguson were two sides of the same architectural coin.

The result was the thesis, central to *Built in Boston* and rather revolutionary in 1978 — illustrated here by Plates 6 and 7 — that the work of McKim and Cram particularly, characterized alike by a cool, severe restraint that still was richly detailed and gravely beautiful, constituted the superb climax to date of the Classical and Medieval traditions in the New World. And that, in turn, nicely fitted with my increasing certitude that the overall cultural history of the 1880–1930 era, particularly in Boston, had been misjudged and undervalued. Unlike such writers as Van Wyck Brooks, I thought New England's Indian Summer had been itself a very great flowering — and that its architecture reflected that fact. Thus the chance offered me by Little, Brown/New York Graphic Society Books to do a full-fledged architectural history of Boston was very welcome. Boston, after all, was sufficiently old and important that its cultural and architectural history often led the nation and thus offered an author the opportunity for more than local attention to his causes. Furthermore, I had a far longer agenda in those days than just righting the modernist-historicist balance.

The other causes I sought to push forward were more local but as keenly held, perhaps because they were more personal. Though I spent my winters as a child at boarding school and my vacations at my parents' summer home, our family house is in Dorchester, on Jones Hill, where my maternal grandparents had settled, after their marriage, in 1908. A great-aunt lived nearby in Roxbury; our doctor lived in Brookline; the awning man was from South Boston; my godparents' home was in West Roxbury; a good friend lived in Jamaica Plain, another in Newton; I had gone to boarding school in Wellesley — and I had not noticed that these areas were notably duller than other places. Yet in book after book that claimed to be about Boston, these neighborhoods and suburbs of the city were as conspicuously absent as the historicist architects were from the art histories, and it seemed to me distorting and impoverishing to ignore those areas at the expense of endless repetitions of the glories of the Downtown–Beacon Hill–Back Bay–Cambridge axis.

I did not then, nor would I now, dispute that this axis is the heart and center of Boston, and as such I naturally had many affectionate associations there. Take one street: my maternal grandfather lived as a graduate student on Mount Vernon Street in 1905–1907; my grandmother's best friend, Grace Turkington, lived on the street in the 1930s — not far from another house on Mount Vernon Street where I spent much of my own college years in the late 1960s sitting at the feet of Professor George R. Ursul, one of my first mentors. I loved Beacon Hill. Similarly, I was at home in the Back Bay; as a youth I spent much time in the old Pierce mansion on the water side of Beacon Street, where my mother managed the practice of a Boston psychiatrist. As for Cambridge, my father was a graduate of Harvard College and had grown up in one of those large and splendid houses in the neighborhood of Brattle Street. Thus I had no quarrel with the axis; rather, I did with so many authors who insisted that it was all there was of Boston worth writing about. Again, what was needed was context — the forgotten and ignored architecture of such places as Roxbury and Newton had to be integrated into the overall Boston scene and find its proper niche and measure.

Another cause was equally dear to me: it seemed dubious that so many *kinds* of Boston's buildings were slighted in books about the city. The splendid theaters of my youth — the Majestic, the Metropolitan, the Oriental, the Colonial — were often not even mentioned; nor were the superb parish churches of the western suburbs, or those endless ranges of three-deckers I used to peer at out of the car window on our trips to and from Dorchester. Well, I was very ambitious! Still, it seemed clear that by integrating historicism and modernism and by dealing with all the various, long-ignored neighborhoods and suburbs of Boston and the equally neglected building types, an architectural history of Boston could be written that would both surprise and stimulate.

That *Built in Boston* continues to do so a decade later and now appears in its third printing and first paperback edition, published, moreover, by a distinguished university press, is very gratifying. But though I am glad to say the book as a whole needs no revision to continue to reflect my view of Boston's architectural history, there are a number of repairs necessary, of which I hope the reader will take careful note.

Two of these repairs embarrass me. First, the Fenway Studios must now take its place in *Built in Boston* as a building of citywide importance. Designed by Parker, Thomas and Rice in 1905, it is the most important Boston landmark in the modernistic Arts and Crafts style. My friends, who know I am an avid collector of Dard Hunter, a leading Arts and Crafts designer, never tire of twitting me for this omission. *Mea culpa.* Even more inexplicable is the fact that I should have ended *Built in Boston* with the Gropius House in Lincoln, totally disregarding Eero Saarinen's M.I.T. Chapel of 1955. This chapel has long been the only "modern" building hereabouts I've really liked (until in 1970 at the Massachusetts Health, Welfare and Education Service Center Paul

Boston's foremost Arts and Crafts landmark, the Fenway Studios on Ipswich Street. The street facade is shown above, the entrance portal and front doors below. Courtesy of Fenway Studios.

The interior of the M.I.T. Chapel. The bronze-toned altar screen is by Harry Bertoia. Photograph by Calvin Campbell, courtesy of Massachusetts Institute of Technology.

Rudolph endowed Boston with a glorious "Baroque" exterior staircase)! I have always been deeply moved at the chapel by the way light enters the interior; filtered through the surrounding trees and softened by the gently moving water of the moat, the light is reflected by the water through the arcades of the moat into the interior, where it reflects and scintillates against the undulating brick walls inside the chapel. No building is at once more dynamic and more dreamlike — striking in contrast with a campus that otherwise seems to consist mostly of unimaginably long linoleum-clad corridors that lead from one parking lot to another.

While on the subject of modernism, I should also like to note that although I tried very hard to do full justice to its history in Boston, ten years ago I did not know (as I do now from reading Elizabeth Sussman's "Taking a Risk" in *Dissent: The Issue of Modern Art in Boston*, the catalogue of three 1985–1986 exhibitions at the Institute of Contemporary Art) that "what appears to have been," in Sussman's words, "the first exhibition to introduce the new [Bauhaus] architecture of Europe to the United States" took place in Harvard Square in 1930. Sponsored by the Harvard Society for Contemporary Art and organized by Philip Johnson, this Bauhaus show, which then traveled to Chicago, preceded by two years the more famous exhibition Johnson and Henry-Russell Hitchcock organized on the same subject at the Museum of Modern Art in New

The interior capitals of the Buick Building are worth a second glance: those are automobile mechanics rather than medieval figures. Photograph by Richard Cheek from *Buildings and Builders* by Nancy Lurie Salzman, Boston University, 1985. Used by permission.

York. Nor did I know until exploring Doris Cole's *Eleanor Raymond, Architect* (Boston, 1981) that Raymond, among the first important women architects, had designed for her sister in Belmont in 1931 a house featured in 1933 in *Architectural Forum* as the first International style house erected in New England.

There are also a number of buildings in the more traditional styles that I neglected in 1978 but wish to note now. Significantly, nearly all are commercial or industrial landmarks, a type of architecture I have never been very interested in, and that would never dominate my work, but one that nonetheless is too important a part of Boston's architectural history for me to continue to neglect. The marvelous enameled terra-cotta Berkeley Building of 1905 by Codman and Despredelle, on the corner of Boylston and Berkeley streets, is one such. Another is the mercantile Gothic Gilchrist Building of 1912 on Washington Street, designed by Bigelow and Wadsworth. Furthermore, I'm afraid I did not in my youth venture into the leather district and did not until recently as a historian see any need to repair the error; thus it came as a complete surprise to me to experience the tremendous sweep and presence of the Melcher Street warehouses and, indeed, to be introduced to the whole Boston Wharf Company area around Summer Street, so much of it the work, ca. 1887–1920, of the company architect Morton D. Safford. In like vein, though I remember my childhood delight whenever I passed the windows of "Fuller's Folly," as the Fuller Cadillac automobile showroom on Commonwealth Avenue was called, I slighted that whole building type as well as the Kenmore Square area where most of Boston's early twentieth-century automobile dealerships were erected. Two buildings particularly need to be noted: the Fuller Building itself, at 808 Commonwealth Avenue, the work in 1928 of no less than Albert Kahn; and the Buick Building at 855 Commonwealth Avenue, yet another work by Arthur Bowditch, designed in 1919 and now the Boston University School for the Arts. The auto mechanics who appear in the Gothic capitals of the Buick Building's interior columns are particularly charming examples of the modernism of historicism.

To some extent, these omissions may be explained by the fact that only recently has much been published in this area by those who know something of such work, and this brings up the whole question of those books which have appeared since 1978 that I wish to add to the bibliography of *Built in Boston*. I learned about the Boston Wharf area from *Boston Landmarks of Industrial and Engineering History: Four Tours* (Boston,

1984); the automobile dealerships are discussed in Nancy Salzman's *Buildings and Builders: An Architectural History of Boston University* (Boston, 1985). Such publications are vital building blocks of urban history. They cause no sensation, but in their plodding, patient documentation of this and that apparently only very ordinary building they add much to our overall knowledge of the city. In Salzman's book alone, to cite some examples: the Dorchester architect of the streetcar suburbs, A. H. Vinal, emerges as "a major architect of the west Back Bay"; the documented interior work of Little and Brown is augmented by new buildings of theirs, including the virtually unknown and amazingly vivid green marble opulence of the Harriet Richards House at 101 Bay State Road, which can now be compared with the Somerset Club's well-known and very refined Directoire drawing rooms; and Shepley, Rutan and Coolidge turn out to have designed at the corner of Bay State Road and Deerfield Street a house for Peter Brooks, he of the Monadnock Building in Chicago, whose severe tastes so influenced the Chicago style. It is appropriately austere. Furthermore, the fact that not only Arthur Little but also Edmund Wheelwright lived in houses of their own design on Bay State Road (increasingly, so it seems, rather an "arty" area at the turn of the twentieth century, comparable to Huntington Avenue around Symphony Hall) enlarges our overall knowledge of Boston's social geography at the time. Salzman's book adds many such pieces to the still far from finished Boston jigsaw puzzle.

No less important is the city's architectural ornament. To the bibliography under Section G, Metalwork, one may add an excellent book: Michael and Susan Southworth's *Ornamental Ironwork: An Illustrated Guide* (Boston, 1978), which has much documentation of the work of Samuel Yellin of Philadelphia, though not enough of Frank Koralewski of the Krasser Company of Boston, who was distinctly in the same class. Also of interest is my own "Johannes Kirchmayer: A Carver of Saints," commissioned by the Goethe Society of Boston, which appeared in *Germans in Boston* (Boston, 1981).

A number of popular books should also be noted, such as *Lost Boston* by Jane Holtz Kay (Boston, 1980); her work, as well as that of Robert Campbell, the *Boston Globe* critic, is always interesting. Then there are two widely available architectural guides to the city, Donlyn Lyndon's *The City Observed: Boston*, published in 1982, and Michael and Susan Southworth's *A.I.A. Guide to Boston*, published five years later. Though each book deals importantly with eighteenth-, nineteenth-, and early twentieth-century buildings and not just with "modern" landmarks, both betray the fact that they were written not by architectural historians but by architects trained in an era when architectural schools preferred to teach urban design rather than architectural history. Nevertheless, both are worth buying. I remember, for example, how startled I was at the Southworths' insight about the Jordan Marsh building of 1948, a building I would not ever have thought anyone could convince me was worth much; "distinct Post-Modernist tendencies" was their surprising and quite inspired conclusion, and this historian was taught thereby yet another lesson about how all of us tend to undervalue the just-past styles of our own lifetimes, to which we are too close. I called Jordan's "an absurd 'Modernistic' Federal Revival" building when I wrote this book ten years ago. I was wrong. Another example, this time from Lyndon's book: he points out (though we cannot know if any distinction should be made between the firm and its senior partner) that the Henry Bigelow of Bigelow and Wadsworth, who designed the marvelous

79 Milk Street, one of two long-overlooked intown office buildings in the modernistic Arts and Crafts mode. Courtesy of the Macomber Company.

fifth floor of the Athenaeum in 1913, one of the finest interiors in Boston, designed the amazingly different Gilchrist Building on Washington Street the year before. That's the kind of weaving together of apparently unconnected threads that advances our overall historical knowledge of the city. Lyndon is surely right, moreover, in noting that the wonderful grotesques of the Gilchrist Building, being the work of the Athenaeum's architect, must be seen as "intentionally droll."

Henry Forbes Bigelow reminds me that amid this discussion of books written I should, perhaps, touch also on books not written that *should* be — soon. Bigelow is such a case. He is one of a number of important architects of regional and even national reputation about whom not nearly enough is known. Were I writing *Built in Boston* today, I would want to study such people more closely, rather as I was able in 1978 to study C. H. Blackhall, then not widely known. There are so many of these architects. Even such firms as the Shepley/Coolidge office and Perry, Shaw and Hepburn fall into this category. One thinks of Bigelow particularly because to his superb Classicism at the Athenaeum must be added not only the stylish commercial Gothic of Gilchrist's but also the most unusual modernistic Arts and Crafts office building of 1904 at 79 Milk Street. This has lately intrigued me because I had not previously noticed the elegantly chamfered corner detail — an oblique void that as it widens toward the top seems to make the building tip backward — and the topmost cornice, which takes the form of a trumpet-shaped cove inset with triangular and pendant green and white terra-cotta plaques. (The raw data for 79 Milk Street, though without any discussion of its unusual stylistic aspect, are found in the *Central Business District Preservation Study* by the Boston Landmarks Commission, an invaluable compendium published in 1980.) Interestingly, when I told my old friend the Boston architect William Buckingham, of Basnight, Buckingham and Partners, about my interest in this building, he remarked that he thought it was the first building erected by the well-known old Boston builders, the Macomber Company. Upon inquiry, they sent me their firm's history, in which 79 Milk Street is in fact described as their "first contract . . . one of the first structural steel buildings in the United States . . . revolutionary in design. . . ." It must indeed have looked revolutionary as it rose at the turn of the century in Post Office Square, then dominated by the old Sub-Treasury and its neighbors, illustrated here on page 42. It is, in Buckingham's words, "second cousin to the Monadnock Building in Chicago." And only thirteen years later. (Another modernistic Arts and Crafts building, pointed out to me by Daniel Coolidge, is 262 Washington Street, the work of Arthur Everett of Everett and Mead in 1901.)

To return to books actually written: three recognized scholars who have given us significant work relating to Boston are Cynthia Zaitzevsky, whose *Frederick Law Olmsted and the Boston Park System* came out in 1982; James F. O'Gorman, whose *H. H. Richardson: Architectural Forms for an American Society* was published in 1987; and William Morgan, who wrote, in 1983, the first full-length study of a famous Boston architect, Henry Vaughan, *The Almighty Wall: The Architecture of Henry Vaughan*. But far and away the landmark books of the last ten years are Abbott Lowell Cummings's definitive *The Framed Houses of Massachusetts Bay 1625–1725*, published in 1979; and *Harvard: An Architectural History* by Bainbridge Bunting and Margaret Henderson Floyd, who edited and much enlarged Bunting's original manuscript. An outstanding scholarly book, the Harvard history was particularly welcomed by this writer because my own principal scholarly work over the last decade (most of it for *Harvard Magazine*) has arisen out of my admiration for the Georgian Revival masterworks at Harvard of Coolidge, Shepley, Bulfinch and Abbott. In this connection, I should also like to note *The Colonial Revival in America* (New York, 1985). Also of very great interest because it touches on so many Boston architects and artists is *"The Art That Is Life": The Arts and Crafts Movement in America 1875–1920* (Boston, 1987). For me this book was a particular pleasure (to round the circle, as it were, of this introduction), for prominently featured in the Arts and Crafts exhibition at the Museum of Fine Arts, Boston, for which the book is a catalogue, was All Saints' Church, Ashmont, Cram and Goodhue's first church and the building, then long forgotten, that first fired up my interest in architectural history fifteen years ago as a young man in Harvard College.

NEW acknowledgments are few but notable. I am glad for the help of both Archie Epps and William Strong in guiding me toward the University of Massachusetts Press and its director, Bruce Wilcox, who has been throughout a pleasure to work with; and of Betsy Pitha, my old friend and now head of the Trade Copyediting Department at Little, Brown and Company, for copyediting this introduction, thus ensuring a necessary stylistic consistency. Tom Parker of the Bostonian Society found for me the illustration I have long coveted for the front cover, and I am grateful to Robert Douglas Hunter and Elizabeth Ives Hunter for directing me to David Loury, who provided the photographs of the Fenway Studios.

I must add that as I now spend more time with the Building Committee for the restoration of the McKim Building of the Boston Public Library than I do writing books, I have good reason to thank Kevin Moloney, Arthur Curley, Victor Hagan, and our architect, Daniel J. Coolidge, for keeping my architectural wits in good order. The cover illustration of this new edition of *Built in Boston*, which shows the McKim Building, is intended to mark the 100th anniversary of its erection, which will be celebrated in 1995, as well as the restoration of this landmark, one of the chief architectural glories of the New World.

Finally, I must enlarge on the last of my acknowledgments of ten years ago, for since my mother's death it is necessary to record a debt to her far greater than I then indicated. The daughter of a learned and dedicated but not very worldly clergyman, Lucien Stanley Groves, and of a brilliant businesswoman, Margaret Shand Groves, who (to put it tactfully) kept the family solvent, my mother in persevering through four years of the Great Depression to her bachelor's degree was herself among a small number of college-educated women in the America of the 1930s. Thus by my arrival it was a family tradition that such things as one's scholarship mattered far more than one's income. The knowledge of so unusual a standard in this materialistic age, and the way my mother believed in me against all odds and helped me in my career as she had my father before me (even to giving up her own opportunity for a graduate degree) is surely the most important acknowledgment of this book. So much was this the case that when Professor Margaret Henderson Floyd used to marvel in the 1970s at my productivity, as one book followed another, culminating in *Built in Boston*, she would say: "Ah, yes, but your mother is your secret weapon." So she was: fundamentally, everything I ever write will always be dedicated to Geraldine Groves Tucci.

D. S.-T.

Shandleigh House,
Jones Hill, Dorchester

26 February 1988

FOREWORD

BY WALTER MUIR WHITEHILL, 1978

T
HE TWO DAYS before Christmas 1977 will stick in my memory because of the
pleasure that I had in reading the manuscript of Douglass Shand Tucci's *Built in
Boston: City and Suburb.* The book moves so skillfully from one thing to another
that it is difficult to put down. One wants to find what is coming next. Moreover, several chapters, based on the author's research in previously unexplored areas, offer new
material and ideas of great interest.

Last year I contributed an introduction to *Architecture Boston,* an excellent book
produced by the Boston Society of Architects with text by Joseph L. Eldredge,
F.A.I.A., which carries the reader around central Boston, Charlestown, Roxbury, and
Cambridge of the present day, explaining skillfully what is to be seen there. As it is a
publication of the Boston Society of Architects, it rightly gives considerable space to
the work of the years since World War II. *Built in Boston* proceeds on chronological
rather than geographical lines, undertaking to show what happened architecturally in
Boston at different periods from the late eighteenth century, and why. Thus Mr. Tucci
often discusses buildings that have disappeared or fallen out of general esteem or even
good repair, like some of the twentieth-century theaters.

Writing in 1945 in *Boston after Bulfinch: An Account of its Architecture, 1800–1900,* the
late Walter H. Kilham, F.A.I.A., observed: "Writers on architecture have usually
avoided saying very much about the work of the nineteenth century, especially in the
United States, but as a matter of fact this era of rapid expansion provides in its architecture a highly instructive picture of the developing culture of the nation."

At the beginning of the nineteenth century the practice of architecture was considered to be within the grasp of any literate gentleman who had a mind to try his hand at
it. When Charles Bulfinch returned from a "Grand Tour" in 1787, he settled in Boston,
"pursuing no business but giving gratuitous advice in architecture," derived from his
travels, as an accommodation to his friends. When financial reverses made employ-
ment necessary, Bulfinch turned to the serious practice of architecture, and within a
few years transformed the face of his native town. Another Bostonian, fifty-five years
younger than Bulfinch, Edward Clarke Cabot, who had raised sheep in Illinois and
Vermont, stumbled into architecture by winning in 1846 the competition for a new
building of the Boston Athenaeum. In his late twenties at the time, he had not been in
Europe. However, he had looked at books owned by the Athenaeum to some purpose.
Although Cabot's brown sandstone facade was obviously of Italian Renaissance inspiration, it only dawned on me last year, when I was writing the catalogue for the American showing of the Palladio exhibition, that it was derived from Palladio's Palazzo da

Porta Festa in Vicenza. When I found among the early nineteenth-century holdings of the Athenaeum a copy of Ottavio Bertotti Scamozzi's great folio *Le Fabbriche e i Disegni di Andrea Palladio* (Vicenza, 1776), in which the facade of that palace figures as plate seven in volume one, then the source of Cabot's inspiration became clear.

During the third quarter of the nineteenth century, architecture in Boston began to assume the air of a profession, as those who wished to practice it sought formal training, rather than relying on travel, books, or apprenticeship in an existing office. The sixteen-year-old Richard Morris Hunt, having been taken to Paris by his family soon after his graduation from the Boston Latin School in 1843, studied at the Ecole des Beaux Arts and worked under Hector Martin Lefuel, who was engaged upon additions to the Louvre and the Tuileries. Returning to the United States after nine years, Hunt opened in New York in 1858 a studio in which he trained younger men in the principles of architecture he had been taught in Paris. William Robert Ware, graduated from Harvard College in 1852, and Henry Van Brunt of the Harvard class of 1854 studied architecture in New York with Hunt, while Henry Hobson Richardson of the Harvard class of 1859 went to Paris to the Ecole des Beaux Arts to get French training at first hand. Ware and Van Brunt, who established a partnership in Boston in 1863, created an atelier in their new office for students on the order of Hunt's. This was so successful that in 1865 Ware was charged with the establishment of an architectural school in the recently founded Massachusetts Institute of Technology. This outstanding new school, which for the first time in the United States offered training in design according to the method of the Ecole des Beaux Arts, caused Ware in 1881 to be invited to found a similar school of architecture at Columbia University.

The American Institute of Architects was established in New York in 1857. A decade later the Boston Society of Architects was organized to seek "the union in fellowship of all responsible and honorable architects and the combination of their efforts for the purpose of promoting the artistic, scientific, and practical efficiency of the profession." Edward Clarke Cabot, who, after his success in the Boston Athenaeum competition, continued to practice architecture, was president of the society from 1867 to 1896, and thereafter honorary president until his death in 1901.

At the beginning of the nineteenth century Boston was a seaport, whose 24,397 inhabitants were almost entirely of English origin. At the end of the century, it was a polyglot industrial city of 560,892. Half of the 1900 population was Irish. A fifth hailed from the Maritime Provinces. Because of the considerable number of immigrants from Russia, Italy, Germany, and other countries, less than 11 percent were what might be considered traditional New Englanders. Even the landscape was changed during the nineteenth century by means of great landfilling operations, undertaken to make room for the burgeoning population. These changes, combined with those in the practice of architecture, make the nineteenth-century buildings of Boston "a highly instructive picture of the developing culture of the nation," as Walter Kilham noted.

In the third of a century since the publication of his book, a generation of younger architectural historians discovered the joys of nineteenth-century buildings, admiring things that their parents either ignored or ridiculed as eyesores. Ware and Van Brunt's Memorial Hall at Harvard is a case in point, although the Harvard Corporation has not yet been persuaded to restore its tower to its original splendor. The neighborhood of

Quincy Market, in jeopardy not so many years ago, has been rescued by the Boston Redevelopment Authority, and is alive with people. The publication of Bainbridge Bunting's *Houses of Boston's Back Bay* in 1967 caused many Bostonians to realize that these buildings were not only the places where their relatives had lived but remarkable examples of nineteenth-century architecture. Mr. Tucci carries his exploration through the first four decades of the twentieth century to the point where the migration of Walter Gropius to Harvard caused an abrupt change in Boston architecture. Now that there is increasing boredom with the austerities of the "International Style," which has moved from *avant garde* to "old hat," it is worth reexamining the traditional architecture that it replaced.

Built in Boston naturally discusses many familiar buildings that have been studied by others, but a good half of the book is based upon its author's personal research and observations. Mr. Tucci has an incurable habit of looking at his surroundings and then trying to discover who built what, and why. As a senior in Harvard College half a dozen years ago, he studied the history of the Harvard Houses. He has written about his own Jones Hill neighborhood in Dorchester. His work in organizing the papers of Ralph Adams Cram and other architects and craftsmen in the Boston Public Library led first to the publication in 1974 of his *Church Building in Boston, 1720–1970* and the next year to a great Cram exhibition at the library, for which he wrote *Ralph Adams Cram, American Medievalist*. A centennial history of All Saints' Church, Ashmont — Cram's early masterpiece in the region — also appeared in 1975. In a secular mood, Mr. Tucci prepared in 1977 a walking tour of Boston theaters, concert halls, and movie palaces for the City Conservation League. In all of these studies he spread so wide and deep a net as to bring up a rich haul of unfamiliar material, which he skillfully presents in this book.

Since the period described is one in which Boston was overflowing its boundaries, Mr. Tucci rightly considers the architecture of neighboring towns, whether or not they were formally annexed to the city. Once public transportation brought places within easy reach of downtown Boston, houses proliferated in the same way in Dorchester, which became part of the city in 1870, and in Cambridge and Brookline, which are independent municipalities. In Chapter 4, "Streetcar City, Garden Suburbs," he gives an enlightening account of this process, using Jones Hill in Dorchester, which he knows intimately, as a point of departure. He indicates that large houses on small lots there were deliberately planned that way from the beginning, and that their proximity to each other and to the sidewalk was not the result of subsequent intrusions. He suggests that this sprang from a memory of the first decade of the nineteenth century on Beacon Hill when Bulfinch was designing for Harrison Gray Otis and others free-standing houses that, due to shortage of land, were later incorporated in solid blocks.

He may well be right, for I have never been able to fathom why, around Brattle Street in Cambridge, on, let us say, Fayerweather Street, people built in the late nineteenth century large, often expensive, and sometimes well-designed free-standing houses on diminutive lots. To me there is more privacy in a Back Bay block, or in one in London, Paris, Rome, or most European cities. But the hankering to have a free-standing house, even if your land is so small that you can look into your neighbor's side windows, is not exclusively a Bostonian or an American folly. In Barcelona, where the Gothic city and the huge nineteenth-century *ensanche* that enfolds it consist of solid blocks of apartments and houses, there is at the head of the Paseo de Gracia a region of luxurious free-standing villas, built on as exiguous pocket-handkerchiefs of land as anything in the Boston suburbs.

Chapter 5 on apartment houses and Chapter 9 on theaters and movie palaces present useful ideas about ubiquitous structures that most Bostonians have simply thoughtlessly taken for granted. The pioneering Hotel Pelham of 1857 and its 1870 neighbor, the Boylston, at the corner of Tremont and Boylston streets, have long since vanished, as have the apartment houses in Copley Square. The first apartment house on Commonwealth Avenue, Ware and Van Brunt's Hotel Hamilton of 1869, was demolished in the last decade by developers who hankered to put a taller structure on the site. As they were foiled by legal action, the lot once occupied by the hotel at the northwest corner of Clarendon Street is still vacant, save as a children's playground. Two blocks up at Exeter Street, the Hotel Agassiz (191 Commonwealth Avenue) of 1872 is still considered a delightful place to live, although it has passed the century mark. Mr. Tucci follows the evolution of the apartment house through Boston and the suburbs, calling attention to significant examples that many of us have passed for years without thinking about.

His account of the theaters particularly intrigues me, for as a child I was taken to see *Ben Hur* in Edward Clarke Cabot's Boston Theatre (of the 1850s) in Washington Street. Then too I delighted in the "crystal waterfall staircase," electrically lighted, with which B. F. Keith had adorned his adjacent Bijou Theatre. When I was in Boston Latin School sixty years ago, my idea of a Saturday morning's diversion was to see a film in the Modern Theatre in Washington Street — then correctly named, for it was built in 1914 — before going on to look for books at Goodspeed's, Smith and McCance, De Wolfe-Fiske's, Lauriat's, and in Cornhill. As the theater district has fallen upon evil days, we tend to forget how many, and how splendid, playhouses were built in the period covered by this book. Unlike the Boston Opera House, most of them are still there, although often in a state of sorry dilapidation.

Interesting as these novelties are, the true point of *Built in Boston* is that it follows local architectural taste from Bulfinch through the Greek Revival, the Italianate, the French Second Empire, and Victorian Gothic to H. H. Richardson; on to the Colonial Revival, the Classicism of Charles F. McKim, and the Gothic vision of Ralph Adams Cram, and makes these transitions seem plausible in relation to the pluralistic culture that emerged during the phenomenal nineteenth-century growth of Boston.

In regard to the eclecticism that prevailed from 1890 to the 1930s, Mr. Tucci observes that "well-traveled and well-educated architects, with well-stocked libraries of measured drawings and photographs of seemingly everything ever built and an endless supply of excellent immigrant craftsmen, coincided with clients equally well-traveled and well-educated and (until 1930) with more money than they often knew what to do with." The Boston Public Library owes much to the mutual understanding and shared enthusiasms of architect and client, for during its construction the president of the trustees was Samuel A. B. Abbott, who later became the first director of the American Academy in Rome. Abbott and McKim egged each other on, enjoyed the process, and obtained superior results. The architect Herbert Browne, who knew Italy intimately and loved to find there marble columns, busts, and bas-reliefs, had a similarly close relation with some of his clients. The design of the music room at Faulkner Farm in Brookline emerged from the combination of four colossal marble columns and a painted octagonal room that he found in Mantua, and a set of tapestries that his client, Mrs. Brandegee, already owned. While the columns determined the height of the room, its length was established by the size of the tapestries, and the Mantua room became a slightly elevated stage where musicians could perform.

Mr. Tucci obviously sympathizes with the belief of the eclectics "that the historical associations of a style were crucial to a building's functional expression, provided all the modern conveniences were worked into it." Mr. Tucci is young enough to be able to do so. The fear of being thought old-fashioned, ill-informed obscurantists led too many of my generation to ignore or deprecate such a masterpiece of traditional eclecticism as Lowell House at Harvard, which still pleases the eye while usefully serving the purpose for which it was designed nearly fifty years ago. Mr. Tucci is free from such prejudices. I greatly like his book. I wish Walter Kilham were still around to enjoy it.

And I wish Walter Whitehill were still around for all sorts of reasons, not the least his many kindnesses to me. I first met him at the Club of Odd Volumes in 1972 when I was a senior in Harvard College, and I will always recall how he welcomed me to those distinguished precincts as if I had just written a brilliant first book. Later that year, when I did send my first book to him — timidly, for it was not brilliant — back from Whitehill came the first of many warmly encouraging letters. Though we were often associated publicly, it is for these more private kindnesses that I will chiefly remember him. Once I had to be in North Andover; nothing would do but that the Whitehills should meet me at the bus stop, drive me to and from my appointment, give me a most handsome lunch, and deliver me back to the bus stop at the end of the day. Then, on Christmas Day of 1977 he called me at home to tell me how much he had enjoyed Built in Boston. *He talked long and eloquently of Boston buildings and Boston friends, nicely relating everything to my manuscript — in part, no doubt, because he must have guessed that there was no one whose opinion of my work mattered more to me. For that reason, when I learned of his death, I asked Dennis Crowley and Stuart Myers, for whom what are now Parts 1 and 2 of this book was written, if I might dedicate the first edition to Mr. Whitehill's memory.*

D.S–T., 1999

BUILT IN BOSTON

1800–1890

PART I

BULFINCH AND THE BOSTON GRANITE ARCHITECTS

TO

RICHARDSON AND OLMSTED

I have always loved building, holding it to be not
only the highest achievement of man but one in
which, at the moment of consummation, things
were most clearly taken out of his hands and per-
fected, without his intention, by other means, and I
regarded men as something much less than the
buildings they made and inhabited, as mere lodgers
and short-term sub-lessees . . .

— Evelyn Waugh
Brideshead Revisited

1

Before and after Bulfinch

IN THE IMAGINATION of the world Boston holds a secure place. Yet what part in this architecture plays, or what kind of architecture, it is hard to say. Samuel Eliot Morison, perhaps the preeminent American historian of this century, likened at least one Boston architect "to a cathedral builder of the thirteenth century [to whom] came visions transcending human experience, with the power to transmute them into reality." But it was not Bulfinch or Richardson that Morison likened to the Master of Chartres; it was Donald McKay, the naval architect. And that "Boston should have carried the clipper ship to its ultimate perfection" was for Morison Boston's, and America's, incomparable architectural achievement. "The *Flying Cloud*," wrote Morison, "was our Rheims, the *Sovereign of the Seas* our Parthenon, the *Lightning* our Amiens . . ." and as the images of these famous ships arise in our minds, his eloquence is irresistible:

A summer day with a sea-turn in the wind. The Grand Banks fog, rolling in wave after wave, is dissolved by the perfumed breath of New England hayfields into a gentle haze, that turns the State House dome to old gold, films brick walls with a soft patina, and sifts blue shadows among the foliage of the Common elms. Out of the mist in Massachusetts Bay comes riding a clipper ship, with the effortless speed of an albatross.

Though Morison naturally pointed in this famous passage from the city itself to its throning harbor, elsewhere in *The Maritime History of Massachusetts* he admitted that he had such respect for Bulfinch that he was "tempted to ascribe his pure taste and perfect proportion to an ocean origin; but," he went on, "curiously enough, land architecture grew steadily worse in Massachusetts as naval architecture reached perfection in the clipper ships." Here, at least, we can disagree.

Consider the relative importance of architecture in Boston when young Charles Bulfinch sailed from its harbor (Figure 4) for his European tour in 1786 and when Henry Hobson Richardson embarked for his trip to Europe not quite a hundred years later, in 1882. Bulfinch left a town by no means rude. Boston's mid-seventeenth-century wooden folk Gothic — of which only the steep gabled Paul Revere House of about 1680 (Figure 5) survives today — had begun to give way to the Renaissance tradition. Christ Church (Figure 6), a kind of "folk Wren," had been followed by the Old South Meeting House in 1729; and at every level from the ca. 1711 Town House (now the Old State House; Figures 206–207) down to simple dwellings like the Crease and Capen houses of about the same time (later, respectively, the Old Corner Book Store and the Old Union Oyster House), the more horizontal Renaissance tradition, increasingly in brick, had made its presence felt more and more. In 1737 Boston was endowed as well with its first stone building, the granite Hancock House on Beacon Hill. And in the mid-

FIGURE 4. Boston from the South Boston Bridge.
Lithograph by Deroy after a drawing by J. Milbert.

eighteenth century, when Boston was both the vice-regal seat and the largest English-speaking community in North America, the town had overcome its Puritanism sufficiently to accept what is called the High Georgian mode. Boston accumulated a number of splendid buildings in this manner, a provincial interpretation of English Palladianism, but strongly influenced by James Gibbs and thus a continuation of the Wren tradition. Perhaps the most famous are Faneuil Hall (see Figure 17), later enlarged but in its original style, and Peter Harrison's King's Chapel (Figure 7), which, involving as it did the introduction into Boston of Anglican liturgical elegance, exercised a wider than merely architectural influence on Puritan Boston.

Boston's Georgian spires nonetheless bravely punctuated the skyline of what was still a basically Medieval town when Bulfinch sailed for Europe in 1786. In fact, Boston's architecture then amounted by any but the standards of the New World to very little. Yet what a different place it was from which Richardson began his European tour almost a hundred years later. One need not share Henry-Russell Hitchcock's enthusiasm to understand the importance of his assertion that Richardson, Boston's leading architect in 1882, was by then "the greatest architect in the world." Bulfinch and Richardson bracket an extraordinary century in the history of architecture in Boston.

Much as one might like to say something new about Bulfinch here, the old and venerable idea that he virtually created Boston architecturally is more or less true. Previously, architecture in Bos-

Seventeenth- and eighteenth-century architecture.

FIGURE 5. Paul Revere House, 19 North Square, North End. Exterior surfaces and interior treatment date from a 1908 restoration by Joseph Chandler, but the structural skeleton is original, ca. 1680. Except for the Medieval street plan still evident in parts of downtown and the North End, this folk Gothic house is all that remains of the appearance of the seventeenth-century settlement.

FIGURE 6. Christ Church, North End, 1723. The steeple of what is commonly called the "Old North Church," the work of William Price, dates from 1740 and has been several times rebuilt. The church was restored in 1912 by R. Clipston Sturgis and Henry C. Ross.

FIGURE 7. Peter Harrison. King's Chapel, 1749. Some of the ornament derives from the first church, including the altarpiece, the gift of King William and Queen Mary in 1696.

ton had been a series of episodes. Bulfinch changed all that dramatically. Stylistically, he continued the English Renaissance tradition, for though it led the political revolution of the colonies, Boston sought no cultural declaration of independence. One sees a reflection of this in Bulfinch's work, which in turn reflected his own admiration of the English Neoclassicists Sir William Chambers and especially Robert Adam. In fact, Bulfinch's style has been called not only "Federal" but "American Adam." But Bulfinch made that manner his own, as is evident in the Massachusetts State House (Figure 8) he designed upon his return from Europe and which was begun some years later, in 1795.

In the State House, frankly derivative of the central riverfront pavilion of Chambers's Somerset House in London, begun in 1778, one can see at a glance how Bulfinch lightened and refined his sources, achieving a more delicate building, the attenuated proportions of which are characteristic of his work. The simplicity of the brick piers and arches of the first floor has been particularly admired: they form, William Pierson has written, "one of the most expressive and lovely passages in American architecture." Inside, Bulfinch marshaled a most distinguished sequence of state rooms. The old Senate, now the Senate Reception Room, is perhaps the handsomest room in Boston: barrel-vaulted and graced by two rows of free-standing Ionic columns, its high-arched windows open generously to Beacon Street and Boston Common. The old House of Representatives, now the Senate, is the grandest apartment, notable for its great sunburst of a dome, whose radiant flat ribs lift gracefully to a lofty apex of delicate fluting (Plate 2). One sees here as throughout Bulfinch's work the elegant spiderwebs of pliant and crisp detail for which he has been so much admired (Figure 14). Its effect is

even more striking in his first Harrison Gray Otis House (1796), where the recent painstaking restoration by the Society for the Preservation of New England Antiquities has yielded unsuspected Federal color combinations — light bluish green with detail picked out in white, for example — that reveal a fine use of color to differentiate and highlight detail.

Bulfinch's chief legacy to Boston was his introduction of Neoclassical town planning. His Tontine Crescent of 1793–1794 was remarkably advanced for its time and not only in Boston (Figure 9). Harold Kirker has observed that although the famous crescent at Bath and perhaps the plan for another in London were Bulfinch's inspiration, not even London had a crescent at this time. The Tontine Crescent must have been a magnificent sight: sixteen brick houses, painted gray and with white pilasters, ranged on either side of a central archway, swept graciously for almost five hundred feet around a tree-shaded park. At the end of the crescent, the shape of which has survived in Franklin Street today, Bulfinch built Boston's first theater in 1794 and in 1800–1803 what became shortly thereafter Boston's first cathedral, Holy Cross Church, erected for the Roman Catholic bishop of Boston, Jean-Louis A. M. LeFebvre de Cheverus. What a whole new world it must have seemed — for in crescent, theater, and cathedral, as in the Massachusetts capitol, Boston was straining for the first time toward an architecture of European finish. Alas, the whole brave parade lasted little more than fifty years, so relentless was the later push of business in this quarter: the theater was destroyed in 1852; the crescent about 1858, and, finally, the cathedral about 1862. But the *idea* of the Tontine Crescent, as we shall see, proved more durable.

Bulfinch's concept of residential design has nonetheless been widely misunderstood. His blocks of row houses

Public buildings by Charles Bulfinch.
FIGURE 8. Massachusetts State House, Beacon Hill, 1795–1798. See also Plate 2.
FIGURE 9. Tontine Crescent (left) and Boston Theatre, 1793–1794, showing the theater as originally designed. Demolished.

Residential architecture by Charles Bulfinch on Beacon Hill.

FIGURE 10. The third Harrison Gray Otis House, 45 Beacon Street, 1805–1808, as it originally appeared, showing also (right) Alexander Parris's Sears House at 42.

FIGURE 11. The same two houses as they appear today, connected by a third house.

FIGURE 12. The second Otis House, 85 Mount Vernon Street, 1800–1802.

always possessed architectural unity; none resembled in any way the massed shoulder-to-shoulder irregularities, for instance, of present-day Beacon Street. As Frank Chouteau Brown pointed out many years ago, Bulfinch essayed connected row house blocks in conjunction with parks — either his own or a public park in the case of Colonnade and Park rows, two splendid ranges of brick town houses, now destroyed, with which he framed Boston Common along Park and Tremont streets between 1803 and 1812. Otherwise he continued to prefer, as did his whole generation, the traditional detached or free-standing town house, set close by the street and the neighboring houses but in its own garden lot. Thus, when the new State House precipitated the development of the adjacent area, Bulfinch's plan was very different in this new quarter. The area was gained by leveling one of the three hills that then rose behind the State House and dumping it into the water where Charles Street now is, the "first instance," in Walter Muir Whitehill's words, "of dumping the tops of hills into coves," and an expedient way of enlarging the small peninsula upon which Boston had been founded that was to become a habit in the nineteenth century. Since this more extensive development called for more than a narrow range of houses facing the Common, Bulfinch imagined here great free-standing town houses. Several survive, but they are easily overlooked because they have usually been subsequently connected to each other (Figures 10, 11). This fate befell the Otis House on Beacon Street, for example, the original appearance of which is clear in Figure 10. That Bulfinch did not foresee its later connection by another house to the nearby Sears House is evident when one notes the ample bay of the Otis House's oval salon, which, in fact, had to be embedded into the connecting house when that

was built. The bay is still there today to document Whitehill's observation that "as we admire the red brick houses around Beacon Hill today, it is well to remember that to Bulfinch, and those of his contemporaries who survived into the 1840's and '50's, these same houses connoted horrid crowding. . . . This was, alas, the penalty of a growing population."

What happened is easily understood. As land became scarcer on the small peninsula, land values increased so alarmingly that no sensible homeowner could for long justify the financial loss involved in keeping his garden. The result has proved charming to our eyes for some time. But it is only on Mount Vernon Street, above Louisburg Square, that Bulfinch's design concept survives — in the splendid house at 85 Mount Vernon, the second that Bulfinch erected for Harrison Gray Otis (Figure 12). Built close by the sidewalk, the carriageway on its eastern flank, its haughty facade of brick and pilaster is felt all the more keenly for its garden setting. And the design concept one sees here, though short-lived on Beacon Hill in the increasingly crowded early nineteenth-century city, was to prove as enduring a memory for Bostonians as that of the Tontine Crescent.

The reader may have been puzzled to observe that Bulfinch built two houses in Boston for Otis. Actually, he built three, for this famous Federalist merchant and sometime congressman and mayor of Boston sought so insistently for more amplitude and greater state that he sold his first Bulfinch house on Cambridge Street, only to sell after a while his second on Mount Vernon Street in favor of the third house, which Bulfinch built for him in 1805–1808 facing Boston Common. (A fourth house, Oakley, also by Bulfinch, was built by Otis as a country seat in Watertown.) Nor was Otis's elegance untypical of the Federalist era. It

9

may well be thought to symbolize as much as crescent, theater, and cathedral the new character of Bulfinch's Boston.

This last Otis house is a culmination in more than one sense of Bulfinch's work, for despite the splendid new Neoclassical vistas he introduced into Boston, some scholars have felt that Bulfinch's designs were really rather unimaginative. Yet Pierson's analysis of the third Otis House is eloquent:

In this superb building all ornamental pretense is stripped away. . . . In actual measurement the façade forms a simple rectangle only slightly wider than it is high. As seen from the street, however, it gives the appearance of being tall in proportion. Bulfinch has created this impression through subtle and expressive means. By spacing the windows more closely vertically than horizontally he has drawn them into five rising tiers. Then he has accelerated this vertical movement by varying the shapes of the windows at the different floor levels. Those in the basement are conventional classical rectangles. On the second — in this case, the principal — floor, however, they are full-length and triple-hung so that in proportion they are very tall and narrow. Those on the third floor are shorter by one sash but still tall; at the top they are conventional rectangles again, identical to those in the basement. The result is a swelling graded sequence from small to large to medium to small which tapers off toward the top. This is the primary rhythm of the façade. But a second rhythm is also found in the vertical spacing of the windows. The closest together are those in the basement and on the second floor, those farthest apart are on the second and third floors. The medium spacing is between the third and fourth floors. Together these two changing sequences form an interlocking gradation both in size and interval which not only increases the sense of verticality but does so with the same qualities of rhythmic grace that are experienced in the controlled curvatures of an oval.

"The shape and location of the windows *are* the design," declares Pierson, who saw in the subtlety and buoyancy of this facade a mature masterpiece: "one of the first creative outbursts by a native architect in American history."

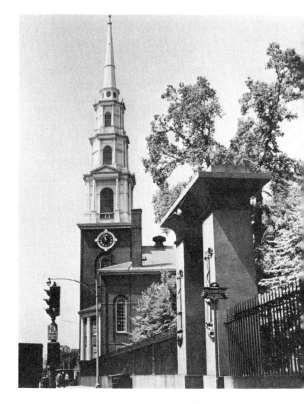

FIGURE 13. Peter Banner. Park Street Church, 1809. The steeple is a splendid example of how Classicists reinterpreted an essentially Gothic form. Solomon Willard's Egyptian Revival gateway to the Old Granary Burying Ground is in the foreground.

Bulfinch inspired a good deal of work in his characteristic style by others. Chief among these was Asher Benjamin, an architect who practiced in Boston after 1803 and is perhaps most noted for his pattern book of 1797, *The Country Builder's Assistant,* the first architectural book both written and published in this country. Among his best-known Boston buildings are the Charles Street Meeting House of 1807 and the Old West Church of 1806. Two other architects of this period who cannot be overlooked are Peter Banner, whose Park Street Church (Figure 13) possesses undeniably the most beautiful spire of its type in Boston, and Samuel McIntire, the famous Salem designer, who so far as is known got no closer to Boston than Waltham, where he designed in 1793 the Lyman House, but whose work is so distinguished that no Bostonian could omit mention of it in any survey, however brief, of this period. Also in Waltham, an environ of Boston then popular for country residences, is Gore Place. Built by an unknown architect in 1805, it is among the finest New England houses of its period. Finally, one cannot forget the housewrights who built in Bulfinch's style so much, for example, of Chestnut Street on Beacon Hill between 1800 and 1830; this street possesses an outstanding parade of fanlights.

Yet nothing can rob Bulfinch of his dominance during this period. Boston was surely his singular achievement. It is impossible not to compare Bulfinch with Wren: what the master did for London in the late seventeenth century, Bulfinch in the early nineteenth century did for Boston. In Joseph Hudnut's words, Bulfinch found Boston "a bewilderment of narrow vistas and left it with a window upon the world."

A SEVERE granite grandeur had by 1815 begun here and there to vary the urbane red-brick Federal streetscapes Bulfinch had created — in much the same way that the wooden Medieval town of the seventeenth century had been in the eighteenth century interrupted by increasing numbers of Georgian spires. But one easily forgets that the bricks of the Tontine Crescent were painted gray — as for that matter those of the State House may have been. Bulfinch probably used stone as little as he did because it was not easily available and consequently very costly; when the Middlesex Canal of 1803 made Chelmsford granite accessible, Bulfinch began at once to use it in his monumental work.

His Suffolk County Court House of 1810–1812 was of ashlar construction. The first of its kind in Boston, it pointed toward the work of Bulfinch's disciples. This was true as well of Bulfinch's last Boston work, the magnificent Chelmsford granite building of 1818–1821 that bears his name at the Massachusetts General Hospital. But it was Alexander Parris, Bulfinch's superintendent on the hospital job, who was to impress upon Boston the latter phase of Neoclassicism to which the Federal genre gave way in the 1820s — the Greek Revival.

The transition from the Federal to the Greek Revival is perhaps best seen in two houses almost certainly by Parris on Beacon Street, now the Women's City Club (Figure 16). Talbot Hamlin has pointed out that at the City Club the Adamesque delicacy of Federal detail has almost completely disappeared in favor of stolid Greek forms. "Of actual Greek detail," he noted, "there is but little . . . but of prophetic hints of its spirit — of its concentrated richness contrasted with broad simplicity, of its feeling for large scale . . . there is a great deal." These houses, Hamlin observed, "can scarcely yet be called Greek Revival, but they show the style in gestation."

A natural enough repercussion of such widely read books as James Stuart and Nicholas Revett's *The Antiquities of Athens,* which brought more and more forcefully to the attention of Europeans and then Americans in the early nineteenth century the grandeur of the Greek architecture that lay behind the Roman Classical achievement, the Greek Revival was also acceptable to Bostonians for other reasons. Their sympathy (though, significantly, in Lord Byron's wake) for the Greeks in their war of independence was only to be expected. Though the War of 1812 had not been at all popular in Boston, the way Americans generally identified with the Greek war of independence may also be seen as

Federal and Greek Revival Design.
FIGURE 14. Charles Bulfinch. 9 Park Street, Beacon Hill, 1803–1804. Detail of doorway. The house is extant but altered.
FIGURE 15. Edward Shaw. 59 Mount Vernon Street, Beacon Hill, 1837. Detail of doorway.
FIGURE 16. Attributed to Alexander Parris. 39–40 Beacon Street, Beacon Hill, 1818, now the Women's City Club. The sumptuous early nineteenth-century interiors of both houses are intact but a fourth floor was added in 1888 by Hartwell and Richardson.

something of an attempt at the long delayed cultural declaration of independence: the Greek fashion was an architecture, as Professor Pierson has suggested, that attempted to reflect the sense of national identity for which Emerson argued in 1837 in his "American Scholar." On the other hand, one wit has opined that the Greek Revival really succeeded because it was egalitarian enough for the Jacksonians and elegant enough for the Federalists, which is probably very close to the truth of the matter in Boston. Walter Kilham's suggestion was even more to the point: "all building committees," he observed, "like columns."

This last remark strikes me particularly because in 1822 Boston had actually become a city, abandoning the town meeting form of government that was scarcely able any longer to bear the burden of shaping its growth. Slowed before the revolution, that growth had begun again in the 1800s, and evidences of it were everywhere. Quite aside from the extensive filling of this period, it was at this time that Boston first availed itself of another device that in the end would increase its size vastly more than land-fill operations; in 1804 Boston annexed the part of the neighboring mainland town of Dorchester that is today South Boston. Meanwhile, bridges flung out more and more routes into neighboring areas (including South Boston, Cambridge, and Charlestown) that it took no prophet to predict would one day also be annexed in one way or another to the capital city. By the 1830s railroads too had begun to open new transportation corridors in and out of the city. Boston was booming; and short of a fire nothing so stimulates architecture.

How revolutionary the new Greek fashion could be can still be keenly felt by anyone who has ever noticed amid the reticent brick facades of Beacon Street the stark white swell-front of the

Sears House at 42, designed by Parris in 1819 (Figures 10, 11). One need also only compare Bulfinch's lovely Federal doorway at the nearby Amory House of 1803–1804, with its wealth of serpentine elegance (Figure 14), with the massive Greek Revival post and lintel doorway of 59 Mount Vernon Street (Figure 15) to see the difference between the two modes. The popularity of the Greek style derived as well, however, from the fact that it was more often easily assimilated into the Federal red-brick residential streetscape. The Greek forms, more massive and substantial and more rectangular than curvilinear in detail, were organized in much the same way as the lighter Federal elements had been, as is evident all over Beacon Hill, where Federal and Greek houses keep very sympathetic company.

But the radical new quality heralded by the sheer granite of the Sears House found its opportunity easily enough in monumental architecture. In 1819, Parris introduced into Boston at St. Paul's Church the most distinctive characteristic of the monumental Greek mode, the full-scale temple front. Five years after St. Paul's, Parris designed the new Quincy Market development, the focus of which is the central market building (Figure 17). The great Greek Revival landmark at the height of that style in Boston, nothing like it had ever been seen in the city before. There had been larger and longer buildings, but the gleaming white granite grandeur of the central market building, which stretches for 535 feet from one great columned portico to the other, was unprecedented in Boston. The project involved the destruction of many older buildings, the filling in of several docks, and the creation of virtually a whole new quarter where long rows of uniform granite buildings yielded a market area of unusual distinction. And within a decade even the market was to be somewhat eclipsed by the

great Boston Custom House (Figure 18), designed by Ammi B. Young.

But if the Greek Revival was thus able to shape both the grandeur appropriate to the city's growing commerce and to assimilate itself more often than not unobtrusively with the red-brick residential streetscape, it also spawned in Boston a radically new kind of architecture that is perhaps best called "architectural construction." This is characterized by the use of granite monoliths in a trabeated or post and lintel fashion; in other words, instead of blocks of granite laid up for perhaps five or more courses on either side of a window, for example, one great monolithic granite post on each side of the window supports a monolithic lintel; thus this use of granite has been called skeleton stone construction (Figure 19). The finest surviving examples today are the two market buildings (1824–1826) by Parris that flank the central market, but the most recent scholarship suggests that monolithic

granite was used in 1810 in Uriah Cotting's Boston Custom House and six years later in his Cornhill business blocks, neither of which are extant. In fact, the first such use of this technique may have been by Bulfinch himself — in 1814–1815 at his Massachusetts Fire and Marine Insurance Building and his Manufacturers and Mechanics Bank, both of which have also been destroyed.

This monolithic granite architecture is also characteristic of the work of the two other architects who importantly influenced Boston at this time — Isaiah Rogers and Solomon Willard. Rogers trained in Willard's office, and once on his own he designed a number of notable Greek Revival buildings in Boston, including in 1842 the Merchant Exchange, the Tremont Theatre (1827), and the Brazer's Building (see Figure 206), where his granite construction was sufficiently innovative for us to discuss it more fully in Chapter 8, under late nineteenth- and early twentieth-century

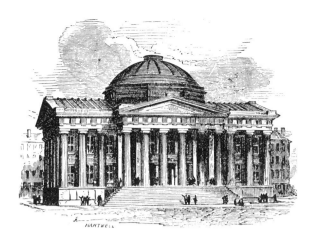

Greek Revival Boston.
FIGURE 17. Alexander Parris. Quincy Market Development, 1824–
1826. Faneuil Hall (1740–1742), as enlarged by Bulfinch in 1805–
1806, can be seen behind the central market.
FIGURE 18. Ammi B. Young. Boston Custom House, 1837.
FIGURE 19. Post and lintel granite construction at Parris's
South Market.

"Modernism." Willard, who like Parris was largely self-taught, worked on several of Parris's buildings: he carved the decorative panels of the Sears House, for example, and the capitals of St. Paul's Church. And it was Willard who more than perhaps any other Boston architect at this time founded his design on monolithic granite by developing explicitly the fondness for Egyptian forms that seems to us today so inexplicable a part of what is supposed to have been, after all, a Greek revival.

Actually, these Egyptian forms are readily explainable. They reflect a persistent stylistic undercurrent throughout the nineteenth century; so much so that there is even a mid-nineteenth-century Second Empire house at 57 Hancock Street on Beacon Hill that rejoices in an Egyptian mansard roof unique in Boston and possibly in America. The fascination with things Egyptian, inspired by the widely publicized archaeological publications that resulted from Napoleon's otherwise rather fruitless adventures in Egypt in 1798, was sustained by the instinctive response of so many to the peculiar quality that things Egyptian seem to invoke in relation to the dead. Thus the great gate of Mount Auburn Cemetery of 1842 by Jacob Bigelow (a replica in stone of an 1832 gate) and Willard's own gate at the Old Granary Burying Ground both exhibit the flaring cavetto cornice on flanking pylons that is perhaps the most characteristic form of American Egyptian Revival architecture (see Figure 13). Willard also executed a notable series of obelisks in Boston during this period: the Franklin monument in the Old Granary Burying Ground of 1827; the Harvard Memorial of 1838, and the immense Bunker Hill Monument of 1825–1843, both in Charlestown. This last, in particular, illustrates the almost superhuman scale and relentless paucity of ornament that is even more pronounced in the Egyptian fashion than in the Greek style.

It is this factor that explains why both seem so similar for all their stylistic differences: in each mode the inherent character of monolithic granite dominated, and this became more and more characteristic of Boston architecture after 1820. In the Bunker Hill Monument the granite courses are two feet seven inches high; at Mount Auburn Cemetery the cornice of the gateway is a twenty-two-foot-long granite monolith; in the retaining wall of the Old Granary Burying Ground there is one piece of granite thirty-three feet long; while the twenty-two columns of the Boston Custom House weigh forty-two tons each, and had consequently to be dragged to the site by no fewer than twelve teams of horses and sixty-five yokes of oxen. Willard, in fact, was so concerned with what might be called construction rather than design that it seems clear he made little distinction: he purchased a quarry in Quincy and he himself supplied the granite used in Young's Custom House. "He was," Kilham notes, "exhilarated by the difficulties of the current fashion which decreed the use of enormous monolithic columns, and spent much thought in devising improved machinery for their handling and transportation." Such was Boston's passion for monolithic granite that it led to what has been called the first American railroad, when Gridley Bryant, the builder of the Bunker Hill Monument, built a kind of tramway to enable him to move huge slabs of granite from his Quincy quarry.

This disinclination to separate design and construction, this insistence on the unity of the two (which appears to have been widespread throughout the east at this time), is reflected as well in the slight differentiation then made between the architect and the engineer. A number of important contemporary works were as much engineering as architecture, including such extant landmarks as the

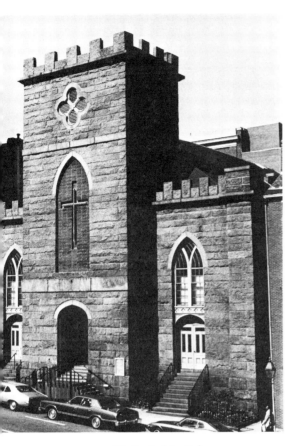

FIGURE 20. Attributed to Solomon Willard. Bowdoin Street Congregational Church, now the Mission Church of St. John the Evangelist, ca. 1831–1833.

great five-sided granite fortress with its massive projecting bastions that was built on Castle Island in South Boston in 1833 by the engineer Sylvanus Thayer, who also was responsible for Fort Warren (1834–1863) on George's Island. Loammi Baldwin's Charlestown Navy Yard dry dock (1827–1833) is another case in point. It is thus often difficult to label people during this period. Baldwin was primarily an engineer; he is often called, in fact, "the father of civil engineering in America." But though at the Charlestown Navy Yard Baldwin worked on the dry dock with Parris, Baldwin himself designed, apparently on his own, Holworthy Hall at Harvard in 1811. Even Parris was listed in the 1818 Boston di-

rectory as both "architect and engineer"; and after having served as Baldwin's assistant he became chief civil engineer of the Navy Yard at Charlestown, where he was responsible for a number of buildings, including the famous Ropewalk (1834–1836), a two-story granite building over one-quarter mile long, which began operation in 1838 and was closed only in 1970. So persuasive a factor was granite construction at this time that during the 1830s the inherent character of this material dominated the new vogue that was beginning to challenge the dominance of the Greek Revival — Gothic.

It is certainly true that if one had chosen to tour Greek Revival Boston in 1840, walking, for example, from the Custom House to the Quincy Market and up past the Merchant Exchange to the Tremont Theatre and down Tremont Street past the Tremont Hotel to St. Paul's Church, one would have seen a government building, a market, a merchant exchange, a theater, a hotel, and a church where the diverse functions of each had been expressed by columned Greek porticos. At its height the Greek Revival was a kind of universal style. And if it seems boring, that is perhaps why the Greek fashion was waning by the 1830s. In its place there developed a taste for Gothic, essayed by Solomon Willard, for example, at his Bowdoin Street Congregational Church (now the Mission Church of St. John the Evangelist; Figure 20).

That style was not new to Boston; the Gothic mode, when not fashionable, seems merely to go underground. Even Bulfinch had attempted a Gothic church, the no longer extant Federal Street Church of 1809, and it is also possible that St. Augustine's Chapel (1819), still extant in South Boston, is by Bulfinch. But early nineteenth-century American Gothic, in its way as literary a taste in its allegiance to Horace Walpole and Sir Walter Scott as was the Greek Revival in its admiration for Lord Byron, did not seek its inspiration in Boston's own seventeenth-century folk Gothic, but in the full-fledged civic and ecclesiastical Gothic of the Middle Ages. And as Gothic principles were scarcely understood at all, these early and distinctly naive Gothic buildings took on the coloration of the Greek Revival as they had of the Federal mode in Bulfinch's day. Thus the Federal Street Church and St. Augustine's seem more Federal than Gothic in feeling; in the same way Willard's Bowdoin Street Church, particularly, seems for all its battlements to possess a peculiarly stolid and massy feeling more akin to the Greek Revival than to Gothic. This was also true of the most exuberant of the Gothic structures that became so fashionable when the public had tired of temple fronts: George M. Dexter's Fitchburg Railway Station of 1847 (near where North Station now stands); Gridley J. Fox Bryant's SS Peter and Paul in South Boston (1845–1853); and even Jacob Bigelow's fantastic chapel at Mount Auburn Cemetery — an 1858 replica of an 1843 building — seem to possess fundamental characteristics that proceed, if not from the Greek Revival, not from Gothic either. Rather, these characteristics proceed from the one thing all these buildings, Greek, Egyptian, and Gothic, have in common: granite itself, whether it built pediments, pylons, or battlements, had really become Boston's dominant style by the 1840s.

The results, insofar as Gothic was concerned, were not happy. Granite Gothic, stolid and ponderous, is not comparable with its English parish church models in the way that Bulfinch's work, for instance, is comparable with Adam's. But that simply reflects the fact that no Neogothicist emerged in Boston in the 1830s or forties whose skill equaled Bulfinch's as a Neoclassicist. In the 1850s such a man would appear — Richard Upjohn. But it is significant that just as Bulfinch's work has often been called "American Adam," scholars have also increasingly concluded that Boston's granite architecture — in whatever "style" — is, in fact, one style — the Boston Granite Style. Sometimes happily, sometimes not, whether through genius, accident, or naiveté, Boston architects had shown by the 1840s that they would shape the common, inherited tradition of Western architecture to their own purposes. This adaptive tradition (evident, for instance, in the way in which Wren reinterpreted the Gothic spire classically) had long characterized Western architecture and it was the background for the architecture of the next hundred years in Boston.

2

THE GREAT TRADITIONS

THE "AMERICAN ATHENS," the epithet that has frequently been applied to Boston as her culture began to mature in the mid-nineteenth century, is not, as one might think, closely related to the Greek style. It is true that Louisburg Square, the famous Greek Revival enclave on Beacon Hill, was built up finally in the 1840s and that in 1850 the square's proprietors erected there a statue (by whom nobody knows) of Aristides the Just, the Athenian statesman and general (Figure 21). But it was for the most part only in residential design that the Greek vogue lingered into the forties. Moreover, the American Athens has seemed to most scholars much more literary and philosophical in essence than architectural or even artistic. Yet whether one looks as did Morison toward the clipper ships being built in East Boston or as would a medical historian to the epochal demonstration of anesthesia at the Massachusetts General Hospital in 1846 or as did Charles Dickens toward such pioneering institutions as the Perkins Institution for the Blind, which began operating in 1832, it is increasingly evident that Emerson, Thoreau, and Hawthorne were but the standard-bearers of a community whose cultural horizons were beginning to broaden in every respect at the beginning of its third century of existence. And architecture in Boston in the 1840s and early fifties — on the eve of the Back Bay — only *seems* less vital. In reality this transitional period heralded the ar-chitecture of the late nineteenth century that is now so much admired.

Since Boston's settlement, architectural design had more or less amounted to keeping up with the unfolding Renaissance. Seventeenth-century buildings, whether one looks at the steep gables of town houses like the Paul Revere House (Figure 5) or at rambling "lean-to" country houses like the Fairbanks House in Dedham (Figure 76), were fundamentally a rude, wilderness reflection of English vernacular Gothic forms: "Folk Gothic," in John Coolidge's words, "survived into the age of Bernini." We often misunderstand this because the Puritans naturally avoided *the* Gothic building type — the church — and built, instead, meetinghouses. (In Anglican Virginia, on the other hand, a recognizably Gothic parish church, begun ca. 1632, survives to this day.) Somewhat belatedly, because Gothic lingered longer in England than anywhere else in Europe, Boston in the eighteenth century gradually abandoned the Medieval tradition: early Georgian design, the High Georgian mode of the mid- and late eighteenth century, and the Neoclassicism of the Federal and Greek periods had in each case reflected the step-by-step evolution from Gothic through the various stages of the Renaissance attempt to repossess the glories of ancient Roman and then of ancient Greek architecture. There was, certainly, a distinct time lag as the Renaissance filtered through in each stage to England and then to America.

FIGURE 21. Louisburg Square, Beacon Hill, 1826–1844.

But by the 1840s, Boston's built environment, an accumulation by then of two hundred and more years, reflected clearly the nature and term of the city's history; it possessed a little folk Gothic and a great deal of English Renaissance architecture, provincial, to be sure, but increasingly distinctive. In the 1840s, however, Boston would begin the process of amassing a great number of architectural forms — early Renaissance palazzos, for instance, and a huge Gothic cathedral — that the New World was too new to have ever possessed.

One might explain this phenomenon by asserting that the Renaissance had by the middle of the nineteenth century exhausted its ancient sources. One need not hazard that controversial assertion, however; it is only necessary to understand that European and American architects began to seek their inspiration at this time not in antiquity, but in the Renaissance itself, and even in the Gothic architecture it had banished. Thus though the emerging Italianate vogue of the forties in America came to this country by way of England, Italianate design was fundamentally a revival in the mid-nineteenth century of the Italian Renaissance forms that had in the fifteenth century attempted to revive ancient Roman forms. At first glance this seems scarcely very sensible. But the key to understanding all of this is to be found in observations long overlooked in this connection, such as Fiske Kimball's, that Renaissance forms "were no more literal imitations of [ancient Roman forms] than the Roman forms themselves had been imitations of Greek forms." As Kimball pointed out: "partly because of medieval survivals, partly because of inadequate knowledge of antiquity, partly even in criticism of the antique, the architects of the Renaissance modified the [ancient Classical] forms so that they are unmistakably theirs." This adaptive tradition, which as we have seen also naturally marked Boston's architecture in the seventeenth and eighteenth centuries, explains why nineteenth-century architects who had come to admire the earliest Renaissance architecture for its own unique architectural character attempted to revive those early Renaissance forms in the Italianate style. Bostonians, conscious that they were no less the heirs of Western culture because they lived on its periphery, claimed all these forms of *their* ancestors as logically as they claimed the common law, for example, or the Christian religion; thus they reached back at mid-century to add to Boston's built environment architectural forms its late settlement had denied it.

However confusing, chronologically, Italianate design may appear, its success was immediate and its influence pervasive. This is not, however, reflected in present-day Boston because a great number of important Italianate buildings have been destroyed. A particular loss was the Boston Museum (Figure 22). One of several new playhouses of the 1840s (called a museum to allay "Puritan" sensibilities), it was designed by Hammatt and Joseph Billings in 1846. Its facade, 164 feet long with rows of gas globes glowing above its iron balconies, must have been the most felicitous sight in Boston. Another Italianate building of importance that has not survived was the Boston Public Library (Figure 23). Designed by C. F. Kirby in 1858, it stood on

Boylston Street where the Colonial Theatre now is, and of all these buildings it possessed perhaps the most characteristic Italianate features: not only a heavy console-supported balcony and balustrade, a projecting and deeply overhanging cornice, corner quoining, and an overall heavy sculptural and arcaded feeling, but also the round arched windows with "Medieval survival" tracery so typical of the early Renaissance. Fortunately, one of the city's earliest and handsomest Italian palazzos has survived — the brownstone Boston Athenaeum (Figure 24), designed by Edward Clarke Cabot, who secured this important commission in rather an interesting way. As Walter Kilham pointed out, the plot to be used was sharply indented at the southeast corner by a triangular projection of the Granary Burying Ground, containing some graves that could not be disturbed. "The other competitors followed the angular indentation, which caused awkward projections into the interior all the way up through the building. [But] Cabot . . . simply carried the rear wall straight across making a segmental arched niche in the basement to accommodate the graves."

Cabot seems also to have been the principal designer in 1854 of the Boston Theatre on Washington Street (Figure 25). A huge and palatial 3000-seat opera house, it was more impressive than the splendid new 2000-seat Music Hall built from the designs of Snell and Gregerson near the corner of Tremont and Winter streets two years earlier. The importance of both halls is evident in Mark A. DeWolfe Howe's remark that it would not thereafter be necessary "to ask a visiting Jenny Lind to sing in the Fitchburg Railroad Station," for both these and the other buildings of the Italianate mid-century we have been discussing expressed architecturally an overall and increasingly cosmopolitan cultural growth at this time — in the performing and vi-

Three mid-nineteenth-century Italianate landmarks.
FIGURE 22. Hammatt and Joseph Billings. Boston Museum, a
playhouse completed in 1846 and now demolished.
FIGURE 23. C. F. Kirby. Boston Public Library, 1858. Demolished.
FIGURE 24. Edward Clarke Cabot. Architect's elevation of the
principal facade of the Boston Athenaeum, completed in 1849. It
is derived from Palladio's Palazzo da Porta Festa in Vicenza.

FIGURE 25. Edward and James Cabot and Jonathan Preston, from
preliminary plans by André Noury. Boston Theatre, 1854, one of
the three great American opera houses of the mid-nineteenth century.
Demolished, although the Keith Memorial Theatre (now the Savoy)
stands in part upon the Boston Theatre's foundations and is almost
identical in overall plan.

sual arts as well as in literature and
thought generally. It was at the Boston
Theatre, for instance, in 1854, that Boston first heard Beethoven's *Fidelio,* three
years before the founding of *The Atlantic
Monthly,* the more often cited symbol of
this lively age. The new Athenaeum also
possessed a sculpture gallery as well as a
painting gallery; the first such extensive
facilities in Boston, they were the seeds
for the Museum of Fine Arts of some
years later. The Boston Public Library
was the first free municipal public library in the world. Like Bulfinch's ensemble of crescent, theater, and cathedral of 1794–1803, Boston's palatial new
mid-nineteenth-century parade of libraries, playhouses, galleries and, perhaps most of all, the immense new
opera house shows how broadly based
was her cultural growth. Nor were the
architectural settings worthy only in
size: the nineteenth-century playwright
Dion Boucicault, for example, thought
the Boston Theatre "beyond question the
finest theatre in the world."

Another reflection of this widespread
growth in all the arts and of its increas-

Re-creation in the Classical tradition.
FIGURE 26. Patrick Keeley and/or Arthur Gilman.
Church of the Immaculate Conception, South
End, 1858. The interior is probably Gilman's
work; the exterior is usually attributed to Keeley,
perhaps in collaboration with Gilman.
FIGURE 27. Possibly by Daniel Badger. McLauthlin Elevator Building, 120 Fulton Street, ca.
1863–1869.

ingly cosmopolitan character was lavish ceremonial and musical splendor, from the beginning a notable feature of the Roman Catholic Church of the Immaculate Conception built in the South End in 1858 (Figure 26). This church is also a splendid example of how the best mid-century American architects translated the Classical tradition into the idiom of their own time just as surely as had the Renaissance architects. The building's design has been attributed to Patrick C. Keeley, a New York designer, and the leading architect in the Roman Catholic tradition in this country in the last half of the nineteenth century. Better known as a Gothicist (one of his earliest churches in the Boston area, St. Rose of Lima in Chelsea, built in 1860–1866, is Gothic), Keeley also designed several notable churches in the Classical tradition, but it is likely that he collaborated on the design of the Immaculate Conception with a well-known Boston architect of the time, Arthur Gilman, to whom the church has also been solely attributed. It is a remarkable building. One sees the "Medieval survival" typical of Italianate design in the tall windows to either side of the central pavilion of the facade and also in the Palladian window of the central pavilion. Similarly, the pavilion is quoined, though the facade itself is adorned at its corners with pilasters. The architect also used both dressed and rough-cut granite on the exterior of this distinguished ensemble of so many historical forms that nonetheless cohere beautifully in one of the handsomest buildings in Boston.

How contemporary this seemingly rather antique Classicism could be in the mid-nineteenth century is particularly evident in the fact that the Italianate vogue lent itself with uncanny distinction to a quite new structural development: the cast-iron facade. These facades were hung in prefabricated sections on the fronts of commercial buildings whose principal source of light (as in the Venetian palaces) was the street (in Venice, the canal). Stylistically appropriate in that this style provided for as many and as large windows as possible, the arcaded Italianate front also suited exactly the requirements of the new structural technique: prefabrication of a number of identical units. This technique was pioneered in New York City but Boston possesses several fine examples: the McLauthlin Building (Figure 27) at 120 Fulton Street is perhaps the handsomest, though the Richards Building of 1867 at 110–116 State Street is more representative of Italianate cast-iron work, even though it has been somewhat altered.

This mid-century "antique" Classicism also took on new life in Boston's environs, and to take the full measure of both the Italianate and Gothic modes one must have recourse to what were by 1850 "bedroom suburbs." It will thus serve more than one purpose to follow the example of Bostonians in the 1850s and enlarge our purview.

W OOD WAS THEN as now the usual residential building material in Boston's suburbs. Although in the Greek Revival period the full-scale temple front was not beyond the carpenter-builder's ability (a quite splendid house of this type, built about 1840, survives today at 2 Dane Street in Jamaica Plain), the suburban carpenter-builder usually simply applied Greek rather than Federal detail after about 1820 to the symmetrical, clapboarded, and detached-house type that had remained virtually unchanged since the early Georgian period. But the Yankee carpenter, in rather an inspired way, was quick to see that by raising somewhat the pitch of the roof and by turning the narrower gable end of such a house to the street he could achieve a kind of temple front that, proceeding directly

Mid-century Italianate and Gothic forms in suburban Boston ca. 1850.
FIGURE 28. 9 Myrtle Street, Jamaica Plain.
FIGURE 29. 9 Brewer Street, Jamaica Plain.

from the conventional gable and corner-boards (rendered as pediments and pilasters), would seem the most natural thing in the world. Such ingenuity, born of trying to reflect in wood a by then essentially masonry style, carried over as well into the carpenter-builder's Italianate work, and was in turn stimulated by the fact that in the suburbs, where freestanding houses and ample lots were still possible and consequently allowed more freedom of maneuver, the transition from the Greek Revival to the Italianate vogue led to a "breaking up" of the traditional symmetrical house.

One can see the effect of this "breaking up" into a more picturesque and broken silhouette at 8 and 9 Myrtle Street in Jamaica Plain where stand Boston's most dramatic Italianate villas (Figure 28). Here, in wood, are many of the conventional Italianate characteristics we saw in brownstone at the Boston Public Library on Boylston Street — paired roundhead windows, heavy, protruding balconies, and a deep, overhanging cornice, significantly not carried across the gable to at-

tempt any form of pediment. This towered, picturesque, suburban Italianate is quite different, however, from that of the rigidly symmetrical boxlike library, and the difference derives not only from the way these asymmetrical houses are massed. It proceeds as well from the character of the fanciful jigsawed wooden brackets that support the cornice and are so keenly felt as a part of the overall design that such houses are often called "Italianate-Bracketed." The Myrtle Street houses show how the carpenter ingeniously applied his jigsaw to the problem of approximating in wood the early Renaissance cut-stone detail of buildings like the old Public Library. Near 8 and 9 Myrtle Street, at 9 Brewer Street (Figure 29), is another asymmetrical house where the picturesqueness of the massing is also equaled by lively wooden detail, but where the jigsaw yielded, not Italianate brackets, but bargeboards and drip moldings; for 9 Brewer Street, built at about the same time as the Myrtle Street Italianate houses, is Gothic. Or, rather, *Gothick*. In this case the "k" added to the word Gothic is the equivalent of adding "Bracketed" to Italianate: both acknowledge the originality as well as the folk quality of the Yankee builder.

Mid-century Gothick cottages closely paralleled the development of the Italianate villa. The Gothick Frederick Sears House of the 1840s or fifties at 24 Cottage Farm Road in Brookline resembles as much as the Myrtle Street Italianate houses those perspectives that appeared in the widely read books of the 1840s and fifties by Alexander J. Downing, the landscape designer and architect who was the great champion of the picturesque at mid-century. In fact, both the Italianate and Gothick modes reflect the beginning of the Victorian search for the picturesque as well as illustrating how ingeniously the Yankee builder endowed both modes (as surely as he had the Greek Revival style) with a new and distinctive character.

The chief Gothic vehicle for the picturesque in the 1850s and sixties was, however, a more sophisticated mid-century American adaption of European forms where both picturesqueness of mass and the use of local material yielded a far more important building type — the Gothic village church — that was becoming increasingly at this time the centerpiece (along with the railroad station!) of the picturesque suburbs. Longwood, in Brookline, was one of the most famous such suburban areas, because it was socially exclusive and laid out and built up according to an overall plan developed by a prominent Bostonian; the same David Sears, in fact, whose Boston town house by Parris we have already discussed. Typically, the railroad station came first. But in 1860–1862, Sears built Christ Church, Brookline, and it is significant that it was modeled by Arthur Gilman after St. Peter's Church, Colchester, England, the Searses' ancestral home — evidence of the way in which Bostonians justified reviving styles that,

while never known in their fullness in the New World, were nonetheless perceived as a part of a cultural heritage common to both Americans and Europeans.

One of the earliest and perhaps the most important of the first generation of picturesque village churches in the Boston area is also in Brookline — St. Paul's Church (Figure 30). It was designed by Richard Upjohn, an English Gothicist who settled in Boston in 1834 and studied for the next five years in Alexander Parris's office. When his close friend the rector of Trinity Church in Boston became rector of Trinity Church in New York City, Upjohn moved there in 1839 to design for that parish perhaps his masterpiece. Yet St. Paul's has, I think, rightly been called by the architect's biographer the "most attractive country church" by Upjohn, who was by 1850 the preeminent Gothicist in America and a leading figure in the High Church Anglican ecclesiological movement that stimulated the Gothic Revival in Augustus Pugin's wake. Like the L-shaped Italianate-Bracketed villa and its companion, the Gothick cottage, St. Paul's was decisively asymmetrical; rather than continuing the axis of the nave, Upjohn's tower stands off center.

One also sees at St. Paul's a distinctive quality that arises from the fact that in the same way that the carpenter-builder used wood in lieu of cut-stone detail on his Italianate villas and Gothick cottages, Upjohn used what was at hand, and probably for the first time in a church — pudding stone. An unusually warm and richly variegated conglomerate that began to be quarried at mid-century in and around Boston, the character of this stone is as distinctive to the Boston area as Quincy granite and for that reason alone St. Paul's seems to belong in Victorian Boston as much as in Medieval England. And because of Upjohn's sensitivity to this material and

FIGURE 30. Richard Upjohn. St. Paul's Church, Brookline, 1848–1851. Boston's great landmark of the mid-nineteenth-century Gothic Revival in pudding stone. Only the exterior survives today.

FIGURE 31. Gridley J. Fox Bryant's Mercantile Wharf Building, 75–117 Commercial Street, 1857. Mostly of large-scaled and rough-hammered granite ashlar with monolithic granite piers, this has been called the masterpiece of what is known as the Boston Granite Style.

because of his strong, quiet massing and fine proportions, St. Paul's also illustrates vividly that local materials imaginatively used by an architect rather than a carpenter might yield not only a strikingly indigenous but also a distinguished and sophisticated architecture. As Gothic, in fact, St. Paul's is in this sense comparable to the best Italianate work in the city itself — Boston's waterfront warehouses — where in this case local granite in the hands of another skillful architect was shaped in the same decade into an even more indigenous and splendid accomplishment.

It was in 1856–1857 that Gridley J. Fox Bryant, the son of the builder of the Bunker Hill Monument and the most prominent commercial architect in Boston, designed the famous State Street Block opposite the Custom House and the equally splendid Mercantile Wharf Building nearby (Figure 31). Each is characterized by a severe granite grandeur. The State Street Block, alas, survives only in part. But as long ago as 1946 Walter Kilham declared that "if a vote were taken for the best piece of architecture in the city, the State Street Block would get mine." Kilham went on to assert — and not just of the waterfront work, but of most of Boston's mid-century Italianate, including the old Boston Public Library and the Boston Museum — that "it was indigenous, not copied from foreign models, and has more right than any other to be considered as a true American style. It was absolutely functional, and if architects had continued with it a style might have developed which would have been as American as a Red Indian." What striking evidence it is of how well Americans adapted the Italianate style that this "seemingly antique classicism," which with its companion Gothic style heralded a century of revivalism in America, was discussed in a chapter Kilham entitled "Plain American." He ad-

mitted that this vogue was "closely related to the 'Italian Villa' style which set the pace for numerous country and suburban houses." But for Kilham that made no difference. Nor is this the last time we shall hear such a lament for this or that manner which, had it only been continued, might have yielded a vital American style. Such a style, increasingly a preoccupation in the nineteenth century, has proved always illusive. In the face of St. Paul's, the State Street Block, and the Mercantile Wharf Building, however, what is clear is that a vital *American* architecture — in the sense of an American adaption and reinterpretation of *any* style common to the Western tradition — was entirely possible.

The next fifty years more than bore this out. The history of architecture in Boston would yield not only a distinguished school of Gothicists led by Ralph Adams Cram, whose work would be acclaimed as an important continuation of Gothic design, but the granite Italianate work is increasingly seen today as an important hinge in American architectural history. The State Street Block, particularly, is notable for its monolithic granite construction, and this construction derived, as we saw in the last chapter, from Bulfinch's work. And as we will see later (Figure 186), it was an important source for Richardson and through Richardson, for Louis Sullivan. When one realizes how picturesque design would flower in the late nineteenth century in Queen Anne work and that the cast-iron facade to which Italianate design lent itself so well was an important precursor of the curtain-wall skyscraper, one can see how seminal mid-century architecture was. It was also in itself a considerable achievement, not unworthy of the American Athens. Confronted with the grandeur of mass and strength of design of Boston's harborfront granite architecture, Henry-Russell Hitchcock has pronounced these ranges of warehouses "hardly equaled any-where in the world." They were the first of Boston's buildings of which that could have been said.

The Italianate Classicism that emerged in the city in the 1850s and the picturesque Gothic church type of the same decade in the suburbs not only evolved simultaneously, but in the 1860s were increasingly if incongruously seen next door to each other in the city proper, where the effect of the Upjohn church type — informal masses of pudding stone or fieldstone about an off-center broach-spired tower — seems to have banished the stolid and symmetrical Gothick church almost at once. This development was universal. At St. Paul's in Dedham, for example, where Arthur Gilman had designed a symmetrically massed, center-tower church in 1845, the same architect, after the first church burned down, designed in 1857 an equally asymmetrical church similar to St. Paul's in Brookline. Perhaps the widest use made of the Upjohn church type in the Boston area was by Alexander R. Estey, a native of suburban Framingham and the architect in 1864 of St. John's Church in that town, who became a leading church architect in the 1850s and sixties. His earlier churches, like the Prospect Congregational Church in Cambridge (1851), continued the old symmetrical, center-tower church type. But by 1867, when he designed two important churches, the Old Cambridge Baptist Church and the Church of Our Saviour in Brookline, both were variations on the Upjohn church type, which was by then the norm throughout Greater Boston. Notable examples are Ware and Van Brunt's First Church of 1865 in Boston (Figure 48) and their St. John's Chapel at the Episcopal Divinity School in Cambridge (1868); the First Congregational Church, Cambridge, de-

signed as late as 1870 by Abel C. Martin; and the Harvard Congregational Church in Brookline (1873–1875), the work of Edward T. Potter, which illustrates how this mode survived into the High Victorian period in more colorful guise.

The result in the city proper was a startling rupture in the architectural unity that had characterized Boston's streetscapes for well over a century. On the one hand, the Classical tradition remained normative for secular architecture generally. Though Italianate could be either sparse or florid in feeling, Classical work generally remained invariably formal and symmetrical in the city, where the academic tradition proved tenacious; the picturesque massing of the Italianate villa and the Gothick cottage were clearly perceived as essentially suburban; the large double house at 70–72 Mount Vernon Street (1847) attributed to Upjohn possesses as severe, symmetrical, and academic a facade as was imaginable. But the more severe and Classical such secular work, the stronger was the contrast with the picturesque Upjohn church. In the Georgian and Federal periods, the church had simply essayed the universal style on a larger scale; its only distinctive feature, the Medieval spire, had been "classicized" after the manner of Wren. And in the Greek Revival period it would have been hard to differentiate several churches from nearby city halls. Even during the 1830s and forties, when Gothick churches in the heart of the city were common, so also were Classical churches. Moreover, the Gothick of this period was almost invariably stolid and symmetrical (Figure 20). But in the 1850s and sixties (and we simply do not notice the incongruity because we are so used to it) Boston built increasingly Classical and symmetrical blocks of secular buildings invariably interrupted at every other street corner by asymmetrically massed Medieval churches of the village type in pudding

Mid-nineteenth-century development in Charlestown, East Boston, and
South Boston.

FIGURE 32. Patrick Keeley. Church of The Most Holy Redeemer, East
Boston, 1851.

FIGURE 33. Patrick Keeley. St. Francis de Sales Church, Charlestown,
1859. In the foreground is the parochial residence.

FIGURE 34. The Loring House, 787 East Broadway, South Boston, 1864,
and, across the street in the background at 788, the Dana House, 1868.

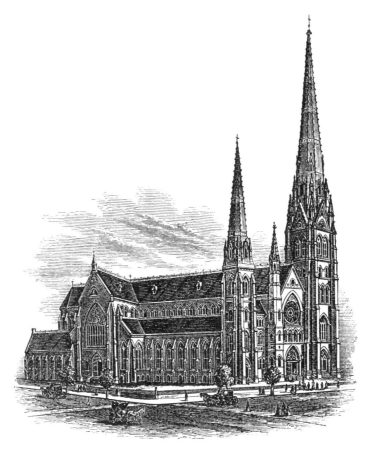

Classical secular architecture punctuated by picturesque Medieval churches was characteristic of the new South End.

FIGURE 35. Patrick Keeley. Cathedral of the Holy Cross, 1865–1875, one of the largest Gothic cathedrals in the world.

FIGURE 36. Columbus Avenue, ca. 1870.

FIGURE 37. Jean Lemoulnier, possibly in association with Gridley J. Fox Bryant. Deacon House, 1846–1848. Demolished. Some interior detail is in the Museum of Fine Arts, Boston.

stone and fieldstone that in such a Classical context were wildly picturesque indeed. Once one thinks of it, this architectural duality emerges as a chief characteristic of the new residential districts that evolved in the city in the 1850s.

The settlement of these areas was undertaken in large measure to counter the movement of so many to the suburbs, which by mid-century was becoming alarming. At first none of the new residential quarters seemed very successful in offsetting this exodus. By the 1850s, Charlestown and South Boston were both connected to Boston by one or more bridges and East Boston by ferry lines, and all three areas (particularly South Boston) offered splendid harbor views from historic old hills that only awaited development. Kilham remarked long ago that why fashionable Boston did not flock at once to "the breezy hills of South Boston with their splendid marine views is one of the unsolved questions in Boston's history. . . . The only answer I can give, is that the Lord in His wisdom saved for His poorer and less fashionable children the beautiful area which their wealthier cousins disdained." Actually, at the summit of these hills, where lovely residential squares with parks were laid out — on Belmont Hill and particularly on Webster Street in East Boston, around Monument Square in Charlestown, and at Thomas Park on Telegraph Hill in South Boston — handsome town houses were built in the 1850s and sixties and many survive today (Figures 34, 231). All three areas were endowed as well in the 1850s and sixties with imposing and picturesque churches. Patrick Keeley designed for the Church of the Most Holy Redeemer in East Boston a Gothic church whose spire is almost 200 feet high (Figure 32). In Charlestown, he designed a similarly lofty stone-towered Gothic church for St. Francis de Sales parish (Figure 33). Still another was erected

from his designs for St. Augustine's parish in South Boston.

The great towered churches, like the hilltop town houses, were quickly surrounded, however, by the extensive manufacturing and harbor-front industries that were naturally attracted to such coastal communities. These had made a sufficient impact by the time all three areas became easily accessible that fashionable residences seemed far less feasible than working-class housing. Thus only such persons of means as had business interests nearby to which they wished to keep close were attracted even to the hilltop enclaves. In South Boston, for example, a still handsome mansion at 788 East Broadway (Figure 34) was owned by Otis Dana, who was certainly a Boston merchant of old family and ample means. But he made his own fortune building up a good deal of South Boston's working-class housing.

Nearby, at 787 East Broadway, Harrison Loring built in 1864 another fine mansion that is still there today. But Loring clearly desired not only a view of the harbor but of his shipyard at City Point. Otherwise, fashionable Boston disdained South Boston, despite the fact that all the older upper-class residential

33

areas developed in the eighteenth and early nineteenth centuries were rapidly deteriorating either because of the expansion of the commercial quarter or because of the need for shelter of the huge numbers of immigrants that were increasingly drawn to Boston in this period. Thus the city had really no choice at mid-century but to widen the still narrow Neck that connected Boston to the mainland and to create on filled land a much-needed fashionable new quarter.

No doubt realizing that this would also make access to the suburbs that much easier, the city fathers made efforts in 1851 to annex the nearest one, Roxbury. These efforts were not successful. But in the meantime the Neck was widened and what is now known as the South End built up steadily in the 1850s and sixties. A brief circuit of this area will disclose that, as in the rest of the city, red-brick Classical residential streets were regularly punctuated with asymmetrical Gothic churches. One of the finest is the Tremont Street Methodist Church (now the Good Hope Baptist Church) designed by Hammatt Billings in 1860–1862, which possesses no fewer than two lofty towers at opposite ends of the building. The most important, however, is the second Holy Cross Cathedral (Figure 35), the plans for which were drawn by Keeley. It was begun in 1867 and the fact that it was not finished until 1875 points up the immensity of the task, for Holy Cross can hold 7000 people, 3500 seated. One hundred seventy feet wide at the transepts, 120 feet high, and 364 feet long, its vast interior encompasses considerably more than an acre and it was with great civic pride that *King's Handbook of Boston* repeated in every edition that Boston's new cathedral was larger than those of Strasbourg, Pisa, Venice, and Salisbury. One is naturally suspicious of Victorian enthusiasms, but Holy Cross is in fact as large as Westminster Abbey. And

though its design is not necessarily superior to the Medieval cathedrals and abbeys it surpasses in size, the fact that Keeley's massive pudding stone exterior remains impressive today even without the planned 200- and 300-foot spires testifies to the basic strength of his design.

When one turns from the cathedral and from the dozen or more smaller churches of its type to the surrounding residential and public architecture of the South End, however, the effect is quite different. The huge Chickering Building (1853) is relentlessly Classical and symmetrical. So too are the houses of the South End (Figure 36). In Chester Square, for example, built up in the 1860s and seventies around a park once much more elegantly garnished, these houses are also substantial and handsome and sometimes even lavishly detailed. But though typical of the mid-century in the Classical context they provided for dozens of Medieval village churches, the houses were not in themselves stylistically progressive for their time; they continued even into the 1860s the by then increasingly old-fashioned Greek Revival swell-front. In overall plan the South End was also conservative. Its best feature was the series of residential squares, modeled after the Tontine Crescent. Worcester Square, in particular, with its gently rounded edges and regular cornice line, is worthy of the comparison. So also is the great sweep of Chester Square, though it lacks the architectural unity of Bulfinch's crescent. But even this feature of the South End plan soon appeared uninspiring in the face of the new architectural fashion that overwhelmed Boston in the early 1860s, the first intimation of which was the outstanding exception to the stylistic conservatism of the South End — the Deacon House (Figure 37).

The work of a French designer, Jean Lemoulnier, probably under Bryant's auspices, this house was built in 1848 quite close to the corner of Washington Street and Massachusetts Avenue. It was not only endowed with remarkably sumptuous interiors — with paintings on walls and ceilings by both Boucher and Fragonard and fittings by Sèvres as well as carved gilt panels from Claude-Nicolas Ledoux's Hôtel Montmorency in Paris, destroyed in 1848 — but it possessed as well the first mansard roof in Boston. (That kind of two-sloped roof, with an almost flat upper slope and a lower one steep enough for windows and often flaring out with a concave curve at the eaves, is named for the two seventeenth-century French architects who popularized it, J. H. and François Mansart.) Yet the pomp of the Deacon House, as of the South End generally, did not long survive. Twenty-three years after its erection the house and its furnishings (some of which may be seen in the Museum of Fine Arts in Boston today) were sold at auction. Indeed, as early as 1863, William Dean Howells's *The Rise of Silas Lapham* portrayed Lapham as having been able to buy "very cheap of a terrified gentleman of good extraction who had discovered too late that the South End was not the thing, and who in the eagerness of his flight to the Back Bay threw in his carpets and shades for almost nothing." Neither fashion nor the mansard style — which by the early 1860s was pretty much the same thing — would flourish in the South End. By then, Boston was flocking instead to the Back Bay.

V ERY slowly in the 1850s and then with a rush after 1860, after more than two hundred years on the periphery of British architectural circles, Boston suddenly surrendered to a passion for things French. The brilliance of the court of Napoleon III exercised, of course, a worldwide influence, as many memoirs of traveling Bostonians in these years testify. And it must be said that the luster of this regime was reflected not only in dress and decor and manners, but more than is perhaps usual in architecture. Paris became under the third Napoleon a kind of universal architectural idol. And of its new buildings none, perhaps, was more admired than the new Louvre of 1852–1857. It directly inspired the Boston City Hall of 1861–1865, with its paired and superimposed columns, rich, sculptural details, and massive, lofty mansard (Figure 38). One of the earliest major Second Empire buildings in America (over which this style swept in the next decade), the City Hall was designed by Gridley J. Fox Bryant, who also designed the now destroyed first Horticultural Hall on Tremont Street in 1865 (Figure 2), and by Arthur Gilman. It was, moreover, followed almost at once by Bryant's handsome plan, now obscured by the destruction of several buildings and the haphazard introduction of others, for the Boston City Hospital in the South End (Figure 39). One senses, in Bryant's explanation of his design to the hospital authorities in 1861, a good deal of the reason Boston surrendered so quickly to things French during this period: "the particular style chosen," wrote Bryant, "is the modern style of Renaissance architecture, a style which stands confessedly at the head of all the forms of modern secular architecture *in the chief capitals of the world*." The emphasis is mine, and it surely discloses the root of this new style's popularity. Boston celebrated its growth into one of the largest Catholic centers in the world by erecting a vast Gothic cathedral. Similarly, in the secular sphere, the city's overall ambition to take its place among the "chief capitals of the world" could only be realized by taking as its secular model the splendors of Second Empire Paris. That was the model which shaped the Back Bay.

The debut of the Second Empire in Boston.
FIGURE 38. Gridley J. Fox Bryant and Arthur Gilman. Boston City Hall, 1861–1865. The building has been recycled into an office building.
FIGURE 39. Gridley J. Fox Bryant. Boston City Hospital, South End, 1861. Only portions of the flanking buildings have survived and these are now surrounded and obscured by later construction.

The Back Bay plan ranks with that of Washington, D.C., as the outstanding
example of city planning in America in the nineteenth century.
FIGURE 40. Commonwealth Avenue, looking east from Exeter Street,
ca. 1885, the centerpiece of the area's spacious and ornamental grid.
FIGURE 41. Charles River Embankment, two blocks to the north of
Commonwealth Avenue, as it appeared ca. 1915. Both the Commonwealth Avenue Mall and the embankment emerged as connections
between the Public Garden and the Fenway, thus forming the first
stages of Frederick Law Olmsted's famous "emerald necklace," the
Boston Park System. See also Plate 1.

Since 1814, this area had been a great mill dam, the earthenwork dike and stone seawall of which are in fact still in place under Beacon Street today, and sewers continued to discharge into the area though it had been cut off from the flow of tide. There was thus more than one reason for its filling. A tremendous undertaking, one of the largest such projects in history, it was a dramatic demonstration of Boston's vitality at this time. Filling began in September of 1857 and as the fill worked its way down the avenues, the houses followed, a block or two behind. So, too, did Boston society. It was to this splendid new quarter that John Lowell Gardner and his new wife, Isabella Stewart Gardner, moved in 1860–1862 to the house at 152 Beacon Street where she began her art collection. Four years later a fine new house at 10 Commonwealth Avenue (Figure 45) was built by Thomas Gold Appleton, a leading figure in Boston society who Oliver Wendell Holmes once remarked "spilled more good things on the wasteful air in conversation than would carry a 'diner-out' through half a dozen London seasons." By 1870 Holmes himself had committed what he called "justifiable domicide" and moved to the Back Bay. Nor is it difficult to understand why.

The contrast to the South End's incoherent plan could not have been greater. As Bainbridge Bunting has pointed out, the Back Bay's great axial scheme constituted "a sharp break from the English cell-like, additive scheme of private residential squares which had previously guided Boston's building. Commonwealth Avenue is probably the handsomest boulevard created in nineteenth-century United States" (Figure 40). Eight splendid blocks long, from Arlington Street to Massachusetts Avenue, 240 feet wide from block to block, with a central mall planted with four parallel rows of trees, Commonwealth Avenue, in Bunting's words, "expressed [Boston's] will to assume a place among the great cities of the world." So too did the whole Back Bay plan, which Lewis Mumford has asserted ranks with L'Enfant's plan for Washington as "the outstanding achievement in American city planning of the nineteenth century." Five parallel axes, formed by the major streets, clearly emulated the Second Empire boulevard system of Paris and attempted to create in Boston an urban environment of truly grand scale (Plate 1). The plan was carried to a kind of extreme in the alphabetical sequence of names of the cross streets — Arlington, Berkeley, Clarendon, Dartmouth, Exeter, Fairfield, Gloucester, Hereford. Furthermore, three-syllable names alternate with those of two syllables.

The new area was also characterized by an extraordinary amplitude and spaciousness: 43 percent of the land directly owned by the Commonwealth was dedicated to streets and parks, a generosity probably unparalleled in mid-century urban planning in the United States. Commonwealth Avenue itself opened off the magnificent new Public Garden, designed by George F. Meacham in 1860. Along with this amenity, over the years a gradually expanding riverfront park was built, beginning with a 100-foot-wide promenade in 1893 (Figure 41) and culminating in this century with the Storrow Embankment. Another important aspect of the Back Bay was its ornamental character; as opposed to the South End, where very few statues or monuments were ever attempted, both the Public Garden and Commonwealth Avenue were embellished with a great number of them. Among the earliest were Thomas Ball's equestrian statue of Washington (1869), widely regarded as one of the finest such works in America (visible in Figure 43), and William Rimmer's statue of Alexander Hamilton (1864) on Commonwealth Avenue. Many more would follow: the Back Bay was to become a

FIGURE 42. The crest of the Classical and Gothic traditions in Boston in the mid-1860s: the corner of Berkeley and Newbury streets in the Back Bay, ca. 1865. Left, William G. Preston's Museum of Natural History, 1863, now Bonwit Teller; right, R. M. Upjohn's Central Congregational Church, 1866, now the Church of the Covenant. These two buildings make an interesting comparison with the two earlier landmarks, St. Paul's Church in Brookline and the Mercantile Wharf Building on the waterfront, shown in Figures 30–31.

French Academic domestic design in the Back Bay in the 1860s.
FIGURE 43. Looking across the Boston Public Garden toward the massed, symmetrical blocks of Arlington Street to either side of Commonwealth Avenue.
FIGURE 44. Attributed to Gridley J. Fox Bryant. 1, 2, and 3 Arlington Street, 1861.
FIGURE 45. 8–10 Commonwealth Avenue, 1864.

symbol of the city as a work of art in its integration of parks, fountains, and statues with both residential and public buildings.

These last added immeasurably to the distinction of the new quarter. Three buildings set a sufficient standard of excellence. William G. Preston's superb Museum of Natural History (Figure 42), now Bonwit Teller, and its long-destroyed companion, the first building of the Massachusetts Institute of Technology (1864), introduced into the Back Bay a restrained French Classicism reminiscent of the Place de la Concorde, while Arthur Gilman's Arlington Street Church (1860) was scarcely less distinguished. Moreover, the houses of the Back Bay were as different in character from those of virtually the same period in the South End as was the Back Bay's monumental axial plan. Approaching the Back Bay along Beacon Street, one can see houses similar to their South End cousins that illustrate this point. Eighty-nine Beacon (1852) is Greek Revival; 96 Beacon, one of two houses remaining of a block of several designed by George M. Dexter in 1849–1850, is a handsome example of the fashionable Italian manner. But once one gains Arlington Street, the change is stunning.

One ought first to look at Arlington Street from the Public Garden (Figure 43), "whose gaudily brilliant flower-beds," Whitehill has written, "like its swan boats, irresistibly recall a French park of the Second Empire." The same spirit animates the streetscape beyond: though ruptured now by one or two later buildings, the majestic, harmonious, mansard blocks of Arlington Street constitute still a splendid frontispiece to the Back Bay, disclosing not only the monumental axial plan of this spacious, ornamental district, but the role these Second Empire blocks were intended to play in this plan. The unity of overall design is striking and beautiful. Every house,

and all of them as a streetscape, is as symmetrical as the spacious grids of the street plan they rise from. Facades are typically axial and flat, from the sheer, uniform planes of which a rigorously chaste, correct, and logical architectonic detail projects crisply to emphasize the crucial structural points of doors and windows. For example, 1, 2, and 3 Arlington Street, attributed to Gridley J. Fox Bryant, are each flat, symmetrical, and architectonic (Figure 44). But these three houses are also conceived clearly as a part of the larger symmetry of the block; which is massed a-b-a — that is, two flanking pavilions projecting so as to frame symmetrically the center house, the whole block tied together by the crowning mansard roof.

Similar compositions occur at 401–407 Beacon Street (1867), designed by Snell and Gregerson, and at 110–130 Marlborough Street (1868) where in a group of eleven houses massed in five parts, not only the two houses at each end project but also the three central houses. A variant scheme, where unity of design is achieved by the regular repetition of the same facade in the same plane used many times over, occurs at Bryant and Gilman's 20–36 Commonwealth Avenue (1860). The smaller the number of houses encompassed, of course, the harder it was to achieve symmetry in the narrow town house lot. Yet 154 Beacon Street, built in 1861, and 17 Marlborough Street, built in 1865, show how ingeniously even one narrow house could achieve an impressive symmetry, though a common device was to design matching houses — as at 8–10 Commonwealth (Figure 45), which are in themselves and as a pair fine examples of the flat, axial facade with correct and sober architectonic detail. This pervasive symmetry also extends to interiors. Insofar as was possible the same axial composition that governs the overall plan of the Back Bay, the blocks of houses, and the individual

house, governs as well the interiors of
the 1860s where mantelpieces, windows,
and doors also are apt to be axially
arranged.

All of this, so reminiscent of its model,
Baron Haussmann's Parisian boulevards, was not only more coherent and
for its time more progressive than the
design concept of the South End, it was
also more disciplined and more theoretical, based as it was on abstract, formal
rules of composition. The South End was
instinctive and intuitive, a continuation
of the Boston tradition; the Second Empire architecture of the Back Bay was academic, and as it was not intuitive to Boston architects, the question at once
arises: how did these architects, suddenly, in the late 1850s and 1860s, learn it
and ultimately master it?

This problem still intrigues scholars,
but the attributions of many of the

houses on or near Arlington Street of the
late 1850s and sixties, which set the
area's tone, are significant: 1–3 Arlington
Street is attributed by Bunting to Bryant;
three houses of 1859, which stood where
the Ritz-Carlton Hotel now is on Arlington Street, are known to have been designed by Richard Morris Hunt; 16 and
17 Arlington were designed by William
Preston; and 20–36 Commonwealth Avenue, quite near Arlington Street, was the
work of Bryant and Gilman. Of these
four architects, who appear to have been
the leading exponents of the French style
in Boston, three studied in Europe —
Gilman, who almost certainly designed
the Back Bay street plan itself, Hunt, and
Preston. The last two are also known to
have studied in France: in fact, Hunt was
the first American student at the Ecole
des Beaux Arts in Paris (where he
worked under H.-M. Lefuel on the new

Louvre), while Preston's elevation for the first Massachusetts Institute of Technology building in the Back Bay is actually signed "Paris, 1863." Preston also points up the fact that the traffic between Boston and Paris was apparently not all one way, for Preston's father, Jonathan, assisted Edward Cabot in 1854 in the final design of the Boston Theatre (Figure 25), and Cabot's design is known to have been based on the work of an otherwise unknown French architect, André Noury, whose presence in Boston at the time Lemoulnier was working on the Deacon House is suggestive. In fact, though little is known about Boston's early French connections, they appear to have been numerous and important.

An especially tantalizing connection, for example, is the painter William Morris Hunt, who settled in Boston in 1862. Many strands met in the career of this artist, of whom it was said that after chatting with him one felt the rest of the world was dead. Very much at his ease among the literati (he was a member of the famous Saturday Club where he forgathered with Emerson and Agassiz and most of Boston's leading lights of the time), Hunt was responsible for the wide patronage by Bostonians of the Barbizon School. The brother of the architect Richard Morris Hunt, whose early French work in Boston has already been touched upon, Hunt's studio was in the same building as the office of two other important architects, Snell and Gregerson, whose French Academic work was frequently distinguished. Hunt's friend Elihu Vedder implied in his memoirs that Hunt knew these architects, and they were certainly the architects of Hunt's Back Bay town house, designed in the French manner for R. M. Pratt in 1867 at 405 Beacon Street.

As scholars have probed more deeply into French influence in Boston in the mid-nineteenth century, it has also become evident that its effect, though epi-sodic, was widespread in Greater Boston as early as in the late forties and fifties. At about the same time he was at work on the Deacon House, Lemoulnier designed at least two other no longer extant French houses in suburban Brookline and Jamaica Plain, while Henry Greenough, the architect brother of the sculptor Horatio, is now known to have designed several mansard-roofed houses in Cambridge in the early and mid-1850s. Nor was the Back Bay the only part of the city proper where the new style dominated. Because the Back Bay has survived, one tends to forget that it was in Post Office Square (where nothing of this period has survived) that in the 1860s and early seventies the French vogue erupted into its gargantuan civic climax. On one side of the square two magnificent insurance buildings stretched for 100 or more feet (Figure 46) — Nathaniel Bradlee's New England Mutual Life Insurance Building and Peabody and Stearns's Mutual Life Insurance Building, both built, like Arthur Gilman's Equitable Building in the adjoining block, just after the Great Fire of 1872. The Mutual Life Insurance Building (1874–1875) was particularly impressive — a sumptuous marble extravaganza; its tower achieved a height of 234 feet and gilded balconies and crests garnished its gleaming white marble. On the other side of the square stood A. B. Mullet's much maligned but undeniably impressive Boston Post Office and Sub-Treasury (Figure 47). Begun in 1869, it was 200 feet long, 100 to 126 feet high, a grandiose ensemble of pavilions and orders and heavily loaded mansards with enormous sculptural groups by Daniel Chester French. Many thought this stupendous ensemble somewhat degenerate. Many more were fiercely proud of it.

In retrospect, the exuberance of this monumental civic array (particularly the tower of the Mutual Life Insurance Building) also illustrates the gradual

FIGURE 48. At first the Back Bay streetscape reflected the same division into Classical residential and institutional architecture and Gothic ecclesiastical architecture that had obtained in Charlestown, East Boston, South Boston, and the South End. Looking down Berkeley Street, ca. 1875: the spire of Ware and Van Brunt's First Church of Boston (1865) appears to the right; in the background is the tower of R. M. Upjohn's Central Congregational Church (1866).

breaking down of the chaste and disciplined Academic style of the 1860s. A few Back Bay houses (Snell and Gregerson's 163 Marlborough Street of 1871, for example) continued the tradition with distinction. But by the early seventies the architectural unity so prized in 1860 was waning. In Boston the strict symmetry and clarity of French Academic design did not survive the decade of the 1860s in which it had reached its zenith. Even the Second Empire style could not for long check the Victorian infatuation with the picturesque.

Actually, it is often forgotten that in one respect the Back Bay was picturesque from its beginning. Like the Immaculate Conception in the South End, Gilman's Classical Arlington Street Church was an outstanding exception in the Back Bay, where the fact that both public and residential Classical design was more academic than in the South End only made the Back Bay's Upjohn-type churches of the 1860s seem all the more wildly picturesque (Figure 48). Significantly, among the first of these churches to be built were two designed by firms whose work in the suburbs has already been discussed — Emmanuel Church (1862) on Newbury Street, still another pudding stone village church by Alexander R. Estey (though extensively enlarged by Frederick R. Allen in 1899); and the Central Congregational Church on the corner of Berkeley and Newbury streets (1866), designed by Upjohn's son, R. M. Upjohn, who increasingly took the lead in his father's office during this period. Admittedly, the Central Church, with its magnificent 236-foot-high spire, is a more formal, urban type of Gothic. But it is still assymetrical, picturesque — and of pudding stone — and the contrast with the Museum of Natural History (Figure 42) of only three years earlier is striking.

But just as Boston was by no means wholly French in the 1860s (for all the logic of the Back Bay street names, the names themselves are aggressively Anglophile), so also even though the strict French mode broke down in the 1870s, Boston's French connections remained a vital cultural undercurrent. These connections, though not yet by any means thoroughly documented, had been deeply rooted and had yielded much more than mansard roofs. As we will see in Chapter 5, for example, the unknown architect (possibly Gilman, perhaps Snell) who designed the famous Hotel Pelham in 1857 is most interesting not because he endowed it with the first mansard in the city proper but because the Pelham was the first "French flat" hotel (that is, apartment house) in America, an innovation the effect of which is still with us today. Similarly, when in 1865 the school of architecture at Massachusetts Institute of Technology was started (two years before the Boston Society of Architects was started), William Ware, who headed the school, not only introduced Beaux Arts methods of instruction into Boston, but thereby founded the first architectural school in

the United States. Less obvious but scarcely less significant is the fact that just as Boston had been led by Hunt to patronize the Barbizon School before many Frenchmen did, so also in the last quarter of the nineteenth century Boston pioneered in collecting the pictures of the French Impressionists. Indeed, Boston's expanding culture yielded a school of "Boston Impressionists." Their work is increasingly admired today and is still another example of what curious alchemies resulted from America's close study of French art and architecture in the nineteenth century. In Childe Hassam, for example, who was born in the Boston suburb of Dorchester in 1859, Boston found a painter whose Impressionist images of the city are as evocative as any of Paris. In his *Boston Common at Twilight* and particularly in *Rainy Day, Boston,* Hassam endowed Boston's Parisian aspirations with a distinction that was at once convincing and indigenous.

The fact that the city Hassam evoked throughout the 1880s and nineties was, as we shall see, considerably more complicated, architecturally and otherwise, than the Second Empire Back Bay of the 1860s only underlies the fact that from her Parisian aspirations of the 1860s Boston steadily evolved toward a more complex and highly original architectural accomplishment and one that would be of world importance. The decade of the 1860s was the eve of Richardson, who from 1859 to 1865, while the Back Bay was beginning to build up, had been quietly at work in Paris, where in 1860 he entered the Ecole des Beaux Arts. Five years later, he returned to the United States and in 1874 settled in Boston, where he had won in 1870 the commission to design yet another Back Bay pudding stone church. By then, however, the metamorphosis of Boston had begun: the French Academic vogue was yielding to the vividly picturesque architecture of the 1870s.

3

H. H. Richardson's Boston

HIGH VICTORIAN BOSTON, richly textured and dramatically massed about picturesque towers, is nowhere better seen or more keenly felt than along Dartmouth Street, between Commonwealth Avenue and Copley Square. Only a few blocks from the regular masses of symmetrical Second Empire houses of the 1860s on Arlington street, this Dartmouth Street vista of the late 1870s and early eighties marks a fascinating shift in taste. It is best seen, perhaps, at the intersection of Commonwealth Avenue, for the two notable picturesque buildings there of about 1880 are actually drastically altered Second Empire buildings of about 1870. At the northwest corner is the Ames-Webster House, which still shows enough of the original mansard house Peabody and Stearns built there in 1872 to set off all the more strikingly the majestic tower, porte cochere, and conservatory that John H. Sturgis and Charles Brigham added to this house in 1882 (Figure 50). Much the same thing happened across the street on the southwest corner a year earlier at the Hotel Vendome, where one can see the nature of this shift in taste even more clearly because there the 1871 building has survived as part of the larger building of 1881 one now sees. Designed by William Preston, this 1871 Second Empire building on Dartmouth Street had a rigorously symmetrical principal facade. But one can see at a glance how, when J. F. Ober enlarged the Vendome in 1881,

without altering the earlier building he massed the new Commonwealth Avenue facade so as to use Preston's building as a part of a much larger and asymmetrical ensemble (Figure 49) which reflects dramatically the Victorian passion for the picturesque.

Subdued for a decade and more (with the exception of the Upjohn church type) by the formal Classical tradition of the city proper and by the French Academic vogue, this passion thereafter erupted again with such force that by 1875 clusters of buildings like Merrill G. Wheelock's Masonic Temple (1867), Cummings and Sears's Hotel Boylston (1870), and Nathaniel J. Bradlee's Young Men's Christian Union (1875) at Tremont and Boylston streets (Figure 51) had endowed Boston in places with not just a picturesque but a startlingly Medieval appearance. Even the Back Bay was transformed. One need only walk up Dartmouth Street toward Copley Square from Commonwealth Avenue to see this. At the northeast corner of Newbury Street is an explicitly Medieval house, built for himself by the architect J. Pickering Putnam in 1878. Opposite stands J. L. Faxon's brilliant red terracotta Hotel Victoria of 1886; startlingly Moorish in its detail, it was not the only building in that style in Boston by the 1880s. On the southwest corner is William Ralph Emerson's Boston Art Club (1881), where the elaborate surface detail does employ Classical motifs, but with an asymmetry as deliberate as that of the building's massing. And behind the Art Club's towered and gabled silhouette rise majestically the lofty polychromatic Gothic tower and greenish copper lantern of Cummings and Sears's New Old South Church of 1874, shaping with the Art Club the most distinguished picturesque ensemble in the city (Figure 52).

This is even more true today than it would have been in the 1870s or eighties, because as one looks across Copley Square toward Trinity Church (Figure 61), that landmark is now only a magnificent episode in a square robbed of its once vivid picturesque architecture. The great symbol of the immense and pathfinding genius of Richardson, whose presence pervades this period, Trinity was mirrored in the eighties by the old S. S. Pierce Building (Figure 60), designed by Edwin Tobey (1887). Behind the church, on the corner of Boylston and Clarendon, stood another Medieval building, Peabody and Stearns's redbrick Hotel Brunswick (1874), and where the Copley Plaza now stands was John H. Sturgis's vivid Gothic Museum of Fine Arts; the building Walter Kilham observed "caused a sensation" when it was completed because it introduced the large-scale use of exterior terra-cotta ornament into America (Figure 53).

Splendid enough without, perhaps the most remarkable aspect of this quarter is within. The decoration of Trinity Church is scarcely less notable than the church's overall design; in Richardson's own words: "a rich effect of color in the interior was an essential element in the design." Moreover, Trinity's decoration has been characterized by James O'Gorman as "a cultural event of the first importance in American history," and by Van Wyck Brooks as marking "the break of the Boston mind with its Puritan past." Certainly, it heralded that break. The work of John La Farge, Trinity's frescoes were the first such work of importance by an American artist, and La

Farge's glass, particularly the great lancets over the west door, are incomparable. They achieve, in the words of Charles Connick, who was not a disciple of La Farge, a "luscious quality of glassiness," while the overall effect of La Farge's glass and murals, and of the glass of Burne-Jones and William Morris amid rich, Byzantine stenciling in red, gold, and green, moved Henry-Russell Hitchcock to compare the interior of Trinity with that of St. Mark's in Venice; Richardson's decoration seemed to Hitchcock to fill the church "with a sort of coloured mist." (Plate 5.)

The decoration of John H. Sturgis's interior at the Ames-Webster House is on a domestic scale almost as remarkable: surmounting the great four-story stairwell is a mural-cycle by the French painter Benjamin Constant, which was also originally enhanced by La Farge glass (Figure 54). Nearby, in the Central Church and the Arlington Street Church, there is also a distinguished parade of stained glass by various of the designers for Louis Tiffany, whose wistful, naturalistic forms and hand-blown iridescent Favrile glass were so characteristic of this period. (Of particular interest is the early and innovative lantern in the Central Church, originally a part of the Tiffany Chapel at the 1893 Chicago world's fair.) This new concern with architectural decoration extended as well to sculpture, and the work of John Evans and his associates is comparable to La Farge's in glass and fresco in that it marked virtually the beginning of architectural sculpture of distinction in this country. Evans, who is of particular interest because his studio was in Boston, executed the carved detail at Trinity as well as at Richardson's Brattle Square Church (Figure 64), where Frédéric Auguste Bartholdi (he of the Statue of Liberty) modeled for Evans the tower frieze whose trumpeting angels have earned the church the affectionate sobriquet

Commonwealth Avenue at Dartmouth Street, Back Bay, in the late nineteenth century.

FIGURE 49. Hotel Vendome, on the southwest corner. The original hotel (now altered since a recent fire), designed by William G. Preston in 1871, stands on the corner; J. F. Ober's enormous addition of 1881 is on the right.

FIGURE 50. Ames-Webster House, 306 Dartmouth Street, across the street, an 1872 house by Peabody and Stearns, seen here as remodeled in 1882 by Sturgis and Brigham. See also Figure 54.

FIGURE 51. High Victorian Boston: Tremont and Boylston streets, ca. 1878. On the left is Merrill G. Wheelock's Masonic Temple of 1867 (demolished); to the right is Cummings and Sears's Hotel Boylston of 1870 (demolished); in between is Nathaniel J. Bradlee's Young Men's Christian Union of 1875, extant but now shorn of its tower.

FIGURE 52. Dartmouth Street, looking toward Copley Square, ca. 1885, perhaps Boston's most picturesque vista of the period. In the foreground is William Ralph Emerson's Queen Anne masterpiece, the Boston Art Club of 1881. Behind it rise the richly detailed tower and lantern of Cummings and Sears's New Old South Church of 1874.

FIGURE 53. Sturgis and Brigham. The first building of the Museum of Fine Arts, Copley Square, as originally envisaged by the architects; designed in 1870. The Copley Square facade (left) was completed in two parts in 1876 and 1879; the principal facade (right) was never built. Demolished.

Back Bay interiors of the 1880s were often as spacious and ornamental as the Back Bay itself, another manifestation of the city as a work of art.

FIGURE 54. Looking up the stairwell of John H. Sturgis's Ames-Webster House, 306 Dartmouth Street, toward *The Justinian Cycle,* the only known murals in the United States by the French Academician Benjamin Constant. The stained glass by John La Farge has unfortunately been removed, but this sumptuous house, which has been called "a Back Bay Queen Anne palace," has otherwise been sensitively recycled into suites of offices.

FIGURE 55. The drawing room of Carl Fehmer's Oliver Ames House at 355 Commonwealth Avenue, on the corner of Massachusetts Avenue, 1882.

"The Church of The Holy Bean Blowers."
Also notable in this period was the work
of the A. H. Davenport Company of
Cambridge (Plate 4), whose wood carv-
ing and joinery adorned not only Trinity
Church but in later years St. Patrick's
Cathedral in New York City and the
White House in Washington. Among
Back Bay houses, Davenport's finest
joinery is probably to be found at the
Mason House (1882) at 211 Common-
wealth Avenue.

La Farge's and Davenport's domestic
work (and also Evans's, for he worked on
many Back Bay houses) is doubly significant, for the sense of the Back Bay as itself a work of art, which we saw developing in the 1860s, was reflected as well in
the decor and furnishing of the Back Bay
house. By the 1880s such houses were
more and more likely to be the abodes of
men and women, leaders in thought and
action, whose drawing rooms, centers of
an elegant and ceremonious life-style,
were as consciously "artistic" as the
statues on Commonwealth Avenue. In
1876, when Charles Wyllys Eliot published his *Book of American Interiors*,
fifteen of the twenty-two rooms described were in Massachusetts and of
these fifteen, nearly half (seven) were in
the Back Bay. One of the most sumptuous was that of the Oliver Ames House
of 1882 on the corner of Commonwealth
and Massachusetts avenues, the drawing
room of which (Figure 55) was described
by William Seale as very much in the
spirit of the 1870s and eighties in that
"every inch of [it] showed the conscious
touch of artistic effort." Nor did all this
represent merely ostentation. Thomas
Gold Appleton, whose house at 10
Commonwealth Avenue (Figure 45) was
touched upon in the last chapter, was
one of the largest subscribers to the
building fund of the new Museum of
Fine Arts in Copley Square, and the
owner of 99 Beacon Street, John Spaulding, left an extraordinary collection to the
museum, including paintings by Manet,
Matisse, Van Gogh, Renoir, Cézanne,
and Degas — all of which had adorned
his Back Bay home.

One may also see in and around the
residential Back Bay the stylistic background of the great picturesque landmarks of this period built in Copley
Square. Forty-one Brimmer Street, built
in 1869 (probably by Ware and Van
Brunt), is an excellent example of what
Bainbridge Bunting has called the "Panel
Brick" style (Figure 56), characterized by
ornament that arises from the bricks
themselves, which project or recede from
the facade (in a stepped corbel table at
the cornice, for example) and yield a variety of planes often in the form of recessed panels. Such detail, being worked
in the facade itself and tending thus to
spread over its surface, creates discreetly the animated and dynamic facade so characteristic of the picturesque
manner. The next step, the use of not one
or two but of several differing and contrasting materials in the same facade, can
be seen at Sturgis and Brigham's Hollis
Hunnewell House of 1869 at 315 Dartmouth Street. One of the first examples
of exterior ceramic decoration on any
Boston building, this work heralded the
same firm's use of ornamental terra-cotta
the next year in the Museum of Fine
Arts. The background of Trinity Church
itself may be seen at Richardson's Brattle
Square Church of 1870. And in the same
block as the church is another herald: the
house that Charles Cummings built for
himself in 1871, on the corner of Clarendon and Newbury streets, the year before he earned the commission to design
the third great picturesque landmark of
Copley Square, the New Old South
Church. There is perhaps no more striking indication in Boston of the force of
picturesque design at this time than that
Cummings's house is more aggressively
Medieval than the Brattle Square Church
itself. In fact, it was the first full-blooded
Medieval house in the Back Bay. Red
brick, black brick, salmon-colored brick,

The architecture of the late 1860s and 1870s was increasingly marked
by facades of contrasting materials and lively detail.
FIGURE 56. A Panel Brick house at 41 Brimmer Street at the foot of
Beacon Hill (1869), possibly by Ware and Van Brunt.
FIGURE 57. Architect's perspective of the same firm's Memorial Hall,
Harvard University, Cambridge. One of the great Ruskinian Gothic
landmarks in America today, Memorial Hall was designed between 1865 and
1871 and completed in 1878.
FIGURE 58. Victorian Gothic in its suburban incarnation could be
as vivid: the Haskell House, 83 Vista Street, Newton, ca. 1870.

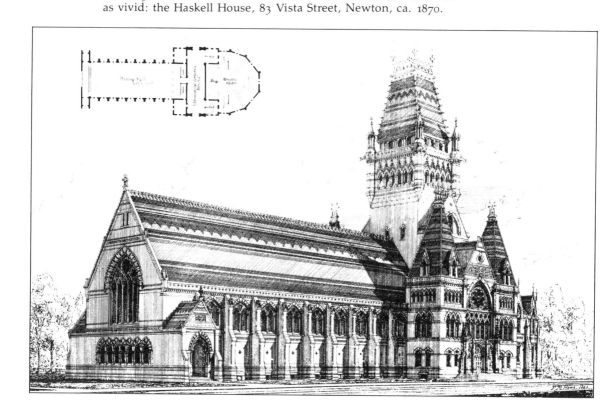

and cream-colored sandstone with polychromatic slate are disposed freely and vividly in the service of huge, cylindrical donjons whose conical roofs compete with a roof structure so elaborate as to defy description.

Not all the background of Copley Square is to be found in the Back Bay. Just as during the Second Empire period the mansard roof appeared first in residential design outside the city proper, the Copley Square Museum of Fine Arts was foreshadowed by Sturgis's Pinebank of 1869–1870 in Jamaica Plain, built for Edward N. Perkins, the chairman of the Fine Arts Committee of the Boston Athenaeum, which first recommended the establishment of the museum. In fact, Boston's earliest and perhaps greatest landmark of the new mode is not in the city proper at all, but in Cambridge — Harvard's Memorial Hall (Figure 57). That extraordinary building was designed by two Boston architects, William Ware and Henry Van Brunt, both Harvard men who had studied with Richard M. Hunt. Along with Sturgis and Brigham and Cummings and Sears, they were leading exponents in Boston of the new picturesque vogue.

L IKE Commonwealth Avenue and Holy Cross Cathedral, each of which in its different way signaled Boston's ambition to rise to the great world and take her place in it, Memorial Hall was Harvard's first attempt to express her rise from a small New England college to a great university. Designed between 1865 and 1871 and finished in 1878, Memorial Hall is 310 feet long and up to 115 feet wide; it rivals in size as much as Holy Cross such great Medieval cathedrals as Lichfield. Stylistically, however, Memorial Hall is quite different from Holy Cross. Walter Kilham tells the story of how in 1911 Abbott Lawrence Lowell took a new profes-

sor of architecture just arrived from Paris (it was Eugène J. A. Duquesne) on a tour of the Yard; Lowell

proudly pointing out the cherished square brick boxes, Hollis, Stoughton, and the rest, Duquesne bowing and saying, "Ah, oui," "très chic," "c'est charmant," etc., and Lowell dreading the moment when they should come to Memorial Hall. Finally they turned a corner and Memorial [Hall] appeared, all its pinnacles shining in the sun, and the gilt clock striking like a band coming up the street. Duquesne stopped short, gesticulated, and exclaimed, "Ah, voilà, quelque chose!" — "Ah, there at last you have something."

How to account for it? The extent to which this vivid new polychromatic vogue swept over Boston reflects the fact that its advent coincided with the Great Fire of 1872, which forced a virtual rebuilding of the business district. Coincidental, too, was the fact that Copley Square began to be built up at this time, as did the streetcar suburbs we will discuss in the next chapter, where some of the most vividly picturesque buildings are found (Figure 58). But what of the new architecture itself? Fundamentally, these buildings of the late sixties and seventies, vividly coloristic, sometimes rambunctious in feeling, yet as often undeniably magnificent, reveal the deep new need of the time in an increasingly industrial and ugly age to dream romantically of a picturesque past. Such was the energy of the post–Civil War period, the dream was necessarily somewhat strident; Memorial Hall *itself* was rather like a brass band stepping up the street. On the other hand, these buildings also revealed how tired Boston architects had become of paraphrasing what had become an academic formula, long mastered. After about 1870, architecture in Boston became increasingly experimental, individualistic, as asymmetrical as it had lately been symmetrical; broken and picturesque in massing and more and more inventive in detail.

Medieval survival and Medieval revival.
FIGURE 59. Triangular Warehouse, built near Dock Square in Boston, ca. 1680. Demolished.
FIGURE 60. Edwin Tobey. S. S. Pierce Building, Copley Square, Back Bay, 1887. Demolished.

And at its best it would also attempt a more sensitive handling of materials and a greater emphasis on good craftsmanship. Because, stylistically, the new picturesqueness of the seventies and eighties was couched overwhelmingly in Medieval terms, which spread from churches to virtually every building type, it can seem to us an even more improbable appropriation on the part of the New World than the Italianate palazzos of the mid-nineteenth century. Yet if one compares the S. S. Pierce Store of 1887 in Copley Square with Boston's Triangular Warehouse of about 1680, one can see that at least one variety of picturesque design would refer in a very real sense to Boston's earliest architectural tradition (Figures 59–60). The Triangular Warehouse was Medieval *survival;* the S. S. Pierce Store was Medieval revival. Notwithstanding the connection of late nineteenth-century picturesque design with Boston's late seventeenth-century architecture, had one inquired in the 1860s or seventies about sources — especially for the polychromatic Gothic of

Memorial Hall — most architects would have pointed to England, whether they liked Memorial Hall or not.

Its detractors, who would seize upon Memorial Hall's contrasting banding and christen it the "streaky bacon" style, united around critics like Clarence Cook, who wrote in the *North American Review* in 1882 that both the new Museum of Fine Arts and Memorial Hall were the products of architects whose heads were "crammed full of remembered bits of Old World architecture and [whose] portfolios [were] stuffed with photographs of more and more bits." They preferred buildings like the University Museum at Harvard, near Memorial Hall. Designed by Henry Greenough and George Snell (two architects of strong academic tendencies) only eight years before Ware's first design (1865) for Memorial Hall and added to by Greenough and Snell in 1871, while Memorial Hall was under construction, the museum is plain and clean-cut, factorylike in its design. Added to repeatedly until as late as 1913 in the same sparse style, it was not, however, a popular alternative. Admired by persons of Cook's persuasion because of its simple functionalism, it was bitterly attacked by others, including Charles Eliot Norton. The first professor of the history of art at Harvard (1874–1899), Norton was, in Martin Green's words, "the Arbiter Elegantiarum of American high culture" during this period, standing "between America and England (and to a slighter extent between America and Europe, and between New England and the rest of America) explaining and evaluating each to each." His evaluation of the University Museum was devastating: "Its bare, shadowless walls, unadorned by carven columns or memorial statues, will stand incapable of affording support for those associations which endear every human work of worth." And though he later came to dislike Memorial Hall (largely because as an economy brick was substituted for masonry), it was Norton who almost certainly played the key role in determining the building's style — which by its admirers was called Ruskinian Gothic, in honor of Norton's close friend John Ruskin, the English architectural critic who in one scholar's words had "bewitched America" by 1870. Ruskin's predilection for Italian Gothic is, in fact, the stylistic background not only for Memorial Hall, but for the Copley Square Museum of Fine Arts and the New Old South Church.

Although Ruskin's preferences were felt with particular force in Boston because of Norton's prestige, Norton was not the only channel of communication between England and America. Margaret Henderson Floyd has pointed out in her discussion of the background of the architect of the Copley Square Museum of Fine Arts that John H. Sturgis's

standards and his architectural education were totally English, and he had fortuitously been acquiring these during one of the most dynamic periods of artistic and architectural thought in England — the 1850's, decade of the Great Exhibition, the Crystal Palace, John Ruskin's *Stones of Venice* and *Seven Lamps of Architecture*, the maturity of the Gothic Revival and the Pre-Raphaelite influences of Rossetti.

Unlike the foreign-born architect, Sturgis as a Bostonian had permanent contacts in both England and America through his father, senior partner of Baring Brothers Banking House, who was living in London, and through his own and his wife's families in Boston. Constant travel kept him in current touch with matters architectural in England on an annual basis, and his talented young partner [Charles Brigham] with a good hand for business proved more than able to manage the firm during his long absences.

In 1876 still another channel was opened — *American Architect and Building News*. Increasingly lavishly illustrated, this journal was the first periodical published in America for the professional architect. Another innovation, in 1883, was the Rotch Traveling Fellowship. Founded through the Boston Society of Architects, it was the first such fellowship endowed in America and greatly facilitated European travel for many who might not otherwise have been able to afford it. The nation's first architectural school; the first American architectural periodical; the first traveling fellowship in the country; all these started in Boston between 1865 and 1885 and testify to how vital an architectural center the city was becoming.

By the mid-1870s, though American architecture was increasingly picturesque and Medieval, it was no longer Ruskinian but Richardsonian. Such was the personal nature of the architectural achievement of the man held by most scholars to have been Boston's — America's — greatest architect.

Born near New Orleans in 1838, Henry Hobson Richardson came

first to Boston with the Harvard class of 1859. Thereafter, as has been noted, he studied at the Ecole des Beaux Arts in Paris, working for a time for the architect Theodore Labrouste, and upon his return to this country he began his practice in New York in the mid-1860s. He moved to Boston in 1874. The massive, robust authority of his Trinity Church (Figures 61–62), reverberated so quickly and so intensely in the imagination of both architects and the public generally that it overwhelmed almost at once every other mode insofar as monumental civic and ecclesiastical architecture was concerned. A free adaption of the eleventh-century Romanesque of Auvergne in Aquitaine and crowned with a tower masterfully adapted from the Old

Cathedral at Salamanca, Trinity was deeply rooted in the Middle Ages; yet in the force of its design it was not only demonstrably Richardson's own, it was comparable in its own way with any Medieval model one might cite for it. Here was, not an American style, but an American architecture that was the master, not the servant, of its sources; a building couched in the terms of a venerable style, but a style suffused with a new vitality and power.

Richardson's architecture was by no means unrelated in this early period to the fashions of his time. Grace Church in Medford (1867), one of his earliest churches, and now the oldest extant church of his design, is demonstrably an outgrowth of the Upjohn church type.

H. H. Richardson. Trinity Church, Copley Square, Back Bay, 1872–1877.
FIGURE 61. The church and the parish house with intervening cloister and garth, from Clarendon Street.
FIGURE 62. The garth from the cloister, showing Richardson's masterful stonework. The interior of Trinity is shown in Plate 5.

One can see as well in his Winn Memorial Library in Woburn, finished in 1877, a banded entrance arch of the sort common to Ruskinian Gothic buildings. But Richardson's Sever Hall (Figure 63) of the next year at Harvard, built in sight of Memorial Hall, illustrates of what a different order was Richardson's work at its best. Sever is more than a masterpiece. Like Trinity, it is both old and new, but in Sever's case Richardson's inspiration was not only Medieval but closely related to the old Georgian buildings of the Yard, with which Sever is, in fact, very sympathetic: Sever's distinction lies chiefly in the fact that its almost Classical serenity of mass catches perfectly the spirit of the dormitories of the old Yard even as its discreet cut-brick detail and low towers and broad-arched entrance establishes its modernity in its own time. Of all Richardson's Boston buildings, however, it is the Brattle Square Church (Figure 64) in the Back Bay and the Crane Memorial Library in Quincy (Figure 65) where one can perhaps most easily identify the fundamental quality that characterizes his work: his remarkable ability to discipline and yet not emasculate the picturesque. One may discern this quality as well in the suburban stations Richardson designed for

the Boston and Albany Railroad in Framingham, Auburndale, Brighton, and Waban. Particularly notable is the Chestnut Hill Station (Figure 66). Wrote Hitchcock in 1936: "By a strict expression of function and material Richardson made asymmetrical design formally monumental instead of merely picturesque." It was, Hitchcock asserted, a "very rare achievement in the long history of architecture."

Richardson was not a theorist. He did not, as Cram would, pour out his ideals and concepts in book after book. One has accordingly to discover Richardson's techniques through the eyes of scholars who have studied his work, and perhaps the best description of how Richardson could discipline the picturesque is Bainbridge Bunting's analysis of the Trinity Church Rectory on Clarendon Street as originally built, before the third story (which does not improve but on the other hand does not destroy the design) was added in 1893 (Figure 67):

The coherence of the Clarendon street elevation results from the complex equilibrium which the architect maintains between a sequence of interrelated though diverse elements. The crux of the design is the placement of the seven second-story windows. Identical in shape but spaced at slightly vary-

H. H. Richardson's Boston.
FIGURE 63. Sever Hall, Harvard University, Cambridge, 1878.
FIGURE 64. Brattle Square (now First Baptist) Church, Back Bay, 1870–1872.
FIGURE 65. Crane Memorial Library, Quincy, 1880–1884.
FIGURE 66. Boston and Albany Railroad Station, Chestnut Hill, 1883–1884.
FIGURE 67. Trinity Church Rectory, 233 Clarendon Street, Back Bay, 1879.
Another story was added by Richardson's successor architects in 1893.

ing intervals, these windows are separated by three panels of cut brick decoration. At each end of the house, two windows enframing a brick decorative panel form a unit of design which aligns with the banks of the windows in the first story and with simple gables on the third level. As the brick panel between the right pair of windows is wider than on the left, there is space for four mullioned first-floor windows on the right side but only three on the left. The larger right-hand gable further reflects this irregular spacing of second-story openings. Two second-floor windows, also separated by a decorative panel, are set symmetrically over the wide arch of the entrance porch. The seventh window of the series establishes the position of the single transomed window of the first story and the smaller dormer in the roof. Thus the unsymmetrical but orderly spacing of these seven second-story windows is echoed in all parts of the facade.

One is reminded here of Pierson's discussion of Bulfinch's third Harrison Gray Otis House, where, as we saw, the placement of windows and their shapes and sequences control utterly that masterpiece. But there is obviously present in the Trinity Rectory another dimension and the key to it is in the words "unsymmetrical but orderly spacing." It is Richardson's inspired adjustment of the features of the facade so as to achieve asymmetrically a genuine reciprocity of parts that establishes something comparable to symmetry and balance but at once more pleasing and more profound — equilibrium. Bunting goes on to explain how this is achieved.

Although the opposing gabled units use identical elements, that on the right is considerably larger than the left, with a wide bank of mullioned windows, larger panel of brick decoration, and bigger gable with round-arched window. This greater size and the way that the right section is isolated from the rest of the facade by the downspout give to it a weight that its counterpart on the left does not have. Counterbalancing this emphasis on the right section, however, is the deep-shadowed arch of the entrance porch and the larger dormer window above it which are located left of center. This equalization of

weights is facilitated by a repetition of identical window shapes in both halves of the composition, a repetition which allows the eye to move freely across the facade in a horizontal direction. Furthermore, the varied window shapes on all floors are unified by the use of window panes of almost equal size. The composition is also held together by four bands of smooth stone which carry across the facade, three related to the first-story windows and one at the height of the main cornice.

Though such subtleties in Richardson's work were naturally lost on most architects, the effect of these buildings, as Kilham remembered, was such that the "arrival of the Romanesque was nothing short of a blitz." Van Brunt and Howe's Cambridge Public Library of 1888, built two years after Richardson's death at only forty-eight, was distinctly Romanesque, *Richardsonian* Romanesque, as the style came to be known, so personal was it to its creator. It is a handsome building. So, too, is the Cambridge City Hall of the same year, by Longfellow, Alden, and Harlow. But these are the exceptional work of outstanding architects. More typical were the increasingly gloomy and soporific Richardsonian Romanesque buildings that succeeded the Ruskinian mode more and more in Boston as elsewhere. It used to be said of Bismarck's successors that they attributed Bismarck's extraordinary success to his habitual dictatorial, bullying manner, which was easily copied, but that they forgot the genius behind the bully, which could not be copied. So it was with Richardson; as he had loved great masonry arches it was easy to conclude that such things were the root of his genius and easier still to go on reproducing them forever. But as we shall see shortly, those who learned most from Richardson — McKim, Cram, Sullivan — almost never couched their work in Richardsonian Romanesque. Nor did that vogue completely dominate even at the height of Richardson's influence.

IN the mid-1870s the evolution of style and fashion in Boston accelerated incredibly. The Cathedral of the Holy Cross (Figure 35) and Memorial Hall (Figure 57) were both designed initially between 1865 and 1867; both were erected in the early seventies and substantially completed in 1874–1875; Trinity Church was built between 1872 and 1877. Any Bostonians who attended the respective opening ceremonies of these three buildings (all of which occurred between 1874 and 1877) could thus scarcely be blamed if they were confused by the wildly different architecture each event celebrated. Upjohn Gothic, Ruskinian Gothic, Richardsonian Romanesque — all reached their zenith in Boston in the mid-1870s — and although the first was to be heard of no more, the second to shine very brightly but only for a moment, and the last to dominate the next decade or more in monumental design, aspects of each lingered on for many years and shaded into one another. Even more confusingly, if the Bostonian who attended these opening ceremonies chanced to be building a house by the late seventies or early eighties, he was probably building in none of these styles. For undergirding the picturesque movement by then and throughout the 1880s was an even more kaleidoscopic vogue, Queen Anne — a term that derives from the work of contemporary British architects (chiefly R. Norman Shaw), whose announced purpose was to recover the English tradition of beautifully crafted buildings that they felt had survived as late as Queen Anne's reign (1702–1714). The effect of their attempts to do so, naturally couched at first in terms of Elizabethan manors and Flemish guildhalls, coincided with the picturesque mood of this country and was apparently felt in Boston as early as 1870 in Weld Hall at Harvard, which Ware and Van Brunt designed midway in their work on Memorial Hall. By the late 1870s, this influence was pervasive.

Less a style than a family of styles, Queen Anne ought really to be thought of as disclosing a state of mind, an *attitude* toward architecture, the innumerable refractions of which defy description. Many scholars, for example, treat both the discreet Panel Brick manner and the Ruskinian mode as a kind of introductory Queen Anne, and these and other picturesque vogues shaded so quickly into each other in the 1880s that it is easy to lose oneself in stylistic confusion. Nor is it enough to say, as did Osbert Lancaster, that the essence of Queen Anne is that its admirers were chiefly driven by "a real loathing for symmetry." It is true that Queen Anne work was usually both asymmetrical in design and Medieval in feeling. But if one searches for its positive rather than for only its negative qualities, it is, I think, true to say that it was most strongly characterized by inventiveness and whimsy. In some way or other it was usually both animated and individualistic — and when such individuality in composition was sought in every dimension, the results were naturally striking (Figures 68–75).

On the exterior, for example, broken, plastic masses, richly textured in surface, often yielded dramatic volumes of space inside — where complex stair compositions, broken into many runs of different direction, typically sought to create a sense of spatial and decorative virtuosity. The use of many varying, richly textured materials on the facade usually reflected a similar disposition of materials within. At 211 Commonwealth Avenue, for example, the reception hall is finished in lustrous mahogany, the library in exuberantly carved quartered oak, the parlor in delicately detailed enameled trim, while the dining room is enhanced by rich, variegated marble. Within and without, design also sought effects we scarcely suspect today. On any one fa-

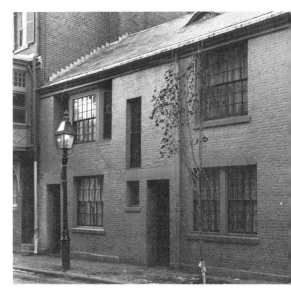

Back Bay and suburban Queen Anne work
by Cabot and Chandler.
FIGURE 68. 12 Fairfield Street, Back Bay, 1879.
FIGURE 69. 1 Melville Avenue, Dorchester,
1880. Demolished.

The many faces of American Queen Anne.
FIGURES 70, 71. 1 Fairfax Street, Ashmont, ca.
1890, west facade and east facade.
FIGURE 72. Clarence H. Luce. 130 Mount
Vernon Street, corner of River Street at the
foot of Beacon Hill, 1878 remodeling of a ca.
1840 house.
FIGURE 73. William Ralph Emerson.
House at 24 Pinckney Street, Beacon
Hill, ca. 1885 remodeling of an 1802
stable.
FIGURE 74. 27 Carruth Street, Ashmont, ca.
1885.
FIGURE 75. Cabot and Chandler. 257 Marl-
borough Street, Back Bay, 1883.

cade, for instance, both materials and planes were frequently distributed so as to annex the sun itself to their purpose through the play of light and shade. This could be all the more vibrant if the sunlight was suffused through trees so as to dapple the textures of the facade with a constantly changing, rippling light. Similarly, quartered oak was particularly popular for interior woodwork because its light blond highlights, running against the darker and more dense grain of the wood, catch sunlight as vividly as the dense grain rejects it. And if this light is suffused not only through trees but through stained glass, a quartered oak staircase dappled in effervescent vermilions and greens on a sunny afternoon is a vibrant and wonderful thing.

Queen Anne design could also be very simple. It was, in fact, enormously diverse — as is sometimes evident in any one building. At 1 Fairfax Street in Dorchester, there is a splendid unattributed house whose principle facade is nothing if not adventuresome: typically pierced by an unexpected and whimsical window, the chimney disappears into a large second-story bay or oriel, only to emerge finally to divide and surmount a dormer window in the roof (Figure 70). On another facade of the same house, however, one sees a similar eccentricity of design expressed in strikingly simple terms through a variation in window size and placement (Figure 71). If one then looks diagonally across Carruth Street to another unattributed Queen Anne house, one can see how both elaboration in mass and variation in window shapes and sizes may be combined in so distinguished a manner that though 27 Carruth Street is asymmetrical and fanciful, its features are so nicely adjusted in every dimension that the architect has achieved a quality of repose (Figure 74).

To attain such an effect was not easy, as so many bizarre Queen Anne houses testify. It was also more difficult to ac-

complish in the connected streetscape of the city proper, where one had usually only one or at best (on a street corner) two facades to work with. Thus perhaps the best Back Bay Queen Anne design is a corner building — Emerson's Boston Art Club (Figure 52). In overall design it is beautifully poised and coherent, but the building is not only asymmetrically massed: it is shaped on Newbury Street into a robust and elaborate design while on Dartmouth Street the effect is much simpler and is chiefly dependent on an ingenious distribution of windows of various shapes and sizes. These Dartmouth Street windows, once one studies them as an ensemble, clearly evoke the Palladian motif; an excellent example of how inventively and subtly the Queen Anne architect often handled historical forms. To best study in the city proper the two approaches we have isolated at 1 Fairfax Street and at the Art Club — the one approach seemingly elaborate, the other apparently very simple — one ought, however, to go to Beacon Hill, where stand perhaps the finest Queen Anne houses in Boston.

The best-known, though it is usually described as a kind of eccentric Bavarian dollhouse, is the conspicuously yellow and red tiled residence that challenges so charmingly the red-brick quarter at the corner of River and Mount Vernon streets (Figure 72). The first floor is built of cement, plastered; the second story is of tiles made in Akron, Ohio, which according to a contemporary report in *American Architect and Building News* were "the first of [their] kind ever manufactured in this country, after an English pattern." It was aptly christened the "Sunflower Castle" by Oliver Wendell Holmes, who thereby caught hold at once of the characteristically optimistic Queen Anne motif, visible here on the second story. Originally built in 1840, the house in its present form was designed by Clarence Luce in 1878 and is somewhat similar to a house by Luce at 76 High Street in Brookline, built two years later. In fact, the "Sunflower Castle" is simply an excellent example in an unexpected place of Queen Anne design. So also is another Beacon Hill curiosity that is strikingly simpler in effect: the so-called House of Odd Windows at 24 Pinckney Street (Figure 73), another remodeling (ca. 1885), in this case by William Ralph Emerson. The fact that no two of its windows are alike intrigues people too much and obscures the superb design of this facade, where one sees how simple Queen Anne could be, and how distinguished in the hands of the architect of the Boston Art Club. Notice the "eyebrow" window that swells up from the roof.

That one of the finest Queen Anne facades in the city should possess utterly no ornament at all is particularly significant because it is often the simplest Queen Anne that has in retrospect been most admired. Indeed, the calibre of design at 24 Pinckney Street (though not this specific house, which was beyond his purview) is precisely that to which Bunting pointed when he remarked that "Boston architectural firms produced some exceptionally good work in the Queen Anne vein. For vigor of design and calibre of craftsmanship, a number of Back Bay residences are comparable to contemporary British work." The Back Bay houses he calls particular attention to — which include 357–359 Beacon (1885) and 505 Beacon (1888) by Carl Fehmer, and 283–285 Beacon (1885) and 257 Marlborough (1883) by Cabot and Chandler (Figure 75) — are singled out not for their exuberance, but because of their sensitivity to proportion and to materials, simply but finely used in compositions of distinction. In both qualities, moreover, Bunting perceived a possible foundation from which "a modern architectural expression" might have been evolved. He observed:

Undoubtedly the Back Bay's most original work was done in connection with a simple use of materials, and, in a sense, this movement symbolizes Boston's artistic maturity. Here her architects produced something of their own. . . . Boston designers stood on the threshold of an indigenous architecture, even as Chicagoans of the same decade were pioneering in the field of architectural engineering.

Bunting's assertion about the best of Back Bay Queen Anne is strikingly similar to Kilham's lament that the best Italianate design in Boston might have developed into a "truly American style." Thus one sees again the way the nineteenth-century revivals, imported perhaps somewhat improbably to this country, proved finally so susceptible to adaptation in the hands of American architects that at their best they seem always to subsequent generations to have been too quickly abandoned with no thought for their potential. This has also seemed true in the case of the Shingle Style, which paralleled Queen Anne work in Boston's suburbs.

ALTHOUGH seventeenth-century Boston Medieval survival had been too primitive to yield ready models for picturesque urban architecture — except, perhaps, for the Triangular Warehouse! — there was in the suburbs a very attractive and indigenous folk medievalism (an example is the seventeenth-century Fairbanks House in Dedham; Figure 76) that triggered in Queen Anne architects a creative response of unusual distinction widely known as the Shingle Style. The Boston architect who most scholars would agree was chiefly responsible for at least the initial development of this style was William Ralph Emerson. He designed a number of large and important houses in suburban Boston — in Canton, Jamaica Plain (Figure 82), Magnolia, and

Medieval survival and revival in the Victorian suburbs.
FIGURE 76. Fairbanks House, Dedham, ca. 1636.
Late nineteenth-century work by William Ralph Emerson in the suburb
of Milton.
FIGURE 77. Misses Forbes House, 7 Fairfax Street, 1876.
FIGURE 78. Glover House, 320 Adams Street, 1879.
FIGURE 79. Emerson's own house, 201 Randolph Avenue, 1886.

throughout the North Shore — but perhaps the best way to gain a feeling for his evolution of the Shingle Style is to focus on three houses that he designed in 1876–1886 in the suburb of Milton.

An early Emerson house, the Misses Forbes House (Figure 77), shows the way in which the wooden house generally could achieve qualities of design and finish equivalent to the brick house (Figure 56). The chief characteristic of such "Stick Style" houses, somewhat (though remotely) influenced by Swiss chalet and Medieval half-timbered work, is the network of wooden framing members that subdivide the facade, a skeletal system suggesting structure though really bearing no relation to it, and yielding, as did Panel Brick work, a series of panels; in the case of the Forbes House this includes diagonal bracing. At the Glover House (Figure 78), one sees emerging the personal idiom of the architect; Vincent Scully's analysis focuses on

the mountainous sweep of the shingled roof, adjusting itself from gable to gable and then gliding down like a deeply sheltering wing over the piazza. . . . Through its continuous adjustment, all the subsidiary masses are pulled together into one plastic and richly surfaced mass, various but coherent, indicative of plastic volumes within, and expressive of shelter.

Finally, if one studies Emerson's own house, one can see by focusing again on the roof the essence of his mature work (Figure 79). Cynthia Zaitzevsky has pointed out that in his own house Emerson achieved "a continuity of roof and wall toward which he had been working for at least a decade, a continuity emphasized by the shingles, which, plain and not fancily cut, stained and weathered a dark brown, uniformly clothe all surfaces of the building." Significantly, the Emerson house is as interesting a comparison with the seventeenth-century Fairbanks House as the S. S. Pierce Building is with the Triangular Warehouse. Yet Emerson's house is by no means a reproduction. Rather, he caught the spirit of the seventeenth-century work and breathed new life into it nearly two centuries later.

The Shingle Style did not always recall seventeenth-century work so explicitly. Kragsyde, erected in 1882–1884 by Peabody and Stearns at Manchester-by-the-Sea, was decidedly a late nineteenth-century building (Figure 80), and an undoubted masterpiece. It is hard to believe that the overall coherence and refinement of this dramatic and mountainous shingled house, astride its majestic crag, could ever have been surpassed. So much so that Scully could not restrain himself from reflecting that the shingled surface of Kragsyde must have seemed "like a thin membrane over echoing volumes, as the boom of the surf below reverberates low and deep through the house." Kragsyde, demolished some years ago, was a kind of apotheosis of the Shingle Style. But Shingle Style houses of importance in Greater Boston survive: for example, the Bryant House in Cohasset (1880) and the Stoughton House in Cambridge (Figure 81), both designed by Richardson, whose work in the view of some scholars decisively influenced the mature Shingle Style. Though Hitchcock points out that the Bryant House proceeds in large part from Richardson's admiration of seventeenth-century work like the Fairbanks House, one can easily see in both Richardson houses — as at the Emerson House and at Kragsyde — characteristics unique to the Shingle Style itself.

The most important of these is the sense of a continuous shingled skin, which is stretched tautly around the structural frame on the exterior and seems to swell out (like the eyebrow window; see Figure 74) or hollow into the house in response to interior volumes, which thus seem to shape the exterior. These volumes, open and informal, are

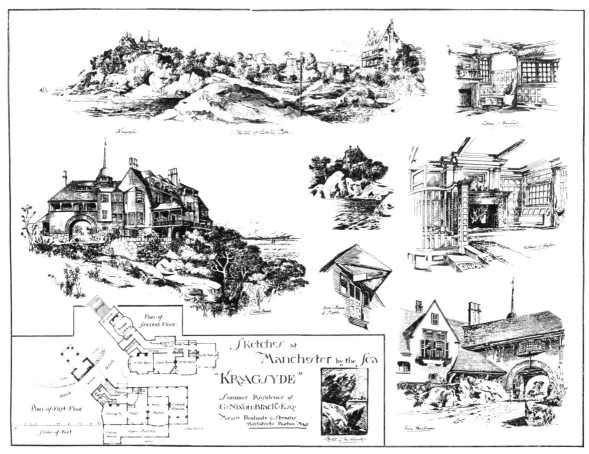

Two Shingle Style masterpieces.
FIGURE 80. Peabody and Stearns. Kragsyde, Manchester-by-the-Sea, 1882–1884. Demolished.
FIGURE 81. H. H. Richardson. Stoughton House, 90 Brattle Street, Cambridge, 1883.

FIGURE 82. William Ralph Emerson worked also in the streetcar suburbs: 101 Forest Hill Street, Jamaica Plain, ca. 1880.

often said to constitute a free adjustment of space to function; and the theory does, indeed, proceed from the Medieval design concept that a building grows organically from within to whatever exterior shape, no matter how odd, the interior needs. But it could not be too odd: unlike the seventeenth-century Fairbanks House, the Emerson House's felicitous exterior shape was not accidental. It was contrived. Informality, as people so often forget today, can be as much work as formality. In fact, architecturally, it is much more work; no architect could lose track of his exterior composition while designing his interior spaces without running great risks, and the Shingle Style was all the more demanding of the architect because of its "free" aesthetic. The interior, for example, ideally developed around a great manorial "living hall," where the main entrance to the house was usually an integral part of an ensemble of entrance, fireplace, and inglenook (a cozy conversational alcove) that was also a common feature of Queen Anne houses generally. This required of a busy architect, who could scarcely repeat himself blatantly too often, a prodigious imagination, and it is not surprising that Richardson's dramatic living hall at the Paine House in Waltham (1884) is perhaps the most famous of its kind in the Boston area. Who does not relish Hitchcock's description of the stairs, which, he wrote, "pour down into the room like a mountain cataract"? At a much more ordinary level, the effect of such an interior could still be dramatic (Figure 104).

The Shingle Style, which was developed by architects who were at the same time shaping Queen Anne design generally in the 1880s, may thus be said to disclose yet again how strong a stimulant to original and indigenous design the various nineteenth-century revivals could be: Vincent Scully has called the Shingle Style "a unique American

achievement, one which has since been acclaimed by the whole world." In this case, however, New England's own seventeenth-century Medieval architecture played a crucial part. This led for the first time to the conscious revival and adaptation of an *American* historical style.

I T WAS Robert Swain Peabody who appears to have first pointed out that the seventeenth-century Fairbanks House in Dedham "would delight Mr. Norman Shaw," the chief luminary of the English Queen Anne movement so closely studied by American architects of similar bent. This interest in early American folk design significantly coincided with the 1876 United States Centennial, which naturally turned many minds toward America's Colonial past generally. The year after the Centennial a group of New York architects, including Charles Follen McKim, of whom more later, undertook a sketching trip along Boston's Colonial North Shore. Peabody himself went on a similar trip with Arthur Little to study Colonial houses in Portsmouth, New Hampshire, and in 1877 Peabody explicitly linked Queen Anne and Colonial in a paper to the Boston Society of Architects and in *American Architecture and Building News.* In the same year Little published the first architectural book on Colonial design: *Early New England Interiors.* Thus in the late 1870s and early 1880s, having discovered that there was in seventeenth-century American folk Gothic an American equivalent of sorts to the Medieval work the Queen Anne movement in England was trying to revive and develop forward, American architects increasingly transferred their attention for the first time to their own architectural history. The result was that as the British Queen Anne movement began to reenact and interpret English architectural history from late Medievalism to eighteenth-century Classicism, American architects tended increasingly toward a parallel reenactment, not of British architectural currents in the eighteenth century, but of the American Colonial architecture that from folk Gothic to High Georgian and Federal had reflected those English currents in a provincial way. The result was a "Colonial" Revival; that is, a revival of the eighteenth-century Georgian architecture that had succeeded folk Gothic.

Boston architects, naturally enough in view of their close touch with the Queen Anne movement, but also because of Boston's important Colonial architecture (which after the 1870s was increasingly admired and restored), were particularly susceptible to such tendencies. Two are of special interest: Robert Peabody and Arthur Little. Peabody was born in New Bedford in 1845, but moved early to Boston, after his father, a Unitarian clergyman, accepted a call to King's Chapel. After Boston Latin School and Harvard College and a brief period in Gridley J. Fox Bryant's office, Peabody studied first with Van Brunt and then in the late 1860s became associated with the Atelier Daumet at the Ecole des Beaux Arts, forming the famous partnership with John Goddard Stearns in 1870 that yielded Peabody and Stearns, a firm that in many ways would be to Boston what McKim, Mead and White were to New York and Burnham and Root to Chicago. Little, who designed a number of striking houses along Boston's North Shore (in Manchester, Swampscott, and Marblehead), was born in Boston in 1852, grew up at 2 Commonwealth Avenue, and after Chauncey Hall School studied at M.I.T. and apprenticed in Peabody's office before opening his own office in 1879. Both men in the late seventies designed early and important Colonial Revival houses. In Peabody's case, his Denny House on Brush Hill Road in Milton (Figure 83) has been called by

Wheaton Holden "a pivotal house in the emergence of the American Colonial Revival," while Little's Cliffs of 1878 in Swampscott has been characterized by Walter Knight Sturges as "the prototypal Colonial Revival House." Cliffs was the more remarkable of the two, for the hip roof and simple rectangular and horizontal shape of its main mass foreshadowed the future of the Colonial Revival. But Cliffs was an episode, however prophetic, and the Denny House (on which Little may have worked) is much more typical of the first stage of the Colonial Revival in the late 1870s and 1880s, when architects began more and more frequently to introduce blatantly Georgian details into houses such as the Denny that remained basically Queen Anne in their complex and asymmetrical massing.

This was not founded in ignorance. Rather, it derived from the fact that architects who had forsaken the French Academic formula for the more "creative" Queen Anne felt themselves quite capable of "improving" the Colonial work they increasingly admired. The frontispiece of the Carey House (Figure 84) at 28 Fayerweather Street in Cambridge, for example, designed by Sturgis and Brigham in 1882, resembles that of the Hancock House in Boston, of which Sturgis had prepared measured drawings; but at the Carey House this frontispiece is off center, and one cannot doubt that Sturgis's asymmetry is deliberate. Nor were such early attempts to revive Georgian forms, generally classified by scholars as "the Picturesque Colonial Revival," restricted to wooden suburban houses. At Rotch and Tilden's 211 Commonwealth Avenue (1882), a house whose lavish and varied Queen Anne interiors have already been touched on, the detail throughout this house is conspicuously Georgian, but is often imaginatively conceived. The front doorway, for example, is thought to have been modeled on a design by Asher Ben-

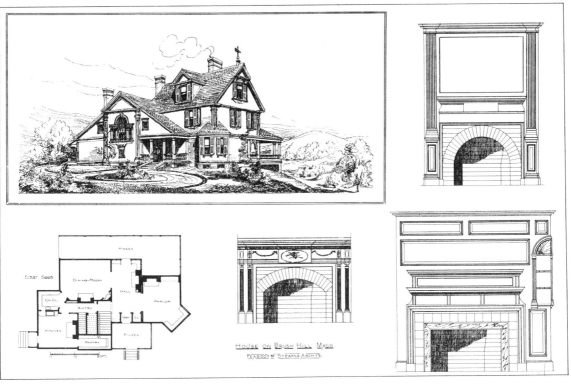

The early Colonial Revival was heavily influenced by Queen Anne asymmetry.

FIGURE 83. Peabody and Stearns. Denny House, Brush Hill Road, Milton, 1877.

FIGURE 84. Sturgis and Brigham. Carey House, 28 Fayerweather Street, Cambridge, 1882.

jamin, but Rotch persuaded Benjamin's composition into a kind of elliptical niche, which makes this doorway very much Rotch's own; so much so that a Colonial purist of the time pronounced the doorway a very bad copy. But that was to miss Rotch's point. He could easily have essayed a better copy. That he did not do so reflects Rotch's taste, not his ignorance of Benjamin's. And today there are not lacking scholars who admire both Sturgis's and Rotch's imagination, or at least respect the ingenious way in which they freely adapted Georgian forms in their own ways.

In such ways did the Queen Anne movement resolve itself finally into a full-fledged Colonial Revival that by the 1890s had shed its Queen Anne auspices altogether and yielded buildings that today are frequently mistaken for Bulfinch's own work. What an endless cycle of shifting tastes is the history of architecture and its telling! The architect who had become bored with French Academic Classicism and yielded to Queen Anne inventiveness so willingly that even when he discovered the charms of American Georgian he could not help "improving" upon it, was led finally by the Colonial Revival back to another kind of academic Classicism, so carefully modeled after Bulfinch's work that no Colonial purist had much to complain of after 1890. But if the purists were happy then, scholars have not been since. Many have argued that architecture in Boston crested in the mid-1880s. At the height of Richardson's career and at the point when Boston architects had achieved a mature local Queen Anne architecture and at the same time pioneered in developing in the city's environs a Shingle Style of unique distinction, Boston was perhaps the most vital architectural center in the country. Accordingly, many have deplored the abandonment of the highly inventive modes of the seventies and eighties in favor of a Colonial and ultimately an overall Classical Revival that seemed by comparison academic and even archaeological. Like Bunting, who concluded that the best Queen Anne work in the Back Bay of the mid-1880s stood on the threshold of an indigenous architecture, Vincent Scully, the scholar who first formally delineated the Shingle Style, has asserted that in the mid-1880s "it is possible that a decisive opportunity for American culture was lost because confidence in invention failed those to whom the opportunity was presented." Instead of developing the Shingle Style, Scully lamented, Boston architects, and Eastern architects generally, abandoned that task — and the future of American architecture — to Frank Lloyd Wright, whose early work is widely thought to have proceeded from the Shingle Style just as much as did the Colonial Revival.

The reader will recall similar reactions as style has succeeded style in these pages. Very often when a shift in fashion leads architecture in a new direction that leaves behind a particularly distinguished accomplishment, such a regret has been voiced by those who see in what was abandoned the potential for that illusive "Americanism" for which American architecture has ever striven. But as we shall see shortly, that same "American" quality, and a profound originality as well, would later on be discovered by other scholars in the Classical and other "academic" revivals that succeeded the Queen Anne and Shingle vogues. Neither taste nor the history of taste stands still.

Before discussing that Classical Revival, however, we must turn to other innovations in Boston's architecture during this period, innovations more fundamental than style.

4

STREETCAR CITY,
GARDEN SUBURBS

To WALK THE LENGTH of Beacon Street from Joy Street to Charlesgate and then walk back from Charlesgate along Commonwealth Avenue to the Public Garden is to trace the history of architecture in Boston in the nineteenth century — from Bulfinch's own work to the most exuberant Queen Anne of the seventies and eighties and the ensuing picturesque Colonial Revival — the development of which we will take up in Chapter 6. But even if one were to extend one's purview to include the few more blocks of houses on Beacon Hill and in the Back Bay that lie behind Beacon Street and Commonwealth Avenue, one can still traverse in an afternoon what was the only first-class residential quarter in the city proper in the late nineteenth and early twentieth centuries. Accordingly, many members of the rapidly growing professional and merchant class who by the 1880s presided over Boston lived elsewhere. Henry L. Pierce, for example, whose bequest in 1896 of over a quarter of a million dollars to the new Museum of Fine Arts was the largest such gift to that institution in the nineteenth century, lived in Dorchester, one of several such suburbs that by the 1870s were no longer independent cities and towns. Pierce did not have to move in 1872 to be elected mayor of Boston, for by then the town of Dorchester had been annexed to the city of Boston. In the later nineteenth century, suburbs were easier to annex than were coves to fill, and this fact trans-

formed Boston at this time and precipitated a revolution in residential design.

The nature and extent of this development is clear in an 1888 publication, E. O. Stanley's *Boston and Its Suburbs*. The first section, "Walks about Boston," includes the business district, Beacon Hill, the North End, and the Back Bay and the nearby factory and working-class areas of Charlestown, South Boston, and East Boston. The title of the second section, "Drives about Boston," which includes Brookline, Brighton, Newton, Jamaica Plain, West Roxbury, Cambridge, Roxbury and Dorchester, Quincy and Arlington, illustrates clearly, however, how completely the old inner suburbs had by then been merged into one enlarged city in contemporary thinking. The distinction made between "Walks" and "Drives" also reflects nicely the nature of this newly enlarged Boston; it was commuter railroad lines (there were ten railroad stations in the city proper in 1888) and ultimately the increasing network of trolley lines and subways that made Boston's expansion possible. By trolley, a Dorchester resident could reach his office in the city proper as easily as could a Back Bay resident. Accordingly, Sam B. Warner, Jr., in his pioneering study of three of these new residential quarters — Dorchester, Roxbury, and Jamaica Plain — christened them "streetcar suburbs."

Another contemporary publication, *Bacon's Dictionary of Boston*, issued in 1883, conveys some sense of the enthusiasm the new suburban residential quarters aroused and notes those that were generally thought to be the most fashionable:

The suburbs of Boston are famed as the most beautiful in the world . . . nature has been assisted by art in a way that has entirely girdled the city with a succession of delightful communities. . . . The most famous and fashionable of all the suburbs lie to the southward and westward, with beautiful rural estates of Boston's merchant princes. Milton, Brookline and Newton, in particular, stand in the front rank in this respect, although but little in advance of Dorchester and West Roxbury. The northern suburbs also contain many delightful estates. . . .

It seemed at first as if the city of Boston would absorb those cities and towns Bostonians began to spill into in the 1850s and then inundated after the 1870s. Ultimately, however, only six voted to join the city: Roxbury (1868), West Roxbury (including Jamaica Plain and Roslindale), Charlestown, and Brighton (1874), Dorchester (1870), and Hyde Park (1912). Newton and Brookline were among many communities that declined annexation. Illogically, stubbornly, they and most of the rest of the suburbs clung tenaciously to their "independence," thus divorcing their political life from their cultural and economic life. As Warner noted in *Streetcar Suburbs:*

No period in Boston's history was more dynamic than the prosperous years of the second half of the nineteenth century. . . . In fifty years it changed from a merchant city of 200,000 inhabitants to an industrial metropolis of over a million. In 1850 Boston was a tightly packed seaport; by 1900 it sprawled over a ten-mile radius and contained thirty-one cities and towns.

Although they could avoid annexation, none of the suburbs could avoid the effects of growth. Few realize that many — including Belmont, Holbrook, Melrose, Norwood, Somerville, West-

wood, Maynard, Winchester, Norwell, Everett, Rockland, and Whitman, for example — were incorporated as separate municipalities only in the 1840–1900 period. Another result of metropolitan growth is the number of suburban towns that became cities in this period: Cambridge and Roxbury did so in 1846, and by 1900 Charlestown, Lynn, Chelsea, Somerville, Newton, Gloucester, Brockton, Malden, Waltham, Woburn, Quincy, Everett, Medford, Beverly, and Melrose had followed suit.

All these communities possessed their own architecture. The seventeenth-century Stetson House in Dover; the so-called Old Castle in Rockport, dating in part from 1678; the eighteenth-century Derby House in Danvers (moved from its original location in Peabody); and the Fisher-Richardson House of the same century in Mansfield may be said to stand for their fellows in almost every town-become-suburb, many of which (the Lee House in Marblehead, for example, built in 1768) are of singular architectural interest. So also are many nineteenth-century buildings. Often, of course, these were designed by local architects: Wesley Lyng Minor, for example, who settled in Brockton in 1882, designed the Brockton City Hall (1890–1891) and a number of fine houses,

In the 1870s and 1880s suburban institutional architecture increasingly rivaled that of the inner city.

FIGURE 85. Hammatt Billings. College Hall, Wellesley College, Wellesley, from Lake Waban, ca. 1885. Demolished.

FIGURE 86. J. H. Besarick. St. John's Seminary, Brighton, 1881–1889.

FIGURE 87. Schickel and Ditmars. The Basilica of Our Lady of Perpetual Help, better known as the Mission Church, Roxbury, 1876. The towers of the basilica were added by Franz Joseph Untersee in 1909.

FIGURE 88. An example of suburban commercial architecture of some distinction: Whitney Hall, the former S. S. Pierce Building, 1324–1334 Beacon Street, Coolidge Corner, Brookline. Designed by Winslow and Wetherell in 1898–1899, it was the suburban counterpart of the S. S. Pierce Building in Copley Square (Figure 60).

including the remarkably preserved Kingman House at 309 Main Street (1886), which possesses extensive mural decoration by Alexander Pindikowsky. Sometimes, too, New York architects worked in Boston's suburbs: P. C. Keeley designed the Church of the Nativity in Scituate (1872; demolished). Nonetheless, most suburban work was done by Boston architects.

The image of picturesque towers lifting from wooded hills by lakes, rivers, or coastline — as well as the crowding in what was increasingly "intown" —lured many institutions to the suburbs, and as many architects. Wellesley College (Figure 85), for example, begun in the suburb of that name in 1875, was largely the work of Hammatt Billings, Ware and Van Brunt, and Heins and La Farge. Most of this development was closer to the city proper. In particular, Brighton and nearby Newton, its hills reminiscent of Rome's, began in the 1880s to take on the character of what has been called a "Little Rome," so extensive was the Roman Catholic institutional development there. St. John's Seminary, its early buildings designed by J. H. Besarick and built in the 1880s of Brighton pudding stone quarried on the site (Figure 86), still crowns the hills above Chandler's Pond, and was surrounded in this century by Archbishop's House and the Chancery; by Boston College, of which more later; and by St. Elizabeth's Hospital, the last two of which moved there from the South End. In Medford the Tufts College Chapel of 1882 by J. Philip Rinn stands at the crest of another hill. As the suburbs grew, many new public buildings were also naturally required. Of town halls, perhaps the most remarkable was the vividly picturesque Wellesley Town Hall and Library by Shaw and Hunnewell (1881) and the dramatically sited Belmont Town Hall, designed in the same year by Hartwell and Richardson. The Arlington Public Library was

designed by Cabot, Everett and Mead (1892); Dedham's Public Library by Ware and Van Brunt (1888); and the nearby railway station (1883) by John Sturgis. Four years later Charles Brigham designed the Stoughton railroad station as well as (with John Spofford) the first of several extant buildings at the Foxboro State Hospital. Other important suburban work by Boston architects includes the Lynn City Hall (1867; demolished) and the Gloucester City Hall of 1869–1871, both designed by G. J. F. Bryant's office.

An enormous number of churches were also naturally built by Boston architects in these new residential areas, for the weekday commuter was much less likely to commute on Sunday morning. Particularly fine examples are the Assumption in Brookline (1878–1886) and Christ Church in Waltham (1897–1898), both by Peabody and Stearns, who did an enormous amount of suburban work, including the Chelsea Town Hall of 1909 and dozens of schools throughout Brookline, Newton, and West Roxbury. Many of these churches were as large and lavishly decorated as any in the city proper. Peter Paul Pugin designed an enormous and elaborate high altar reredos for Sacred Heart Church in East Cambridge (1883); and the Church of the Most Precious Blood in Hyde Park, designed by Charles Bateman in 1885, was endowed with a rich interior of variegated marble and lustrous woodwork. The most ambitious was the Mission Church in Roxbury (Figure 87). Boston's basilica (in fact as well as name: its official name is the Basilica of Our Lady of Perpetual Help) is an enormous and impressive church, begun in 1876 and completed in 1910. Designed by Schickel and Ditmars with towers by Franz Joseph Untersee, it holds 4000 people and seats 2000. Much smaller, but as important because it is an outstanding example of High Victorian picturesque design, is Ware and Van

Brunt's St. Stephen's Church (1880) in Lynn.

So extensive was Victorian suburban development that one could go on in this vein indefinitely. The commercial architecture of the new areas is also worthy of attention. At Quincy Square and at Coolidge Corner in Brookline (Figure 88), there are splendid late nineteenth-century half-timbered retail and business blocks that ought to be carefully preserved and restored. In Dorchester, the Walter Baker Chocolate complex, designed for the most part by Winslow and Wetherell in 1888–1892, is an impressive red-brick complex that extends for nearly a block on each side of a large intersection. A great deal of excellent sculpture also adorns the suburbs: one thinks of Henry Hutson Kitson's figure of Sir Richard Saltonstall in Watertown, Bela Pratt's Soldiers and Sailors Monument in Malden, and Cyrus Dallin's *The Hunter* in Arlington. Sometimes the only work in Boston of important sculptors is in the suburbs. This is true of Albert Atkins, whose best-known local work is his War Memorial in Roslindale, and of Lee Lawrie, the sculptor of the famous *Atlas* at Rockefeller Center in New York, whose only Boston commissions will be found in Forest Hills Cemetery in West Roxbury and at Richmond Court in Brookline. The most important suburban landmarks, however, have either been touched on already or will be later in this book. The streetcar suburbs are interesting chiefly for their houses.

Most of these were built in by far the largest of Boston's suburbs, Dorchester. A quiet rural town when it was annexed to Boston, by the First World War it was challenging Providence and Worcester in population. In fact, Dorchester became the largest community in New England except for Boston itself, of which it remains the largest part; its population within fifty years of annexation jumped from scarcely 12,000 to nearly 200,000. It was an unprecedented expansion, which like the filling of Back Bay shows the city's extraordinary vitality in the late nineteenth century. So huge and so diverse is Dorchester that it is a kind of microcosm of all the streetcar suburbs, and is thus perhaps the best introduction to their design concept.

How little we understand the architectural history of Boston is evident in the assumptions that will usually arise in any comparison of an early nineteenth-century streetscape (Beacon Street across from Boston Common, for example, the evolution of which we discussed in Chapter 1) with a late nineteenth-century streetscape, such as lower Cushing Avenue on the western slope of Jones Hill at Upham's Corner in Dorchester, one of the few areas in the streetcar suburbs that has been sufficiently researched to serve as a case study. Stylistically, the two streetscapes reflect the different fashions of the early and the late nineteenth century. But insofar as the streetscape — the relation of one house to the other — is concerned, just as most people assume because of our present-day definition of "town house" (connected to a similar house and built nearly on top of the sidewalk) that Beacon Street was meant to look the way it does today, so also because of our present-day definition of the suburban ideal (amply set back and widely separated houses obscured by trees and grounds and hidden along curvilinear streets) we assume that on Cushing Avenue later houses must have been inserted between the original houses, resulting in the densely packed housing characteristic of the streetcar suburbs. But these assumptions are both untrue. As we have seen, Beacon Street's character today derives from later houses that connected what

Lower Cushing Avenue, Jones Hill, Dorchester.

FIGURE 89. Looking eastward; from right to left are the Southworth House (designed by Sylvester Parshley, 1899); the Chamberlain House (attributed to David Chamberlain, 1875); the Hoadley House (Henry J. Preston, 1886); the Sylvester Parshley House (Sylvester Parshley, 1893; see also Figure 117); the Chadwick House (William G. Preston, 1895; see also Figure 91); and the Gallier House (W. H. Besarick, 1894). To the far left is St. Mary's Church (Henry Vaughan, 1888; chancel and transepts by Hartwell and Richardson, 1893).

FIGURE 90. Subdivision plan of lower Cushing Avenue after it had been largely built up, including the houses that appear in Figure 89. Because houses were often owned by wives and because of changes in ownership, the Southworth House (directly behind the Dyer House) appears on the map as owned by Sarah F. Parshley and the Chamberlain House as owned by S. Parshley.

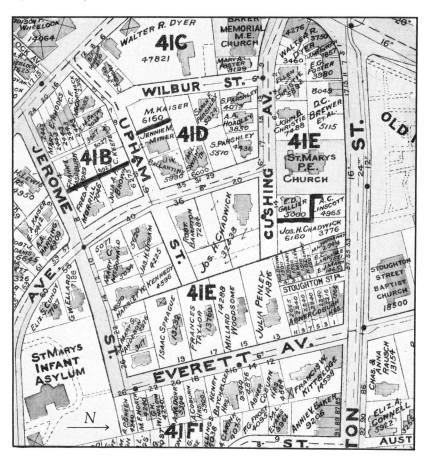

had been free-standing town houses into the present-day blocks (Figures 10, 11). It is the Cushing Avenue streetscape (Figure 89), however at odds with our present-day definition of suburban these densely massed houses may be, that appears today exactly as its designers and first residents intended. This becomes clear when one studies its development.

The first person to comment upon it was David Clapp, head of one of the old Yankee families that had dominated the town of Dorchester between its founding in 1630 and its annexation to Boston in 1870 in much the same way that a number of Boston families had wielded great influence in the capital city. Clapp's family had lived on Jones Hill since the early 1700s. Yet when he noted in a history of the hill he wrote in 1883 that on the nearby Dyer estate "instead of three or four scattered farmhouses, one may now see scores of beautiful dwelling houses," this venerable Dorchesterite was delighted, remarking how fortunate it was that the hill had attracted homeowners with "the means and capacity to improve and adorn a naturally fine location." Clapp, to be sure, profited from it; in 1889 he broke up his own estate into house lots and made a great deal of money. But he not only proudly named the new street he laid out after the Devon estate (Salcombe) from which the Clapps had come to Dorchester in 1630; he also built a house on one of his new lots for himself and three nearby for his children. And Clapp's enthusiasm reflected Micah Dyer's, whose subdivision of his estate Clapp approved of so heartily.

"The venerable Micah Dyer," as Justin Winsor called him in *Memorial History of Boston*, was a graduate of Tilton Seminary and Harvard Law School and a descendant of a seventeenth-century Massachusetts settler. Though his wife belonged, like Clapp, to an old Dorchester family (Mrs. Dyer's grandfather had helped fortify Dorchester Heights during the Revolution), Micah Dyer was from a leading Boston family. Contemporary biographical directories noted particularly Dyer's role as a pioneer in women's professional education in this country: he was the first president of the Female Medical College of Boston, which merged with the Boston University School of Medicine to become the first medical school in the United States to grant a full medical degree to women. Mrs. Dyer, a leader in Boston social and club circles, was herself a founder of the Women's Charity Club, under the auspices of which began the New England Hospital for Women and Children and the first school of nursing in the country. The Dyers were thus "old money" insofar as both the city of Boston and the town of Dorchester were concerned and when Dorchester was annexed they were ideally suited to subdivide their estate — where their continued presence as houses rose all around them between 1875 and 1900 not only lent great prestige to the new residential area but illustrated that, like Clapp, they regarded such development as an improvement. (So also did their son, who lived in the Dyer House until his retirement in 1918.) Moreover, the fact that Micah Dyer sold his Union Park town house in the South End in 1865, and moved to Jones Hill and the Dorchester house that thereafter was his only Boston residence, indicates that Dyer intended all along not to create a country estate but a new residential quarter of the enlarging city.

He seems at first to have envisaged connected row houses. When he first subdivided his estate in 1874, retaining what had been the estate house for himself (on a much smaller lot), the subdivision plan he filed showed narrow, 2000-square-foot lots, usable only for row houses. But although a long, curvilinear street, Cushing Avenue, was laid out through Dyer's land in 1881 to provide access to St. Mary's Infant Asylum, which had located at the hill's summit, in twelve years Dyer attracted only one buyer, and that buyer had bought *two* lots and erected in the center of them one clapboarded, free-standing house very similar to Dyer's own. Accordingly, in 1886, a new subdivision plan was filed that abandoned the narrow lots and provided for large 5000- and 6000-square-foot parcels that could serve only the large, free-standing houses now standing on them (Figure 90). However small the Cushing Avenue lots now seem, they are thus more than twice the size Dyer had originally intended and as they all sold at a regular rate throughout the 1880s and nineties it is clear such lots were what was wanted. But, one wonders, by whom?

A hundred years later one cannot exactly reconstruct the population of any neighborhood. But the unusually intensive research undertaken in this area has yielded a good deal of data about Dyer's new neighbors. On or facing these two short blocks of fifteen houses on lower Cushing Avenue between Wilbur Street and Upham Avenue, developed by Dyer, the original homebuilders of 1875–1900 included eight persons of whom something is known. James Humphreys Upham, who built 40 Cushing Avenue (Figure 116) in 1895 and lived there until his death, was the last chairman of the Board of Selectmen of the Town of Dorchester, a trustee of the Boston City Hospital, and treasurer of the Grand Commandery of the Knights Templars of Massachusetts and Rhode Island. One of the leaders of Yankee Dorchester (he was a descendant of the merchant after whom Upham's Corner had been named around 1800), Upham illustrates as did Clapp and Mrs. Dyer that old money as well as new would put down roots in the new subdivision. Upham was also the chairman of the Dorchester Committee of Robert Treat Paine's prestigious As-

FIGURE 91. William G. Preston. Chadwick House, 20 Cushing Avenue, 1895.

sociated Charities, and Paine's youngest son, George Lyman Paine, the rector of St. Mary's Episcopal Church, was Upham's neighbor at 21 Cushing Avenue, across the street.

Paine and his wife rented from Sylvester Parshley, who built 21 Cushing in 1900 next to his own home, which he had built at 17–19 Cushing Avenue in 1893 (Figure 117). Parshley was among the foremost builders in New England. One of three partners in the firm of McNeil Brothers, one of Boston's major builders in the late nineteenth century, Parshley superintended the building of many of the great houses of the Back Bay, Fifth Avenue, and Newport, where the firm built the Vanderbilt estate, Rough Point, for Peabody and Stearns. They rebuilt 46 Beacon Street into Eben Jordan's palatial residence, built 199 Commonwealth Avenue for McKim, Mead and White, and were also responsible for a whole range of public buildings: including the R. H. White department store on downtown Washington Street, several buildings at Harvard, and the great Sub-Treasury and Post Office building in Post Office Square (Figure 47). Parshley's own chief work was the

Senate Reading Room in the Library of Congress in Washington.

Behind his own house, Parshley built a third house in 1897–1898 for his son, Wilbur, after whom the adjoining street was named. Eventually, from about 1900 to 1921, Parshley rented this house to James Edgar Southworth, for whom Parshley built the adjoining "automobile house" in 1910. A prominent Boston merchant of old family (listed in the Social Register), Southworth was general manager of the Wheat Export Company and of the United States Grain Exchange and, according to his *Transcript* obituary, "handled all the grain shipped from the port of Boston during the First World War." Another house, 35 Cushing, was built for himself by the Reverend John Ballantine, the pastor of the nearby Pilgrim Congregational Church; the house next door was built in 1896 by Amanda Loguee, treasurer of the Clifton Manufacturing Company of Boston, New York, and Chicago. And across the street, 20 Cushing was built in 1895 by Joseph Houghton Chadwick (Figure 91). The president of the Chadwick Lead Company and a founding trustee of Boston University, Chadwick was described in a contemporary report in the Boston *Traveler* as the "Lead King of Boston." Finally, 36 Cushing Avenue was built by Robert Bampton, Chadwick's partner.

These eight residents of both sides of the curving streetscape erected on Dyer's land — Upham, Paine, Parshley, Southworth, Ballantine, Loguee, Chadwick, and Bampton — having all been (like Dyer) persons of some consequence in Boston, are easier to "reconstruct," biographically, a hundred or so years later, than their neighbors. But, since Warner has documented the fact that the "one basic pattern" organizing these suburbs was "segregation by income," we can assume the neighbors were Bostonians of a similar type. All but one

were Bostonians, as opposed to pre-annexation Dorchesterites; every resident but one of these fifteen houses maintained his principal business address in the city proper. All were Yankee, Protestant, and relatively wealthy. As had been true on Beacon Hill at the beginning of the century, when the patriot Federalists had succeeded to the state of the exiled Loyalist gentry, most of the residents of newly built up Cushing Avenue at the end of the century also represented new money, which tended here as in the Back Bay to build more pretentious houses than did the scions of the patriot families that by the 1890s represented old money. The older families, though fewer, were, however, more important: it was the old money on Jones Hill, the Clapps', the Dyers', the Uphams', the Paines', and also St. Mary's Episcopal Church's, that naturally attracted the new money. And it is also clear that throughout the area, a web of personal connections among homeowners, developers, and architects (who were sometimes the same people) determined the shape it finally took.

The Dyers, for example, were among the most prominent Methodist families in the city: and this cannot be unconnected with the fact that at the foot of Cushing Avenue, next to the Dyer House, a large, towered stone Methodist church was built in 1890. Boston University was the centerpiece of Methodism in Boston, and Chadwick, who built 20 Cushing five years after the church was built, was, as we have noted, a founding trustee of the university. Chadwick, like Parshley, bought all the lots around his house and started to develop his land, inviting his partner, Robert Bampton, to build 36 Cushing in 1897. Bampton, however, was Episcopalian, doubtless the more easily drawn to Cushing Avenue by the erection there in 1888 of a new St. Mary's Church for the famous parish where Bishop Phillips Brooks had been confirmed and where Governor

Henry J. Gardner had been a parishioner. And it was St. Mary's that evidently prompted Parshley to build 21 Cushing, which, immediately it was built, was rented successively by the two rectors of St. Mary's of this period. A third church in Upham's Corner, Pilgrim Congregational, yielded, as we have seen, another of these houses, built by its pastor.

As Irish Catholic families began to appear in these blocks after the turn of the century, St. Margaret's Hospital, which evolved out of St. Mary's Infant Asylum, was increasingly a part of this web. Patrick McDonald, who lived at the corner of Cushing and Jerome, a state representative and close friend of Mayor John Fitzgerald, was treasurer of the hospital; Edward J. O'Neil, senior partner of O'Neil and Parker of Boston and sometime president of the Massachusetts Casualty Underwriters Association, who bought Chadwick's mansion in 1914, was McDonald's successor as the hospital's treasurer. Similarly, John Arthur Foley, who bought 2 Wilbur Street in 1918, was clerk of the corporation and president of the medical staff at St. Margaret's. A graduate of Harvard College and Harvard Medical School, Foley was also president of the New England College of Pharmacy and professor of clinical medicine at the Boston University School of Medicine. When one recalls that throughout the whole twenty-five-year development of these blocks virtually all the lots for sale were owned, successively or simultaneously, by Dyer, Upham, Parshley, and Chadwick, and sold with deed covenants requiring houses of similar character to those alrady built ("not detrimental to a first-class residential area"), one begins to suspect how carefully the development of these two blocks was controlled by a group of people whose mutual connections and interests are so evident. This is reflected, too, in the architecture of Cushing Avenue.

Chadwick's house (Figure 91) was designed by William G. Preston, whose important Back Bay work we have already noted. Preston, who probably also designed Bampton's house next door, had designed many buildings for Boston University, as well as the Chadwick Lead Building itself, still extant in downtown Boston on High Street. Four Cushing Avenue houses were designed by W. H. Besarick, the city architect of Boston. They stand, significantly, to either side of St. Mary's Church, of which Besarick was a parishioner. In fact, Besarick, Preston, and Parshley (who was his own designer) designed nine of the fifteen houses on these two blocks. That and the fact that other architects working in the area were well-known designers and that these were expensive houses (averaging about $10,500 each) account in large part for the area's architectural quality.

Another factor was St. Mary's Church. A Gothic church of national importance (William Morgan has noted that it possesses "probably the finest timber roof of its kind in the United States"), St. Mary's was the first and only parish church in the city designed by Henry Vaughan, one of the original architects of Washington Cathedral. Half-timbered and very domestic in feeling, St. Mary's established a superb anchor for Cushing Avenue, which sweeps down gently to the church from the corner of Upham Avenue, where stands a Medieval house of 1894 (Figure 116) by another British architect, Herbert Moseley. Across the street from St. Mary's is a fine Medieval house, designed by Henry J. Preston in 1886 (Figure 92). Next door, Parshley's own home at 17–19 Cushing (Figure 117) is a Queen Anne house of great distinction and coherence of design whose Georgian detail effects a superb transition to Chadwick's house, which like all the rest of these houses is decisively Georgian. In fact, the houses of William and Henry Preston, Parshley, and

Besarick, clustering about Vaughan's church, form one of the finest architectural ensembles in the streetcar suburbs. And every house stands exactly today as far from its neighbors as its first home-builders and architects desired! Clearly, wealthy and prominent citizens insisted upon such densely massed houses. Chadwick and Parshley, for example, bought up most of Dyer's remaining lots and built upon them (next door to themselves) other large houses on equally small lots — though both owned enough land to indulge, had they wished to, in "estates." It was a design concept created by the homeowners themselves.

The best way to discover why this apparently curious design concept was preferred on Dyer's land to either estatelike spaciousness or connected town houses is to inquire briefly into what may have lured these homeowners to Dyer's lots in the first place. This is not as difficult to determine as one might think. First, these houses were all built after the 1876 Centennial in an area whose important Colonial landmarks received much attention in Boston's guidebooks of the time. An 1885 guide to the city, for example, noted that the burying ground at Upham's Corner, on the other side of St. Mary's Church, dated from 1634, that Richard Mather was buried there, and that a few blocks away stood the Blake House (ca. 1650). The same guide, noting of Upham's Corner that "nowhere else can be seen the blending of old and new than here," went on to point out that the prestigious quality of the area was being maintained and that "a great number of beautiful mansions have been erected in recent years." Nor were more practical things overlooked in this guide; no prospective homeowner could have failed to notice that fifteen of the eighteen stores listed in the Dorchester section of the guide were in Upham's Corner, or that it was also a crossroads of several rail and trolley lines. If this sounds more like

building a city than a suburban refuge, that fact is significant. The crest of Upham's Corner commercial development came quickly, in the early 1920s, and it was very urban indeed: it was there, within two blocks of Parshley's home, that John and Paul Cifrino developed a store that was "unique in the history of food stores" and one that Professor William Marnell describes at length in his fascinating *Once Upon a Store: A Biography of the World's First Supermarket*. He admits it is a perilous claim but points out that no one has challenged it.

Another sign of the area's growth was the new Columbia Road parkway. This road, the principal access to Dyer's side of the hill (its parklike character was destroyed in the 1950s in favor of more traffic lanes), connected Franklin Park and the Dorchester Bay waterfront: the first, the largest park in New England, the second, a yachting center of importance. And its effect seems to have preceded it. Dyer, who had gladly yielded land for Cushing Avenue, similarly encouraged the construction of the new parkway: in his *American Series* biography, in noting that Dyer's progressive tendencies were frequently the incentive to active measures for the public good, Dyer's biographer cited as the best example of this that "anticipating the ultimate construction of Columbia Road some years prior to the commencement of work upon that splendid thoroughfare, Dyer, at considerable personal expense, set back the ancient trees upon the street line of his fine estate at Upham's Corner in order to facilitate the improvement." Dyer's lots also possessed splendid views of not only the parkway but the Dorchester waterfront it extended to: *King's Handbook of Boston* throughout the 1870s described the Jones Hill view as "overlooking Boston and its thronging suburbs and the island-strewn harbor and the open sea beyond, as in a bird's-eye view."

Unfortunately, no real estate advertisements have been discovered in further support of all this, but on April 27, 1870, an advertisement did appear in the *Transcript* for one of the adjoining Jones Hill subdivisions that stressed that the estate house would remain, to set the tone of the area; that the ocean views were "unsurpassed"; and most important of all, that these Jones Hill lots were "the finest property *within three miles of State Street* now on the market" (my italics). Thus it is not surprising that, when one turns to the houses themselves, their design reflects most of these factors.

In some respects, this is obvious: most houses, for example, have lookout towers, glass-enclosed "sky parlors," or third-floor porches to take advantage of the view. As the area built up, twelve of the houses were increasingly Colonial Revival, not only recalling the general fashion of the day but, of course, reviving the historical Colonial image of the area. All the houses are free-standing in garden settings, thus reflecting the same concern with preserving and enhancing the landscape evident in the adjoining Columbia Road parkway, itself the result of Bostonians' determination to halt the progressive obliteration of the landscape that had been under way in Boston since the early nineteenth century, when even the small gardens around Beacon Hill houses had fallen victim to the scarcity of land. And if one notices not only their garden settings but also the regular alignment to each other and to the street of all these densely massed and similarly scaled houses, it will be evident that their design reflects more than anything else their proximity (by trolley) to State Street — indeed, to the business district of the city proper. In fact, this proximity explains the whole curious design concept of large mansions on seemingly tiny lots. Today, what distinguishes these densely massed houses in our perception is their lack of land: what distinguished

them in the minds of those who built them was that they possessed any kind of grounds in the first place, for these houses — built by men who were not Dorchesterites so much as Bostonians — were not in our sense of the term suburban houses at all. Cushing Avenue's increasingly Colonial Revival houses were a more profound and fundamental "Colonial Revival" than we suspect. They were an attempt to revive in the vast new lands of the city the ideal town house — detached, and on its garden lot — that had been so characteristic of Boston until the scarcity of land had begun to obliterate that ideal in the 1820s (Figures 10, 11). In fact, several homeowners on Cushing Avenue possessed country homes — but not on Cushing Avenue.

T HAT parks and parkways, as well as trolleys, knit the streetcar suburbs into the city is very important. These areas were called "garden suburbs" long before they were christened "streetcar suburbs" because Boston's park system was closely related to them. The work of Frederick Law Olmsted, who was by the 1870s the foremost landscape designer in this country and perhaps in the world, the development of the park system, like the Back Bay itself an outstanding example of nineteenth-century urban planning, has been described by Cynthia Zaitzevsky:

From 1878 until his retirement in 1895, Olmsted helped the Park Commissioners refine their 1876 master plan for a park system, as well as designing the individual parks. The core of the park system was its continuous portion or the "emerald necklace," consisting of five major parks (Back Bay Fens, Muddy River Improvement, Jamaica Park, Arnold Arboretum and Franklin Park) and their connecting parkways. Commonwealth Avenue connected the new park system with the existing Common and Public Garden. In 1897 Columbia Road was widened and joined to

The design concept of the streetcar-suburb detached townhouse: the Hoadley House, 15 Cushing Avenue (1886), a representative upper middle-class single-family house. FIGURE 92. The house is shown flanked by other large detached houses, massed closely and regularly to each other and to the street, and is seen past the block-long retaining wall that frames the "block park" — a terraced garden setting common to all the houses, whose lots are significantly unbroken by fencing or planting on lot lines. FIGURE 93. Detail of Hoadley House tower, showing the proximity of the house to the civic and commercial towers of nearby Upham's Corner (see Figure 90), already a busy retail center by the 1880s.

the Dorchesterway and the Strandway, linking Franklin Park with Marine Park in South Boston. Individually, the five major parks are among the most important and innovative of Olmsted's designs. Together, they form a five-mile corridor of continuous parkland that has long been recognized as a landmark of urban planning [Plate 1].

A major factor in the development of the parks was the fact that however well designed new "garden" suburban subdivisions might be, their effect in the long run would be to dramatically cut down open spaces if these new subdivisions were not connected by parkways and adjoining parklands, generously dispersed. As Edwin Bacon pointed out:

When the desirability of parks in the sense of New York's Central Park, Brooklyn's Prospect Park and Philadelphia's Fairmount Park, was suggested here, it was common to say: "But

Boston does not need parks; look at our suburbs! They are parks in themselves." Early in the 'seventies of the nineteenth century the rapid changes in the suburbs caused by the expansion of the city . . . made increasingly evident the importance of doing something.

Today, when the park system itself has barely survived in some places and when the small gardens of a street like Cushing Avenue seem a very pale reflection of that system, it is hard to see their connection. One can do so easily, however, by studying Figure 101 (the Jamaicaway) and then Figures 92 and 93 (Cushing Avenue). Notice that shrubbery along Cushing Avenue more often hugs the house than marks the lot lines, where fences seldom occur and were, in fact, sometimes prohibited by deed restriction. Notice, too, that the effect of this landscape design is to create a kind of large "block park," visually a *common*

85

setting for *all* the houses of the block. The effect was often greatly heightened (as on Cushing Avenue) by retaining walls running uniformly around all the houses of the block and yielding a block-long grassy terrace from which the houses rise. The point is that it was a garden setting — with its corollary: light and air on all four sides of a house — that the detached town house wanted; not yards or gardens of any size for any purpose such as recreation or food growing; this would have been absurd one block from a major commercial center, Upham's Corner (Figure 93). Actually, the houses on Cushing Avenue and other such streets have just about as much land on all four sides as houses on Commonwealth Avenue have on one side (Figure 158).

A problem here is that we have lost track of a continuing factor in residential design in Boston that can be traced back to Boston's first important row houses. When Bulfinch was forced by his financial failure to abandon the second crescent he had planned to build facing the Tontine Crescent and built instead a series of free-standing double houses, it was the free-standing houses that became the most fashionable, according to Frank Chouteau Brown, "even though the side yards were *very narrow*." The italics are my own and point to how deep-seated in Boston was the preference for even the narrow yards of semi-detached houses as opposed to the block of connected houses, two walls in each of which had to be windowless. Admittedly, the Tontine Crescent inspired Bostonians to emulate it for generations. But this was at least partly due to scarcity of land and not because the detached house had ceased to be the ideal. Thus, in 1838, E. C. Wines noted that on what is now downtown Summer Street the gardens of the houses were such that "Town and Country seem here married to each other." And a half-century or more later

this ideal was still very much alive. How vibrantly is clear from Edward Everett Hale's observation in 1893 that

As late as in 1817, in a description of Boston which accompanied a show which a Frenchman had made by carving and painting the separate houses, it was said, with some triumph, that there were nine blocks of buildings in the town. This means that all the other buildings stood with windows or doors on each of the four sides, and in most instances with trees, or perhaps little lanes, between; as all people will live when the Kingdom of Heaven comes.

For Hale, for countless thousands more, the Kingdom *had* come, so to speak, in the streetcar suburbs. And just as the Tontine doubles, when compared with the Tontine Crescent, looked more desirable, despite their small yards, so also did Cushing Avenue when compared with a street of connected town houses (Figures 110, 111). Significantly, Edward Everett Hale lived, not in the Back Bay, but in Roxbury Highlands.

In 1878 this area was described in *King's Handbook of Boston* as a quarter "sought by those 'well-to-do' citizens who desire to establish their homes not too far from 'down-town' and where the advantanges of both city and country can be agreeably combined" — echoing, however unconsciously, in an 1878 description of the Highlands E. C. Wines's comment in his 1838 description of Summer Street, which by the 1880s was a bustling shopping area. Another contemporary source, Edward Stanwood's *Boston Illustrated* of 1872, described the Highlands in these terms and at the height of the Back Bay's prestige:

. . . on Elm Hill Avenue, and between it and Walnut Avenue, some of the best houses are located. Many of these are veritable palaces, representing all styles of architecture and varying in cost from $12,000 to $60,000. Many of them are surrounded with trees, shrubbery, flower gardens, or grassy lawns, adding to the beauty and attraction of the streets and

Both attached and detached town houses were characteristic of the streetcar suburbs.
FIGURE 94. J. Williams Beal. Harris Wood Crescent, Fountain Square, Roxbury Highlands, 1890.
FIGURE 95. One of the houses finally built on Townsend Street, at 140–142, one house removed from the Harris Wood Crescent, ca. 1890.
FIGURE 96. Another connected residential block in the streetcar suburbs, again facing a park. Murdoch Boyle. 1791–1821 Beacon Street, Brookline, 1907.

avenues as excellent driveways. Walnut Avenue, Humboldt Avenue, and Elm Hill Avenue all lead up to Franklin Park, and the two latter end at Seaver Street, which skirts its northern side.

A particularly elegant area, two blocks from Walnut Avenue, grew up around Fountain Square, where on the Harold Street side, J. Williams Beal, a well-known Boston architect of the period, designed a block of houses that must rank among the most lovely ensembles of picturesque connected town houses in Greater Boston (Figure 94). They still survive in fair condition. Built at a cost of about $160,000, this block constitutes a kind of Queen Anne Tontine Crescent of fifteen attached brick and half-timbered town houses, the architectural unity of which is not equaled by any Queen Anne group anywhere in the city. Still another example of the way the Tontine Crescent persisted in Bostonians' imagination, this splendid block is not, strictly, a crescent; significantly, however, it was originally called Harris Wood Crescent. The houses of the next few years on Townsend Street alongside this block were often equally picturesque, particularly 140–142 and 148 Townsend (Figure 95); this last, like the Harris Wood Crescent houses, is brick on the first floor with full half-timbering above. These houses were also fashionable; the 1897 street directory shows the president of the Odorless Excavating Company living at 148; the treasurer of the E. T. Cowdrey Company at 136; the treasurer of R. J. Todd Company at 146; and the president of the Bay State and Boston Gas Illuminating Company at 140, all with business addresses in downtown Boston. But these Townsend Street houses were also as radically different from the Back Bay as the crescent was similar, for all of them, like those on Cushing Avenue, were free-standing and in garden lots. And if this design concept of large free-standing houses set in garden lots *not* facing a park, together with town houses that *were* connected facing the park, sounds familiar, it should — it was Bulfinch's design concept of one hundred years earlier.

Nor are Harris Wood Crescent and Townsend Street unique in this respect. At 1791–1821 Beacon Street in Brookline, from Dean Road to Clinton Path, a block of fifteen red-brick connected houses (Figure 96) was built in 1907 by Murdock Boyle, a Dorchester designer who worked also in the Back Bay. But these connected houses facing the Beacon Street parkway give way to detached houses if one follows either Dean Road or Clinton Path (both of which, like Cushing Avenue, have no parks) away from Beacon Street. In fact, when we have at last integrated the history of the streetcar suburbs into the larger history of the expanding Victorian city, it will surely emerge that where the city grew by annexation, the significance of streets like Townsend Street and Cushing Avenue lies in the fact that developers were able in the much enlarged late nineteenth-century city to reverse the trend established in the small, early nineteenth-century city when large, densely massed but detached town houses on ample lots were abandoned in favor of narrow lots and attached houses.

Two streets, of course, make a small case study. But it seems clear that neither Cushing Avenue nor Townsend Street was eccentric in its design concept. The same principle is evident along all upper middle-class Dorchester streets. The lavishly detailed Queen Anne house with its unusual stained-glass arched window at 35 Melville (Figure 97) on the corner of Allston was designed in 1882 by the then city architect of Boston, Arthur H. Vinal, as his own home. As grand a house as Upham's or Chadwick's on Cushing Avenue, it is similarly sited, a few feet from the sidewalk. So too are the neighboring houses that Vinal also built, ap-

Representative upper middle-class streetcar-suburb town houses.
FIGURE 97. Arthur H. Vinal. Vinal House, 35 Melville Avenue,
Dorchester, 1882.
FIGURE 98. Samuel J. Brown. Mitchell House, Walnut Street
between Highland Avenue and Austin Street, Newton, ca. 1885.
FIGURE 99. Wright House, Pearl Street, East Somerville, ca.
1890.
FIGURE 100. 369 Harvard Street, Cambridge, 1877.

parently to stimulate development and control it carefully by establishing the street's character. These houses, 29, 35, 37, and 39 (this last an attribution) together with 33, designed by L. Underwood in 1886, constitute one of the most sumptuous ensembles in the city of late nineteenth-century streetcar-suburb architecture. Diagonally across the street from Vinal's house, at 96 Lyndhurst Street, is another large house (designed in 1896 by A. B. Pinkham), the interiors of which are among the most lavish and unusual in the city.

The same design concept is also evident along Carruth, Alban, and Ocean streets at Ashmont. The most famous house in this area, a great mansarded mansion on Welles Avenue, purchased by Mayor John F. Fitzgerald after his rise to prosperity, has been torn down. But for our purposes 61 Alban Street is more significant, for here again one finds the house of another well-known architect, Harrison Atwood, who was at one time city architect of Boston. Atwood's house, which he built for himself in 1881, possesses a splendid interior and is also sited close to the sidewalk and to neighboring houses, some of which Atwood also built himself. On nearby Beaumont and Carruth streets (Figure 74), two of the grandest residential streets in the city, the same design concept is again evident in the parade of fine mansions by such architects as W. Whitney Lewis, Longfellow, Alden and Harlow, Willard M. Bacon, and Edwin J. Lewis, Jr.

Study the streetscapes illustrated in Figures 89, 90, 92, 95, 97, 99, or 106. Notice the regular alignment of these houses, each to each other and to the street; notice their similarity of size, scale, and finish; observe that their garden setting — for reasons we have already touched on — yields no quality of cottage or lane. Instead there is a public, formal aspect. These are front-facing, densely massed, regularly aligned,

similarly designed and scaled town houses — built by a generation determined to breathe again, in a more livable residential city where they would be delivered from the tyranny of the windowless wall and the narrow row house. And no doubt because clapboards and shingles can be painted varying colors, thus offering whatever scope for individuality was wanted, one sees on such streets not only a generally uniform setback but a relentless uniformity of cornice line maintained through all the stylistic changes of the period far more rigorously than in the Back Bay.

This design concept spread rapidly, as any circuit of Boston's suburbs will show. Not only Newton (Figure 98) but Melrose and Watertown possess many areas of this sort that have yet to be documented. Cambridge abounds in such streets, notably Harvard Street (Figure 100). Two eighty-four is a splendid detached town house designed in 1887 by Hartwell and Richardson; so also are 280, designed in 1886 by C. J. Williams, and 298, designed in 1888 by John Hasty. Farther up the street is a large Colonial Revival house at 340 that was designed in 1897 by Arthur Vinal. Like Vinal, Hasty worked also in Dorchester, where he designed 30 Pleasant Street in 1897, though perhaps his best house of this type that is known is 20 Highland Avenue in Cambridge. Other fine examples of this house type may be noted on Pearl Street in Somerville (Figure 99), and in Jamaica Plain (Figures 82, 101).

So persuasive did this design concept become that even where houses faced parks in the streetcar suburbs such houses were increasingly not attached (as at Harris Wood Crescent) but freestanding. Notable examples are Emerson Garden in Brookline, and Wellesley Park (Figure 102), Mount Bowdoin, and Sunset Circle in Dorchester, but whole streets were sometimes also laid out on this principle. One of these is on Avon

Boston's streetcar suburbs were as often called "garden suburbs."
FIGURE 101. Jamaica Pond neighborhood of Jamaica Plain, typical of
upper middle-class suburban subdivisions of the late nineteenth and
early twentieth centuries. Notice the relationship between the garden
lots of such detached town-house streets and the nearby park, one of
many of Olmsted's Boston Park System, which by 1900 extended from the
Back Bay through Jamaica Plain, West Roxbury, Roxbury, and Dorchester
to Dorchester Bay.
FIGURE 102. An even stronger relationship between the park system and
streetcar-suburb subdivisions is evident in such enclaves as Wellesley
Park in Dorchester, 1885–1900, one of a number of ensembles of detached
houses built around small private parks of the sort favored by Bulfinch
and found in the 1840s and 1850s on Beacon Hill (Figure 21) and in the
South End. So great was the extent of land in the streetcar suburbs
that while attached housing was often built facing such parks (see
Figures 94, 96), detached housing was increasingly preferred whether
or not the houses were massed around a park. Another residential park
is shown in Figure 105.

FIGURE 103. Samuel J. Brown. Fottler House, 389 Washington Street, Dorchester, 1900. A splendid example of the upper middle-class streetcar-suburb detached town house. For other work by Brown, see Figures 98 and 104.

Hill in Cambridge, where on Walnut Street, despite the fact that there is an ample fifty-foot setback on a parkway seventy feet wide, the houses are not attached but free-standing.

The extent to which the design concept of huge town houses, massed closely to one another and to the street, was carried is evident in the Fottler House of 1900 in Dorchester (Figure 103), located on the crest of Washington Street, overlooking the city and the harbor. It would be absurd in the face of its pretentiousness to believe its owner could not have afforded more land. Nor, in view of its proximity to the sidewalk, can one conclude this mansion was a country house. In fact, like most Bostonians of this class — including Mayor John Fitzgerald, who summered in Hull — Fottler possessed a summer residence, in Harwich Port. In both its design and siting, his Dorchester residence is unmistakably a detached town house.

T HROUGHOUT this discussion of the streetcar suburbs I have stressed upper middle-class houses for a number of reasons. Warner pointed out that of "the richest 1 percent of the population" of Boston,

the richest among them sometimes purchased an expensive town house in the Back Bay, sometimes built estates in the country, sometimes even owned both. Many, however, took advantage of their greater control over hours of work and the fashion for suburban life to build big houses on the best streets and finest prospects of suburban Boston. Such houses appeared both at great distance from Boston where railroad transportation had to be relied upon, and closer to town in the old high-priced pockets of land where former estates had been cut up into large and expensive parcels. Sections of Jamaica Plain and Roxbury highlands throughout the last third of the nineteenth century enjoyed a steady building up of such enclaves. Dorchester and most suburban communities came to contain at least a few streets and houses of Boston's wealthy.

He also noted that "in the 1840's and 1850's when relatively small numbers of middle class families had moved to the suburbs they had done so out of a clear preference for a rural setting," but after 1870 "the new commuter's choice of the rural ideal was a less clear one . . . he desired an architecture which would provide some of the effect of the row house facade — the public presentation of an impression of wealth and social standing." Warner cited Townsend Street as an example. But in an overall, general, nonarchitectural study such as his, streets like this naturally were touched on very briefly. In an architectural history, their importance is obviously much greater.

In the first place, it was naturally the upper middle class who could afford to build the most interesting houses in every style during this period. Many such houses are cited throughout this book. The craftsmanship of Parshley's house at 17–19 Cushing Avenue (Figure 117) for example, was not uncommon; nor was that of 102 Ocean Street at Ashmont (Figure 104), designed by Samuel J. Brown. Such examples might be multiplied all over the streetcar suburbs. Particularly interesting are the lavish interiors of 16 Sacramento Street in Cambridge (1883), probably the work of Ware and Van Brunt, and of 70 Salem Street in Malden (Plate 4). The fact that the Cambridge house was the residence of the president of the Shaw Furniture Company and the Malden house the home of the owner of A. H. Davenport Company and that the ornament of both houses was done by those famous woodworking firms (just as Parshley's firm detailed his house) is significant: because many of Boston's leading designers and craftsmen lived in the streetcar suburbs, one

FIGURE 104. Samuel J. Brown. 102 Ocean Street, Ashmont, 1899. Detail of the stairwell, an example of the lavish interior detail typical of the better streetcar-suburb house.

Central middle-class streetscapes in the streetcar suburbs reflected the fashions set by upper middle-class streetscapes.
FIGURE 105. Oakview Terrace, Jamaica Plain.
FIGURE 106. Hampshire Street, Everett.

finds there a great deal of their best work. But I have stressed upper middle-class houses chiefly because the wealthy were free to do what they wished in terms of housing as the middle and lower classes were not. When one discovers that the "Lead King of Boston" built his 1895 mansion, not set back in the center of his several lots, but close by the sidewalk, on only one lot; that he then sold another lot to his partner for another and similar house; and that Parshley and Vinal and Atwood did the same thing; one wonders if the middle class in the streetcar suburbs and even to some extent the lower middle class were following a fashion established by the upper middle class in their densely massed houses, rather than only succumbing to a necessity.

Middle-class residential architecture was naturally less expensive and more apt to be designed by speculator builders. One block from Cushing Avenue, for example, William Wight built up a new street, Mount Cushing Terrace, in 1914, with a number of small two-family houses that cost about $4,000 each, or less than half the price of the big Cushing Avenue houses of fifteen to twenty years earlier. Nor does the slightly varying exterior decor of these two-families obscure the fact that each is the mate of the other. Close by a prestigious street like Cushing Avenue, a good class of buyers was to be expected, however; and throughout the streetcar suburbs, middle-class developers naturally sought proximity to upper middle-class areas. Just as the Back Bay speculator sought to emulate the design concept of the fashionable Back Bay connected town house, so the streetcar-suburb speculator sought to emulate the more fashionable houses of the streetcar suburbs. The houses of Mount Cushing Terrace, so poor in land and so densely massed as to seem a cruel joke played on the working class by a greedy speculator, seem actu-ally to have been a reflection of streets like Cushing Avenue.

Perhaps the best example is Oakview Terrace in Jamaica Plain (Figure 105). The fact that the first house built there, 28 (1892), was designed by Longfellow, Alden and Harlow, may indicate an initial attempt at an upper middle-class street. But in the event, Oakview Terrace, as built up in the 1890s, was decisively middle class. As opposed to the houses of the 1890s on Cushing Avenue, which had cost an average of $10,500 each, the nineteen houses built in the same years on Oakview Terrace cost with one exception between $5500 and $6500. Yet Oakview Terrace, which not only emulates upper middle-class density but rises to a small, circular, parklike cul-de-sac, is utterly charming. A tree-shaded and altogether delightful street, it illustrates superbly how at half the cost the middle class could enjoy the amenities of the detached town house. This meant much more for the middle class, whose only alternative to streets like Oakview Terrace was South Boston or East Boston or Charlestown (and not on their lovely hilltops) or marginally respectable and declining lodging-house areas like the South End. And behind those areas there were only the close-packed tenements of the slum districts. (Some idea of what these were like is evident in Mayor Andrew Peters's report in 1918 that while the density of population in Jamaica Plain and West Roxbury was 2500 per square mile, in the North End the figure was 125,000.)

How fundamentally we have misunderstood the streetcar suburbs is clear if one studies for a moment Beals Street in Brookline, where the house at 83 may not at first impress. But this was the first home of Joseph and Rose Kennedy after their marriage, where President John F. Kennedy was born. It is, of course, a modest house, suitable for a young couple starting out, and not at all the equal of Mayor Fitzgerald's Ashmont mansion. But Joseph Kennedy was a rising banker, his wife the daughter of Boston's mayor, and their choice indicates the regard in which such small, middle-class, streetcar-suburb houses were held.

T HE design concept of the streetcar suburbs could contract (usually on the middle-class level; Figure 106) but it could also expand, especially at the upper and upper middle-class level. On Melville Avenue in Dorchester, while Arthur H. Vinal was establishing the densely massed streetscapes we have been discussing, several other architects at the other end of the street were developing a more spacious variant with more generous setbacks and circular drives leading under porte cocheres to large barns. Established in 1879 by E. A. Poe Newcomb in his design of 6 Melville, this more ample design concept was firmly established in 1880 by Cabot and Chandler in their design for 1 Melville Avenue (Figure 69). The same firm built another house of this type at 3 Melville in 1881; George Meacham had designed 10 Melville across the street along similar lines in 1880; and Cummings and Sears followed suit at 5 Melville in 1884. As the class level was demonstrably the same at both ends of the avenue, it is not at all clear what to make of this more generous concept. Stables, a sure sign of wealth in one sense, were also odorous and it was no doubt for that reason that they were sometimes prohibited on upper middle-class streets. It was only about 1910, when automobiles came into use among the upper classes, that, where there was room, the successor to the carriage house, the "automobile house" (with chauffeur's quarters), appeared on Cushing Avenue and Townsend Street. Previously, horses and carriages were kept at nearby commercial stables, as on Bea-

con Hill and in the Back Bay. It is thus unclear whether stables on Melville Avenue necessitated the larger lots or were simply a repercussion of them. And it is also unclear what either the larger lots or the stables may mean otherwise.

This more spacious concept is naturally only found in upper-class and upper middle-class areas, but even in those areas it is usually the exception rather than the rule. Two houses designed by Julius Schweinfurth illustrate the lack of any correlation, for example, between the size of a house and its setback. A very large house of his design for James Hathaway in Brighton, built in 1898, is set back in spacious grounds. Yet his Frederick Coffin House of years later in Brookline, though as large as the Brighton house, is set close by the street, on the sort of terrace we saw on Cushing Avenue and on Melville Avenue. And just as really large houses of "estate quality" were sited right on the sidewalk, small houses might have enormous setbacks. The key, perhaps, is to be found in this evocation of Newton from an 1888 Boston guidebook, which also illustrates the enthusiasm the newly emerging suburbs aroused.

Newton, the most favored and delightful among the many attractive suburbs of Boston, is distinctly a city of beautiful homes. It has been appropriately designated the "City of Villas." . . . Newton is noted for its magnificent country seats and luxurious dwellings, its superb drives, exquisite scenery and elegant surroundings, its beautiful lawns, gardens and conservatories, and is the home of many of the foremost and wealthiest of Boston's merchants, manufacturers, scientists, artists, literary and professional men, who after the hours of active pursuits, retire hither to their palatial residences to enjoy the health imparting air amid the luxuriant surroundings of fruit, flowers and foilage. This is, in short, an ideal American community, and represents the highest development of New England civilization — the very apex of our social structure, so-to-speak.

"City of Villas," of course, refers to the

Two Newton houses, ca. 1890–1900,
showing the variety in design concept
and particularly in setback of upper
middle-class streetcar-suburb housing.
FIGURE 107. Haskell House, 888 Beacon
Street, ca. 1890.
FIGURE 108. Julius Schweinfurth. Dennison House, Newtonville, 1900.

FIGURE 109. Alexander W. Longfellow,
Jr. 115 Brattle Street, 1887. Designed by
Henry Wadsworth Longfellow's
nephew for the poet's daughter, this
house is but one house removed from
its famous progenitor, the Vassall-
Longfellow House of 1759, and the
newer house represents a much more
profound Colonial Revival than many
suspect. Few realize that more of Brattle Street is Colonial Revival than Colonial.

densely massed house type: "villas" was also the term used by the *Rand McNally Guide to Boston* to describe the houses of Jones Hill, though like so many favored terms of those days it is not very appropriate. We are also told that Newton possessed "magnificent country seats" — to which, however, commuters returned every night — which means they were not in the usual sense of the terms country houses as opposed to town houses. What it may mean is that these quite large houses on many acres were fall and spring houses. Many wealthy Bostonians of this period maintained three houses: Colonel Oliver Peabody, for example, possessed a town house on Commonwealth Avenue, a country estate in Maine, and a third house on Adams Street in Milton that was used in the spring and fall but was regularly described in Bacon's *Boston: A Guide Book* as "the fine country seat of the late Oliver W. Peabody." Many of the more generously sited houses of this period in the inner suburbs may have been of this type. On the other hand, others may represent an attempt to combine in one house both a winter town house and a country summer house, an option the suburbs allowed.

Several Newton and Brookline houses are of interest in this connection. One was built by Edward H. Haskell, the president of the Haskell-Dawes Machine Company in Boston. Haskell, who was president of the New England Baptist Hospital, a director of the First National Bank of Boston, and the donor of a number of buildings to several colleges, appears to have been close to being a millionaire. Like Chadwick, however, he built his house at 888 Beacon Street in Newton (Figure 107) scarcely a few yards from the sidewalk. Charles S. Dennison, on the other hand, who owned the Dennison Manufacturing Company of Boston (with offices all over the country and in England), chose a more spacious de-

sign concept for his Newton house, designed by Julius Schweinfurth in 1900 (Figure 108). Robert Peabody, the architect, essayed a similar spaciousness when he built his house of 1876 at 50 Edgehill Road on "Pill Hill" in Brookline. Set in nearly two acres, it scarcely sounds like a town house. Yet that was its function. When Peabody moved to another house of his design in the Back Bay in 1901, he sold the Brookline house but he did not sell his summer home at Peach's Point in Marblehead. Clearly, all one can conclude is that tastes differed, so much so that palatial estate mansions continued also to be built in this period in the inner suburbs. For instance, the Brandegee House at Faulkner Farm, on the Brookline–Jamaica Plain line, designed by Little and Browne in 1895–1899, contains seventy-two rooms and is set in a terraced Italian garden, one of the first works of Charles S. Platt.

This wide diversity of design concept in the inner suburbs is all the harder to define because, according to how subdivisions were landscaped and how the houses were sited, houses on one street can seem more estatelike or rural than houses on another street, even though the lot sizes are similar. Where the streets are curvilinear, the siting of houses informal and irregular, and the planting so disposed as to emphasize these features, there is naturally a more informal and even rural quality. Style is also important in this respect, as one can see on Brattle Street in Cambridge.

That Brattle Street should figure in this discussion of the Victorian detached town house will doubtless surprise many people. But just as we mistake the character of early nineteenth-century Beacon Street and late nineteenth-century Cushing Avenue, so also do we mistake the character of Brattle Street, which is actually more Victorian than Colonial. In fact, between Brattle Square and Elmwood Avenue there are only six pre-

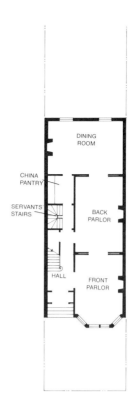

Representative attached and detached upper and upper middle-class town-house plans and lots, 1880–1920.

FIGURE 110. Plan of an attached house, 25 feet wide, in the Back Bay, where, Bunting notes, the great majority of houses were 25 or 26 feet wide. Note that in all but corner houses, light entered from only two sides and in the case of this typical plan, one reception room was without any windows whatsoever.

FIGURE 111. Plan of a detached house, 20 Cushing Avenue, Dorchester. In *Streetcar Suburbs,* Warner estimated that the ca. 1850 South End house covered 50 percent of a 2000–3000-square-foot lot; and that the expensive Back Bay house of the 1860s to 1890s used two-thirds of a 2300–2600-square-foot lot. By contrast, even a moderately priced middle-class streetcar-suburb single covered only 20 to 30 percent of a 4500–6000-square-foot lot. At the lower and lower middle-class levels, cheap intown row houses and tenements of the pre-streetcar era covered 80 to 90 percent of 600–1400-square-foot lots, while even cheap two-families and three-deckers in the streetcar suburbs used only 50 percent of 2400–2700-square-foot lots.

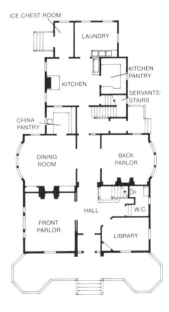

Revolutionary houses; and only eleven more were built between the Revolution and 1854. Thirty-three houses along this magnificent street were built in the last quarter of the nineteenth century and the first years of the twentieth. The pre-Revolutionary houses, however, are in a sense as important to our discussion as the late nineteenth-century houses, for even before the Revolution Brattle Street was close enough to Boston to have emerged as perhaps the first example of the attempt to combine the pleasures of both town and country. Bainbridge Bunting and Robert H. Nylander have described Brattle Street in the late eighteenth and early nineteenth centuries:

One cannot write categorically, but for most of these families their Cambridge estate seems to have been a principal residence. Men like East Apthorp and David Phips appear to have lived here the year around. William Brattle, John Vassall, and Richard Lechmere owned houses in Boston, but the locations suggest that these were rental properties. Only John Vassall seems to have owned what might be called a proper town house (the former Faneuil House), but that was not acquired until 1772.

There is thus a very good reason to conclude this discussion of the streetcar suburbs on Brattle Street.

All the disparities in design concept we have discussed are evident on and just off this famous street: Longfellow Park was laid out (by Charles Eliot) rather formally in 1883 and its houses built up in a fairly regular alignment; Hubbard Park nearby, on the other hand, was laid out more informally (ca. 1886), achieving a much more picturesque and irregular quality. On Brattle Street itself, some large houses are informal in design and yet massed quite close to the sidewalk, including H. H. Richardson's Shingle Style masterpiece, the Stoughton House of 1883 at 90 (Figure 81), which Hitchcock has called "the best suburban wooden house in America." Other, more formal houses, such as the Colonial Revival house of 1887 at 115 (Figure 109), possess more ample setbacks and even circular driveways. And the fact that 115, designed by Alexander W. Longfellow, Jr., a nephew of Henry Wadsworth Longfellow, for the poet's daughter, derives stylistically from the poet's own house at 105 Brattle, built in 1759, is significant: as the Queen Anne and Shingle styles gave way throughout Boston in the late 1880s to the more formal and urban-looking Colonial Revival, the town house character of these "suburban" streets emerges more clearly to us, particularly on Brattle Street, where stand a number of the eighteenth- and early nineteenth-century prototypes of the Victorian detached town house.

Despite the disparities in design concept, one sees here as throughout the streetcar suburbs, when the trees are bare, that Brattle Street discloses the fundamental factor common to all the late nineteenth- and early twentieth-century suburbs: save for a few last-of-their-kind houses in the Back Bay, a hundred years after the Tontine Crescent it is evident that Bostonians at every class level rejected utterly the connected town house block and turned back instead to some version of the eighteenth- and early nineteenth-century ideal of the garden lot and the free-standing town house.

5

FRENCH FLATS AND
THREE-DECKERS

IN THE LATE NINETEENTH CENTURY Bostonians not only set their architects the task of reviving the free-standing town house; at the same time they required of them a violently contradictory achievement. Thus the architects who dutifully pulled the connected town house block apart into separate houses on garden lots in Newton and Dorchester were at the same time in the heart of the city more and more often expected not only to put the block back together again, but then to stand it up in the air, as it were; eight, nine, and ten stories high, and climbing every year a little higher, the apartment house was as far from the free-standing garden house as one could get. While there was for the latter a deep-seated, almost venerable precedent, there was scarcely any precedent at all in the United States for the apartment house when the first such building, the Hotel Pelham (Figure 112), appeared in Boston in 1857, on the corner of Boylston and Tremont streets. (It should be noted that most of the early apartment houses were called Hotel this or that, but such "apartment hotels" were quite distinct from commercial hotels catering primarily to transients. Though several commercial hotels encouraged permanent residents, apartment hotels did not seek transient guests, although they were popularly described as the habitats of the "newly wed and the nearly dead.")

Although Calvert Vaux had argued in an address in New York to the American Institute of Architects, in the year the Pelham opened, for the introduction of flats into this country, there seems no way at all to explain why Boston should have been endowed with America's first apartment house except by reference to the French influence we discussed in Chapter 2. That it *was* the first of its kind in any American city (except perhaps for New Orleans) seems clear, for the apartment house did not appear in New York City — where it would achieve its Victorian apotheosis in such buildings as the Dakota and the Ansonia — until 1869. Nor is it surprising, given the radical nature of the idea the Pelham heralded, multifamily occupancy, that it seems (with one possible but undocumented exception) to have been the only apartment house in Boston until the late 1860s; the first New York apartment house, R. M. Hunt's Stuyvesant Flats, was also unimitated for a decade. It is significant as well that one of the first four apartment houses built in Boston after the Pelham, Cummings and Sears's Hotel Boylston of 1870 (see Figure 51) was erected opposite the Pelham. The three that followed, however, were all in the Back Bay: Ware and Van Brunt's Hotel Hamilton at 260 Clarendon Street and the Hotel Kempton at 237 Berkeley, both built in 1869, and Weston and Rand's Hotel Agassiz of 1872 at 191 Commonwealth Avenue. Interestingly, the Hotel Vendome (Figure 49) on Commonwealth Avenue, a commercial, transient hotel that nonetheless catered to

FIGURE 112. Possibly by Arthur Gilman. Hotel Pelham, Boylston Street at the corner of Tremont Street, 1857. The Pelham, since demolished, was probably the first apartment house built in the United States.
FIGURE 113. Hotel Oxford, Huntington Avenue, Back Bay, ca. 1885.

permanent tenants, appeared about the same time, in 1871.

Thereafter, a great number of apartment houses appeared in Copley Square itself — notably J. Pickering Putnam's Hotel Cluny (1876), Levi Newcomb's Hotel Bristol (1879), the Copley (1882), and the Hotel Westminster, designed by Henry C. Cregier of Chicago in 1897. Throughout the 1890s the Copley Square concentration tended to spread toward Massachusetts Avenue up Huntington Avenue, where were built the Hotel Oxford (Figure 113) and the Hotel Ilkley (1890). All these have been torn down, but during the same period the residential Back Bay spawned twenty-three similar apartment houses, nearly all of which have survived, including the Aubry by William G. Preston at 149 Newbury in 1883, the Imperial at 308 Commonwealth Avenue in 1889, and the Royal, the first apartment house on Back Bay Beacon Street (at 295) in 1885, both designed by Samuel D. Kelly. The new fashion was also felt on Beacon Hill, where in 1885–1887 the Tudor, an immense apartment house designed by S. J. F. Thayer, was built on the corner of Beacon and Joy streets, and it was felt too

in the streetcar suburbs, where the earliest important apartment house of this period appears to have been the Warren, designed by Carl Fehmer (1884), in Roxbury Highlands. In the 1890s, these clusters of hotels throughout the city increased dramatically. But the supremacy of the Back Bay was reinforced by the erection of such deluxe apartment houses as the Marlborough by Willard T. Sears at 416 Marlborough Street in 1895; two apartment houses designed by McKay and Dunham, the Hotel Lafayette of 1895 at 333 Commonwealth Avenue, and the Tuileries of 1896 at 270 Commonwealth Avenue; and the huge Hotel Cambridge, designed by Willard Sears in 1898, at 483 Beacon Street on the corner of Massachusetts Avenue.

The evident movement toward Massachusetts Avenue flowered into another cluster at Charlesgate, in the mid-1890s — where the Hotel Charlesgate, designed by J. Pickering Putnam, opened in 1891, closely followed by the Colonial at 382 Commonwealth (1895) and the Torrington (1896–1899) at 384–388 Commonwealth (both designed by Arthur H. Vinal), and in 1897 by the large Hotel Somerset, a commercial and mainly transient hotel by Arthur Bowditch that catered to permanent residents. It was from Charlesgate that the apartment house spread into the Fenway and along Audubon Road through Audubon Circle to its principal suburban flowering on Beacon Street in Brookline. At the same time these fashionable clusters naturally precipitated a legion of middle-class apartment hotels. The *Boston Street Directory*, which first set off such hotels from the primarily transient type in 1878, listed 108 in that year. By 1890 more than five hundred were listed throughout the city, the chief middle-class hotels for the most part having been erected on Columbus Avenue in the part of the South End closest to the Back Bay. There one such, the Hotel Albemarle, designed in 1876, still stands in fairly good exterior condition on the corner of Columbus and Clarendon streets. It is not difficult, however, to differentiate the fashionable hotels, and a survey of the Boston Social Registers between 1890 and 1920 (in which years the number of apartment dwellers more than doubled) documents the important role Boston society played in the rise of the apartment house.

Although in the 1890s and later there grew up along the "Gold Coast" on Mount Auburn Street near Harvard Square a dozen or more fashionable apartment houses for young men of wealth at Harvard, most Social Register apartment dwellers in 1890 lived in or around Copley Square, particularly in the Victoria and the Brunswick, both commercial hotels, and in the Ludlow, the Cluny, and the Bristol, which were strictly apartment hotels. In the residential Back Bay the most fashionable place of residence was also a commercial hotel, the Vendome, though the Agassiz was very popular, as was the Oxford on Huntington Avenue. By 1919, however, much had changed. The Back Bay remained preeminent, but a perceptible

shift is evident: the Huntington Avenue apartment houses had declined by 1920 in social standing, and Charlesgate had emerged as the most prestigious address. Not only the Charlesgate itself, but the Colonial, the Torrington, and the Hotel Somerset possessed by far the most Back Bay Social Register tenants, while society generally was clearly following the march of the apartment house up Beacon Street into Brookline, where the most fashionable concentration was between Carleton and Powell streets (mostly at Richmond Court Apartments and the Wolloton) and between Summit Avenue and Lancaster Terrace (in the Stoneholm, the Colchester, and Brandon Hall). By 1920, the middle-class apartment house concentration had also shifted, from the South End to the Fenway.

The lead Boston society took with respect to the apartment house is even clearer when one notes that among the earliest tenants of the Hotel Hamilton, one of the first apartment houses erected, were Major and Mrs. Henry Lee Higginson. The head of Boston's leading banking house and the founder of the Boston Symphony Orchestra, Higginson lived there only four years. But when he moved in 1874 it was in order to occupy a suite in his own apartment hotel, the Hotel Agassiz, which he built on Commonwealth Avenue in 1872. Like so many Back Bay residents, Major Higginson moved at various times of the year: the summer found him at his home in Manchester-by-the-Sea, the fall at Rock Harbor on Lake Champlain, and the winter in his Back Bay apartment. Similarly, the new building type early attracted distinguished architects: not only Thayer, Preston, Fehmer, and Ware and Van Brunt, whose work has already been noted, but Clarence H. Blackall, who designed the Dana Chambers on Dunster Street and Oxford Court, both in Cambridge; McKim, Mead and White, the ar-

chitects of the fashionable block of bachelor flats at the corner of Charles and
Beacon streets; and both Cram and
Richardson, whose work of this kind we
shall discuss shortly. Architectural quality not unnaturally followed social quality. But I have stressed the high social
standing of the first apartment houses in
Boston for another reason. It is crucial to
understand that apartment living was
very much still another new *fashion* in
the late nineteenth century for the upper
classes, and as we have seen it is usually
a mistake to look at residential architecture generally without noting what effect
fashion as well as necessity may have
had. In this case, as with the streetcar-
suburb house type, the matter is crucial,
for the miles upon miles of new middle-
class apartment houses that marched out
of Boston in every direction after 1900,
up Commonwealth Avenue into Brighton, for example, dramatically changed
the city's scale and overall appearance.

SOMETHING of the design concept of
the city's first apartment houses as
understood during this period can be
gleaned from the 1885 edition of *King's
Handbook of Boston.*

The "French flat," or Continental system of
dwellings, sometimes called "family hotels," — a single tenement occupying the
whole or part of a floor, instead of several
floors in a house, — gained its foothold in
America by its introduction in Boston. Before
the annexation of the surrounding districts,
Boston is said to have been the most densely
populated city in America; and there was a
natural demand for economy in space. The
first building of the "French flats," or "family
hotel," class was the Hotel Pelham, at the
corner of Tremont and Boylston Streets, built
by Dr. John H. Dix about twenty years ago.
. . . This style of dwelling rapidly increased
in popularity, and now their number is so
great that it is hardly practicable to mention
them here. They range from the most palatial
and elegant structures, equally beautiful in
exterior and interior decorations, to plain and
comfortable houses adapted for people of
moderate means.

Rather unconvincing with respect to
origins — it was not until *after* the annexation of the surrounding districts that
the apartment house developed in Boston beyond just the one example of the
Pelham — this paragraph nonetheless
conveys much of the sense in which the
apartment house was early understood
in Boston, where the terms "French flat"
and "family hotel" were used throughout the late nineteenth century along
with "apartment hotel" to distinguish
apartment houses from commercial hotels. The crucial sentence, however, is
the first — "a single tenement occupying
the whole, or part of a floor, instead of
several floors in a house" — for the comparison of the individual "tenement" or
"apartment" or "suite" with the several
floors of the town house is the key to understanding this revolutionary new
building type. Unlike so many even
quite costly apartments today, the
upper-class apartment in this period attempted to *duplicate* the three- or four-
story single-family town house in most
respects and to *surpass* it in one respect:
the greater amplitude of the reception
area, which on one floor without a staircase could be contiguous and spacious
in a way impossible in the usual connected house of two or at most three or
four rooms on each floor. At the Cluny,
for example, the second floor suite (Figure 114) offered a reception area of five
contiguous rooms, four of them (reception room, parlor, library, and dining
room) off a central hall with coatroom
and water closet — and a fifth (a smoking room) off the dining room. There
were also seven bedrooms and two full
bathrooms with kitchen and service
areas. All this and fifteen closets on one
floor! Not all apartments were this large:
the Marlborough's suites were seven
rooms and bath; but five rooms and bath

Two Back Bay apartment houses by J. Pickering Putnam, one of the leading apartment house designers in late nineteenth-century Boston.

FIGURE 114. Hotel Cluny, Copley Square, 1876. Plan of second-floor suite. Demolished.

FIGURE 115. Haddon Hall, Commonwealth Avenue at Berkeley Street, 1894.

were the absolute minimum at the upper middle-class level. Indeed, how spacious such apartments typically were is evident in a 1923 request for a change of occupancy at the Hotel Gladstone in Dorchester (designed by J. H. Besarick in 1887): "put in new partitions in apartment on 6th floor so as to divide apartment into *three* small apartments" (my italics).

Such buildings also offered before they were common a host of luxuries: in 1895 the Marlborough, for example, advertised electricity in all rooms, twenty-four-hour telephone service, and all-night elevators. A great many possessed elegant dining rooms: *King's Handbook* noted, for example, that though the Oxford was mainly an apartment hotel it possessed a "first class restaurant." Others offered private kitchens, and *Ba-*

con's Dictionary of Boston noted that in many such buildings "the kitchens [of all suites] are clustered at the top of the [apartment] house," thus dealing with cooking odors. A report of 1917 at the Building Department documents the fact that at 187–189 Huntington Avenue, a small apartment hotel designed by A. H. Vinal in 1895, there were "janitor's and maid's rooms in basement," a practice followed at Richmond Court. Services also varied. In the bachelor flats at 66 Beacon, designed by McKim, breakfast was served in one's apartment, but lunch and dinner were presumed to be at one's club. Even middle-class apartment blocks in the South End, like the Hotel Albemarle (1876), at the corner of Columbus Avenue and Clarendon Street, possessed full bathrooms in each of their many suites, a luxury in the 1870s even at the upper-class level. Such technological improvements, including central heating, were a key factor in the development of the apartment house. So also were elevators. Documentation is naturally spotty, but Bunting notes that there was an elevator at the Hotel Hamilton in 1869 and two at the Agassiz in 1872, and in 1886 *Bacon's Dictionary of Boston* noted that even "many of the less pretentious [apartment houses] have passenger elevators."

If one looks at Haddon Hall (Figure 115), a luxurious apartment building on the corner of Commonwealth Avenue and Berkeley Street designed in 1894 by J. Pickering Putnam, the need for an elevator is apparent. But the great height of most early apartment houses (which derived, of course, from the profit motive as well as from the increasing demand for suites) was a problem more easily solved on the inside than on the outside, where such buildings seriously marred the established scale of town house streetscapes (see Figure 158). Thus, although the individual apartment on any floor early achieved social parity with the town house, to which it was comparable and in some respects superior, the apartment building as a whole (in terms of its exterior appearance) was not widely welcomed. Ironically, if only the French flat fashion had caught on in Boston twenty years earlier, Commonwealth Avenue might have been a Parisian boulevard indeed; but by the time apartments were fashionable the low four-story town house had established a scale unsuitable to blocks of flats. On commercial thoroughfares there was no problem, which is no doubt why so many such apartment blocks were erected in Copley Square and on Huntington Avenue between Copley Square and the splendid new civic center — rivaling Copley Square in many ways — that emerged at the intersection of Huntington and Massachusetts avenues with the erection be-

tween 1900 and 1910 of Symphony Hall, Horticultural Hall, the St. James Theatre, the Mother Church, and the New England Conservatory of Music. In fact, apartment houses in Copley Square and on Huntington Avenue often had stores on the first floor, creating a distinctly cosmopolitan and even Parisian ambience compared with the rather staid appearance of Commonwealth Avenue. The same design concept (now being revived and sometimes thought to be quite radical) was often followed in nineteenth-century apartment blocks: the quite handsome apartment house John Hasty designed (1888) that still stands next to the Cambridge City Hall on Massachusetts Avenue provided one entrance to the first-floor shops and another to the apartments above. So had the Pelham, in 1857. But Commonwealth Avenue was not a commercial thoroughfare, and although Haddon Hall duplicated the side-hall-and-bay-window town house plan, it piled up this plan ten stories high. Nor were double-bayed apartment houses like the Imperial much more attractive, though they could be less high. They were scathingly called the "dumbbell" type.

An even more difficult problem confronted the apartment house designer in the streetcar suburbs, where on only a few main streets (Massachusetts Avenue in Cambridge, for instance, or Columbia Road in Dorchester) could the tall apartment block possibly be used. Yet so popular did this "horizontal" rather than "vertical" life-style become that by the 1890s there was a demand for it on the residential single-family streets of upper middle-class areas in the streetcar suburbs. Thus the ingenuity of the Victorian architect was taxed still further: obviously there were families of some means who preferred apartments to houses and renting to owning; but many of these families wished to enjoy these benefits not in huge intown apartment

French flats in the streetcar suburbs: two apartment houses on Jones Hill in Dorchester.
FIGURE 116. Herbert Moseley. 23 Upham Avenue / 41 Cushing Avenue, 1894. Across the street from this two-suite house is the single-family designed in 1895 by Edmund Freeman for James Humphreys Upham at 40 Cushing.
FIGURE 117. Sylvester Parshley. 17–19 Cushing Avenue, 1893, surely the most splendid two-suite house in the city.

blocks but in detached houses on garden lots in the streetcar suburbs. Could a suburban apartment house be contrived where each apartment would equal the streetcar suburb's detached town house in the way the Back Bay apartment house equaled the connected town house, which meant in the streetcar suburbs no windowless walls and on the exterior (so as not to disrupt the scale and overall appearance of the streetscape) the illusion of a single house? In fact, such a house type did evolve in the 1880s and nineties in the streetcar suburbs, and so well was the illusion of a single-family house preserved that we have in fact seen the result already without noticing anything amiss: on Townsend Street in the Highlands one of the four detached houses discussed in Chapter 4 was not a single-family house — it was an apartment house of two suites: 140–142 Townsend, the home of the president of the Bay State and Boston Gas Illuminating Company (Figure 95). Similarly, in Micah Dyer's two-block development on Cushing Avenue in Dorchester only six of the twelve houses we discussed were actually single-family houses. The rest were apartment houses of two suites!

On these two blocks it is important to note the same social parity of single-family house and apartment house we saw in the Back Bay (see Figure 116). Though the first houses on these two blocks were singles, thereafter singles and two-apartment houses were built simultaneously. In fact, Joseph Houghton Chadwick, the Boston lead magnate, built his High Georgian mansion of 1895 (Figure 91) next door to one two-apartment house and across the street from another, for Sylvester Parshley's own house of 1893 was a two-suite house (Figure 117). Actually, of Parshley's three houses in these two blocks, two were apartment houses. Typically, both the single-family that he built next to his own house and the two-apartment house he built around the corner possessed Social Register tenants: the Paines (in the single) and the Southworths (in the two-suite house). What was important in the streetcar suburbs as in the Back Bay was not renting versus owning or single house versus apartment, but the overall quality of the neighborhood and of the living unit itself; its spaciousness, interior finish, and, in the case of the apartment house above all, privacy.

One of these Cushing Avenue houses, the Loguee House of 1896, may be cited as an example of the first and unsuccessful attempt to evolve an apartment house in the streetcar suburbs that would possess the general appearance of the detached single house (Figure 118). It is, in fact, a conventional double or semidetached house of the kind built since Bulfinch's day. But though each unit was open to light and air on three as opposed to only two sides as in all but corner houses in the Back Bay, there was still the one windowless wall between the two "houses," which in the streetcar suburbs was definitely second rate. Most important, the narrow, connected town house plan of each unit imposed the old two-room reception area off a narrow railroad track hall that the detached town house (and also the French flat) was specifically designed to avoid. Significantly, this is the only conventional double in these two blocks: all the other two-suite houses are designed on a quite different basis, the principle of which will be clear if we compare the Loguee House with the two-apartment house that Parshley rented to the Southworths and both with

a multifamily Brookline apartment block designed by Charles Newhall and all three apartment houses with the Chadwick House at 20 Cushing Avenue (Figures 118–120, 111).

Chadwick's single-family house may be taken as the upper middle-class streetcar-suburb norm: there is a spacious five-room reception area — a parlor, sitting room, dining room, and library off a large central reception hall. The back of the first floor is given over to the service area, the second floor contains bedrooms, and the third floor has a billiard room and servants' quarters. As in the Back Bay apartment house, fewer bedrooms and servants' rooms were necessary in an apartment, but absolute parity in reception areas was crucial: even elderly couples would expect to entertain according to the spacious fashion of the day. Thus by dividing the two-suite house *horizontally* instead of *vertically*, not only could one get light and air on four sides, one could also evolve exactly an equivalent of French flat spaciousness. Parshley's house (Figure 119) thus possesses a five-room reception area (off which also opened two private porches) with light coming from every side; a startlingly superior plan to that of the Loguee House, Parshley's plan is comparable to the apartment house plan (Figure 120) in Brookline in spaciousness and superior insofar as light and air are concerned. However, one or two bedrooms were insufficient even for the apartment dweller, who would also require at least one bedroom for a live-in servant; and there thus arose the supreme test for the apartment house architect in the streetcar suburbs. It was easy enough for Parshley to lay out two spacious reception areas on the first and second floors for two separate apartments, creating reception areas comparable with those in either a single house or the apartment block French flat, but no building in the streetcar suburbs that

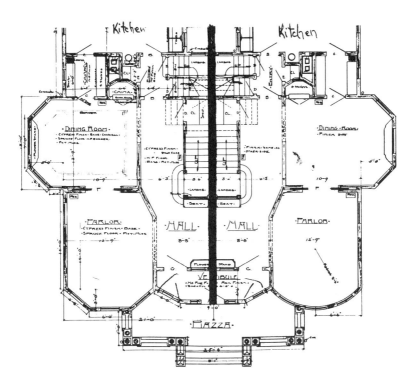

French flat apartment house plans in Boston, 1890–1910, compared with
conventional detached double or duplex plans of the same period.
FIGURE 118. William Smith. First-floor plan of a conventional
double house on Jones Hill, Dorchester, ca. 1895.
FIGURE 119. Sylvester Parshley. Second-floor plan of detached
two-suite house on Jones Hill, Dorchester, ca. 1896.
FIGURE 120. Charles A. Newhall. Second-floor plan of part of an
attached apartment house block on Beacon Street in Brookline, ca. 1910.

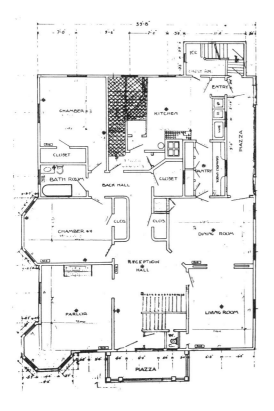

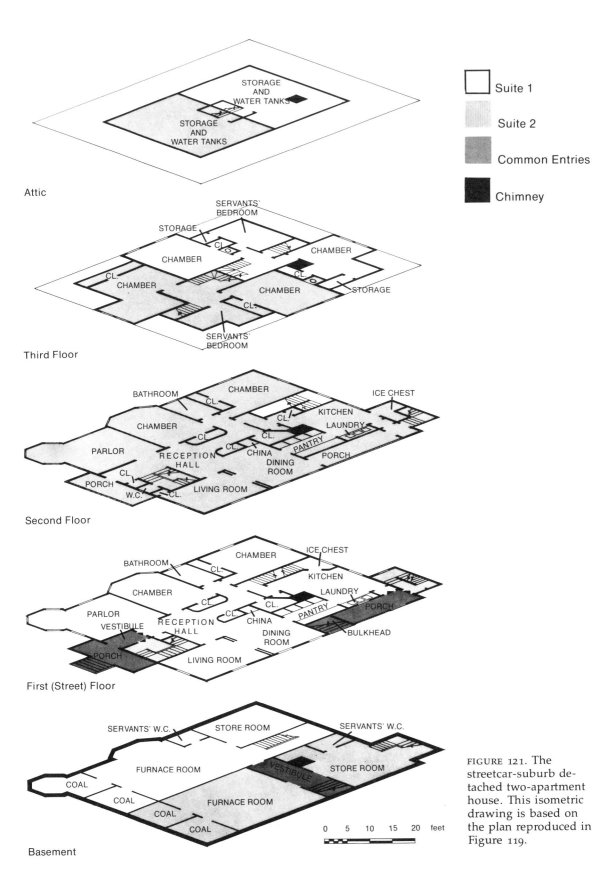

FIGURE 121. The streetcar-suburb detached two-apartment house. This isometric drawing is based on the plan reproduced in Figure 119.

preserved the appearance of a single house could manage, as did the Cluny, to accommodate four or five bedrooms as well on the reception area floor. Thus, the crucial problem: how in such a horizontally divided house could one contrive the access each apartment needed for additional bedrooms on the third floor and, indeed, for the necessary service, mechanical, and storage space each apartment required in both cellar and attic, while maintaining the absolute multifloored privacy of the conventional vertical double?

An ingenious solution was found: so ingenious it is difficult to illustrate in only two dimensions although there is no particular mystery about it (Figure 121). Each apartment had to be pierced vertically (in the way any house is pierced by chimneys, for instance, whose presence is not always obvious in plan) with several stairwells so arranged that staircases entirely private to the apartments they originated in led only to those portions of the cellar, the third floor, and the attic allotted to each apartment. But if the principle is not mysterious, its application was complex, called certainly for much ingenuity, and was also very expensive. The horizontal two-suite house required almost twice as many staircases — a costly part of construction — as the single-family, and two of everything from reception area mantlepieces to kitchens, bathrooms, and heating plants. In Parshley's house, as originally designed, one could go from the cellar to the attic in each apartment, but one could *not* go from one apartment to the other without leaving the house and ringing the front or back doorbell of the other apartment. It is also clear why the *second*-floor suite was the preferred suite in such houses, invariably the owner's if he lived on the premises. The second-floor *piano nobile* tradition enters in here; and as in any apartment house — at the Cluny, for in-

stance — the space lost to a common hall or vestibule made the first floor somewhat less spacious. The second-floor unit was thus larger (particularly the reception hall, which gained not only a large adjoining stair hall at the expense of the first-floor unit's hall, but any space used downstairs for a common vestibule), while the first-floor entrance and service porches became on the second floor private living porches that extended the reception area significantly. The higher elevation gave also more light and air, and frequently magnificent water views in the case of hilltops. Lastly, the second-floor unit was one flight rather than two removed from each suite's "second floor" on the third floor.

Notice, however, that these advantages were unavoidable in the horizontal two-suite apartment house. And the first floor, being the first floor, possessed (traditionally) its own advantage. But if absolute parity between suites was not possible, an approximate parity *was* acceptable: an inevitable compromise that no expense could rectify. Where possible this parity was also expressed on the exterior: where two facades (in the case of a corner house) allowed separate entrance porches, outer doors, and vestibules for each apartment, such facilities were invariably provided on the front as well as at the back of the house. Indeed, two separate street numbers were used even when the same street turned the corner (as at 17–19 Cushing Avenue) to emphasize the double occupancy. Only in mid-block, where more than one entrance porch and outer door on one facade was obviously impossible if the scale of the streetscape and the appearance of a single-family were to be maintained, was one shared room permitted, as in any apartment house: a common entrance hall or vestibule. Even in mid-block, however, two numbers for one house, if it was a two-suite house, were frequently used,

111

despite the common vestibule. That in itself was a minor compromise. It was in the matter of space of reception area and *multifloored privacy* that compromise was never possible if the horizontal two-suite house was to equal single-house living in a way the vertical double never could. By comparing the plans of another two-suite house, designed by J. Winslow Cobb in 1908 in Winthrop (though where in that town I cannot discover), with Parshley's house, and by extending the comparison to other apartment houses in both the Back Bay and in Brookline, some sense of the ingenuity required in the design of multifamily housing will be evident.

ALL the conventions and proprieties of single houses in a ceremonious and hierarchial age applied to any first-class apartment: separate bathrooms were required for servants, for example; dining rooms and kitchens had to be connected by china pantries; access to all rooms without having to go through other rooms was insisted upon. No relaxation in such standards was considered. Apartment house design was extremely complex, and many architects accordingly made it a specialty. In Boston it would seem that the chief apartment house architects between 1870 and 1900 were Samuel D. Kelly, McKay and Dunham, and J. Pickering Putnam. Putnam's practice was apparently the most extensive at the upper and upper middle-class level. Born in Boston in 1847, a graduate of Boston Latin and Harvard College, Putnam not only studied at the Royal Academy of Architecture in Berlin but was among the first Boston architects to study at the Ecole des Beaux Arts, in the late 1860s. His major Boston apartment houses include the Cluny, the Copley, Haddon Hall, and the Charlesgate, where his room layouts are brilliant, developing to

the maximum the inherent flexibility of "same floor houses" so as to allow contiguous reception areas and even whole apartments to expand or contract as required (Figure 123). One can see how flexibility of plan also appears in Parshley's plan (Figure 119): one of the four rooms opening off the central hall of the reception area opens also off the rear hall and depending upon which door is used this room can be either a fifth reception room or a bedroom. Moreover, Parshley connected four reception rooms with each other through three wide doorways, organizing spacious diagonal vistas the whole width of the house. Yet each of the four or five reception rooms is clearly differentiated, and they unfold in a highly logical and functional sequence: the stairs point one directly to the parlor, from which a long diagonal vista draws one to the dining room, from which there opens generously the "postprandial" living room or library, from which another door delivers one back to hall and staircase — without having to retrace one's steps, go through one room to gain another (except the hall, of course), or, indeed, to ask one's way at any stage. And it will be at once evident that the Putnam and Parshley apartment plans are in all these respects superior to the plan of Cobb's Winthrop house (Figure 122).

A particularly vexing problem in the apartment house plan was how to segregate decisively a contiguous reception area (adjoining a dining room and kitchen) with a contiguous bedroom area (adjoining a bathroom) without recourse to Cobb's long and narrow railroad track hall of door after door. Cram's discussion of the design of Richmond Court, an apartment house he designed in 1898 on Beacon Street in Brookline, touched on this problem at some length.

Each suite consists of nine rooms, not including halls or passageways, all with outside light and air, among which are a large reception hall, parlour, library, dining-room, and

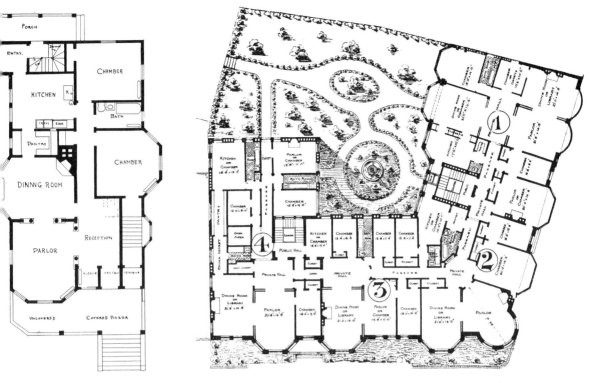

Examples of how reception, service, and sleeping areas might be segregated in apartment houses.

FIGURE 122. J. Winslow Cobb. First-floor plan by this well-known Shingle Style architect for a two-suite house in Winthrop Highlands, ca. 1908.

FIGURE 123. J. Pickering Putnam. Second-floor plan of the Charlesgate, 535 Beacon Street, Back Bay, 1891.

FIGURE 124. Cram, Wentworth and Goodhue. Plan of second floor (third and fourth floors are identical) of Richmond Court Apartments, 1213 Beacon Street, Brookline, 1898.

kitchen, this last being thoroughly isolated from the rest of the apartment, though communicating directly with the servants' staircases. . . . By means of an ingenious arrangement it has been possible to place the bed-rooms with their closets and bath, on a private passage separated by a door from the reception room and staircase hall; this device ensures the cessation of all those *contretemps* — often amusing indeed, but more often unpleasant — so familiar to the dweller in apartments; the entrance of a strange guest into one's bed-room under the impression that he is decorously making his way to the parlour; the tramp past a long range of mysteriously closed doors to the dining-room, or the apparently hopeless prominence given to the bath-room, being instances.

Cram's plans (Figure 124), however, though not guilty of the almost full-length railroad track of Cobb's design, still depend on admittedly short but still evident railroad tracks in each apartment. Parshley's, on the other hand, is much better. By *turning* the railroad track between the reception area and the bedroom area, he decisively separated the two areas (which cannot even be seen from each other) and at the same time by rounding the walls he used the reception area end of the railroad track to enhance the length of the reception hall, balancing, as it were, the other "wing" of the reception hall, which leads to the second-floor front porch. And by rounding both corners of the wall to the left of the railroad track, he introduced into the reception hall a kind of pavilion that adds enormously to its spatial excitement. It is a tour de force of planning.

Another important aspect of apartment design was that it should achieve parity with the single house in finish and detail as well as in privacy and spaciousness. In Parshley's houses, marble floors and lavish quartered-oak–paneled stairwells and reception rooms point up the fact that apartment houses, large and small, often offered reception areas as beautifully detailed as in any single-family house. At the Hotel Royal on

Beacon Street, for example, there were parquet floors in the parlors, and at Richmond Court Cram noted that "the vestibules and staircase halls . . . are finished in oak, panelled for about two-thirds of the height of their walls, the stairs themselves . . . with elaborate newel posts and balustrades." In the individual apartments he pointed out that

The reception-rooms . . . have been wainscoted with oak to a height of five feet and six inches. The parlours are finished in enamel and the dining-rooms in oak, with a wainscot two-thirds the height of the walls. The bed-rooms are finished in white, and the bath-rooms in enamel-tiled wainscoting and floors, the plumbing appliances being the best of their several kinds, with porcelain tubs, nickel-plated trimmings, and fixtures of the most approved patterns. The kitchens and pantries are finished in hardwood.

It may be argued that though the streetcar suburb's two-suite apartment house was a more harmonious part of its streetscape than the Back Bay "dumbbell" apartment house, this effect was purchased through a dishonest facade, a factor that much exercised many people, then as now. Actually, as has been noted, where it was possible to express the two-suite horizontal house on a corner lot where each of the street facades could have its own entrance porch, this was nearly always done. Moreover, such "dishonesty" was frequent at all levels during this period. William H. Jordy points out that McKim, Mead and White's famous Villard Houses complex in New York of 1883, "concealed within its noncommittal palazzo elevations no less than six separate houses of varying sizes . . . one for [the owner], the rest for rent." Nor is every Back Bay town house what it seems. As Bunting notes, 326 Dartmouth Street is, so to speak, T-shaped, "with the wide bar toward the street and the stem at the rear, where the house narrows down to a single room fifteen feet wide" to allow the two neighboring houses to push into its sides. At 8 and 10 Commonwealth Avenue (Figure 45), to cite another example, the two apparently similar houses are really quite different: the library of 10 actually extends the whole width of the back of *both* houses on the second floor.

Just as the prestigious Back Bay apartment house spawned legions of middle-class apartment houses throughout the Fenway and on the main commercial streets of the expanding city, so also the characteristic upper middle-class two-suite apartment house of the streetcar suburbs must have influenced its ubiquitous middle-class variant — the two-family house, a type perhaps nowhere better seen than on Oakview Terrace in Jamaica Plain, which, as was noted before, constitutes generally a splendid middle-class streetcar-suburb comparison with upper middle-class streets. Again, on Oakview Terrace (Figure 105) only seven of the nineteen houses we discussed in Chapter 4 were singles: all the rest were two-families. And as was true of single-family houses, the two-family houses on Oakview built in the 1890s cost, with one exception, between $5500 and $6500 to build, or about half the cost of the Cushing Avenue two-suite houses of the same decade. The Oakview Terrace houses are, of course, much smaller. But their lesser cost also reflected the omission of several costly features of the two-suite house. Typically, for example, middle-class two-family houses had a common back staircase, thus compromising the principle of multifloor privacy. In the class-conscious 1890s this made a big difference. And it is significant that whereas on Cushing Avenue some of the grandest and costliest singles were built next door to already extant two-suite houses, on middle-class Oakview Terrace there was *not* the same parity between apartments

and single houses one sees at the upper middle-class level. The singles came first, then the two-families. Out of seventeen one- and two-family houses, between 1892 and 1895 all houses built (six) were singles; between 1897 and 1900, only one single was built, nine were two-families, and one was a three-family. Yet the two-families of Oakview Terrace, which provided garden lots massed about a circular park to persons who would otherwise probably have lived in one of the tenement districts described in the last chapter, are by no means intrusions architecturally in a singularly charming residential quarter.

N EITHER the Back Bay apartment house, nor the streetcar suburb's two-suite apartment house, nor their numerous middle-class progeny, were entirely satisfactory solutions, however, to the increasing need for multiple-family housing at all class levels in late nineteenth- and early twentieth-century Boston. The Back Bay apartment house was outlandishly big; significantly, it was a Haddon Hall type of apartment house, built about 1900 on Beacon Street, that caused the furor that led to the imposition of height restrictions for buildings in Boston. On the other hand, though the two-suite apartment house in the streetcar suburbs was harmonious enough in that setting, two-suite houses at any class level could not meet the increasing demand for apartments. Nor were they as profitable as three- or four- or even six-family houses.

The seemingly logical solution to the Back Bay problem — small three- or four-family houses only three or four stories high — was only occasionally attempted there. Two four-apartment houses at 187–189 Huntington Avenue have already been touched on; another was designed by Putnam in Copley Square in 1885, and two more were built

FIGURE 125. J. A. Halloren. Sutherland Appartments, a block of eight double three-deckers at 1714–1742 Commonwealth Avenue, Brighton, 1914, front and rear facades.

at 497 and 499 Beacon Street in 1888–1890. A few six-family houses were also built, notably the very fashionable trio at 384–386–388 Commonwealth Avenue in 1896–1899. But these stacked six apartments in six stories, rather than in only three in a wider house. Only at Audubon Circle are double three-deckers evident (Figure 126). It is in the same square, a too often overlooked and remarkably harmonious red-brick ensemble clustering about Cram's Second Church, one of the city's handsomest churches, that one may see Boston proper's most handsome three-decker, now the Eastman Funeral Parlor (Figure 127), designed by Kilham and Hopkins for Judge Henry S. Dewey. One could wish that such three-deckers and not "dumbbell" apartment houses had been built more often in the Back Bay. Widely published, this flat-roofed three-decker loaded three similar apartments one on top of each other, each with such amenities as eight fireplaces per suite. Each possessed a living room, sitting room, and dining room off its own hall, three bedrooms, kitchen, pantry, maid's room, and two baths, with a servants' common sitting room in the basement along with other service rooms. There

was a built-in "automobile room" accessible from the alley, and there was also a passenger elevator. But only three apartments, however harmonious in appearance in the Back Bay, were, in that heavily populated, highly taxed, and very fashionable area, rather a poor investment. Even double three-deckers were hard to justify in the Back Bay. Instead, the problems associated with the Back Bay apartment house found their resolution on Beacon Street in Brookline, where Olmsted's splendid tree-shaded parkway of 1886–1887 naturally attracted fashionable builders. Here, too, the tall dumbbell type was introduced (one of the most fashionable, the Wolloton, was of this type) but in Brookline there was sufficient space to encourage the development of a much more acceptable type — the courtyard apartment house.

Richardson appears to have had this type in mind for a Back Bay apartment house he began to design but never built. Henry-Russell Hitchcock, in *The Architecture of H. H. Richardson and His Times*, noted that the plan was "rather skillfully disposed about a central court. Thus there would have been more light than in the deep apartments of the new and disgraceful 'dumbbell' type actually

Three- and six-deckers at Audubon Circle on Beacon Street in the Fenway, a few blocks from the Brookline border.

FIGURE 126. Benjamin Fox. Double three-decker at 459–461 Park Drive, 1900.
FIGURE 127. Kilham and Hopkins. Three-decker apartment house, 896 Beacon Street, built as the residence of Judge Henry S. Dewey, ca. 1905. First-floor plan.

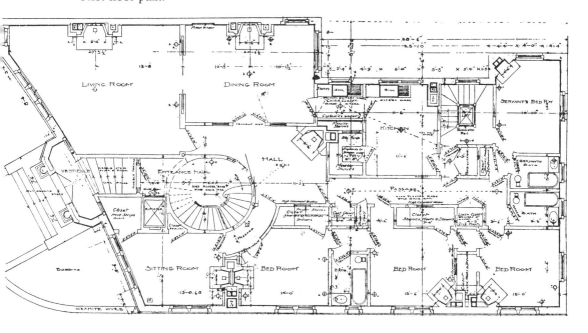

FIGURE 128. Cram, Wentworth and Goodhue. Perspective by Goodhue of Richmond Court Apartments, 1213 Beacon Street, Brookline, 1898. Probably the first apartment house in the northeastern United States massed and detailed like a great Tudor manor about a courtyard open to the street. The floor plan is reproduced in Figure 124.

erected in this decade on Commonwealth Avenue." In the event it was Ralph Adams Cram and Bertram Grosvenor Goodhue who appear to have introduced this building type into Boston — at Richmond Court on Beacon Street in Brookline (Figure 128). They explained themselves in the elegant brochure announcing the opening in 1898 of what is still, three-quarters of a century later, one of Boston's handsomest apartment houses. Cram wrote that a plan had

been chosen quite unusual in this country, though frequently found abroad. The apartments are grouped about three sides of a large open court, which is separated on the fourth side from the street by a light iron railing with tall brick and stone posts at intervals, and elaborately wrought ornament about the gateways, of which there are four, two larger ones for carriages, and two smaller for foot passengers. It has been the intention of the owner to render this court as beautiful as possible, and in befitting accordance with its situation on Beacon Street, perhaps the most beautiful as well as the most elegant of boulevards, and to this end it has been laid out and

adorned, like similar small private parks abroad, in the formal Italian fashion, with low box-hedges, clipped yews, flowers, and terraces. In the centre of the circular space formed by the driveway is set a fountain, from the cup of which rises the slight, graceful figure of a nymph in green bronze, modelled especially for its situation by [the distinguished American sculptor, Lee] Lawrie. From each suite a number of windows open on this court, and the view therefrom will be very different from the usual city prospect. Below lie the shrubbery, walks, and fountain, on the opposite side rises another wing of the building, while just without the enclosing *grilles* of wrought iron one sees all the life and motion of a brilliant thoroughfare.

Cram discussed particularly the problem of size.

Perhaps the chief objection brought heretofore against all apartment-houses, both city and suburban, has been their height — certain examples readily recalling themselves with horrible distinctness to the mind of every one, their monotonous stories being piled one above the other like veritable chimneys. The Richmond Court buildings are of quite another sort, however: but four stories in height, the effect of a large English Manor has been obtained, together with all its desirable qualities of strength, dignity, and repose, while the court is not forced into fulfilling the ignominious function of a mere light-well.

Thirty-six years later, when the relatively unknown architect of 1898 had become internationally distinguished, Cram asserted in his memoirs that Richmond Court had been "the first attempt to camouflage an apartment house through the counterfeit presentment of a great Tudor mansion" and if only because he lamented the fact, this is strong evidence for Richmond Court's having been the prototype. "From then on," continued Cram, "this sort of thing has run riot in multifarious exaggeration all over the Eastern seaboard, and I have wondered many times since, if a measure of guilt does not attach itself to us for what, unwittingly, we had done." Yet, as in the case of the "dishonest" two-suite house, there was good and in this case even venerable precedent: apartments for courtiers, after all, had always been a standard feature of palaces. And Boston is fortunate in many of the local apartment houses that were inspired by Richmond Court: the most conspicuous and grandiose example, begun in 1900, is Riverbank Court Apartments (now Ashdown House), designed by Henry B. Ball and H. E. Davidson on the other side of the Harvard Bridge, but perhaps the best is Burton Halls in Cambridge, built at 10 Dana Street in 1909 and designed by Newhall and Blevins. Here the way the elements of Richmond Court have been reorganized on an oddly shaped lot is imaginative. Certainly the grandest courtyard apartment house, however, is the Stoneholm in Brookline (Figure 148).

If the low, courtyard apartment house resolved the problem of the huge Back Bay type of apartment building, it obviously was not a solution to the need for larger than two-suite streetcar-suburb

apartment houses. On residential streets of. detached and usually wooden houses there was overwhelming opposition to any kind of sizable apartment house and always the chance of losing one's investment if one altered the street's character too abruptly. Even in middle- and lower middle-class areas, four-story apartment hotels, whether of brick or wood (around Central Square in Cambridge, for example, on Norfolk Street), came so close for all their architectural interest to being tenements that very few were erected. Imaginations were stretched, as a few surviving oddities suggest: 382–392 Harvard Street in Cambridge, designed in 1889 by Richards and Company, probably the apartment house specialists who worked also in the Back Bay, is a most interesting attempt to organize a number of units with private street doors into one wooden building whose scale is not disruptive. Another imaginative solution — building three connected houses as one unit, a development of the old semidetached vertical double — can be seen at 103–105 Raymond Street in Cambridge, designed in 1898 by Blaikie and Blaikie, another architectural firm that specialized in multifamily housing and did work in the Back Bay. This type of three-family house, though undeniably impressive, was evidently thought too wasteful of land and was only rarely attempted. Such houses also required at least one windowless wall per unit.

The problem of the more than two-family house in the suburbs seems to have amounted to this: whether to bring back the windowless wall in three or more connected vertical units or to break the two-story cornice line and pitch roof streetscape with a full third story. Given how strongly opposed to the windowless wall the streetcar suburbs were, it is scarcely surprising that the second choice was almost universal and that the three-decker emerged as the smallest

119

possible dwelling of more than two apartments where the essence of street-car-suburb design — light and air on four sides of each dwelling unit — could be preserved. By 1878 photographs of the Mission Church in Roxbury disclose great ranges of these three-deckers on every side. In the city of Boston it is estimated that between 1870 and 1920 over 16,000 were built — over 20 percent of all the city's dwelling units today. "Boston's weed," someone has called them; but that is far from true. The much maligned three-decker for which Boston is so notorious is a fascinating building type, too long overlooked and unsung.

Anyone who knows Tennyson's stirring line — "the rushing battle-bolt sang from the three-decker out of the foam" — will know that the pre-architectural usage of the term "three-decker" was chiefly naval, like "sky-scraper," which meant originally the topmost sheet of sailing vessels. Much nonsense has been written to explain the extension of the term to three-story houses, but the logic of the extension is surely clear: a "three-decker" was in the first place "a line-of-battle ship carrying guns on *three decks*" (my italics), to quote from the *Oxford English Dictionary,* and there have thus been by extension "three-decker novels" (novels in three volumes); even a "three-decker brain" (in Holmes's *The Professor at the Breakfast-Table*); and as devoted followers of the *Forsyte Saga* may recall, Jolyon Forsyte, on the occasion of his third marriage, to Irene, was christened a "three-decker" by an unkind relation. The term also has had other architectural uses: New England, for example, is full of "three-decker pulpits."

The actual origin of the house type itself has mystified scholars. In its characteristic form, the three-decker is a three-story house with one apartment of six or seven rooms on each floor, opening off common front and rear stairwells. It appears in varying forms throughout the country, but seems to have originated in New England. In *Housing Problems in America,* Prescott Hall recounts the tale of a Worcester architect who, having badly underestimated the cost of a mansard house of his design, persuaded his builder to recover their profits by omitting the mansard and carrying up the walls of the house on each side to a flat roof. Like Mrs. O'Leary's cow, the story is on the one hand of a kind too easily spread and on the other hand is just possibly true. Certainly, the mansard roof (first used in downtown Boston, significantly, on an apartment house: the Pelham; Figure 112) provided virtually a full third floor, and there are three-deckers here and there throughout Boston that seem to disclose a relationship between the mansard house and the three-decker. In East Boston, many of the earliest three-deckers are mansard-roofed on the front, while the side and rear walls are carried up the full three stories: at Edward Everett Square in Dorchester there is a house still with its side and rear mansards whose front facade (presumably later) was carried up the full three floors. Nearby, at Everett Avenue, is also a most interesting block of three-story connected mansard houses (ca. 1875) that look very much like prototypal three-deckers because the mansarded third floor is not continuous and gives way in places to the sheer three-story facade. Yet the 1885–1886 *Dorchester Blue Book* discloses that these were connected, single-family houses.

The problem of the origin of the three-decker has been compounded, moreover, by scholars who have concentrated on lower-class three-decker construction and having isolated these from their wider architectural context seek the origin of the three-decker house type *only* in the tenement reform legislation of the 1870s that made lower-class three-decker construction more profitable for speculators than tenements, and in the expanding trolley network that allowed the lower classes increasing access to the suburbs. What has been widely overlooked, however, is that the three-decker *as a building type,* at all class levels, is the streetcar-suburb version, on the detached town house streetscape, of the French flat apartment house.

One of the few scholars who have noticed this is Robert Bell Rettig, who, on the basis of his own research into this subject for a projected but unfortunately never completed study, pointed out in his *Guide to Cambridge Architecture: Ten Walking Tours* that the Stanstead, a four-story 1887 apartment house on Ware Street in Cambridge, reflected "the emerging type of 'decker' apartment house." Later on, in the same work, he noted while touching on the Kensington, a huge 1902 apartment house of six stories on Magazine Street in Cambridge, that it was organized "on the 'decker' or 'French flats' principle," thus equating the two terms. Consider Haddon Hall in this light — and it requires very little imagination to perceive this apartment house (Figure 115) as virtually a "ten-decker" and then to imagine it, shorn of its upper seven stories, as a three-decker. Nor is this notion fanciful. As we have seen, Haddon Hall would thereby have been as harmonious a part of the streetscape as Judge Henry S. Dewey's three-decker at Audubon Circle (Figure 127) and have caused no furor, although in the Back Bay it would have yielded too few rents to be profitable.

The same close relationship is also evident if one compares a typical Back Bay "dumbbell" apartment house, such as the Imperial or the Belvoir, to the conventional double three-decker: each stacks two long flats running from flanking bays at the front to the rear on each floor off common halls. In fact, not surprisingly, the same architects often designed both types: just as Samuel Kelly's wooden decker at 20–24 Meacham Road (1894) in Cambridge is identical in design concept to his brick four-flat building (1889) at 423 Marlborough Street in the Back Bay, so also, on a larger scale, John Hasty's brick "apartment house," the Templeton (Figure 130) at 367 Harvard Street in Cambridge, is identical with his wooden double three-decker, the Lowell (Figure 131) at 33 Lexington Avenue in Cambridge, built five years later.

American Architect and Building News always reported the erection of wooden streetcar-suburb three-deckers as "3-story frame apartments." In an article in *The Brickbuilder* in 1905, entitled "Boston 'Flats,' " after discussing many of the latest and most fashionable French flat apartment houses in the Back Bay, the author observed that "the flats which are being constructed are nearly all in the line of small buildings, mostly of three stories, located in the outlying parts of the city. When not built of wood, these structures are commonly built of ordinary red brick." The article was surely referring to three-deckers. This is not surprising, for the use of "flat" and "decker" as equivalent appears to have been the norm at the turn of the century. In Russell Sturgis's *Dictionary of Architecture and Building*, published in 1901–1902, occurs this note: "The term 'flat' is entirely general and applies to any domicile on one story of a large building."

Judge Dewey's Back Bay three-decker, complete with elevator and working fireplaces, and the Lowell in Cambridge are also evidence for a related and too often overlooked fact: there was a social and therefore an architectural hierarchy of deckers as there was of every other residential type in this period. It is certainly true that most three-deckers were built (and not remarkably well) for the lower middle class and the lower class.

Three-, six- and eight-family apartment houses in the streetcar suburbs.

FIGURE 129. William H. Smith. Three-decker apartment house, 18 Church Street, Meeting House Hill, Dorchester, 1905.

FIGURE 130. John Hasty. The Templeton, double four-decker apartment house, 367 Harvard Street, Cambridge, 1895. Not surprisingly, Hasty also designed wooden deckers:

FIGURE 131. The Lowell, double three-decker apartment house at 33 Lexington Avenue, on the corner of Brattle Street, Cambridge, 1900.

Wooden three-deckers of unusual distinction exist throughout the streetcar suburbs, particularly in Jamaica Plain, Dorchester, Brookline, and Roxbury Highlands.

FIGURE 132. C. A. Russell. 801 Centre Street, Jamaica Plain, 1894.

FIGURE 133. Gardner Bartlett. 128 Davis Avenue, Brookline, 1904.

FIGURE 134. James T. Ball. Three-decker near Franklin Field, Dorchester, ca. 1908.

FIGURE 135. Charles E. Wood. 119 and 121 Dale Street, Roxbury Highlands, 1891.

So also were many apartment buildings — and many single-family houses
were mean and cheaply built singles
Judge Dewey or the residents of the Lowell would not have lived in for a moment. Just as there were elegant singles
and cheap singles, there were elegant
three-deckers and cheap three-deckers.
Fortunately, the cheap apartment houses
and two-families and singles did not dis-
credit those house types the way cheap
three-deckers have discredited that
house type; otherwise, we should be left
with scarcely any choice at all between a
castle and a hovel! The Lowell and Judge
Dewey's are outstanding examples.
But there are a great many more fine
three-deckers than most imagine.

Some of the finest reflect the picturesque vogue, such as 174 Elm Street (ca.
1891) in Cambridge and 801 Centre
Street (1894) in Jamaica Plain (Figure
132), where C. A. Russell, the designer,
attempted to mitigate somewhat the effect of the break in the streetcar-suburb
cornice line that resulted from the full
third story. Another most imaginative
Jamaica Plain three-decker is shown in
Figure 3. The classic and flat-roofed
three-decker could also be rendered with
distinction, as at 18 Church Street in
Dorchester (Figure 129). Perhaps the
most unusual three-decker thus far documented is at 128 Davis Avenue in Brookline (Figure 133). Designed by Gardner
Bartlett in 1904, this shingled house
has the expected porches only to the rear:
its facade is massed about a stuccoed entrance bay with half-timbering and dia-
mond-paned windows. When we look at
the very different but as handsome
three-deckers that adjoin it at 122 and
124 Davis (ca. 1900), it is not difficult to
see how mistaken are those who conclude that as a building type the three-
decker is worthy of little attention.

It is also a great mistake to assume that
three-deckers were never architect-
designed or were invariably designed by
inferior architects. The "Building Intelligence" column in *American Architect*
documents the fact that many well-
known architects designed as many
deckers as they did all kinds of apartment houses. And it is overlooked completely that several architects made a distinct specialty of three-decker design,
providing plans of excellent quality
for builders and developers and subsequently publishing them. One such
pattern book, published in 1908 by *Architects and Builders Magazine,* discloses
that one of the most influential was a
Dorchester architect, James T. Ball, who
submitted to the compiler of the book
the photograph reproduced here (Figure
134). Ball wrote:

Until the advent of this house in the vicinity of Boston, all three family houses had
been built on the narrow deep plan, say from
22 to 28 feet broad and 50 to 75 feet deep. A
builder, realizing how much easier it had
been for him to sell his broad two family
houses, made the request for this type in a
three-flat, and immediately it sprang into
favor and has been extensively copied
throughout this section. . . . In this design
we have a Colonial house both inside and
out. The rooms lead off from a useful large
square central hall, not from a long, narrow
dark corridor, as was the practice. There are
five rooms — bath and back piazza all enclosed under the one roof. All rooms are light
and sunny. . . . Finished plainly, this house
can be built for $6,000 complete, while $500
added would give the rich appearance presented by the accompanying illustration.
There are a dozen of these houses renting for
$25 to $30 per flat.

Each of the dozen houses of this design built (and in the event, no doubt,
many dozens more) would have been an
improvement on almost any street. But
Ball's three-deckers were not expensive.
In *Streetcar Suburbs,* Warner pictures a
most handsome pair of three-deckers in
Roxbury Highlands (Figure 135); subsequent research discloses that both
houses (at 119 and 121 Dale Street),
which Warner rightly observes are the

equal of much speculator building in the Back Bay, were designed in 1891 by Charles E. Wood and cost $7500. The disparity in prices of four Jamaica Plain three-deckers built in the ten years between 1892 and 1902 will document the wide range of the three-decker hierarchy: 40 Paul Gore Street, designed by Jacob Leopold in 1895, cost $3000; 38 Paul Gore, built by Joseph Bulley in 1892, cost $4500; at 46 Creighton, a particularly handsome pitched-roof three-decker was built by Robert A. Watson in 1902 for $5500; while C. A. Russell's decker at 801 Centre Street in 1894 cost $6500. Similarly, in Dorchester, at 8 Montello Street, T. Edward Sheehan, a local architect, designed a three-decker in 1892 that cost $7500 and another at 2 Montello (1897) that cost $12,000!

This hierarchy of three-deckers is reflected to some extent in what little is known of contemporary attitudes toward them. On Townsend Street in Roxbury Highlands, the rather elegant area (discussed in Chapter 4) just beside the Harris Wood Crescent, largely developed by Robert and Jessie Todd (who occupied 140 Townsend), also includes three-deckers built by the Todds themselves, who built single-family houses (at 144 Townsend); doubles (at 150–152 and at 166–168 Townsend); and a double three-decker at 170–172 Townsend in 1915. This last decker, however, was of brick; had a pitch rather than a flat roof; cost $20,000; and was given a setback of twenty feet. Nor is it clear that the introduction of three-deckers led invariably to a decline in the overall character of a street. In Brookline, for example, when a number of three-deckers were built about 1900 across the street from the Davis Avenue home of Charles Rutan, a partner in the prestigious firm of Shepley, Rutan and Coolidge (H. H. Richardson's successors), Rutan did not move; he was still there in 1913. On the other hand, at the same time the Todds

were building their three-deckers on Townsend Street, Cushing Avenue's residents made a point of insisting that the adjoining Mount Cushing Terrace of 1914 *not* be built up with three-deckers, and there is evidence that Chadwick's mansion was sold only on the understanding that the land behind it out of which Mount Cushing Terrace was created would be subdivided only for middle-class two-family houses. The data with respect to the acceptability of deckers are thus inconclusive. Nor do the often quoted protests of the time against three-deckers, which led by the 1920s to zoning changes in the city and suburbs that virtually prohibited them, at all clarify the matter.

A frequent charge — that three-deckers deteriorated rapidly, were fire hazards, and involved high maintenance — is substantially true of any wooden house; we know this now that so many streets of wooden mansions improperly cared for have become slums. The more serious charge — that they led to a decrease in land values — was never demonstrated; in fact, B. J. Newman followed that charge with the rather contradictory assertion that they also increased land values so that single houses were prohibitively costly in areas where much more money could be made by building apartment houses. This second charge also points up the fundamental and rather romantic predilection all the anti–three-decker forces shared for the single house: Newman's attack on deckers makes plain the fact that the prejudice against three-deckers was one part of an overall prejudice against *any* kind of apartment house. Newman thought, for instance, that "where many families use one entrance, the approach to the immoral home in a multiple building is less conspicuous than in a dwelling," and he indulged in the rather remarkable observation that "sex morality often is by subtle ways weakened through long established apartment house living." Such buildings, he concluded, were often "a shield to the lewd man and woman," and as marital discord was the more easily overheard and consequently the more embarrassing, he announced that "it is a short cut from the apartment house to the divorce court!" If none of this calls to mind the staid middle-class three-decker streets of the Highlands, neither does it seem to recall the Hotel Agassiz. Apartment dwellers, wrote Newman, were usually "nomads" characterized by a "lack of civic interest." Clearly, he did not know Major Higginson. He also pointed out that three-deckers were ugly because they were monotonous: by this standard, Louisburg Square would scarcely survive Mr. Newman's remarks.

Every charge leveled against three-deckers really fell of its own weight: if most were cheap, of what house type was this not also true? If most were speculator-built, so also were most houses, including many, for example, in the Back Bay; if they were expensive to maintain, so were all frame houses, however elegant; if deckers followed the streetcar, what didn't in the streetcar suburbs? If they were densely massed, so also were the houses of Melville and Cushing avenues. At a housing conference held in Boston in 1918, Charles Logue even went so far as to call the three-decker "an ideal type of house," and Marion Booth and Ordway Tead wrote in 1914 that even at the lower middle-class level,

the values which the tenant receives in this modern flat in the three-decker are so little short of luxurious that it is no wonder that they are in demand. A flat which rents for from $20 to $25 a month includes a parlor, dining room, kitchen with set tubs, cook stove with water heater attached, two bedrooms, front and back piazza, hot air furnace, electricity and hard wood floors.

That the data should be inconclusive with respect to the contemporary attitudes toward deckers surely points all the more directly to the effect of the three-decker hierarchy we have been discussing: how acceptable deckers were obviously bore some relation to what kinds of deckers were involved.

This decker hierarchy is, however, often misunderstood. The flats-over-the-corner-store variety, for example, was not necessarily the meanest type of flat housing. As we have seen, flats over shops were not unusual at the Social Register level in the Back Bay. What was important was what kind of flats over what kind of store and in what kind of neighborhood. Buildings of shops and flats on the corners of pleasant retail streets from which led upper middle-class residential streets offered far better accommodations than the barely detached rows of entirely residential three-deckers in South Boston. Nor is the space between three-deckers and their setback any guide at all to their quality; in fact, many three-deckers were built in connected blocks. Some of the most picturesque are in Brighton (Figure 125).

Such blocks are difficult to document because connected three-deckers look very much like connected single-family town houses. Indeed, just as many of the Cushing Avenue houses in Dorchester turn out to be two-suite houses, so also the row of handsome brick connected houses built in 1907 between Dean Road and Clifton Path on Beacon Street in Brookline, which we discussed in the last chapter, are, in fact, three-decker houses (Figure 96) and they are as elegant as their location would suggest. The residents of this block in 1914 included Mr. and Mrs. C. P. Seaverns (he was the president of Howe and French on Broad Street in Boston); Mr. and Mrs. Charles Lindsey (Mr. Lindsey was the manager of the Parker House, then perhaps Boston's leading hotel); several doctors and lawyers with business addresses on Beacon Street in Boston; and a number of what would today be called "junior executives." Each of these three-deckers reflects this class level. Every eight-room flat possesses four reception rooms opening through wide doorways into one another, and because the deckers are joined at their *narrow* rather than at their wide ends (a luxury unknown even in the most elegant single-family town houses) three reception rooms overlook Beacon Street and one scarcely notices the two short windowless walls. There are also two bedrooms, a kitchen, and maid's bedroom. A serving hatch between dining room and kitchen also documents the presence of servants. Each three-decker has marble staircases and elaborate tiled floors and each flat has a dining room paneled to a height of six feet in oak with a wood-burning fireplace. Brookline and Dorchester, particularly, abound in connected brick three-deckers, and one can always distinguish the class level at once according to whether they are connected at the narrow or wide sides.

Such buildings not only look like single-family row houses; as an ensemble they also look very much like one large apartment house. Yet this element of illusion may well be misleading. What is the difference between an apartment house and a block of connected three-flat houses? Having sought the origin and evolution of the three-decker in the French flat fashion, we may now find it instructive to work our way back from the three-decker to the clearly recognizable courtyard apartment house. One of the earliest of these is the Peabody in Ashmont (Figure 136). It bears one of the most august names in Boston, that of Colonel Oliver Peabody, a senior partner in Kidder, Peabody and Company, one of Boston's most important bankers, and a scion of a leading Boston family. It bears his name because he erected it to protect the church next door, All Saints, of which he was a parishioner. Situated

in one of Dorchester's upper middle-class areas, across the street from a railway station (later replaced by Ashmont Station on what is now the Red Line) and next door to a famous church, and the proud possessor of a celebrated name, the Peabody was designed as well by a distinguished architect, Edwin J. Lewis, Jr. Its multitude of picturesque chimneys are indicative of its amenities, which include working fireplaces in every apartment. Another amenity is that one gains access to the building principally through charming half-timbered porches that jut into the courtyard around which this brick ensemble is massed.

As we will see shortly, All Saints had been designed by Cram for the Peabodys, his first major patrons, and the Peabody apartment house, begun in 1896 while Cram was still working on the church, may well have been the inspiration for the full-fledged Tudor manor of Richmond Court, the courtyard apartment house Cram designed in Brookline two years later, the widely emulated design of which solved the problem of the ungainly Back Bay dumbbell type. Yet its four different building permits document conclusively that the Peabody is actually *four brick three-deckers,* connected to each other at their narrow ends just as are those on Beacon Street in Brookline, but massed in the case of the Peabody about a courtyard. The much maligned three-decker, whose origins we have sought in the French flat fashion of the 1870s and eighties, may thus in turn have inspired the eventual flowering of the French flat into its most plausible and distinguished form, the red-brick and "Tudor Manor" courtyard apartment house.

THE sense of illusion or pretension that has turned up again and again in this discussion of multifamily architecture — where all sorts of tricks were apparently played to make two-families look like one-families and three-deckers like apartment houses and apartment houses like Tudor manors — is, finally, a kind of clue that we have misunderstood the social conventions and therefore the architectural problem of Victorian multifamily housing.

How greatly we have misunderstood the social conventions can perhaps best be illustrated by comparing the Peabody to the Albemarle Chambers on Albemarle Street, in the South End, another red-brick courtyard ensemble of connected three-deckers (twelve in this case) built in 1899. The closeness of Huntington Avenue, then the dividing line between the fashionable French flat apartment house district and its middle-class and lower middle-class South End cousins, no doubt accounts for this complex, which is located off St. Botolph Street, which was respectable but certainly not fashionable. But the Albemarle Chambers, designed by Israel Nesson, was not only built two important blocks away from fashion but also directly next to very busy railroad tracks, and its social standing was naturally vastly inferior to that of the Peabody. Such indices of the time as *Clark's Boston Blue Book,* which included a directory of members of Boston's clubs and a visiting list of the residents of the better streets, listed every resident of the Peabody. The Albemarle Chambers (indeed, Albemarle *Street*) was scrupulously avoided; as was St. Botolph Street. Aside from location and such amenities as room layout and working fireplaces, the Peabody and the Albemarle Chambers are virtually identical. But it was precisely such amenities, and privacy and spaciousness of living unit allied with the social calibre of the neighborhood (and not the relative proximity of one's fellow tenants or any question of ownership or renting), that counted. Thus by

the social conventions of the time, the Peabody was an apartment house and the Albemarle Chambers a tenement. And that was not an illusion.

Freed of the social misconception (that the gulf was between single and multioccupancy structures rather than between the costly and the cheap of each type), we are thus liberated from the architectural misconception — that multifamily architecture was increasingly misleading in appearance because it was perceived to be inferior to single occupancy. The multifamily architect was forced to misleading exteriors because while the demand for apartments rose dramatically at all class levels year after year, the scale of every type of residential streetscape in Boston was unfriendly to the apartment house. Haddon Hall, for example, was quite honestly an apartment house, but its type provoked a furor — not because it was an apartment house, but because it was not harmonious with the streetscape. Neither Richmond Court nor the Peabody provoked any furor at all. Each was misleading, as was the two-suite house, but each provided for the new horizontal life-style in a manner harmonious to already built-up single family streetscapes. Interestingly at the end of this thirty-year evolution of the horizontal flat or decker, the last few enclaves of connected single-family row houses built in the first years of the twentieth century in Boston — Charles River Square (Frank Bourne, 1909) and West Hill Place (Coolidge and Carlson, 1916) — can in each case be easily mistaken for an apartment house (Figure 137).

Each of these ensembles of connected red-brick town houses reflects Bulfinch's precept, discussed in Chapter 1, that connected dwellings should ideally face or enclose open space. But so also does Richmond Court. And that is the point. When the multifamily architect was able through the courtyard apartment house to build in the traditional scale of the

FIGURE 136. Edwin J. Lewis, Jr. The Peabody, 195 Ashmont Street, Dorchester, 1896–1897, an apartment house that consists of four connected brick three-deckers with servants' quarters under the roof. Two of the four entrance porches to each three-decker are visible in the courtyard. The ground-story apartments of the two three-deckers whose narrow ends face Ashmont Street were designed for doctors and incorporate waiting rooms and offices, features common to both intown and streetcar-suburb apartment houses. Patients entered through the private street-front entrances.

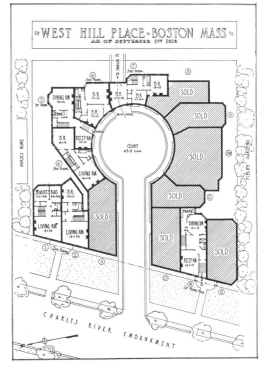

FIGURE 137. Coolidge and Carlson. West Hill Place, off Embankment Road at the foot of Beacon Hill, 1916. First-, second-, and third-story plans of single-family connected row houses on overall site plan.

FIGURE 138. De Vos and Company, et al. Longwood Towers, originally Alden Park Manor, Brookline, 1922.

single-family row house streetscape and to apply to the apartment house Bulfinch's precept about open space (that is, the courtyard), he achieved for those who preferred a horizontal rather than a vertical dwelling unit and to rent rather than to own an ensemble of horizontal dwellings as gracious in appearance as any row house square and as harmonious with Boston's traditional streetscapes. The misleading multifamily facades of Victorian Boston were not the problem: they were the solution to the problem of how to organize a great number of such horizontal dwelling units in streetscapes that were unfriendly in both the city proper and the streetcar suburbs. Moreover, once one thinks of it, the shift in fashion from the vertical dwelling unit to the horizontal dwelling unit had also importantly undergirded the revival of the detached streetcar-suburb town house: such houses, like French flats, which emerged during the same period in Boston, sought always for one-floor spaciousness in reception area and as much light and air as was possible. Significantly, at Longwood Towers (1922–1925) in Brookline, called originally Alden Park Manor and designed by K. M. De Vos and Company, with George R. Wiren and Harold Field Kellogg as consulting architects, the development of the apartment house in Boston reached its climax in another red-brick Tudor design that went Richmond Court one better and broke up the courtyard apartment building into several detached buildings (Figure 138) ranged about a garden setting similar to that of the streetcar suburb's detached town house.

An apartment house luxurious enough that the president of Lever Brothers was counted among the tenants for many years, even its corridors are endowed with linenfold oak paneling. Like Richmond Court, which is divided into five halls — St. Albans Hall, for example, or Grafton Hall — Longwood Towers is divided into smaller sections with very British-sounding names — Arling Cross, Belden Cross, and Charing Cross — but at Longwood Towers these divisions are not entries off a courtyard but separate tower buildings of many apartments each, which rise from a huge three-story underground parking garage (no doubt the first such facility in Greater Boston) that is hidden from view by the garden setting. And in rather an uncanny way the design of Longwood Towers foreshadowed the future of Boston in the twentieth century.

1890–1950

PART II

———

McKim and White

to

Cram and Goodhue and Gropius

6

CHARLES MCKIM
AND THE CLASSICAL REVIVAL

BY THE 1890s, over a million people lived within a twelve-mile radius of the State House. And whether one lived in a huge apartment block, a conventional single-family house, or the most vernacular of three-deckers, if it was stylish in the nineties, it was relentlessly Classical. Nor was the fact that architectural style, after splintering into many modes in the Queen Anne period, had resolved itself through the picturesque Colonial Revival into a full-fledged academic Classicism unrelated to Boston's enormous growth. City and suburbs had become metropolis, and it was not unnatural (especially in the wake of the Colonial enthusiasms aroused by the 1876 Centennial) that once Boston's architects focused on their Colonial and Neoclassical heritage, they began to feel that a revived Classicism was what Boston no less than New York needed to order its growth in the late nineteenth century and to ennoble its aspirations. Aspirations? Most scholars have concluded that by the 1890s the "New England Renaissance" was dying. Yet New England's "Indian Summer" seems to have been rather more vigorous than we have been led to believe, and in order to understand this new Classicism we must accordingly reexamine the cultural background of late nineteenth- and early twentieth-century Boston, which was the context for the building that heralded the American Classical Revival — the Boston Public Library, built in 1888–1895 in Copley Square (Figure 139).

John Jay Chapman once asserted that he could "attach to almost every portrait in Venice an honored Puritan name." Similarly, Kenneth Clark's discussion of early fifteenth-century Florence is strikingly applicable to late nineteenth- and early twentieth-century Boston. For the puzzle we must now explore — why and how at the behest of hard-headed Yankee trustees the Boston Public Library arose in Copley Square in gleaming white Classical rebellion against its dark Ruskinian and Richardsonian Medieval environment — is akin to a paradox posed by Lord Clark. Given the character of the men who had made Florence so rich — "the bankers and wool merchants, the pious realists" — it seems at first glance baffling that suddenly out of the dark, narrow fifteenth-century streets arose those light, sunny Renaissance arcades that "totally contradict the dark Gothic Style that preceded and to some extent still surrounds them." Yet Lord Clark pointed out:

For thirty years the fortunes of [Florence], which in a material sense had declined, were directed by a group of the most intelligent individuals who have ever been elected to power by a democratic government . . . the Florentine chancellors were scholars, believers in the *studia humanitatis,* in which learning could be used to achieve a happy life, believers in the application of free intelligence to public affairs, and believers, above all, in Florence.

Commercially, nineteenth-century Boston also had been declining for some

FIGURE 139. McKim, Mead and White. Boston Public Library, Copley Square, Back Bay, 1888–1895. The principal facades.

decades. But that is not to say that Bostonians had forgotten Emerson's declaration: that Boston was "not an accident, not a windmill, or a railroad station, or cross-roads tavern, or an army barracks grown up by time and luck to a place of wealth; but a seat of humanity, of men of principle, obeying a sentiment and marching loyally whither that should lead them," and, as so many have observed in earnest and in jest, believing as they marched, above all, in Boston.

Admittedly, the comparison seems forced at first. Yet Whitehill has insisted that it has been the always renewable supply of "literate and responsible Trustees and treasurers [that] has done more than anything else to make Boston a center of civilization," and the comparison of late nineteenth-century Boston with fifteenth-century Florence is surely implicit in the way he dealt with the Bos-

ton volume in the University of Oklahoma Press's Centers of Civilization series, which was dedicated to cities that have "exercised a radiating influence upon the civilization in which they have existed." To the announced titles — *Athens in the Age of Pericles, Rome in the Augustan Age,* and *Florence in the Age of Dante* — Whitehill added, not Boston in the Age of Emerson, but *Boston in the Age of John Fitzgerald Kennedy.* When the book was published in 1966, he explained his choice by pointing to the fact that it was after 1870 that Boston had grown "far richer in the elements of civilization," citing the observation of Alfred North Whitehead in 1942 that "insofar as the world of learning today possesses a capital city, Boston with its various neighboring institutions approximates to the position that Paris occupied in the Middle Ages." In fact, it was precisely in the 1870–1900 period that Boston began to develop the galaxy of institutions for which it is now known the world over and to build in the New World, to which the balance of power was slowly shifting, the great center of Western learning and culture it remains today.

The list is astonishing. In the last half of the nineteenth and the beginning of the twentieth centuries there were founded in Boston a dozen or more universities, colleges, and schools of national importance: Tufts University, the Massachusetts Institute of Technology, Boston College, Boston University, Radcliffe College, Northeastern University, Simmons College, the New England Conservatory of Music, Wellesley College, and much of Harvard, including the schools of architecture and business administration, to name only perhaps the most distinguished. No less astonishing is the number of museums founded during this period; five at Harvard alone (including the Fogg and Busch-Reisinger museums), as well as the Gardner Museum and the Boston Museum of Fine Arts, this last (along with the Metropolitan Museum in New York, incorporated in the same year) the first true art museum in America in the modern sense of the term. Wherever one looks — at education, medicine, museums, music (the Boston Symphony Orchestra was started in 1881) — it is clear that no other period in Boston's history of three and a half centuries can equal for vitality this one.

All this has been greatly obscured by Van Wyck Brooks's conclusion, in *New England: Indian Summer, 1865–1915*, that by the 1890s "the Boston mind appeared to have lost its force." But in the very next sentence — "it was yielding, inch by inch, to the Catholic Irish" — one sees what Brooks meant. And when he cited as evidence of this decline the fact that by the early years of this century "the most prominent objects in Boston were the Catholic Cathedral, the dome of the synagogue [probably Temple Israel] and the dome of Mrs. Eddy's Mother Church," his point cannot be mistaken. The Boston that Brooks's study chronicles (especially the literary tradition upon which he focuses) *was* deteriorating. But a new Boston was evolving at the same time and it is a mistake to read into Brooks's record of decline the idea that because the new and evolving Boston was more pluralistic culturally it was inferior.

Late nineteenth-century Boston, which by no means lacked for Yankee building blocks (one thinks of Henry Lee Higginson's Boston Symphony Orchestra or of President Eliot's Harvard), was enriched immeasurably by the newer groups; Brooks himself instances Louis Sullivan, "a Boston boy born and bred — one of the first fine shoots of the Boston Irish." But Brooks could have said much more, relating not just the Catholic Cathedral to Louis Sullivan but the synagogue, for example, to a Lithuanian Jewish boy who had immigrated to Boston with his parents in 1875: the legendary scholar Bernard Berenson, who in 1952 at the age of eighty-seven wrote in his diary, "I still consider Boston my home." One wonders too, in connection with Christian Science, how much the fact that its founder, Mary Baker Eddy, was a woman enters in here. Certainly Mrs. Eddy was not the only woman whose achievements at this time were not taken very seriously. The same might be said for the pioneer women architects during this period, several of whom studied and practiced in Boston: Marion Mahoney Griffin, for example, who became Frank Lloyd Wright's chief draftsman, graduated from M.I.T. in 1894; Minerva Parker Nichols designed the Browne and Nichols School in Cambridge (1894); and Lois Lilley Howe, the first licensed woman architect in the country, was a lifelong resident of Cambridge. Whatever Brooks's motivations, however, in singling out so critically the Catholic cathedral, Temple Israel, and Mrs. Eddy's church, another person than Brooks might well have written quite another kind of book, as Whitehill ultimately did.

How ethnically diverse Boston was becoming is evident in Whitehill's estimate that by 1900 only 11 percent of the city of Boston's population were Bostonians of "traditional New England origin." Even in the suburbs one sees unmistakable evidence of this growing diversity: between the late 1850s and the early 1870s, for example, Protestant meeting houses in the suburbs of Stoneham, Danvers, and even in historic Lexington were remodeled into Roman Catholic churches: respectively, St. Patrick's, the Church of the Annunciation, and St. Brigid's.

Today, when this more pluralistic Boston, "the Boston of John Fitzgerald Kennedy," has become as much "Boston" in our minds as Mather's or Emerson's city, one can see, as have Howard Mumford Jones and Bessie Zaban Jones, that despite the city's late nineteenth-century literary and commercial decline, "to infer from this that the 'Boston mind' had weakened is mistaken."

The decaying "Indian Summer" image we have of the late nineteenth and early twentieth centuries in Boston persists because it is enshrined in our literature under august auspices. One thinks of T. S. Eliot and of Henry Adams — above all, one recalls Henry James, standing at the foot of Beacon Hill, gazing toward the Back Bay and the expanding metropolis beyond it. Wrote James:

It is from about that point southward that the new splendors of Boston spread, and will clearly continue to spread, but it opened out to me as a tract pompous and prosaic, with which the little interesting city, the city of character and genius, exempt as yet from the Irish yoke, had had absolutely nothing to do.

Even James, however, as we will see, found much that was impressive in the nineties in Boston. Nor is this surprising; the Joneses point out that Boston had become by the turn of the twentieth century "the cultural capital of the United States." And while one would not wish to carry the comparison to the Renaissance too far, or to extend its point carelessly to architecture, Vincent Scully has observed that the Queen Anne movement "recreated the whole process of the English Renaissance itself" in the direction that it took from "a late medievalism toward an eventual 18th century classicism." Furthermore, how one evaluates the increasingly Classical architecture of the 1890s will depend importantly on whether one sees it as shaped by the declining culture or by the aspiring and maturing culture, each of which paralleled the other in the same period.

Bainbridge Bunting's conclusion that the Georgian Revival he chronicles in the Back Bay illustrates a declining and complacent culture thus proceeds from a review of the overall cultural background of the 1870-1900 period in which he emphasizes three events: Cleveland Amory's "curfew" for entrance into Boston society in 1879; H. G. Wells's conclusion that by 1875 the "filling up" and closing of the Boston mind was complete; and the removal, also in 1875, of the executive offices of the Burlington Railroad from Boston to New York. Lewis Mumford, on the other hand, insists that "it is not by accident that Harvard's rejuvenation in science and scholarship under Charles Eliot coincided with the constructive enterprises of the Back Bay, in the generation between 1870 and 1900." Whereas Bunting cites the fact that in 1913 Boston could "overlook the Armory Show with genteel equanimity," Mumford notes that it was at the Museum of Fine Arts in the Back Bay that "the fresh world of color opened up by the French Impressionists was displayed long before either the Metropolitan Museum or the Chicago Art Institute were in a position to show similar work." And Mumford concludes that it was not only during this 1870–1900 period but "in the Back Bay that Boston first established itself as one of the centers of world culture in the arts and sciences."

In this light the increasingly Classical and Georgian Back Bay takes on a very different aspect that is surely applicable to the whole metropolis. Consider, for example, how George Santayana's boyhood memories of the Great Fire of 1872 document unconsciously at one and the same time Bostonians' growing pride in the 1870s and the increasing dissatisfaction of Santayana's generation (which matured in the eighties and nineties) with the picturesque seventies. He recalled in *Persons and Places:*

the contagious excitement and even pride felt by Bostonians at having had such a big fire. People would not speak of the London fire any more; they would say the Boston fire. Unluckily, for Boston, Chicago had had an even bigger fire; and more unluckily in my opinion Boston had no Wren to rebuild the town. That was the era of an architectural medley of styles imitated from picture-books by professional speculators and amateur artists.

Unconsciously, Santayana's boyhood thoughts echoed those of many of Boston's rising young architects. Four years after the Great Fire, Robert Peabody was already lamenting the effect of what he called the "bric-a-brac style"; by the 1880s this view was widespread. Considering Commonwealth Avenue in 1888, which as we have seen had grown into a very picturesque street during the Queen Anne period, C. H. Blackall found Boston's grand boulevard "about as disappointing as anything could be," its "once stately aspect" (that is, its French Academic buildings of the 1860s) having deteriorated into "a continual ka-

leidoscopic change of style and detail from house to house." What had seemed a charming and individualistic diversity at the height of the Queen Anne mode in the 1870s was increasingly perceived by the late eighties as fussy and strident, even degenerate.

This was the context of the Boston Public Library, which may also be taken as a sign of the underlying continuity between the old and exclusively Yankee culture and the new, more pluralistic culture then beginning to evolve. The old culture, Brooks admits, found no difficulty in the new library's Italian Renaissance architecture: Boston, he observes, "prayed over the Florentine library . . . and even made Florence and Venice Bostonian somehow because of its regard for Italian culture. . . . the Library seemed quite at home in a town where Italian studies, fostered by Norton and Longfellow, by Perkins and Lowell, were a part of the atmosphere all men breathed."

But it is perhaps more important, given the role of the public library movement, that the new Copley Square library marked a cultural achievement that was Boston's own; and one distinctly related to the city's increasing immigrant population. Today, opposite the library, in the center of Copley Square, is a memorial to one immigrant for whom the library was very important — Kahlil Gibran, the young Lebanese from Boston's South End who was so deeply influenced by the Boston Bohemia of the 1890s, discussed in Chapter 7, and who became one of the most widely read poets of the twentieth century. On the other side of the library is another monument — the new addition to the library, designed by Philip Johnson. Few realize that a significant part of its cost came from a million-dollar trust fund established by John Defarrari. Probably he was not the barefoot newsboy reading in the old Boston Public Library whose presence there so impressed Matthew Arnold on his visit to Boston in 1883, but Defarrari was, indeed, in the 1880s a poor newsboy of immigrant stock, whose access to the library's books on economics enabled him to rise to great wealth and, in fact, prompted his generous gift to that institution.

These two penniless immigrant boys — the Lebanese poet-to-be and the Italian millionaire-to-be — are, as it were, the vital context of the Renaissance library. There was thus a function, and certainly a future, but there was no precedent for such an institution: the architects were asked to create for the first time in the world a huge metropolitan library for the general public as well as for the scholar. And the building itself, a commitment to this rather radical undertaking, seemed to many upon its completion a success "secured for civilization as well as for Boston." The new Public Library not only recalled architecturally the glories of the Renaissance; it marked one of several large nineteenth-century Boston achievements not unworthy of the association.

T HE first plans for the Public Library were, in fact, what a flaccid culture might well have been content with. Years later, Cram remembered that these plans (by the city architect) showed "a chaos of gables, oriels, arcades and towers, all worked out in brownstone" and that it had required "a growl of rage and indignation" before they were scrapped, a protest one of the library's trustees later pointed out was "started by [the city's] architects." A particular plea was made by Arthur Rotch, the architect to whom Cram was then apprenticed; there was "the keenest anxiety," insisted Rotch, "that this opportunity of making a building worthy of our far-famed public library should not be

lost." Freed of the city architect by the force of the public outcry, the library trustees chose the New York firm of McKim, Mead and White, largely, it would seem, because of the enthusiasm of one trustee, Samuel Abbott (who was a cousin of Mrs. McKim), for the Italian Renaissance Villard Houses in New York, then the most conspicuous evidence of that firm's commitment to what Joseph Wells called the "classical ideal." Wells, an influential designer in the New York firm, defined that ideal simply: "clearness, simplicity, grandeur, order and philosophical calm."

Actually, the trustees might have looked much closer to home for Italian Renaissance by McKim, the partner in charge, as it turned out, for nearly all the firm's Boston work, for the Andrew House of 1883–1884 at 32 Hereford Street (Figure 144) was among their earliest work in that mode, a reflection of the fact that though practicing in New York, McKim was closely connected with Boston. He had entered Harvard College in 1867 and remained there a year before going to Paris to study architecture and upon his return to this country he had been apprenticed to Richardson. Boston's architecture also strongly influenced McKim. He thought Bulfinch the greatest American architect and one of McKim's partners asserted years later that the leaning of the office toward the Classical dated from McKim's sketching trip to Boston's North Shore in 1877. McKim also married into a distinguished Boston family, the Appletons. Moreover, according to his biographer, "the plan and the general outline of the design [for the library] began to shape themselves in McKim's mind" at the Appleton House on Beacon Street, where he established a small, private office after he had received the library commission.

Not everyone liked McKim's plans. When the model of the new library went on exhibition in 1888 one newspaperman thought the design recalled a warehouse; the *Globe* compared it to the City Morgue. As the building rose, the *Herald,* in the spring of 1889, deplored the design: "What opportunities for splendidly broken skylines that western background affords the architect, but this flat-backed, flat-chested structure, promises to crush them to the earth." But the significance of McKim's design seems to have been felt at once and in ever-widening circles. As Leland Roth has pointed out, the promise of the Villard Houses was

fulfilled beyond expectation when the [library] was opened in 1895. Here all the resources of the architecture of the past were gathered together, fused with modern construction techniques and embellished with the finest works of art. Its interior was a virtual palace and the exterior drew together and gave final definition to the vast open space of Copley Square. . . . The Library also demonstrated the kind of public splendor that could be achieved when architects, painters and sculptors worked in concert. Here was a building which demonstrated that in America, as in Europe, the city would be a work of art.

Not only did the library exhibit, in the words of Cram, " a serene Classicism, reserved, scholarly, delicately conceived in all its parts, beautiful in that sense in which things have always been beautiful in periods of high human culture"; but its architectural art prompted Ernest Fenollosa to call the building "our first American Pantheon." In fact, a chief purpose of the building, wrote Charles Moore, was "to create a visible manifestation of the civic consciousness of Boston," and the result was an ensemble of decorative art that remains distinguished to this day.

McKim was a master of the dinner of persuasion, and he cajoled trustees, politicians, private donors, and artists into rising repeatedly to his costly enthusiasms. How difficult a process lay behind this splendor may be seen in his rela-

tions with Puvis de Chavannes. Moore notes that a witness to McKim's first meeting with Puvis in Paris in 1891 recalled: "the price was very generous indeed; the artist was evidently staggered. I noticed that he trembled and the silence became oppressive. Mr. McKim quietly urged the matter, praising the artist, who finally said: "the offer is princely, but the undertaking is great. Boston is distant, I am an old man; in fact, I am afraid. *Enfin, j'ai peur.*" Puvis finally accepted but later declined under pressure of another offer in France. McKim tried again. He had a model made of the staircase, and sent it in 1892 to John Galen Howard, then studying architecture in Paris, pressing Howard to "call upon M. Chavannes and represent to him for the Trustees and this office our desire to have him undertake the work at his own price." Back in Boston, the library's growing cost called a halt to the negotiations, but McKim determined "to renew the attack upon Chavannes" while in Paris in the winter of 1893, and this time he succeeded. The result was the great sequence of murals on the main staircase, created by the artist with actual pieces of the marble before him, and with the graining of the marble painted as a guide on the bottom of each canvas, work William Jordy has recently pronounced as "among the outstanding examples of mural decoration in the country" (see Plate 6).

There were many failures. Projected work by both Whistler and La Farge was for one reason or another never realized; nor were Saint-Gaudens's sculptures for the facade. What was done was also unusually controversial. Many know that McKim's own gift, Frederick MacMonnies's *Bacchante,* proved too daring for Boston; but few remember that Sargent's *Synagogue* in his third-floor gallery cycle *Judaism and Christianity* so distressed many Jews that the legislature attempted to effect its removal. What was achieved

FIGURE 140. Boston Public Library, the Delivery Room. The doorways are of blood-red marble, *rouge antique,* with variegated red and green Levanto marble; the *rouge antique* mantelpiece they flank is 11 feet high, brilliantly polished, and superbly carved. Above the entablature is one of a series of murals by Edwin Austin Abbey entitled *The Quest of the Holy Grail,* which endow the Delivery Room with a rich Pre-Raphaelite pageantry still much admired today. The Delivery Room opens off the stair hall (Plate 6).

was, however memorable: Bela Pratt's much maligned but splendid figures of Art and Science at the main door (Figure 141); Daniel Chester French's bronze doors, ornament enough for a vestibule where also stands MacMonnies's figure of Sir Henry Vane; Augustus Saint-Gaudens's three facade panels and his superb medallion bust of Robert Billings (a Boston merchant and library benefactor) in the north arcade of the courtyard; Domingo Mora's facade colophons; Puvis de Chavannes's serene pastorale on the Grand Staircase; Edwin Austin Abbey's murals in the Delivery Room (Figure 140); the great mural cycle by Sargent (Figure 142) in the gallery that bears his name; even the work by lesser-known artists would be notable in any other building. The rich red Pompeian Lobby by Elmer Garnsey, the New York artist whose work can also be seen at the Library of Congress; the Venetian Lobby opposite, sea-green and bright with gold, the work of Joseph Lindon Smith, a Boston muralist; the *Triumph of Time* on the ceiling of the Elliott Room, which takes its name from the artist, John Elliott; all contribute to an ensemble of architectural art perhaps unequaled in nineteenth-century American architecture.

Yet at the heart of the library's splendor is what Royal Cortissoz called McKim's passion for "the pure structural character of a well-laid course of stone." To McKim, Cortissoz wrote, "building materials were what pigments are to the painter; he handled them with the same intensely personal feeling for their essential qualities that a great technician of the brush brings to the manipulation of his colors and he left upon his productions the same autographic stamp." Cortissoz remembered:

During the building of the Boston Library certain sheets of marble were to be put in the entrance hall — Numidian, I think they were — and their dimensions were determined by McKim with the utmost care. He regarded those dimensions as essential to the ensemble, but when the marble was delivered it was found that they had not been rigidly followed. Forthwith the sheets were rejected. The contractor argued at tremendous length and almost wept, but McKim was harder than the Numidian itself. He was dealing in marble as an artist deals in paint. . . .

The marble of the staircase was particularly hard to procure. Moore noted that McKim demanded " a certain, golden-yellow stone called *Monte Riete,* or Convent Sienna," which was available only "from a quarry owned by a religious order who only had a block or two taken out by primitive methods when the convent needed money." McKim not only needed some four hundred tons of this marble but also had to choose it carefully with respect to color, for the lightest marble in color is at the bottom of the staircase; the marble gets gradually darker and darker as one ascends; a superb example of the subtlety of his work here.

Insofar as the library as a whole is concerned one must discriminate. Who is not grateful today for its courtyard? Bates Hall is certainly one of the noble rooms of America. The scholars who point out that neither is a masterpiece are perhaps judging the building only by the lofty standards of facade and stair hall. Varying opinions of the different cycles of murals in the library will also probably continue to shift back and forth from good to excellent to awful so long as art historians draw breath. But the enduring merit of the Public Library is undoubted. It is not in some ways supremely functional. But the fact that there was no precedent for such a building must not be forgotten; nor Charles Moore's defense that a chief function of the building *was* to express civic pride: in 1888 the trustees had stated clearly that the library was to be "a palace for the people." It was also in some ways innovative. The tile vaults on the ground story by the Guastavino firm of New

FIGURE 141. Boston Public Library, detail of the principal facade, showing the figure of Art, one of two statues by Bela Pratt that grace the platform upon which the library stands.

FIGURE 142. Boston Public Library, south end of the Sargent Gallery, showing Sargent's lunette and frieze of *The Redemption*, mixed media on canvas, 1903. Although Sargent's great crucifix is not as vivid or blatant as Cram's similar Calvary at All Saints, Ashmont (Plate 7), Sargent's murals are more provocative than most realize, exhibiting in places what Martha Kingsbury has called a kind of "exalted delirium," evoking "sexuality, danger and perversity." But Sargent's work did not shock Boston: his points were made through innuendo, not anecdote. Beginning in 1893, Sargent worked for nearly thirty years on these murals, several of which were exhibited at the Royal Academy in London before their installation in the Boston library.

York and Boston (whose factory was in the Boston suburb of Woburn) constitute, according to Hitchcock, the first extensive use of such vaulting. But in the end each person will find his or her own reasons for liking (scarcely ever for disliking) the library and will find them in different places: in the dark splendor of the Sargent Gallery or in the sunlit courtyard, or, perhaps, in the pomp of the great doorways and mantlepiece of the Delivery Room. The last word, though, must be ceded to Henry James. Detained by the view from the windows of the staircase landing into the courtyard, which seemed to him, he wrote, like "one of the myriad gold-colored courts of the Vatican," he turned back readily enough to the great staircase, marveling at "its amplitude of wing and its splendor of tawny marble" and at what he characterized as its "high and luxurious beauty." At the library Boston found the grandeur it had mislaid on Commonwealth Avenue.

Until recently, that observation could only have been quoted with tongue carefully in cheek. Indeed, it used to be said of Richardson that he was building for the ages, and of McKim, Mead and White that they were building for the eighties! But our sense of the library's greatness as architecture has been growing now for almost a hundred years. Jordy's recent and brilliant analysis of the library's facade actually *adds* somewhat to McKim's presumed sources, but at the same time increases one's respect for McKim's handling of them. Calling it "thrice-sanctioned," Jordy concludes that the Roman Colosseum can have been only a starting point, that the other well-known source for the library's facade, Henri Labrouste's Bibliothèque Sainte-Geneviève in Paris, furnished only the most specific composition readily available, and that Leon Battista Alberti's San Francesco (Tempio Malatestiano) at Rimini certainly encouraged

McKim in his linear refinement of Labrouste's scheme and suggested as well motifs for detail. Jordy also agrees with Hitchcock that the general compositional scheme derives from a contemporary American source — Richardson's Marshall Field Warehouse of 1885–1887 in Chicago. These varied sources only hint at the complexity of the creative process by which such sources sifted through McKim's mind to their final resolution.

Writing generally of McKim, Mead and White's designs, Leland Roth has analyzed the extent to which the firm's designs differed from their models and drawn a startling conclusion.

The horizontal lines are strongly emphasized, multiplied or otherwise stressed, binding the whole design together. . . . The model is regularized, complex rhythms are simplified and variations made uniform, so that the design as a whole is more easily comprehended and given greater apparent unity. . . . The number of elements or components found in the model is reduced, simplifying the composition. Details become harder, sharper, crisper, and the entire building becomes tauter. The building's relationship to the ground is strengthened by the use of broad podiums, terraces, fans of stairs and similar devices. Ornament is most often confined to distinct areas where it approaches the point of saturation, setting up a sharp contrast between the blank wall surfaces and the enlivened zones of ornamentation.

Roth emphasizes in his discussion that "the underlying themes of strong horizontality, clear statement of component parts, tautness and strong relationships to the ground we can observe in the work of McKim, Mead and White are also characteristics of the architecture of Frank Lloyd Wright" and in every instance, he continues, "they are qualities that have been identified as uniquely American in feeling." Not unnaturally, Europeans may sometimes see this more clearly than we do: Roth quotes Le Corbusier's observation — "in New York . . . I learn to appreciate the Italian Ren-

Three Back Bay houses by McKim, Mead and White and a streetcar-suburb house by Julius Schweinfurth.

FIGURE 143. 303 Commonwealth Avenue, 1895.

FIGURE 144. Andrew House, 32 Hereford Street, corner of Commonwealth Avenue, 1883–1884.

FIGURE 145. 413–415 Commonwealth Avenue, 1890.

FIGURE 146. Julius Schweinfurth. Leighton House, Roxbury Highlands, 1894, a wooden detached house comparable with 32 Hereford Street.

aissance." In its American incarnation he thought it possessed "a strange new firmness which is not Italian but American." It is a refrain we have heard before, from the mid-century Italianate to the Shingle Style. And it is hard to mourn the rise of the Classical Revival in the face of the Boston Public Library, or to dispute the assertion of the plaque in McKim's memory there — that "in this building enduringly is revealed the splendid amplitude of his genius, an inspiration to all men."

I T was in the wake of the library that at the great World's Columbian Exposition held in Chicago in 1893, in part McKim's work, the gleaming white Classical court of honor, with its evocation of urban order and grandeur, dazzled America. In Jordy's words, the Boston Public Library "heralded the main impetus in American architecture from the nineties to the thirties." Boston's architects accordingly set out to shape the metropolis in the library's image.

Naturally, very few attempts were made to introduce this kind of monumental Classicism into residential Boston. McKim himself did so at the Algonquin Club at 219 Commonwealth Avenue in 1887 and at 303 Commonwealth Avenue (Figure 143) in 1895 with conspicuous success. Yet perhaps only one other Back Bay house, 297 Commonwealth Avenue (1899), designed by Peabody and Stearns, achieves a comparable distinction. Instead, the domestic reflection of the revived Classical tradition was usually Georgian Revival — the Weld House (1900) at 149 Bay State Road, by Peters and Rice, is by far the grandest — or, by the 1890s, explicitly Federal in feeling. Two of the handsomest houses in the Back Bay, Arthur Little's own house at 57 Bay State Road, designed by him in 1890, and the double

house at 413–415 Commonwealth Avenue (Figure 145) by McKim, fall into this category. Edwin J. Lewis's 240 Ashmont Street in Dorchester (1912) and Julius Schweinfurth's house for George Leighton in Roxbury (Figure 146) (so similar in feeling to the Andrew House; Figure 144) are excellent illustrations in the Georgian mode of the streetcar-suburb type in both brick and wood.

Such houses, which show the outcome of the picturesque Colonial Revival that we noted evolved out of the Shingle Style, not only constitute a kind of domestic mirror of the overall Classical Revival of the 1890s but also significantly reflect Boston's own early nineteenth-century Neoclassical work. Bunting has noted that the Andrew House is reminiscent of "Boston's old Greek Revival vernacular," and Roth has gone so far as to assert that the same house recalled Parris's double-bowed brick facade (1818) at what is now the Women's City Club (Figure 16). That house seems also to Bunting strikingly similar in its entrance composition to McKim's 199 Commonwealth Avenue, while Roth suggests that the McKim house at 303 Commonwealth Avenue (Figure 143) echoed the Sears House of 1819 (Figures 10, 11). The inspiration of West Hill Place and Charles River Square is also clear: each is yet another reincarnation of the red-brick residential square that had charmed Boston since the Tontine Crescent of 1794. In fact, in West Hill Place, Boston's architecture seems as circular, historically, as is this charming enclave in plan, and this reenactment in the early twentieth century of the architecture of the early nineteenth century can seem at first very perplexing. Yet Bunting remarks that not only are many Back Bay houses the "artistic peers" of their Beacon Hill prototypes, but also one might question whether Boston's late nineteenth- and early twentieth-century Georgian Revival is a case of "Georgian

The more flamboyant Renaissance-derived styles did not flourish in Boston, but there are two outstanding exceptions. FIGURE 147. Charles Brigham. Burrage House (now Boston Evening Clinic), 314 Commonwealth Avenue, Back Bay, 1899. FIGURE 148. Arthur Bowditch. The Stoneholm, one of Brookline's most fashionable apartment houses, 1514 Beacon Street, 1907.

revival or *survival*" (my italics). He admits that one might reasonably argue that Georgian forms had never really utterly disappeared from Boston, citing 58–60 Commonwealth Avenue, a full-blown Georgian Revival house of 1866. Daniel Selig has made the same point, arguing that for this reason "it is not truly accurate to speak of such revivals in Boston" where Georgian and Federal forms had "appeared consistently and appreciably throughout the nineteenth century." And if one sees the domestic Georgian mirror of the Classical Revival as a continuation of an unbroken local tradition, one can see too why the overall Classical Revival was perceived in Boston in the 1890s not as a sign of backsliding, but as a revivification, even an enlargement, of an accumulated and indigenous local heritage of form and detail that was clearly susceptible to new and vital life in the hands of men like McKim. It is perhaps for these reasons that the Classical tradition in Boston only very rarely differentiated itself into the more exotic Renaissance-derived modes. Such buildings, however, being exceptional, are all the more valuable today.

Two Back Bay châteaux, for instance, are outstanding. The earliest, the design of Carl Fehmer for Oliver Ames in 1882, stands on the corner of Commonwealth and Massachusetts avenues, and its brownstone detail includes a series of panels that depict activities (reading, playing the violin, dining, for example) appropriate to the room over the windows of which they occur in the facade. At 314 Commonwealth Avenue (Figure 147) is deservedly the most famous of this type in Boston. The work of Charles Brigham, who designed this house after the manner of the châteaux of Chenonceaux, its extraordinary cut-stone detail, deeply undercut so as to hold shadow, is highly ostentatious by Boston's social standards, but one must be grateful for its superb craftsmanship. A number of French interiors are also notable: chiefly Little and Browne's double drawing room at the Somerset Club, sumptuously detailed with gilt daggers and eagles in the Directoire style, and Parker, Thomas and Rice's ballroom addition to the Baylies House at 5 Commonwealth Avenue. In the realm of public buildings there is also Winslow and Wetherell's French Renaissance Hotel Touraine (1899–1900) on the corner of Tremont and Boylston streets. Still handsome, though disfigured by first-floor alterations, it took its inspiration from the great royal château at Blois.

Not all the Renaissance-derived styles appeared under French auspices. In the Back Bay, for example, Bunting notes a Schweinfurth house (1895), characterized by sixteenth-century Spanish ornament, at 304 Commonwealth Avenue; a Jacobean-inspired house of 1903 by Chapman and Frazer at 240 Commonwealth Avenue; and a full-fledged Tudor manor house of two years later by the same architects at 225 Bay State Road, a type that naturally abounds in the suburbs. There are also a very few examples in Boston of the exuberant, lavishly sculptural, and dramatic Beaux Arts manner. As Daniel Selig has pointed out, "the Boston Beaux Arts often seems timid and meek, especially in comparison to the high fashion Beaux Arts of New York," but Schweinfurth's two houses at 426–428 Beacon Street, built in 1904, are distinguished and there are also two opulent Beaux Arts Baroque facades at 128–130 Commonwealth Avenue, built in 1905. One wonders if Arthur Bowditch could have been their architect? Certainly they are similar to his little-known Stoneholm apartment house at 1514 Beacon Street in Brookline (Figure 148). Built in 1907, the Stoneholm is the most magnificent building of its type in Greater Boston — a splendid Baroque extravaganza that holds the high ground above Beacon Street with great distinc-

Two comparisons with the first Museum of Fine Arts, shown in Figure 53.

FIGURE 149. Henry J. Hardenberg, Clarence H. Blackall, Associated. Copley Plaza Hotel, Copley Square, Back Bay, built in 1912 on the site of the first museum.

FIGURE 150. Guy Lowell. The second Museum of Fine Arts, the Fenway, 1909. Transverse section.

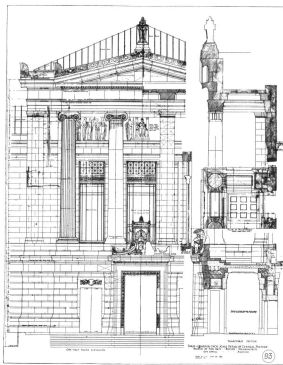

tion. Only the opulent, theatrical Baroque and rococo of the downtown theaters (see Chapter 9) is comparable.

How immediate and widespread was the Classical passion aroused by the library is perhaps most evident if one compares the old Museum of Fine Arts in Copley Square (Figure 53) with both the building that displaced it in 1912 — Henry J. Hardenberg and C. H. Blackall's superb Copley Plaza Hotel (Figure 149) — and with the new Museum of Fine Arts in the Fenway, designed by Guy Lowell, which opened in 1909 (Figure 150). Severely Classical (the second museum's great staircase and its Fenway facade rank in each case as the most monumental Classicism in Boston), the museum was but one of many vast, axial, and "imperial" structures erected by Boston institutions in the library's wake. Harvard's schools of law, medicine, and architecture, and its Widener Library and first Fogg art museum, the Boston Symphony Orchestra, the Massachusetts Institute of Technology, Chil-

dren's Hospital, the Boston Opera Company, Tufts University's Forsyth Dental Infirmary, the New England Conservatory of Music, the Christian Science Church, the Peter Bent Brigham Hospital — all sought, like the Museum of Fine Arts, to emulate in their buildings the library's pomp.

Very few architects attempted the overwhelming monumentality of Richard Morris Hunt's Fogg Museum of Art (1893; demolished) or of Edward T. P. Graham's Forsyth Dental Infirmary and Boston City Hall Annex (Figure 151). More typical is Kilham and Hopkins's Massachusetts College of Pharmacy (1920) or McKim's Symphony Hall (1892–1900), where the much richer ornament proposed was never carried out. Equally austere were the New England Conservatory (1901) and the Boston Opera House (Figure 152), both designed by Wheelwright and Haven; so chaste did the latter seem to one wit that he christened the new hall "the first Unitarian opera house." Even more severe

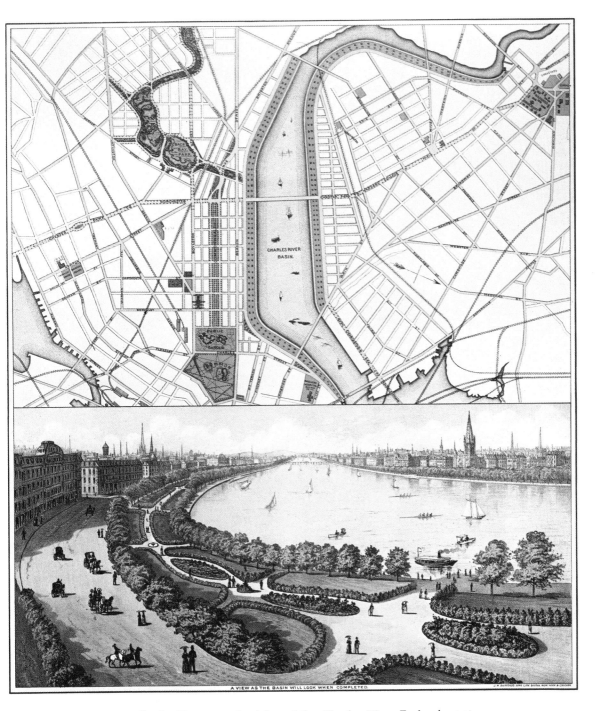

PLATE 1. Charles Davenport's vision of the Charles River Embankment, 1874. Although the Cambridge side (to the right) never quite lived up to these expectations, the grandeur of the Back Bay (to the left) as finally realized is evident in the plan, where its spacious axial grid stands out clearly. One can also see the Back Bay's relationship to Frederick Law Olmsted's Boston park system, the "emerald necklace" of parks that connects the Back Bay with downtown Boston at the Common and with the streetcar suburbs. Beyond the "Back Bay Park" at the top this system of parks was continued through Jamaica Plain and Roxbury to Dorchester Bay.

A century apart, Charles Bulfinch's interiors in the Massachusetts
State House (opened in 1798) and Clarence H. Blackall's Colonial
Theatre (completed in 1900) illustrate the range and diversity of
Boston's architecture. PLATE 2 shows Bulfinch's House of Representatives,
which has been the Senate Chamber since 1895. PLATE 3 shows the
principal lobby of the Colonial Theatre, one of the most admired of
Blackall's playhouses.

PLATE 4. The Back Bay was not the only new residential quarter of the expanding nineteenth-century metropolis to attract wealthy Bostonians. In 1891, A. H. Davenport, for example, built his home, designed by Chamberlin and Austin, at 70 Salem Street in Malden. The superb detailing of the quartered-oak stair hall and its furniture is typical of the work of Davenport's firm, which made most of the furniture designed by Charles McKim in 1902–1903 for the White House.

PLATES 5 through 8 show the principal interiors of the four great landmark buildings of late nineteenth- and early twentieth-century Boston. In themselves a fascinating comparative study (many of the same artists and craftsmen worked on two or more or all of them), the oldest is Trinity Church (PLATE 5). Built in 1872–1877, Trinity takes its acknowledged place among the great churches of the world. The frescoes were executed in 1876–1877 by John La Farge; the apse windows are by Clayton and Bell. Richardson's successor architects designed the chancel stalls (made by A. H. Davenport and Company), the chancel parapet (carved by John Evans) in 1902, and the pulpit (also by Evans) in 1916. The high altar and its ornaments (1938) were designed by Maginnis and Walsh, who also redecorated the entire chancel. Ernest Pellegrini of Irving and Casson modeled the bas-reliefs under the apse windows.

Charles McKim's work and Ralph Adams Cram's, both the issue in differing ways of Richardson's, constitute the crest of the Classical and Gothic traditions in American architecture. In the case of both men, Boston possesses the landmark building that became the national model in each tradition: McKim's Boston Public Library in Copley Square, begun in 1888; and Cram's Church of All Saints at Ashmont,

begun in 1891. PLATE 6 shows the great stair hall of the library,
throughout which McKim achieved a marriage of art and architecture
unique in this country in the nineteenth century. PLATE 7 shows the
chancel of All Saints, where Cram and Goodhue and their artist-
collaborators realized one of the most distinguished ensembles of
Gothic Revival art in the world.

PLATE 8. Isabella Stewart Gardner's Fenway Court is perhaps best known for its collection of old masters. Yet pictures were also painted *at* Fenway Court (by John Singer Sargent, for example), and not only the personality of the collection but above all its uniquely organic setting moved Henry Adams to say to Mrs. Gardner: "You are a creator, and stand alone." "A masterpiece of its kind," in Aline B. Saarinen's words, the ingenious design of Fenway Court was a revised and enlarged version by the architect Willard T. Sears in 1899 of plans he had prepared for "Mrs. Jack" in 1896 for a proposed home on Beacon Street, "the design [of which]," wrote Morris Carter, "was entirely Mrs. Gardner's."

are the original courtyard buildings of the Massachusetts Institute of Technology, designed by Welles Bosworth (Figure 153), though the site undeniably invites the effect. Seen from the Harvard Bridge, this great low-lying mass responds superbly to the spaciousness of the river's sweep. Siting, in fact, was a key factor in "imperial" architecture. It is not so much that great space was necessary as that it was a function of such architecture to organize and define its surrounding spaces. Thus South Station (1899), designed by Shepley, Rutan and Coolidge, may not be thought a finer building than the same firm's Langdell Hall (1906) at the Harvard Law School; but Langdell Hall can never really be seen because of its siting and landscaping. South Station, on the other hand, sweeps up the two streets it fronts upon to a majestic finale in Dewey Square that is felt by those who know it, so much motion is there, even when only part of the station comes into view down Summer Street. Similarly, Harvard Medical School (Figure 154), which is so magnificent that it annexes a 100-foot–wide boulevard with twenty-foot setbacks to its axial splendor, can be felt the minute one turns onto Avenue Louis Pasteur; one waits as one progresses up this tree-lined street for the flanking screens of trees to give way and disclose the square that spreads out in tribute to the massive white marble quadrangle. Designed by the Shepley office in 1906, it is as severe as Classicism usually was in Boston, but the glistening white marble and the high, balustraded terraces of the great court all lend an undeniable grandeur to the composition. Today, it still seems, as it did to Sylvester Baxter when it was first built, "like a fragment of the memorable White City at Chicago." All around the Fenway it is echoed in building after building — particularly in O'Connell and Shaw's Boston Fire Department Alarm Building (1925).

At the Massachusetts Institute of Technology, Boston was endowed with the dome of the Pantheon in Rome. At Harvard Stadium (1903–1910), designed by McKim, Mead and White, Boston gained a building reminiscent of the Roman Colosseum. At Union Station in 1894 (Figure 208) the Shepley office essayed a grandiose triumphal arch on the Roman model — now demolished but similar to the frontispiece of Commonwealth Pier. And in 1904–1906, Charles Brigham and Solon S. Beman erected for the First Church of Christ, Scientist, in the Back Bay a florid and grandiose basilica, the splendid dome of which lifted the Classical Revival up to dominate the city's skyline (Figure 155). It remained only for three architects — William Chapman, R. Clipston Sturgis, and Robert D. Andrews — to attach white marble Classical wings to the Bulfinch State House in 1914–1917. Its brick was painted white and thus yielded Boston a great axial capitol building, gleaming white (Figure 156). Such was the city's enthusiasm for the Classical ideal. In 1928, however, the powers that be happily had second thoughts and restored the original red brick. Even before the new white marble wings were added, however, the State House had grown in 1889–1895 by way of an enormous addition behind the Bulfinch building. Because the Bulfinch building had been painted yellow since 1855, this rear extension was of yellow brick. The dome had been covered with gold leaf in 1874, with the result that since 1928 the whole complex has become a kind of bird of paradise, with a red body, gold head, white wings, and yellow tail. Such are the dangers of an expanding sense of civic grandeur.

The State House extension, designed by Charles Brigham, is without question Boston's most maligned building. Cram could not tolerate it for a moment. In his memoirs he remembered that when he

Monumental Classicism in Boston.
FIGURE 151. Edward T. P. Graham.
Boston City Hall Annex, 1914. The
four colossal figures were modeled
by the sculptor Roger Noble Burnham.
They have been removed, but
Burnham's decorative panels on the
main doors of Graham's Forsyth
Dental Infirmary of the next year in
the Back Bay survive, as does his
architectural sculpture on the facade
of the Busch-Reisinger Museum at
Harvard.
FIGURE 152. Wheelwright and Haven.
Boston Opera House, Back Bay, 1909.
The decorative sculpture was the work
of Bela Pratt. Demolished.
FIGURE 153. Welles Bosworth.
Maclaurin Building in the Great Court
of the Massachusetts Institute of
Technology, Cambridge, 1913, looking
across Harvard Bridge from the Back
Bay.
FIGURE 154. Shepley, Rutan and
Coolidge. Harvard Medical School,
the Fenway, 1906.
FIGURE 155. Charles Brigham and
Solon S. Beman; completed by Brigham,
Coveney and Bisbee. Extension of
the First Church of Christ, Scientist,
Back Bay, 1904–1906.

FIGURE 156. The Boston State House as it appeared ca. 1920, after the red-brick Bulfinch building had been painted white to match the two white marble wings added in 1914–1917 by William Chapman, R. Clipston Sturgis, and Robert D. Andrews.

won the second prize in the competition he had been told that, for a consideration, the job could be his. In Cram's words, after the building was finished,

and what is sometimes known as the "fried egg" and sometimes as the "yaller dorg" extension had revealed itself before the gaze of an astonished public, I have sometimes wondered if I should not have been justified in waiving all ethical considerations and yielding to the plausible lobbyists, just on the chance that something a little less trying might have been attached to the admirable old Bulfinch front. In any case the actuality has served one minor purpose, for while I served my time as an instructor in architecture at Technology I could use it as the best existing example of a structure in which every line, in which mass, detail, and material, together with the composition as a whole, was exactly and ingeniously wrong.

Today, this building's setting has been so barbarized by the turning of its balustraded park into a parking area that few would disagree with Cram. Yet of all the attempts to rival the spatial splendor and architectural art of the Public Library the Brigham extension is of particular interest because, like George Clough's Suffolk County Court House (1886–1895), it is contemporaneous with the library.

The Court House possesses an enormous lobby — nearly five stories high — that is endowed with an elaborate

FIGURE 157. Henry Forbes Bigelow. Addition to the Boston Athenaeum, 1913–1914. Fifth-floor reading room. The Athenaeum's interior is unique. Wrote David McCord: it "combines the best elements of the Bodleian, Monticello, the frigate *Constitution*, a greenhouse and an old New England sitting room."

parade of life-size allegorical figures by Domingo Mora. This great space is handled so ineptly, however, that it seems only wasteful and pompous, a startling reminder of what the Public Library might have looked like. But the State House extension is another matter entirely. The interior often recalls the library in its forms and detailing (the triple arches and balustrading of the Senate Staircase Hall) and in its materials (the Siena marble of the Hall of Flags), and though it does not in these respects achieve the distinction of the library, it is comparable both in plan and in its provision for architectural art. Brigham's well-thought-out ceremonial sequence of Sen-

ate Staircase Hall, Hall of Flags, and House Staircase Hall, this last rising spaciously to an enormous pillared lobby that leads into the House of Representatives, is unique in Boston, and the attempt to integrate mural decoration with figure sculpture is evident throughout the building. None of the murals has been widely admired, but the building's figure sculpture is frequently distinguished. Two figures are by Daniel Chester French: the statue adjoining the Senate Staircase Hall of the Civil War hero William F. Bartlett, and the heroic bronze figure of Governor Roger Wolcott that is backed by Richard Andrews's mural in the great hall outside the House

151

Shaping the "City Beautiful."
FIGURE 158. Charlesgate at Commonwealth Avenue, ca. 1900. Arthur Shurcliffe designed the balustrading (still extant, but overshadowed today by an access ramp to Storrow Drive); the statue of Leif Ericson is the work of Anne Whitney. Dedicated in 1886, the figure originally stood farther down the avenue.
FIGURE 159. McKim, Mead and White and Augustus Saint-Gaudens. The Robert Gould Shaw Memorial, Boston Common, 1897.

Chamber. The Senate Staircase Hall also possesses two sculptures by Bela Pratt, a large bronze relief of General Thomas G. Stevenson and the Army Nurses' Memorial, a powerful work unveiled in 1914.

Many more of Boston's Classical buildings sought to emulate the library's design concept with respect to architectural art. C. H. Blackall's Tremont Temple of 1896 possesses murals by Edmund C. Tarbell; Sargent himself executed murals for the staircase of the second Museum of Fine Arts and for Widener Library, as did N. C. Wyeth for R. Clipston Sturgis's Federal Reserve Bank of 1922. Another and very successful attempt of this sort was made by Henry Forbes Bigelow in his superb fifth-floor reading room (1913–1914) at the Boston Athenaeum, where he provided innumerable niches and broken pediments for the display of portrait busts (Figure 157). Nearby, at Congregational House, a series of facade reliefs by Mora show that the attempt to integrate art into architecture extended also to the exterior of buildings. This tendency had begun, as we saw, in the 1870s, and by the 1890s such work, though never common, became widespread. Not only the library but also the Opera House and the Museum of Fine Arts were endowed with exterior sculpture by Bela Pratt, and even business blocks were sometimes so adorned: William G. Preston's bank at 145 Milk Street, completed in 1906, rejoices in a number of allegorical figures by Max Bachman.

Many efforts were also made at this time to integrate sculptural embellishments into an architectural setting that in turn would integrate buildings into the landscape to produce a more formal and splendid cityscape. Perhaps the most extensive such effort was made at Charlesgate, where Commonwealth Avenue, as it crosses the bridge, was elegantly balustraded by Arthur Shurcliffe (Figure 158). Another was the Larz Anderson Bridge, designed in 1912 by Wheel-wright, Haven and Hoyt, and built of brick surely in anticipation of the subsequent red-brick ranges of Harvard buildings it now links so beautifully, even though it has been ruthlessly shorn of its gilded lamps. Johannes Kirchmayer, the well-known architectural sculptor, modeled its sumptuous gilded mantlings, so sadly tarnished today. Most of these efforts were the results of collaborations of architects and sculptors. It is not generally known that Henry Bacon and Daniel Chester French, whose collaboration at the Lincoln Memorial in Washington in 1922 constituted perhaps the climax of the American Classical Revival, worked together on several important early twentieth-century monuments in Greater Boston, including the Longfellow Memorial off Longfellow Park in Cambridge (1914); the Parkman Memorial in Olmsted' Park in Jamaica Plain (1906); and the White Memorial (1924) in the Boston Public Garden. Similarly, McKim, Mead and White and Saint-Gaudens collaborated on two Boston monuments: the Phillips Brooks Memorial (1910) in Copley Square, which has never (and for good reason) been much admired, and the Shaw Memorial opposite the State House (1897), which is on the other hand one of the most distinguished such ensembles in the country (Figure 159). The two trees that were planted within the Shaw Memorial between the Common and Beacon Street were actually a part of McKim's design and illustrate the way in which such ensembles sought to knit together into the streetscape not only architecture and sculpture but features of the natural landscape as well.

Nowhere else was the city balustraded so splendidly in the service of a great public building as at the Shaw Memorial. Looking up the steps to see the white marble wings of the State House rather than the Bulfinch portion, one would think one was in Washington —

but only for a moment — because although Boston possessed several architects at this time who instinctively thought in terms of monumental buildings and grand vistas and who longed to remake Boston in this pattern, they never succeeded in endowing even so conspicuous a place as Copley Square with the plaza and fountains it so desperately needed. The only such vista (except for Avenue Louis Pasteur) realized in Boston was the mall at Franklin Park, where a number of marble columns were salvaged from the interior of the 1837 Boston Custom House (when it was being rebuilt to support its tower in 1913) and erected into a lofty gateway. Only when French's sculptural groups from the Boston Post Office were placed at the other end of the mall in 1929 when that building was destroyed did Boston achieve a suitably grandiose Classical vista.

THE Classical Revival is easily ridiculed. But it was Vincent Scully, no disciple of McKim, who best expressed its value to us when he pronounced a valedictory on McKim's Pennsylvania Station in New York at the time it was brutally torn down. Now, one arrives in the new underground Pennsylvania Station and rides an escalator up to the street; in other words, wrote Scully, "one scuttles in today like a rat" — whereas through McKim's great vaulted concourse "one entered the City like a God." Boston has been more fortunate: the great Renaissance staircase of the Boston Public Library invites every man still to proud ascent, and that is not a bad definition of what the Renaissance was

all about in the first place. Nor can one forget that other remarkable building of this period, Fenway Court (Plate 8), completed eight years after the Public Library opened. Although it was too personal a creation to become an architectural prototype in any real sense, the setting Isabella Stewart Gardner and her architect, Willard T. Sears, created for the collection she bequeathed to the public moved one historian to exclaim that it seemed almost as if "the Venetian Renaissance had been reincarnated in Boston." Traditionally, of course, most art historians have been more impressed by Mrs. Gardner's paintings than by their setting; many would agree with Martin Green that it shows late nineteenth- and early twentieth-century Boston culture as more aquisitive and interpretive than creative. Yet that these are mutually exclusive values has not always been clear, especially when one remembers that Mrs. Gardner not only purchased Raphaels and Rembrandts; she also patronized Sargent, who surely caught the image of Boston in his time as definitively as did Stuart or Copley in theirs. Today one might well conclude, moreover, that Mrs. Gardner's unique ensemble of art and architecture, a Venetian palazzo "turned inside-out," is as much a work of art as any individual treasure in it. Even then, Henry James admitted as much: he called Fenway Court a "tour-de-force — no Evolution at all — but pure Special Creation in an adverse environment." Yet his last words are increasingly suspect as we begin to understand how much this "adverse environment" yielded Boston at the crest of her own renaissance.

154

7

RALPH ADAMS CRAM AND
BOSTON GOTHIC

T HE RICHNESS AND VITALITY of Boston's cultural life in the 1890s was
such that not even the force of the
Boston Public Library and the Chicago
world's fair of 1893 was able to narrow
Boston's vision of herself or her architecture to only the Classical vista and colonnade. In 1891, even before the Public Library was completed, at an architectural
exhibition held in the library, the plans
of two totally unknown young architects
for the small and then not very important
Episcopal parish, All Saints in the Ashmont section of Boston, plans that were
decisively Gothic, provoked for that reason a startled interest. One wonders how
many people guessed then that by 1918,
when Dean George H. Edgell of Harvard
and Fiske Kimball published their history of world architecture, the church
built from these plans (Figure 160) would
be one of the four Boston buildings illustrated in that book and that like the other
two late nineteenth-century buildings
pictured, Trinity Church and the Boston
Public Library, this Ashmont church
would be seen by the authors as another
national prototype — of a new Gothic
Revival. One suspects that very few people, standing in the as yet unopened library, which at that very moment had
eclipsed Trinity Church and Medievalism generally, could have seen this. Yet
such was the force of the new vision
and of the two Boston architects who
launched it — Ralph Adams Cram and
Bertram Grosvenor Goodhue — that
right through to the 1930s this Gothic Re-

vival would parallel the Classical Revival
in extent and importance and its leader,
Cram, would become the Boston architect of his generation who most importantly shaped architecture not just in
Boston but throughout the country.

Two important churches may be
thought of as significant bridges, as it
were, between Trinity Church and All
Saints, Ashmont. The first to be built
was Sturgis and Brigham's Church of the
Advent, designed in 1875 and finished
by R. Clipston Sturgis, one of Cram's
early mentors. The interior of the Advent
(Figure 161) is not at first glance anything
like that of Trinity. Yet actually, the two
churches (built at almost the same time)
are very alike in plan: both are more
nearly Greek than Latin crosses, with
short, stubby naves and enormous chancels and transepts to each side with balconies — in other words, both are in
plan auditorium churches, designed
about a central area, without the long,
narrow Medieval nave. In detail, although the Advent possesses nothing
like Trinity's frescoes, its original
stained glass (by Kempe and by Clayton
and Bell, two famous English makers) as
well as its splendid later glass by Christopher Whall is of high quality and the
figure sculpture in stone and wood
throughout the interior has no parallel at
Trinity. Most important, Sturgis's manipulation of interior space at the Advent is brilliant. The crucial factor is
that he persuaded the conventional
arches flanking the high chancel arch to

very different disclosures: the arch to the right opens out grandly for its full height into a large Lady Chapel, while the arch to the left is filled in with the organ casework and opens out only below for one story through a heavy arcade into a much smaller chapel. The addition of low oak screens (executed some years later but obviously intended by Sturgis) between the arches into the Lady Chapel gave a wholly new dimension to the ingenious equilibrium. These densely carved screens hold to the planes of the walls below, while the arches above open out into a lofty secondary apse, thus foiling the left flank of the chancel, where the organ casework *above* holds to the planes of the walls. Volume and void are nowhere better handled in any Boston church.

rium. The effect of the two interiors as Cram and others (T. S. Eliot, for example) saw them on Sunday morning was even more striking, for the Advent was designed by Sturgis as a stage, not for preaching, but for the musical and ceremonial pomp of the Anglican Solemn High Mass. The Advent, not Trinity, was the cutting edge of the break with the Puritan past in Boston.

As was nearly always the case in late nineteenth-century Boston, the sources were English. The parish of the Advent was founded in 1844, eleven years after the start of the Oxford Movement in England, and its artistic ornament and liturgy caused a sensation in Boston. The boy choir of 1849 was among the first in the country and for some years the Epis-

Unlike Trinity, the Advent also possessed from the beginning a conspicuous high altar and reredos of Sturgis's design to which was added in 1892 the large openwork screen by Sir Ernest George and Harold Peto, in each case the gift of Isabella Stewart Gardner. The effect is not just more interesting than that of Trinity; in the way the Advent focuses finally on the high altar and at the same time spreads out at the church's flanks into a variety of perspective and light and shadow, its plan is transformed: the Advent is a temple; Trinity, an audito-

copal bishop of Massachusetts refused to make his annual visitation to the parish because, in Phoebe Stanton's words, the Advent had scandalized him "in using art." By the 1880s the Advent's rector was Charles Grafton (a founder of the Cowley Fathers, the first post-Reformation Anglican monastic order), who had been sent to Boston by the great Tractarian leader, Edward Pusey. Under Grafton the Advent's "Pugin-Medieval" pageantry and ornament became virtually a tourist attraction, "widely famous," in the words of *King's Handbook*

FIGURE 160. Cram, Wentworth and Goodhue. Perspective by Goodhue of All Saints' Church, Ashmont, 1891–1894. How could Cram and Goodhue in their first church achieve such a masterpiece? In fact, Thomas Tallmadge thought it an essential achievement for an architect like Cram, "who aspires to be a prophet." There must be, wrote Tallmadge, not only the element of surprise, but such an architect's first work must swiftly "swim into the ken of an astonished and needy world."

FIGURE 161. Sturgis and Brigham. Church of the Advent, Brimmer Street at Mount Vernon Street, at the foot of Beacon Hill, designed in 1875–1876. The church was completed after John Sturgis's death in 1888 by R. Clipston Sturgis in association with Henry Vaughan, who designed the pulpit and supervised the design of the west window; Ralph Adams Cram and Bertram Grosvenor Goodhue, who designed the interior of the Lady Chapel and much other interior ornament; and Sir Ernest George and Harold Peto, who designed the great openwork screen of 1891–1892 that surmounts Sturgis's high altar reredos.

FIGURE 162. Henry Vaughan. Chapel of St. Margaret's Convent, Louisburg Square, Beacon Hill, 1882. St. Mary's Church, Dorchester, Vaughan's only parish church in the city, is visible in Figure 89.

of Boston, "for its imposing ritual . . . large surpliced choirs and processionals [and] richly adorned and lighted altar." It is significant that the Advent's only rivals in the 1880s were the huge new Roman Catholic Cathedral of the Holy Cross and the Jesuit Church of the Immaculate Conception nearby.

The Advent's vivid Medievalism was echoed on a much smaller scale, by the other new High Church Anglican center of this period in Boston, St. Margaret's Convent in Louisburg Square. Its small but handsome chapel (Figure 162) is, so to speak, the second bridge between Trinity and All Saints, for it was designed by Henry Vaughan, a devout Anglo-Catholic who had been chief draftsman to George Frederick Bodley, the great English Gothicist. As Cram's chief mentor, Vaughan was thus able to introduce him at first hand to the English Gothic Revival, and in Vaughan's own work and in the English work Cram first saw during his trip to Europe in 1886, Cram perceived at once the same sort of creative spirit in the Gothic mode that had been evident to him in the Romanesque manner at Trinity. Converted to English Gothic, Cram converted also to Anglo-Catholicism in Rome in 1887 and upon his return to Boston was baptized and received into the Episcopal Church.

The effect the Oxford Movement had on Boston in the 1880s is suggested by the fact that Cram, the son of a Unitarian minister, was by no means the most prominent offspring of a Unitarian clergyman to become an Anglican. Two others were Colonel Oliver Peabody and Mary Lothrop Peabody, the daughter of the preeminent Unitarian divine in Boston at this time, Samuel Kirkland Lothrop. It was, in fact, a herald of sorts that it should have been Lothrop who commissioned Richardson to design a Medieval church for his congregation — the Brattle Square Church (Figure 64). That commission established Richardson

in Boston. And it was Oliver and Mary Lothrop Peabody who startled Back Bay Boston by leaving King's Chapel, perhaps the city's most prestigious Unitarian church, and converting to Anglicanism at All Saints, Ashmont, where they became Cram's first patrons and largely built for the parish Cram's first church in 1891–1894.

How Cram met them we do not know, although it may have been through R. Clipston Sturgis, who has been credited with designing the Peabody town house at 25 Commonwealth Avenue. But as it turned out the commission to Cram was as important as the one to Richardson, for All Saints signaled a new direction for the Gothic Revival in America and for American religious art generally: in Cram's wake that revival became not only more Medieval but explicitly Catholic. It was also an unmistakable sign of how the city was changing. Puritan Boston, by 1900 one of the largest Roman Catholic dioceses in the world and one of the seedbeds in America of the Oxford Movement, was by the early twentieth century also the center of a full-fledged revival of Medieval Catholic art — from churches to vestments — which by the 1930s had revolutionized the visual image of American Christianity. Culturally, the Puritan tradition was dying at its heart and would wither increasingly in the course of the twentieth century. So too, after the Second World War, would the Catholic artistic tradition, but in the meantime it stimulated Cram to an architectural achievement comparable with Richardson's and McKim's.

Cram insisted that All Saints constitute "a complete reversal" of American architectural design. He was determined, he wrote in 1899, that it "must have nothing of the artificial savagery of 'modern Romanesque'; nothing of the petty trivialities of those buildings that have been tortured into chaotic fantasies in the wild desire for an aggressive picturesqueness." But the fact that Cram led American church architecture at All Saints away from Richardsonian Romanesque as decisively as McKim did in the realm of secular design at the Public Library is less important than the fact that Cram insisted All Saints must not be "simply a study in archaeological experiment; it must be essentially a church of [the late nineteenth] century, built not in England, but in New England."

Cram asserted vigorously all his life that though architecture must naturally evolve out of the past, "if it remains in bondage to this older art, if it wanders in the twilight of the precedent or, in fear and trembling, chains itself to the rock of archaeology . . . it ceases to be art — ceases? no; it has never even begun; it is only a dreary mocking of a shattered idol, a futile picture puzzle to beguile a tedious day." Yet his illustration of this point of view was rather paradoxical — beginning with All Saints, he designed in the late nineteenth and early twentieth centuries a long parade of Gothic churches — thus posing starkly the underlying problems not only of his own work, but of revivalism as a whole and of both Richardson's and McKim's work particularly. As we will see in the next chapter, Louis Sullivan's early achievements in Chicago paralleled both McKim's Public Library and Cram's All Saints in Boston. From the perspective of today, Cram's insistence that All Saints was a building of its own rather than of some past time thus reads like a riddle. It is the riddle of explicit revivalism generally, which was the driving force in American architecture until the 1930s.

The underlying problem here is that we lose sight of two facts: first, that Cram was an avowed disciple of Richardson; second, that it was not Richardson's style that impressed Cram, but the way Richardson (and Vaughan and the English Gothicists) handled style. Like McKim, Cram repudiated Richardson's style but *not* Richardson himself, who Cram was correct in thinking would in future years be venerated not for the style but for the vitality he introduced into American architecture. We also overlook the fact that for Cram as for Richardson and McKim, modernity lay not in style but in how style was used. Thus Cram, at age twenty-two in 1885, in his diary, put his finger exactly on why he thought Richardson had so easily overwhelmed Victorian Gothic: American Gothicists "not only copy the deficiencies as well as the beauties [of Medieval Gothic] but they make modern necessities conform to Gothic forms. . . . It does not seem," wrote Cram to himself, "as though such servile copying is true art." Cram's definition of modernity emerges clearly: modern necessities ought not to conform to Gothic forms; it must be the other way around; the modern necessities must shape new Gothic forms. And this premise — that old styles cannot only be copied and adapted but can also be re-created — explains why Talbot Hamlin could call Cram's Gothic work "epochal" in the twentieth century and why Claude Bragdon (an ardent admirer of Sullivan) could in 1907 compare Cram with Sullivan: Cram, wrote Bragdon, could design Gothic churches "without dragging a train of absurd archaisms in their wake."

Though the distinctions between copying and adapting are clear enough, between adaptation of a style and its re-creation into new forms the topography is harder to chart. Montgomery Schuyler, a leading architectural critic at the turn of the century, put Cram's thesis this way: "the Gothic principle is the very principle of progress, and faithfully applied to modern conditions would result in an architecture as unlike in form [but] as kindred in spirit to the medieval building in which thus far it has found its most triumphant expression." Cram himself — so clear did all this seem to him — could not understand why Victorian Gothicists, instead of trying to take up the Medieval threads and logically develop them, chose to study to death the old Medieval forms, as if they were all the life Gothic could ever have. The question Cram posed had thus to do more than anything with *what was and what was not Gothic.* His primary contention was that it was organism, not form, that should be studied, "principles . . . not moldings." The American Gothic Revival, Cram thought, had exhibited invariably either a perverse scholarship in dead forms, un-Gothic because such a copybook Gothic had no artistic integrity; or a perverse spontaneity in new forms, un-Gothic because they did not arise from Gothic principles of design and construction. The former was a case, Cram thought, of careful reproduction: the latter of careless reminiscence.

It was not, significantly, Pugin's view, or the view of his disciples, like Upjohn. Pugin had held that Gothic "had gone its length" by the Reformation and that "it must necessarily have destroyed itself thereafter." Cram, on the other hand, in the little booklet describing the plans for All Saints that the parish issued in 1892, held that "beautiful as were the results of the religious builders of the 15th century, they themselves had almost infinite capacity for still nobler works," but that this capacity was never realized, for by the early sixteenth century "churches were no longer built, but destroyed instead"; and that modern Gothicists should emulate Richardson's capacity for original design and rather than building churches "that shall pretend to have been built in [the sixteenth] century [should] work steadily and seriously towards something more consistent with our temper and the times in which we live." Gothic was not dead, concluded Cram, only moribund — and misunderstood. The difference between Pugin and Cram is the difference between adapta-

tion (few talented architects *can* copy) and re-creation. Cram, wrote Charles Maginnis many years later, "pleaded without ceasing for an honest architecture of blood and muscle for the scenic mimicry of historic form."

All Saints was Cram's first attempt to achieve this ideal, and it is only his genius that misleads one at first into thinking that it is a careful "period piece" Perpendicular essay. In fact, Cram would have been bored to death with the picture-postcard replica of an English village church we imagine we see at Ashmont, as well as ashamed to have copied such a church. Not everyone liked everything about All Saints; Charles Eliot Norton wrote to Cram in 1892 that though the design seemed to him "well thought out," he wondered how Cram would "justify for our modern needs so heavy a tower?" Yet in 1916 one of Cram's partners told only the truth when he wrote that All Saints "formed the foundation of [the firm's] career and reputation." The famous view of the church — which probably appeared at one time or another in every American architectural journal of the period — is from the southeast (Figure 160), a point of view from which one can easily see why its grandeur of mass seemed to many to yield a kind of robust New World Perpendicular, all the more persuasive for "the skill with which," wrote Schuyler of the windows, "the depth of the wall is revealed." Though explicit in its reminiscence, All Saints is profoundly original. Inspired by English Perpendicular parish churches in its overall design and detailing, the Ashmont church also owes much to Trinity Church in its sense of disciplined picturesqueness. But the authority with which the great tower of All Saints leaves the ground, the dark grandeur of its tremendous volume, and the enormous, quiet majesty and striking simplicity of the whole church — all this was new in American architecture and

Cram, Wentworth and Goodhue. All Saints' Church, Ashmont.
FIGURE 163. The Great Tower, 1894.
FIGURE 164. The nave, 1892, looking toward the north aisle and the chancel.

very much at odds with the "gilded age" (Figures 163, 164). The sense of mass and masonry, utterly unadorned and robustly laid up, is by no means oppressive; John Coolidge has observed that the rough-textured and random-coursed walls of All Saints are ordered with such delicacy of feeling that they seem the work of an artist rather than of a mason, unconsciously echoing Cortissoz's analysis of McKim's use of marble in the stair hall of the Public Library.

Within, All Saints must have seemed even more astonishing: this great church is more simply conceived than many small wooden chapels of the time. "Serious and simple to excess! is it not?" Henry Adams's query might well have been applied to the All Saints nave. Though it was not immediately inspired by the Cloth Hall at Ypres, Cram's description of that hall is significantly the best description of his Ashmont nave: "a simpler composition could hardly be

imagined," he wrote, "or one more impressive in its grave restraint. . . . Its great quiet elements are left alone, not tortured into a nervous complexity. . . . The great hall [is] broken only by columns and arches and roofed with a mass of oak timbering like an ancient and enormous ship, turned bottom up." For a nave, of course, the simile is even more apt. All Saints was a remarkable achievement for a first church; so much so that of its type — the suburban as opposed to the city or cathedral church — it is almost universally regarded as his masterpiece. Some have gone further; John Coolidge once observed: "so much of what one admires at All Saints' survives dehydrated in Goodhue's solo performances; and so little in the later works of Cram."

How was it done? One needed to know Gothic so thoroughly and to think in it so naturally as to be able to use it as a kind of language, the vocabulary and grammar of which could then grow as it

161

was stretched by the "modern necessities" Cram wrote of. He called this "creative scholarship." It might take many forms. Typical of his architectural programs, for example, was his conclusion that because fifteenth-century English design had "acquired its richness and fluency at the expense of certain [thirteenth-century] qualities of reserve, formalism and classical gravity," much might be evolved by applying "the lessons of suppleness and adaptability learned in the 15th century [so as to develop] through modern forms some of the qualities of composition, proportion, development and relation" that had characterized Gothic in the thirteenth century. One might argue that this was more scholarly than creative, but in other architectural programs of Cram's the scale seems to tip more clearly to creativity alone. The downtown church, for example, fascinated Cram. Because it had by his time to contend with soaring skyscrapers amid which the loftiest towers were futile, such conditions (he wrote in 1899), "being essentially modern and almost without precedent," offered the church architect his most exciting challenge in the twentieth century. Yet where adaptation ceases and re-creation begins is easier to define in theory than it is to explain in practice.

Cram's solution to Boston's apartment house problem, discussed in Chapter 5, is a case of adaptation; Richmond Court (Figure 128) was not, as we saw, without some stylistic justification and was both innovative and successful. Significantly, it does not possess battlements, Cram having concluded that these were scarcely necessary for an apartment house. (Lest this seem obvious, it should be stated that a later apartment house next door, Hampton Court, does possess battlements as did many twentieth-century apartment houses inspired by Richmond Court.) It is a small thing, but the lack of battlements discloses a crucial factor in Cram's work: whatever the architectural program, he insisted that worthwhile architecture, much less a creative scholarship, was impossible in any form unless it was rooted in a quality he early perceived in Medieval cottages: "Frank and simple and direct," he wrote, "built for use . . . they possess in the highest degree perfect adaptation to function, and therefore absolute beauty." Originality in design was only posturing for Cram, unless it arose from a structural need that in turn arose from function.

This principle did not result from a timid mind that sought refuge in the tried and true: yielding an innovative adaptation at Richmond Court, it is the root of Cram's re-creation at All Saints. There, the nave is not just simply conceived — it actually repudiates all the usual Gothic conventions of height to width to length. It is too wide for its length and too low for its width. Such originality is all the more striking upon discovery because though one feels a new quality at Ashmont, it is so quietly achieved that it is hard to identify. The reason, as Robert Brown observed, is that All Saints is original in design "not from any desire to be 'original,' but simply to honestly meet . . . present conditions." In this case the new condition was that the whole congregation expected to see both altar and pulpit. This compelled so wide a nave that Cram reduced the aisles to narrow ambulatories, a change in plan that suggested to him a change in elevation: he made the aisles very low, endowing instead the clerestory with the principal windows and consequently with an unusually lofty quality that discreetly reversed the usual Medieval proportions in both plan and elevation. The change in plan was adaptation. To have then expressed this plan so perfectly in elevation, thereby shaping a nave that was *finer* because of its unusual dimensions, the breadth and height of which imply and control the famous tower — that was re-creation. The result was a most "un-Gothic" nave by the standard of the copybook, but a nave of exceptional strength and amplitude that foretold many of Cram's later triumphs, including his masterpiece — the nave of St. John the Divine in New York (1916–1926), which startled A. D. F. Hamlin into admitting that it exhibited "such originality and boldness of invention as to form in reality a new and distinctly American chapter in [Gothic] development." It so moved Kingsley Porter, the Harvard medievalist, that he called Cram's nave "a tenth symphony."

It had happened before. Bates Lowry has written of the sixteenth-century attempt to revive the Classical architecture of antiquity — "Suddenly, in Bramante's work, buildings appear that seem to be *continuations* of the [ancient] Imperial Roman style rather than reinterpretations or copies of it." My emphasis illuminates the nature of the achievement of both McKim and Cram, whose work, like Richardson's, in whose vitality it was rooted, may be seen as two sides of the crest of nineteenth-century American architecture — when the adaptive tradition we have seen develop throughout that century flowered at last into an American architecture that was able to transcend adaptation.

McKim figures importantly in Boston architectural history because of the Public Library. But it is Cram's work — though only his Boston buildings can be discussed here — that is Boston's contribution to the climax of nineteenth-century American architecture.

O NLY recently have scholars begun to assess the impact of Cram on his time. Never popular among the architectural establishment because he did not admire the Ecole des Beaux Arts and decidedly unpopular in many circles because of his Socialist leanings and passionate Medievalism, Cram, scion of an old, distinguished, but not well-off Unitarian family, came to Boston in the 1880s as an architectural apprentice to Rotch and Tilden. A leading light of the Boston Bohemia of the 1890s, Cram, along with Bertram Goodhue, Alice Brown, Bliss Carman, Fred Holland Day, Herbert Small, Louise Imogen Guiney, and Richard Hovey (often in league with Ernest Fenollosa, Daniel B. Updike, and Bernard Berenson), was a vital part of this fin-de-siècle movement, which influenced so many currents of thought. During this period, Cram himself was art critic for the *Boston Evening Transcript*. His first appearance in that journal had been under the prophetic heading "Have We a Ruskin among Us?" and by the First World War Cram had indeed become not only the architect who represented Boston to the world, but a kind of "American Ruskin" whose earnest and controversial views surfaced everywhere in the 1920s, from the novels of F. Scott Fitzgerald to the Encyclopaedia Britannica. After he and Goodhue won the prestigious competition to design the United States Military Academy at West Point in 1903, Cram's reputation rose like a tidal wave and overflowed into a dozen vocations.

He and his designing partners (Goodhue from 1892 to 1914; Frank Cleveland and Alexander Hoyle from 1914 to 1942) designed well over fifty churches in over forty states and overseas for virtually every denomination and in nearly every imaginable style; a great many houses, libraries, and schools; and collegiate buildings at the University of Southern California, Rollins College, Notre Dame, Bryn Mawr, Wellesley, Princeton, Sweet Briar, West Point, and Rice University. In many cases they designed or supervised the design of whole campuses. The firm dominated American church archi-

FIGURE 165. Cram, Goodhue and Ferguson (Boston Office) with Okakura Kakuzo and Francis Gardner Curtis for Guy Lowell. Japanese Garden Court, Museum of Fine Arts, Boston, 1909, as originally furnished.

tecture between 1900 and 1940 and exercised an enormous influence upon American architecture generally and on the allied decorative arts particularly. In the meantime, though he had never gone to college, Cram became a distinguished Medievalist. He prefaced Henry Adams's *Mont-Saint-Michel and Chartres.* He was a founder of the Medieval Academy of America. As a Medievalist, he enjoyed a transatlantic reputation; no journal tackled his detractors more vigorously than did the *Times Literary Supplement* when it pointedly observed in 1916 that Cram "does not enjoy Gothic romantically or talk romantic nonsense about it; he hears its living music." He was also a scholar in Japanese art and a member of the visiting committee of the Japanese collection at the Museum of Fine Arts in Boston. His *Impressions of*

Japanese Architecture and the Allied Arts remains in print today and is a standard source in the field. For many years professor of the philosophy of architecture and head of the School of Architecture at the Massachusetts Institute of Technology, he was also a social theorist of some importance who strongly supported Franklin Roosevelt's New Deal; Albert Jay Nock once asserted that it was only Cram's reputation as an architect that had "overshadowed [his] claims as a philosopher." Finally, Cram was the foremost ecclesiologist of the Anglican Communion.

Cram established himself in all these fields through more than two dozen books and an avalanche of scholarly and polemical articles in upward of fifty journals in the United States and abroad, including five journals of which he was either a founder or editor, among them *Commonweal*. Indeed, Cram seems often to have created in his books the demand he and his partners then met at their drafting boards. But his writings are perhaps important today chiefly because neither Richardson nor McKim wrote very much, and it is only in Cram's books that one can discover the specific techniques of the "creative scholarship" he held was necessary to re-create rather than only adapt. It will thus serve more than one purpose to relate here these principles to his important Boston work, which constitutes the best case study imaginable in explicit revivalism and the many forms it could take. There is, for example, no more striking instance of how fundamental to Cram's work and how widely applicable was his theory of "creative scholarship" than the Japanese temple room and garden court (Figure 165) he designed in collaboration with the curatorial staff at the Museum of Fine Arts in Boston at the time of the opening of the present building in 1909. For generations his work there has been studied and admired: writing in 1910, Julia de Wolf' Addison marveled at the way in which Cram's rooms achieved "a wonderful harmony of great verisimilitude without being a servile copy of any existing building," while in 1928 G. H. Edgell pronounced these rooms "masterpieces . . . an achievement unsurpassed in American work or, for the matter of that, abroad." Here again, as at McKim's library, there lay behind Cram's work a timely and also an original purpose: timely in that these interiors were a setting for what was already the most distinguished collection of its kind in the world, and original in that, as Addison pointed out, "not until such a museum as this is seen, may a visitor fully understand the message of Japanese art as displayed in this way."

It is significant that the "inspiration" Addison thought the root of Cram's tour de force at the museum was exactly the aspect Whitehill emphasized in his own analysis of those rooms in 1970 in his *Museum of Fine Arts, Boston: A Centennial History*. In an attempt to explain how such strikingly appropriate interiors could have been created "without attempting to reproduce Chinese or Japanese interior decoration," Whitehill pointed to the use of "natural wood and plaster in a structural relation that has always pleased the *sensibilities* of the Japanese." The emphasis is my own. Not only does Whitehill's statement point to Cram's insistence that re-creation depended on studying the underlying motives and principles of a style rather than only its past forms, but also his analysis as a whole illustrates how keenly sensitive Cram was to where and with what materials he was working.

In the town of Westborough, for instance, when he converted a barn into a church in 1900, he insisted the painted red boarding of the exterior be left alone, refused to introduce pointed windows or even stained glass, and installed Venetian blinds only to filter the light. Yet he more than rose to the opportunity offered him in the same year by the dramatic site on which he built St. Stephen's Church in Cohasset (Figure 166), the massive Gothic tower of which rises majestically from a great crag overlooking the ocean. Similarly, the stone and half-timbered Atwood House (1917) and the nearby playhouse and art gallery (1916) Cram designed in Gloucester are built on great weatherbeaten rocky ledges and of the same rock. In the case of the house, entrance is gained through a kind of porte cochere that tunnels through the rocky foundations and the first floor of the house, from the middle of which a stone staircase leads up through the stone ledges to the main living floor, where the same rough stone is used for the fireplace. On Beacon Street in Brookline, however, near Richmond

Three parish churches in Boston by Cram and his partners.

FIGURE 166. St. Stephen's Church, Cohasset, 1899–1906.

FIGURE 167. All Saints' Church, Brookline, 1894–1926. Perspective by Goodhue showing the tower, which was never built.

FIGURE 168. Second Unitarian Church of Boston (now Ruggles Street Church), Audubon Circle, the Fenway, 1913–1917.

Court, his Gothic design of 1894 for All Saints' Church (Figure 167) at the corner of Dean Road is decidedly less robust and far more delicately conceived, and at nearby Audubon Circle, Cram reacted to that urbane red-brick apartment house square by making his Second Unitarian Church there (1913) the handsomest Georgian church in twentieth-century Boston (Figure 168).

This sensitivity to both site and materials proceeded as well from yet another controlling principle, without which all these buildings would have seemed only a kind of mimicry to Cram: his buildings are what they seem to be. If they possess vaults, they are *real* vaults of self-supporting masonry — as surely as Cram made no attempt to disguise the barn wall, he made no attempt to disguise construction generally. His great timber truss roofs, his vaults, everything in his work reflected his conviction that false construction could only be "ostentation," that the beauty of a thing was what it *did* beautifully. "The foundation of good architecture," Cram asserted, "is structural integrity." Anything else, he thought, was "scenepainting." A splendid illustration of this principle is St. Anne's Chapel at the Anglican convent of that order in Arlington (Figure 169), where the evocative character of the chapel derives in large measure from the rough but carefully designed random-coursed stonework, both within and without. But Cram's constructional honesty was not any more archaeological than his design. He was grateful for steel, and there *is* steel in some of his churches. But it is frankly used *as steel,* in the same way stone is used as stone. No material was unacceptable to Cram; he invariably used whatever material, ancient or modern, could honestly best serve his purpose. For example: he often wanted vaults, but he wanted also to answer the new need of his own time for better acoustics. Thus he stimulated

Wallace Sabine and Rafael Guastavino to undertake their pioneering acoustical experiments, which resulted in the first patent on an acoustical ceramic tile.

Another and crucial idea undergirded all Cram's work from the earliest rendering of a Gothic church we possess by Cram himself, dated 1888. This rendering, which established the fundamental design concept of his firm's first decade (including that of All Saints, Ashmont), shows an architecture of mass and proportion, simply composed and articulated. It documents Cram's assertion that "the trouble with most architects is that they do not know when to stop when they get through." This is perhaps the particular principle that triggered his creativity. Like Richardson, Cram had no faculty for designing detail; that was Goodhue's task. But he was a master of mass and scale, the quality that is most evident in the rough elevations by Cram himself — which contain as it were the genetic code of his buildings — from which Cram's designing partners developed the detail. The towers of All Saints, Ashmont, and St. Stephen's, Cohasset, are evidence of this. So also is his strikingly simple Ellingwood Chapel at Nahant (Figures 170, 171).

On a grander scale he only enlarged upon the same principles. The notion that Gothic must be characterized by great height is never found in his writings. Rather, he knew that its invariable characteristic was the varied organization of "perspective through perspective," as Kingsley Porter put it. This was accomplished best, Cram wrote, by a nave and chancel of "utmost simplicity of design, gravity of massing, refinement of proportion [and] classicism of composition," set within a larger space enclosed by "bounding walls following varied lines, giving space, distance [and] variety." This manipulation of space, he went on, should coincide with an analogous distribution of "clear, diffused light

Two suburban chapels by Cram and Ferguson that are among their most admired work.

FIGURE 169. St. Anne's Convent Chapel, Arlington, 1914–1916.

FIGURES 170, 171. Ellingwood Mortuary Chapel, Nahant, 1917–1920. Both were inspired by Cram's own chapel in Sudbury (Figure 176).

FIGURE 172. Cram and Ferguson. Conventual Church of SS Mary and John, Monastery of the Order of St. John the Evangelist, 980 Memorial Drive, Cambridge, 1935–1938. Cram's last major work in Boston. The nave makes an interesting comparison with his first nave, at All Saints, Ashmont, in 1892 (Figure 164).

St. Paul's Cathedral in Boston shows the nature of Cram's revolution of the visual image of American liturgical art.

FIGURE 173. The chancel as it appeared in the late nineteenth century.

FIGURE 174. The same chancel after Cram's remodeling, 1913–1927.

dying away into shadows" in the great central space and an "infinite variety of light and color" beyond the arcades or, perhaps, the reverse. All these factors of space, detail, light, and color must subtly develop toward a flowering, as it were, at the chancel arch — where the church must at one and the same time "draw in, concentrate, until it converges on the high altar," and yet "open out, expand, reveal vistas." It was the nave arcades, Cram pointed out, that organized this design concept. By continuing to the altar their main lines invariably converged there, while their voids disclosed the expanding variety of perspective beyond, whose "profound shadow and sudden lights" were for Cram the fundamental decoration of a Gothic church. His wonderfully strong interior, with its rugged stone walls, at the Chapel of the Cowley Fathers Monastery in Cambridge, one of his last major works, is a splendid illustration of his evocative manipulation of interior space (Figure 172).

For Cram this *was* architecture, and he once suggested that every architect should eschew even "one atom of detail" for five years in order to learn this lesson.

They would learn, too, he thought, other lessons: that while detail was not necessary it could greatly deepen a building's significance if still other principles were followed. "Richness," wrote Cram in 1899, "must be backed up by fine, solid and simple architecture. The finer and franker the lines [of the building], the more reserved and powerful the parts, the greater the richness of detail that may be allowed" — so long, that is, as such detail was absolutely subservient to the building that it decorated. Stained glass, he argued, should never utilize perspective or modeling: it must be entirely flat, entirely decorative, entirely architectural, never assertive; never a hole in the wall, but, rather, the wall rendered translucent. Finally, such detail, though reticent, must be allowed only if it were of superb quality. Thus, such was the Cowley Chapel's strength and large simplicity that Cram felt able to fill the windows with jewellike glass and to articulate the various interior volumes with exquisite wrought iron and finally to introduce into the sanctuary a magnificent marble baldachino over the high altar. His remodeling of St. Paul's Cathedral in Boston is as well a vivid example in the Classical tradition of how different was a Cram chancel from a Victorian chancel because of these principles (Figures 173, 174). Similarly at one of his most distinguished Gothic churches, the First Unitarian Church in West Newton, he designed a tower of great elaboration. But a close study will disclose that the exquisite cut-stone detail grows perceptibly out of a very strong and simple mass as the tower rises (Figure 175).

Inevitably, some of Cram's Boston work is not successful. His First Universalist Church in Somerville (1916–1923) is curiously bland. Several other churches, having never been finished, lack coherence. This is particularly true of St. Paul's in Malden, probably designed in 1905 and started ca. 1911. All Saints in Brookline (begun in 1894), like Christ Church in Hyde Park (1892), suffers also from the fact that its tower was never built. Even the few elevations Cram himself did for Boston University in the late 1930s (most of the design of Boston University was by Cram's partners) must be pronounced failures; Cram admitted himself he was sad to have left so large a mistake behind him in his home town, a mistake later rendered ridiculous by mock-Gothic towers. Cram's Boston skyscraper was also a disappointment (Figure 216); he complained that after he had signed the contract for the Federal Building of 1930–1931, he discovered that the government expected him only to design a masonry veneer for another architect's steel frame. But it is not true, as so many assume, that most of Cram's finest work is elsewhere: the Bos-

ton area parish churches we have discussed here are among his best work in a vein many scholars think prompted Cram's most convincing achievement. Of this type Greater Boston possesses two buildings by Cram that are unique.

One is St. Elizabeth's Chapel in Sudbury, built by Cram in 1914 on his own estate for his family, friends, and neighbors and now the local Episcopal parish church (Figure 176). It is a masterpiece of straightforward but remarkably evocative church design, where mass and proportion and simple materials, sensitively handled, disclose the root of Cram's genius. It is in fact in such simple churches that one sees why Cram could handle so superbly the great masses of St. John the Divine in New York, which is the largest cathedral in the world. The second of these two works is, again, All Saints, Ashmont, for this church leads, as it were, two lives: not only did it herald Cram's Gothic Revival in the 1890s, but because Oliver and Mary Lothrop Peabody dedicated their fortune to its embellishment and endowment, Cram was able to develop and expand All Saints over a forty-year period into a uniquely distinguished example of his work. In the first place he was able to add to the church (in 1912 and 1929) two chapels, evolving an ante-choir in between, and thus to endow what was already an unusually lofty suburban church with the spatial grandeur of a great city church. But it is the decorative splendor of All Saints that is chiefly notable, for one may see at Ashmont work by most of Cram's important artist-collaborators, including the two who developed most under Cram's patronage and direction: the sculptor Johannes Kirchmayer and the glassman Charles Connick, two Boston artists who dominated American architectural art in their fields in the early twentieth century and whose work is the climax in Boston of the decorative revival of the 1870s we first saw in the Back Bay.

171

Two important Cram churches in the western suburbs.

FIGURE 175. The tower of the First Unitarian Church in West Newton (1906) is among the most striking in Greater Boston. The church was also notable for its cloistered garth, until it was ruthlessly obliterated by an extension of the parish house.

FIGURE 176. Built as Cram's own chapel, St. Elizabeth's Church, Sudbury (1914), is of its type Cram's masterpiece.

Connick, whose studio Cram helped to establish in 1910, was a master of expressive line. Though his glass was entirely decorative and architectural, that quality only enhanced Connick's often distinguished portraiture. Stained glass, for Connick, was pure translucent color, whose function it was, through the filtration and radiation of light passing through color in its utmost purity, to yield what he called an "adventure in light and color" — in the "balancing of light and shadow in dissolving color as it functions in changing lights," the light vibrating through "eloquent spaces patterned in stone." Connick's work, which moved the poet Earl Marlatt to describe Connick glass as "darkly murmurous as stars or ships on gull-illuminated seas," can be seen throughout Greater Boston. His best local work is probably at the Cowley Fathers Monastery in Cambridge, and his first representative window is at All Saints, Brookline. But All Saints, Ashmont, is the best place to study his characteristic style because here one can see his glass as nowhere else alongside the earliest and largest of only a few American windows by Christopher Whall, the great English glassman whose vitality decisively influenced Connick.

Kirchmayer's work at Ashmont may be his masterpiece. As persuasive an artist in wood as was Connick in glass (though on its own Kirchmayer's work shows a difficulty with scale that only Cram seems to have been able to control), Kirchmayer was quite different from Connick. He wrote almost nothing. But his Lady Chapel triptych at Ashmont (Figure 177), like all his work the result of chisel and mallet on a solid balk of wood with no model (only the nude in charcoal and the drapery in crayon on the balk itself), is sufficient to document his reputation as the preeminent American architectural sculptor in wood in this century. Inspired by his Detroit Cathedral reredos

of 1910 — which was exhibited in the rotunda of the Museum of Fine Arts in Boston, such was its distinction — the All Saints triptych was itself exhibited in Boston, before its installation in 1912, at the St. Botolph Club Gallery on Newbury Street. Notice how in the central panel Kirchmayer quietly persuaded the Virgin's robe into two small praying angels. It is a small thing, but it knits the central figure even more closely into the whole composition. This triptych, an undoubted masterpiece of the American Gothic Revival, is easily overlooked, however, because it is the decoration of the chancel at Ashmont by these and other artists between 1897 and 1918 (under Cram's overall direction) for which the church became so notable in the early twentieth century. Some of the planned decoration was never carried out. Sir Edward Burne-Jones died before he was able to undertake the altarpiece; the pavement was never tiled; the murals and stained glass Cram wanted in the chancel have never been attempted. But one notices these things only when they are pointed out.

Within the chancel arch is a lofty rood of Byzantine splendor. Conceived by Cram as a great "icon" to dominate the interior, it caused almost as much controversy when it was installed in 1911 as had the *Bacchante* at the Public Library in 1896. But though strenuous efforts were made to remove it, this vivid crucifix, which marks the triumph of Medievalism in Puritan Boston, is still there today. Behind it opens out the best example anywhere of Goodhue's genius for decorative detail as restrained and integrated by Cram into architecture (Plate 7). The stone figure sculpture was modeled for John Evans by Domingo Mora — sculptors whose work we first saw at Trinity Church and at the Public Library — while the gold plate of the high altar (Figure 178) was modeled by Kirchmayer, who also executed the

For forty years after the erection of All Saints, Ashmont, Cram continued to lavish upon it some of his most distinguished architectural art.

FIGURE 177. Detail of altar and triptych in the Lady Chapel, 1912; one of the outstanding works of art of the American Gothic Revival, it has been called the masterpiece of Johannes Kirchmayer.

FIGURE 178. Detail of elevation by Goodhue of the high altar cross, modeled by Kirchmayer in 1899 and executed by Thomas McGann in gold plate on chiseled brass. For the entire chancel see Plate 7.

superb carvings of the oak paneling by Irving and Casson. The altarpiece, *The Enthronement of the Virgin,* was painted by George Hallowell and was exhibited in London to critical acclaim in 1904. The tabernacle is the work of the Boston goldsmith James Woolley.

This sumptuous detail, which was widely published in its own right, is conceived as an integral part of the Caen stone reredos. Inspired by the great medieval screen at Winchester Cathedral, it in turn inspired Goodhue's famous reredos at St. Thomas, Fifth Avenue, and is comparable with both. The provision for oil paintings within the cut stone and for free-standing pedestals flanking the altar gives an unusually multidimensional feeling to this ensemble, which is so faultlessly detailed and proportioned that it enhances and sets off the altar, rather than crushing it. Indeed, the overall decoration of the chancel shows the last of the major principles from which Cram's vitalization of Gothic design proceeded — that though a strongly designed interior might be endowed with very elaborate detail, such detail had not only to be well crafted, it had to be organic and functional. There is no better illustration of Cram's strict functionalism: All Saints was designed as a setting for liturgical worship in the Catholic tradition, which is essentially corporate in nature. Thus its architectural art reflected this function. It was designed to be visually corporate, each detail calling attention not to itself but to an overall and organic unity of design that Cram insisted must pervade not only the architectural setting but all the elements of what John Henry Newman called "the sacred dance" of the High Mass — including even such things as altar frontals and processional crosses, which Cram and Goodhue designed here as elsewhere.

Cram did not pioneer this concept at All Saints. It is evident in his and Good-hue's first important decorative work, their Lady Chapel interior (1894) at the Church of the Advent. It also animates Cram's much simpler chancels at St. Luke's Chapel, Roxbury (1900), and at St. Michael's Church, Milton (ca. 1914), and his interior remodeling (1910–1930) at St. John the Evangelist on Beacon Hill, where Cram, who was a parishioner there, formed a kind of partnership with the choirmaster, the well-known American composer Everett Titcomb, that yielded a standard of liturgical art for which St. John's was known throughout the country. But the Ashmont chancel became as much the national model for church interiors in the Catholic tradition as had the church itself for exteriors because Cram and Goodhue and their artist collaborators achieved at All Saints one of the most distinguished ensembles of Gothic Revival art in the world.

I T is a measure of how vital a center of explicit revivalism Boston remained until the 1930s that two other local firms specializing in both Gothic and Classical church design emerged in Cram's wake after 1900 and achieved a national reputation. The most remarkable was Maginnis and Walsh, whose senior partner, Charles Donagh Maginnis, became the leading Roman Catholic architect in this country.

Boston is fortunate to possess perhaps Maginnis's masterpiece: the Church of St. Catherine of Genoa on Spring Hill in Somerville (Figures 179, 180), built from 1907 to 1916 through the generosity of a son of Boston's first Irish and Roman Catholic mayor, Hugh O'Brien, to whom a chapel of St. Catherine's is dedicated. The fact that Maginnis himself had first come to Boston as an immigrant from Ireland underlines the increasing importance at this time of the Irish Catholic contribution to Boston's cultural as well as its political life. (Maginnis, who near the end of his life was awarded the Gold Medal of the American Institute of Architects, the highest award the institute confers, may in the long run be accounted a more important figure in Boston's history than Mayor O'Brien.) St. Catherine's is admittedly flawed in two respects: its marble columns hide steel and its lofty campanile was never built. Probably neither flaw is due to Maginnis, and it is in other respects so fine a church that Cram published it frequently and Sylvester Baxter called it "one of the most beautiful churches in America." Few would quarrel with that assertion. Though the exterior today has been disfigured with some kind of paint, the high barrel-arched nave leads still to a sanctuary splendid with Mexican onyx and gray and white marble whose somewhat silvered hue contrasts beautifully with the rich gold ground of the half-dome above the high altar. The two side chapels, St. Hugh's and St. Catherine's, have reliefs by Kirchmayer, and the high altar was almost certainly the inspiration for Maginnis's altar and chancel of 1938 at Trinity Church in Boston, which Hitchcock has pointed out completed Trinity much as Richardson wished to in the first place (see Plate 5). Nor did Trinity's magnificent new high altar occasion any controversy. Though in 1913 President Eliot of Harvard had been scandalized by Cram's "Catholic" chancel for the Second Unitarian Church in Boston, by the 1930s Cram was designing high altars for Protestant churches all over the United States.

Maginnis (who was also a fine illustrator; see Figures 197–200) endowed many parishes in the Boston archdiocese with singularly beautiful churches. These include Our Lady of the Presentation in Brighton (1913); St. Aidan's in Brookline (1911), Maginnis's own parish; St. Julia's in Weston (1920); and the chapel at St. John's Seminary in Brighton

(1899–1902). Particularly notable are three Gothic churches: St. Catherine of Siena, built in Norwood in 1909 and noted also for extensive stained glass by Connick; St. Paul's (1920) in Dorchester; and St. Theresa's in West Roxbury, designed in 1929 and graced with figure sculpture by George Aarons. What is now Emmanuel College in the Fenway was also designed by Maginnis in 1916. But even these seem to pale before the beautiful Gothic buildings he began to design for Boston College in 1909 (Figure 181). Somewhat unappreciated today, his work there constitutes the most dramatic Gothic Revival ensemble in Greater Boston and was a strong factor in his widening reputation. On the other hand, for all his skill as a Medievalist, Maginnis was most persuasive as a Classicist. His design for the Jesuit chapel in Weston, assured, regal, and filled with splendid stained glass by Earl Sanborn, is the most distinguished example of twentieth-century Classicism in Greater Boston (Figure 182).

The other major Gothic firm in Boston was Allen and Collens. Like Maginnis and Walsh, whose work ranged from a much admired Carmelite convent in California to the sumptuous high altar of St. Patrick's Cathedral in New York City, Allen and Collens enjoyed a national reputation. They designed, for example, Riverside Church in New York City. As they were much given to compromising the structural integrity Cram insisted upon by using hidden steel framing, one is grateful that they did not do this in Boston at their Lindsey Chapel at Emmanuel Church on Newbury Street (Figure 183). This chapel, with its ornamental ironwork by F. Koralewski and its fine high altar and stained glass by Sir Ninian Comper, is exquisite. Other local work by Allen and Collens includes what is now St. Clement's Church (ca. 1920) in the Back Bay (which has lost its handsome tower) and the Second Church in

Newton (1909–1916). Nor should one forget that Henry Vaughan, despite the demands of his work on the Washington Cathedral, continued to design parish churches around Boston, including St. John's Church in Newtonville (1902–1903) and the Church of the Redeemer in Chestnut Hill (1913–1915), the handsome tower of which was added in 1920, after Vaughan's death but from designs prepared by him. Other architects essayed important Gothic work in Greater Boston that included R. Clipston Sturgis's Perkins School for the Blind in Watertown (Figure 184), and Shaw and O'Connell's Immaculate Conception Convent in Malden (1930). Non-Gothic church work of merit by able local architects must also be noted: particularly fine is Charles Greco's Blessed Sacrament Church in Jamaica Plain (1910–1917), with a reredos by Henry H. Ahl and Stations of the Cross by Kirchmayer, and two churches by Edward T. P. Graham: St. Paul's (1915) near Harvard Square (see Figure 201) and the Church of the Holy Name (1938–1939) in West Roxbury.

Often suburban ecclesiastical architecture, however little known, is of considerable interest. For example, the Church of the Blessed Sacrament (1911–1913) in Walpole is one of the best of the "modernist Gothic" type in Greater Boston. St. Paul's, Natick (Brigham, Coveney and Bisbee, 1919), includes chancel carvings by Charles Pizanno and glass by both Joseph Reynolds and Earl Sanborn. Connick glass not already mentioned will be found at the Harmony Grove Chapel, Salem, and at St. John's Church, Hingham, where one may also see glass by Wilbur Burnham, another early twentieth-century Boston craftsman of national reputation, whose best local work is probably in two West Roxbury churches, Holy Name and St. Theresa's. Glass by Margaret Redmond is extant at St. Peter's, Beverly (as well as at Trinity

Church, Boston), and the only building in Greater Boston whose facade is honored by the work of the distinguished British sculptor John Angel is Archbishop Williams High School in Braintree.

All religious groups felt the force of this Boston school of church design, and not only Cram designed churches for widely differing groups. C. H. Blackall, for example, designed both Temple Israel (1907) on Commonwealth Avenue near Kenmore Square and Temple Ohabei Shalom (1928), a richly Byzantine synagogue on Beacon Street in Brookline, as well as the Episcopal Church of Our Saviour (1889) in Roslindale and the Baptist Tremont Temple on downtown Tremont Street in 1895. Cram's own influence was most keenly felt in the mushrooming early twentieth-century suburbs around Boston, where modern Gothic churches abound. Sometimes they are small, like St. Joseph's in Needham (1918) or Sacred Heart in Watertown (1913); quite large Gothic churches, however, such as the Church of the Immaculate Conception in Everett (completed in 1908) or St. Theresa's in Watertown, begun as late as 1939, were not exceptional. Particular examples of Cram's influence include two churches in Winchester — the Church of the Epiphany (Warren, Smith and Biscoe, 1904) and the Unitarian Church of Winchester (George Newton, 1898) — and the First Baptist Church in Melrose, also by George Newton (1907), and Edwin J. Lewis's All Souls Church (1901) in Braintree. Churches that were more Romanesque than Gothic continued to be built — St. Anthony's in Revere (1924), for example — and one can see in Wellesley (at Carrère and Hastings's Wellesley Congregational Church, 1921–1923) that Georgian continued to be popular; but the Cram-type Gothic parish church was far more widely favored: both the First Congregational Church of Wellesley

The Boston work of Maginnis and Walsh, the leading American Roman Catholic architects of the early twentieth century, includes three buildings of national importance.
FIGURE 179. Church of St. Catherine of Genoa, Somerville, 1907–1916.
FIGURE 180. Interior of St. Catherine's.
FIGURE 181. Boston College, Newton, 1909, the most dramatic and extensive collegiate Gothic in Greater Boston. The pond is now built over.
FIGURE 182. Chapel of the Jesuit Novitiate, Weston, 1929. Maginnis's design is surely the most distinguished example of twentieth-century Classicism in Boston. His chancel at Trinity Church, Copley Square, is shown in Plate 5.

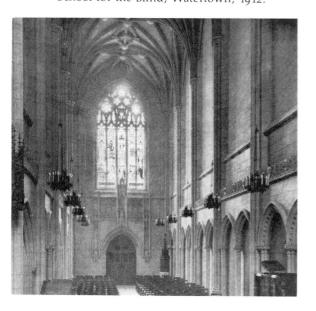

FIGURE 183. Allen and Collens. Leslie Lindsey Memorial Chapel, Emmanuel Church, Back Bay, 1920–1924.

FIGURE 184. R. Clipston Sturgis. Perkins School for the Blind, Watertown, 1912.

Hills (George Newton, 1901) and St. Paul's Roman Catholic Church in Wellesley (Joseph Maginnis, 1917) are thus typical of this period in that they were closely modeled on All Saints, Ashmont.

One could go on indefinitely: nearly every town around Boston as everywhere else has its memorial to Cram's influence. One wonders, however, if there was any deeper meaning to this. Was there an idea behind All Saints, Ashmont, as far-reaching for America in its sphere as the idea that lay behind McKim's Public Library? Beyond architectural reform, when he began All Saints in 1892, Cram made no such claim. Yet one looks naturally for a larger meaning in this triumphant twentieth-century Medievalism centered in once-Puritan Boston. It may well be found in the fact that both a Congregational and a Roman Catholic church in Wellesley as well as a Unitarian church in Winchester and a Baptist church in Melrose are by no means exceptional in having all been inspired by Cram's church at Ashmont, it-self an attempt to re-create a pre-Reformation English Gothic style. And as we have seen, by the twenties, the interiors of such churches were likely to be as similar to one another as their exteriors. In retrospect, the fact that Cram (unlike Richard Upjohn, who in the mid-nineteenth century refused even a Gothic exterior to a Unitarian parish in Boston) ultimately persuaded almost everyone in America in the early twentieth century to a common Christian architecture is surely not unrelated to the enthusiasm with which Americans of so many different religious traditions ultimately welcomed the ecumenical movement after the Second World War.

CHARLES MAGINNIS observed once that "in the austere quality of his mind and the logical enterprize of his pencil one detects [in Cram] a resemblance to McKim as certainly as one perceives the analogy between Goodhue and Stanford White." For Boston the first analogy was more important: McKim was the partner in charge of all his firm's Boston work, including the Public Library, and it was Cram who decisively shaped the important work of his office in Boston, including All Saints, Ashmont. Designed and built simultaneously, the Copley Square library and the Ashmont church paralleled each other from the beginning. Both the outgrowth of Richardson's work, each was so distinguished an example of "re-creating" a historical style that church and library shaped the dominant modes in American architecture until the Second World War.

That both these pivotal examples of "creative scholarship" should have been built in Boston is significant. That Boston's leading architect from the early 1900s to the 1930s was a man who did re-create a vital Gothic architecture is of even more importance. As Kenneth John Conant has pointed out, Gothic "trigger[ed] an inventive personal reaction in Cram as a designer. Under him the Gothic which he loved had an afterlife so vigorous that it is unfair to think of him as merely a revivalist." Conant, in fact, makes the same point about Cram's architecture that the *Times Literary Supplement* made of Cram's writings on Medieval Gothic: Cram succeeded. McKim had also succeeded. In a more personal way, so had Isabella Stewart Gardner. In a letter to Mrs. Gardner about a proposed visit by her to his Sudbury chapel, Cram emphasized that it was not only *his* chapel and that it was regularly open to the public. Indeed, Fenway Court and Cram's chapel are very comparable buildings: it was scarcely less outrageous for Cram to build a "twelfth-century chapel" on his estate than it was for Mrs. Gardner to build a "Venetian Renaissance palace." It is perhaps more to the point that in the case of both chapel and palace, as also at the Public Library and at All Saints, sincerity and taste — genius, if you will — yielded convincing and distinguished results.

It was these characteristics that ennobled so much that might otherwise be thought ostentatious in the legacy of beauty left to Boston. In each case these buildings reinforced in Boston particularly an attitude toward art and architecture that had for centuries been taken for granted. In their distinct and several ways the Public Library, Fenway Court, All Saints, and Cram's chapel sought to advance a whole range of cultural values in a society newly pluralistic enough to make good use of all of them and vital enough to have nurtured men and women equal to the creation of the kind of beauty that would express those values in a distinguished way. Architecturally, this involved recalling the Renaissance palazzo and the Medieval church. But these were perceived as building types that could stimulate the creative architect to his own personal and timely achievement in the same way that the Renaissance attempt to recover the architecture of antiquity had stimulated Bramante. That this centuries-old tradition of revival and re-creation found such vital champions in the 1890–1930 period, and that one of these, Cram, was the Boston architect who exercised the widest national influence in his time, was a crucial factor in Boston's architectural history during this period. A vital Boston culture, secure at the turn of the century in the glories of the Renaissance and Medieval revivals, withstood easily the violence of Louis Sullivan's fierce attack on what has often since been called "historicism."

8

THE SHADOW OF
LOUIS SULLIVAN

FOR BOSTON, Louis Sullivan will always be the man that got away. Actually, as Sullivan entitled his memoirs *Autobiography of an Idea*, one might better say that he will always stand for the *idea* that got away, which is rather loosely called "Modernism." Like so many architectural terms, it is not luminous, but Whitehill is one of the few people who have had the courage to point out that "it is no good at all trying to describe a building as an example of 'modern architecture.' Modernity evaporates overnight." Because it still has a polemic meaning, the word has stuck, however, to a movement in architectural history that began nearly one hundred years ago.

The son of immigrant parents, Sullivan was Boston born and bred — in 1856 at 225 Bennet Street, as is announced by the plaque on this site, which is now a part of the Tufts New England Medical Center. Sullivan did not like Boston. Nor has Boston ever really claimed Sullivan, and there is no work at all by him in his birthplace. Sullivan in Boston recalls irresistibly Conan Doyle's famous lines in "Silver Blaze," when the inspector asks Sherlock Holmes:

"Is there any point to which you would wish to draw my attention?"
"To the curious incident of the dog in the night-time."
"The dog did nothing in the night-time."
"That was the curious incident," remarked Sherlock Holmes.

What Sullivan did do in Boston seems somehow unreal today. Imagine a young man, uniformed and hoisting a Springfield rifle with fixed bayonet, tramping Tremont Street the night after the Great Fire of 1872, a part of the M.I.T. Battalion charged with defending what was left of Boston's business district. Behold the prophet and genius of modern architecture in America, in Boston in 1872 — before Charles McKim or Ralph Adams Cram; before even H. H. Richardson had come to live in Boston.

In his autobiography, which is written in the third person, Sullivan's impressions, as a boy and as a young man, of Boston were set down with a startling vehemence. "As a conglomerate of buildings," he remembered, Boston had "depressed Louis Sullivan continuously since he became engulfed in it." Yet the one building that overwhelmed Sullivan was perhaps the least likely — the Gothic Revival Masonic Temple on the corner of Tremont and Boylston Streets, designed in 1867 by Merrill G. Wheelock (see Figure 51). Sullivan passionately loved it. It seemed to him, he recalled:

a message from an unseen power. Thus immersed, he returned again and again to his wonder-building, the single one that welcomed him, the solitary one that gave out a perfume of romance, that radiated joy, that seemed fresh and full of laughter. How it gleamed and glistened in the afternoon sunlight. How beautiful were its arches, how dainty its pinnacles; how graceful the tourelle on the corner, rising as if by itself, higher and higher, like a lily stem, to burst at last into a wondrous cluster of blowering pinnacles and a lovely, pointed finial.

That he should also have admired Richardson's tower at the Brattle Square Church is more understandable (Figure 64).

After attending the public schools, young Sullivan began the study of architecture at M.I.T., having formed, he later remembered, his ambition to be an architect while talking of architecture with a builder one day on Commonwealth Avenue. But he liked M.I.T. no better than Boston; the curriculum seemed to him a "misch-masch of architectural theology" and after a year he departed, unnoticed, ultimately for Chicago, where his family had previously moved. The Boston of Richardson and of McKim's library and then of Cram did not mourn the loss. But as Sullivan's fame spread, his work and that of his disciples continually shadowed both the Classical and Gothic Revivals and all the modes in between during the 1890–1940 period in Boston as elsewhere, for behind the diverse pomps of traditional design, a perhaps revolutionary new force was increasingly evident after the 1890s; whatever style was chosen, working underneath and behind style (which was becoming, as it were, a kind of skin, not always nourished by underlying structure), there was often to be found — the steel frame.

Except in very tall buildings, its presence was (and is) only vaguely felt. Indeed, structural innovations often went unnoticed. Who suspected then, or knows now, that in the Shepley office's Chamber of Commerce Building of 1890–1893 (since become the Grain and Flour Exchange) "the floors and ceilings of the offices in the sixth and seventh floors over the Board Room," according to Charles S. Damrell, "are suspended from [the] roof" (see Figure 195)? In fact,

the least distinguished buildings "architecturally" in Boston in 1890–1940 are often those most famous for innovative structure. The New England Mutual Life Insurance Company (1939) is a case in point. Its design by his partners drove Cram to near despair and David McCord to a scathing clerihew:

> Ralph Adams Cram
> One morning said damn,
> And designed the Urn Burial
> For a concern actuarial.

But underneath lurked a tour de force; the so-called floating foundation (occasioned by the fact that this is all made land) that William Le Messurier called "an example of brilliant engineering."

What effect such structural innovations ought to have on design was much disputed in the 1890–1940 period. Cram wrote in 1914:

The steel frame is the *enfant terrible* of architecture, but like so many of the same genus it may grow up to be a serious-minded citizen and a good father. . . . If we can make it realize that it is a new force, not a substitute, we shall do well. When it contents itself in its own proper sphere . . . then it may be a good servant. Like all good servants it makes the worst possible master; and when it claims as its chiefest virtue that it enables us to reproduce the Baths of Caracalla, vaults and all, at half the price, or build a second Chartres Cathedral with no danger from thrusting arches, and with flying buttresses that may be content beautifully to exist, since they will have no other work to do, then it is time to call a halt.

"A new force, not a substitute" — Boston's leading "traditionalist" seems to have understood very well the driving force behind Sullivan's determination to break out of the historical circle of revivalism and eclecticism and create instead the steel frame's own aesthetic. But Boston as well as Chicago had a great fire in the early 1870s, which, as we have seen, Sullivan saw the effects of at first hand;

FIGURE 185. Proposed interior treatment (1895) of the Boston subway system, the first in the United States. The designer is unknown, but Peabody and Stearns, Alexander W. Longfellow, Jr., and Edmund Wheelwright are all known to have designed rapid-transit stations in the early 1900s. Nonetheless, *The Brickbuilder* complained in 1898 that architecturally the new subway was "about as enlivening and cheerful as a second century catacomb."

Boston as much as Chicago was bursting its narrow confines. Why then did Boston's vitality in the late nineteenth century — which is seen in its tremendous landfill operations and in such revolutionary new developments as America's first subway (Figure 185) — seem so uncongenial to Sullivan? Why was the Chicago Style of the 1880s and 1890s not, instead, the Boston Style? Was it, perhaps, for the same reason that in Scully's view the New England Shingle Style was left to Frank Lloyd Wright to develop? It is not quite so simple.

Quite aside from our new appreciation of the work of McKim and Cram, William Jordy has observed:

For those who would take an overly provincial view of the Chicago achievement, for instance, how puzzling that two of the principal clients for Chicago commercial buildings were the Boston financiers, Peter and Shepard Brooks, who seem to have been exceptionally forceful in instructing their architects (through their Chicago real estate agent,

Owen Aldis) on the virtues of architectural austerity. The Brooks brothers not only financed the Portland and Montauk, but the Monadnock, Rockery, and Marquette buildings, among others, all of them key buildings in conditioning what is conventionally tagged as the "Chicago" point of view. Yet the Brooks' exhortations seem to have been powerless to effect anything in Boston comparable to the Chicago achievement.

This is all the more interesting because, as Thomas Hines has pointed out, in their rationale for the Monadnock's severity — that it was "for use not ornament" and that "its beauty will be in its adaption to use" — these two Boston financiers unconsciously formulated the Chicago aesthetic. Moreover, it has long been argued that Richardson's work was a crucial influence on Louis Sullivan: Richardson's Ames Estate Store on Harrison Avenue (1886; demolished), for example, suggested a treatment Sullivan was to develop for the expression of the steel-skeleton skyscraper. Wheaton Holden has also documented an important inspiration for the Ames Store in Peabody and Stearns's R. H. White Boston Warehouse Store of four years earlier. He notes that Peabody and Stearns's design, "a milestone of its time" and the most widely published of their buildings, almost certainly was known to John Root when he designed his very similar McCormick Office and Warehouse Building in Chicago in 1885–1886 and that "Louis Sullivan may even have owed a lingering debt of thanks to Robert Peabody in his Walker Warehouse in Chicago [1888–1889]."

Still another new factor appears in Margaret Henderson Floyd's recent study of the Copley Square Museum of Fine Arts (Figure 53), where, as we have seen, Sturgis and Brigham introduced into this country the large-scale use of terra-cotta. Mrs. Floyd observes:

The importance of iron and steel construction to nineteenth-century architecture has long been known, yet the revival of ceramics plays a more important role than is generally recognized. Louis Sullivan's terra-cotta sheathing of the Wainwright Building in St. Louis (1890–1891) or his Guaranty Building in Buffalo (1894–1895) are acknowledged today as the finest designs of their time. They would hardly have reached reality, however, without the prior development of a terra-cotta industry in America for the reproduction of the material, or continuous experiment to perfect the relatively sophisticated technology of its application.

"Technologically," she concludes, "the [Copley Square] Museum of Fine Arts, Boston, was the bridge between London and Chicago."

To root these things in an even more venerable past, here are two further examples of what is increasingly surfacing. Cynthia Zaitzevsky recently discovered a long-overlooked building by Richardson (Figure 186), which because of its post and lintel construction on the upper floors suggests a relationship between Richardson's work and the mid-nine-teenth-century Boston Granite Style. Moreover, Winston Weisman has pointed out that a number of mid-century Philadelphia buildings may well have been important sources for the principles Sullivan applied to the tall metal-frame skyscraper. One building is thought by Weisman to be especially significant: the Jayne Building, whose front — "conceived as a stone skeleton with glass panels stretched between the ribs" — Weisman traces back to Isaiah Rogers's Boston work. He notes:

Isaiah Rogers seems to have first suggested the solution in his Merchants' Exchange of 1842, setting four monumental four-story Corinthian piers in antis as an ornamental screen for the business spaces behind. These are tied together at the various levels by deeply recessed floor strips. Windows fill the space between the vertical and horizontal elements. In the Brazer's Building [Figure 206], erected at the same time, Rogers transforms this ornamental scheme into a structural one while preserving its vertical character. In this instance, the granite piers of the ground story carry a lintel and then continue on through the second and third stories without interruption as a result of the way in which the spandrels are recessed between the piers.

Weisman goes on to point out that Sullivan, who worked in the vicinity of the Jayne Building when employed by Furness and Hewitt in 1873, is likely to have seen this and other buildings and he asserts that two early Sullivan buildings are "more or less identical" to the Philadelphia buildings. As such evidence accumulates, it surely bears out Jordy's observation.

On the other hand, now that the Modern movement has floundered somewhat, it will doubtless occur to many that Boston and not Chicago was building the better and more humane city in the 1880s and 1890s and that the 125-foot limit restricting the growth of the skyscraper in Boston was wise; that Boston was correct to draw back from the skyscraper. Norris K. Smith, for example, has written disparagingly of one scholar who,

like most historians, accepts the conventional notion that the tall building was somehow made necessary in Chicago (but not, for some reason, in Paris or London or Vienna)|or Boston|, by economic and utilitarian considerations; yet I think it reasonably clear that the one motivating force behind the invention was simply greed. The skyscraper, with its fabulous multiplication of rents, was made for those same greedy exploiters who were slashing down the magnificent forest of Michigan and Wisconsin, all but exterminating the buffalo and the Indians, and polluting the rivers and the air (as Burnham outspokenly declared) in their heedless and headlong pursuit of wealth. William Jordy has taken the time to ascertain that the invention of the tall building was the work of uneducated architects — men who, to a man, had had a high school education at best, together with some instruction in engineering, and had little or no grasp of the traditions in support of which the art of architecture had long functioned.

In his recent and provocative *Form Follows Fiasco*, a play on Sullivan's famous dictum "form follows function," Boston architect and critic Peter Blake has concluded that Modernism after all was "a religion as irrational as all others, from snake-handling to psychoanalysis." But here again, it is not so simple a matter.

In the first place it is significant that Bostonians tunneled America's first subway under the sacred sod of the Common but nonetheless restricted the height of skyscrapers: one could not *see* the subway; it did not intrude visually on the streetscape. Skyscrapers did. And there is a strong tradition that the erection of a Haddon Hall type of tall apartment building (A. H. Vinal's twelve-story building of 1903 at 48 Beacon Street) precipitated the height restriction formulated finally in 1904. Strongly contested, the legislation had to be upheld by the United States Supreme Court. But it was thought then — as it would be now — to be highly progressive legislation in that it was "preservationist" in its

point and also distinguished between the business district, where buildings 125 feet high were allowed, and residential areas, where the limit was 80 feet. The first such comprehensive height-of-building law in the country, it had actually more than anything else to do with zoning. As we shall see, it was altered when the 125-foot limit proved a hindrance to the growth of the business district. Furthermore, the steel frame — and even a reflection of its aesthetic expression — appeared in Boston in the same year that the Classical Revival heralded by the Public Library went west with a vengeance and overwhelmed Chicago — indeed, the whole country — at the Chicago World's Columbian Exposition of 1893. In that year, while the Boston Public Library and All Saints at Ashmont were nearing completion, Boston was endowed with the Winthrop Building.

WITHOUT at all suggesting that Boston got the better of the exchange, it is nonetheless true that however much the city lost to Chicago with Sullivan's departure, Boston gained not a little back when Clarence H. Blackall of Chicago, who had not only taken both his B.S. and M.S. degrees at the University of Illinois but also studied at the Ecole des Beaux Arts, decided to settle in Boston. He is said to have taken a walk down Washington Street and been scarcely more impressed than Sullivan. Unlike Sullivan, however, Blackall saw opportunity; he became a draftsman for Peabody and Stearns. The first Rotch Scholar (in 1884), he was also the first president of the Boston Architectural Club and ultimately enjoyed a national distinction.

Blackall's work has not subsequently been given the attention it deserves. Few know that it was Blackall who carved out

FIGURE 186. H. H. Richardson. Hayden Building, Washington at La Grange streets, Downtown, 1875–1876.

FIGURE 187. Clarence H. Blackall. The Carter (later the Winthrop) Building, 7 Water Street, between Washington and Devonshire streets, Boston's first entirely steel-framed office building, 1893–1894; looking from the lavish tripartite glazing of the second floor to the rich, overhanging cornice.

of several Beacon Hill tenements in the 1920s the imaginative Primus Avenue Apartments off Phillips Street, that he was in fact a leading apartment house and hotel architect (among the first, at Oxford Court in Cambridge in 1926, to provide a parking garage integral to an apartment house), and even fewer realize the great number of innovative theaters he designed (discussed in Chapter 9). Even less is known about his early years in Boston. Yet Blackall in the 1880s and nineties was a conduit of sorts between Boston and Chicago. He continued to work there (he designed several buildings for the University of Illinois at Urbana in the early 1900s) and in 1888 he was explaining Boston to Chicago in a series of articles in *Inland Architect* while at the same time explaining the Chicago innovations to Boston in a similar series of articles in Boston's periodical, *American Architect*. Nor was he content merely to explain: it was Blackall who in 1893–1894 startled Boston by designing and erecting the city's first steel-frame building, the Carter (now the Winthrop) Building, between Washington and Devonshire streets (Figure 187).

It seems quite clear that this is *the* first such Boston building. When the subject of steel framing has come up in the past it has only been in passing, and perhaps for that reason the terminology employed has not been exact. Hitchcock, in *The Architecture of H. H. Richardson and His Times,* observed that Richardson's successors, "in building the Ames Building on Washington Street [the still extant skyscraper of 1889, not to be confused with Richardson's own earlier Ames Estate Store of 1886 on Harrison Avenue], were the first to bring the new skyscraper construction to [Boston]. This was in the same year, 1889, in which Bradford Lee Gilbert first used skeleton construction in New York for the Tower Building on Broadway." Some years later, in his *Guide to Boston Architecture,*

Hitchcock noted the Ames Building's "bearing walls of solid masonry," but he still overlooked the Winthrop Building and pointed instead to the Iver Johnson Building of 1908 as "almost the only example of early skyscraper design in Boston." Of course, "skyscraper construction" and "skyscraper design" can mean many things. The Sears Building of 1868 on the corner of Washington and Court streets appears to have been the first office building to have possessed an elevator in Boston, and both Peabody and Stearns's Fiske Building (1887), now destroyed, and the fourteen-story Ames Building of 1889, which has survived to challenge in distinction of design every subsequent tall office building in Boston, can certainly be called skyscrapers in the sense of having been dependent on the elevator (Figure 188). But insofar as steel framing is concerned, only two buildings have been advanced as possibly predating the Winthrop Building: the Exchange Building of 1887 by Peabody and Stearns (for whom it should be remembered Blackall was a draftsman) and the second Brazer Building by Cass Gilbert. But Colonel W. Cornell Appleton, Peabody and Stearns's last chief designer (who told Wheaton Holden of the steel framing in the Exchange Building), insisted it was only used in part and that the Winthrop Building marked the first time in Boston steel framing had been used throughout a building. And Walter Kilham, who suggested the second Brazer Building, also noted that the Winthrop Building could have been erected first. In fact, an examination of the respective building permits shows the date of Gilbert's design to have been 1896, three years after the Winthrop Building.

This is reflected in extant correspondence at the Building Department between Blackall and the city engineer, with whom Blackall argued a number of technical questions about the proposed

The skyscraper in Boston before and after Blackall's Winthrop Building (see also Figure 46).

FIGURE 188. Shepley, Rutan and Coolidge. The Ames Building, 1889. The fourteen-story Ames Building dominated the Boston skyline until 1914. To its left is the Sears Building (1868; Cummings and Sears), later enlarged; probably the first office building in Boston to have been dependent upon the elevator.

FIGURE 189. Carl Fehmer. The Worthington Building, 33 State Street, 1894; this was among the first steel-framed office buildings in Boston to follow the Winthrop Building's lead.

FIGURE 190. Julius Schweinfurth. The Garden Building, 248 Boylston Street, 1911.

steel-frame construction. Interestingly, Blackall's first application (dated 1892 and later abandoned) was for a masonry structure, while the second application, which for the first time shows that Blackall was the owner as well as the architect, is conclusively for a steel-frame structure. This second permit specifies steel under "external walls," "floor timbers," "headers and trimmers," and "rafters," while under "materials of front" the specification is "steel frame, brick and terra cotta covering." That this is the historic document, recording as it does the first use in Boston of the steel frame, is also substantiated by statements made only two years after the building's erection by the second-in-command at the Building Department, Charles S. Damrell. In his *A Half Century of Boston Building*, in this case surely the best testimony, Damrell wrote:

Few Boston buildings have received the attention that has been given to the structure upon the irregular tract of land bounded by Washington, Water, Devonshire Streets and Spring Lane . . . the first structure to be erected in Boston in which the skeleton system of steel construction has been used. . . . It consists, in brief, of a steel frame with brick and terra cotta simply as a filling or skin. Supporting columns are made of four pieces of steel, the cross section of one of which is like the letter Z, all riveted to a center plate. These columns extend through the walls and are joined rigidly by beams in each story, and are also connected by horizontal trusses on the floors and vertical trusses in the partitions in such manner that the whole structure is rigid. . . .

Damrell's attitude also documents the fact that the innovative Winthrop Building by no means "snuck in" Boston's "back door"; its significance was at once appreciated. Damrell not only illustrated the building in his book; he devoted his longest article to it. It was also published in *Inland Architect* in 1893. And Cram remembered forty-three years later in his memoirs that the Winthrop Building had been in the 1890s in Boston "the source

of curiosity and doubting amazement."

Today the Winthrop Building is no longer amazing, though it is still handsome, with its pale golden buff brick and terra-cotta "about the color of slightly burned toast," to quote from a mid-nineties description. More importantly, its exterior design is as interesting as its steel frame, for the two *are* related, and in a way that illustrates nicely the extent to which Blackall both agreed and disagreed with Louis Sullivan's steel-frame aesthetic. Blackall discussed this question at some length in his "The Legitimate Design of the Architectural Casing for Steel Skeleton Structures" in *American Architect and Building News* in 1899, where he rejected what he called the "post-and-girder" mode, as well as the "aqueduct style," and argued instead for a frankly Classical casing such as one sees in the Winthrop Building. He did conclude that steel-frame buildings should be expressed through a strong base, a plain shaft, and a rich, crowning cornice, but he made precisely the analogy to the base, shaft, and capital of the Classical column that Sullivan rejected. Yet there is about the Winthrop Building as a whole, particularly in its lavish first- and second-floor glazing, a striking expression of its steel-frame construction. This is all the more evident if one compares the Winthrop Building with Carl Fehmer's 1894 design for the Worthington Building at 33 State Street (Figure 189), for although the clean-cut window and door openings (as well as the building's overall profile) show that Blackall was not the only Boston architect of the period alive to the challenge of the Chicago School, at 33 State Street the steel frame is not so noticeably expressed as at the Winthrop Building.

Each of these buildings — two of many similar Boston buildings of the late 1890s — ought, however, to be compared with the Garden Building of 1911 (Figure 190), designed by Julius

Schweinfurth, who, like Blackall, had been employed in the office of Peabody and Stearns in the 1880s. Stephen Neitz and Wheaton Holden have pointed out that the glass panes of the Garden Building's first-floor showcase windows were joined at the building's corners without any intervening structural member and that it was in the same year, 1911, that Walter Gropius featured the "glass corner" in his famous Fagus Factory at Alfeld on the Leine. It would be easy to exaggerate the importance of this fact. None of these buildings exercised the national influence in the 1890–1930 period of the Boston Public Library or All Saints, Ashmont. But the Winthrop, Worthington, and Garden buildings illustrate very clearly that in the year the Classicism heralded by the Public Library achieved its triumph in Chicago, and throughout the next two decades, the historic architectural innovations of the period were felt in Boston with greater force than most have suspected.

I F very few Bostonians remember that Louis Sullivan was born and grew up in Boston, probably even fewer realize that in the mid-1870s Frank Lloyd Wright, who would become Sullivan's most famous disciple, was playing with his "Froebel blocks" in the Boston suburb of Weymouth, where his father was minister of the First Baptist Church from 1874 to 1878. Wright departed the Boston area at age eleven, however, and it is not too much to say that however much his early domestic work may have been rooted in the New England Shingle Style, he was scarcely ever heard of in Boston again until the 1930s. A few weak echoes of the Prairie Style exist; there are a few of what can only be called "Stucco Style" houses, and it is interesting that some of the best of such houses, characterized by straightforward

geometric forms, uncluttered by ornament, were built by architects for themselves: in Cambridge, for example, H. Langford Warren's home at 6 Garden Terrace, built in 1904, and Charles Greco's home of six years later at 36 Fresh Pond Parkway. All sought a more modern idiom. One Cambridge stucco house — 16 Berkeley Street, designed by Harley Dennett in 1905 — does reflect more clearly some of the same design elements one sees in the Prairie Style — the blocky, geometric form, the horizontal quality strongly reinforced by low, lidlike, and wide projecting roofs, the banked windows, while flat stucco wall surfaces avoid "historic" style or detail (Figure 191). Also in Cambridge, at 114 Irving Street, built in 1911, is a cement-walled house of the "Craftsman" type, so called because such houses were popularized by the magazine of that name, edited between 1901 and 1916 by Gustav Stickley, who argued for a greater emphasis on well-crafted practicality and simplicity in residential design. There are also some early examples of the low-sloping "California Style" bungalows that were perhaps the Prairie Style's chief competitors. Boston's Building Commissioner Patrick O'Hearn designed one for himself in 1904 on Melville Avenue in Dorchester. Another of this type was built eight years later, at 71 Avon Hill Street in Cambridge. In the Back Bay, perhaps the most "progressive" design of this period was the facade of 395 Commonwealth Avenue (Figure 192) by A. J. Manning in association with Louis Comfort Tiffany, who designed the mosaic work of the facade and also decorated the staircase hall.

Concrete was also used increasingly at this time. Harvard Stadium was, in fact, one of the earliest large-scale buildings of reinforced concrete. A number of concrete warehouses and a fine concrete viaduct and train barn (see caption to Figure 201) were also built in the early 1900s and

New directions in domestic and commercial design in the 1900s.

FIGURE 191. Hartley Dennett. 16 Berkeley Street, Cambridge, 1905.

FIGURE 192. A. J. Manning in association with Louis Comfort Tiffany. Frederick Ayer House (now the Bayridge Residence for Women), 395 Commonwealth Avenue, 1899–1900.

FIGURE 193. Coolidge and Carlson. Store front, 1304 Massachusetts Avenue, near Harvard Square, Cambridge, 1907.

Modern construction did not necessarily imply what we should today call "modern" design.

FIGURE 194. Coolidge and Carlson. The Colonial filling station (now a fruit market), Massachusetts Avenue at Northampton Street, South End, 1922, is more "traditional" than Boston's only surviving nineteenth-century gasholder (right).

FIGURE 195. Peabody and Stearns. Custom House Tower, 1911–1915, built on top of the original Custom House (Figure 18). In the right foreground is Shepley, Rutan and Coolidge's Grain and Flour Exchange, 1890–1893.

FIGURE 196. Daniel Burnham and Company. Architect's perspective of Filene's Boston Store, Summer and Washington streets, 1912, the last major work of one of the architects of the Monadnock Building in Chicago.

even a few concrete block churches (stylistically Gothic) were built, an innovation pioneered in the Boston area by Frank Bourne. His first such experiment was at St. Luke's Church in Chelsea in 1907. The idea did not, however, achieve any wide currency.

Nor did Boston rally particularly in the early years of this century to the latest European import. Tiffany's popularity notwithstanding, the full-fledged curvilinear forms of the Art Nouveau style occur seldom: the best example is Coolidge and Carlson's altogether charming Art Nouveau storefront near Harvard Square (Figure 193), surely one of the few of its type to have survived in this country. But one has to search hard for such "progressive" currents; and like the curiously Sullivanesque entrance arch to the Hotel Somerset (Arthur Bowditch, 1897), these things mean more now than they did then. Even distinctly new building types sought traditional forms: one has only to discover, unbelievingly, the delightful old gas station (Figure 194) that still stands at the junction of Massachusetts Avenue and Northampton Street in the South End to see how tenacious what is now called "traditionalism" was in Boston. Designed by Coolidge and Carlson in 1922, this Classical pavilion is of cement block construction, its eye-catching red dome supported by concrete columns. But the best example is Peabody and Stearns's Custom House Tower, dedicated in 1915 (Figure 195). (The 125-foot limit on Boston buildings did not pertain, the property being owned by the federal government.) Boston's first really startlingly tall skyscraper, nearly five hundred feet high, the tower took the form of a granite Classical campanile that Burchard and Bush-Brown complain looks like "a vast chimney stack rising from a Roman temple."

The Custom House, like the gas station, is representative. Aside from office buildings, and even in that building

type more and more discreetly, Boston's architectural vitality at the turn of the century diverged from the Classical and Gothic norms only to seek an increasing eclecticism. Admittedly, critics like Dean Edgell thought they saw in some few local buildings — such as Coolidge and Shattuck's Boston Lying-In Hospital of 1923 — "something of the modernist expression that we associate with the work of Sullivan and Wright," but Edgell admitted that the architects of the hospital would probably have denied any such intent "indignantly."

Even in Chicago, traditionalism remained rampant, and it had more to do with local pride than any devotion to Modernism that when Shepley, Rutan and Coolidge designed the monumental Classical Art Institute of Chicago in 1892, that city's architects retaliated by renaming the Boston firm "Simply, Rotten and Foolish." Twenty years later the same attitude surfaced in Boston when one of the architects of the Monadnock Building, Daniel Burnham, was commissioned to design Filene's Boston store. R. Clipston Sturgis went even to the length of writing a letter to the Boston *Herald* to protest not the Filene design but the choice of Burnham.

One of a series of five major stores by Burnham — Marshall Field's in Chicago, Gimbel's in New York, Wanamaker's in Philadelphia, and Selfridges's in London — Filene's Boston store (Figure 196) was significantly more advanced technically than stylistically. A frame of light-gray terra-cotta encloses on each of the principal facades a generous olive-green terra-cotta grid of windows that does emphasize (as Burnham intended it should) the importance of light and air to the building's function. The color contrast is also handsome. But the gray outer frame is richly detailed Italian Renaissance stylistically, and the fact that it was characterized in *The Brickbuilder* in 1912 as "a frank expression of modern ideas" says much for how many meanings the word "modern" may have. Actually it was an example, all the more striking for Boston given its designer, of modern technology endowed with traditional Classical pomp. In our meaning of the word, Filene's stands not for Modernism, but for the traditionalism that through an increasing eclecticism would continue to dominate Boston architecture for the next twenty or more years.

I N the early years of the twentieth century the Classical of McKim and the Gothic of Cram were only the dominant strands of many in Boston, which in a sense was beginning as a whole to look like the Bayley House at 16 Fairmount Avenue in Newton, designed in 1883–1884. Each of the ground-floor reception rooms of the Bayley House was in a different period style and by 1920 the same could be said of Boston's buildings generally. Cram himself, as we have seen, designed buildings in every style under the sun. Indeed, most of Cram's collegiate work in Massachusetts — at Wheaton College and Williams College — was in the Classical tradition. And any one work is likely to disclose its own eclecticism: Talbot Hamlin noted that Cram's Second Church of Boston in Audubon Circle (Figure 168) was as "distinctly English" to one side of its tower (the church) as it was "distinctly American" on the other side (the parish house).

How eclectic Boston was becoming in the 1890s and 1900s is perhaps best illustrated by the work of one important local architect in a very short period of time: Edmund March Wheelwright, the then city architect, whose *Reports of City of Boston Architect Department* for 1891–1894 include designs of his that range from red-brick Georgian to full-fledged half-timbered Medieval villages and Oriental temples (Figures 197–200). Although mu-

nicipal architecture might be expected to be rather conservative, hardly any historical style was safe from Wheelwright, or, indeed, any one building; his admiration for the Palazzo Vecchio in Florence is evident, for example, in his Fire Department Headquarters (Figure 197). The Oriental shelter and duck house he proposed for the Fenway was never built; but a similar building by Charles Austin (The Bird House) exists in Franklin Park. Nor was Wheelwright, whose work was then and still is much admired, any less eclectic in his private practice. His splendid Longfellow Bridge (1907) was inspired by one he had admired in the then Russian capital of St. Petersburg, while his Horticultural Hall (1901) may be the handsomest English Baroque building in the city. And though he was more than capable of stately masses (he designed the New England Conservatory, the Massachusetts Historical Society, and the Opera House), he was also able to rise to the only occasion I know of in the history of Boston's architecture when an architect was asked to design a building that would be something of a joke: the Lampoon Building on Mount Auburn Street near Harvard Square (Figure 201). This "jolly brick midget of a building," in William Germain Dooley's words, "smiles at you like a caricature of a face — circular windows for eyes, hanging lantern for a nose, a domed roof for a hat with a birdcage tassel, Gothic windows for ears, classical pilasters, gargoyles and what have you." For all this, it is by no means a silly building; although it is more ingenious than beautiful, it sits jauntily astride a flatiron-shaped island in the middle of Mount Auburn Street, mediating elegantly between the huge Jacobean and Georgian piles that surround it and tying together the streetscapes into one of the most charming urban vistas in Greater Boston.

One might illustrate a similar variety

Edmund M. Wheelwright's work illustrates vividly the breadth of his eclecticism.

FIGURE 197. Boston Fire Department Headquarters, South End, 1894, now the Pine Street Inn.

FIGURE 198. Ferry head house proposed for East Boston, 1893.

FIGURE 199. Lunatic asylum at Pierce Farm, West Roxbury, 1893.

FIGURE 200. Shelter and duck house proposed for the Fenway, 1895. The sketches are all by C. Maginnis, then Wheelwright's draftsman.

FIGURE 201. The Lampoon Building, Mount Auburn Street, Cambridge, 1909. In the background is the campanile of E. T. P. Graham's St. Paul's Church, 1915. It would be unfair to forget, however, that Wheelwright was concerned with much more than style. He was an authority on schoolhouse design (his Brighton High School of 1894 was nationally influential), and he designed the robust reinforced concrete and iron viaduct and train barn at Forest Hills Elevated Station, West Roxbury, in 1909.

CITY OF BOSTON — PUBLIC INSTITUTIONS DEPT

LUNATIC ASYLUM AT PIERCE FARM, WEST ROXBURY.

EDMUND M. WHEELWRIGHT, CITY ARCHITECT..

— BLOCK PLAN —

CITY OF BOSTON — SHELTER AND DUCK HOUSE — BACK BAY FENS

EDMUND M. WHEELWRIGHT CITY ARCHITECT

in the work of almost any of the leading Boston architects of the period. A recently discovered full-fledged High Georgian mansion of 1895 on Jones Hill in Dorchester by William G. Preston strikingly contrasts with his forbiddingly Medieval First Cadet Corps Armory of the same year in Park Square. Looking at these contrasts in the work of the same architects, one thinks of Walter Kidney's observation that after 1900

a house was usually Georgian, Tudor, or Cotswold (Anglo-Saxon home atmosphere), unless it was a mansion and intended to look like one, in which case it might have been Jacobean or one of the Louis (aristocracy of wealth). A church — if not Colonial — would, for an old and ritualistic sect, be Gothic (Christian heritage); if it was for some new sect, like the Christian Scientists, it might be decently but non-committally wrapped in something classical. A synagogue, in absence of a true Hebraic architecture, was usually Byzantine or Moorish. A school was Tudor or Jacobean (Oxford, Eton). A theatre was either Louis XV (courtly diversions) or — especially if a movie house — something utterly fantastic, with some sort of high-pressure Mediterranean Baroque providing the norm (palace of illusions). For the center city, classicism was long the near-universal solution; a cluster of styles, rather than a single style, it clothed the museum, the library, the memorial structure in cool eternal beauty, but broke into rustications, ressauts, and swags, giant orders and Renaissance cornices for the more worldly office buildings, the bank, the apartment house, the theatre, the clubhouse, and the town mansion.

Quite distinguished architects even went so far as to essay one style on the exterior and another on the interior. Arthur Bowditch's extremely sparse exterior and vaguely Sullivanesque entrance arch at the Hotel Somerset does not prepare one for Little and Browne's opulent gilt Louis XIV ballroom within. Nor does the red-brick Georgian exterior of the second Fogg Art Museum, designed by the Shepley office in 1925, hint at the sixteenth-century Italian courtyard inside. To us this may seem incongruous,

but we vastly enjoy it. The truth is that the eclectics' creed is by no means dead.

Kidney's parenthetical asides — "Anglo-Saxon home atmosphere," "Christian heritage," "courtly diversions" — are the key to understanding the eclectics' creed. It is true that during this period well-traveled and well-educated architects, with well-stocked libraries of measured drawings and photographs of seemingly everything ever built and an endless supply of excellent immigrant craftsmen, coincided with clients equally well-traveled and well-educated and (until 1930) with more money than they often knew what to do with. It is also true that building beauty, as it were, was the high goal of many dedicated architects whose clients, insecure nouveaux riches, sought to build a kind of instant baronial heritage. But all these factors do not explain the stylistic diversity we are discussing. Kidney's asides do, for in Boston as elsewhere, just as the pervasive stylistic unity of the Greek Revival, for example, had reflected a homogeneous culture, so architectural eclecticism reflected the increasingly pluralistic culture that emerged at the end of the nineteenth century. Within the context of this cultural pluralism eclectic architects —meaning, substantially, all architects between 1890 and 1930 — argued that no one style could possibly be expressive and thus functional in every case for every building. One might continue to design Classical government buildings for the same reason Bulfinch had, because of Classicism's associations with Athens and the Roman Republic. Gothic churches were another example. But the eclectics pointed out that the country was far too diffuse culturally to rally as a whole in every case to any one style —including Sullivan's or Wright's. They did so because until the 1930s most continued to believe that the historical associations of a style were crucial to a building's functional expression, provided all the modern conveniences were worked into it. That was the eclectics' creed, and it proved an extraordinarily resilient idea: Everyman's definition of form follows function for many years, it was abandoned by architects only amid the financial trauma of the Depression and it has not been entirely abandoned yet — as numberless "Tudor" motels and "Colonial" restaurants attest — by the general public.

Only recently, however, have critics and scholars begun to take this controversial assertion seriously again and to try to judge eclecticism by its own standards. There are signs that the results may be startling. Some argue, for instance, that many of the innovations of the Shingle Style survived after all into the 1920s in the much maligned eclectic "Period House" in the suburbs. Jonathan Lane has asserted: "the early Period House took over with little modification the most advanced planning of the shingled houses of the eighties" and that between 1890 and 1930 the design of the Period House was marked by a gradual development from which

emerged three concepts in residential planning which survived the reaction against Eclecticism in the early thirties to influence profoundly the further evolution of domestic architecture in the United States — the open plan, the use of rambling, one-story designs [the horizontal dwelling unit whose development was also traced in Chapter 5], and the provision of outdoor living areas. The introduction of these ideas has been generally associated with the work of those architects who rejected eclecticism in the early thirties and who, at least initially, drew much of their inspiration from contemporary European architecture. It has not been fully recognized that these innovations first achieved considerable currency here at a time when the influence of eclecticism was paramount . . . !

A factor that contributed strongly to the integrity of this eclectic architecture was the remarkable contribution made by the artists' crafts (the Boston Society of Arts and Crafts, founded in 1897, was the first such society in the country). The superb quality of craftsmanship and of the artistry of the Public Library (Figures 140–142); of the chancel and Lady Chapel of All Saints at Ashmont (Figure 177); of Little and Browne's interiors at the Somerset Club, the Brandegee House at Faulkner Farm, and the Hotel Somerset; the finish of the Lindsey Chapel (Figure 183); the decoration of the Colonial Theatre (Plate 3) and the cut-stone detail of the west porch of Trinity Church (with figure sculpture for the Shepley office by Hugh Cairns and Domingo Mora under John Evans) — such things were seen then as they are coming to be seen again as very beautiful. Nor were such splendors restricted to great civic and religious buildings. Evans did superb cut-stone detail for the Ames Building. Such architects as Carrère and Hastings, McKim, Mead and White, and Cram and Ferguson designed a number of elaborate mansions on Boston's North Shore, discreetly hidden at the ends of private roads (particularly in Beverly, Manchester, and Gloucester). Hitchcock divulged a well-kept Boston secret when he remarked of these houses that "together they almost rival Newport." C. Howard Walker's interiors on the tenth floor of the Ditson Building (1916) at 178–179 Tremont Street include architectural carving by Kirchmayer himself. Henry Wilson, whose doors at St. John the Divine in New York have been so much admired, modeled a set of bronze doors (Figure 202) made by Gorham in 1929 — showing the history of the tea trade — for the Salada Tea Building near Park Square in Boston, designed by Densmore, Le Clear and Robbins. Overlooked by most today, these doors earned a Silver Medal at the Paris Salon in 1927. Undeniably the most magnificent of their type in Boston, they are among the major works of a distin-

FIGURE 202. The great bronze doors of the Salada Tea Building on Stuart Street near Park Square are the work of British sculptor Henry Wilson and were cast by the Gorham Company in 1929. The panels depict the Ceylonese tea trade, and the framing figures represent Indian deities. The cut-stone detail around the doors, the work of French sculptor Caesar Caira, is dominated by statues of Demeter, Triptolemus, and Persephone.
FIGURE 203. Allen and Collens. Newton City Hall, 1932.

guished British sculptor who did very little work in the United States.

Thus between 1890 and 1930 Boston accumulated many variations of many things: ranging from the Classical dome of the Pantheon at M.I.T. (Figure 153) to the Romanesque Church of St. Trophîme at Arles that was the inspiration for the Shepley firm's west porch at Trinity Church. Nor was any secret made of such things — though sometimes the aptness of the model might be questioned. There is in the January 1916 issue of the *Boston Society of Architects Journal* a solemn protest against the convenience station newly erected on Boston Common, and judged to be "a fairly close copy of the Music Pavilion in the Gardens of the Petit Trianon at Versailles." Several architects protested that it was "an impropriety to copy one of the most elegant architectural monuments of the

past for a public urinal." (Just which historical model might have been more appropriate does not seem to have been considered; Osbert Lancaster points out that the ecclesiastical baptistry was a widespread model for British convenience stations — but not approvingly.) Usually, however, the historical association of a style was a clear guide. The Georgian Revival, for example, reached its climax in Boston not in domestic work but in public and collegiate design in the 1920s and 1930s.

The patriotic associations of Georgian naturally made that style particularly popular for civic buildings, especially in suburbs that wished to avoid monumental urban Classicism. Boston's suburbs abound in such buildings: two particularly fine Georgian examples of this period are the Weston Town Hall (1917) designed by Bigelow and Wadsworth, and that of Needham (1930) by Winslow and Bigelow. One of the most extensive is the Newton City Hall and War Memorial Building (Figure 203). It was designed by Allen and Collens and includes a spacious Aldermanic Chamber modeled on Independence Hall in Philadelphia. Indeed, the passion for things Colonial peaked in the 1920s in a number of remarkable ways. Henry Ford's much publicized restoration in the mid-1920s of the Wayside Inn in the Boston suburb of Sudbury was one local repercussion of a national movement Boston strongly influenced. It was a Boston architectural firm, Perry, Shaw and Hepburn (the designers in 1926–1928 of the Roxbury Latin School in West Roxbury and also in 1929 of Longfellow Hall at Radcliffe in Cambridge), who began in the 1920s the restoration at Williamsburg that has subsequently exercised so wide an influence on American taste. Both the Henry Francis du Pont Winterthur Museum at Winterthur, Delaware, and the American Wing at the Metropolitan Museum of Art in New York, which opened in 1924, were decisively influenced by Henry Davis Sleeper's remarkable ensemble of period rooms and artifacts at Beauport, his Gloucester home. In Boston this Colonial enthusiasm also coalesced with a similar passion for things maritime in the really extraordinary new "counting house" opened on State Street in 1928 by the State Street Trust Company, where one may yet transact one's affairs, in a building where oak and pine paneling, antique lanterns, and ship models combine to create an environment virtually unique in Boston business. The building itself was designed by Parker, Thomas and Rice; the interiors by Richardson, Barott and Richardson.

Greater Boston also possesses a Medieval reconstruction, Hammond Castle (1928) in Gloucester, designed by Allen and Collens, who also built The Cloisters in New York. But it is for its Colonial enthusiasms that the 1920s are best known, and their effect has been long-lasting; so much so that the chaste Colonialisms of Royal Barry Wills remained popular into the post–World War II period. Work in this vein by Wills and others (including many by the Shepley office) may be seen throughout Greater Boston: in Wilmington, Hanover, Bedford, Dover, Randolph, Medfield, the Bridgewaters, Abington, and particularly in Scituate, Lynnfield, Sharon, and Needham. No "period house" was as popular as the "Colonial" house, and this was especially so in the famous old Colonial towns-become-suburbs such as Lexington. More buildings in such towns than many visitors realize — for example, Frohman, Robb and Little's Trinitarian Congregational Church in Concord — date from the twentieth and not the eighteenth century. Vivid commercial variations on a Colonial theme have also survived the war, and some of these have become almost indelible images of vernacular America in the twentieth century. Perhaps the best-known such image to have originated in Boston during the twenties and thirties is Joseph Morgan's Colonial Revival design for the roadside restaurants of Howard Johnson; one of the earliest of these (ca. 1938) to feature the now ubiquitous orange roof (originally the idea of the designer Maurice Gianni) still stands at 2790 Washington Street in Canton. But throughout this period the most distinguished Georgian venture in Boston was undertaken at Harvard, so much so that this work is a excellent case study in the methods and mores of eclecticism.

H ARVARD YARD, venerable even in 1900, by which time it had served America's oldest college for nearly 270 years, was distinctly imperiled at the turn of the twentieth century. The once peaceful enclave was increasingly surrounded by noise and bustle. And more had fled, a great many thought, than just peace and quiet. No one regretted the fact that Eliot had by his pioneering emphasis on postgraduate study transformed Harvard from a small college into a great university; the foundation, in fact, of Boston's new greatness. But many, including Eliot's successor, Abbott Lawrence Lowell, regretted deeply that the more continental university tradition (which offered students only lectures, otherwise encouraging them to fend for themselves) was undermining what was left of Harvard's British collegiate tradition of communal living and learning. A crucial factor in a liberal arts education, which sought to instill values as well as facts and to encourage a broad cultural awareness, this tradition had languished under Eliot. At the same time many others felt, as the Overseers noted in 1894, that Eliot's rather erratic architectural development of the university had resulted in buildings so "inharmonious in style" that it was destroying Harvard's character. A number of people concluded that the two problems were not unrelated; that the haphazard character of the school's architectural development was closely related to Harvard's increasing diffusiveness as the collegiate tradition languished.

It was in this context that Charles McKim introduced the Georgian Revival into Harvard in his design of 1889 for the Johnston Gate. The gate's location, between Massachusetts Hall (1718) and Harvard Hall (1764), seemed to McKim to invite a Georgian design, and he endowed the new gate (and several more in the Yard he designed thereafter) not only with his usual excellence of design but with the same concern for materials that is characteristic of the Boston Public Library. Charles Moore noted that the "color and texture and form on the New Hampshire brick were the subject of ex-

periment and repeated trials, with results so satisfactory that the term 'Harvard Brick' came to be applied to them." Nor did McKim make any secret of his desire to "bring Harvard back to bricks and mortar" and to just appreciation of her oldest Colonial work, where "simplicity, appropriateness and proportions were cardinal features." It was this lead that the Shepley office followed four years later in its design of two dormitories, Perkins and Conant halls to the north of the Yard on either side of Oxford Street in 1893. These were Harvard's first Georgian Revival buildings. The new mode reached a climax, however, in 1900 in McKim's Harvard Union, where the goal of restoring the "collegiate way" first coincided with a full-blooded, lavishly detailed Georgian Revival.

Again, an important new idea lay behind the Union: the second such facility to be built in this country and the first actually to be called a "union," McKim's huge and elaborate dining hall (which clearly inspired Parker, Thomas and Rice's dining room of 1912 at the Harvard Club of Boston on Commonwealth Avenue) was intended to revive the collegiate way at Harvard. One gets a keen sense of how important a role the Union's architecture played in its function from Santayana's remark (not suprising in view of his dislike of Queen Anne design) in a letter to a friend about "the chorus of praise we are raising about the big new room at the Union. It is the only noble room in the college and will give many people here their first notion of what good architecture means." The movements in aid of "Harvard Brick" and Harvard College seemed thus to coincide perfectly, and whichever may have begat the other, the results, both social and architectural, doubtless seemed too felicitous to be only coincidence. The adherents of the collegiate way, pining for the cohesion of the eighteenth-century Yard, did not resist

Coolidge, Shepley, Bulfinch and Abbott. The
Houses of Harvard College, Cambridge.
FIGURE 204. The Great Court of Lowell
House, 1929.
FIGURE 205. Right to left: Dunster (1929),
Leverett (1925–1930), and Winthrop
(1913–1930) Houses as seen from the Charles
River. To the right of the bridge is McKin-
lock Hall at Leverett House.

McKim's admiration for the Yard's eighteenth-century architecture; once, that is, he had demonstrated at the Union that the spirit of the old work could be plausibly caught on the much larger scale required by twentieth-century Harvard.

Henceforth, for three and more decades, Harvard Brick and Harvard College became synonymous, almost sacramental; the former the outward and visible sign of the inward and spiritual grace. The Yard itself was closed to traffic and screened from the noisy streets around it by long rows of harmonious Georgian dormitories and gates erected in 1924–1930 by the Shepley office. When Lowell determined that the only way to preserve the collegiate way was to build a series of freshman halls (in 1913) along the Charles River and was then able to develop around these halls a whole new series of "colleges within the college," he commissioned Charles A. Coolidge of the Shepley firm virtually to re-create the eighteenth-century Yard all over again along the river, but on a much grander scale and around a series of Georgian quads, the architectural harmony of which he hoped would exhibit a "dignity and grace of a kind to impress and refine those who enter [its] courts, dining halls and libraries." Yet there was more to the new Houses than gracious communal living. Again, as at McKim's Public Library there was a new and vital idea behind it all, for the "Houses," as these small colleges within Harvard College are called, were an integral part of radical academic innovations by Lowell, built around a new tutorial system. Similarly, Coolidge did more than re-create the old Yard.

It is not hard to see that the river Houses not only recall the Yard, but often relate as well quite clearly to specific buildings there. The elaborate mantling on Dunster House is similar to that of Holden Chapel (1742); the Lowell House Dining Room is reminiscent of the Fac-

ulty Room in University Hall, designed by Bulfinch in 1813. Precedents from further afield are also evident: the Old State House (Figure 206) in Boston is startlingly apparent (see Figure 205) at McKinlock Hall; Lowell's tower seems to have been modeled on that of Independence Hall in Philadelphia; Eliot's cupola derives from that of the New York City Hall; and the river front of Gore Hall will seem very familiar to anyone who has even briefly seen Wren's seventeenth-century palace front at Hampton Court. Despite this, Bainbridge Bunting and Robert Nylander note that "the remarkable thing is how individualistic yet how harmonious" the whole range of houses seem and how hard it is to believe that they were built within sixteen years by one firm. Their analysis of Lowell House (Figure 204), for example, justly conveys the quality of Coolidge's work.

Since Lowell House consists of two quadrangles completely enclosed by massive buildings, the result could have been confining and monotonous. Such a feeling is skilful exploitation of natural irregularities in the topography and by the masterful way the massing of buildings on different sides of the quadrangles are varied. The entrance under the tower is at the highest elevation, and here also the block of buildings is at its greatest height: four stories, a raised cornice, and a high basement. . . . The dining hall and [common room] on the opposite (south) side of the court not only rise from lower ground but are of a single story in height. In this manner one seems to look over the roof of these lower buildings when entering the enclosure. Units on the east and west sides of the court are placed at intermediate levels so that there is constant variation in floor heights, and the wing on the east is lower than the other because it forms one side of the smaller quadrangle. The master's house in the southwest corner is also differentiated in massing. Furthermore, the two courts are connected by interesting vaulted passageways which change levels; thus the spaces of these quadrangles are varied and flowing rather than static and restrictive.

Eliot House, with its great hexagonal

court, is also distinguished. Nor do we pay enough attention to the fact that Hicks House at Kirkland (now the House library) and Apthorp House at Adams (the Master's Residence) are early and significant examples of not only saving eighteenth-century structures but using them in new and imaginative ways. At Adams House the Shepley office also sensitively incorporated not only Apthorp House but — what is remarkable for the 1930s — two rather exotic late Victorian apartment buildings as well as their own new Georgian work into a most improbable but in the end very successful ensemble. Adams House, all the Houses, are a notable architectural achievement. Not only did the Shepley office improve on the old Yard; they referred to one of the Yard's own models and H. A. Yeomans did not exaggerate when he wrote that "anyone who stands today on the Western Avenue Bridge and looks upstream will see something that may not unfitly be compared to the spires of Oxford." Indeed, the gathering Houses of Harvard, their towers lifting among the trees and reflected in the long sweep of the river, form the most magnificent architectural vista that Greater Boston affords (Figure 205).

The parallel vista along the Allston side is in no sense comparable, for the Harvard Business School (1924) by McKim's successor office (still under the name of McKim, Mead and White), though beautiful in the effect of its great court, does not possess the character and distinction of the Shepley Houses. The eclectic creed, that the successful building needed to be couched in a style whose historical associations expressed the building's function, was like all architectural creeds dependent in the event on the skill and vitality of the designer. The Shepley office simply designed the better ensemble. And from the eclectic point of view their reminiscences of eighteenth-century buildings were not disappointing. For the shapes one recognizes are quite differently organized; the details one has seen before are quite differently dispersed; and both are only a part of volumes and voids, of spaces and of plans that are the architect's own. The Harvard Houses are a singularly beautiful adaptation whose quality remains important to Harvard College today. And they reflect the fact, now often overlooked, that though the eclectic considered himself heir to an accumulated architectural vocabulary of many centuries, it was in his own mind his vocation to be the master and not the slave of that accumulated treasury of forms and details. Thus he saw no more need to invent a new vocabulary than does the poet, who does not invent new words or even necessarily new forms in order to write new poetry. For the eclectic, all the varying modes of the architectural vocabulary he had inherited, whether Classical or Gothic, were fundamentally timeless.

9

THE BOSTON RIALTO

THE EXPANDING METROPOLIS had yielded Boston by the early twentieth century two dramatic new "built environments": vast sprawling streetcar suburbs such as Dorchester and Jamaica Plain and densely built-up apartment districts such as on Commonwealth Avenue in Brighton, Park Drive in the Back Bay Fens, and Beacon Street in Brookline. In response to these, a third new "built environment" emerged in the heart of the old city, the scale of which would have astonished any previous generation; for by 1900, from Tremont Street toward State Street, Boston had transformed itself into a great metropolitan rialto. On Beacon Hill, in the Back Bay, in the South End, the old scale remained. But downtown, what remained after the Great Fire of 1872 of Boston's eighteenth- and nineteenth-century buildings no longer seemed quite the same. The elegant Old State House of 1711–1747, for example, began in the 1880s to be dwarfed on every side by great ranges of office buildings that by 1900 towered over it menacingly (Figures 206, 207).

The result was a network of canyons whose real style was "downtown." Some of the consequences of this we will touch on in our discussion in the next chapter of the ways in which the skyscraper sought sunlight. At this point it is simply the sheer size and radical new scale that concerns us. Peabody and Stearns's Exchange Building on State Street, for example, was built to include 1100 offices in 1887 — more offices in one building in 1887 than there had been brick houses in all of Boston 165 years earlier. Many such buildings were built to be little towns of sorts: the Old South Building, on Washington Street between Milk and Water streets, designed by Arthur Bowditch in 1902, and the Little Building, on the corner of Tremont and Boylston streets, the work of C. H. Blackall in 1916, are excellent examples. Each was designed with lavishly detailed exterior shops and extensive interior arcades on the lower two floors: filled with small shops then as they still are now, these and such later examples as the Park Square Building (1923), designed by Densmore, Le Clear and Robbins, are among the most successful and exciting urban spaces in Boston. It is to be hoped they will survive long enough to be restored one day — now that the Quincy Market has revived our interest in this time-honored urban amenity.

Other building types that illustrate the tremendous new scale of intown are the railroad station (Figure 208), the department store, and the hotel. R. H. White's store, designed by Peabody and Stearns in 1877, and Jordan Marsh, whose main store was the work of S. J. F. Thayer in 1880, are gone, but something of their pomp survives in Filene's (Figure 196) and in the R. H. Stearns Building, designed by Parker, Thomas and Rice in 1908, and in the Paine Furniture Company Building at

Park Square, the work of Densmore and Le Clear in 1912. (Even less remains of the elegant street-floor shops of this period, more of which are obliterated each year. Only one original shop survives at the Little Building. It is to be hoped that the nearby shop fronts on Boylston Street of what was lately the Wurlitzer Store and of the Boston Music Company will survive, and every effort should be made to preserve the handsome Victorian shop fronts — one including protruding glass display windows enhanced with stained glass — at the Old South Building.) Boston's late nineteenth- and early twentieth-century hotels have fared somewhat better. This is particularly fortuitous because Boston has a long tradition of distinction in hotel design reaching back to Isaiah Rogers, "the father of the American hotel," whose Tremont House of 1828 (it stood opposite the Parker House; see Figure 1) was credited by Jefferson Williamson with being "indisputably the first definitely recognized example of the modern first class hotel." It amazed Charles Dickens, who thought it possessed "more galleries, colonnades, piazzas and passages than he could remember or the reader believe."

In the late nineteenth and early twentieth centuries there followed a series of magnificent hotels, the most important of which — the Vendome (1871, 1881), the Touraine (1897–1898), the Somerset (1897), the Copley Plaza (1912) — have all been touched on previously. These, in turn, were then in some sense surpassed by Blackall's Hotel Kenmore of 1915 and by the three major hotels that opened between March and May of 1927: the new Parker House, designed by Desmond and Lord; the 1100-room Statler Hotel (now the Park Plaza), the work of the noted New York firm G. B. Post and Sons; and the Ritz-Carlton Hotel. Not only have all these survived, but also, in the case of the Copley Plaza and the Parker House, so have their splendid interiors. Both have lately been compromised in places by spurious "restorations" (which included at the Parker House *removing* the crystal chandeliers of the main dining room), but one can at least be grateful that so much of each hotel has survived. Victorian interiors also endure in several Boston restaurants and shops unconnected with hotels: the most important is the lavishly detailed mahogany dining room of 1886 at Locke-Ober on Winter Place, but Wirth's on Stuart Street also possesses some handsome late nineteenth-century woodwork. Other nineteenth- and early twentieth-century interiors include the Marliave, on Bosworth Place, which still retains many original features, and Slagle's, an almost perfectly preserved Victorian lunchroom on Spring Lane, established in 1877 as Wyman's. Its present interior dates from 1902. (Another interior and front of note survive at Little and Rogers's Singer Sewing Machine store at 55 Temple Place.)

Other intown building types one might explore are the massive bank buildings so characteristic of the financial district, such as York and Sawyer's now demolished First National Bank (1924) and McKim, Mead and White's New England Trust Company (1905), and the distinctive "downtown" church type, built in office-building fashion right upon the sidewalk, often with stores on the ground floor. Tremont Temple, designed by Blackall in 1895, is the best example. But the building type that perhaps best illustrates the new function of "downtown" as a metropolitan rialto is the theater. Focusing on theaters is also an excellent way to conclude this discussion of revivalism by touching on the exuberant Baroque manner characteristic of theater design, an aspect of Boston's architectural history that was nationally influential and has for too long been overlooked.

A dramatic illustration of the changing scale
of nineteenth-century Boston: the Old State
House and its environs.

FIGURE 206. About 1870. The second building
from the left is the Brazer's Building.

FIGURE 207. About 1900, looking down State
Street from Broad Street.

FIGURE 208. Another example of the city's rapid growth in the late
nineteenth century: the great Union Station on Causeway Street. The three-
turreted structure to the left, behind which stretched a 700-foot-long
train shed, was designed by E. A. P. Newcomb in 1871–1878 as the Lowell
Station. To the right is the enlargement of 1894 by Shepley, Rutan and
Coolidge, which created the Union Station by linking the old Lowell Station
with yet another station to the far right. The entire Union Station was
demolished in 1927, when North Station and Boston Garden were erected.

Boston's first theaters, including the famous halls touched on in Chapter 2, invariably reflected the dominant style of their period. Bulfinch's Boston Theatre of 1794 (Figure 9), the first American theater designed by a native professional architect, was, as we saw in Chapter 1, a splendid Neoclassical landmark. The Tremont Theatre of 1827 by Isaiah Rogers was Greek Revival, with the full temple front characteristic of that style. The Howard of 1847, also by Rogers, was a notable theater long before it became (as the Old Howard) perhaps the most famous burlesque theater in the world. Though its Gothic facade was probably unique in the history of American theater architecture, it also reflected the fashion of the period. And the Boston Museum (Figure 22), designed in 1846 by Hammatt and Joseph Billings, was one of the most elegant Italianate buildings of its time. Even the High Victorian period left its mark on theater building in Sanders Theatre. A part of Ware and Van Brunt's Memorial Hall at Harvard (Figure 57), Sanders was modeled freely on the Sheldonian at Oxford, and has been called the "finest Shakespearean theatre in the world." By 1900, however, eclecticism was characteristic of theaters as of all building types in Boston.

Between 1900 and 1935, twenty-four major theaters and concert halls (leaving aside dozens of minor theaters and halls) were built along the intown rialto — startling evidence of how the theater district and "downtown" generally were growing during this period. Thirteen of these were clustered in the new Theatre District that emerged during this period on lower Tremont and Washington streets. Another concentration of halls appeared uptown, revolving around the Symphony Hall–Jordan Hall–Opera House cluster of 1900–1910. Two of the handsomest of the new playhouses were chiefly Georgian in inspiration — the

Wilbur on Tremont Street, designed by Blackall in 1914, and the Repertory (now the Boston University Theatre) on Huntington Avenue, designed in 1925 by J. Williams Beal's Sons. The Wilbur (Figure 209) is itself, however, a fine example of discreet eclecticism: its three well-proportioned portals and the scheme of two engaged columns framed in pilasters and pediments often seem familiar to Bostonians — who can be forgiven for not realizing why: the portals derive from a well-known Beacon Hill landmark, the Thomas Bailey Aldrich House of 1837 at 59 Mount Vernon Street (Figure 15). (Perhaps Blackall knew that Aldrich was one of Edwin Booth's closest friends.) Yet the Wilbur's facade is not merely derivative. One critic observed that the blind windows, for instance, were "something between cleverness and inspiration." The interior is as fine; the auditorium is in its chaste way the handsomest of any Boston playhouse. Steinert Hall, on the other hand, built on Boylston Street in 1896 from the designs of Winslow and Wetherell, is more monumental in its Classicism, while many of the forms and details of the Shubert on Tremont Street, designed in 1910 by Thomas M. James, reflect that architect's admiration for the Petit Trianon at Versailles. But the flamboyant and opulent Classicism so characteristic of theater design was early essayed at those two remarkable theaters built within three years of each other on either side of the corner of Tremont and Boylston — Blackall's Colonial Theatre and John Galen Howard's Majestic Theatre.

The erection of the Colonial, in 1899–1900, was enough of an architectural event to have been marked by a long series of articles by Blackall in *American Architect* and by a special tour of the new theater by Blackall for the Boston Society of Architects. After the tour, according to *The British Architect* in London, which reported the event, both

Two distinguished Downtown playhouses.
FIGURE 209. Clarence H. Blackall.
Architect's perspective of the Wilbur Theatre,
252 Tremont Street, 1914.
FIGURE 210. John Galen Howard and J. M.
Wood. Majestic (now Saxon) Theatre, 219
Tremont Street, 1903. Proscenium
boxes show original and no longer
extant lambrequins.

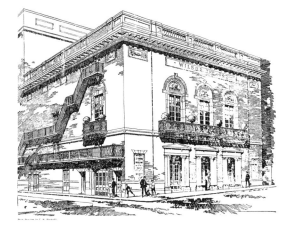

Blackall and H. B. Pennell (who decorated the interior) gave papers on the Colonial's design at a meeting of the society. The oldest theater of any sort in Boston continuously operated under the same name, was ever a name less apt? Far from evoking Boston's venerable Colonial architecture, this now richly storied playhouse, celebrated for its associations with Irving Berlin and Sigmund Romberg, where Ziegfeld launched his Follies and where Rodgers and Hammerstein opened so many triumphs, is as sumptuous and elegant as any of the productions that have played there (Plate 3). Its lavish carved detail is the work of the John Evans Company, whose other Boston work includes the cut-stone detail at Trinity Church and much of the exterior and interior detail of the Boston Public Library and All Saints, Ashmont. The extensive sequence of murals is in type and period unique in any Boston theater or concert hall and represents an attempt to introduce into theater building in Boston the integral architectural art of the Bos-

ton Public Library. It includes three paintings in the lobby after the style of Boucher by Newton Wells and a series of landscapes above the door-heads by Victor Durando. Another and better-known artist, Marian Peabody, executed the work over the door-head in the ladies' room, where an otherwise unknown B. Tojetti did the ceiling panel. The great frieze in the dome of the auditorium (the three standing figures represent Tradition, Truth, and Inspiration, between pairs of figures representing the dances) was painted by Herman Schladermundt, who is perhaps best known for his mosaic vaults at the Library of Congress in Washington. Schladermundt and his assistants also executed the four seated female figures in the adjoining circles, which are entitled "Epic Poetry," "History," "Tragedy," and "Comic or Pastoral Verse." Pennell himself painted the act-drop. The effect of all this, amid satinwood paneling, blue-green satin wall hangings, and delicately toned and subdued gold, must have been stunning in 1900. It still is. And since the Colonial is the oldest Boston theater to survive intact, as splendid now as it was nearly eighty years ago, it would be hard to exaggerate its architectural importance. It was, incidentally, at a performance of the Ziegfeld Follies at the Colonial that John Singer Sargent selected three chorus girls to pose for the Danaïdes, who carry water jars in his lunette above the entrance to the library in the great staircase hall of the second Museum of Fine Arts.

Around the corner on Tremont Street, the Majestic Theatre (now the Saxon) is by no means as well preserved, for the Numidian marble lobby (with murals by the well-known New York painter William de Leftwich Dodge) has been covered over by a modern veneer. Enough survives, however, to make the Majestic (Figure 210) unique. The second of three benefactions to Boston (the others were Jordan Hall and the Opera House) by Eben Jordan, the owner of Jordan Marsh, the Majestic is the only known local work of John Galen Howard, who, after M.I.T., the Ecole des Beaux Arts, and an apprenticeship with H. H. Richardson, sought his opportunity out West, where he became professor of advanced design and head of the School of Architecture at the University of California at Berkeley. Howard was already well-known when he designed the Majestic, and it cannot have hurt his growing reputation. He did not attempt the refined elegance of the Colonial. Instead, behind a florid, monumental facade, he designed a playhouse Elliot Norton once called a theater of artifice and exaggeration; a theater whose lavish rococo auditorium, unmatched in Boston, was also in its day innovative in its exploitation of electricity. Rather than simulating older forms of illumination (candelabra, for instance), the electric fixtures are integrated into the architectural fabric, anticipating the movie palace genre of some years later. The interior is chiefly lit (as originally designed) by softly

glowing glass globes set into garlanded arches that bend sensuously over the auditorium, which for this reason seems to resemble an inverted bowl — an effect that is all the more intimate for its lavish detail. In a very real sense the Colonial and the Majestic were sufficiently sumptuous that nothing else of the same scale could have surpassed them. But another and much grander scale became necessary as Boston grew and it was on this scale that flamboyant Classicism — "Mediterranean Baroque" as Walter Kidney called it — erupted in the 1920s into the astounding architecture of the movie palace, the building type above all that illustrates most vividly the growth and importance of the downtown rialto.

The huge hall of several thousand seats was by no means new to Boston in the early twentieth century. As we saw in Chapter 2, in the mid-nineteenth century Boston was endowed with two huge halls: the 2000-seat Music Hall (now the Orpheum) of 1852 and the 3000-seat second Boston Theatre (now destroyed) of 1854 (Figure 25). At the Music Hall Bostonians thronged to see such notables as Oscar Wilde (in 1882) and to hear such important musical events as the world premiere of Tchaikovsky's Piano Concerto no. 1 in 1875. It was at a concert in this hall that Henry Lee Higginson discovered what Walter Muir Whitehill has called "the key to his great design," the founding of the Boston Symphony Orchestra, which played its first concert at the Music Hall in 1881. The New England Conservatory of Music, the first college of music founded in the United States, was started at the Music Hall in 1867.

In terms of drama and opera, the same significance attaches to the Boston Theatre, the grand staircase of which on opening night was once described as "a confusion of beauty, splendor and fashion." Virtually every important star of

211

the time played the Boston, including Sarah Bernhardt, Maurice Barrymore, Lillie Langtry, James O'Neill (Eugene O'Neill's father, and Edwin Booth, who was appearing at the Boston, in fact, the night his brother shot Lincoln. Paderewski also played there, and Victor Herbert in some of his earliest appearances. It was, however, for opera that the Boston is chiefly remembered. In size and splendor it was an opera house and it was at the Boston Theatre that Bostonians first heard *Die Walküre,* in 1877; Massenet's *Manon,* in 1886, only one year after its American premiere in New York; *La Bohème,* in 1899, three years after its world premiere; the complete *Ring of the Nibelung,* in 1899; and in 1910, *Tosca,* ten years after its world premiere in Rome. The Metropolitan Opera first played the Boston Theatre in 1883, in the year of the Met's founding, and in subsequent years under this and other companies' auspices all the legendary divas, including Calvé, Melba, Gadski, and Lehman, sang at the Boston. Gustav Mahler conducted *Don Giovanni* there, and Caruso made his local debut on the Boston's stage. Memorable civic events also occurred at the Boston, including the Grand Ball given for the future King Edward VII during his visit to Boston in 1860 while still Prince of Wales.

The man who more than anyone else brought the whole of Greater Boston flocking downtown in the 1880s and 1890s was Benjamin Keith. A door or two away from the Boston on Washington Street, in 1883, he and another young man, Edward Albee, started a storefront "museum" of curiosities that eventually revolutionized American entertainment. The only eyewitness account of Keith's storefront museum is that of George Upham, who remembered that "Keith himself introduced the acts in this house and Mrs. Keith kept it clean." The underlying reason for Keith's increasing success was that he seized upon the preference of most Bostonians for family variety shows no minister or priest could object to and at the same time insisted upon first-quality acts that were not only decent but exciting. Moreover, because of his revolutionary concept of "continuous performances" he was able to do so at low prices. It was a winning combination, and in 1894 Keith was able to build right next to the Boston the B. F. Keith Theatre that would become known in later years as "the mother house of American vaudeville."

Conventional enough in appearance, the new Keith was revolutionary in concept. The first attempt (much ridiculed at the time) to appropriate the splendors of the opera house for "lowly, despised variety entertainment," the new theater (only a part of the lobby of which survives today) was designed by the New York architect J. B. McElfatrick, whose remodeling of the Metropolitan Opera House had been so much admired. A stunning success, the Keith was a landmark in the history of American theater building. Such palatial theaters became a crucial part of the Keith vaudeville formulas, and a phenomenon that in its own right and in terms of its later effect on movie design exercised an enormous influence on American vernacular culture in the first decades of the twentieth century. Eventually, there were nearly four hundred, including the famous Palace in New York — and one of these was the proud old Boston Theatre, which finally surrendered to Keith in 1909. At the same time Keith endowed the Bijou (a second-floor theater that was between the Keith and the Boston) with its famous "crystal staircase" made of glass. Underneath, lit by multicolored electric bulbs, was a cascading waterfall. Thus he created a three-theater complex that seated 7000 people. It seems today to have been the immediate prototype of the movie palace.

The first of these movie palaces to be

FIGURE 211. Clarence H. Blackall. Modern (later the Mayflower) Theatre, 523 Washington Street, Downtown, 1914. The theater, including the facade shown here, is a remodeling of the lower floors of an earlier building designed by Levi Newcomb.

FIGURE 212. Thomas Lamb. B. F. Keith Memorial (now the Savoy) Theatre, between Washington and Tremont streets, Downtown, 1928. This theater is built in part upon the foundations of the famous Boston Theatre of 1854 (Figure 25) and largely follows the plan of the Boston, itself a successor to Bulfinch's original playhouse of 1793–1794 (Figure 9), which was Boston's first theater.

created was the old Music Hall. When a plan to cut a street through seemed to threaten its existence, no one rushed to its defense; instead, the chance was seized to build Symphony Hall. The projected street was never built, however, and doubtless to the embarrassment of many, the old Music Hall survived and prospered, as a vaudeville theater, of all things, complete with an elaborate new stage and two new deep balconies, designed by Little and Browne in 1900, that incorporated the long, shallow concert-hall balconies into rows of boxes. In 1904 Arthur Vinal undertook another remodeling, enclosing the boxes in elaborate enframements, and the following year he designed the still extant Washington Street entrance and lobby to mark the Music Hall's new name — the Empire. In 1906 the present name was adopted, and it remained the Orpheum even after it had caught the eye of Marcus Loew, who bought the theater and commissioned Thomas Lamb in 1915 to remodel it into a movie palace. The result, though stylistically Adamesque, nonetheless included a crystal proscenium arch lit by hundreds of electric lights that has survived to this day. Boston's first concert hall is thus also her first movie palace, and its occasional exuberance — particularly in the imaginative use of electricity — can now be seen as early indications of how enormously movie palace architects would enlarge Keith's concept of a palace for Everyman. Other and smaller movie houses of the time — Blackall's Modern Theatre of 1914 on Washington Street (Figure 211), Lamb's Fenway Theatre of 1915 on Massachusetts Avenue, and Funk and Wilcox's Strand Theatre (1918) at Upham's Corner in Dorchester (probably the city's first movie palace built from the ground up as opposed to a remodeling) — sought a chaste Classical elegance. So too had the first downtown "deluxers," the Washington Street and

Scollay Square Olympias (1912 and 1915). But their sensuously undulating marquees, the more exotic for their introduction to the Boston rialto of electricity as a part of exterior design, were significant. In the early 1920s another Adamesque movie palace, Loew's State, was designed by Thomas Lamb. Then, in the "roaring Twenties," the rialto erupted into a rich "Movie Palace Baroque" splendor, unprecedented in Boston and comparable with that of any other American city, in the Metropolitan Theatre of 1925 and the B. F. Keith Memorial Theatre of 1928 (Figure 212).

Keith not only influenced, even dominated, American entertainment, he was also a much beloved civic benefactor; his legacies to the Boston Archdiocese, for instance, were enormous. It was thus not surprising that after Keith's death, Albee and Joseph Kennedy (who had become chairman of the board of the Keith successor firm) announced in 1925 a memorial that was astonishing even for the 1920s. They would build across the street from the Boston Theatre a new Boston Theatre of substantial impressiveness (now the Essex) that would keep the Keith shows running in Boston while they closed the Keith Theatre *and* the Boston Theatre and erected in their stead a magnificent new B. F. Keith Memorial Theatre. There was much dismay. What could honor all the accumulated and venerable associations of these two theaters more fittingly than the two as they stood? Albee, a showman, answered simply: "The most beautiful playhouse in the world."

Designed by Thomas Lamb, the B. F. Keith Memorial Theatre (now the Savoy) was built in 1928 in part on the granite foundations of the Boston Theatre and with the same floor plan. Its Baroque opulence is still intact. Certainly, it is one of the most beautiful movie palaces in the world. Unlike so many, it is what it seems to be: the sixteen great marble columns of the lobby *are* marble; they were quarried in Italy and polished in Vermont, and each weighs seven tons. The walnut paneling is by C. H. Rugg, whose interiors at the Parker House are so admirable. The molded plaster detail was executed by the John Evans Company. Frederick Bucher, the Newport art dealer, recalled in 1957 that one of the paintings in the lobby, Josef Israels's *The Young Mariner*, had cost Albee $27,000 and that he had had to outbid William Randolph Hearst to get it. And as for the immense auditorium, A. J. Philpott of the *Herald* did not exaggerate the morning after the opening: it was, he asserted, "a dazzling, architectural dream in ivory and gold." It is that still.

T HE Boston rialto — and flamboyant Classicism — reached its extravagant climax at the immense and storied Metropolitan Theatre (Figure 213). Then as now one of the largest theaters in the world, the Metropolitan (now the Music Hall but soon to revert, one hopes, to its old name) is not the most refined theater in Boston in detail nor the most distinguished in finish. But these distinctions are overwhelmed by its grandeur of space and line and its splendid scale. Every American metropolis had something of the sort by 1930, but only the great cities were endowed with huge flagships like the Metropolitan, which it was no exaggeration to call "cathedrals of the motion picture." Blackall's last Boston theater (designed with several lesser-known associated architects), the Metropolitan is historically the most important Boston landmark of the roaring Twenties; of that astonishing era when Adolph Zukor, in town for the Met's opening, could promise Bostonians a 5000-seat theater of "mountainous splendor; a movie palace of fabulous grandeur and stupendous stage

presentations" — for 35¢ a ticket and no more than 75¢ on weekend evenings. Nor did first-nighters notice that there were only 4407 seats. Like so much about the age of exaggeration, the exaggeration was so slight as to be unimportant. The *Globe* the morning after the Met's opening (attended by some 20,000 people) willingly conceded on page one that the Met was an "Architectural Marvel." Bostonians, said the *Advertiser* some days later, were still "rubbing their eyes and wondering if it was all a dream."

It wasn't. The Metropolitan was the closest thing to a sort of dignified Disneyland Boston had ever seen. Not one but four lavishly detailed marble lobbies opened out behind the marcelled blondes in the box office — a block-long parade of marbled halls that Blackall handled superbly, drawing the audience through a first and second and then a third lobby, each elaborate but low-ceilinged, and then through even lower entries that yielded, suddenly, to a dramatic Grand Lobby, five stories high and dazzling, encircled by three tiers of promenades, the gold, marble, and crimson decor scintillating in the light of huge crystal chandeliers. Brilliant ceremonial and social planning is the chief characteristic of these lobbies, which in the best Beaux Arts manner unfold in a supremely logical way. One can never lose one's way at the Met. And even today, after many years of neglect, the mezzanine promenade of the Met's Grand Lobby discloses one of the great spaces of Boston, the view of which during any intermission is in itself worth the price of a ticket to almost any show.

The Met was overwhelming; yet it was not *only* designed to overwhelm. These huge lobbies and promenades could hold thousands of people because it was an essential component of the Met's continuous performance policy of lavish stage reviews alternating with first-run movies every few hours every day of the week that the auditorium be emptied of 4407 people and filled with 4407 more twice each afternoon and evening during relatively short intermissions. While the first show was on, the audience for the second had to be filling up the lobbies and lounges — the Grand Lobby alone is nearly a block long — which were intended not only to hold but to fascinate. There were fresh flowers every day; bridge hostesses sought to arrange card parties; there were Ping-Pong tables; a telephone room; an outdoor promenade and loggia; a wood-paneled smoking room for gentlemen, six sumptuous lounges for ladies; five checkrooms for coats and packages; and after 1932 there was a chic Art Deco restaurant as well — the Platinum Salon. There was a regular Met radio show, broadcast from the theater on WEEI. There were two orchestras: one played on the balcony overlooking the Grand Lobby; another, the Met Collegians, played nightly for dancing in the Grand Lounge. There was a "Taxi Room" at the Hollis Street door, from which cabs could be summoned, and if you became ill, no need to leave: there was a Red Cross room off the lobby, staffed by a professional nurse. Nothing like the Met had ever been seen in Boston (the manager's office even boasted a small private theater for screening films). The sumptuous decor of the theater's lounges and their varied activities and solicitous attendants were, so to speak, the first act. Just getting from lounge or restaurant to the auditorium was another; particularly if one's seats were in the balcony, for Blackall took care to make this usually dismal prospect the best adventure of them all. Balcony patrons at the Met never saw a staircase until they departed. Instead, they were whisked effortlessly up five stories by large passenger elevators — then as now unique in any Boston theater — to the highest promenade of all, where the view down seventy-five feet through the

great chandeliers to the Grand Lobby below was (and still is) stunning.

Movie palaces today, like Newport palaces yesterday, are not often taken very seriously. It is the immense and not easily duplicated seating capacity of the Met's auditorium that now fuels most of the plans to restore it. Yet the Metropolitan was in its day a serious architectural achievement. (Today it would be an impossible one.) Its handsome bronze details were the work of the Gorham Company, and the auditorium murals were perhaps the major work of Edmund Kellogg, a student of Frank Duveneck and well-known in his day. The Met itself was also widely and admiringly published, not only in contemporary architectural journals, but in R. W. Sexton's *American Theatres of Today* and in G. H. Edgell's *American Architecture of Today*, where the former dean of the School of Architecture at Harvard devoted a page to this latest work by the country's leading theater architect. While he thought the Met's Grand Lobby "as impressive as Versailles," he observed pointedly:

There is something jarring in the sight of commonplace crowds in overshoes hurrying across a lobby which, despite its occasional use of spurious materials, is worthy of Mansart, while the elegantly dressed visitors to the Boston Opera-House stroll during the entr'actes along a corridor scarcely more imposing than that of the city jail. None the less, this is typical of America and perhaps not an unhealthy phenomenon.

Blackall, who had achieved as successful an effect in the chaste auditorium of the Wilbur as in the opulent Colonial, really knew very well how to manage Movie Palace Baroque in Boston. "Atmospheric" theaters (with ceilings that simulated moving clouds) never got any closer to the downtown rialto than East Boston (where the Seville Theatre indulged in Moorish mystery) or Malden (where the Alhambra attempted the same thing) or Mattapan (where the Ori-

FIGURE 213. Blackall, Clapp and Whittemore, et al. Metropolitan Theatre, 268 Tremont Street, Downtown, 1925. Auditorium, with murals by Edmund Kellogg. One of the largest theaters in the world, the Met has recently been renamed the Music Hall, but when it is restored as a successor to the now destroyed Boston Opera House, the old and historic name will almost certainly be revived.

ental essayed the Chinese type) or Brighton (where the Egyptian only slightly varied the formula). Boston's rather staid Opera House (Figure 152) was simply another illustration that Boston would rather be dull than ostentatious. It is doubtless for this reason that the Met's Grand Lobby is not as voluptuous as similar movie palaces in other cities; the New York Paramount, for example. Blackall nonetheless took as his model for the Met not the Boston Opera House but the extravagant and opulent Paris Opera House (1861–1875) by Charles Garnier. And when the Met becomes Boston's opera house (the first one having been torn down) Boston will — by accident — have saved perhaps the handsomer interior.

The auditorium of the Metropolitan is not as stately as the Grand Lobby, but it possesses its own and comparable character. Though it is one of the largest auditoriums in the world, it is surprisingly warm and inviting. There is to be sure a wonderful amplitude as one moves down the orchestra floor, which achieves a distinct grandeur closer to the proscenium and its colossal flanking portals with their enormous reclining nymphs. But the scale of these portals also mitigates the sense of vastness, even as the horseshoe of loge boxes — an operatic touch unique in any Boston theater — gives a sense of enclosure rather than of limitless size. And when one mounts to the balcony, the side walls of the auditorium are now seen to bend generously toward each other to create something like the enclosing "inverted bowl" of the Majestic. Here, though, the enclosing feeling does not oppress the balcony, for the proscenium and overhanging sounding board bend too and all coalesce high above in an ample dome that breaks through the top of the "inverted bowl" to create an open and almost airy feeling above the immense balcony. The soft, burnished gold detail,

the rich hangings and the dull sheen of the black glass mirrors, all enlivened by the lambent polychromy of electrical color effects that glowed from the thousands of lights hidden throughout the dome and along the arched mirrors and from behind shadowed niches, created a stunning setting for the great stage and the silver screen it was the Met's function to glorify.

Both were worth glorifying. The Met's Grand Orchestra was conducted by Fabian Sevitsky. The corps de ballet and the 100-voice chorus were thoroughly professional. The organ was an immense Wurlitzer. The stage shows were spectacular. The Met produced its own shows; John Murray Anderson, a brilliant producer whose reviews appeared also at the Alhambra and the Hippodrome in London and at Radio City Music Hall in New York, staged many of them. Moscow once burned to the ground on the Met's stage, which of its type was then quite a flexible facility, incorporating, for instance, no fewer than four elevators. No wonder that when the banks of spotlights flooded down through the glowing auditorium to the gold curtain there was a perceptible hush before the Met's Grand Orchestra rose majestically into view on its forty-foot-wide elevator, signaling with the thundering Wurlitzer the start of still another spectacular stage show. These were so spectacular that the Met's management leased the Wilbur next door for additional rehearsal and scenery areas.

B Y 1930, Boston's intown theaters altogether seated nearly 50,000 people — and many a night they were all filled. So extensive were the amenities of the Boston rialto that two underground networks of luxurious tunnels and lobbies were built between 1890 and 1920 to facilitate access to several of the more important theaters. Robert Shackleton was rather amazed to report in 1916 that the Boston Theatre on Washington Street could be reached from Tremont Street "through a long tunnel-like foot-passage, and then an actual underground passage beneath a building; and another theatre, close by, has an entrance even more interesting, this being a hundred yards or so of subterranean passage, lined with mirrors, not only under buildings but underneath a narrow street." Similarly, in 1918 C. H. Blackall designed another network of tunnels and underground lobbies, still extant though unused, which connected the Boylston Street subway station and the Little Building with the Majestic and Plymouth theaters.

Thus the exuberant Classicism of the Paris Opera House proved as adaptable in the case of the movie palace as had the Georgian Revival at Harvard — an odd comparison, but perhaps each environment is a striking evidence of the success of the eclectic creed. Behind style, there was, however, much invention along the Boston rialto. Quite aside from Keith's revolutionary concept of a palace for Everyman, Boston was very nearly the leading center of theater design in the early twentieth century in the United States.

C. H. Blackall, whose work at the Winthrop Building documents his adventuresomeness and whose Colonial, Wilbur, Modern, and Metropolitan theaters document his eclecticism, was widely regarded as the most experienced theater architect in the United States. It is also often overlooked that Wallace Sabine of Harvard "found the solution of a difficulty thousands of years old" (to quote from the Harvard faculty's minutes at the time of his death) when his work with McKim, Mead and White on Symphony Hall in 1900 yielded the first concert hall in the world built according to a definite acoustical formula; even today Symphony Hall is in this re-

FIGURE 214. Arthur Bowditch. Paramount Theater, 549 Washington Street, Downtown, 1932. The magnificent "moderne" marquee and upright are extant but covered over.

spect internationally distinguished. Though Blackall clearly knew little or nothing of Sabine when in 1900 he wrote the long series of articles on the Colonial in which he insisted acoustics were a matter about which one could only guess, Blackall subsequently collaborated with Sabine on several Boston theaters, including the Scollay Square Olympia and the Modern. Both men also embarked on a most creative collaboration with a third Bostonian of note, George Pierce Baker of Harvard. Few realize that Baker, who is best known for his "47 Workshop" at Harvard (Eugene O'Neill and Thomas Wolfe were among his students), was as interested in the perfect playhouse as in the perfect play. Indeed, the "47 Workshop," an outgrowth of a number of ideas in local theater circles catalyzed by the American premiere in Boston in 1911 of *The Playboy of the Western World* by the Abbey Theatre, mounted productions at both the Brattle and Agassiz theaters in Cambridge and led Baker to study a number of downtown Boston and Cambridge playhouses carefully. His idea was to build *the* perfect playhouse at Harvard, and, naturally, Blackall and Sabine collaborated with him on this project. Though their ideal theater (designed by Baker and Blackall; Sabine was then dead) was not built until 1925 and then at Yale (whither Baker had gone), this creative Boston school of theater design ought not to be lost sight of in any discussion of Boston architecture.

It was, of course, precisely that the results of such innovative thinking were regularly cloaked in "historical" styles that so infuriated the early Modernists. But even in the 1930s the only concession Boston theater design made to this view was to take up the Art Deco style we will discuss in the next chapter, in which vogue the last of Boston's movie palaces, the Paramount, was designed by Arthur Bowditch in 1931–1932 (Figure 214). At the Paramount, however, the significant factor from our point of view in this chapter is the marquee and its upright sign. An integral part of the theater's "moderne" facade, as signs and graphics of all kinds were in that period, the Paramount marquee and upright (which survive today, though the marquee has been covered over with an ugly new veneer) are really better symbols than any skyscraper of the excitement of "downtown" in the early twentieth century. Marquee and upright alike were magnificent multicolored electrical extravaganzas whose thousands upon thousands of dancing light bulbs endowed Boston's theater district with a kind of incandescent splendor that typified "downtown." By the 1930s many such marquees lit the Boston rialto. Like fireworks, they bedazzled the metropolis.

10

TOWARD GROPIUS

ECLECTICISM AND MODERNISM appeared by the late 1920s and early thirties to have achieved in buildings like the Paramount a kind of truce, the terms of which were Art Deco. Actually, this new vogue only expanded the range of styles available to the eclectic architect, who continued to believe that a building should be couched in a style whose associations expressed its function but was increasingly faced with buildings whose function was without precedent and that seemed, therefore, to require a style whose associations were simply new — or, in the vocabulary of the time, "moderne."

This appears to have been more a theoretical than a practical matter. Baroque opulence had proved more than expressive of the movie palace because that building type was really something old — an opera house — called something new — a movie palace. On the other hand, once the houselights dimmed to disclose the flickering images of the silver screen, *that* was so incredibly new that the architectural setting seemed to some perhaps by contrast too old. No doubt the streamlined automobile pulling up in front of the Classical domed gas station (Figure 194) set up similar vibrations; though one could presumably service a car under a dome as well as under anything, there was a sense of incongruity in doing so. Significantly, though it could flower into an exotic decoration, Art Deco was chiefly characterized by a sleek, streamlined,

machine-age geometry and it was thus particularly useful to architects like George Bartlett when faced, for example, with the task of designing something like the Colonial Air Transport Hangar and Depot Building, ca. 1928, in East Boston, where Boston Airport (now Logan International Airport) opened in 1923. Another new building type of the 1930s was the drive-in movie theater. The first of these in the Boston area (and probably in New England) was the Weymouth Drive-in Theatre in the suburb of that name; terraced so as to allow each car a better view, it was built in 1936 by Thomas Domara.

Although very often understated in Boston, Art Deco was not only widespread, ranging from Washington Street shops to movie palaces, but important for its chic, fashionable connotations: some of *the* fashionable places in Boston — the Ritz-Carlton Hotel, the Junior League Building, Shreve Crump and Low — were by 1930 discreetly Art Deco. And in 1929 the style sufficiently intrigued Boston's architects that the entire Boston Architectural Club yearbook of that year was given over to Art Deco design.

A fair amount of it was in Boston proper, including four dramatic new skyscrapers, all four of which survive: the Public Services Building at 60 Batterymarch Street (now the Batterymarch Building) of 1928 by Harold Field Kellogg; the United Shoe Machinery Building of Parker, Thomas and Rice at

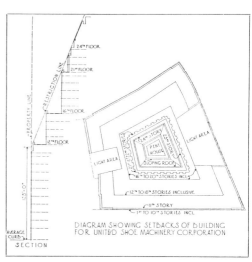

The Art Deco skyscraper in Boston.
FIGURE 215. Parker, Thomas and Rice. United Shoe Machinery Building, 138–164 Federal Street, 1929. Exterior perspective and diagram showing setbacks.
FIGURE 216. Cram and Ferguson and James A. Wetmore. Boston Post Office and Federal Building, Post Office Square, 1929–1931. The United Shoe Machinery Building is 24 stories and 298 feet high; the Federal Building is 22 stories and 345 feet high.

138–164 Federal Street (Figure 215); the State Street Trust Building at 70–75 Federal Street by Thomas M. James; and the Post Office Building by James A. Wetmore and Cram and Ferguson in Post Office Square (Figure 216). Of these four the United Shoe Machinery Building made the most important contribution to the skyline: its strong vertical ribbons of recessed windows and majestic stepped-back massing endowed Boston with a fine example of the characteristic skyscraper of the period, which took advantage of a 1928 revision of the Boston height restriction law that allowed much taller buildings if these were "stepped back" sufficiently to admit more sun into increasingly dark downtown canyons. The Batterymarch Building, on the other hand, was one of the first buildings in this country to seek an illusion of constant sunlight in the way Kellogg shaded the color of the bricks from dark heather brown at the bottom to lighter (and sunnier!) buff at the top. Whatever the differences in design concept, all four buildings virtually doubled the scale of downtown Boston, with some distinction; and it has thus always been something of a mystery to me why so many in dealing with the skyscraper in Boston pass at once from the Custom House Tower, completed in 1915, to the post–World War II John Hancock Building by Cram's successors.

Of all Boston's architects, Strickland, Blodget and Law were perhaps the most adept at Art Deco. In addition to quite large buildings such as the blatantly Art Deco Junior League Building of 1929 (now the Katharine Gibbs School) on the corner of Arlington and Marlborough streets and the nearby and more understated Art Deco-cum-Federal Ritz-Carlton Hotel, which opened in 1927, they did a number of fashionable Newbury Street storefronts. Two that survive more or less intact today are Mam'selle (1927) at 83 and the Kidder, Peabody office (ca.

1928) at 69, the polished black granite facade of which now announces Roberts Furs. Their most exquisite detail, including silver-gray and emerald-green murals by Jacques Carlu of M.I.T. and his wife, Natacha, was at the Ritz (Figure 217), the famous dining room of which was endowed with silvered detailing on the columns and huge silvered circles containing the signs of the zodiac on the ceiling.

Nearby, at Shreve Crump and Low, on the corner of Arlington and Boylston streets, William T. Aldrich, who remodeled this building in 1930, also used a silvered ceiling. But at Shreve's the exterior detail is what is important: the "pilasters" and "capitals" of the facade — flat, streamlined, stylized, and quite unlike the Classical forms they derive from — are superb examples of the inventiveness characteristic of Art Deco (Figure 218). But perhaps the most elaborate and characteristic Art Deco detail still visible in Boston is the metal work in the United Shoe Machinery Building lobby and in the Franklin Street foyer of the State Street Bank and, most of all, the exotic inlaid ebony and walnut chevron woodwork of the Paramount Theatre; highlighted by aluminum and gold decorations, this woodwork and the sleek, streamlined geometry of the Paramount interior generally are now unique in Boston.

The most important single Art Deco ornament in the city, the famous Bigelow Kennard clock (Figure 219), is no longer, alas, where it should be (protruding from a facade), though it has at least been preserved and is now in the Museum of Fine Arts. Nor is there, unfortunately, any work in Boston in this mode (though there are, as we have noted, earlier works) by Lee Lawrie, the American sculptor who was so influenced by Art Deco. There is, however, quite fine modernistic sculptural work at the East Cambridge Savings Bank (Figure 220) by the

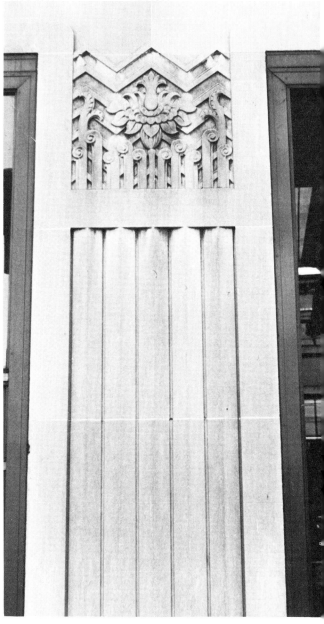

Art Deco details.

FIGURE 217. Strickland, Blodget and Law. Ritz-Carlton Hotel, 15 Arlington Street, Back Bay, 1926–1927. Interior of function room showing murals (now destroyed) by Jacques and Natacha Carlu.

FIGURE 218. William T. Aldrich. Remodeled store for Shreve Crump and Low, 330 Boylston Street, Back Bay, 1930. Detail of facade.

FIGURE 219. Cast bronze and aluminum clock designed by Roland Baldrey and installed in 1933 over the entrance of the Boston jewelers and metal-workers Bigelow Kennard and Company, and now in the collection of the Museum of Fine Arts, Boston. Apollo, the sun god, is depicted riding across the heavens, the waters of time beneath. The passage of time is symbolized by the "wings of time" in flight at the top of the structure, while the swiftness of time is suggested by the bent bow and raised arrow that connect the structure to the facade.

well-known New York sculptor Paul Fjelde. The bank itself, Italian Romanesque in feeling but with strong Byzantine overtones, was designed by Thomas M. James in 1931 and its modernistic detail well illustrates how the newer mode could be combined with more traditional forms in the same building and by an architect whose earlier Classicism we have noted at the Shubert Theatre.

James's Cambridge work points up as well the fact that the "moderne" was not restricted to intown, though it chiefly flourished there. In Cambridge, one may see in the Sears, Roebuck store at Porter Square, designed in 1928 by George C. Nimmons and Company, a more modest version of Nimmons's huge Boston store in the Fenway (Figure 221), which opened in the same year. Probably the finest of several suburban buildings of this sort is the miniature skyscraper J. Williams Beal's Sons designed in the mid-1920s for the Granite Trust Company at Quincy Center. One may also see in both city and suburbs fine examples of a characteristic new element of design in this period, the use of stylized lettering (usually the name of the firm or of the building) as an integral element in the design of the facade. Aside from the Paramount, the most splendid example in Boston was Shephard and Stearns's I. J. Fox Company facade on Washington Street (1934), recently devastated, first, by a new street canopy that ruins the front, and, secondly, by new owners who have removed the lettering of the facade. In Cambridge, along the Charles River on Memorial Drive, the BB Chemical Company building (Figure 222), by the Shepley office, has been much more fortunate: Polaroid Corporation, which recently bought the building, has shown great sensitivity in the way it carefully substituted its own name on the facade.

Sparser versions of more traditional styles paralleled Art Deco work in Boston. At Wellesley College, Charles Z. Klauder designed an extensive modernistic Gothic complex in 1927–1931. A kind of stripped-down Classicism is also evident in Ralph Harrington Doane's Motor Mart (1927) in Park Square (Figure 223) and even more so in his Rindge Technical High School (1932) in Cambridge. But in hindsight the firm whose work during the 1930s was perhaps most progressive was the Shepley office, Richardson's successors, who have turned their hands to everything over the years from Romanesque churches to Logan International Airport. In 1930, while at work on Harvard's Georgian houses, they designed the first "modern" building at Harvard and perhaps the first really distinguished building in Greater Boston that sought to shed completely traditional "historical" ornament — the Biological Laboratory at Harvard (Figure 224).

Built of reinforced concrete, though it is finished in brick to honor its older brick neighbors and retains as well the basic Classical mass of colonnade and entablature, the building has crisply cut vertical panels of windows very much in the new spirit. So also is the architectural carving, which is inspired: a great herd of elephants sweeps across the topmost part of the building, carved in the brick by Katherine Ward Lane, who also modeled the rhinoceroses that flank the main entrance. It is really this carving that still gives this building distinction. How much it was admired in the thirties is evident in the fact that in 1936 Henry-Russell Hitchcock (who thought Shepley's Harvard Houses "parodies" of the eighteenth century) compared the Biological Laboratory with Sever Hall in its attempt to catch the spirit of older work nearby while striking out in a distinctly modern way. The laboratory was "certainly not the best example of contemporary style in America," Hitchcock wrote. "But there was," he continued, in 1930 "in the field of college architecture

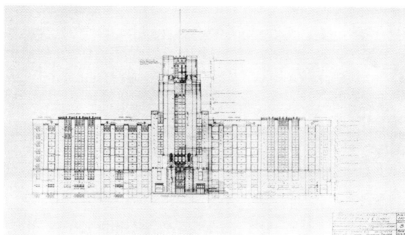

"Moderne" design in the 1920s and 1930s.
FIGURE 220. Thomas M. James. East Cambridge Savings Bank, 1931.
FIGURE 221. George C. Nimmons and Company. Sears, Roebuck store, the Fenway, 1928. Elevation of principal facade.
FIGURE 222. Coolidge, Shepley, Bulfinch and Abbott. BB Chemical Building (now Polaroid Building), 780 Memorial Drive, Cambridge, 1937.
FIGURE 223. Ralph Harrington Doane. Motor Mart Garage, Park Square, Back Bay, 1927.

FIGURE 224. Coolidge, Shepley, Bulfinch and Abbott. Biological Laboratories, Harvard University, Cambridge, 1930.

in America no building of comparable significance, just as there was none at the time of Sever."

The Shepley office attempted more or less the same effect, on a much larger scale and this time in white brick, at Northeastern University, the competition for which work they won in 1934. On the other hand, they did not abandon traditional forms: the Littauer Center at Harvard (1938) is a full-fledged adaption of the Bulfinch Building of 1818–1823 at the Massachusetts General Hospital. It was the first building erected by Harvard after the appointment of Walter Gropius to the faculty of the Graduate School of Design in 1937.

G ROPIUS's appointment, which has been called "an epoch-making event," brought to Boston one of the outstanding figures in modern architecture and design. Until the rise of Hitler had driven him first to England and then to America, Gropius had at the famous German school of architecture, the Bauhaus, led in formulating what is called the International Style. Characterized by flat-roofed and blocklike masses with no ornamentation of any kind, how revolutionary the "machine aesthetic" of this style must have seemed in Boston is evident if one considers the series of buildings Gropius and others of similar conviction embarked upon in the Boston area in the late 1930s. Among the earliest and most influential was a house Carl Koch designed (nominally with Edward Durrell Stone) at 4 Buckingham Street (Figure 225) in Cambridge in 1937. Bunting and Nylander describe it thus:

When first occupied, the house was a great curiosity, and the many people who came to see it were generously received by the owners. Tastefully furnished with contemporary furniture and fabrics, in large part imported from Sweden, the visual effect it created was warm and inviting, and it proved to many skeptics beyond a doubt that modern architecture was not necessarily cold and impersonal. Indeed, the Koch house played an important role in converting a whole generation of architectural students at Harvard and MIT to the cause of modern architecture.

Two years later M.I.T. possessed its own example of the International Style in the Alumni Swimming Pool of 1939, designed by Anderson and Beckwith, two alumni of M.I.T. (Figure 226) and during the same period Boston was endowed with several innovative buildings by Hugh Stubbins. These include the Troy House at 11 Wyoming Avenue in Needham (1936) and a dental office at 775 Main Street in Melrose (1936), both designed in association with Royal Barry Wills; and a 1939 remodeling, with Marc Peter, Jr., of the Telepix Cinema in Park Square, which John McAndrew described in 1940 as "the most thoroughly modern design for any movie theatre in the country."

It was, however, the work of Gropius himself, who formed a partnership with a former Bauhaus colleague, Marcel Breuer, in 1937, and of Walter Bogner, an associate of Gropius at the Harvard Graduate School of Design, that naturally attracted the widest attention in Boston in the late thirties. Bogner designed two houses: 45 Fayerweather Street (1940) in Cambridge and his own house (1939) on Wood's End Road in Lincoln. Gropius's own house of 1938 is on Baker Bridge Road in the same town (Figure 227). With Breuer, Gropius also designed the Haggerty House (1939) on Jerusalem Road in Cohasset (their first work in this country); the small Chamberlain cottage (1940) in Wayland; and the former Ford House (1939) in Lincoln, which like Bogner's own house and Breuer's own (1939) stands on Wood's End Road in Lincoln, a quiet suburban lane whose importance in Boston's architectural history in this period is seldom suspected.

Early landmarks of the International Style in Greater Boston.
FIGURE 225. Carl Koch and Edward Durrell Stone. 4 Buckingham Street, Cambridge, 1937.
FIGURE 226. Anderson and Beckwith. Alumni Swimming Pool, M.I.T., Cambridge, 1939.
FIGURE 227. Walter Gropius. Gropius House, Baker Bridge Road, Lincoln, 1938.

Significantly, the Chamberlain cottage sought to state the International Style in New England terms (by using wood) as did Bogner's 45 Fayerweather Street, which was built of bricks recovered from the destruction of a Back Bay house. And Carl Koch made a similar effort — using not only wood but also pitched roofs — in a group of five houses (the Gordon, Cushman, Hartshorne, Wissmann, and Koch houses) on Snake Hill Road near Pleasant Street in Belmont, that he designed in 1940. None of the modernists proposed tearing down Boston — as Le Corbusier had once considered leveling Paris. But the stark cubes of the International Style announced a revolution nonetheless: in 1948 Gropius would write of the need for an architecture that was "radiant and naked, unencumbered by lying facades and trickeries . . . an architecture adapted to our world of machines, radio and fast motor cars." The Gropius House, in Ada Louise Huxtable's words, "was a clarion call to the future."

Boston's response was uncertain. The fact that such leading modernists as Walter Bogner, Louis Skidmore, and Edward Durrell Stone had all been Rotch Fellows in the late twenties; indeed, that Gropius, whom Burchard and Bush-Brown would call "the most influential single man in planting modern architecture firmly in America," should have been asked to teach at Harvard, shows the lively intellectual climate of Boston during this period, echoed, for example, in the great amount of modern music premiered by Serge Koussevitsky and the Boston Symphony Orchestra in the thirties. Curiosity, however, does not always imply enthusiasm, as Burchard and Bush-Brown point out:

Gropius's appointment to Harvard in 1937 excited derision among many older architects, such as Charles Killam, Professor of Architecture Emeritus at Harvard, who wrote bitterly against the appointment of "social reform-ers," "mere critics," "specialists in domestic work of low-cost housing," "extreme modernists." . . . Conservative communities such as Lexington, Massachusetts, thought that all the modernists who were settling on Six Moon Hill or in nearby Lincoln in modern houses must be liberals, even radicals, probably intent on violent reform.

The same authors, noting that Cram was perhaps "the most outspoken critic" of modernism, admitted, however, that "there was much folly Cram could point to in the modern movement" and that "an exhibitionist like Salvador Dali did not help matters when, on his arrival in New York in 1936, he announced his desire to live in a 'fur-lined uterus.' "

But there had also been much folly in the Gothic movement; few of Cram's "disciples" honored his ideal of constructional honesty, for instance. Moreover, Cram's response to Modernism, earnestly sought not just in Boston but throughout the country (for Cram by the 1930s was the last of the great traditionalists), was more subtle than strident, though consistent. He had warned as early as 1914 that when criticizing new forms American architects were on uncertain ground because "as a matter of fact, we are bound hand and foot to a traditionalism that is Byzantine in its rigidity and mounts often to the level of an historic superstition." He wondered repeatedly in his writings how one could "build a gymnasium like a medieval abbey," for example, or design a "Gothic" skyscraper, and despite the fact that Raymond Hood (who had been apprenticed to Cram) was a close friend, he once compared such anomalies to a "Byzantine motor car." In fact, no one attacked traditional architecture more fiercely than did Cram: "the astute archeology of some of our best modern work, Classic or Gothic," he wrote in 1914, "is stupefying and leads nowhere." What had happened, of course, was that Cram saw his own disciples and

FIGURE 228. Richard Shaw. St. Clement's Church, Somerville, 1946 remodeling.

FIGURE 229. Alvar Aalto. Baker House, M.I.T., Cambridge, 1947.

FIGURE 230. The Architects Collaborative (Walter Gropius). Harvard Graduate Center, Cambridge, 1949.

McKim's increasingly perpetuating the same sort of bloodless clichés Richardson's disciples had been guilty of in the 1880s. All Cram could do was to point out that it was natural that a "technological civilization . . . should show itself in an adequate art" and that if that art was ugly, as he frequently found it, it was because technological civilization was itself ugly. He did protest vehemently that only at great peril to their identities and values could the church or the home embrace the new technological aesthetic. But when he cautioned Modernists that "the force that destroys can never under any circumstances rebuild," Cram admitted too much for the traditionalists. Just as conservatives despaired of him when he publicly supported Franklin Delano Roosevelt, Cram really offered neither side much comfort. He was always his own man, prophet or crank according to one's view. The traditionalists were at least spared the knowledge that when Cram and Gropius, having expressed a desire to meet, commandeered the library of a mutual friend for a chat of several hours at a Sunday house party in suburban Boston in the late thirties, all that the curious guests overheard through the closed door was hearty laughter.

Charles Maginnis, who outlived Cram (who died in 1942) by over a decade, ultimately mounted a more vigorous attack on Modernism, but though persuasive he too was damning the age as much as its architectural expression when he wrote in 1945:

The mathematical system that is being proposed to us is superbly adequate to the challenges of realism, but it has yet to rise convincingly above the topicalities. Simplicity might well have been its largest gift, but it is presented to us, not as a gracious excellence, but as a by-product of a biting logic, a harsh and defiant emptiness. Its content is too thin, its temper too immediate. It is fitting for the things that end tomorrow. Why shake off the tyranny of history to take on the tyranny of the passing hour? . . . It is needful that architecture have the gift to express our ideals no less than our realistic habit. What is utility but an end that can be seen by the shortsighted? All the great ends lie further. . . . In a dramatic detachment we are expected to find our gratifications henceforth in the atmosphere of our machinery. The idea is too violent.

Maginnis's eloquence, however, was not matched by the architecture of his fellow traditionalists. The history of the J. Harleston Parker Gold Medal in the late thirties and early forties is ample evidence of what was happening. In 1939 it was awarded to Cram's Cowley Fathers Monastery in Cambridge (Figure 172); in 1943 it was given to Perry, Shaw and Hepburn for their Houghton Library at Harvard. Yet these were virtually the last buildings of distinction in Boston to earn this award in either the Gothic or Classical mode. The next award, in 1946, to Richard Shaw's St. Clement's Church in Somerville (Figure 228), represented a startling descent, and shows how under the pressure of Modernism, the traditionalists were driven to fatal compromises that were more violent by any traditional rubric than Modernism. A similar building, which essayed an absurd "Modernistic" Federal Revival style, was designed by Perry, Shaw, Hepburn and Dean for Jordan Marsh on Summer Street in 1948–1951. How striking by comparison were Gropius's Harvard Graduate Center (Figure 230) of 1949 in the North Yard or Alvar Aalto's Baker House (1947) along the Charles River at M.I.T., the serpentine plan of which allows every room a river view (Figure 229). About St. Clement's and Jordan Marsh there was a sense not only of compromise and uncertainty, but of apology and decline, even of decay. The Gropius and Aalto buildings, on the other hand, though more shocking in form, made no apology; indeed, they exuded a sense of confidence that this was to be the future. Whatever one's tastes, the sense of what was decaying and what was beginning must have been irresistible. In another sense, the same thing must have seemed true of another retail complex of the late forties — Shoppers World in Framingham, a pioneering suburban shopping center by Ketchum, Gina and Sharp (1949–1951). Perhaps even more startling was the technologically innovative house for Amelia Peabody in Dover designed by Eleanor Raymond in 1948; described then as a "sun-heated house," today it would be called a solar house.

Thus did the ground begin to shift under architecture; after the Second World War with the force of an earthquake. In the event, Boston not only accepted Modernism, but with open arms: Martin Myerson and Edward Banfield pointed out in their *Boston: The Job Ahead* that the post–World War II work in and around the city by Aalto, Belluschi, Gropius, Koch, Le Corbusier, Pei, Rudolph, Saarinen, Sert, Stubbins, and Yamasaki constituted "a greater concentration of work by outstanding living architects than is to be found anywhere else in the world." But that is another book. And if in the seventies we are again somewhat unsure of our footing, today we are all preservationists! Indeed, the planned preservation of the Gropius House by the Society for the Preservation of New England Antiquities prompted Ada Louise Huxtable to reach what is perhaps the only conclusion of this survey of what has been built in Boston until the eve of our own era:

There is first, the lovely, subtle paradox of the Gropius House, that clarion call to the future, as an authenticated antiquity. How inexorably time turns the avant-garde into history! And how much delicate irony can be obtained from the fact that this house marked the conscious rejection of history in terms of emulations of past styles (indigenous tradition was a superbly rationalized substitute) and the declaration of a new esthetic and a brave new world. The new esthetic is the norm, and the brave new world grows old. The landmark takes its place as part of the history that it spurned, and the movement that rewrote history becomes history. Always history wins.

Ultimately, the post-World War II architectural revolution has yielded a new respect for the architecture of the past.
FIGURE 231. Restored town houses, Monument Square, Charlestown.

1950–2000

PART III

———

TAC AND SERT TO PEI AND KALLMANN AND McKINNELL

11

Heroic Modernism

THE MODERNIST CENTURY — at least insofar as architecture is concerned — has nowhere been more Modern than in Boston in the years since Gropius's advent.

Of course, just what *Modern* (as in Movement), or *Modernist*, or, indeed, *Modernism* may mean in the first place (even whether or not one or all of these words should be capitalized) has always been a matter about which opinions differ. Is Modernism correctly or even aptly likened, as Alfred Barr famously did, to a torpedo moving relentlessly through the always advancing present and trailing behind it the art of — what?— twenty-five or fifty or a hundred years previously? Does what's Modern have an expiration date, like produce or medicine? When does Modern (big *M*) become classic (small *c*)? There are, surely, Modern classics! And if Modern (or is it modern?) is not just a synonym for contemporary, to be out-grown eventually, is it on the other hand a clear-cut historical style, corresponding to a clear-cut historical period, perhaps ill-labeled (like Gothic or Italianate) but fixed in time and recognizable — to be followed in that case by Post-Modern, and more or less the same argument all over again about whatever *that* term means?

This is for me one of those games (no theorist I) not worth the candle. Sufficient to say my view here is that while many things — including Gothic, even Italianate — may have in the twentieth century mod-

ern incarnations, when the word *modern* is used all alone it means in twentieth-century American architectural history something quite specific, which had, so to speak, three lives. For me, in fact, there is not one, but three Modernisms.

There is, first, American Modernism of the 1890s and 1900s, a label not everyone would agree to but which I insist on be-cause while not unrelated to the Art Nouveau style (and distinctly indebted to the Arts and Crafts style), what I call American Modernism *should* be so labeled because it achieved distinctive and lasting expression, both in the Chicago School of Louis Sullivan and the Prairie School of Frank Lloyd Wright. However, it is an expression of less importance to us here because it found only very faint echoes in Boston, echoes detailed in Chapter 8, "The Shadow of Louis Sullivan," where I have suggested that this Modernist master will always be for Boston, where he was born and inspired to architecture as a boy (and even, briefly, trained—at M.I.T.), the "man who got away."

But this was hardly true of the Modernist idea generally. When the second of our three Modernisms, what we call today Art Deco or Moderne, came to the fore in the late 1920s and 1930s, Boston's architects this time showed more initiative. In *Rediscovering Art Deco USA*, a recent guide to that period, Cram and Ferguson's 1928 Federal Building in Post Office Square, for example, is described by the authors as the centerpiece of "a splendid Art Deco vista [that] is unparalleled in the U.S.A." That is to be enthusiastic to a degree (I would have thought: Rockefeller Center?), but it does underline how wholeheartedly even Ralph Adams Cram, Boston's leading Gothicist, embraced the Moderne style in the late 1920s and 1930s. This was true as well of the Coolidge/Shepley office, H. H. Richardson's successors; indeed, that firm in some ways went even further than Cram, especially in their 1934 design for Northeastern University, the design of which verged on our third Modernism.

That third Modernism was a far more radical Modernism — fulminating before World War II, flowering just after it. Its advent in New England is touched on just briefly in *Built in Boston* at the end of Chapter 10, "Toward Gropius," and is generally referred to as the Modern Movement. Itself divisible into two modes — the dominant European mode (what has come to be called the International Style) and the persistent, ongoing American mode (which is to say, the ever-renewing vision of Frank Lloyd Wright) — of this third Modernism it may well be said that architecture in its wake was fundamentally changed. And it is the European mode of this third Modernism, the dominant mainstream Modernism of the twentieth century, that Bostonians took up with such fervor that Ada Louise Huxtable would write, "Boston may be known as the cradle of liberty, but it is also the cradle of modern architecture in this country."

That fact has grown in significance as the late twentieth century has unfolded and Modernism, and its unruly progeny, Post-Modernism and so on, has become virtually the only architectural tradition of our time, pointing, moreover, more and more insistently to a twenty-first-century architecture that is likely to be nothing less than astonishing.

Make no mistake, however: though architecture has changed mightily under the stress of Modernism, in Boston's architectural history there has been less discontinuity than might at first seem to be the case, not the least reason why Boston was so welcoming, for example, to the International Style, the twentieth-century aesthetic of which was often called "Puritan" after the aesthetic of Boston's seventeenth-century settlers.

Indeed, it was a welcome well grounded in history. The place Boston first earned in the annals of Western architecture, when Charles Bulfinch urged its sturdy eighteenth-century provincial Georgian into the distinctive New World Adamesque we call today the Federal style, took on a transatlantic dimension with the emergence of Boston's incomparable Granite Style architecture of the mid-nineteenth century, a mode of building we now know influenced later in that century America's greatest architect of the time, Henry Hobson Richardson, whose work first turned toward the Puritan capital the eyes of lovers of architecture the world over, work that along with that of his Brookline neighbor, Frederick Law Olmsted, greatly influenced both Sullivan and Wright. It was an influence acknowledged even by European Modernists like Sigfried Giedion who — to close the circle, so to speak — highlighted Boston's mid-nineteenth-century Granite Style architecture in a seminal mid-twentieth-century book of radical modernist thought, *Space, Time and Architecture*, written by Giedion while he and Gropius were colleagues at Harvard on the eve of the Second World War.

There it was, of course, as we saw at the end of the last chapter, that Gropius came so quickly to be seen, with respect to the Modern Movement in architecture, as its great herald in the New World — if, that is, you discount Frank Lloyd Wright!

Many did. Although it is perhaps hard to credit today, until relatively late in his life, though Wright's work was by many much admired (including by both Cram and Gropius), by many others it was for years determinedly discounted. And nowhere more so than in conservative Boston, where Wright, like that other presiding genius of Modernism, Picasso, was for a very long time pretty widely disparaged.

Even today, Boston is Gropius's town, not Wright's. But given our perspective in 2000 it would be misleading to take up the tale of Modernism in Boston where it was left here so many years ago with Gropius's advent and to follow it forward into our own time, when Wright has come, rightly I believe, to be seen as so dominant a figure, without harking back and enlarging on Chapter 8, where in 1979 I touched on Wright I now believe too lightly, myself then somewhat an example of what I now complain of! Even in Eurocentric Boston, before there was Gropius, there were Sullivan and Wright, and, before there was European Modernism there was *American* Modernism. As Ralph Adams Cram himself tartly pointed out in 1929, it was "the architectural joke of the century that we are raving over the flat planes and horizontal lines of the Dutch and German designers, most of which [planes and lines] first saw the light [in the early 1900s] in the town of Oak Park, Illinois."

F RANK Lloyd Wright in Boston — which he first remembered, he once told Bruce Pfeiffer, as a boy of nine (that would be in 1876), standing in front of the Jordan Marsh department store on downtown Washington Street: "look at that young boy with his cap set at so assiduous an angle" — this from two passersby according to Wright, a fugitive memory (characteristic of Wright) of childhood visits to the big city that would likely have stood out for a boy whose suburban childhood on Boston's South Shore was decidedly a mixed business. "The little preacher-family was desperately poor," Wright would later recall, and the center of his daily life "a modest, gray, wooden house near a tall and white brick church in drab old Weymouth."

Modest? Gray? *White* brick? Drab? *Historic*? These were not good memories for the World's Greatest Architect! Indeed, in his old age Wright would declare, Bruce Pfeiffer tells me, that Philadelphia was the ugliest city in America "unless it was Boston."

Still, Wright's youth in Boston was not all grim. It was at another downtown store (Milton Bradley, Wright said) that his mother had bought the Froebel blocks Wright famously played with as a boy, and it was in the Weymouth house that he learned to love Bach and Beethoven, listening to his father play the piano late into the night.

Bach, Beethoven, and Froebel blocks are, of course, a very short story. And after his youth Boston seems hardly to figure much in Wright's life. But that is to speak of Boston as a *place*. As an *idea* — several in fact — Boston is all over Wright's life. There was the dubious business of Wright's supposed relationship to the Boston poet James Russell Lowell; in aid of which, though no such link can be found, Wright added *Russell* to his father's name. Even more puzzling was Wright's reaction to another New England notable: "Henry Adams, Boston Brahmin, would dislike Louis Sullivan and Walt Whitman," insisted Wright. "His [Adams's] frame of reference was never theirs, *or mine* [emphasis added]." Similarly, in a review of a book on Japanese art and architecture by Ralph Adams Cram, Adams's ally and Boston's leading architect in the 1900s, Wright called the author "Edificer Cram," a sour enough usage. Poor Cram. He actually admired Wright's work and said so in print more than once. Perhaps Wright actually learned something about Japanese art from Cram's book, a thing Wright would take care to obscure.

Poor Adams. He, too, had the misfortune, perhaps, to have been one of Wright's sources! Wrote Brendan Gill, Wright's best biographer: "Wright's autobiography is a direct imitation of Sullivan's, as Sullivan's was of Henry Adams.'" And had not

Adams famously commissioned to build his own house Richardson himself, who had no greater admirer than Louis Sullivan, Wright's mentor and youthful master? Speaking of which, wherefore this ugly Boston of Wright's experience? Wright, as much as Sullivan, in his designs if not in his words, repeatedly disclosed in his early work in the Chicago suburb of Oak Park, where he settled as a young architect, how highly he thought of the leading designer of Boston's buildings in those days. Scholars, subsequently, have not disagreed: "The ground-hugging repose that Richardson sought . . . was to inspire the horizontal Prairie style architecture of Frank Lloyd Wright," James O'Gorman has written; so was "the sheltering roof, geometrical clarity, horizontal proportions, and natural materials of Richardson's work." Margaret Henderson Floyd went further, writing of "the American tradition of architecture in the landscape, epitomized in the collaboration of H. H. Richardson and Frederick Law Olmsted and leading to the designs of Frank Lloyd Wright."

Yet out of all this inconsistency what emerges is a pattern, a pattern of conflict. Wright, in the apt phrase of Gill a man of "many masks," was clearly conflicted about Boston. How much so is painfully obvious in the way (probably untruthfully but still significantly) Wright in his *Testament* recounted how a professor of aesthetics, Kuno Francke, "came from Harvard to Oak Park (1909) . . . to see the work I had done of which he had heard at Harvard. Astonished and pleased by what he saw . . . he urged . . . 'Your people are not ready for you. Your life [in America] will be wasted. . . . Fifty years, at least, will pass before your people will be ready for you.'" Indeed, when he dined in Boston with Gropius thirty years later, the prediction had held up well enough for Wright to complain bitterly to Gropius, according to a letter of the German master years later to Vincent Scully (quoted by Reginald Isaacs),

that he (Wright) had never been offered such a position as Harvard had offered Gropius.

It is to miss the point to insist Wright would hardly have been happy at Harvard, or at any school. After all, there's no evidence he *liked* James Russell Lowell's poetry either. Similarly, it is to miss the point to complain of inconsistencies in Wright's visual memories of the Boston area.

Think Concord, not Weymouth! And consider carefully Wright's assertion that he had found after all in drab old Weymouth "the transcendentalism of Concord . . . in the books of Channing, Emerson, Theodore Parker, and, yes, Thoreau"— names over a half century later Wright would blazon in a kind of shrine-niche in his famous Unitarian church in Madison, Wisconsin. "All Bostonians!" Bruce Pfeiffer mused to me recently, wonderingly.

Notice too that Unity Church, Oak Park, one of Wright's most celebrated buildings, was Unitarian —"the Boston religion" Mark DeWolfe Howe called it — of which Wright was himself a leading member. (Oak Park itself, in fact, is described by Gill as "a utopian suburb [that] drew its high intellectual aspirations from New England.")

Boston's influence on Wright would seem to have been, in fact, more various and more significant than has previously been thought. It may thus surprise less that, however Wright obscured his response to that influence, at least once the influence went the other way.

Cram was not the only Bostonian with whom Wright was linked by a mutual passion for the art of Japan. Most closely of all, Wright was allied in this cause with two Boston Brahmins, Beacon Street bred and Harvard educated, both wealthy collectors of Japanese prints: William and John Taylor Spaulding.

Wright himself was a collector, and it was his friend, Frederick Gookin, who introduced Wright to William and John Taylor Spaulding when they visited

Chicago in 1912. Wright never forgot the result: in early January of 1913, he later remembered,

About ready to return to Japan I received a telegram from the Spauldings inviting me to come to Beacon Street. . . . I gladly went. At dinner that evening . . . "Would you consent to try to find prints for us in Japan, Mr. Wright? . . . We feel we can trust you completely. . . ."

I said, "I will take whatever money you want to spend, spend it and divide what I buy. I'll keep what I think I should have, and you shall have the others."

"Well," said John as he laughed, "that's hardly a business proposition, is it, Mr. Wright?"

I said, "No, I am not a businessman, Mr. Spaulding."

They wanted to know why I would not do it on commission. I said, "Too much bookkeeping." We left it at that and went to bed.

Prone as Wright was to embellish and even to invent, one must take this story with a grain of salt. As Julia Meech points out, it was not quite so simple, for while the Spauldings "were impressed by the flamboyant architect's reputation as a connoisseur . . . they were shrewd Yankee businessmen, able to give as well as they got."

Even so, it was an extraordinary business. I doubt in the first place if Frank Lloyd Wright spent many overnights on Beacon Street. He was by 1913 not only a famous architect, but a notorious one, having conspicuously deserted his wife and children in 1909, fleeing Oak Park for a life of scandal; indeed, he made the 1913 trip to Japan not with his wife, but with his then girlfriend.

Nor is it likely many Beacon Street Brahmins ever slept on such a proposition as Wright had put to the Spauldings. Seemingly, Wright carried the day:

Next morning [Wright went on] John and William said they had thought it over. "We will be glad to accept your offer. You will find twenty thousand dollars to your credit in the Yokohama Specie Bank when you arrive in Tokio."

There was no scratch of a pen to record the agreement.

The twenty thousand was soon gone. . . . I would cable for money from time to time as "finds" turned up. . . . The money always came, no questions asked. Nothing from me except excited demands for more money until I had spent about one hundred and twenty-five thousand Spaulding dollars. . . .

A superb collection, quite beyond price — most of it now in the Boston Museum of Fine Arts, a gift from the Spauldings.

Extraordinary, to be sure, but not unprecedented, and as superbly Bostonian as Wrightian if one pauses and considers the matter. For during the China trade Captain Robert Bennett Forbes (the Forbeses' town house faced the Public Garden only a block further up Beacon Street from the Spauldings') in all his dealings with the legendary Chinese merchant, Hoi Kuai, never exchanged scrap of paper either.

Which is not to say, as Meech has documented, that William Spaulding did not keep close tabs on Wright in Japan, at one point writing him: "You know, my good Mr. Wright, that many of us feel that your ideas of the value of prints is upon a *pretty* lofty pedestal, and we do not attempt to keep this feeling a second from you." Nor was he always so subtle: the same year he challenged Wright pretty directly in pointing out that "the amount we have invested is at least four times the sum we had any idea we would be called upon to expend." Spaulding did not realize, perhaps, that none of Wright's clients ever had any other experience of him! But he surely guessed they always got good value from Wright. If Gookin was correct to call William Spaulding the "prince of American collectors," William hardly exaggerated when (after Wright returned to Boston in July 1913, bringing to Sunset Rock, the Spauldings's great North Shore house at Prides Crossing, the fruits of his labor) he pronounced Wright the "Father of our collection." Like Bernard Berenson

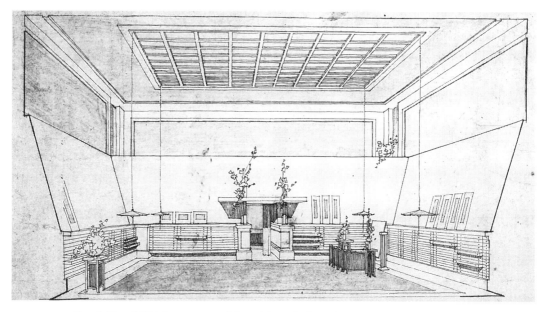

FIGURE 232. Frank Lloyd Wright: proposed Spaulding Gallery for Japanese Prints. Back Bay, 1914. Probably Wright's design was intended for Boston's Museum of Fine Arts.

with Isabella Stewart Gardner, Wright had not only helped to amass but also to shape his clients' collection: "You have been the means," wrote Spaulding to Wright, "of making our collection as great — or very nearly so — as any in the world — and you should be extremely proud of your child."

So proud, and so much more the designer than anything else, that by February of 1914 the architect was already at work on Boston's first radical Modernist architecture, designed by Frank Lloyd Wright for the Back Bay area (inspiring thought) an art gallery or print room for the storage and exhibition of the Spaulding collection. "You must tell us of the plans for the Museum print room as they take shape," wrote William Spaulding to Wright ardently. "Our conversation on the subject has made us so eager to have a room of our own and to know our treasures are in safety that I wish we could start building tomorrow."

The intimate character of the room (Figure 232) notice the low armchair and adjustable, slanted easel for studying specific prints — may mean it was designed for the top floor or as a rear addition of the Spauldings' town house at 99 Beacon Street, with which Wright was, of course, familiar. On the other hand, the reference to the "Museum print room," with a capital M, suggests a more institutional setting, surely Boston's Museum of Fine Arts, to which the Spauldings seven years later gave the collection, and which in this era — having recently occupied a vast new building — encouraged just such flair and artistry in the design of the Japanese Department's galleries particularly. Witness Cram's celebrated garden court and temple room of 1910, illustrated on page 164 (Figure 165).

Wherever in the Back Bay area of Boston the gallery was intended to be, the uncertainty of those days at the start of World War I surely waylaid the idea. That and yet more scandal attaching to Wright! Notorious already for having abandoned his wife and children, Wright found himself in the summer of 1914, just after start-

240

ing work on the Boston gallery, the center of a lurid and unsavory mass murder when a crazed servant killed the woman Wright was living with, her children, and others, and set fire to Wright's country house. Beacon Street must have been horrified. What certainly did *not* derail the project was the "fact" (quite mistaken) that the Spauldings had Japanese prints in common with Wright and not Modernism; John Spaulding's collection of Modernist painters would be by 1925 a notable one, and included the work of Cézanne, van Gogh, Matisse, Gaugin, and Prendergast. Many were among the earliest examples of the artists' work to enter the collection of Boston's Museum of Fine Arts when these works too were given to that institution by Spaulding, who was in the 1920s also a patron both of the Boston modernist painter, Margaret Sargent, and of the Harvard Society of Contemporary Art, of both of which more soon.

Nor could there have been much fault to find in Wright's design, which is exquisite. As Meech points out, it was "ideally suited to the small size and intimate character of Japanese prints . . . . The perspectives reveal Wright's clever and practical solution for print viewing. . . . Prints . . . lean against slanted walls above the cabinets. Wright also designed a skylight to allow viewing by natural light . . . an adjustable slanted easel was available for studying individual prints while seated."

So highly did Wright prize this design he later offered it to the Metropolitan Museum when his own collection went there, and the Boston gallery has also been cited by William Jordy as a source for among the last and one of the greatest works of Wright's career, the Guggenheim Museum in New York. In fact, at least one major American museum has considered in recent years recreating Wright's wonderful print room.

Why, one wonders, should not Boston's Museum of Fine Arts do this? The response of America's greatest architect to one of Boston's — and the world's — greatest collections of Japanese prints is a priceless artistic and intellectual legacy that ought to be fully realized. Of course, neither the assembling of the Spaulding Collection nor the designs for the Spaulding Gallery are exactly unknown; they're just tales to be found in very different books, so to speak, books not often consulted together. Yet now that Wright's own stature in his field has come to equal the Spaulding Collection's in its field, what a coup it would be for Boston's Museum of Fine Arts (which surely seeks a Wright room anyway — who doesn't? There's one today even in so far distant and venerable a clime as the Victoria and Albert Museum in London) to be able to install a Wright interior that may well have been designed for the Boston Museum, and was certainly designed for one of the museum's greatest collections.

The Frank Lloyd Wright Foundation, which carries out Wright's unbuilt work when circumstances permit, is not uninterested. It won't resolve Wright's love-hate relationship with Boston. But what a brilliant way for Boston's museum to greet the new century. I propose a millennial gift for Boston.

RADICAL Modernism in Boston proper in 1914 got very little further than the never built Spaulding print room. Indeed, the year previously, in 1913, the Armory Show, which introduced Picasso and company to Boston, had disclosed only too well the city's conflictedness toward Modernism. On the one hand, the same percentage of people in Boston cared enough to attend the show as did New Yorkers in that city. But there were many fewer buyers in the Puritan capital. However, if it seems as if Boston rejected Picasso in 1913 only to reject Wright in 1914, the tale is, again, more complicated. In outlying areas both of mind and place, away from the public glare, more Bostonians than the Spauldings gave evidence of

FIGURE 233. Purcell, Feick and Elmslie: Bradley House, Woods Hole, 1911. The first Wrightian architecture actually built in Boston's orbit.

stirring. A small stirring, but close at hand, and prophetic, was that in 1911, for instance, Margaret Sargent, the notable Modernist artist of the next decade, then in her youth and quite unknown, painted her Back Bay bedroom "the color of cement," in her biographer's words, and was thought very outré. A much larger stirring but way out of town occurred when in the very same year Harold and Josephine Crane Bradley actually achieved the first Wrightian landmark in Boston's orbit, a summer bungalow in the seacoast town of Woods Hole south of Boston designed by Wright's (and Sullivan's) friend, sometime assistant, and disciple, George Grant Elmslie, after Sullivan and Wright perhaps the greatest master of the Prairie Style, and William Purcell (Figure 233).

Now we have expanded our definition of Boston (see the preface to this new edition). This house arises here as it did not in the first edition, which dealt only with those echoes of early American Modernism closer to Boston proper. In fact, Modernism, as we'll see here time and time again, arises first in suburban Boston.

One of three houses commissioned by the Bradleys (one by Louis Sullivan, the other two by Purcell and Elmslie), the Woods Hole bungalow, a summer residence, and one of only four East Coast works by the firm, is arguably their best-known house anywhere. Built on a high, grassy knoll jutting out into the ocean, the dramatic setting is beautifully exploited, the picturesque coastline fully commanded. There is a boldly rounded first floor, semicircular living room, behind and above which is a hardly less striking form, an elegantly elongated second floor of bedrooms, of which H. Allen Brooks exclaims, "The horizontal sweep of the elevated bedrooms makes them appear to hover, almost like a sea gull, above the point of land."

The shingling is also deftly contrived so as to create an effect quite similar to that of the long, thin Roman brick Wright was so apt to project every few courses in order to underline an overall pattern of horizontality, a pattern made more evident by deeply raked out continuous horizontal joints (as contrasted with vertical joints of flush, butted bricks that hardly registered visually at all). Purcell and Elmslie achieved strikingly similar effects.

So much so to our eyes today, however, it is hard to believe and therefore necessary to point out that although it is historically of the highest importance as the earliest radical Modernist work of the American school in Boston's orbit (or, indeed, on the East Coast), and was by no means in its day unnoticed (it was widely published in contemporary architectural journals), the influence of the Bradley House was felt hardly at all in Boston.

This was not, I suspect, entirely because of the Prairie Style's controversial forms. Nor was it that Frank Lloyd Wright's work was universally disliked in Boston. Avant-garde taste is a minority taste everywhere, even Paris! Consider, for example, Cram's observation in 1916 that "the low stretch of the Western plains has been symbolized in the parallel lines . . . characteristic of the work of Frank Lloyd Wright." Admiringly, Cram allocated two out of eight illustrations in his "Promise of American House Building" that year to Wrightian houses, one — the Boynton House in Rochester, New York — by Wright himself. For Cram, however, and for other Bostonians (Easterners even), I suspect the western plains were one thing, Boston quite another.

As always, thankfully, Boston enjoys the priceless boon of not having to depend entirely on its establishment, architectural or otherwise; always, in every field, there are the revolutionaries, or at least the next generation! At least one M.I.T. student, for instance, in 1914, according to that architecture school's history, undertook a project "inspired by the Midway Gardens in Chicago designed by Wright." Indeed, throughout our discussion here, there will be not only architects but also architectural students to consider, even brilliant undergraduates: in this case Lincoln Kirstein, Edward M. M. Warburg, and John Walker III.

In the 1920s (the First World War distracted everyone until then), these three, aided by Agnes Monghan and Philip Johnson, founded the Harvard Society of Contemporary Art, the intention being to "supplement the work being done by the Boston Museum of Fine Arts and the Fogg Museum of Art" in respect of radical Modernism, which was, of course, in the conservative Boston of the 1920s, precious little — the whole point to the society, which was "the first organization in the country," in Nicholas Fox Weber's words, "to devote itself to an ongoing program of changing exhibitions of recent art." Years later John Coolidge would write that the Harvard Society's purpose was "to pick up the torch lit by the Armory Show of 1913 and to introduce younger Americans to the arts of the early twentieth-century and of our own time," a fascinating observation when one recalls that of the three cities in which the Armory Show appeared, Boston, thought generally to be the most hostile, was finally where the show's bright beacon of Modernism was actually relit in America.

Headquartered, student fashion, in two hired rooms overlooking Harvard Square at 1400 Massachusetts Avenue (the walls of which were white, the ceiling silvered with squares of tea paper, and the furnishings of tubular steel chairs and such), the society, established in 1928, did not confine itself to exhibiting Picasso, Matisse, Miro, Brancusi, Calder, Hopper, and Diego Rivera. Architecture, too, intrigued — including Wright, Buckminster Fuller, and even Walter Gropius and the Bauhaus. Indeed, the society is chiefly significant in Western architectural history for having dared in conservative Boston (prophetically) to mount in 1930 the first exhibition in the world outside Germany of the architecture of Gropius and the Bauhaus (see illustration on page xi). Moreover, like the Armory show, the Bauhaus exhibition also traveled, for the first time in America introducing New York and Chicago as well to the Bauhaus aesthetic and all its new forms and striking compositions —

243

demanding, challenging, drawing the eye back again and again.

If the fact that the spirit of the Armory Show was rekindled in Boston is significant, so is the fact that it was by the academy, and that Modernism was at first very much more gown than town in Boston. Even the success — and distinction — of the Harvard Society of Contemporary Art at first hardly made a dent in the obstinate conservatism of the Museum of Fine Arts and the overall art and architecture community. The essential and inevitably somewhat adversarial but always fructifying dialogue between the city and the academy, upon which Boston's preeminence as the country's intellectual center has ever been based, is seen here in very high relief. Nor did the Great Depression help, finally dooming even the Harvard Society. Conservatives rejoiced.

Indeed, so virulent was the rejection by Boston's establishment of Modernism in any form (except for a brief revolt, quickly quashed, at the Boston Art Club), that the pent-up enthusiasm — and frustration — the Harvard Society had disclosed soon hemorrhaged as far away as one could get from Boston proper and still be in New England — in Hartford, Connecticut, of all places. Caroline A. Jones tells the tale in *Modern Art at Harvard* — a work that nicely brings all these threads together — about A. Everett ("Chick") Austin of Harvard's Fogg Art Museum, who

became the new director of the Wadsworth Atheneum and transformed one of the oldest American art museums into the newest with the 1934 opening of the Avery wing. Striving for the "hovering horizontals" and smooth planes of the International Style, the new addition included an atrium that echoed — in a modern idiom — the Fogg's own Renaissance courtyard. Opening with a ground-breaking Picasso exhibition and the world premiere of the Gertrude Stein/Virgil Thomson opera Four Saints in Three Acts, Chick Austin's museum "forced modernity on New England for good and all."

Austin's modernism and the Stein/Thomson

opera . . . had a catalytic effect. . . . As Agnes Mongan tells it, groups of Boston cognoscenti went down for the glittering opening; on the drive back, an inspired Nathaniel Saltonstall (a Boston architect and a trustee of the Museum of Fine Arts) said, "Agnes, why can't Boston do something about contemporary art?" As Paul Sachs had responded to Lincoln Kirstein a few years earlier [the result being the Harvard Society], she advised Nat to organize.

America, not just New England, had achieved something of an apotheosis at the Athenaeum in 1934 — not in New York's orbit, but in Boston's, though at its outer limits. Further, the bright lights of Harvard's next generation who ignited the happening in Hartford followed up by mounting not just the historic Picasso show, but the first American museum purchase of the work of Mondrian, and the American premiere of a work by Satie. Finally, they showed movies as art in Hartford seven years before the Museum of Modern Art did in New York. Shades of Isabella Stewart Gardner, whose Matisse was the first to enter an American museum, and who had heard Satie at Fenway Court. But who since in Boston?

The International Style version of the Fogg court notwithstanding, not as many architects as artists seem to have figured prominently in all this. Indeed, not many Boston architects come to mind in this connection as at all "advanced." Two, no longer well known, were George W. Brewster and G. Holmes Perkins. Even more obscure was George Sanderson, who designed in 1930 for the artist and critic George L. K. Morris a studio in Lenox, in the Berkshires, inspired by Le Corbusier's studio for the sculptor Amade Ozanfont, with whom Morris, a New York artist, studied (Figure 234). Two others were Harvard-trained Boston Brahmins of admittedly some repute, but in other fields. One was Nathaniel Saltonstall, whose influence was felt chiefly with respect to contemporary painting, not architecture (he was instrumental in starting Boston's Institute

FIGURE 234. George L. K. Morris Studio, Lenox, 1929–30 According to an article in the *Berkshire Eagle* in Morris's lifetime, Morris's architect was "George A. Sanderson of Littleton, whose work is quite familiar in the Boston area." A sculpture commissioned in 1934 from Gaston Lachaise adorns the grounds.

of Contemporary Art); the other John Wheelwright, the son of the quite important architect whose work is discussed in Chapter 6. The younger Wheelwright designed little, however, beyond a house or two and his own famously "red-and-black Pompeian chambers on upper Beacon Street" (Lincoln Kirstein's words) and then, as today, was chiefly known as a Modernist poet. Only the third, Eleanor Raymond, though handicapped in that era by being a woman, achieved very much in this respect.

Raymond, along with Lois Lilley Howe (an early M.I.T. graduate best known for designing the Women's Building of the 1893 Chicago World's Fair), Eleanor Manning (notable for her leading role in the design of Old Harbor village in South Boston of 1937, Boston's first public housing project and one of the first in the country), and Mary Almy, all three the partners in one of the four earliest firms of women architects in American history, was a luminary of a circle of gifted artistic women (another was the sculptor Amelia Peabody) centered on the College Club in the Back Bay. A graduate of Wellesley College, Raymond went on to study at the Cambridge School of Architecture and Landscape Architecture, a pioneering school for the training of women, founded in Cambridge in 1915 and merged in 1930 with

Smith College, from which Raymond received her master's degree in architecture.

Though most of her work was quite traditional, Raymond had the repute, according to Doris Cole, her biographer, of being "a pioneer in contemporary design." Though it was only in her last years that mainstream media like *Newsweek* would hail her as "a dazzlingly prolific innovator," especially in the area of energy conservation, as early as in 1931 *Architectural Forum*, the leading professional journal of the day, credited Raymond with having designed "probably the first modern [International Style] house in Massachusetts," the background of which Cole describes thusly:

While traveling in Germany Raymond recalls how interested and impressed she had been with the new buildings of the Bauhaus School architects. Upon her return she was anxious to try her hand at these new forms, . . . the opportunity arose when she began designing a house for her sister [in Belmont] . . . in 1931. . . . The Raymond House did have flat roofs and horizontal lines, but in her hands this international style was . . . transformed into her own style suited to New England.

House Beautiful explained further: "Built of cedar-matched boarding . . . the usual stark white exterior walls [are] . . . transformed into a gray-green, with the front

FIGURE 235. The debut of European Modernism in Boston's orbit. The first International Style house in New England of note, and one of the first in the country: the Rachel Raymond House of 1931 in Belmont, designed by Boston architect Eleanor Raymond for her sister.

door, iron railings, and posts supporting the roof . . . painted red" (Figure 235).

Subsequently, others (Bainbridge Bunting, for instance, in his work for the Cambridge Architectural Survey) have been less impressed with Raymond's Modernist work, but I think it needs to be explored more fully. Particularly interesting is the fact that Raymond designed for Amelia Peabody a whole series of innovative buildings, including in 1933 the Peabody Studio in Dover and the solar house noted in Chapter 10. A sculptor who had studied under Archipenko in New York and also in Paris, Peabody (whose best-known work in Boston is probably her *Mother and Child*, a bronze of 1931 at the Mugar Building at Northeastern University) was not as a sculptor a radical Modernist, but was much more Modernist in her taste as a client and patron. She was

a trustee and benefactor, for example, of Boston's Institute of Contemporary Art, yet more evidence that architecture, especially if controversial, is always as much a matter of the client as of the architect.

Both the Spaulding Gallery and the Bradley House in Woods Hole testify to that as much, of course, as Raymond's work for Peabody, and that sculptor was far from Boston's only "progressive" client. Another was Margaret Sargent, a Bostonian of old family (she of the cement-colored Back Bay bedroom of 1911), whose paintings were shown by the Harvard Society of Contemporary Art. By 1936 Sargent had overwhelmed the historic architecture of her Commonwealth Avenue town house, where she had in the 1920s entertained (and plotted and collaborated with) both George Luks and Alexander Calder, with a new drawing

246

room described as "black and white, with stark chrome furniture." More importantly, she by then owned both a Gauguin and a Picasso, perhaps the first in a Boston collection.

Often Modernism — especially in Boston proper — first showed itself in those days in interior design. Indeed this was true of the most important client of them all, that princely patron of so many good causes, John Nicholas Brown, the eighth generation New England patrician of fabled wealth (the richest baby in the world, he was once called), though in the 1920s he showed his hand only very discreetly, as was his style: "I designed a modern bedroom in my mother's [Commonwealth Avenue] house in Boston," Brown wrote Richard Neutra once, "which, I believe, was the first modern room in New England." Tantalizingly, he does not describe his design, nor according to the Brown Center in Providence does any record of it survive. But Brown's Modernist Boston bedroom was (as was his membership in the Harvard Society of Contemporary Art) chiefly significant as a portent: after his marriage, when Brown and Anne Kingsolving Brown began to summer on Fishers Island, New York, off the Connecticut coast between Rhode Island and Long Island, they commissioned Neutra himself to design for them in 1936 a summer residence (Figure 236) even more striking than the pre-war Woods Hole bungalow of the Bradleys.

One of the first of the European Modernist designers to come to America, in 1923, Neutra, steeped in the Vienna school of Modernism and with experience of the Bauhaus too, had also spent the better part of a year studying with Wright. Neutra, in fact, in Thomas Hine's words, "bridge[d] perhaps better than any other architect the frequently polarized worlds of [Wright's] Taliesin and [Gropius's] Bauhaus," in other words the worlds of American and European radical Modern-

ism. His house for the Browns was the first great work of the European Modernist school in Boston's orbit, and therefore comparable to the Woods Hole house, the first great landmark in that orbit of the American Modernist school. In form it was an arresting design — more like a train than a house, felt the four-year-old son of the family, Carter Brown, who in later years also saw how romantic even so astringent an International Style house as Neutra's could be: "Especially [Carter] loved the way the silver-gray aluminum paint reflected the changing sunlight. Indeed, he recalled, when the western façade caught the late afternoon sun the house turned red." Was it a very different red from Eleanor Raymond's!

Neutra's design did strike rather more deeply: perhaps just because of its hard-edged rationality, the Brown House did succeed, in Neutra's words, in "expressing the spirit of [its] time and the puritanic character of New England." Intuitively, Brown, as much of a Modernist as Neutra, had supplied surely the one side of the equation Neutra lacked, for Brown was as much a New Englander as a Modernist, and there is certainly a sense in which Neutra's house tries, as Wright's gallery really had not and as Elmslie's bungalow had only to a limited extent, to be as New England as it was Modernist in character.

"Windshield," as the Browns called the house (which was destroyed by fire in 1975), unlike the Spaulding Gallery or the Woods Hole house proved very much a portent, and one for which the Boston/Harvard elite were clearly ready. Reported Brown to Neutra in 1936: "There is already a tremendous interest in the house. . . . I was dining with the Department of Fine Arts at Harvard last week. Those connected with the Architectural School seemed most excited over the event of a Neutra house in the East. I feel the house will cause a tremendous stir."

More of a signpost than a spark as it turned out, Windshield actually caused

FIGURE 236. The designer of New England's first Modernist room — in the 1920s in the Back Bay — John Nicholas Brown became in 1936 the client of Richard Neutra, who designed "Windshield" for Brown and his wife on Fishers Island, New York, "one of the most spectacular houses," in Thomas Hines's words, "of the early modern movement in America."

less of a stir probably than Brown had in mind: unlike his Modernist bedroom in Boston, Windshield was very far off from the center of things. And if it was not the effect of Wright's American Modernism but of the European Modernism of figures like Neutra that in Boston was to be transforming, it was, again, not an outsider, but a Boston architect who would have to do the deed.

Moreover — and this goes to the heart of Boston's role, historically — in one way every bit as self-centered and provincial as New York or Washington, Boston is never, however, local in its intellectual focus: Boston architects look outward, typically, not inward. If it would have to be a Boston architect it would have to be one who had won his spurs elsewhere. Or, perhaps, a pilgrim from afar seeking new life no less than had the Puritans. Behold — Walter Gropius! From the announcement of the fund to preserve his house by the Society for the Preservation of New England Antiquities: "Educator, social philosopher, and perhaps the most potent architectural force of the twentieth century, Walter Gropius brought a fresh, new spirit to the art and science of design. He has rightly

been called 'one of the few actual inventors of modern architecture' and 'the most influential architectural teacher alive.' He literally helped to change the face of the world."

What Bostonian could resist? (Wright would have raged to read it.) Echoes here of the American Revolution, of Abolition, of Women's Rights (of Platonism, of course, fundamentally, and, indeed, of do-good-erism, and arrogant reformist zeal). The words might have been taken from an honorary degree citation — or from the press release announcing that in 1937 the Father of the Bauhaus himself was coming to Harvard. And all of a sudden this tale of Modernism in Boston is no longer one of half-forgotten landmarks, however important, or of obscure prophecies, but of the conversion of America by the Apostle of Modernism, for so Gropius quickly became.

A student then at Harvard, Karl Koch recalled that while he had spent his first year "reverently drawing the numerous plaster casts of Classical details . . . by my third year [the newly arrived] Gropius let it be known [they] . . . were free for the taking."

Is it any wonder that at a Cambridge

dinner party not long after Gropius's advent Harvard professor Kenneth Conant and a group of his friends, including John Coolidge, founded the American Society of Architectural Historians? That too was very Bostonian.

INTERESTING, to pursue this theme for a bit, the different directions taken in Boston and in New York in the wake of the Harvard Society of Contemporary Art's Bauhaus show of 1930: in New York, to which the Harvard show traveled, it has been widely seen as an important stimulus to the founding of the Museum of Modern Art, while in Boston it seemed rather to prepare the way in retrospect for the coming of the Bauhaus master to Harvard's architecture school. To be sure, Columbia has a fine architecture school and there would be an Institute of Contemporary Art founded in Boston, while Harvard's collection of modern art would by the end of the twentieth century become one of the most notable. But the original emphasis in New York and the emphasis in Boston could not have been more different, nor more characteristic of each city.

Gropius, for his part, worked quietly. It was his way, well described by Reginald Isaacs:

[At Harvard, Gropius] faithfully appeared twice each week at each student's drafting table. . . . His comments attracted nearby students, who frequently benefited more than the nervous individual whose new design was being criticized. His demeanor quiet, his words were few and his sketches still fewer, Gropius nevertheless elicited a response from every student. A gesture, a line from a stubby pencil out of his vest pocket, or a few questions were sufficient to direct a new attack. Frequently, he appealed to the entire student group to concern itself with the realities of the housing problem and the requirements of the legislation then being shaped in Washington. He asked that they examine earlier experience, and experi-

ment in construction methods. Each student was inspired to find a personal expression and interpretation of any project. Gropius also encouraged collaborative efforts, perhaps of two architects with a city planner and a landscape architect.

If it was a revolution, and it was, in Boston it was more persistent than noisy. Though Gropius was by no means ignored (within a week of his arrival at Harvard in April of 1937 *Architectural Record* published his views on education extensively), the New York museum was always the bigger story. And Boston's side of the revolution accordingly more difficult to measure. It is thus fortunate that our best witness to the Boston side of this history is the influential *New York Times* architecture critic of the 1960s, Ada Louise Huxtable, who has often addressed the subject of how European Modernism triumphed so completely in America. Characteristically, the pivotal event was a widely acclaimed 1932 Museum of Modern Art show curated by Philip Johnson and Henry-Russell Hitchcock, a show that gave the new architecture a name — the International Style. And equally characteristically the MOMA show was a further development of the Bauhaus show of two years previously in Boston, while the two curators of the New York show were both Harvard graduates. (Johnson, in fact, had lent to the Harvard Bauhaus show many of the objects exhibited.)

But there was more to it, of course, than one show, or even two. In fact, even the genius of Wright and disciples of his like Elmslie amounted — historically, in the 1930s — to relatively little, as, too, did Neutra's fine work in California, compared to the work of converting to the International Style the East Coast intellectual and social elite. As Huxtable declared, "It was the conversion of the Eastern establishment to the new architecture that determined the course of serious building in this country from then on." As is so often the case with the wise old city on a hill, forever weighing and judging and testing and pulling back and pushing forward, that conversion was to be the task of the old New England capital, its cutting edge the Harvard cohort already touched on here. The result? For Modernism, wrote Huxtable, 'What happened in Boston was the architectural shot heard round the world.'

It was a nice compliment for New York's leading critic, in a column of September 1980, to proffer the old Puritan-become-Victorian city, which by the Second World War seemed so exhausted-looking. For Huxtable's image struck deep under the surface of what looked then to be a tired-seeming city in its comparison to another shot heard in the environs of Boston some centuries previously that also resonated far and wide.

Huxtable, moreover, allowed herself to ruminate on why all this should be so, observing that even before modern Boston's constellation of educational institutions had been founded, it had become "a city where ideas have always flourished; the tradition-conscious conservatism and sense of continuity of its cultural establishment have been coupled with a delight in open inquiry and a high priority for the life of the mind. Come to think of it, that is probably a perfectly good working definition of civilization."

Interestingly, a half century or so previously, before the Second World War, Alfred North Whitehead pronounced Boston a center of civilization for just that reason: it was analogous in the modern period, he thought, to Paris in the medieval period. Whitehead, indeed, saw Boston's great galaxy of universities as the chief reason for this, and four decades later it was the two preeminent institutions of that galaxy that Huxtable fixed on as the key stimulants of the history of Modernism in Boston. Most of the glories of Boston's

Modernism, she wrote, "were brought to Boston by something else that the city's intellectual leadership has specialized in — enlightened patronage. Strictly speaking, Boston's great educational institutions, Harvard and the Massachusetts Institute of Technology, were the real crucible in which American modern architecture was formed." Gropius particularly led the way, his supreme distinction being that he was to be delayed only somewhat by the Second World War in "transforming the Harvard Graduate School of Design into the harbinger," in Donald Lyndon's words, "of modernism in the United States."

TRYING, however, as I have here to keep an eye on both background and foreground, on clients as well as architects, on architectural students as well as their masters, we ought perhaps to consider another arrival in town in this era, in 1935, just two years before Gropius's, that of an utterly unknown young Chinese student, one of innumerable aspirants to architecture to be seen between the two world wars daily crisscrossing Copley Square in more or less complete obscurity to lectures and studios at M.I.T.'s School of Architecture, located then in the Back Bay on the square's eastern edge, on Boylston Street between Clarendon and Dartmouth Streets. There it was, in fact, that the eager young student — as much a refugee really from communism as was Gropius from Nazism — discovered in the perverse way of all students another if more distant modern master than "the Silver Prince" (as Paul Klee used to call Gropius, so "suave" was the guiding light of the G.S.D.) — no less than Le Corbusier — the man himself, and in Copley Square!

It is an old story. Conservative, stagnant Boston (never more so than in the 1930s, during the Depression) — such tired soil, one is told, always so unfriendly to new ideas of any kind. Yet what revolutionary revelations seem typically to erupt, historically, in such unfriendly soil! No more than most of Boston's architects and artists cared for Gropius, did they care then for Le Corbusier, who one suspects would have been then at least as roundly condemned as Wright and Picasso in Boston had he been then as well known. The painter, at least, had not proposed as Le Corbusier had to destroy Paris, substituting for it his "radiant city" of parkland punctuated by skyscrapers. But, no less than Harvard's dean of architecture, M.I.T.'s dean knew his duty to his students (among whom we know the young Chinese student already stood out) and thus it was, to the delight of Ieoh Ming Pei, that the great French master was invited to come and lecture at M.I.T.

Strange apparition, indeed — Le Corbusier in Boston's Back Bay. It was only for two days. But decades later an older and by now world-famous I. M. Pei would remember his experience of "Corbu" in Copley Square in 1935 as "the most important two days in my professional life."

An episode, to be sure: the incendiary French Modernist master in Boston; an episode in one sense that would hardly be comparable to the steadily growing influence of the creator of the Bauhaus in Harvard Yard. But Le Corbusier would return to Boston. And by the 1960s, when Huxtable would conclude that Pei might "very likely be America's best architect" (something no one would ever venture of Gropius), the Hancock Tower Pei's firm designed in Copley Square was no episode: Pei's gift to Boston would become the signature landmark of Boston in the modern era.

It was one of many gifts, each far more gratefully received by Bostonians than those Gropius would proffer. But that is to be very provincial, and I am allowing the Bostonian in me too much to break through here. And the teacher! Because in any era I am less interested in other teachers than in students: like Pei, in whose young mind no less than in Gropius's middle-aged mind modern architecture was coming alive — even in Copley Square in the 1930s.

Yet, after all, the student must have teachers. And Gropius by most accounts was a great teacher, a "born teacher" Giedion called him, not less because he listened as well as taught. Indeed, Pei too would, after M.I.T. and Le Corbusier, cross the Charles and study to very good point at Harvard with both Gropius and Marcel Breuer, then Gropius's partner in practice, and in the end a hardly less celebrated master (he of UNESCO in Paris, the Whitney Museum in New York, and the H.U.D. Headquarters in Washington) who early joined Gropius on Harvard's faculty.

So did many others for larger or shorter periods of time, most notably Sigfried Giedion, who spent his Harvard year exploring eighteenth-century Salem houses, leading a seminar on mid-nineteenth-century Boston Granite Style architecture, and writing *Space, Time and Architecture*, one of the most influential architecture books of its time, a milestone in modern thought and an ardent apologia for the Modern Movement. (Indeed, as William Jordy has pointed out, it was not until Giedion's book that "the early Chicago office buildings receive[d] their due.")

How heady were these early Modernist days at Harvard is clear when one recalls the Norton professor in 1939–40 was Igor Stravinsky. Only Mies van der Rohe (between whom and Gropius no love was lost) resisted the siren call of Boston and elected Chicago instead. Still, the first book on Mies's work was by Philip Johnson, who took up the study of architecture at Harvard in 1942 very much as Mies's acolyte. Indeed, students as well as professors thrived in Cambridge. For young Pei, for instance, it cannot have been less important that it was there he met Henry

N. Cobb, who would later become Pei's partner, in fact, the lead designer, years later, of the Pei office's Boston Hancock Tower.

Cobb was a native Bostonian, born in Brookline; Pei a transitory one, a native of Shanghai. And eventually both would be based in New York. Yet, we associate Pei no less than Cobb with Boston, very much the way we think of Charles McKim, one of the first, historically, of a new breed of "Boston graduates" as I call them: men and women in the modern era of Boston's educational fame who, wherever they ultimately settle, because of long, formative school years spent in the New England capital (nearly a decade in Pei's case) become imbued with the culture of Boston, becoming honorary Bostonians.

Like McKim, Pei was a Harvard man who met his future wife in Boston and had many Bostonian friends or relations (McKim's brother-in-law was speaker of the Massachusetts House of Representatives; Pei's friend and classmate at M.I.T. was Massachusetts governor Frank Sargent). Pei also, much like McKim, would do important work in Boston.

To be sure, "the mandarin [and] the Boston Brahmin," as Pei's biographer calls Pei and Cobb, began in very different places. But they were well met in Boston in a larger historical sense too; because Cobb's ancestors were in the China trade, he and Pei in some sense stood witness again to the long-standing affinity between Boston and the Orient, of which the greatest mark is, of course, the fabled Asian collections of Boston's Museum of Fine Arts, where when he would one day design the east wing, Pei in some sense rounded the circle in the fascinating way that such things happen in ancient, deeply layered, and lively cultures like Boston.

If those kinds of links in one way or another would eventually conduct Modernism in architecture over the years into Boston's psyche all the more naturally,

it must still be admitted that not only in the late 1930s and in the forties but even into the fifties, Gropius and company, the Modernist spearhead, had really a harder time, seemingly, converting Boston than the New World as a whole! Although one of Gropius's two sponsors when he applied for American citizenship was no less than Henry Shepley of the venerable Coolidge/Shepley office, H. H. Richardson's successors, the oldest architectural firm in America and Harvard's official architects, and although Gropius at the 1937 meeting of the American Institute of Architects (in Boston that year) had been given a standing ovation, it is equally significant that the Modernist master, who had come to Harvard in the rosy afterglow of the dedication of the Coolidge/Shepley office's magnificent Georgian Revival riverfront residential colleges at Harvard, had to wait more than a decade for the university to offer him a commission.

ONE reason for Gropius's long wait was the appearance of the so much more graceful Scandinavian variant of the International Style, which first got its foot in the door in Boston in the very year of Gropius's arrival, when Eliel and Eero Saarinen began a most significant relationship with the Boston Symphony Orchestra. Commissioned in 1937 to prepare the master plan for the orchestra's new summer home, the Berkshire Music Center at Tanglewood, the splendid country estate of an old Boston family given for that purpose to the BSO, Eliel Saarinen designed a great symphony pavilion, or, as it has come to be known, the Shed (Figure 237).

According to BSO historian Mark DeWolfe Howe, the project was "entrusted to Mr. Eliel Saarinen, the Finnish architect of Detroit, with whom, as with his compatriot, Sibelius, it was clear that Dr. Koussevitsky [the BSO's legendary conductor of the time and the founder of

FIGURE 237. The Boston Symphony Orchestra's Koussevitsky Music Shed of 1938, the design of which was a collaboration between Eliel and Eero Saarinen.

FIGURE 238. Tanglewood opera house and chamber music hall of 1942 was designed entirely by Eero Saarinen, his first work in Boston's orbit.

253

Tanglewood] felt a natural affinity." Indeed, Koussevitsky, who was Russian and a promoter of international modernism in music, knew Finland of old, and as Saarinen was a close friend of Sibelius, whose work Koussevitsky particularly admired, there is a deep-rooted, cross-cultural, and interdisciplinary dimension to the Tanglewood commission.

Some claim the design is not Saarinen's because it was somewhat modified by the engineer Joseph Franz, who supervised its construction. However, Albert Christ-Janer, Eliel's biographer, quotes Saarinen as saying, with respect to Franz's changes (which were not many, and only one of which, the introduction of pillars, Eliel lamented), "But this is not a bad thing, because conditions change and a plan should not attempt to frustrate the forces of change. There must be flexibility." Notes Christ-Janer, "The form of the structure . . . is in keeping with the plan which [Eliel] drew up, the basic idea in agreement with the concept which he and Koussevitsky formulated." One can see this, moreover, from Saarinen's original model, reproduced in Christ-Janer's study.

If there is a hand other than Eliel's evident in the Shed it is that of Eliel's son, Eero, which Craig Miller documents in his essay on both Saarinens in the *Macmillan Encyclopedia*. The "powerful sculptural forms" of this period of the younger Saarinen he refers to are very apparent in the sweeping contours and majestic profile of the gigantic steel structure (it seats six thousand), and even more so in the case of Tanglewood's opera house of seven years later. Of this last, almost entirely Eero's work, a critic has written that "the tied, bow-string arches of the wooden opera house . . . constituted a step in [the] direction of a most important strain of development in Eero's development in the forties . . . [of] a functionalist, economical architecture, liberated from pictorial considerations" (Figure 238).

As for Gropius, if he did not enjoy the sort of institutional support from Harvard that the Saarinens did from the Boston Symphony Orchestra, it was characteristic of him that he soon made his own opportunity, also to the west of Boston, in the suburb of Lincoln, just the sort of outlying setting in which previous Modernist modes had debuted. It was to be his own house.

As Reginald Isaacs, Gropius's biographer, tells the story, Henry Shepley made it all possible by raising the matter with Mrs. James Storrow, who a critic describes in terms no one familiar with the perennial Boston "blue-stocking" of legend (another had given Tanglewood to the BSO) will dispute: she was, he writes, "an elderly, civic-minded, and progressive person who knew little about modern architecture but was interested in learning about it. . . . She was persuaded that a newcomer should have the opportunity to show what he could do. If the result was nonsense, it would die. If successful, it would be a contribution." Anxious it should be a fair fight, she also funded the erection nearby Gropius's new domain of a traditional Colonial house "so that the old and new could be compared." It was so Bostonian. In the event Gropius's design pleased Coolidge so much she gave other house sites nearby to other Modernist architects, including Breuer, who built nearby in 1936. Nor does it take anything away from Coolidge's benefactions from the Boston point of view that Storrow evidently had her eye too on the future subdivision of her great estate, which she asked Gropius to take up in 1942.

As with any building of the stature of the Gropius House, there are several ways to approach it and the best is not necessarily the most exhaustive. Elsewhere I have stressed Gropius's social teachings. But the Gropius House is a masterwork that begs for formal analysis, and I like best that of Sherban Cantacuzino.

Rooting his analysis in the 1927 house at Garches by Le Corbusier, who Canta-cuzino feels was "as much a painter as an archi-

FIGURE 239. Walter Gropius and Marcel Breuer: Haggerty House, Cohasset. In the 1930s and forties Breuer led students on "pilgrimages" to such early Modernist milestones. Preeminent among them was Gropius's own house in Lincoln. See figure 227.

tect," he observes, "Cubism attempted to show simultaneously the front, back and inside of objects," but that "it was left to architecture to demonstrate the existence of time as a fourth dimension [for] . . . only in a building is it possible to appreciate the many-sided quality of space by moving from one point to another." It is in this context that he writes of the Gropius House:

In a formal sense the house is a cube with some parts pushed out and others cut open. The handling of space is entirely contemporary as in Le Corbusier's house at Garches, but, unlike that house, realized in traditional materials. . . . Gropius [has] created a masterly three-dimensional composition reminding one that the origins of the modern movement lay as much in the formal preoccupations of the cubist and abstract painters as in functionalist doctrines.

Figure 239 conveys just this sense of the cube both expanding and contracting in another such house to the point that one almost does feel one sees "the many-sided quality of space."

Gropius and Breuer were both partners in architecture as they were colleagues in teaching. And one of the high points of their work in the late 1930s and early for-

ties was the Hagerty House in Cohasset (Figure 239); other works included the Ford House in Lincoln, the Chamberlain House in Sudbury, and another in Wayland. Moreover, as William Jordy points out, "the practice which Gropius and Breuer established together had almost as much impact as their teaching." Indeed, these two masters and their disciples would not just make Cambridge but several of Boston's western suburbs a kind of Modernist refuge. Noted Jordy, "Like psychiatrists of the period, modern architects tended to cluster; they often stayed close to the architecture schools. . . . They enjoyed one another's company in what was then a rather lonely point of view."

They also included their students in all this. In fact, the student in at least one case designed the house: years later Pei recalled how he was among the first dinner guests invited to Philip Johnson's own house on Ash Street near Harvard Yard, designed by the precocious young Philip in 1942 for his own use while he was a student at Harvard's Design School. Plainly a precursor in many ways to his famous Glass House, the house's design was also brilliantly impertinent in the best patrician

FIGURE 240. Frank Lloyd Wright: Baird House, Amherst, 1940. It is a house that has inspired two famous Wright scholars.

tradition of Harvard, obvious homage, after all, to Mies van der Rohe, Gropius's great rival!

Pei was also in his student days invited as well, of course, to Gropius's own house ("a revelation" for students, who, as Michael T. Cannell, Pei's biographer, notes, had "mostly admired modernism in magazines"), and as well something of "a taste of avant-garde Weimar within walking distance of Walden Pond," in the words of one critic. It was a heady combination, for the Gropius House was naturally a must-see station on the international Modernist "railroad." Had not Stravinsky himself, at Harvard in 1939–40, with his new bride, Vera de Bosset, turned up at the Gropius's scarcely an hour after their wedding? In the same period, Frank Lloyd Wright came on a visit (this was the occasion when he complained so bitterly of Harvard's neglect of him).

It was at least a Harvard man who was responsible at that time for the first design of Wright's actually built in Boston's orbit, the Baird House of 1940 in Amherst (Figure 240), only an hour's drive or so from Gropius's house (and perhaps one reason Wright was in Boston), one of a dozen or so houses of 1939–41 which

showed generally the renewing effects even on Wright of the International Style, and more specifically, in Brendan Gill's words, the "strong influence that Mies van der Rohe was having upon Wright."

With its striking "car port," an invention of the architect's then hardly six years old, this Amherst residence proved in its own way rather a romantic and very Wrightian project. It was an idea born in the mind of an Amherst College professor of English in only his late thirties, Theodore Baird, who, while he thought very little of the literary quality of Wright's autobiography, loved the architect's description of what a house should be. Hoping against hope, Baird wrote Wright to ask about a modest house design. Impressed doubtless by the professor's spunk, and perhaps because Wright was in a sentimental mood (his father had been a student at Amherst College), Wright met Baird in New York and spent three hours with him finalizing the project.

Although Wright's design (one of about a dozen house projects he did on the eve of World War II) certainly was not in the same league with Gropius's house, Baird's house was, in Gill's words, a "superb" design, by no means minor work. Indeed, minor works don't set hard-headed scholars dreaming, as the Baird House did Harvard professor Neil Levine, who explains in the preface to his monumental study, *Frank Lloyd Wright*, that once when he and John Coolidge were planning a student field trip west of Boston, Coolidge

recalled that the Baird House in Amherst was quite nearby other things we were to see and suggested we include it on our itinerary. When I objected on grounds of relevance, he insisted, saying that it would be inexcusable to deny the students such an extraordinary opportunity. I assume he was also thinking of me, and for that I shall always be grateful to him. The night following the visit, I dreamt about the building, and then again the night after that. I could not get the image of it out of my mind.

To have inspired in this way is more than most architecture can boast, and the Baird House played the role more than once; as a young man, Worcester native Bruce Brooks Pfeiffer often visited the Baird House before setting off to join Wright's fellowship at Taliesen. A distinguished Wright scholar today, he presides over the Frank Lloyd Wright Foundation at Taliesen West.

Another west-of-Boston work of the early forties by Wright was his "Cloverleaf" housing development of 1942 for the Berkshire town of Pittsfield. An evolution from Wright's mostly unbuilt Suntop Houses of 1938, the name of the Pittsfield project derives from Wright's ingenious and striking quadruple house designs, an adventuresome three-dimensional exploration of some ideas in town house and multifamily design first touched on here in Chapters 4 and 5. Certainly Wright's most brilliant such design in Boston's sphere, the Cloverleaf was all but built when some local politician lived fully up to his job description and killed off the proposal, protesting that a job in Massachusetts had been given to a Wisconsin architect! The mind boggles.

The genius of Wright's four-family clusters, of course, was that any one of the four in each cluster looked from almost any vantage point more or less like a freestanding suburban house — indeed, rather a grand one (each had a two-story living room) — and it is not at all beside the point here that whilst this tale of ours is certainly closing in on the core city, the 1937–42 Modernist architectural eruption we are detailing (Gropius, Wright, the Saarinens — all working west of Boston within that five-year period, and all making their Boston debut there in terms of built work) took place entirely in the suburbs.

Notice too what we would call today the multicultural (if still predominantly Eurocentric) nature of that suburban web being woven around old Boston by these Modernists. There was Koussevitsky and the Saarinens and Sibelius, the Russian-Finnish connection; Pei and Cobb forging for the future their own Chinese-Boston connection; above all, there was Gropius, the German Jew, who seems, however, to have met the Boston Brahmin on the same ground, where neither had any difficulty spotting the very clear-cut affinities of the aesthetic of each. The multicultural and the indigenous were conspiring together. Indeed, early Modern architecture in Boston is a play, I sometimes think, with few enough characters — clients like John Nicholas Brown, designers like Gropius, and a Greek chorus standing about of diverse students and disciples with, perhaps, a critic or two: Lewis Mumford, for instance, who when he first visited the Gropius House wrote in the guest book, "Hail to the most indigenous, the most regional example of the New England home, the New England of a New World."

The exuberant response of a grateful guest, sympathetic to his host's point of view? Only a few years later, in 1940, in his *Introduction to Modern Architecture*, J. M. Richards wrote of "the New England school of domestic architecture, employed by Gropius and Breuer and aiming at a modern equivalent of the white-boarded farm house, with its fieldstone fireplaces."

Pointedly, Richards contrasted this New England School with the "California School, of which Richard Neutra is the chief exponent."

And, in truth, in the wake of Gropius's and Breuer's pioneering early houses south and west of Boston, John Nicholas Brown's Fishers Island house by Neutra does look somehow suddenly *less* "New England."

Gropius himself was clear about all this, both in his design and in his explanation of it. And his house, in fact, can only be understood as a response of Bauhaus principles (architecture seen as an organic harmony of arts and crafts mediated through new industrial techniques) to New England's own architectural traditions, which in Gropius's houses included his use of fieldstone and clapboards (though vertically and indoors) and even a screened-in porch. The design exemplified the idea of "fulfilling regional conditions," Gropius insisted, "rather than international precepts."

Perceptive students of his work, moreover, have been quick to agree. William Curtis again: "Gropius sensed in the stripped forms of the early Massachusetts vernacular a concentration on essentials akin to his own." And although Sigfried Giedion recalled well enough how when he was "staying with [Gropius] in the autumn of 1938 crowds of visitors used to come over every weekend, and often on weekdays as well, to see the newly finished 'modern house,'" what seemed to impress Giedion most of all was the beauty and seemliness in the New England landscape of Gropius's and Breuer's work. Their house of 1940 in the nearby suburb of Wayland, for instance, particularly moved Giedion: It "hovers," he wrote, "over the ground like a butterfly."

Thirty years later Huxtable would sing a very similar song, praising Breuer's work particularly: "In the New England of the thirties and forties, a small, elite group knew his houses — shelter as simple, expressive geometry in fieldstone, glass and taut, white surfaces, cantilevered over the countryside."

The multicultural dimension is evident too in Wright's work in Boston's orbit in the 1940s and early fifties, which included two in Massachusetts (the Grieco House of 1945 in Andover and the Schuck House of 1956 in South Hadley), one in Warwick, Rhode Island (the Slater House of 1946), and two in Manchester, New Hampshire (in 1950 the Zimmerman House and five years later the Kalil House). This is particularly the case with the last two, the only ones built.

A superb example of his late Prairie Style, and set in grounds beautifully landscaped by the architect, the very long and unusually spacious Zimmerman House includes a thirty-six-foot, clerestory-lit living room, the entire structure sheltered under an astonishingly elongated roof, one dramatic roofslope which is, in fact, as much Shingle Style as Prairie Style in feeling. Very fitting, of course, given the New England roots (through Richardson and Sullivan) of Wright's Prairie Style. Yet that only in this one of his six New England house designs did Wright revert to the full-blown Prairie Style suggests also a conscious reflection of the program of his clients, a prominent Manchester physician, Isadore Zimmerman, and his wife.

Russian Jewish immigrants, the Zimmermans had every reason to be very appreciative of "the American way of things," and that was in the first place likely a key reason for their choice of Wright, than which there was arguably no more American an architect anywhere. Another reason, however, was perhaps that for all their love of America the Zimmermans seem to have been made to feel distinctly outsiders, and Wright's work was more challenging of the New England context than that of Gropius or Breuer. The Zimmerman House, for example, however Shingle Style it is, is more American than New England.

Zimmerman, who left his house (with all its furnishings by Wright, some unique) to Manchester's Currier Gallery (which operates it today as a museum), first sought Wright out in 1949, meeting him in New York. The New Hampshire physician had been much moved — in just the way Theodore Baird had been (he of Wright's first New England house of 1940, in Amherst) by the master's writings about architecture. Also like Baird (indeed, like Wright's first Boston clients before World War I, the Spauldings), Zimmerman was a graduate of Harvard, which if it never offered Wright the job he thought himself worthy of, at least yielded America's foremost architect of his era many admirers, and not a few clients. Was there something in the Harvard air that bred Modernists?

It would seem so. Indeed, the more important story in Boston in the mid-1940s was not so much about Wright, predictably, but about Gropius, and the founding in 1945 of the Architects' Collaborative, which in Reginald Isaacs's words, brought together "Gropius' experience, wisdom and renown, coupled with the vigor and fresh ideas of young associates [to] establish the basis for a practice that would become world encircling and world famous." Behold, the second generation of Modernists.

The founders of TAC, as it was at once called, were eight: Gropius and seven of his disciples — five men (Robert MacMillan, Norman Fletcher, Chip Harkness, Ben Thompson, Louis McMillan) and two women (Sally Harkness, Jean Fletcher). It was all very modest at first, Norman Fletcher recalled:

Our first office was in what . . . is now the Harvard Square Theater. . . . We all had equal pay—we put in the same small amount of capital at the beginning. We got basic maintenance, which was very little at that time. We also decided that if a family had children, a new child would warrant $50 extra per month. So as the families grew, everybody was getting $50

more except Gropius, who didn't have any children. He began to feel a little itchy about this after a while, so we raised him and everybody was even again.

There was, in truth, very little money to go round originally, for this now legendary Modernist firm suffered through long and lean years at first. Yet in design it very quickly became the gold standard of American Modernism; even its failed projects became prototypes for an entire generation of architects everywhere.

Early designs were, of course, very suburban, like the Attleborough (Massachusetts) High School, an important model for schools everywhere. And this was true as well of one of the most widely admired works, Six Moon Hill in the town of Belmont.

Out cross-country skiing one day, some of the young men and women among Gropius's students and disciples had discovered a wooded and as yet undeveloped hillside tract and fallen at once in love with it. Forthwith, five of the original eight TAC associates bought up the land and developed it into a kind of semi-Utopian community that had as much to do with Emerson as with Gropius (significant comparison). Twelve families eventually, mostly Harvard people, mostly architects, bought into the idea, jointly building the one road, a cul-de-sac, along both sides of which, on half-acre lots, they built very straightforward "start-up" houses. The original investors drew lots as to which land would be theirs, and sold off the remaining lots at the same price they had paid for them originally, all in the context of a nonprofit corporation in which all held stock. Fletcher again: "There was no provision for co-op bylaws in Massachusetts at the time, so we founded a nonprofit corporation and adopted bylaws, many of which were fashioned after Quaker communities, namely, equal votes for everybody, with two votes per household, so that the wife can vote differently than

259

the husband. No discrimination of race or creed. Common land, that sort of thing."

Not surprisingly, however, plenty of discrimination was shown architecturally, and there was from the first an agreed-upon Modernist aesthetic: all houses had to be designed by an architect who lived on Six Moon Hill and approved by a community review board. And although the aesthetic was as creative as one might expect — the plastic bubble-dome skylight was invented at Six Moon Hill — it was a very spare aesthetic befitting start-up homes for young families; only if it were looked at closely, for example, would the visitor notice the very Wrightian profile of most of the roof overhangs.

In this matter of the small Modernist suburban house, individualism, however, played its part, for the tradition of the "Architect's Own House" — however plain, after all, such a house was necessarily all but a cult object to his followers — thrived in early Modernist Boston. In Lincoln alone there were three: Gropius's, Breuer's, and that of Walter Bogner, a Harvard colleague and an ally of Gropius. In Cambridge there were others, for not all the younger generation submitted to the restraints of Six Moon Hill. Several built quite striking houses of their own, including Carl Koch and Hugh Stubbins, who also followed Gropius and Breuer into suburban Boston house-building, a field so attractive for Modernists young and old alike that Henry-Russell Hitchcock's guide to Boston architecture of 1954, the first written from a Modernist point of view, reported that while there were only four modern houses in what Hitchcock called Boston's "inner ring" (all in Cambridge, none in Boston proper or Brookline), only five on Boston's South Shore (in Hingham and Cohasset) and only two more on the North Shore (both in Swampscott), there were already a whopping hundred or more in the western suburbs.

Actually, the national rather than region-al perspective of sociologists James and Catherine Ford (clients and neighbors of Gropius) in their 1940 book, *The Modern House in America*, best discloses the situation, for there were, in fact, in 1940, more modern houses judged publishable by the authors in Boston (thirteen) than in Maine, Connecticut, Pennsylvania, New York, Delaware, South Carolina, and Florida — which is to say the whole Eastern Seaboard, where any such houses existed at all. Indeed, there were more such modern houses in Boston at that time than in any *state* in the union except California, which led decisively with twenty-three to Boston's thirteen. New York, the state with the third largest number of modern houses, had only four.

Indeed, so much was the small house a focus of early Modernist architects, the Museum of Modern Art mounted an exhibition about the building type as early as in 1945. Significantly, not only masters like Wright and Gropius and Breuer were included, but also up-and-coming designers, including both Koch and Stubbins, whose work enlarged significantly on the Modernist-New England unity.

Koch's first house (Figure 225), designed (nominally with Edward Durell Stone) for his parents in Cambridge at 4 Buckingham Street in 1937, was very urban and formal, and actually not noticeably sensitive to the New England architectural tradition. But Koch's eye, as was the case with so many of these early Modernists, was less for city than for suburb, especially the outlying, more rural suburb, and in 1941 he designed a cluster of small "start-up" houses on Snake Hill, Belmont, including one for himself, that became so famous that a student named Robert Venturi at Princeton within the decade cited it in his master's thesis ("Context in Architectural Composition") for the way it "recognize[d] the natural qualities of the site," a wooded suburban hillside with a stunning view all the way to Boston Harbor.

Koch, who like all ambitious young architects perpetrated books (the best-selling *At Home with Tomorrow*) as well as buildings, was perhaps most notable for the much larger development of a hundred houses on two hundred acres of prime woodland and meadow in the suburb of Concord of a residential community he called, with Thoreauvian fervor, Conantum. Begun in 1953 and one of the first uses of cluster siting, the design concept was that "land plays a greater role than architecture." Indeed, an acquaintance, Robert Mack, who grew up at Conantum, ascribes a life-long love of hiking to the experience. Forty acres, nearly a quarter of the Conantum's acreage, were set aside as common land, through which ran hiking trails, while the houses Koch designed for the site, pre-fabricated and based on a standard module, were very inexpensive start-up houses — out of which came Koch's famous "Techbuilt house," found eventually in thirty-two states.

Koch's design was in the first place very pleasing, managing to be both very modern in feeling (particularly in the glazing) and also traditional (each had a steep-pitched roof). (The most easily accessible example of Koch's Techbuilt house stands at 23 Lexington Avenue in Cambridge, not far from Koch's first house.) Not far from that, at 199 Brattle, is Hugh Stubbins's own house, which is in its woodsy elegance a more high-style fusion of the modern and the traditional house, but uncannily New England in feeling as well, a reflection surely of Stubbins's very facile design skill, honed in of all places the office of Royal Barry Wills, that master of the Cape Cod house who Margaret Floyd once aptly credited with a "structural understanding of the timber-frame house . . . as deep as Ralph Adams Cram's of the Gothic."

Wills had even less reason than Cram to panic in the face of Modernism of any stripe: in a 1939 *Life* magazine competition

between modern and traditional architects Wright himself was famously trounced by Wills, whose work was vastly popular. But the Colonial Revival master nonetheless thought it only prudent to enlist the services of a younger associate to conceive a "modern" variant on the "traditional" Wills product. He chose Hugh Stubbins. And Stubbins, as he worked out his thoughts, found that the suspected affinities seen in high-style works between the Bauhaus and the New England aesthetic were strong enough to survive at even the vernacular level. The result was a series of widely published Modernist work by Stubbins and Wills, most notably in 1937 the Smith House in Milton, the Adams House in Brookline, and, above all, the Troy House in Needham, this last a brilliant synthesis of a Wills small house design with Modernism.

Koch and Stubbins, both so gifted at grafting Modernism into both New England architecture and landscape, at the middle-brow level, were, interestingly, the two in Gropius's circle of disciples or nearly who decided to settle permanently in Boston. Yet both also over the years became progressively more identified with M.I.T. than with Harvard.

So does the Bauhaus/Scandinavian polarity, already introduced here, arise again. The Saarinens, in their work at Tanglewood, had collaborated with an M.I.T. acoustician. It was perhaps a link they developed. But fully a decade before Eero Saarinen's work at M.I.T., that school of architecture recruited an even greater Modernist master (only slightly less famous than Gropius, though of the next generation), today — certainly as a designer — vastly more renowned. Having already seized the day and stolen a march on Harvard by erecting an International Style collegiate building far ahead of its revival — the Alumni Swimming Pool of 1940 illustrated on page 229 (Figure 226) — M.I.T. that same year brought to America from Finland as visiting professor no less than Alvar Aalto. Within the decade Aalto would endow M.I.T. with perhaps Boston's most glorious Modernist landmark.

The focus of activity of the Modern Movement in Boston was shifting from west of the core city to Boston's inner ring, from the outlying suburbs — where Modernism, however suburban, was not just an affair of houses after all: witness Harrison and Abramowitz's elegant Brandeis University Chapels of 1953 in Waltham (Figure 241) — to the academy's Cambridge heartland, just as a decade or so later, in the 1950s, the focus would shift again, this time to the beckoning skyline of Boston proper.

FIGURE 241. Harrison and Abramovitz: Catholic, Jewish, and Protestant Chapels, Brandeis University. Waltham, 1954.

12

THE "NEW BOSTON"

T HE INTERNATIONAL STYLE, in its purest form, was a kind of religion, certainly an ideal, and one which brooked no compromise. Witness its appropriation of the very word "Modernism." Art Deco or Moderne, for instance, was by the acolytes of Gropius utterly despised. Yet while a work like the Gropius House — the first Modernist building in Boston of international stature — was sufficiently a masterpiece that its lucid beauty silenced critics, no one would have called it (as one well might so many deco buildings) graceful; and something there was in even the modern psyche, in even the Puritan aesthetic, that missed the gracefulness. Thus it was that in the 1940s, the influence of Gropius's Harvard began to be mitigated somewhat by the influence of Aalto's M.I.T.

Though the Finnish master first arrived in Cambridge in 1940, the Second World War disrupted his and everyone else's plans, and it was not until after the war that he returned to M.I.T. By then, moreover, his increasing anti-Americanism (which stemmed from what he saw as the indifference of the United States to Finland's wartime devastation) caused him to entirely alter his plans to relocate his family to America (he had even enrolled his son at Taliesen), and as it turned out he never established himself at M.I.T. in any way comparable to Gropius at Harvard. But Aalto's presence at M.I.T. in the first place was a reflection of an overall vision

of William Wurster, who in 1944 became Dean of Architecture at M.I.T.

A California architect trained at Harvard and the creator of San Francisco's "Bay Style," Wurster, a close friend of Aalto (the two men had considered forming an architectural research institute together), had a vision for M.I.T. based, in Margaret Floyd's words,

on an American rather than a European program, but one which would match the forward-looking emphasis of the Bauhaus system then in place at Harvard. . . . Wurster . . . had been much influenced by the alternate Modernism of Scandinavia's Alvar Aalto and its alignment with the American tradition of architecture in the landscape, epitomized in the collaboration of H. H. Richardson and Frederick Law Olmsted, and leading to the designs of Frank Lloyd Wright. This deep affinity in American architecture had been carried from Boston to California [in the 1900's] by Greene and Greene, who attended M.I.T. . . . Now through Wurster it would return to Boston newly invigorated by the Bay Style concept.

In this vision Lawrence Anderson shared. Head of Design at M.I.T. in the 1940s, Anderson had met Aalto in Finland; and notwithstanding the fact that because of the war whatever plans he and Wurster may have had to wed M.I.T. and the Finnish architect more permanently had gone awry, Aalto's stature was such that a very little of him, so to speak, went a long way. Just illustrations, for instance, of the Villa Maias in Finland, the masterpiece of

FIGURE 242. Alvar Aalto, Baker House, M.I.T., Cambridge, 1949. "Boston, which was," in Meredith Clausen's words, "then [in the 1950s] the architectural capital of the country, with even MOMA in New York in effect being run from there," rallied around Aalto's design. It is perhaps the region's greatest landmark of the Modern Movement.

Aalto's residential work, with its innovative spatial effects, attracted house designers all over the United States, where watered-down versions of Aalto's ideas soon appeared in both architect-designed and builders' tract housing in the postwar building boom. Moreover, Wurster and Anderson did succeed in one of their chief goals: the design by Aalto of an important work at M.I.T. — Baker House.

It did not disappoint. If the Gropius House is a masterwork of the Bauhaus/ International Style aesthetic, Baker House is as masterful a landmark of the Scandinavian/International Style aesthetic. And Baker House is not hidden down a country road west of Boston: M.I.T.'s senior residence hall, it stands along the Cambridge bank of the Charles River overlooking Boston proper — where still today it takes its place with the Gropius House as the preeminent Modernist landmark of New England.

Baker House for Boston is what the Guggenheim Museum is for New York. Indeed, the essential comparison in my mind about Baker House is not so much with Gropius's work as with Wright's, and the comparison that always arises in my mind with Baker House is Fallingwater itself. Wright's great house of 1937 outside Pittsburgh is chiefly notable to me for how Wright brilliantly humanizes the natural landscape with his relentlessly International Style "trays," if I may call them that, a man-made form strikingly poised to enhance the natural setting.

Aalto at Baker House, it seems to me, though facing a much more challenging program than a private house and in a much more complicated urban environment, rivals Wright's achievement by incorporating into the form of Baker House what at Fallingwater is both form *and* setting, for Aalto's own concrete International Style "trays" — the dining room and common rooms — are beautifully poised, not as at Fallingwater over and against the natural landscape, but against

a "landscape" of Aalto's own design, his daringly curvilinear "wave"— the dormitory proper. Though it is far from being lyrical, in the sense that the "wave's" purpose is obviously to seize the most river views by increasing the perimeter overlooking the Charles, the effect of Aalto's work *is* lyrical beyond dreaming—all the more so as his great "wave" catches subliminally the watery motif of the river it overlooks. No wonder even critics so unforgiving as Manfredo Tarfuri and Francesco Dal Co declare Baker House to be (along with the Vuoksenniska Church in Finland) the greatest of Aalto's works (Figure 242).

All this, furthermore, takes account only of the riverfront: the entrance façade on the other side, with its remarkable cantilevered twin straight-run stairways, is as magnificent and arresting a composition as American architecture in this period can boast (Figure 243).

Historically, the greatest significance of Baker House is the way it expresses Aalto's legacy to architecture today. Wrote one critic:

Sigfried Giedion has given this master from Finland the unusual position . . . of achieving the "organic humanization" of modernism. . . . Giedion's perspective can also be discerned in Henry-Russell Hitchcock's 1951 essay, "The International Style Twenty Years After" [a centerpiece of which is an analysis of] "Aalto's [Baker] House at the Massachusetts Institute of Technology . . . [a] notable post-war structure . . . at the extreme limit of the International Style [because of] the expressive irregularity of the plan . . . and [such] details as the willful roughness of the brickwork." . . . Both Giedion and Hitchcock felt it important to link Aalto with the definition of modern architecture, to defend it and help it to survive.

Thus the catalogue of the MOMA retrospective exhibition of Aalto's work would refer to "the truly universal appeal of his personal version of the International modern movement." Indeed, without Aalto, the International Style might have to be

FIGURE 243. The campus-front façade of Baker House. Although Boston's seminal role in the history of the Modern Movement came in the Harvard Society of Contemporary Art's 1930 exhibition (the first in the world) of the art and architecture of the Bauhaus, in terms of built architecture Baker House scored a tremendous triumph.

pronounced a failure. Certainly significant is the contemporaneous response to Baker House of Robert Dean of Perry, Shaw and Hepburn: Aalto's "sense of materials and textures differentiated his brand of international modernism from that of the German Bauhaus." Dean wrote, "Aalto was an immediate success in Boston."

The contrast with Gropius could not have been more harshly put. Harvard, moreover, added greater insult to great enough injury when in 1947, not content with having commissioned the Coolidge/ Shepley office yet again over Gropius to do a major building, the Lamont Library, they sought out, not Gropius, but Aalto to design an important interior of the library, the Lamont Poetry Room. (With its recording and listening equipment this was a pioneering effort, the first such in the

country, for which Aalto designed an exquisite blond wood interior.) Not content, they then commissioned Shepley to do another and even more modern building — Burr Hall. Perhaps it was finally more embarrassment than anything else when the powers that be at Harvard in 1948, two years after Aalto's M.I.T. commission, finally agreed to give to Gropius and TAC the job of designing the Harkness Graduate Center there.

Gropius had to ask, however; it is known that he went personally to Harvard's then president and to Provost Paul Buck to urge TAC be given the job, which it is thought Buck finally arranged. But to what avail? Margaret Floyd's analysis, a comparison of the Graduate Center with the contemporaneous Burr Hall by the Coolidge/Shepley office, tells the tale best:

FIGURE 244. Shepley, Bulfinch, Richardson and Abbott: Arthur Fiedler Footbridge, 1954, an example of the effect on a Boston firm otherwise past its prime of M.I.T.'s liaison with Scandinavian Modernism.

When erected [1948–52] the [Harkness Center] complex was one of the few examples of adequately understood International Style architecture in the country. . . .

The aesthetic impact of the complex comes from the informal but structured grouping . . . ranged about two small quadrangles and a sunken mall. The geometry is clean and sharp . . . . The whole has a feeling of clarity and lightness, a feeling enhanced by the thin canopies that shelter walkways. . . . Its character is of a sparse puritanical functionalism. . . .

The university's other early modern building, Allston Burr Lecture Hall (1951) . . . by Coolidge, Shepley, Bulfinch and Abbott (with Jean Paul Carlhian as designing architect) in close approximation of the International Style, . . . showed more verve and originality than the contemporaneous Graduate Center. . . .

The organization of strong geometric forms . . . provided the principal aesthetic interest [of Burr Hall]. . . . At the same time the Baroque undulation of its façade, enlivened by the shifting shadows of trees, was extraordinarily successful.

Floyd's analysis is devastating. While the overall extent of Gropius's influence on twentieth-century architecture is monumental, his brilliance as a designer, unarguable before 1940, had begun to decline. In 1953 it was Burr Hall that won the J. Harleston Parker Gold Medal.

It was about this time, according to contemporary report, that Gropius, unusually, was seen to lose his temper one evening at a meeting of the Boston Society of Architects: during a presentation of the new Jordan Marsh Company design — an astonishing combination of Modernist cantilevering, Moderne form, and Historicist (Federal Revival) detail, all skillfully combined in what we'd call today a Post-Modernist essay — Gropius called out loudly, "This building sets modern architecture back twenty-five years."

An explanation for this outburst, for Gropius was typically among the most courteous of men, is that the presenter of

267

FIGURE 245. Eero Saarinen, M.I.T. Chapel and Kresge Auditorium, 1955. With Baker House they constitute a veritable New World Acropolis of Scandinavian Modernism. For the interior of the chapel, see the illustration on page xxii.

the Jordan project was Robert Dean of Perry, Shaw and Hepburn, Aalto's associated Boston architects in the design of Baker House, the influence of which can be seen, for example, in the Fiedler Footbridge (Figure 244) of the Shepley office. Gropius might well have felt beset on every side! To be sure, Aalto did not linger at M.I.T. But the Scandinavian Modernist aesthetic did, and in Aalto's place there now appeared Eero Saarinen, who in 1955 designed buildings of great importance for the school, buildings that were far more influential at the time than Gropius's work.

First came the Kresge Auditorium (Figure 245), an early example of what William Jordy called "the curvilinear drama of reinforced concrete," a drama that reached its apogee in Wright's Guggenheim Museum in New York. In fact, Kresge was the first large-scaled concrete shell edifice in the United States: it is pure geometric form, based on an eighth of a sphere cut triangularly so as to rest on only three supports nearly 150 feet apart. The effect is dazzling, especially from the lobby inside, where the splendid fan-shaped pendentive of the dome shapes space dramatically as it sweeps down to its pinpoint, for so it seems, of support. How moving is Saarinen's recollection: "We tried spanning this one-room building with a dome supported at three points— the shape of one-eighth of an orange. At first it seemed strange, but gradually it became the loved one."

Then came the chapel nearby (Figure 245), an awesomely beautiful building — "a synthesis of structure, geometry and poetic intuition," in Curtis's words, where "abstract intentions were reinforced by rich modulations of light, space and texture," ideas inspired by Saarinen's memory of a moonlit night in a mountain village in Sparta during a student visit to Greece. Thus his ingenious combination at M.I.T.'s chapel of top and bottom lighting.

But architecture is always a risky business (during the design of Kresge,

268

FIGURE 246. Peitro Belluschi: First Lutheran Church, Back Bay, 1954, the best Boston work of a master of Modernist church design.

Saarinen's marriage broke up), and while in one decade M.I.T. had collected three masterworks from Aalto and Saarinen (as opposed to Harvard's one less-than-masterful work from Gropius) the M.I.T. buildings as an ensemble do not cohere. One can only hope some future landscape design will resolve this, for Baker House, Kresge, and the chapel constitute a kind of New World Acropolis of high-style Scandinavian Modernism, an Acropolis that deserves a splendid setting.

THIS rather more graceful Modernist version thrived at M.I.T. throughout the 1950s, in no small measure because of a new dean who came on the scene in 1951, Pietro Belluschi, a distinguished architect who not only supported Saarinen's work at M.I.T. — which at the time, of course, was highly controversial — but did so forcefully: "Creative masterpieces do not come easily or by timid approach," Belluschi insisted, arguing that both Kresge and the chapel were worth the trouble.

So was Belluschi's own work, itself very much in the Aalto-Saarinen tradition. Belluschi made a specialty of ecclesiastical work, and his Boston area commissions include three superb examples: Trinity Church in Concord, Temple Israel in Swampscott (with Carl Koch), notable for its splendid high hexagonal clerestory, and (his finest Boston work) the First Lutheran Church at Marlborough and Berkeley Streets in the Back Bay (Figure 246). Commissioned in 1954, First Lutheran was a work Belluschi (who lived on nearby Fairfield Street) paid special attention to. Its elegantly arched, thin-shell concrete roof is a superb foil to nearby Victorian pomps, the enclosed court a serene refuge, and the deft detailing of the church's lovely salmon-colored brick on the Marlborough Street façade (say I who walk past it daily) a wonderful gift for tired eyes at day's end as the sun moves across it. Harvard's Dean Joseph Hudnut illustrated First Lutheran in an *Architectural Forum* article on Modernist western church design, and so highly did he think of it that Belluschi's church was

269

one of only three illustrated; another was Le Corbusier's Pilgrimage Chapel at Ronchomp!

At the same time, it must be said the continuities and harmonies of the streetscape of perhaps America's foremost nineteenth-century residential quarter were rudely disrupted by First Lutheran. Even though Belluschi, for all that he was a newcomer, knew his Boston (Matisse possibly; Picasso never; Gropius was truest, like the New England winter; Aalto best, more humane; as for Wright, no thank you) he nonetheless offended, even in the excellencies of his design. Two or three or four of such things as First Lutheran and the Back Bay's design cohesion were going to be lost. If you were inclined to be wary of Modernism, as most Bostonians then certainly were, what was bad about Belluschi's Back Bay church was very bad, and what was good was not good enough.

In architectural circles, however, the detractors of Modernism by the early 1950s were in retreat, and as Aalto and Saarinen moved on and Gropius stayed, not everyone even at M.I.T. welcomed the new dean, nor his admiration of the Scandinavian Modernist aesthetic, which I must not, by the way, mislead the reader into thinking was the only face of M.I.T. either in those days. Less visible than Kresge or the Chapel or Baker House, and more typical, was the hard-edged, mainstream International Style Modernism of the Compton Laboratories of 1957, the work of M.I.T. alumnus Gordon Bunshaft of the New York office of Skidmore, Owings and Merrill. Indeed, so divided was M.I.T., there were some before Belluschi's appointment in 1951 who lobbied instead for the appointment of José Lluis Sert. As it turned out it was Sert, a brilliant Spanish modern architect and protégé of Le Corbusier, who two years later succeeded Gropius at Harvard, where he and Dean Hudnut, increasingly at odds (over teach-ing architectural history chiefly), finally came to a parting of the ways.

Here, certainly, though it was slow to disclose itself, was a cultural watershed for Boston. Recall how fiercely, for example, Bostonians rejected Picasso from the first time his work was seen in Boston in 1913 right through the 1920s and thirties (when it was a brave Boston collector who even privately hung on his walls the by-then already legendary Spanish artist). It was not until 1941 that Picasso's work was exhibited at the Fogg ("Fantasmagoria or Plain 'Nuts'?" trumpeted one Boston paper); 1949 before the Museum of Fine Arts bought its first Picasso print; 1952 before the Fogg purchased one of his paintings; and 1958 before the Museum of Fine Arts followed suit—thirty years after the founding of the Harvard Society of Contemporary Art. Indeed, as late as in 1964 Boston's museum was making it a point to buy Picassos, "in view of the fact," as its director of the time drolly put it, "we can't anticipate the bequest of major works of Picasso from Boston collectors."

Sert, who when he came to Boston in 1953, proceeded in the time-honored way to design and build his own house — a sparsely elegant affair arrayed around several patios at Francis Avenue in Cambridge — hung proudly there the work of Picasso as the work of a friend and colleague; for the new guiding light of architecture at Harvard in the 1950s was not only Picasso's friend (gasp), but the designer of the 1937 Paris World's Fair Spanish Pavilion for which Picasso painted *Guernica*. Sert made it no secret that he and Picasso were once "very much together; I used to see Picasso and a group of friends in the café [in Paris] every evening." Miro was also a friend; Sert designed the painter's studio. And before Sert departed Boston, so greatly had things changed, the President and Fellows of Harvard College (more gasps) would avail themselves of a patron's offer to commission for Harvard — for the penthouse dining room of a

Sert-designed building — a cycle of paintings by no less than Mark Rothko, that brilliant, melancholy Transcendentalist. Behold, the Golden Age of Modernism in Boston, finally about to burst upon the Puritans!

Alas, the manner in which it did burst in the 1950s could not have been more unfortunate for all the best laid plans of the biggest names of Harvard and M.I.T. on the eve of Sert's appointment — Koch, Stubbins, Belluschi, and TAC with Gropius himself in the lead. They called themselves the Boston Center Architects. Their idea was that where there had long been only railroad yards (between the Back Bay and the South End) a huge new complex would be built, centered on a lofty forty-story slab tower. The first stirrings of civic renewal in the core city in decades, Back Bay Center was to have been, Donald Lyndon would write, "splendid evidence of what large-scale development in the hands of modern Boston architects could bring to the city's future." Indeed, the design attracted national attention, winning the *Progressive Architecture* award for outstanding project of the year, and becoming the subject of a Museum of Modern Art exhibition in New York, largely at the behest of an enormously impressed Phillip Johnson.

Supposed to be the great triumph of advanced Modernism finally arrived at Boston's heart, it was not to be. Both business and labor, wary of change, felt threatened by the plan, which languished. Instead, at decade's end, when the Prudential Insurance Company gained control of the project, Boston suddenly found a Los Angeles architect in charge whose aesthetic was very different: well might Paul Goldberger call the result, the Prudential Center, "perhaps the worst piece of corporate-sponsored late 1960s urban renewal in the country."

That was hardly the only disaster. There was the utter destruction, beginning in 1958, of a whole neighborhood, the West End, involving the displacing of thousands in aid of replacement architecture — Charles River Park — even worse than the Prudential Center. Then there was the central artery, a six-lane elevated highway that, also in the 1950s, rammed through downtown Boston with hardly any regard at all for the violent destruction of much of the city's most significant architecture. It was a catalogue of catastrophe.

Yet while it gave Modernism or whatever a bad name for a long time, suddenly, in one year, 1960, the professors and the politicians were seen to be finding common ground after all, common ground and high purpose. And it is not hard to see why. Into what was a really very depressing situation stepped a newly elected mayor of the core city, John Collins. A visionary who would be the first Boston mayor awarded a Harvard honorary degree in the twentieth century, Collins's first action was to place at the head of the city's redevelopment authority another visionary, city planner Edward J. Logue. The politicians, suddenly, had fielded a team that was more than up to the professors.

Gropius, ever the resident master in Boston, would be an important player. He was really the star of Boston Modernism's first chapter in outlying Boston — north, south, and west of the core city — in the late 1930s and forties, just as Aalto and Eero Saarinen were alike stars of Boston Modernism's brilliant second chapter in the academy in the late 1940s and fifties. Now in the core city in the 1960s there would be a new star: that young student at M.I.T. who had been so happy to encounter Le Corbusier in Copley Square decades previously — I. M. Pei. First, however, let it be said of the collaboration between the academy and the core city that it now flowered at the deepest level; its roots were to be found in a considerable achievement of Sert — the commissioning of the foremost Modernist architect of the world — Le Corbusier — to design a building for Harvard.

L E Corbusier at Harvard was bound to be for Boston a seminal event, and one not easily carried off. But just as Boston had a new mayor, so Harvard had a new president: Nathan Pusey, a man very interested in advanced Modern architecture. And although Le Corbusier had distinctly a love-hatred for America, admiring its technology but despising its architectural conservatism, and in consequence "haggled over the Harvard contract and took his patrons to the brink of humiliation," in William J. R. Curtis's words, the great French master responded ardently to the program Harvard set before him for what became the Carpenter Center for the Visual Arts (Figure 247). Not only did the program recall to Le Corbusier his own education; it "appealed greatly to the architect," Curtis wrote, because of its "lofty intentions to do with harmonizing the head and the hand."

Furthermore, having a great concern for his position in history and very much aware too of the place's "special link to the modern movement, as both Walter Gropius and Sigfried Giedion had taught at Harvard before Sert [himself Le Corbusier's old friend and sometime assistant who proposed the Harvard project to him]," the French master, Curtis concludes, did not have to be too much convinced that at Harvard a "Le Corbuiser building [was] needed to take its place in a miniature museum of architecture, crystallizing the best of contemporary expression."

Arrived in Boston in November of 1959, Corb was more ambivalent than ever when he was taken to the cramped Cambridge site: famously, he shrugged; it was, he said, "such a small commission from such a large country." His eye searching for breathing space, he spied from a Faculty Club window Harvard Yard; in *that* the architect was seen to be quite intrigued, particularly in the pathways as they filled up with students criss-crossing the yard between classes. And in his discussion of "the many intentions and levels of meaning in the Carpenter Center" as finally realized Curtis (in his *Le Corbusier: Ideas and Forms*) focuses on just the effect of the Yard's design on the building's design: "The first idea for the Carpenter Center actually emerged in writing as a short prose poem in [Le Corbusier's] sketchbook. Circulation was the generating force: '. . . the spiral from the roof of the museum must become a track of gardens and dense rockeries in the landscape and forming landscape. . . . [It was] a literary response to the paths of the Yard."

A three-dimensional response! And while the idea of the spiral proved impractical, the *S*-ramp that grew out of it in Corb's mind proved to be the heart of the design that he developed through many sketches and ideograms throughout 1960 and early 1961. He flew to Boston again in June of 1960 to present his plans and model, and such was their success Harvard administrator Arthur D. Trottenberg spoke of an overall "state of euphoria."

Ultimately, "His one building in the United States is a private diary of life-long themes written," Curtis insists, "in a half-veiled code." Tim Benton expands on this in Raeburn and Wilson's *Le Corbusier: Architect of the Century*:

What makes the Carpenter Center interesting is that Le Corbusier seems to have self-consciously anthologized his own architectural development. The building can be read as a sort of dictionary of Corbusian discoveries, from casual observations fifty years before through a lifetime's restless *recherche patiente*. Perhaps because he was keenly aware that he was being employed as an "old master," as a "great architect at work," perhaps because he responded warmly to his old friend Sert and their many

FIGURE 247. Le Corbusier's only work in the United States: the Carpenter Center for the Visual Arts at Harvard, Cambridge, 1961.

shared experiences, and possibly even because he was "teaching" the young Jullian de la Fuente, the design of the Carpenter Center became explicitly self-referential.

The entire project claimed Le Corbusier's constant attention, sometimes maddeningly so. "Do these plans so that they will think [at Harvard] I am a real architect," he self-consciously told his assistant, who prepared drawings Tim Benton calls "among the most eerily beautiful produced in [Corbu's] atelier in these years." And although endless disputes over this and that ultimately sapped Le Corbusier's enthusiasm (he declined to attend the dedication, which would have meant flying to Boston directly from India), Tim Benton notes, "In the finishing of the building, Le Corbusier insisted on the highest standards"; for example: "demanding a smooth surface for his béton brut [raw concrete]."

There is for all this in the final work the same ambivalence discernable in the architect's initial response to the idea and in his subsequent response to the site. Curtis admits, "Le Corbusier knew that this was to be his one American building. He had hoped for more. . . . He had hoped to build an example of his disalienated utopia of the future, 'The Radiant City,' as a replacement for Manhattan; he ended up building a complex urbanistic metaphor on Quincy Street."

Sigfried Giedion was at once more critical and more understanding. "The Carpenter Center," he wrote, having in mind every dimension of linking head and hand, "is an attempt to penetrate the unknown." An apt image, of course, considering the building's "ramp-paths." However, perhaps because the tremendous dynamic force exerted by the work (despite the "interior" quality of the penetrating ramps) is primarily an affair of the exterior only — leaving me, so to speak, unappeased — I never experience Le Corbusier's Harvard building without wanting at once to go and see another building; a work that will take us again "north of Boston," in Robert Frost's words, Louis Kahn's masterful Phillips Exeter Academy Library of 1965–72 in southern New Hampshire (Figure 248).

Like the Carpenter Center, one of the two last works its architect lived to see completed, the library has been called the earliest example of "the simplest and strongest architecture of [Kahn's] career"

by David Brownlee and David DeLong in their study of the architect. They write:

By the late sixties Kahn [who spoke often of his work in terms of "form" and "design," or "belief and means"] came upon a favorite formulation that was more mysterious: silence and light. In November 1967, in what may have been his first public explanation of these newest terms, he told a Boston audience [whilst at work on the design of the Exeter Library] that architecture was created at a point that lay between a silent ideal and the illumination of the real.

Kahn often spoke that way. In another speech, the year before, also in New England (to the Boston Society of Architects), he declared, "There is no such thing as modern since everything belongs to architecture that exists in architecture and has its force." Indeed, it was in no small measure because Kahn talked that way — in terms at best opaque and frequently beyond understanding — that although he was one of the front-runners when the Kennedy family summoned a number of leading architects in 1964 to Boston's Ritz-Carlton Hotel to be vetted for the Kennedy Library commission, he did not get the job.

An architect worthy of comparison even with Wright and Aalto and Le Corbusier, Kahn, who was Philadelphia-based, but taught in 1956 at M.I.T., was worth trying to decipher. And his Exeter library — with its strong concrete forms suggesting an affinity with the Carpenter Center — is also a building equally mysterious. So much so that Brownlee and DeLong hardly exaggerate in seeing in the library, which as it turned out is Kahn's only New England work, "an almost alchemical integration of mass and space." This central "room" at Exeter, each of its four elevations framing immense five-story-high concrete circles (which brace the corner piers and disclose through the circles floor upon floor of book stacks) is rivaled only by Wright's great room at the Johnson Wax Building.

FIGURE 248. Louis Kahn: Phillips Exeter Academy Library, Exeter, N.H., surely one of the great interiors of the world.

L̲ᴇ Cᴏʀʙᴜsɪᴇʀ in Boston in the 1960s was a great event. "At Boston's Logan International Airport the exact time of his arrival had not been announced," Giedion recalled; "nevertheless the entire [Harvard] School of Architecture was at the airport to greet him." Boston feted the Master, rejoicing in having extracted from the great form-giver of twentieth-century Modernism a great prize, and a vigorous spur to creativity at a time when Collins, Logue, and Pei had clearly, in Donald Lyndon's words, "set out to make a world of their own" in Boston. A new world!

In this all three men were ambitious but not imprudently so: "An alignment of the political planets appeared in the sky in those days," *Boston Globe* architecture critic Robert Campbell would write ratherly biblically — three of Boston's sons being at that time president of the United States (John Fitzgerald Kennedy), Speaker of the United States House of Representatives (John McCormack) and Massachusetts senior senator (the president's brother, Edward Kennedy). Indeed, Collins, Logue, and master planner Pei doubtless took not a little inspiration from the fact that they had but to ask and federal dollars seemed to all but rain down upon them. The politicians and the professors, each side now a formidable force, joined forces too with banking and big business in a way never possible in the prewar years, when Yankee-Irish tensions ran high under controversial Mayor James Michael Curley. Moreover, it was characteristic of Boston that the leading spirit of "the Vault," as the elite leadership circle of Boston business and finance was called, was a Coolidge of the same family as the Coolidge/Shepley architectural firm responsible for Harvard's splendid Georgian Houses. "Beauty once flourished in Boston," declared Logue. "It must again." And so it would.

The centerpiece of the "New Boston," as it was called, was to be a splendid new Government Center to replace what had become the sleazy honky tonk of Scollay Square. But the urban planners of the academy, like the architects, had even bolder ideas.

First, there was the "Walk to the Sea." Second, the "High Spine." And while a number of figures — Robert Sturgis, Hideo Sasaki, Jack Meyer — contributed importantly to both ideas, each would seem chiefly to have been the progeny of Kevin Lynch, whose seminal book, *The Image of the City*, was published in 1960, that watershed year in the history of Modernism in Boston. Of Lynch's book, David Crane wrote, "To understand Lynch's audacity, one must go back to 1953, the year when he began his studies in perception . . . when respectable planners were concerned with anything but the exploration of urban form. It took a rebellious young teacher . . . fired by the inspiration of F. L. Wright (his sometime mentor) to turn the tables." Lynch had, indeed, spent a year as a student of Wright before coming to M.I.T., where, first as a graduate student and then as a faculty member, his path-finding work in urban planning played nicely into the process of the new Harvard/M.I.T. Joint Center for Urban Studies. Founded in 1959, the center published *The Image of the City*. Forty years later it is still in print, its understanding of urban form still influential.

The "Path to the Sea" envisaged opening the heart of downtown Boston's business and governmental districts to Boston Harbor. The "High Spine," part of the "Architects' Plan for Boston," advocated the building of more office towers in the Back Bay, but that they be, in Robert Sturgis's words, "restricted to a narrow corridor from the Fenway to the Harbor, giving the city a recognizable form when seen from the various highway 'gates' or from the various neighborhoods."

Collins and Logue turned to Pei to take the lead in the overall design of the Government Center. Ably aided by

Harry Cobb, Pei took up the task eagerly, determined not to repeat the mistakes of the West End. William Osgood recalls a lunch with Pei and Whitehill at Patton's restaurant, for example, Pei all the while sketching on the place mats, trying to find a way to incorporate the Old Howard Theatre into the new center. Whitehill, too, relied on Pei, finding in him "a singular appreciation [of Boston's] essential qualities." Though as the demolition of Scollay Square proceeded, nerves began to fray. The story is told of Cobb's father, who lived at the head of Chestnut Street and walked over Beacon Hill and through Scollay Square to his downtown office every day. "Harry," he is said to have queried his son, "What have you done with Boston?"

What indeed? He had begun to open up the walk to the sea, for one thing, with the great opening that cuts through Welton Becket's Center Plaza, linking Pemberton Square to City Hall Plaza. For another, to anchor one end of the high spine with Gropius's Kennedy Building (Figure 249), the major work in Boston of the master who had put the city on the Modernist map in the first place — for by 1966 Gropius's twenty-six-story tower stood finished before the city's surely astonished gaze. Like a vision it must have seemed — sleek, machined, so gleaming white and confident — it had risen out of the rubble of old Scollay Square with a conviction and an assurance worthy of the era.

From the beginning, however, Gropius's building disappointed many. The one player the Collins-Logue tyranny could not push around was the federal government, which in turn was often at odds with Gropius over aspects of the design — the number of elongated, baylike projections on the façade, for example. (Gropius got only one, the cafeteria — he wanted many more.) The position of the tower relative to the other projected landmark of the center, the City Hall, also

aroused controversy; there are reports of strained meetings between Cobb and Gropius (his old professor, after all), who according to Norman Fletcher was "emotionally attached to the scheme, his first tall building in the United States." Yet the design, though striking for Boston, was less so for the rest of the world of architecture. To comments about the lack of original form, Gropius replied in Miesian fashion, "We cannot make a new architecture every month." This, from Gropius! — who had always argued Modernists did not study history, they made it. But Gropius was by now nearly eighty, and is said by Reginald Isaacs to have been chiefly proud that he had lived to design work for so grand a setting designed by one of his students — Pei.

One aspect of Gropius's building about which approval was widespread in design circles was his insistence (against much governmental inertia) on art! One of the joys of the much-maligned Harvard Graduate Center is the common room mural by Miro, for example; now at the Kennedy Building there was to be another mural, by Robert Motherwell, and — most conspicuously — sculpture (*abstract* sculpture — gasp!) by Dimitri Hadzi.

A Greek-American émigré, of wide repute today in his field, Hadzi's first public sculpture anywhere had been commissioned for M.I.T. in 1963. A disciple of Henry Moore, and, even more fundamentally, of Picasso and the cubists, Hadzi at the Kennedy Building confronted Boston with a work of great power but notable controversy. Located not in the building's colonnade as Gropius had first envisaged, but right in front of the building's main entrance, presiding over a vast new plaza, Hadzi's great fifteen-foot-high bronze, a work of intricate spatial complexity, was entitled *Thermopylae*, its vigorous silhouette and menacing, combative shapes a reference to the famous battle of the fifth century B.C.E. in which the heroic Leonidas of

FIGURE 249. The Architects' Collaborative/Walter Gropius, Norman Fletcher, partners in charge: John Fitzgerald Kennedy Federal Building, Government Center, 1961. Visible on the plaza is Dmitri Hadzi's *Thermopylae*. The major work in the city's heart of the master who put Boston on the world's Modernist map, the Kennedy Building is today seriously threatened by proposals for reshaping the City Hall's plaza.

Sparta was defeated by Xerxes of Persia, a visualization in symbol and form inspired by Hadzi's reading of John F. Kennedy's *Profiles in Courage*. "I wanted," wrote Hadzi, "to convey the complexity and paradox within a vital, vigorous personality through symbolic, abstract shapes . . . while . . . stressing the idea of stability and strength."

Hadzi's work, more than most sculptors', Peter Selz has written, grew out of "the paradox of art that attempts to be both democratic and elitist," a paradox that bedevils modern art particularly, and it is perhaps for this reason that few give this great work the attention it deserves, although it is historically the first public Modernist sculpture in Boston (another gift of the academy to the city, for Hadzi, like Gropius, taught at Harvard) and even today is by no means the least moving. If for most Bostonians it meant learning a whole new language of art, that just deepens its significance.

Thermopylae depends for its effect not on readily understood symbolism, but on its formal relationships. It is perhaps best studied in relationship with another bronze commemorating another battle situated a short distance away on the edge of the Boston Common — the Shaw Memorial — a greater work, but comparable. Writes Selz:

Like Hadzi, Saint-Gaudens spent time in Rome [Hadzi spent nearly twenty-five years in Rome before his decade and more in Boston], and the Shaw Memorial is exquisitely modeled in the style of the military reliefs on the Trojan Column. . . . Above the realistically rendered group, Saint-Gaudens placed an allegory of Victory — located in a position similar to Hadzi's shield in *Thermopylae* — thus fusing naturalism with idealism. . . . Those who study the work understand its historical context as well as [its] general meaning.

Construing such historical and aesthetic links, in this case between antiquity, our own Civil War, and the Kennedy era, is doubtless a burden for many. For some

FIGURE 250. Kallmann, McKinnell and Knowles, Boston City Hall, 1962, arguably the great building of twentieth century Boston.

FIGURE 251. Interior of stairhall.

it is a joy. It must be admitted, however, that Gropius and Hadzi confronted core Boston with a great deal all at once.

But what on earth, Virginia, was that strange, almost Mayan or Aztec building rising across the plaza? "Chandigahr on Scollay Square," trumpeted *Progressive Architecture*. Actually, it was the new Boston City Hall (Figures 250, 251), the work of two twenty-something architects from Columbia, Gerhard Kallmann and Michael McKinnell, who against all odds won the 1962 competition for a building

that has in subsequent years become perhaps the most widely admired and the most widely hated building in America.

The new City Hall wasn't just Modernist — it was Brutalist. And its confrontation with Gropius's International Style Kennedy Building is as striking a confrontation of the Modern period as the Richardsonian Trinity Church was in the Victorian period with the Classical Revival Boston Public Library in Copley Square. And, like the library of the 1880s, the City Hall of the 1960s heralded tremen-

279

dous change in Boston's architectural history. Modernism was evolving dramatically.

The term *Brutalist* derives from the rugged concrete exteriors characteristic of Le Corbusier's late work (hence Chandigahr, Gropius's famous government center in India) though Boston's City Hall was actually more closely inspired by another late work of that architect, his monastery at La Tourette. The style yielded two landmarks in the Government Center: the new City Hall and, on the other side of Gropius's Federal Building, the State Services Building.

Both buildings remain controversial, as, indeed, does Brutalism itself. Approaching from Tremont Street I find the City Hall majestic and uplifting, at once lofty and welcoming, disclosing (as M. F. Schmertz has noticed) the influence of Kahn as well as of Le Corbusier. I agree with Donald Lyndon's judgment that "there are few buildings to match it in architectonic daring and spirit," and I share his appreciation of how the building discloses itself:

From the intermediate lobby, glass doors (now locked) lead sideways into the bottom of a great light court. Here the building is most like a Piranesi fantasy. You stand on top of the brick platform base with its concourse underneath, below a concrete framework that supports stepped terraces of office space overhead, and between mammoth piers and quadrupled columns that hold the whole thing aloft in the open air. Ramps lead up to this space across the plaza face of the building, and a narrow stair plummets down the other side to Congress Street. . . . It is an amazing place.

On the other hand, it is not (nor ever was, never mind that the American Institute of Architects voted it so in 1976) the sixth greatest American building (whatever *that* means). But neither would one say such a thing about the Bulfinch State House. It is, perhaps, enough to say Boston's City Hall is a great and worthy landmark: "As fine a building of its time

and place," said Whitehill, "as Boston has ever produced." Moreover, as winning the commission for Trinity Church attracted to Boston from New York the greatest Boston architect of the late nineteenth century, Henry Hobson Richardson, so winning the City Hall job brought to the New England capital the men who founded perhaps Boston's leading architectural firm of the second half of the twentieth century — Kallmann and McKinnell, of whom more later.

Alas, the same cannot be said of the architect of the third landmark of the Government Center, Paul Rudolph.

Harvard-trained, Rudolph's best work was incomparable. His magnificent Jewett Arts Center at Wellesley College, for example: the ascent of the exterior stair up through and out into the old neo-Gothic quad above and behind it is one of the great experiences of Boston architecture. A well-considered view was that of Mildred Schmertz, who called the work of Rudolph

a synthesis of the ideas of Le Corbusier, Wright and Kahn. It is heroic, humanistic and sculpturally alive. His buildings are powerful interventions, creating new scale relationships in their surroundings. They are gateways, bridges, rallying points, creating great swirling outdoor environments and dynamic, intricately juxtaposed interior spaces. According to Ulrich Franzen: "He started the first real dialogue about architecture in the context of the city . . . this was a new approach to analyze problems of form and scale, space and function, as urban problems, rather than in the context of individual buildings." His two most spectacular exercises in urban form are the Boston Government Service Center and the Southeastern Technological Institute [in South Dartmouth, Massachusetts].

The Institute particularly is more than vigorous (it has been called overly aggressive); it is also very beautiful — while the *Boston Government Center State Services Building* (a group of three separate structures) is not only very beautiful but in

FIGURE 252. Paul Rudolph: Massachusetts Health, Education and Welfare Service Center, Government Center, 1970, one of a number of staircases that are hardly equaled beyond Baroque Rome.

places uniquely visually rewarding (Figure 252). Everywhere there is Rudolph's signature corduroy-textured poured concrete, rendered even more "brutal" by the way the raised edges of the "corduroy" are hammered so as to disclose the aggregate stone within the material. But it is not brutal to me in the sense that I understand the word; in fact, it is richly ornamental, tapestrylike. And out of this material, furthermore, Rudolph shapes curvaceous contours, sinuous lines, cylindrical towers — indeed an entire landscape, inside and out, that to me is more romantic than brutal, more picturesque than hostile — a landscape that encompasses within perhaps the finest stair in the city, and then, outside, two other staircases, each of which surpasses the interior staircase! Such incredible bravura is worthy of Baroque Rome.

The Government Center in some respects remains controversial even today, and perhaps it will add something here to search out a more international than provincial perspective, and a highly critical one at that, the view of Manfredo Tafuri and Francesco Dal Co in their *Modern Architecture*. In their work, which covers *world* architecture from the 1920s to the 1970s, Boston is singled out just because of its "most sensational" Government Center, for the stature of the design advisory committee (including no less than Sert, Stubbins, and Beluschi) that supported Pei, Gropius, and the Kallmann/McKinnell office, and — though the Kennedy Building is found wanting — for the fact as well that "among the new public buildings were two of genuine high quality: the *Boston Government Services Center* by Paul Rudolph — and the [Boston City Hall] . . . by Kallmann, McKinnell and Knowles."

It may help to add that more may be going on in the case of both buildings than is readily apparent. Consider Jencks's analysis of the City Hall:

By varying the size of the unit and the rhythm of the voids, quite a syncopated melody could be played as in the Boston City Hall. Here we find a steady beat of top windows (a, b, a, b, etc.) amplified below in larger windows (A, B, A, B, etc.) while it both continues (on two levels) and is interrupted (on one). This interrupted rhythm and fugal counterpoint were inspired by Stravinsky's music, among other sources. The clash of opposing themes, in all its sculptural weight, is reminiscent of Michelangelo.

Michelangelo. Stravinsky. These are portentous names to drop in old Scollay Square. But the new City Hall, once built and resplendent, justified much. Downtown Boston's first landmark of the radical Modern Movement is at once one of America's foremost landmarks — though for this accolade there was, historically, the usual heavy price to pay. Just as there was hardly a city in the United States without some version of the Old North Church or the Bulfinch State House, or of Trinity Church, Copley Square, or All Saints, Ashmont, or the Boston Public Library, so now critic Nathan Silver of the *New Statesman* would write of "the winning design of the Boston City Hall competition of 1961, following which half the towns in America got little Boston City Halls."

The problems with the Government Center are otherwise. The too great distance of Center Plaza from the plaza is one. The other is the way the plaza design beautifully integrated with buildings and streetscapes on the Sears Crescent side of the City Hall goes on to expand more and more aimlessly, on the other side of the hall, only to spring a leak, finally, alongside the Kennedy Building, where the plaza more or less just falls off the face of the earth. Nor does the lovely long-range vista of the Old North Church thereby disclosed redeem the short-range failure at ground level.

That said, it should be noted that the background of current dissatisfaction with the City Hall Plaza is what critic Alan Tempko calls the battle of "'usable' public

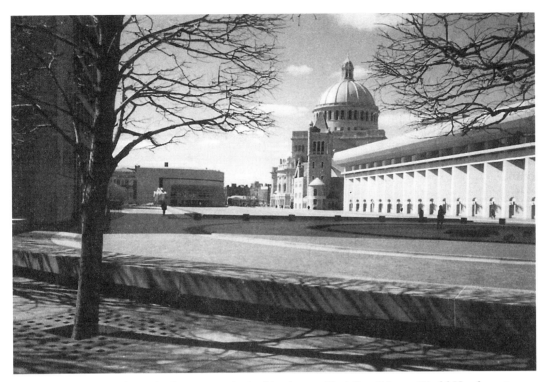

FIGURE 253. I. M. Pei/Araldo Cossutta, principal in charge: Christian Science World Headquarters, Back Bay, 1963, as much a triumph of the Corbusian vision as Charles River Park is a disaster.

space (as opposed to unpeopled, abstract plazas)." In other words, the dissatisfaction is as much an affair of taste as of style, the core issues being part and parcel of a perennial conflict in all styles between elite culture, so often concerned with refinement and taste and very comfortable with spare elegance and formal space, and mass culture — with its pop taste, distinctly uncomfortable with spare, formal settings, and so apt to want to "warm things up" in a way some would call "homey," others "schlock." When the space in question surrounds public buildings, the politics of such a situation is obvious.

Indeed, with two other settings by Pei similar to City Hall Plaza, the fact that hardly any fault is found in them can be attributed not only to perhaps better design, but also to their being located in private settings.

Beginning in 1962 with the highly sculp-

tural but still very refined twenty-one-story Green Building (the Dreyfus Building followed in 1967; the Landau Building six years later), Pei designed a trio of buildings in and around Killian Court on M.I.T.'s Cambridge campus of particular interest because the architecture is set off by, and in turn itself beautifully sets off, superb modern sculpture by very great masters indeed. Beginning with Alexander Calder's *The Big Sail* of 1965, M.I.T. gradually added Louise Nevelson's *Transparent Horizon* and Henry Moore's *Three-Piece Reclining Figure, Draped*, while nearby was placed Picasso's concrete sculpture, *Figure d'écoupée* (Cut-Out Figure), cast by Carl Nesjar.

Pei's second project was the Christian Science World Headquarters, begun in 1963 in the Back Bay, for which Araldo Cossutta was partner in charge (Figure 253). Here the centerpiece is not a bold new landmark like the City Hall, but an old one — the huge, domed Mother Church of Christian Science: Chandigarh on Scollay Square has become the Vatican on Huntington Avenue! But Le Corbusier's great work in India did indeed inspire the architect's splendid 525-foot-long colonnade, each pier forty feet high, which together with an administration tower and Sunday School Building make up the heart of the complex, a collaboration with Boston's famous firm of landscape architects, Sasaki, Danson and Demoy. Their contribution is crucial, for as Christopher Jencks points out, at the Christian Science Center the "landscaping literally becomes part of the buildings. Water in two reflecting pools is treated as a flat, architectural plane to double the images."

Donald Lyndon has also noticed the "flawlessly formed and finished concrete for which the Pei office is renowned" at the Christian Science Center, and that it is "cast in sections, carefully stacked upon each other in a manner reminiscent of the severe granite-slab buildings of the waterfront." It is a fascinating link with Boston's mid-nineteenth-century Boston Granite Style this critic suggests. He has, perhaps, put his finger on one reason why Walter Whitehill found Pei's work so sympathetic to Boston.

Not everything in 1960s Boston in the wake of the Carpenter Center was inspired by Le Corbusier's work. Neil Levine suggests in his study of Wright, for instance, that Gund Hall, the arresting profile of which is so apt for Harvard's Graduate School of Design, the work in 1968 of John Andrews, is very much more Wrightian than has been imagined. Comparing Gund to Taliesen West in Arizona, Levine concludes that "the sections of the two buildings are almost identical."

But the 1960s were without question Corb's decade in Boston and never to a finer point than the Christian Science Center, which is easily the most serene architectural experience in the city; the one

experience (when not tripping over kids in fountains or warning signs) in which the essence of the overall Modernist vision can be felt in all its power. To walk along the plaza's 200-foot-long pool, the water elegantly spilling over the rounded marble edges, or on a hot day to walk under the shade of the colonnade, is to feel — as on a beach alone — how small humankind is, but (as one does *not* on a beach) how grandly humanity can project of so much into the artful shaping of the environment. Here as nowhere else in Boston one finally sees some merit in Corb's urban planning. Having had the worst of it in the West End, in the Christian Science Center, Boston got the best of it.

The depth and importance of Le Corbusier's influence on Boston was, however, more subtle than the obvious allusions to the master's work in Kallmann and McKinnell's work and in Pei's in the 1960s. Which was only to be expected. Le Corbusier was never other than a guest in Gropius's town.

Le Corbusier in Boston —"Boston," he muses in his *Quand les cathédrales était blanches*, "city of thought and meditation." Yet he tells this story:

Today I am dining alone at the Copley-Plaza in Boston. I am bored and have time to observe. In the dining room of this excellent hotel there is a religious silence. Opposite me are three men who are certainly engineers. Every five minutes one of them speaks. Silence and mastication. The three men have handsome heads, characteristic of their country: balanced, strong, energetic. One is old, one young, one middle-aged. The meal is finished. Coffee. Silence. Then after a long time conversation begins. Unquestionably they are talking about their discoveries, but without passion or excitement. They masticate their words, speak quietly and reflectively. I should even say that they seem as if they were under the influence of a religious event. Those men won me with their handsome faces. I think: what a grave and serious country! When such men take hold of an idea or begin to act, they do not let go. But, on the other hand, if they are undoubtedly happy in their serenity, they have not yet tasted the joys of thought — not of thought which is a line of conduct, an ethic (they certainly have that), but of active, ardent thought, which contains the joys of a profusely flowered field.

A day or two later, in New York: "Observations of the same sort. . . . Engineers at work . . . the urban crime of frightfully extended city regions. . . . I begin to put my reflections together. . . . Americans who live in cities often say: 'We are the victims of an inferiority complex. . . .' Thus those thousand-foot skyscrapers."

It is, of course, necessary to keep one's perspective here: Le Corbusier in Boston is only one aspect of Le Corbusier everywhere, so worldwide was his influence by the 1960s. From the perspective of the formidable British architectural historian, David Wakin, for example, the discussion of the "brutal character [of] Le Corbusier's most striking later works: the chapel . . . at Ronchamp [in France] . . . ; the government buildings at Chandigarh, India; the Dominican monastery of La Tourette [also in France] . . . ; and the Carpenter Center [in America]" makes plain just in its geographical spread Le Corbusier's worldwide influence. Of course, that one of his four major last works (the last, actually) was built in Boston cuts both ways: but we are concerned here less with the influence of Boston landmarks elsewhere and more with influences on Boston's own architectural history. And the influence of the Carpenter Center, as might be imagined, in a town whose architects were so committed to Modernism, would be hard to exaggerate. My friend Robert Bell Rettig for instance, a graduate student at Harvard when the Carpenter Center was under construction, actually rented an apartment on Prescott Street to get a good view of the action — never mind it meant living virtually in the middle of a noisy construction site. Such devotion! Perhaps it should not

surprise, then, that some of the next generation should have seen Le Corbusier's late aesthetic as contributing importantly to a "Boston School" in the 1960s.

The idea, though very carefully hedged about, would be advanced by William Curtis, a most distinguished scholar:

The historian who is determined to define a "Boston School" of architecture will have the most luck if he looks at the work produced by local firms in the sixties. But the categories stretch very thin and the shared features tend to be superficial. Even so, one notices a pre-ponderant tendency to employ plain geometrical forms; to adhere to simple rectangular concrete frames and skeletons; to detail buildings in a "no-nonsense, no frills" manner; and to adopt bare concrete finishes. Looking at the matter in a larger perspective, one might hazard the guess that Gropius-inspired common sense was being clothed in a rough skin derived from Le Corbusier.

Curtis cites a number of examples of buildings that could possibly be catalogued as "Boston School," and as we'll see soon enough here, it was a case of rounding up the usual suspects: Gropius/TAC, Ben Thompson (ex-TAC), Cambridge Seven (which could almost have been called then "Younger TAC" or "TAC-in-waiting"), and another Cambridge firm, Ashley, Meyer & Associates (later Arrowstreet). Wrote Curtis in 1980:

TAC, Gropius' own . . . seemed to prefer well-organized architectural prose to the extremes of architectural poetry . . . includ[ing] the John F. Kennedy [Federal Building] in the Government Center (1967) with its large slab and repeating façade system and the more recent Josiah Quincy Community School (1976) at South Cove. . . .

In his Design Research Building of 1967 [FIGURE 254], Ben Thompson, once a member of TAC, used the open façade, free plan and cantilever principles to create an airy, light-filled shop window. . . .

In the same period, Cambridge Seven, a firm younger than TAC, designed the aquarium on the Boston waterfront as an unpretentious,

FIGURE 254. Architects' Corner, Harvard Square, Cambridge. Sert's building is on Brattle Street at the far left; Gropius's TAC Building is on Story Street on the far right; in between on the corner is Benjamin Thompson's Design Research Building.

inward-turning box, with a ramp spiraling around the main fish tank at its center. A similar combination of sobriety and logic informed Ashley, Meyer & Associates' competition-winning entry for the Boston Architectural Center where the studios were made simple, free-plan spaces, while the library at the top and the exhibition area, meeting room and entrance at the bottom were accentuated through changes in mass and projections. The affinities between these three schemes are obvious.

One can already see much of this "Boston School" in an important book of 1965, the first on Modern design in Boston, *New Architecture in Boston* by Joan E. Goody, who is now a well-known Boston architect. Although Goody's book is full of the optimism and idealism of the Modern Movement, it documents Curtis's view only through illustration; Goody saw then "no characteristic common to all the new architecture which could be called distinctively Bostonian."

But perspective helps. Fifteen years later (in 1980) Curtis hazarded seven works. And thirty-five years later, more than Curtis's seven "Boston School" buildings stand out for me in Goody's book. I'd add (along with all of Pei's Boston work) Frederick Stahl's 70 Federal Street of 1968, Rudolph's Blue Cross/Blue Shield

Building, all of Stubbins's illustrated work (particularly the Charlesgate Apartments and the Countway Library), much of Koch's, and two garages: TAC's Children's Hospital Parking Facility of 1964 in Roxbury and the M.I.T. West Parking Facility of 1964 in Cambridge, in the design of which Marvin E. Goody and John M. Clancy were associated with another firm. Significantly, moreover, of the thirty-odd architects whose work is discussed and illustrated in Goody's book, only seven are not from Boston, and three of those (Breuer, Pei, and Johnson) were all closely linked to the New England capital by long residence. And by far the largest number of works Goody touched on (nine) are those of Curtis's first "Boston School" firm, TAC.

Whether or not there really was in the 1960s a Boston School only recognizable later in historical perspective, there certainly was a kind of sanctum sanctorum that symbolized Boston's architectural establishment of those days and its place on the Modernist world map — "Architects' Corner," as it has always been called, at the intersection of Brattle and Story Streets, a block from Harvard Square (Figure 254).

Here it was that TAC, whose determination to reform all departments of human life had already found its residential expression at Six Moon Hill, extended its domain to the world of daily office and studio as well, building the TAC Building (8 Story Street) in 1966. Sert followed suit in 1970 with a building of his own (where — appropriately enough — the Charette firm [drafting supplies and such] is to be found today), while TAC alumnus Earl R. Flansborough built a building at 44 Story. All were grouped around an intimate interior courtyard where in 1975 the legendary "Bauhaus style" Harvest restaurant was established as something of a social center.

There was also a retail dimension at Architects' Corner to this expanding Bauhaus world that compassed home and hearth as well as office and studio (a world that had too its "Greater Bauhaus"; Karl Koch, he of Conatum, etc., had his office just up the street from Architects' Corner), and this dimension was in many ways the one that most penetrated the public consciousness, the name of the store alone — Design Research (or D. R. as it's always called) — becoming all but synonymous with the Modern Movement. Housed in one of the most exemplary of Curtis's "Boston School" buildings, D.R. had its precursor (the more fashionable Rapson's in the Back Bay) and, too, its more mass-oriented progeny of today (Crate and Barrel), but D. R. in its prime became a major directing force in American culture.

Perhaps the best way to comprehend the store's significance is to consider the description of it by *New York Times* architecture critic Herbert Muschamp, who in 1998, nearly thirty years after he had been as a young man a clerk in the New York City branch, wrote of D.R. as

long famous as the only retail establishment in New York where you could buy the objects on view in the design collection of the Museum of Modern Art. Founded by Benjamin Thompson . . . who would later pioneer the concept of the

festival marketplace in Boston, San Francisco and New York, the store stocked the classics of modern furniture by Thonet, Aalto, Mies van der Rohe, Breuer, Magistretti Hoffman and [Charles] Eames. It also introduced innovative work by young Italian designers like Joe Colombo. . . .

The store's esthetic embodied principles that began with Arts and Crafts and continued with the Bauhaus . . . functionality, truth to materials, simplicity of geometric form, the use of new materials and methods.

That Muschamp is talking about the New York branch rather than the Boston original is particularly significant in the light of our discussion in the last chapter of the way the pioneering stages of the Modern Movement in America diverged in different if complementary directions between Boston (where the cutting edge was Gropius at Harvard) and New York (where it was the founding of the Museum of Modern Art), vectors characteristic of each city. Now one sees how both coalesced in a retail thrust common to both places.

In terms of strictly architectural influence — though the "Boston School" would persist, and, in my view, achieve its apotheosis in the Perry office's Wellesley College Science Center of 1972 (Figure 255), of which more later — it was primarily Sert's work that was the big story at Architects' Corner, and — early Kallmann and McKinnell aside — Sert's was certainly the most arresting architecture of the 1960s in Boston.

Sert's impact on Boston was fourfold. First, the design of his own house at 64 Francis Avenue in Cambridge, "setting the precedent," in Margaret Floyd's words, "for the patio house, derived from indigenous Latin American domestic forms that [Sert] had developed while working with Le Corbusier and Paul Weiner," had its effect on Boston as elsewhere. Second, there was Sert's overall involvement in Boston's architectural affairs — advising on the Government Center, for example, or

FIGURE 255. Perry, Dean, Stahl, Rogers and partners: Wellesley College Science Center, Wellesley, 1972. An "unacknowledged sibling," in Nathan Silver's words, of the Pompideau Center in Paris, its straightforward concrete grid makes it an outstanding example of the "Boston School" tentatively identified by William T. R. Curtis.

FIGURE 256. Sert, Jackson and Gourley: Boston University Law School Tower, West Back Bay, 1961. Sert's striking towers at Harvard and at Boston University unify both banks of Boston's Charles River.

attracting Le Corbusier to Harvard. Third, his Holyoke Center of 1965 to the south of Harvard Yard and his Undergraduate Science Center of 1970 to the north brought order out of chaos on Harvard's main campus, effectively integrating the historic Yard, the North Yard, the South Yard, and Harvard Square into an organic unity. Fourth, Sert's work affected Boston's "little skyline" — the one along the river, not the harbor. Sert, uniquely, designed riverfront architecture for Harvard, M.I.T., and Boston University.

The quality of the work at B.U. (Figure 256) is particularly outstanding. Sert was faced with very restricted terrain dominated by Moderne Gothic by Ralph Adams Cram that most Modernists would have

thought very unfriendly. Yet Sert succeeded in reorienting the university to the riverfront, and also incorporating decisively new buildings without harming the old ones. Indeed, strikingly Modernist as Sert's work was ("structural elements are stressed rather than masked," notes Nancy Salzman, "while modular proportions provide a human scale, reflecting the influence of Sert's master, the French architect, Le Corbusier"), this new work not only gained something from Cram's work but added to it; the large, quarter-round clerestory structures on the roof of the Law Library, for example, superbly echo the arches of the chapel arcade. The School of Law tower that is the focus of the B.U. work is, moreover, a visual link between

288

the B.U. campus downriver and the Harvard campus on the opposite bank upriver, where three more towers make up Peabody Terrace of 1964, surely Sert's masterpiece. Of all this work William J. R. Curtis has written:

One may see Peabody Terrace as an extension of Le Corbusier's communal prototype, the *Unité d'Habitation* at Marseilles. Such inherited principles as the street-in-the-air, the sunbreaker and the roof terrace, have been fused with the local courtyard tradition for student residences, and the imagery of light wooden balcony attachments of nearby buildings. A utopian vision of an alternative city, in which an ideal harmony of man, nature, and urban existence was implied, has thus been modulated, rendered less absolute, and wedded with a preexisting context. In the same period Sert applied similar principles to the design of Holyoke Center and to the new nucleus of Boston University. Gradually a distinctive style began to emerge in which interior streets, irregular massing, textured facades, silhouettes of service towers, grill-like treatments of fenestration, silver-grey concrete and bright primary colors, all played a part.

Well might Gropius hail his colleague, when in 1969 Sert retired from Harvard, in a grandiose hymn of praise, as "a cultural leader of broad international scope" and as "a great architect" who had "united the Mediterranean spirit with that of the New World, giving the age-old patio idea of the dwelling a new meaning." He continued, "Prototypes of your own creative work grace Europe, the Middle East and South America, and you have greatly enriched the skyline along the Charles River for Harvard and Boston University." It was the German émigré at his most Bostonian: cheerfully devoting one of two sentences to Sert's work in Boston while the other sentence dealt with his remaining work on three continents! Alas, this was perhaps the last time so international a scope could be claimed for a Boston architect. The year Sert retired, 1969, Gropius died.

If Sert's work in the 1960s was evidence enough of how fructifying the influence of Le Corbusier could be in the case of a thoughtful architect, other developments in Boston proper disclosed just as surely how destructive the French master's influence could be in the case of greedy developers. Although it is hard to credit these many years later, in 1963 a citizen's committee of the Back Bay felt it necessary to present to Mayor Collins a plan to preserve that area from the threat of skyscraper apartment towers on alternate corners of Commonwealth Avenue, "an echo," Margaret Floyd pointed out, "of Le Corbusier's Voisin plan for Paris."

One such tower — Carlton House of the Ritz-Carlton Hotel, on the corner of Arlington Street, the work of Skidmore, Owings and Merrill — was actually built; two others appeared on the river side of Beacon Street. But no more and no matter. What happened to the West End would not happen to the Back Bay. In that watershed year of 1960, from whence we have already traced here the saga of Pusey and Le Corbusier and Sert and their various works, and, too, the parallel saga of Collins and Logue and Lynch and Pei and theirs, there also began a third line of development, hardly less important at all — the historic preservation movement — which was to be the most powerful influence on American architecture of any force since the advent of the Modern Movement itself. Spurred by Jane Jacobs's seminal book of 1961, *The Life and Death of Great American Cities*, which rediscovered the genius of the inner city neighborhood in a era when a corrective to Modernist planning was necessary, preservation quickly became the cause of the day. Playing as it did more or less equally both to Boston's strengths and to its weaknesses, the preservation movement was one in which Boston would quickly take a leading role in America.

The movement's best days and ways, at least in Boston, were its earliest. Recall Harry Cobb's father's query to his son? That was *not* exceptional. For whatever reason, all true Bostonians are inveterate walkers (Boston proper is very small and very much still a walking city), and many keep a sharp eye out whilst doing so. Of no one was this more true in his day than historian Walter Muir Whitehill. Infuriated, as were so many then, by the scandalous destruction in 1958 of the Boston Opera House (which had an effect in Boston not unlike the destruction of Pennsylvania Station in New York), Whitehill, whose daily round took him down Beacon Hill from the Athenaeum (of which he was the director), through Scollay Square to the Faneuil Hall markets (thereat to pick up his dinner at Sanborn's Fish Market), and thence to North Station and the train to suburban Andover (the day's catch carefully stowed in his briefcase), no more liked what he saw than had Cobb's father.

Nor did architect Frederick Stahl, who had just moved into his splendid Beacon Hill house (which he was restoring), and who on his daily walk to and from his own downtown office found himself focusing — like Whitehill — on the deteriorating buildings which adjoined the site of the new Government Center.

To historian and architect one must add as well a businessman, Roger Webb. A 1961 graduate of Harvard Business School turned house-mover and restorer-developer, Webb, a disciple of Whitehill, was also observing with concern the developing scene. He approached Logue and was at once put in touch with Stahl, who in the meantime had alerted to his worries the board of Boston's venerable old Society for the Preservation of New England Antiquities, which was, of course, the sort of cohort with which Whitehill kept in close touch. (Boston has a long prehistory of preservation, after all: the society's founder in the early 1900s, William

Summer Appleton, has been called America's first professional preservationist.) Stahl and Webb hooked up, Logue commissioned a report, and the idea of preserving the Faneuil Hall markets (Figures 17, 19) was born, the joint progeny, be it noted, of ardent scholar, Modernist architect, savvy developer, and visionary city official.

Whitehill's varying path to the fish market in those days also took him past another threatened landmark, the eighteenth-century Old Corner Bookstore, beloved in the 1850s of Emerson, Hawthorne, Thoreau, and company. In this case Whitehill joined forces with William B. Osgood and others and founded something called Historic Boston, Inc., still today a force in preservation. And in due course the old store was bought and saved from destruction.

Osgood, another Harvard Business School graduate and a young trust officer at the State Street Bank and Trust Company (though he was best known around town as something of a collector of Boston prints and such), fell heir after the death of the State Street Bank's legendary president, Allan Forbes, to the task of curating Forbes's famous corporate collection of Boston maritime prints, paintings, and ship models, a pioneering example of the Bostonian's traditional combination of historical and scholarly interests with a no less dedicated interest in the corporate image. It was a tradition that had much to do with the saving of the markets and the Old Corner Bookstore, the latter instance being, in fact, the first time in the United States a historic building was preserved not as a museum but as a still tax-producing building, in this case through the tenancy and financial aid of the *Boston Globe*. Similarly, the same combination of history and business (and many of the same men, including both Whitehill and Osgood) rescued the Old Wayside Inn (of Longfellow's tale) in Sudbury. City or suburb, it was the Boston way.

Meanwhile, Stahl, too, was busy preserv-

FIGURE 257. Stahl Associates: State Street Bank Tower, Financial District, established a standard of design elegance, along with Edward Larrabee Barnes's 28 State Street Tower, seldom lived up to since.

ing old Boston. The center of his activities was Beacon Hill, where an attempt to tear down the Boston University Chapel and Theological School caused a furor that Stahl resolved: "For the first time in Boston, I believe, a case was prepared," he later recalled, "based upon proving the feasibility of converting existing buildings [to housing] with restoration of the exteriors."

When not occupied as a preservationist, however, Stahl was, in Whitehill's words, himself "conjuring" the money (in London, so little confidence did Boston money have then in its downtown) to finance (with the enthusiastic support of Whitehill, concerned with "assur[ing] the continued integrity of the State Street region as the financial center of Boston") the building of Boston's first advanced Modernist office tower. It was the projected corporate headquarters for — of course — the State Street Bank (Figure 257). If history and business

seemed to go hand in hand in Boston, so also did Modernism and preservation.

This balance, indeed, was carried even into Stahl's actual design for the new tower, the plan for which he recalled in later years was based upon a "review of the evolution of high rise office building planning, needs of local office users and a desire to emulate the 'impressive austerity' of the older masonry buildings of the waterfront. . . . The computer analysis of the steel frame, was, we believe, the first undertaken in Boston." In a similar vein, in 1965, Alfred Duca's *Computersphere*, a Cor-ten steel sculpture at the Government Center Post Office on New Chardon Street, was, according to Marty Carlock, probably "the first work ever done from a computer-generated design." The form of this sculpture is believed to deliberately resemble the wrecking balls that demolished the West End and Scollay Square.

291

Another architect who combined Modernist design with a sense of history and was also keen on property development was Belluschi. Through M.I.T., Belluschi met the developer Norman Leventhal, a graduate of the institute and the founder after World War II of the Beacon Companies, to whom Belluschi opened up a whole new architectural vision. Aided by Robert Brannen, who led Belluschi's back-up team for many years (out of which developed the large Boston firm of Jung, Brannen & Associates, founded in 1968), Belluschi first took on Leventhal's Wellesley Office Park, a very ordinary 1950s affair. The result was that rare thing, a beautiful suburban office park, so beautiful that it was just the sort of thing that worried Logue and Whitehill into reviving State Street before it emptied out into such sylvan suburban business enclaves.

Soon enough, though, Belluschi was introducing the same high standards to the downtown skyline in his Keystone Building of 1968 at the corner of High and Congress Streets. Intended, as Donald Lyndon observes, "like those of [Stahl's] State Street Bank . . . to be similar in scale to traditional building forms" nearby, Belluschi's windows in the Keystone Tower have their own character, however: they are abstracted and arranged in groups of three to constitute the building's principal exterior motif of the three-sided bay, a ubiquitous feature of traditional Boston architecture. Belluschi's bays, however, ripple elegantly around the entire building.

As much sensitivity to historical context as Stahl and Belluschi showed, both Hugh Stubbins and Paul Rudolph showed even more: the former in the Beacon Street façade of his 330 Beacon Street high rise, where he varied the window treatment every three floors vertically so as to reflect the basic three-story module of the Back Bay townhouse; the latter at his Blue Cross/Blue Shield Building of 1960, a work whose exterior façades relate very

strongly to Boston's nineteenth-century Granite Style.

Some of the best of Harvard's architecture at this period reflects a similar aesthetic, as at the Shepley office's Andover-Harvard Library of 1960, where, in Margaret Floyd's words, "although the design makes no attempt to duplicate Collegiate Gothic shapes and details, it complements them admirably by the scale and shape of its fenestration." Similarly at Quincy House the same architects carefully made the proportions of the steel casements of the bedroom windows of the same proportions as those of the older buildings nearby. Yet it was no less significant that every third floor Shepley's designer, Jean Paul Carlhian, endowed Quincy's sitting rooms with large and very modern expanses of plate glass.

Such early Modernist efforts fascinate in exactly the way they so often defer thoughtfully to historic buildings while invariably succeeding in terms of their own stylistic modernity. Stahl famously carried this standard even to the extent, so important a principle did it seem to him, of designing in the early 1970s for the late nineteenth-century Hotel Vendôme (Figure 49) an addition that was rigorously International Style, and interiors that fused historic preservation and new work meant to spur the revival of the Back Bay, then under such development pressure that after a major fire razing the Vendôme was a distinct possibility — as was a skyscraper tower on the site!

Another example is Karl Koch's addition of 1965 to Lewis Wharf, where the new cantilevered balconies Koch added on to the original granite lower stories — their steel brackets and concrete slabs quite in key with the old granite construction — are very effective. The same thing is true of the undoubted masterworks of the genre, Stahl's elegant 1974 parish house addition to the Park Street Church of 1809 (Figure 259) and Paul Rudolph's almost Wrightian 1971 addition to the ruins of the First and

FIGURE 258. F. A. Stahl's stylish architecture of 1971 at the Hotel Vendôme. His two-level retail concourse and five-story residential "Galleria" were carved out of old lightwells. Intended to revive not only the historic hotel but also the then languishing Back Bay, Stahl's Modernist design encompassed historic interior detail such as the columns of the Vendôme's once magnificent Victorian lobby, a detail which, though it survived a disastrous fire, was ultimately obliterated by a dumbed-down white-brick décor in the postfire reconstruction.

Second Church in the Back Bay (Figure 260). Both designs document conclusively that Historicism (Federal or Victorian Gothic) and even the most insistent Modernism can abide beautifully to the greater glory of both.

This aesthetic extended into every sphere of design, whether in interior design (Leslie Larson's imaginative use of original historic detail in a Modernist way, for example, in his design at the Old City Hall of the Maison Robert restaurant) or landscape design outside. At the Boston Waterfront Park by Sasaki (which completed the "Walk to the Sea" in 1976), the granite-columned wood trellis was intended according to Melanie Simo as "an abstract

representation of the wharf structures that once occupied the site."

The intellectual background of this Modernist/Preservationist sensibility is not yet entirely clear. Stahl himself speaks of the influence on him of architectural history at Dartmouth in the 1950s, and his reading of Giedion and Mumford, implying that the lack of such teaching was one reason he departed Harvard after only one year, 1952–53.

That, however, was on the eve of the rejuvenation of Harvard's design school by Sert, whose own more sympathetic view toward architectural history was evidenced by the fact that within two years of his appointment as dean he hired Eduard

293

FIGURE 260. Paul Rudolph: First and Second Church of Boston, Back Bay, 1971. A brilliant work, almost Wrightian in feeling. Other Back Bay Modernist works include 113 Commonwealth Avenue of 1937—Moderne going International Style on Commonwealth Avenue—very similar to Hillel House at Boston University, designed like 153 Marlborough Street, another Modernist house, by the Harvard-trained architect, Jacob Krokyn.

294

Sekler, who with Sert's blessing over-turned Gropius's banishment of architectural history to the Fogg. Indeed, by the mid-1950s it was again a required course.

The key here was Sekler's own very unusual background. Trained as a professional historian, he was also a practicing — and very Modernist — architect, as well as a widely influential teacher.

In a very real sense this Modernist/Preservationist aesthetic had an effect as well on the design of the 28 State Street tower, which followed Stahl's State Street Bank Tower by only a few years, establishing a much sleeker, high-style model for the downtown financial district in 1969.

The design of Edward Larabee Barnes, a Harvard-trained architect already of national repute, 28 State Street showed that just as a Modernist addition to an old building could set off an old structure harmoniously — more so, perhaps, than a Historicist addition — so in even the most sensitive of locations (in the case of 28 State Street right on top of Boston's elegant old nineteenth-century Royal State House) a skyscraper immensely larger than the older building could complement the historical landmark to very good advantage. The tower at 28 State, elegant in its sleek pink granite cladding and superbly proportioned, still makes that point today. However, Barnes's aesthetic, though widely influential in the subsequent era of massive skyscraper development downtown (witness, for example, TAC's Shawmut Bank Tower of 1975), did not please everyone. Among the dissatisfied was Gerald Blakely of Cabot, Cabot and Forbes.

This firm, perhaps the preeminent American industrial and commercial property developer of the post–World War II era, though founded in 1904, really came to the forefront with the New England Industrial Park in Needham, the first of more than a dozen such developments in the 1950s and sixties that created Boston's legendary Route 128, America's high-tech highway (another thing Logue and Whitehill worried about). Then, in the 1970s, it was high-rise office projects on which Cabot, Cabot and Forbes concentrated, the first being Technology Square in Cambridge.

By far the grandest work of the period by these developers were two new downtown skyscraper towers that joined with Barnes's 28 State Street to form a kind of arc around the Old State House: the Boston Company Building of 1970 designed by Pietro Belluschi at the corner of Washington and Court Streets and 60 State Street of 1977 designed by Skidmore, Owings and Merrill at the corner of State and Congress Streets. Both were very different in their aesthetic from Barnes's tower.

Belluschi, in the Boston Company Building, chose not only a distinctive palette (and rather a sour one — bronze-colored anodized aluminum with bronze-tinted glass), but also made the radical decision to take the engineers' basic structural bracing of the building as the principal motif of his façade design. Indeed, this bracing, triangular in form, of course, shows itself dramatically in the façade in the pattern of blocked openings.

It was an idea hardly anyone, then or now, has liked. Even Belluschi protested the manner in which his idea was distorted by the last-minute decision to lop off the top three stories. But he also defended the finished design. A notable designer of skyscrapers, after all, he called his design a long overdue "dialogue with the engineer," pointing out that the best high rises were always a matter of "extracting whatever beauty may be hidden [in structure] while doing it in an understated way." Moreover, the Boston Company Building figured importantly in the publicity surrounding Belluschi's winning in 1972 of the AIA Gold Medal, an honor that Boston's architectural community could hardly not be proud of, however unim-

FIGURE 261. Hugh Stubbins and Associates: Federal Reserve Bank Tower, downtown, 1977, a work of wonderful strength and clarity.

pressed most were with the Boston Company Building, or, indeed, with what many saw as Belluschi's too-frequent compromises with his developer friends.

Skidmore, Owings and Merrill, for 60 State Street, the second of the two towers that with 28 State Street arc around the Old State House, chose, like Belluschi, a very much more assertive aesthetic than had Barnes. Built as Cabot, Cabot and Forbes's own corporate headquarters, 60 State consists of two very slim, tubelike masses, clad alike in a tight granite grid, both of which attempt a kind of minimalist sculptural effect in their topmost silhouettes, neither very convincingly.

By the late 1970s, however, it was not only at the head of State Street that the early efforts at a distinctive Modernist aesthetic sensitive to the historic city was being abandoned. In 1971 even so venerable an institution as the First National Bank of Boston was responsible for an astonishingly bombastic tower by Campbell, Aldrich and Nulty, the heavy, dark red granite, bulging middle range of which is difficult to explain and impossible to defend.

Whitehill and Stahl and their cohort, if they had won the day for a vital downtown whose effect would be both historic and Modernist, had sowed seeds that would grow not so much weeds as — to change the image — monsters.

Two skyscrapers of truly inspiring form did rise to gift the city in the 1970s: the Federal Reserve Bank Tower downtown (Figure 261) and the John Hancock Tower uptown — the first, a masterwork of Hugh Stubbins; the second, equally a masterpiece, the work of the Pei firm.

"Boston's show-stopper architect," Margaret Floyd called Stubbins; "one of the most notable American architects of the twentieth century." And if his Citicorp Center in New York or his Congress Hall in Berlin are better known, his Boston bank was hardly less distinguished. Indeed, all his Boston work showed just that

296

coveted ability to wed innovative Modernist design with a high respect for and a sure response to the historic fabric. Of an entirely different range of work by Stubbins for Harvard, for example, Floyd wrote, "In the Loeb Drama Center he adjusted the mass of his design to the scale of the Brattle Street environment and initiated bold new use of the metal grille. At the Countway Library [at Harvard Medical School in the Fenway] his towering construct carried off a difficult assignment with panache. At Pusey [Library] he abandoned an assertive posture entirely to produce an elegant contemporary building in Harvard Yard."

Stubbins's work extended into so many areas. Consider, for instance, just his suburban Boston schools, which were celebrated in *Progressive Architecture* in 1963: the Maimonides and the Heath Schools in Brookline, the East School in Hingham, the Peabody in Cambridge, and the Royal School in Beverly, this last serene enough to evoke pastoral Japanese landscapes, and all of them deliberately spacious and often built around courtyards.

Yet Stubbins could also design so boldly "high-tech" a building as the Boston City Hospital Mechanical Plant — and, in 1977, so gorgeous a tower as the Federal Reserve Building. This great work, its two massive towers rising majestically, supporting and framing a ladderlike façade of striking louverlike sunshades, is entirely clad in aluminum with the color and sparkle of champagne, the surface of which, depending upon the light, glows sometimes hot pink, other times almost pure white, and in between every shade of gold, rose, and vermilion; this is "a true landmark building in the modern mode," Naomi Miller and Keith Morgan have written, "conveying the power and poetry of high technology."

At the other end of the "high spine" — uptown — in the Back Bay, the story that decade was the Hancock Tower (Figure 262) by I. M. Pei (Harry Cobb the partner in charge). And in this case the

story became an astonishing one wherever in the world it was told, for reasons, let it be said, both good and bad.

"The story of the Hancock Tower is endless, and wherever you probe it, there's no limit," critic Robert Campbell has written, "to the disasters and tragedies and miscalculations and beauties and wonderful examples of professional conduct by engineers and architects. It is a door opening into a room with another door and another door and another door." Very few of these doors can be opened here. Suffice it to say that it was a nearly fatal commission for Pei, a commission that could easily have destroyed him, as one problem after another arose in one of the most excruciating fiascoes in the history of architecture. Yet it was a fiasco that became a triumph.

The design itself was widely condemned. Its construction severely damaged Trinity Church nearby. The first winter's storm of 1973 yielded hundreds of damaged windows and flying shards of glass in Copley Square, roped-off streets, and a façade as much of plywood as of glass. Walter Cronkite on the CBS Evening News, *Time*, *Newsweek* — all reported the disaster around the world. Pei, his career in shambles, admitted it was all "humiliating."

In the end though, the flaw was thought to be in the glass, not the foundation. And the drama of it all, of a building "nearly defeated by its own ambitions"— at once audacious, even dangerous — a building even now remarkable for its engineering, and for its complicated monitoring system to detect deflections in the glass (including something called a "tuned mass damper," a rolling weight on a film of oil on the fifty-eighth floor to counter high wind stresses), captured the popular, even the architectural, imagination.

It is the exterior, of course, once so controversial, that now arouses almost universal praise. Intended, of course, to defer to Copley Square's historic architecture — a "skywedge" Curtis calls it, that must be read "as a plane in space, not as a volume"

FIGURE 262. I. M. Pei/Henry Cobb, principal in charge, John Hancock Tower, Back Bay, 1972. Cobb's goal, he has written, was "to achieve a symbiosis between the church, the tower, and the square . . . that might animate rather than oppress the urban scene.

— it seems to Pei himself a case of Cobb "play[ing] with light . . . with illusion."

Who says it best? Curtis: "On some evenings it rises pristine and glistening above the city like some elegant, minimal sculpture." I, who live with it all the time (like my friend who rented his Cambridge apartment to behold the Carpenter Center, I bought my Back Bay condo for its view of the Hancock), can vouch for this, for Pei's own biographer's analysis ("almost spiritual in its cool, prismatic detachment"), and for another critic's words: "What the church steeple is to the New England village, the Hancock is to the Boston metropolitan area. It signals presence, magnetizes space."

Arguably the last and best expression of the Modernist skyscraper, the Hancock Tower is the triumph song of the Modern Movement in America.

13

THE POST-MODERNIST REACTION

EVERYTHING FAMOUSLY speeded up in the 1960s. Even as the Boston of Le Corbusier, Sert, Kallmann and McKinnell, and I. M. Pei was coming into being — as well as the pioneering historic preservation efforts of Whitehill, Stahl, and company — all were increasingly overtaken by larger events as the cultural sea change of the sixties gathered force, at once troubling and enabling, and like everything else, greatly impacting architecture.

Certainly it became clear, somewhere between the anti–Vietnam War movement and Watergate, that Modernism, so nearly triumphant, was no longer "the answer" its idealistic advocates had assumed. And nowhere was the disillusionment fiercer than in Boston, especially at Harvard, where architecture students were in the forefront of student unrest in the late 1960s and early seventies.

This is not the place to mount any considerable discussion of why all this came about. Alan Balfour has perhaps put it most succinctly in our context here in his discussion of Ben Thompson's work: "One's pleasure in [Post-Modernism] . . . has to do with Modernism's having lost its freshness. . . . If only," he added, "Aalto had come [to stay] instead of Gropius."

Then, too, in most timely fashion, the fathers of Modernism all departed from the stage. Wright had died in 1959. In 1965 Le Corbusier died; four years later Mies and Gropius, both in 1969. With all the high priests gone, the disciples wavered. Wayne Andrews, a critic with whom I have seldom seen eye to eye, got one thing right:

The two most influential architects in the New England of the twentieth century are Ralph Adams Cram and Walter Gropius, who preached doctrines that are difficult to reconcile but were as one when it came to being dogmatic. . . .

The German Walter Gropius, who came from the Bauhaus to superintend Harvard's School of Architecture in 1937, was hailed as the herald of a new era; like Cram, however, he was worried if students glanced around. "When the innocent beginner," Gropius announced, "is introduced to the great achievements of the past, he may be too easily discouraged from trying to create for himself."

Truly, the new ideals of the 1960s were increasingly as different from Gropius's as they were from Cram's — behold, not priests, but rebels, iconoclasts all. For Robert Venturi and Denise Scott Brown, for instance, the text of their new homily was a celebrated book of the period — *Complexity and Contradiction in Architecture.* "Less is more," Mies had insisted; to which Venturi rejoined, "Less is a bore." Institutional and corporate America might continue to seek out Pei; in the architecture schools it was Venturi's ideals to which the students thronged.

Actually, Venturi as an undergraduate at Princeton had admiringly absorbed Historicism from Cram and others, and in due course, Romanticism from Eero Saarinen, but in Rome he was much attracted to Mannerism. To many the result seemed crazy or chaotic or both, and wherever he worked (it was his mother's house in Philadelphia that first brought him to wide repute), was controversial, no less so in Boston's orbit; for example, two 1971 houses of his on Nantucket, the Trubek and Wislocki houses.

Of these Tarfuri and Dal Co in one book complain that Venturi "in his shrewdly subtle cottages . . . stakes all on banality, on usual and obvious forms, where form is reduced to a caustic comment on that banality," which is a harsh judgement whatever is meant! Yet Carter Wiseman in his book sees in the same two houses "a witty excursion backward into the New England salt box vernacular." Venturi, Wiseman felt, "fiddled with the standard window treatment, upsetting the traditional symmetry just enough to remind the visitor that an architect had been at work, but not so much as to break the associative link. . . . In the end, however, it was the *idea* of fiddling with the expected, rather than the visual appeal of the buildings themselves, that had the greater impact."

In Boston's core, predictably, Venturi turned up the heat considerably. In his 1966 design for Copley Square, entered in that year's competition but not found worthy, he conceived what he called "a sort of maze of tree-lined pedestrian streets, activated by changes of level, and including a replica of Trinity Church with various other features like 'an alphabet,' numbers and nursery rhymes in giant encased characters" — distinctly *not* what would ever have been envisaged by the august directors of the Hancock Company on the eve of their commissioning Pei to design the corporate icon.

Indeed, Venturi's explanation of all this was opaque enough: of the toy Trinity he declared, "the miniature imitation is a means for explaining to a person the whole which he is in, but cannot see all of." Sensing, perhaps, he'd not quite got his idea across, he added, "Trinity Church

is duplicated as a toy in the middle of Copley Square" — an idea to which the governing body of Trinity Church was even less likely to respond to sympathetically than the board of the eventual toy-maker (or so we are entitled to believe), the Hancock Company.

What a missed opportunity it all seems! Yet another aesthetic confrontation in the square formed by the Romanesque Trinity and the Classical Revival Boston Public Library — a mid-twentieth-century debate this time — between the corporate grandeur of Pei's Hancock Tower and Venturi's mocking, anti-establishment design for Copley Square. Boston's architectural history is the poorer for the loss. One can only be amazed that six years later a similar impertinence, the notorious but delightful "rainbow" gas tank graphic by Sister Corita Kent (she of the LOVE stamp) was actually realized on Boston Harbor in Dorchester Bay — despite many seeing in her rainbow a profile of Ho Chi Minh!

In Copley Square, however, there was surely never even a hope for Venturi's scheme; certainly not with, in the same year, the return to the Boston scene of Philip Johnson, the announced designer not of an elegant Miesian house in Cambridge this time but of what has subsequently come to be called the Johnson Building of the Boston Public Library (Figure 263). Pei, in fact, almost got that job as well as the Hancock according to Johnson, who recalled it was only his professed admiration (to the library's board) for the Historicist splendors of the library's McKim Building that earned him the accolade.

Indeed, from the point of view of a critic like Christopher Jencks, it hardly mattered which of these "authoritarian" formalists landed the job, for if Pei was the chief luminary of what Jencks calls "the Harvard formalists" of the day, architects to a besieged establishment, Johnson must have seemed to Jencks a shooting star

coming on only too fast in the same galaxy. Some there were who saw in Johnson's design for high granite bollards fronting the new library's ground-floor windows a protective shield against the riotous 1960s. Certainly I remember at least one Harvard Square bank in my student days replacing its plate glass front with a solid brick façade. (Robert Twombly, similarly, saw Boston's City Hall as "a 1960s icon of the state under siege.")

Certainly Jencks wrote of the Boston library addition that "such pompous formalism was characteristic of American civic centers of the sixties . . . criticized for falling, heavily, between classicism and modernism."

What, precisely, *was* that between Classicism and Modernism? Ever the lookout on the crow's nest, Johnson had perpetrated Post-Modernism.

Mᴏʀᴇ immediate signs of the times were to be found in such places as Boston's South End. Three projects stand out.

The first, Villa Victoria, was begun in 1972 by developer John Sharratt. An inter-esting experiment involving a small Latino enclave in a kind of participatory architecture — the low-rise, arcaded, inward-looking, village character of this residential development has won both praise and blame; very satisfying to its original (first-generation immigrant) residents, later (and perhaps more assimilationist) generations have been quick to notice how the development's design repudiates the overall South End community.

The second project, the Harriet Tubman House of 1975, by Stull Associates, was designed to be as open to the surrounding community as Villa Victoria was closed, reflecting another experience of a different urban minority community, African Americans. The Tubman's façade, still one of the liveliest and most graphic in the city a quarter century and more later, is intimately related to the building's plan and the institution's purposes. Wrote William J. R. Curtis:

A center for welfare offices, place to hang about, crèche garden, etc., in a multi-racial community, [the Tubman House] takes its cue from not only the surrounding street directions and the grain of local materials but the social context as well. The device of screen-like layers

FIGURE 264. The Architects' Collaborative: Josiah Quincy School and Community Center, South End, 1976. An ingenious work designed to be open to its surrounding neighborhoods and to draw them together.

of planes in the façade is . . . here employed gradually to blend the life of the street with the life of the main atrium of the building, as an equivalent to the desired openness and informality of the institution.

The open-minded attitude Curtis notes was central as well to the third and most ambitious of these South End landmarks characteristic of the period, the Josiah Quincy School of 1976 by TAC (Figure 264). The design makes the school one element in a very outward-looking urban landscape of paths and terraces (decorated by an abundance of porcelain-enamel murals with inscriptions in Chinese, Spanish, and English) connecting with a myriad of surrounding streets, a reflection of the diversity of this public school of not one but many communities.

Architecture was changing in the downtown core as well. Pointedly, a building of 1972 adjoining the Government Center — the Capital Bank — can be seen as mocking not just the architecture of the 1960s but also Boston's major icon of the previous decade — the City Hall — within sight of which the bank's designers, Anderson, Notter (notable preservationists!) committed lese majesty in three

dimensions by designing a rather topheavy cut-out corner, surely an architectural pun, as Susan Michael Southworth suggested, on Kallmann and McKinnell's nearby masterwork.

Modernism — always confident, not infrequently authoritarian — did not decline gracefully. But decline it did in the 1970s, and nowhere more fatally than in Boston, though it was undoubtedly an event of 1972 in St. Louis that symbolized for the general public the demise most decisively. Wrote Charles Jencks:

Modern Architecture died in St. Louis, Missouri on July 15, 1972 at 3:32 P.M. (or thereabouts) when the infamous Pruitt-Igoe scheme, or rather several of its slab blocks, were given the final *coup de grâce* by dynamite. . . .

Without doubt the ruins should be kept. . . . Pruitt-Igoe was constructed according to the most progressive ideals . . . and it won an award from the American Institute of Architects when it was designed in 1951.

The Pruitt-Igoe's architect, Mioru Yamasaki, had not spared Boston in his long and distinguished career (or New York, where the World Trade Center is his), and I do not doubt many at Harvard yearned then (even now?) to stage their own demolition party for Yamasaki's William James Hall of 1963 — as awkwardly sited north of Harvard Yard as the Carpenter Center is to the Yard's east, but with none (*none*) of the latter's redeeming genius. But though Boston did later stage only a slightly less spectacular demolition of an early Modernist landmark (when the Traveler's Insurance Company Building, a sixteen-story skyscraper, was blown up in 1988), the storming of the Bastille in the puritan capital was more diffuse — seen in the mounting revolt of the public against one skyscraper project after another that seemed heedless of the city's character. It was always Cobb's father's question!

As was only to be expected in Boston, there was a book. It was the idea of Peter Davison of the Atlantic Monthly Press. Ever alert to the zeitgist as a good editor should be, the traumas of the Modern Movement in architecture prompted Davison to provoke Peter Blake to write (the year after the Wagnerian scene in St. Louis) *Form Follows Fiasco: Why Modern Architecture Hasn't Worked*.

Beginning with an article in Boston's most prestigious journal, the *Atlantic Monthly*, in September of 1974, which Blake later recalled modestly, "caused something of a stir in the architectural establishment in the United States and elsewhere" (in fact, it caused a firestorm in architectural circles the world over), Blake excoriated Modernism. Were the chairs of this designer beautiful? Certainly. But were they comfortable? Never. Was the ideal modern urban streetscape striking? Of course. Yet, Blake winked, "no people are in sight, and none are wanted." It was unfair in many ways. But in many other ways it was true.

Blake cast, of course, a much wider net than Boston, but the "cradle of Modernism" was for that reason only too full of examples of Modernism's trauma. Blake had a field day. Did Modernists attempt more than was possible, their vision (irresponsibly) ahead of available technology?

One might have cited Wright's use of tubular Pyrex instead of conventional glass at the Johnson Wax Building. But instead of attacking that icon of American architecture, it was (of course) Boston's Hancock Tower that Blake cited. Were vast plazas and reflecting pools inhumane (even in Boston, un-Bostonian), which is to say problematic in a city of fierce winter winds? So much for the Christian Science Center.

Indeed, Pei came off not very well at all in Blake's book. Nor Le Corbusier! For instance, Blake illustrated old Acorn Street, surely Boston's most popular "post card," a narrow, rough-cobblestoned mews of old two-story red-brick houses from the early nineteenth century, the Beacon Hill equivalent, say, of Neuschwanstein Castle in Bavaria, and just about as relevant to modern housing design. Tellingly, however, Blake illustrates on the facing page Boston's worst urban renewal nightmare of the 1950s — the West End. The caption of these two scenes is not subtle: "A street on Boston's Beacon Hill and a 'street' in Boston's Charles River Park, a Radiant City that replaced a community not unlike neighboring Beacon Hill." Anyone who knows the truth of the matter knows that this was to paint with a very broad brush indeed. But broad brushstrokes their contribution make. Especially when Blake went on to compare Le Corbusier's Radiant City to Florida's Disneyworld, outside Orlando, a "new town" Blake loved, about which he struck chord after sympathetic chord.

Thus fueled, the rebellions of those days, which peaked in the early 1970s, were notable. Yet often, as in the case of the controversy over the Park Plaza project in Park Square — which if completed would have plunged the Public Garden into sunlessness, for example — the controlling issues had more to do with philistine capitalists and only incidentally with the architects. One fight, however, stands out as having had a conspicuous architectural

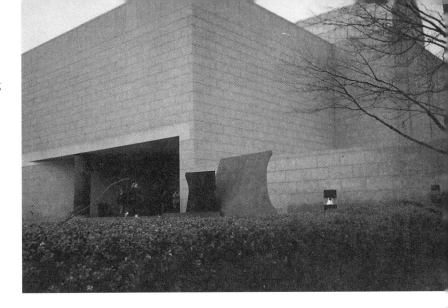

FIGURE 265. I. M. Pei's severely elegant west wing of Boston's Museum of Fine Arts. This most Bostonian of designs dates from 1981.

FIGURE 266. I. M. Pei's original design of 1967, blocked by neighborhood activists, for the Kennedy Library at Harvard. It was dominated by Pei's great glass pyramid. According to one of the architect's biographers, many "Cambridge residents were later amused to see [the pyramid] reappear more than a decade later at the Louvre in Paris." Lovers of architecture at least were more ashamed than amused that Greater Boston's loss was Paris's gain, a great symbol now of the French capital's vitality and sophistication.

dimension: the Kennedy Library. Again, the architect was I. M. Pei, who first achieved national stature because of this commission, but must have wondered more than once if he would survive it —or the Hancock Tower fiasco.

Some Bostonians wondered, of course, if *Pei* was worth the trouble! Even the Hancock Tower has always had its detractors, including Manfredo Tarfuri. And David Watkin has cited examples of Pei's work in both Washington and Boston as "vast and bombastic public buildings," a view some Bostonians would share, concerned as they are that Pei's work altered too much

Boston's traditional scale and form.

Walter Whitehill, as already noted, disagreed. So do I. No more Bostonian a work of art exists, for example, than Pei's gravely elegant and superbly understated entrance façade at the Museum of Fine Arts (Figure 265), its austere granite wall arcing elegantly inward under its massive lintel, almost as if driven by a Boston wind, pulling one into the museum. And the Kennedy Library itself, with its abstract, white geometry of parallelogram, cylinder, and pyramid, over and against Boston Harbor, has an almost timeless quality, worthy of a location that on first

FIGURE 267. I. M Pei: the Kennedy Presidential Library, Dorchester, 1977. For the original Cambridge design, see figure 266.

sight prompted Mrs. Onassis to exclaim that it was "the most beautiful place I've ever been."

But what a price was paid and what a loss sustained. And how characteristic it all was of the 1960s.

First planned for the banks of the Charles at Harvard (Figure 266), a site of John F. Kennedy's own selection, Pei's design appeared just as Vietnam, Watergate, Chappaquiddick (and, in Boston, the West End) all conspired to batter a beautiful project to death. Pei, often to be found at work at an impromptu office at the old Kennedy apartment on Beacon Hill (not far from where Charles McKim set up a similar staging ground in the 1890s, during his design of the Boston Public Library), found himself beleaguered by neighborhood activists violently opposed to the Kennedy project.

Philistines, of course, are ever with us. But in this matter a far larger and more diverse array of good citizens, wary of traf-

fic and tourists, took up the cause. Hopeless to point out that cities *thrive* on congestion and traffic, of course, or that more often *too much* open space destroys them, not too little. Many who did not want the Kennedy Library, after all, would just as soon not have Harvard itself. Equally hopeless to suggest the peace and tranquility of Cambridge in times past is now to be found not in the city but in the country. A few tried anyway. As Robert Campbell has so aptly put it in a discussion of why "pedestrianizing" city streets in the 1960s so often had failed, "Removing the colorful moving cars from American streets was like stripping the bright rotating toys from a baby's crib. Sensory deprivation ensued, and the streets died. . . . Planners had forgotten that congestion is a virtue, not a vice, of cities."

Pei himself, asked about the experience years later, put the architectural problem of the 1960s and seventies bluntly: "They all wanted a say, and, of course, they were

306

all very anti-establishment." In fact, Pei insisted, the architecture of the thing hardly mattered at all: "I don't think the community in the Cambridge area . . . was that much interested in the design . . . , [but in] the number of cars that would have come into the area."

Now I believe the harbor site reinvigorated Pei, as it certainly did Mrs. Onassis. Boston did gain a superb landmark (Figure 267). Yet what a loss. The Kennedy School finally built in Cambridge certainly "represents better environmental planning," wrote Margaret Floyd in her history of Harvard's architecture, but she also saw that the original "Pei design . . . would have added a stunning gem to the architectural diadem of Harvard." Its central feature, a lofty glass pyramid, turned up in Pei's design for the Louvre years later. Boston's loss; Paris's gain.

B Y THE time in the 1970s that both those world-class disasters, the Hancock Tower and the Kennedy Library, had resolved themselves, that decade had found in Boston both its focus — the Bicentennial of 1976 — and an architectural expression that was nothing if not characteristic of the era — Faneuil Hall "festival marketplace," which opened in the bicentennial year to almost unprecedented acclaim. "The Faneuilization of America is proceeding apace," Progressive Architecture would proclaim a scant five years later. Somewhere, probably, it still is.

It had been gathering momentum, of course, since the first stubborn, brilliant responses of the early 1960s to the threat of those days to historic structures by Whitehill and Stahl and Webb and Company. And though the most far-seeing of their early dreams, the marketplace, had proved elusive, finally the idea was taken up — and thanks to the genius of a most remarkable developer, James W. Rouse, carried out, despite nearly everyone else's position that the idea was, in Anna

Borgman's words, "downright outlandish." (People were then still fleeing cities.) Rouse, however, had the vision to undertake what Jane Thompson called "a monumental act of pioneering" in developing in effect the country's first indoor shopping mall (Figure 268). The result, in the wake of such followers as New York's South Street Seaport, was that the Faneuil Hall market concept of a "festival marketplace," in Borgman's words, virtually "transformed the landscape of the nation." And for Boston, wrote Stahl, it also represented "a watershed for preservation."

At first Whitehill, as ever, stood at the center of things, inspiring, arguing, protesting, encouraging, pushing here, pulling back there. In the late 1960s he had taken the lead in insuring the survival of the Back Bay from threats already touched on here. Not only was there suddenly a great exhibition on Back Bay architecture at the Museum of Fine Arts ("The City as a Work of Art") but in 1967 Whitehill had persuaded Harvard University Press to publish the thesis of Harvard scholar Bainbridge Bunting, which duly became *Houses of Boston's Back Bay*, still in print today. It was a seminal book; its purpose — and Whitehill's — was very clear: in 1955, the east slope of Beacon Hill had been made a protected historic district; in 1967, Back Bay would be made another, its architecture forever preserved.

Thereafter, in the 1970s, building on the increasing interest in Boston's inner ring of suburbs like Brookline, Roxbury, Dorchester, and Cambridge (the seminal book here, also published by Harvard University Press, has been Sam B. Warner's *Streetcar Suburbs* of 1962), Whitehill turned his attention to Cambridge, historically with Beacon Hill and Back Bay Boston's heart and soul. Bunting, like bishops of old, was suddenly translated; in this case from the Back Bay to Cambridge, where yet another public-spirited State Street lawyer and friend of Whitehill's, Albert Wolfe, the founder of

FIGURE 268. Benjamin Thompson and Associates: Faneuil Hall Markets, downtown, 1976. In its wake critics spoke of the "Faneuilization of America."

the Cambridge Historical Commission, appointed Bunting its director.

It was an era of many such organizations. Of Historic Boston we have already spoken. Agitation having already generated national as well as local preservation legislation, formidable regulatory bodies also came into being: the Massachusetts Historical Commission in 1963, the Boston Landmarks Commission in 1965. The Society of Architectural Historians, whose founding at Harvard in the 1940s in the face of Gropius has already been noted here, gained a Boston chapter, founded by Robert Bell Rettig in 1971. A citizens' watchdog group called the Boston Preservation Alliance also arose to vex the philistines.

The Cambridge Historical Commission, however, quickly became the gold standard. Under Bunting it set standards hardly equaled anywhere in the country. The most important contributions were a scholarly but highly accessible series of five architectural survey reports issued

between 1965 and 1977 which documented Cambridge thoroughly, a full-scale architectural history of Harvard (again a Bainbridge Bunting book from Harvard University Press, completed by Floyd after Bunting's death) and a popular architectural walking tour by Rettig (this time the publisher was M.I.T. Press). Whether it was Victorian town houses in the South End, sycamore trees on Memorial Drive in Cambridge, or the CITGO rooftop sign in Kenmore Square (a splendid post–World War II neon work of art), by the 1970s some organization could be depended upon to defend it, even to the extent in one case (a unique-to-Boston Art Nouveau Harvard Square shop front of 1907, illustrated in Figure 193) of convincing the owner to agree to covenants that required that the shop front be given to Boston's Museum of Fine Arts if all in situ preservation efforts failed.

The first edition of *Built in Boston* in 1979 was a part of the same movement, incorporating not only material on Cram churches, Harvard Georgian Revival, Art Deco, early Modernist work in Boston but also studies of Boston's streetcar suburbs, apartment houses, movie palaces, town houses, Colonial landmarks, and even three-deckers which many found shocking then to consider in the company of Bulfinch and Richardson. It was, perhaps, a little ahead of its time. Indeed, no sooner had I noticed a building of 1911 at 248 Boylston Street (see page 189) as the first in Boston to boast a glass corner than the architectural firm of Hoyle, Doran and Berry disgraced themselves by destroying it and substituting phony rustication. Nor did the Ritz-Carlton take any notice at all of my illustrating one of their function rooms that boasted gorgeous emerald green Art Deco murals by the distinguished French architect and co-designer of the Palais de Chaillot in Paris (the centerpiece of the Paris Exhibition of 1937), Jacques Carlu, who was for many years a professor at the M.I.T. School of Architecture, only a block removed from the Ritz. (Decades later, the murals languish still under many coats of paint in a boring Ritz function room that could be splendid.)

If corporate Boston was slow to see profit in preservation, architects themselves were not. Here too is an aspect of Pei's "imprint on Boston" too little taken note of, for the Government Center Plan of the early 1960s had established one precedent after another in aid of preservation, reflecting the Pei-Whitehill partnership. Not only was a large 1816 business structure preserved as one boundary of the center (becoming the inspiration, moreover, for another new boundary building) but the antique gilded teapot so beloved of Bostonians (a shop "sign" originally, which still "steams" today) was carefully moved a door or two up the street to serve as a design focus. Most important were the terms of the new city hall competition itself, one vital purpose of which, Pei has recalled, was to save the scale of Faneuil

Hall: "In the competition program for city hall, we ruled out a tall building and specified that it must be a horizontal building . . . . It was written into the program for the first time in a competition in America." Suddenly, all sorts of things were possible: preservation was hot, restoration hotter, and naturally the spotlight first focused on great Victorian landmarks such as Memorial Hall at Harvard (which the university would probably have torn down in the 1970s had it not been for Whitehill's tireless watch over it), landmarks which in the last decades of the twentieth century would achieve the one hundredth anniversaries of their erections. Above all there were the three Copley Square masterworks: Trinity Church, the New Old South Church, and the McKim Building of the Boston Public Library.

All were restored brilliantly by the city's leading restoration architect, Daniel Coolidge of Shepley, Bulfinch, Richardson and Abbott, as Coolidge's father's old firm had become. Although the Shepley office was better known in this period for the work of their most distinguished designer, Jean Paul Carlhian, Coolidge was by no means unoriginal in his domain. "Careful in craft, original and beautifully reasoned," is the way Ann Beha has described Coolidge's work, which earned for him a National Award for Preservation from the American Institute of Architects. Beha calls Coolidge a "scholar's architect," as this scholar can well attest, having directed with him the first phase of the restoration of the library. One story in particular I think discloses Coolidge's gifts.

In Bates Hall, great, blind arches intended for murals (for which money was never found) begged for some solution that at one and the same time avoided modern murals (like Chagal's, at the Paris opera, for instance), that would have offended purists, but equally avoided perpetuating what are now great, staring blanks that give a majestic space a very funereal aspect. Coolidge came up with the idea of filling those blanks with mirrors fitted into bronze muntins according to the design of McKim's in the great arched windows facing Copley Square — an idea both daring and deferential and supported by both the then-president for the board, Kevin Moloney and the then-Director, Arthur Curley, and approved — such was Coolidge's repute — by the Massachusetts Historical Commission. Alas, much smaller minds, not able to compass Coolidge's brilliance, have (for now at least) defeated it.

Few buildings, of course, merit full-scale restoration, and what above all distinguished the preservation movement of the 1970s and thereafter is what came to be called "adaptive reuse." In this area two architectural firms stand out: Childs, Bertman, Tseckares, Casendino and Graham Gund Associates.

CBT as the firm today is called first came to wide attention for their pioneering and exemplary restoration in 1969 of the Ames-Webster House, the grandest of the mansions of Commonwealth Avenue)the sixty three foot-long hall culminates in a stairhall endowed originally with stained glass by John La Farge and murals by Benjamin Constant), where to this day and in the hotel Vendôme across the street CBT maintain their offices, bursting with more skyscrapers than restorations, alas, such has been their success.

But it is for their long and honorable record of adaptive reuse of historic structures — like the Fire Department Headquarters in the South End they transformed into the Pine Street Inn for the homeless — that CBT is most well known. This is especially true in the Back Bay, where in the years since Whitehill and Bunting CBT have sometimes seemed that area's secret weapon in transforming itself back into Boston's most fashionable quarter, albeit now as much with respect to retail as residential life. In 1974 they transformed the old Exeter Street Theater into Waterstones;

in the next decade they world reconfigure the old Museum of natural history into Louis Men's Store. It is not surprising then, that the firm has followed that evolution into designing such new work as the NIKE store of recent days, a handsome commercial structure, and the first new building on Newbury Street in many years.

A similar evolution is evident in the architecture of Graham Gund. His first widely praised work was his adaptive reuse in 1975 of an old Back Bay police station, out of which Gund shaped the galleries of what became Boston's Institute of Contemporary Art. And then eight years later, in 1983, at Church Court in the Back Bay, he ingeniously inserted a series of apartment blocks into the ruins of a burned out stone gothic church. Yet the contrast with Paul Rudolph's similar 1971 project at the First and Second Church (Figure 260) could not have been greater: whereas Rudolph's was a stunningly original Modernist composition still worth study today, Gund's was a cheerfully vulgar Historicism few would give a second thought to.

It was, after all, only a matter of time before all this emphasis on preservation led to a return to outright Historicism, for which preservation had become increasingly really a kind of substitute (even camouflage, as we'll see soon), and most architects reacted predictably. Not only did Historicist motifs begin to surface in their work, but in just the way Victorian architects of the 1880s (such as Rotch and Tilden: see pages 70–72), trained in Queen Anne techniques, approached the Colonial Revival sure in their confident Victorian way they could *improve* upon it and do *better* Colonial than the original of their (so admirable but so limited) ancestors, so also a hundred years later, in the 1980s, Modernist-trained architects were quite sure, thank you, they could improve on Historicism or eclecticism or traditionalism or whatever one called it.

FIGURE 269. James Stirling's controversial Sackler Museum at Harvard, Cambridge, 1979–1985. A masterwork within, its glazed brick striped exterior (intended to respond to Memorial Hall; see FIGURE 57 on page 52) has found few defenders.

PHILIP Johnson, back in Boston, in dialogue with Hilary Lewis and John O'Connor about Johnson's still highly controversial addition (Figure 263), completed in 1973, to McKim, Mead and White's Boston Public Library:

Do you recall what the public reaction was in Boston?

No, I don't think the public reacted. The students and critics reacted; it was horrible! The professors at Harvard — everybody — said it was the worst thing they had seen. . . . The classicists said, "It's not enough like the [McKim] library." The modernists said, "It isn't modern." You know who liked it? Ada Louise Huxtable of the *New York Times*. So you never know.

We both had the same reaction. . . . It feels like it was built in the 1980s. . . . It certainly feels ahead of its time. . . . In general this project seemed to mark that interesting transition between modern and postmodern.

Yes, I was chosen over I. M. Pei because they thought I was a Renaissance man. I was interested in history. No other modern architect whom they interviewed would talk about it. . . . I loved McKim. . . .

If you were forced to cast this building as either modern or postmodern, how would you respond?

It's postmodern, but it's certainly . . .

Right on the cusp.

Yes, it's right on the cusp, that's the word, right, I think that's why nobody likes it. . . .

It's interesting that you say it's a cusp building, because in fact the *BPL News* of 1967 says: "in the case of the new addition, the result has been an inauguration of a completely new style, one which, it is hoped, will prove to be a milestone in architectural history.

Well, maybe it is the beginning of post-modern.

That, of course, is more plausible to us a generation later — the *BPL News* not withstanding — than it was in the 1970s, when all eyes in Boston not riveted to the Hancock Tower or the Kennedy Library were fixed firmly on the Faneuil Hall markets. But Johnson's library of 1966–1973 *was* more prophetic by far than any of them. Whether or not Johnson is correct to assert that his Boston library really is the beginning of Post-Modernism in America, it seems certainly in retrospect the most dramatic of signposts in Boston in the 1970s of what was coming. Another signpost was the way the Boston Architectural Center was "born again" (no other term will do) four years after the library's completion when at the behest of its then-director, that perennial provocateur, Peter Blake (he of *Form Follows Fiasco*), the plain-spoken "Boston School" landmark suddenly in 1977 through the offices of muralist Richard Haas became — on one side at least — a fully articulated and beautifully detailed Renaissance illusion! Haas's mural, an astonishing multi-story illusionist work entirely covering the top four floors of one façade of a building in the Brutalist concrete style, was more than a signpost; it was a billboard for Post-Modernism, which within two years would yield its Boston masterwork in James Stirling's controversial Sackler Museum of 1979–1985 at Harvard (Figure 269).

To be sure, the Sackler is a flawed masterwork — the slick, glazed orange and blue gray brick exterior banding is problematic, and the entrance pylons, without the bridge to the Fogg across the street they were meant to support, present a difficulty with no clear solution (just rejoice in them, I say). Inside the building, however, Stirling hit a home run.

One of only four American works by this master (and winner of the Pritzger), the Sackler has been analyzed best by Margaret Floyd. Particularly fine is her description of its interior:

The enormous height of the flagstone entrance hall, lighted at night from behind its four megalithic columns, evokes . . . the Hypostyle Hall of the temple of Karnak. . . . On the staircase walls are embedded ancient sculptural reliefs. . . . One of the most creative elements of the building, this staircase slashes up the full height of the structure at a width of only seven feet, producing a sense of compression and movement equal to that of the grand gallery leading to the King's Chamber in the Pyramid of Cheops at Gizeh. . . . Stirling has produced a masterpiece in this interior.

This is surely the grandest modern staircase in Boston, excepting only those by Rudolph in the Government Center; and aside from McKim's staircase at the Copley Square library, the Sackler's is the greatest stair in Boston of any style. Even Naomi Miller and Keith Morgan, who savage Stirling's design generally, admit that the staircase posed beneath its glass roof has become "an object of wonder . . . an ingenious tour de force, an animated street whose neon-light installed handrail provides warmth on winter days."

If Johnson's library addition, Haas's beaux-arts illusion, and Stirling's museum seem a confusing entrance for Post-Modernism to make here, there is, in fact, good reason. Progeny as it was of Modernism, and admiring, too, of Historicism, Post-Modernism as it began to try to articulate itself only grew more confusing. Most clear to me was the explanation of Philip Johnson, whose important contribution to Boston's architectural history at the library is all the more important to acknowledge in view of the problematic nature of so much of his later Boston work. Johnson, at least, tried (in connection with his Boston library actually) to distinguish what he saw as two very different kinds of Post-Modernism. He pointed out that the library commission had come to him not only at a particular point in time, historically, but also "by way of a board [of trustees] thoroughly aware of history and wanting a historical addition and my wanting a modern one. And [the Johnson Building] is the end result. This is the postmodernism I approve of in a way. We twist it enough so that we have to ask, 'Is it a modern building?' I don't know. It doesn't fit; it's on the cusp. Later, postmodernism became more of what Robert Stern does. . . ."

And what, you ask, does Robert Stern do? Too much, or not nearly enough, according to one's point of view. This controversial architect — on the one hand widely lampooned as the "Ralph Lauren of architecture," on the other recently honored by the deanship of Yale's architectural school — came early to be known in the architects' jargon of the late 1970s and eighties as a "Gray," as opposed, that is, to a "White," labels worth perpetuating, perhaps, in aid of trying to sort out Post-Modernism.

The "Grays" reached back behind the Modern Movement for their inspiration (does this sound familiar? See here, or anywhere, under Pre-Raphaelite, Queen Anne, Cram Gothic, etc.) — back to the Historicist work the early Modernists disdained (though it is only fair to say that some of it — Arts and Crafts work, for example — seems to me now *proto*-Modern in feeling). The era the Grays especially identified with and in which they saw much they thought they could make something of, was the late nineteenth-century Shingle Style (discussed in Chapter 3), with its great, simple masses and gray-shingled palette — hence "Grays."

The "Whites," on the other hand — so does history never stop repeating itself — reached back to excavate what by the 1970s had become, indeed, a historical period like any other — the period of just those heroic early Modernists who had ultimately vanquished Historicism, led, of course, by Gropius, Mies, and above all by Le Corbusier himself, he of all those pristine white buildings — hence "Whites."

Leading the Whites were the "New York Five," as they were sometimes called, themselves led by Peter Eiseman. More adept as a theoretician perhaps than as a designer, Eiseman not surprisingly cultivated Boston connections. He taught for a time at Harvard, where he was not, however, given tenure. One of his famous series of four houses (all of them, Carter Wiseman insists, "notorious for their uninhabitability"), House II of 1969, was the Falk residence in Hardwick, Vermont; and all four of them are reputedly connected in part to Eiseman's fascination with M.I.T. professor Noam Chomsky's studies in linguistics.

More architecturally productive were three other Whites: Richard Meier, Charles Gwathmey, and Michael Graves. Meier's aesthetic, especially elegant it always seems to me at seaside — white metal skin, glass block, pipe railings — is by now iconic of its era; but although two of his prototype designs (his "Suburban Prototype House, Concord, Massachusetts" and his Olivetti branch office) were designed for Boston, his closest major realized work is quite at the outer fringes of Boston's orbit, in Connecticut.

Gwathmey, however, whose interest in Le Corbusier's work is less in the pristine white of the master's forms and more in their spatial and proportional complexities, has achieved three handsome Boston buildings distributed between the Back Bay, Cambridge, and Cape Cod, where in 1968 he designed one of his first characteristic works, Cooper House (Figure 270),

313

FIGURE 270. Gwathmey Siegal: Cooper House, Orleans, 1968. Among the earliest work in Boston's orbit of perhaps the most distinguished of the Post-Modernists.

the design of which is closely related to the Gwathemy House that launched his career, especially in its sense of interpenetrating volumes.

Graves, finally, who trained at Harvard as well as elsewhere, has produced two Boston-area works: his two schemes for the Health, Fitness and Wellness Center at St. Paul's School, Concord, New Hampshire, and the Pura-Williams House in Manchester-by-the-Sea on Boston's North Shore, both in 1994. The design of the Manchester house reflects Graves's increasingly sceneographic and decorative interests — Disneylike in their palette of conspicuous if muted color — and, indeed, by the 1970s Graves was more gray than white. Ah, Post-Modernism!

"Grays," though much thicker on the ground (Shingle Style Revival has been a popular style in New England for obvious reasons), have always, however, been harder to define, a sympathy for shingled houses being only one if the most conspicuous strain of "Graydom." Robert Stern (he of just such worthy shingled essays as Chilmark of 1979 on Nantucket and Red Oaks of 1992 in Cohasset) is only one architect of same, while even Stern's work has been varied enough. His library for St. Paul's School is more than just a fantasia on a theme of one Victorian Boston designer (Richardson); it is a deft homage, by no means antique in feeling, to another (Vaughan). Stern may be a Historicist, but he is not a nostalgist, at least not here, where he mediates beautifully between disparate things at an idyllic, fragile point of St. Paul's historic campus. Moreover, he is also capable of so stylish a work as Point West Place of 1983 in Framingham, the polychromatic stripes which surely must, as they were intended to, register forcefully on swiftly passing traffic.

Another shade of gray, so to speak, perhaps the most important shade, has derived more from Venturi's work, and is worth a moment because some Po-Mo was saved by wit, not a little of which was Charles Moore's. Alas, there is little of that

314

fine architect's work in Boston's sphere, but what there is is very good: an addition of 1985 to the Dartmouth College Art Museum and another to Williams College's museum of two years later, both the work of Centerbrook, perhaps Moore's best-known firm.

All things considered, however, the best of both shades in Boston is to be found in one building by Stern — the Houghton Mifflin Building at the corner of Boylston and Berkeley Streets in the Back Bay. Built in lieu of the second part of an earlier building at Boylston and Clarendon — a building by Philip Johnson that proved so offensive an intrusion into Copley Square (and provoked such public outcry) that the client changed architects midstream — Stern's design is not just deft urban theater. That its corner motif derives from the 1948 Jordan Marsh Building by the Perry/Dean office (according to Stern himself, to me) is a lovely touch. That "proto Post-Modernist" building having been, as I've noted, quite ahead of its time and that Gropius so disliked it (what he would have thought of Stern's building — or of TAC's Heritage on the Green a block away! — does not bear thinking about) only adds here to our sense of history's always passing parade. So too does the reason I suggest Stern on Boylston Street may stand not just for Stern but also for Moore: Stern managed there much better than the over-scaled windows and by-now heavy-seeming wit of Jordans. The entrance vestibule motif on Boylston Street, for example, is a full-fledged, tempietto, rather freely rendered replica on the Boston State House's upper reaches and golden dome. It almost makes up for the loss of Venturi's toy Trinity Church from Copley Square.

Much less elegant than either toy State House or toy Trinity was the Sankey bottle, Boston's one full-fledged Venturi moment of those years: a fifty-foot-high roadside replica of a milk bottle built as a roadside ice cream stand in suburban Taunton in the early years of the automobile era, circa 1933, this surviving example of folk art was brought to Boston and installed in 1976 on the Congress Street Wharf by the entrance to the Children's Museum. It was the closest Boston came to *Learning from Pop*, or was it *Learning from Las Vegas*? Whichever: Boston, like Post-Modernism, had come a long way.

ANOTHER way of looking at it would be to conclude that architecture in Boston — in the largest meaning of the word — had pretty much come to the end of its rope. Form-givers no more, Boston's architects in the 1980s increasingly were seen as contrivers of pleasant urban environments; exterior decorators, so to speak, taking their cues from past masters and contemporary society.

Even TAC compromised. Certainly Gropius's old firm in 1986 perpetrated what can only be called a kind of Victorian Revival at 855 Boylston Street, and a more stolid design (the Historicism of which Gropius would have abominated) it would be hard to find even along nineteenth-century Beacon Street. Three years later at 1 Bowdoin Square, Graham Gund attempted Sullivanesque Revival, no less, and it would not be too much to say that Art Deco Revival soon followed and abounded (101 Federal Street, for example, designed in 1988 by Kohn, Pederson, Fox Associates; or 265 Franklin Street of 1984 by Goody, Clancy).

In this last style the results, admittedly, were more interesting. At 265 Franklin, for example, Goody, Clancy's design seems to reflect (whether consciously or not I do not know) a cardinal principle of pre–World War II American Historicism, since then usually forgotten: that, as Ralph Adams Cram put it, in the case of Gothic design the intervention of the Renaissance could not help but (and *should*) make "modern" Gothic necessarily different, however subtly, from medieval Gothic. Naomi Miller, in

315

her analysis of 265 Franklin, has picked up on this idea: the building, she writes, "conflat[es] the architecture of the twenties with that of modernism . . . a series of stepped setbacks rise. . . . The pattern is reinforced by the use of such materials as rough-hewn rose granite on the lower stories and polished rose granite on the upper stories. A relatively ingenious rectilinearity dominates all. Subtle planar distinctions are evident." Thus Deco design after (European) Modernism does indeed seem here to have rather a different character than (pre-European) Modernist Deco design had. The lobby, moreover, rejoices in the most beautiful of Boston's ubiquitous office-building fountains.

Whether curiously or not, the closer to the time of the design of the historical style being revived, the better the design usually turned out to be. Witness Gwathemy, Siegal's Knoll Building in the Back Bay, of which no less than Ada Louise Huxtable wrote, "This suave and sophisticated reinterpretation of the International Style brings modernism full circle, as innovative force, established orthodoxy and creative renaissance." Or was that Po-Mo, too?

To be sure, Huxtable's hymn to the Knoll Building documents that even the most explicit revivalism of the Post-Modernist period was by no means without architectural merit in the judgment of a most exacting critic. But if Huxtable could not say enough for the Knoll Building, more than enough just about summed up the apparently exasperated response, for example, of Huxtable's counterpart at the *Boston Globe* to the Science Discovery Museum in suburban Acton. Robert Campbell noted that designers E. Verner Johnson & Associates used "motifs cribbed from such high post-modern icons as Robert Venturi (his mother's house) and Michael Graves (numerous works of the late 1970s)." Campbell added, "Inside, there's a lot of Charles Moore." Understandably dizzy, the *Globe*'s architecture critic pronounced the museum "Post-

Modernist Revival" — whilst Post-Modernism, of course, yet reigned. If things had begun to speed up in the 1960s, by the eighties the acceleration was dizzying.

The finale, surely, was something called "façadism." Witness 99 Summer Street (Goody, Clancy, 1986), 125 Summer Street (Kohn, Pederson, Fox Associates, 1989), and Exchange Place of 1981 by the WZMH Group, to cite just the most conspicuous examples of this favorite ploy of the Post-Modern era, which either preserved and enhanced or emasculated and destroyed historic landmarks according to one's point of view. My view is, perversely perhaps, the brassier the better: the buffed Victorian white marbled grand stair of the Exchange Building, for instance, glistening in its vast new lobby of mirror and glass. Certainly, too, it is as apt an architectural expression in Boston of the "Massachusetts Miracle" of the 1980s as of Post-Modernism itself, which it can be said suited the era very well, and not least in the theatricality of the style, which achieved its apotheosis in Boston at Rowe's Wharf, Adrian Smith's fantasia of 1987 on the waterfront.

No one approaching downtown Boston from the sea (by water taxi from Logan International Airport across the harbor, for example) ever forgets the drama of the great six-story arched gateway of Rowe's Wharf, which is eighty feet by eighty feet, or the rotunda beyond. Even a walk along its quay can be memorable. But while Rowe's Wharf is undeniably glorious urban theater, the best in Boston of its ilk, whether or not it is architecture is another matter entirely.

Certainly most such building of the period in Boston was nowhere near so interesting. The worst? Philip Johnson's International Place is an easy target. Too easy. To walk along Atlantic Avenue is to realize how much better Johnson is than many others. As for Johnson's glitzy parody of the Boston Public Library's marble and ironwork within, it is worth remembering that it is just the sort of thing (which we cherish today) that Newport cherished in the gilded era, not to say Bavaria! I think of Henry James's remark that he found he could stand a good deal of gold leaf.

There are, furthermore, worse things than vulgarity. What was not developers' glitz in the 1980s was usually much worse — which is to say tasteful: bland red brick and white trim infill buildings that were every bit as soul-destroying in their vapidness as the vulgar towers, and hardly less destructive of the city's character. (Better to die of outrage than boredom, I say.) Again, TAC's offenses stick most in the throat: for example, their Heritage on the Garden of 1988, the worst sort of "contextualism."

Nor did preservationists offer better. Especially problematic was the way they favored the idea of Boston as a sort of historical theme park — Beacon Hill, for example, as Bulfinch Village.

The architectural character of the hill as it appeared in the 1920s and thirties, when first its charms began to persuade the citizenry that its fabric ought to be preserved, arose in no small measure from the diversity of both its architecture and of the overall culture of the hill (aristocratic to bohemian) of which it was a reflection. The two, moreover, fed into each other nicely: semi-public building use (clubs, publishers, cafés, charitable foundations, convents, and such) meant that in a limited way (befitting a basically residential area) the public historically had had some access to the hill's splendid architectural interiors. The nonresidential use, furthermore, often kept intact the house's interiors in ways residential conversion might not have. (A mansion converted to lawyer's offices, for instance, preserved the spaciousness of the main floor of reception rooms, each of which became an office; the hall the waiting room, in a way condominium conversion could not have. It was a point Whitehill made often.)

Despite the benefits of nonresidential use, the powers that be on the hill increasingly have pursued a policy on the south slope of apparently encouraging the "cleansing" of the area of both architecturally "unfortunate" Victorian excretions and of socially "unfortunate" nonresidential uses. "Restorations," for example, of a house to its earliest appearance, involving removal of "later" elements and the addition of phony new "Greek Revival" features, has increasingly been encouraged. Yet what Pickney Street or even Chestnut Street would be without its picturesque Victorian additions does not bear thinking of. Consider, for instance, the gift the Sunflower Castle (Figure 72) is to its streetscape.

Similarly, there are Modernist contributions on Beacon Hill that later eras will cherish: 34 Hancock Street, for instance, a 1974 design by James McNealy and John Bennet, who when an old building burned down showed how Modernism could bring its own gift to the hill. As one critic has observed:

Its form keeps the rhythm of flat front entry and projecting bay windows by using large windows in the flat part over the entry and a bay that is not round but is instead a skewed polygon with one angle more acute than the other. One side of the bay is blank for most of its height, the other is notched by [large unpaned] corner windows. The bay stops two floors short of the top to make a balcony for one floor and to leave the highest floor free for a full-windowed penthouse. It is a modestly eventful brick building and does not fawn on the past; a seemly neighbor.

Of even greater value is the Modernist stained glass at the entrance to St. John's Church, Bowdoin Street. "Eagle," the symbol of St. John and of the Cowley Fathers, whose historic church this was, reflects the important aesthetic and intellectual contribution of the Cowleys (whose tastes have characteristically tended to the avant-garde) to Beacon Hill and Boston generally at the time of the development of Government Center. It is, moreover, the design of Gyorgy Kepes, the abstract expressionist painter and New Bauhaus artist who in 1946 founded the Center for Advanced Visual Studies at M.I.T. Yet two prosaic wooden doors ("historically accurate," of course) may soon obscure this significant work of art, unique to the area, by a notable artist — frequent collaborator of Belluschi, for instance, in some of his best-known churches throughout the country.

In many cases, clubs, publishers, cafés, charities, and such, if not forced out, have been eased out in periods when real estate prices are such that sale is an attractive option for a needy nonprofit. Historically, perhaps the most dramatic example of this pattern occurred at the Women's City Club, which allowed the public in a limited way to see the bowfront parlor, in which Longfellow married Fanny Appleton, and the house's magnificent architectural interiors, so long celebrated in Boston. But when it was proposed, the club being no longer able to maintain itself, that the Suffolk University Faculty Club take over the buildings (hardly a boisterous use) so negative was the reaction on the hill of influential citizens that the idea seemed hardly worth pursuing. The club reverted to residential uses, as too, since then, has Little, Brown's headquarters building a few doors up Beacon Street, another literary and architectural landmark no longer accessible, that has become some rich person's private house. To be sure, Beacon Hill is *not* yet quite a gated community, nor is it entirely a Bulfinch Village, but it's not hard to catch the drift of things.

Similarly, in the Back Bay several Modernist buildings — 113 Commonwealth, 153 Marlborough Street, Boston University's Hillel Center — are at risk from the apparent policy of the Back Bay Architectural Commission that allowed very harmful alterations to the International style part of the Hotel Vendôme while carefully protecting the Victorian part.

As in the city, so in the suburbs. The Minute Man National Historic Park in Concord has begun to seek to turn back the clock, not this time to the entirely residential and Georgian Beacon Hill of the 1800s, but to the revolutionary period of the 1770s. All of this is, or course, the worst sort of "falsified history," in Huxtable's words. But everything so unfortunate as to have been built since then has ever since been in danger from preservationists who adhere to what Temple University professor Michael Wallace rightly calls "Mickey Mouse History."

Some there are, of course, who would apply that judgment to Post-Modernism of the 1980s as a whole. But in the cracks between developers' glitz, infill bore, and preservationist theme parks, some architects and planners stand out as having tried — often necessarily in connection with fairly modest work — for more.

A Boston architect whose career bridged Modernism and Post-Modernism, was Joseph Maybank of Architectural Resources Cambridge. The recollections of Maybank, a graduate of Harvard College trained as an architect at M.I.T., of his time as a young architect at TAC and then on his own, show how the changing face of architecture in this period had as much to do with technology as with theory and in any case with convictions Maybank tried to uphold but in connection with which he had to develop a certain flexibility.

There was at TAC, Maybank recalled, "a kind of Bauhaus mantra [about] 'honesty.' It had to do, among other things," he continued, "with the expression of certain kinds of materials. . . . One had to have a sense of the *nature* of [poured concrete or whatever]. It had also to do with structure," Maybank insisted: "One could never *fake* structure." He went on:

As the years wore on . . . building codes and costs began to make this kind of honesty more and more difficult. . . . Ironically, in order to express the true nature of the structure, it often became necessary to fake it. For example, one couldn't show the real steel structure (now almost universally used because of its economy) because it had to be covered in fireproofing. So, in order to express "structure," architects had to cover the real load-bearing members with other materials. . . .

The days of cast-in-place concrete and load-bearing masonry were over: the age of sheetrock and hung ceilings had begun. . . . What, after all, were the "plastic qualities" of sheetrock? This new architecture of veneer seemed to be about images — not literal images, but token images, even ironic images. façades were façades again. . . .

One of the products of this new approach is the architectural style we now call "Post-Modernism" . . . [not just a reaction] to the routine, clichéd Modernism we began to see in the late 1960s . . . [but] also a necessary response to changes in building construction . . . to rising costs. . . . [For example] we had to rediscover the aesthetic of the past [as increasingly architects] no longer could use huge sheets of glass but had to make solid walls and punch them with windows again.

Maybank's own work by the 1980s illustrated his point of view very well. Certainly his use of glass was a signature element in the design of two of his best buildings of that decade: the Cabot Center at Tufts University in Medford and the Belfer Center at the Kennedy School at Harvard, the upper reaches of which are finely conceived abstractions (as much of glass as brick) of the conventional but elegant Georgian Revival Kirkland House across the street.

If architects in the 1980s were increasingly trying to regain old skills, the best of them were also trying to avoid the sort of boilerplate increasingly typical of the huge corporate architectural firms and to forge new alliances, in an era of increasing "contextualism," with landscape architects, who, with the outstanding exception of the always formidable Hideo Sasaki (his smashing waterfront park has already been touched on) became noticeably more conspicuous in this period.

Consider the striking series of new rapid transit stations of the 1980s on the Orange Line, especially Stull and Lee's Ruggles Street Station, a tubular-framed, high-tech structure, the Forest Hills Station by Cambridge Seven, with its distinctive 120-foot-high white metal clock tower, and the light-filled, glass-roofed Alewife Station by Ellenzweig Associates, who also (with Roy Mann Associates, the Hilgenhurst office, and Stull and Lee) were responsible for the Southwest Corridor Park that connects all these Orange Line stations — running four or more miles from city to suburb, in lieu of another expressway that community protest had stopped dead.

Ellenzweig was also involved with Craig Halvarson Associates in surely the most splendid new city square and park in Boston in generations, Post Office Square, in the Financial District. Conceived by a group of civic-minded businessmen in 1983, the Friends of Post Office Square achieved a most imaginative project whereby an existing garage was destroyed and on top of a new multistoried underground garage a superb new park was created; the garage's ventilation shafts, for instance, are incorporated into latticework garden pavilions with copper-clad pitched roofs. The design won the Parker Medal in 1992.

Halvarson did an equally imaginative small work near Harvard Square, Quincy Square, where the shape of the spiral is followed through many media. In Salem, furthermore, Halvarson achieved with architect James Cutler and environmental artist Maggie Smith a memorable work in the Witch Trials Memorial. It is a deeply moving design, laid out as a greensward around which are granite walls and benches inscribed with victims' names and their protestations of innocence, gathered from court records. Just beyond the walls, in an old graveyard, the seventeenth-century tombstones of some of the trials' participants stand as mute witnesses. (One so wishes those responsible for Boston's Irish Famine Memorial had achieved so distinguished and moving a recollection of another tragic historic event.)

The character of these 1980s cityscapes

319

discloses very well the changing values and tastes of this era, which tended very much away from the stately and dignified (seen often as pompous) and toward a sometimes startling informality. This was even true of quite the best work in the heart of downtown Boston, Post Office Square, and also of the 1989 design of Dean Abbott with Clarke & Rapuand for Copley Square. In both cases the design is clearly more park than square in the traditional sense of those words, and a very naturalistic, informal park, too. So casual is Copley Square (its splendid fountain aside) it hardly comes as a surprise when one stumbles (as many literally do) on the little bronzes of the hare and the tortoise, an allusion to the over one-hundred-year-old Boston Marathon, which traditionally ends in the square.

Indeed, art underfoot became suddenly pleasingly widespread in Boston: Lilli Ann Killen Rosenberg's *City Carpet*, a ceramic, brass, and stained concrete work that recalls old-fashioned games in a hopscotch pattern, in front of old Boston City Hall, is a much more imaginative historic marker (in this case of the old Boston Latin School) than the usual bronze wall plaque or statue. Even more interesting are two other works downtown: *Asaroton* by Mags Harries, and *Boston Bricks* by Gregg Le Fevere. The latter consists of a series of a hundred bronze "bricks" inset into the pavement of Winthrop Lane, their subject matter ranging from the arts to politics; the former (*Asaroton* means "unswept floor"; the reference is to an ancient Greco-Roman mosaic technique) consists of bronze detritus, inset into the asphalt pavement cast from real leftovers in the market area. Similarly, near Harvard Square at Massachusetts Avenue and Garden Street, brass hoofprints designed by Robert Neiley inlaid in the pavement perpetuate imaginatively the famous ride of Paul Revere's associate William Dawes to alert patriots in Boston's environs to British intentions in the opening days of the American Revolution.

Civic sculpture itself was also marked by informality in this period. Whether it is Penelope Jencks's superb bronze of Samuel Eliot Morrison in front of the St. Botolph Club on Commonwealth Avenue (perched atop a huge rock in his sailor's slicker), or Lloyd Lillies's marvelous bronze, erected six years later at Quincy Market, of the legendary Boston Celtic's coach Red Auerbach (shown courtside, lighting his victory cigar), the point is clearly to draw the viewer into the work. Indeed, Lillies's memorial to Mayor James Michael Curley (two bronzes this time: the orator on his pedestal and the "people's friend" on an adjoining bench) purposely leaves room — on the bench — for the people!

The very definition of sculpture in this period changed fundamentally: the Tanner Fountain in front of Harvard's Science Center, for instance, is the work of designer Peter Walker and of Joan Brigham, a "steam sculptor." Equally innovative is Robert Amory's polyethylene and aluminum *Helion* at Church Green near South Station. A kinetic or moving sculpture, it consists of twenty-four orange disks (hence "Lollipops," its nickname) mounted on ball bearings; ever moving at the wind's whim, it is a colorful grace note on the cityscape.

An architectural firm that brought many of these spheres together, a firm noted as much for their urban design and planning as for their architecture was Koetter-Kim, which since its founding in 1978 was a leading exponent, first in Boston and then abroad (in London particularly, where Koetter-Kim's first studies of Canary Wharf date from 1988) of a movement in town planning called the "new urbanism." A movement much influenced by the Cornell architectural historian Colin Rowe, new urbanism was rooted in Rowe's teaching that the best Modernism existed in deliberate continuity with the Renaissance, and Koetter-Kim early showed a commitment to this ongoing "humanistic" tradition.

Indeed one of their most successful projects was the beautifully composed school complex of 1986 they designed next to St. Paul's Church near Harvard Square, where they suavely fused the antique brick Lambard style of the church with the very different aesthetic of the great stucco mass of the building facing it (itself apparently undistinguished, but a key part along with the church and Adams House in one of the handsomest cityscapes of the Boston area), into a building complex whose style would be hard to name but of the success of which there is no doubt at all. In no small measure because of an unusually sophisticated client, the parish rebuffed the usual archdiocesan hacks, the building committee having been convinced by Tim O'Donnell theirs was a "publishable" project, given St. Paul's proximity to Harvard. The commission was thus given to architects of some distinction on the cusp of their first critical success (at Codex, of which more soon). The result was excellent.

However, more characteristic by far of the work of Koetter-Kim was their plan of the early 1980s for Storrow Terrace, a range of connected terrace housing over Storrow Drive that would have "completed" the Back Bay grid and restored to the core city a traffic-free park and promenade along the Charles River. Alas, the idea was never taken up, though in addition to influencing the firm's later Canary Wharf work in London, its effect is also discernible in their master plan for University Park in Cambridge, where Koetter-Kim again carefully continued the grid of surrounding streets right through their plan, this time for an urban office park.

Fascinatingly, their greatest success in Boston was achieved in another such park and not in the city but in the suburbs; specifically in two suburban office malls, the Codex world headquarters of 1983 in Canton and the Apple Hill complex of five years later in Tewksbury. Of them Fred Koetter has written:

Codex and Apple Hill are two pieces of commentary upon two aspects of the contemporary suburban situation. Codex turns its back to the highway — reestablishing a fragment of vanishing landscape. . . . Apple Hill embraces the highway.

We imagined a building [at Apple Hill] that was . . . literally of the highway. Sited at the prow of a triangular site defined by the intersection of a major local road and Boston's heavily traveled outer ring road, the building lent itself to this intention. By pushing the building as close to the highway as possible, we intensified its relationship to the highway.

The building is . . . characterized by long, horizontal lines. . . . One could identify with the act of moving past this building at high speed. . . .

The suburban office park as a building type has hardly yielded anything better in Boston since, for the first of which jobs the Boston Society of Architects gave Koetter-Kim the Parker Gold Medal.

That being the only time a suburban office center has ever been so honored by the Parker jury discloses the generally low repute of that building type, of course; a repute shared with suburban retail centers and with shopping malls in either city or suburb. Only one such mall in Boston since Belluschi's day has won noticeable praise — the Cambridge Side Galleria by Arrowstreet — the design of which is of interest for attempting for once to open up a mall to its surrounding neighborhood.

That said, there is another mall, Copley Place in the Back Bay, its overall glitz not- withstanding, of which there is this much good to say. A real effort was made at something like high quality civic sculpture, the dominant element of this "mallscape" being Dimitri Hadzi's 1984 *Fountain*, a sixty-foot-high granite, travertine, and marble sculpture, the palette of which (unlike the exterior of Copley Place!) nicely captures inside the mall something of the exterior Ruskinian browns of old Copley Square, endowing Copley Place (otherwise quite deadly in its sense of nowhere — or, perhaps, everywhere) with at least some sense of place.

The most notable Hadzi in Boston is

outside, however: his 1985 *Omphalos* in Harvard Square.

An "omphalos" or "world navel" was the ancient marker of a spiritual center, and Hadzi's in Harvard Square (of mixed granites, twenty-four feet high) is wonderfully rich in symbolism. Critic Joseph Masheck queries, "Cosmic world tree? Revolutionary 'Liberty Tree'? Memorializing abstract stand of doomed American elms?" and wonders as well about a whole hierarchy of meanings ranging from its representing "the shifting vertical planes of the often sculpturesque weathervanes of Harvard" to "a multi-directional sign at a New England crossroads" to, perhaps most significantly (thinking of our earlier discussion of Boston as seen by Alfred North Whitehead and Ada Louise Huxtable), "Boston itself, that 'Hub,' or 'omphalos' of the Universe," intellectually a claim best staked, of course, in Harvard Square.

In architecture, however, despite the many praiseworthy efforts catalogued here, it was by 1985, the year of Hadzi's Harvard Square monument, a dubious claim. When Ben Thompson won the AIA Gold Medal in 1992, the first Boston architect to do so since Sert, it was for work he had begun back in the 1970s. And when Harvard professor Alex Krieger and architect Andrea Leers (of whom more later) took the measure of the architecture of the 1980s in Boston in an article notable alike for its clear-sightedness and fair-mindedness, it was clear from their conclusions that Boston's years of leadership in American architecture had long since passed.

Singling out many of the profession's most ballyhooed pomps of the 1980s in Boston — including Philip Johnson's New England Life Building and International Place, Graham Gund's 75 State Street (with Skidmore, Owings and Merrill), Rowe's Wharf (entirely by Skidmore, Owings and Merrill), John Pedersen and Fox's 75 Federal Street, and TAC's Heritage on the Garden — Leers and Krieger did not mince words:

Each of these clearly set out to redress the abstract and alien character of their immediate modernist predecessors. If the merits of a considered, historically-based, contextural response is evident in these projects, then so is the beginnings of a formulaic traditionalism. These are large mixed-use projects generally with substantial budgets. Far more numerous are buildings . . . in which safe compositions of red-brick, some surface decoration and a historic motif or two at the entry or cornice presume to satisfy a "Boston style."

Yet again here a "Boston style" is posited, and, alas, not the least likely. It has, whatever it is called, Krieger and Leers conclude in a devastating analysis,

reduced much new architecture in Boston to a benign if not downright stilted conventionality. Elaborate design review under the control of a powerful city agency (the BRA) with the participation of many special interest and preservation groups, further reinforces conventional notions of contextuality while discouraging originality.

The very attractions of a balance forged between progress and preservation have brought new pressures for large-scale development and rebuilding. This continues to threaten or overwhelm the irreplaceable physical evidence of the city's past. At the same time a crisis of architectural identity tends to equate contextual appropriateness with the veneer of historicism.

But that is not the only legacy of the 1980s, though it remains a potent drag on Boston even today. In the Post-Modern 1970s and eighties one Boston firm (mostly) avoided the pitfalls of those years and gradually emerged as a kind of gold standard, and for more than Boston — Kallmann, McKinnell and Wood.

Architectural partnerships, like long-lived marriages or great friendships, like nations and even religions, if they are notable enough, have always their founding legends. Behold, Kallmann and

McKinnell's nativity narrative.

The scion of an intellectual Jewish family in Weimar, Gerhard Kallmann, his legal studies cut short in the 1930s by the rise of Hitler, took refuge in England. After study at the Architectural Association in London and a stint in an editorship at *Architectural Review*, stymied still even after World War II by lack of opportunity in Britain, Kallmann again translated himself to newer climes, this time to New York City, where, teaching in the early 1960s at Columbia's school of architecture, the by now middle-aged professor met Michael McKinnell, a young British student from Manchester, who had taken his first degree in architecture there and was pursuing graduate study in America.

Despite a formidable age difference (Kallmann was forty-something, McKinnell twenty-something) each was so drawn to the other that in 1961 they decided to throw in their lot together and begin the practice of architecture in America as a team. The story goes that during a long walk all but the length of Manhattan Island they agreed to seek out competitions to enter — the time-honored way for architects to get ahead — and resolved that if by their fifth they hadn't won one they would give up the idea.

They won the very first, with a design almost immediately famous. And although it was the first building either man had designed in his own name, it was built just as it came from their boards — in the office of a friend, Edward Knowles, with space to spare and a registration stamp — hence Kallmann, McKinnell and Knowles (soon to become Kallmann, McKinnell and Wood when in the course of erecting their building they fell in with a Boston engineer, Henry Wood). The building, of course, already much discussed here, one of the most admired by American architects in the postwar era, was the present Boston City Hall (Figures 250, 251).

Like H. H. Richardson, who nearly a hundred years before, in 1874, had been drawn to Boston after winning another competition for Trinity Church in Copley Square, Kallmann and McKinnell doubtless came the more easily because of Harvard, Richardson's alma mater and the source of many of his clients. Certainly both Kallmann and McKinnell found themselves soon enough members of Harvard's faculty of architecture.

Doubtless too the stability engendered by their teaching positions accounts for the new firm's survival after the City Hall, the wake of which was more problematic than one might think. Their few (though splendid) jobs then — the Boston Five Cent Savings Bank of 1964, for example, and the Phillips Exeter Academy gymnasium of 1965 — continued in the vein of the Brutalist concrete aesthetic of the City Hall and, in an era of decidedly changing architectural fashion, the office's survival was certainly in question. And while it is almost too much to have to say that yet again the gods intervened, so crucial (and unexpected) was the commission of 1977 to design the Cambridge house of the American Academy of Arts and Sciences, a venerable and distinguished Boston institution of scholarly leaders in many fields, and so dramatic was the change in Kallmann and McKinnell's aesthetic when challenged by the Academy to eschew exposed concrete, that it is hard to know what else to say.

Actually, as Kallmann points out, the plan of the Academy is very similar to that of the City Hall, and given the Cambridge commission was to design what was essentially a country house on an almost rural wooded hilltop site, the stylistic change was natural enough. Nonetheless, their new posture seemed sufficiently Post-Modern to some that Kallmann and McKinnell's supporters rallied to their defense conspicuously. One critic, Mildred Schmertz, protested that just because, in the Academy's design (as opposed to the

City Hall's) the architects went "back further in time than Le Corbusier for their inspiration [to the Arts and Crafts style], Kallmann and McKinnell have justly or unjustly been labeled post-modern." The label was inaccurate, Schmertz argued. They had "drawn upon memory and recollection not in the post-modern spirit of recondite codes and pedantic one-upmanship, but joyfully in response to a great chance."

It was rather a strained defense: Le Corbusier was a living, contemporary master at the time his late work inspired the design of the City Hall; when the Academy was designed the Arts and Crafts style had been for sixty years a receding memory of pre-World War I vintage. And as for Kallmann and McKinnell's "memory and recollection" ("joyfully"!) versus "recondite codes and pedantic one up-manship," this was surely a matter of liking one thing and not liking another and choosing carefully what one calls each.

Similarly, Robert Campbell is equally determined (in his discussion of a later work, the Hynes Auditorium) to protect Kallmann and McKinnell from being identified with eclecticism, that dirty word so redolent of the Pre-Modern era of Classic and Gothic Revival and whatever: Kallmann and McKinnell are "eclectic in inspiration but never in expression," Campbell insists, "because the sources are always digested, abstracted, and transformed." Unless Campbell means to perpetuate the 1920s Modernist caricature of eclecticism, that is surely, however, to assert Kallmann, McKinnell and Wood *are* eclectics like Charles Coolidge (look at the Harvard Houses) or Ralph Adams Cram (look at Cambridge's Cowley Monastery) — eclectics who certainly "digested" and "transformed" (and even "abstracted," in Cram's case, as Modernism loomed at the end of his career) in just the way Kallmann and McKinnell do.

Of course, there were *bad* eclectics, architects who perpetrated, for example, the many clones of Coolidge Georgian or Cram Gothic or McKim Classicism that litter the landscape. But if we are to hold Cram and Coolidge and McKim responsible for those, there are surely already some progeny of the Boston City Hall for which to hold Kallmann and McKinnell responsible, and by no means are they of the quality of the most notable Boston building influenced by the City Hall, Hugh Stubbins's Countway Library of 1963 at Harvard Medical School. The Shepley office's Fanny Mason Wing of Harvard's music building, built in 1970, makes one wish its designer had never heard of Kallmann and McKinnell, to say nothing of the Boston City Hall. And that is just in Boston. In Kansas City, as Alex Krieger has pointed out, the annex to that city hall, very much influenced by the Boston original, is a case of "imitation not always resulting in flattering forms."

Good eclectics, bad eclectics, Post-Modern or whatever — the reason then as now these were fighting words in Boston's architectural community is clear: by the 1980s, what Kallmann and McKinnell's work was called mattered to everyone after the success of the American Academy, because it had become the gold standard in architecture in Boston, even for those who thought they were headed in the wrong direction stylistically.

And no wonder. Their work of the late 1970s and the eighties marked a decade and more of outstanding architecture and more than one near-masterpiece — some of it (their gorgeous Becton Dickinson Headquarters of 1981 New Jersey, for example) beyond our ken here, but enough of it in Boston to assert that it is not too much to say Kallmann and McKinnell endowed city and suburb in this period with a body of work rivaled in the last one hundred years only by McKim and Pei.

324

Six works stand out: the American Academy, Back Bay Station of 1976, the Hynes Convention Center of 1982 in the Back Bay, the 1985 Harvard Business School Fitness Center (Shad Hall), the Newton Public Library of 1986, and the Asian Export Wing at Salem's Peabody Museum of 1984 — six works in nine years, works architects, academics, critics, and even the public seem never to tire of talking about, whatever they called them.

Post-Modernists Kallmann and McKinnell have never been, actually, but historically the debate will inevitably focus on that topic if only because of the contemporary debate in the 1980s. And because, too, so much of Kallmann, McKinnell and Wood's mature work was done in that era, it is through a Post-Modernist grid that their designs will register most immediately and most forcefully.

The measure of Post-Modernism has best been taken to my mind by Allan Tempko, the brilliant architecture critic of the *San Francisco Chronicle*. By no means unaware of the dead end the International Style called Modernism is, or that what he calls "commercialized architecture" in the vein of Disney can be "shrewd urban design" (in Boston think Rowe's Wharf), and even admiring at times of the king of glitz, architect John Portman ("there is no denying its barbarous energy," Tempko has written of San Francisco's Hyatt Regency), Tempko has nonetheless been relentless in his critique of Po-Mo.

Not just for its "fakery" and propensity for "stage sets" in lieu of architecture; not just for the often "vulgar flash of the detailing"; nor only for the frequently "conflicting lines and clamorous details," has Tempko savaged Post-Modernism. The phrases in quotation marks disclose his gift for the deft cut (best of all are "the brontosaurus of glass-covered atriums" and his comparison of another design to "Pontiacs, pro-football, and chewing gum"). But Tempko has, unlike so many

other critics, gone way beyond name-calling in his analysis.

In fact he gets quite to the heart of the matter, protesting the "glitzy, shallow and ruthless manipulation of popular taste" characteristic of Po-Mo, which typically tricks the unsophisticated mercilessly while denying them even the palest echo of the real thing. Indeed, Tempko nails the thing utterly when he zeroes in on what he calls "the reactionary sentimentality of Post-Modernism, the architectural counterpart of Reaganism in politics." But Kallmann and McKinnell's work stood apart.

I like the way Mildred Schmertz approaches the matter. "Four principal themes," this critic writes, characterize [Kallmann and McKinnell's] architecture — dramatization, compositional rigor, the primacy of movement, and the expression of structure. These are the keys which open the mind," Schmertz declares, "to an understanding of their distinguished work"; these and any number of their "studied imperfections," as Alex Krieger calls them, which I find elegantly illuminate most of Schmertz's themes as well as Krieger's:

At the Harvard Business School Fitness Center [Shad Hall], an expressive steel lintel makes possible the doubling of a typical bay at the building's entrance, but the lintel is unexpectedly supported at its center. . . .

The architectural-shaped trusses at the Back Bay Station suggest the bearing of much weight, but they actually support only a thin flat roof. As if in acknowledgment of this modest role, they . . . rest on small brackets.

Examples such as these . . . are not the product of formal virtuosity, witticism, self-indulgence or carelessness. In each instance . . . a sensibility is jarred or an expectation denied. Coming to terms with these buildings requires alertness and patience. Neither easy admiration for the immediately apparent craft in detailing, nor the opposite — dismissal of the building's idiosyncrasies of form — is the best springboard for what the intellect will confront and what the senses will eventually enjoy.

To extend this dialogue from Schmertz and Krieger to Elizabeth Padjen is to take up Krieger's challenge that what begins with the intellect in Kallmann and McKinnell's work will win through to the senses, for how differently Padjen reads the significance of that so expressive steel lintel and column at Shad Hall's entrance: "an enormous lintel spans the entry," she writes, "supported by a single column with an outrageous gilded capital, a 'gilded fist' that the architects thought was an appropriately muscular metaphor for an athletic building on a campus where cupolas display 'gilded crania.'" Marvelous! Notice how the unnecessary column (without ever explaining itself, so to speak) nonetheless justifies itself for Schmertz so that, the senses appealed to, the intellect is, indeed, appeased.

These bare steel lintels and uprights, which (along with their wide, flaring cornices and "ragged edge" corners, as at the Newton Library) have become characteristic of KMW's stone façades, rather fascinate. So far as I can tell they derive less from a study of the work of Mies, who famously used steel in this very direct, exposed way, and more from an affinity for Aldo Rossi. Certainly KMW does not intend them as Post-Modernist gestures like the clumsy stone "lintels," for instance, that appear rather ridiculously in the glassy façades of the 1988 addition to the United Shoe Building in Boston by Stubbins Associates. Moreover, KMW's steel "posts and beams," far from seeming inappropriate or out of place, instead play a most eloquent role in their design.

Critic John Morris Dixon has studied this use of steel and sees it as a part of something larger: there is, in Kallmann and McKinnell's mature work, he suggests, "A tension between exposed members and applied wrappings, between Modernist elements — which often carry references to precedents such as, say, nineteenth-century iron framing — and

Historicist elements, which are always considerably abstracted. The design partners, Gerhard Kallmann and Michael McKinnell, consider themselves Modernists, but their respect for historical precedents comes up repeatedly in discussion of their work."

Notice how richly layered, each layer almost doubled, this analysis has become: it is Kallmann and McKinnell's Historicism that is most Modern (always so abstract); it is their Modernism that is most Historicist (which is to say, nearly always precedented): text on subtext on text.

If only because he has been a keen student and expositor of this firm, it is timely to extend the critical dialogue here (which I'm trying to make reflective in these pages of the year-in and year-out dialogue KMW generates) to include Robert Campbell, who has always been intrigued by what he calls

a certain angst that has persisted in the work of this remarkable team of architects . . . [whose] buildings are always far more than accommodations of the client's program. Like good poems, they offer a dense compaction of possible readings and metaphors. . . .

The Hynes [Auditorium in the Back Bay] has that metaphoric richness. The red third floor hall [lined with huge black doors on both sides], suggest[s] the set for a dramatization of the Masque of the Red Death. . . . [There is] the more hopeful movement of rising up through [the main staircase of the great full-building-height rotunda] from darkness into light. . . . Though KMW's work always seems tectonic and fully built, as opposed to pictorial or narrative, it is amazingly rich in ghostly messages, references, metaphors, and demarcations.

Elsewhere, in this connection, Campbell dwells on exactly the use of bare exposed steel that we've focused on here. Observing at the Hynes that the principal element (especially at ground level) of the Boylston Street façade (Figures 273, 274) is granite

FIGURE 271. In the year of Carlo Scarpa's death, Gerhard Kallmann contrived this homage to the great Italian master: a fireplace surround inspired by a design motif characteristic of Scarpa's work in the Kallmann, McKinnell and Woods house for the American Academy of Arts and Sciences in Cambridge.

"cut into shapes that recall, in a diagrammatic way, the details of the building's Boston past," Campbell continues:

As the eye moves upward, strange things begin to happen. Granite gives way gradually to steel and glass, materials more expressive of our own time. At the top, simple blue-black steel girders, almost like those of a bridge, span the windows and support the roof. It's as if the Hynes' granite were being peeled away, story by story, to reveal the modern steel skeleton that actually supports the building. The history of Boston commercial architecture is recapitulated in this one façade. Its narrative quality makes clear what Kallmann means when, for once, he tries to sum up the meaning of architecture in a single sentence.
 "Architecture," he says, "in distinction from building, is the presentation to the viewer of the act of construction."

Yet again, the fructifying quality of the Boston Granite Style comes to the fore, and no wonder. These designers, who still work together in a private studio distinct from their drafting rooms, seem to have been drawn together importantly in the first place by their shared love for a very un-Po-Mo idea indeed — an architecture strongly expressive of its structural means. Neither man is fundamentally a theorist (though Kallmann, if one can get past his

guard, is an eloquent architectural thinker), but designers and builders, albeit highly intellectual. Indeed, Robert Silver recalls that at Harvard students often called them Column and Mechanical!
 Yet it is no secret from most that, leaving aside questions of secondary structure (the support within the façade just of itself), though the exterior stone, steel, and glass walls of so much of their work — for example, of the Hynes — in our modern sense of the word's meaning are certainly "structural" (suspension from an enclosing steel frame is a structural system, after all), they are in the traditional load-bearing sense suggested by the disposition on the façade of stone and steel not structural. One sees stone on stone and steel on stone, the steel lintels toothed into stone on either side of the openings they span. But the granite stones, despite the pattern of their placement, are suspended by clips from the underlying steel frame, and only some of the exposed steel beams (those supporting the gabled roof, for example) are supportive of primary structure.
 Now the vertical *I*-beams Mies famously used on the exterior of Lake Shore Drive Apartments in Chicago aren't structural either (they are welded to the uprights of the steel frame so as to project from the

FIGURE 272. Gerhard Kallmann's drawing of his Peabody Essex Museum façade, Salem, 1984. Wrote Jean Paul Carlhian: "Until the creation of the International Style . . . architects continually searched the past for sources of inspiration. There is, however, a world of difference between borrowing and imitating, with the former bearing all the attributes of a creative act and the latter presenting all the characteristics of a stale, safe attitude."

surface), and the rationale for these modern "pilasters," in William Jordy's words, is that the exterior *I*-beams "not only record the technology [of the towers' construction] but celebrate it. Both the material and the process by which the tower is built become vivid." But horizontal *I*-beams in a masonry façade, despite Campbell's apt image of the "peeling away" of the façade, seem a more complicated question.

Pressed somewhat (and in a conference room overlooking just this façade of the Hynes), Kallmann is at his Socratic best. Of course, architects have their secrets. Should one expect of buildings more than one expects of people? (I think of John Coolidge's defense of Cram's aisle pier buttresses at All Saints, Ashmont, to me disappointing. Their *function*, my old teacher insisted, was decorative.) At his board Kallmann makes a similar point. "The eye, Douglass, the eye: architecture is a metaphor" — otherwise it's *just* construction, *just* engineering. The eye. Always the eye.

I wonder if Picasso was right then? "Art is a lie," he says somewhere, "that tells the truth." No, retorts Kallmann, "not a lie — an artifice."

As a matter of fact, I'm not sure I entirely agree — of which more later — but I have

learned something (one is always learning with Gerhard Kallmann), and not just about his architecture. And I discover soon enough that such explanation as there is for designing minds so wonderfully perverse as his and McKinnell's is to be found in Kallmann's writings, wherein he revealed himself as long ago as in 1959 as "contemptuous of agreeable and acceptable aesthetic effect," espousing vigorously "an architecture of more stern construction!"

His fundamental attitude toward Modernism (at just the point it was waning) is an attitude that is by no means unfriendly. No less than Peter Eiseman has declared, "if modern architecture lives in America, it lives in the minds, the hearts, the eyes and hands of [Kallmann and McKinnell]." But it is an attitude that has always been stubbornly independent: certainly to his fellows in Kallmann's youth, architects of Modernism's second generation and the direct inheritors of the heroic Modernist masters, Kallmann preached the necessity of not succumbing to the pursuit of "elegant variations on the themes of the modernist patriarchs." Nor was it enough, he declared, in a memorable phrase, to "stun the eye but remain bored forever after."

For Kallmann and McKinnell this attitude seems to have been from the start neither a matter of history as such, nor of

FIGURE 273. Kallmann, McKinnell and Wood, Hynes Auditorium, Back Bay, 1982. Elegant and assured, it stands nobly alone amid the architectural glitz of Boylston Street.

architectural style (especially of the architecture adjacent to a project of theirs). Rather, it seems to have depended for them on the nature or "mind," as it were, of the overall culture of the place to be built in, and of what in that culture seemed to them most characteristic and enduring, even in some ways unchanging, and in the response to this culture of the architect. This is what I believe Kallmann means when he speaks (in a Jungian way?) of "memory" — both collective (of the place and culture) and individual (of the architect) — "memory" that is the point of departure for, ideally, entirely original form, which at its best will not only achieve the newly designed building's own purposes, but give new and expanded meaning to the place being built in.

This is surely why Eduard Sekler insists that Kallmann and McKinnell's work "reveals itself only to those observers who penetrate beyond the surface appearances to the fundamental constituents — to the most basic, essential experiences of architecture: space and light, structure, construction and tectonics; and, equally important, time — time in the experience of movement through space, or time in its flow from past to future, creating the experience of history."

Creating the experience of history. Kallmann and McKinnell do that. In ways as small as the American Academy mantelpiece — with its figure of the cornice of Brion's tomb in San Vito d'Altivole, an originally Wrightian motif Carlo Scarpa transfigured — Kallmann's homage to Scarpa in the year of his death (Figure 271). In ways as large as the marvelous, richly layered façade of the Peabody Museum's Asian Export Wing, where (doubtless influenced by the zeal of that indefatigable lover of architecture, the Peabody's then-curator of Asian exports, H. A. Crosby Forbes) Kallmann and McKinnell achieved something Campbell, with his great affinity for KMW's work, has described very well:

This façade has several layers. The first is a Chinese-looking white stucco wall, topped by green tiles and pierced by a round, traditional Chinese Moon Gate. One perceives this wall as the enclosing wall of the garden rather than as part of the building. At one point the wall seems to have been eroded, revealing an octagonal window of the new wing behind it. The erosion doesn't look real but looks like the deliberate, abstract representation of an erosion, making the wall into a playful ruin.

The next layer is a sort of false front. . . . It's

329

FIGURE 274. Kallmann, McKinnell and Wood's Hynes Convention Center of 1982 is architecture both distinguished and exciting, its high-style interiors, such as the top floor gallery, full of dash as well as dignity.

very flat and is made of brick and limestone trim. . . . Three big rectangles at its upper level frame only empty air. . . .

Seen another way, the Export Wing façade is a little anthology of logical ways to span openings in brick. Steel girders cross the big square holes, while flat brick arches span the tiny square windows beneath them. This unique façade, elegant and logical but as playful as a puzzle of puns and anagrams, plays nicely against the romantic Oriental garden wall.

So it does. Not knowing what it was (shame to say I'd never been to Salem until a field trip for this book), I admired Kallmann's original drawing of this façade (Figure 272) in the firm's waiting room only to forget it through a long interview, at the end of which, when I asked Kallmann if there was something I'd left out he especially liked of his work, he promptly led me out the door to the drawing I had so admired!

For so reserved a man of so reserved buildings, it was a moment. Kallmann and McKinnell are quintessentially Bostonian. Kallmann: "I do *not* design buildings that shake hands with people." McKinnell: "Years ago a colleague warned us that neither of us had a single self-promotional bone in our bodies." You could not be more Bostonian.

So too with their architecture. I am thus

tempted — Curtis, Serenyi, Krieger, all having invoked here the idea of "Boston Style" — to pronounce on the matter finally for Kallmann and McKinnell, whose claim to such a thing is very great. And in more than just reticence. There is also gravitas and finesse, neither unrelated to how they create what Sekler calls the experience of history.

Standing in Copley Square at the Boylston Street corner of McKim's Boston Public Library of 1888, one can see quite clearly (I'm sure deliberately) the end façade of the Hynes Convention Center of 1982 up the street. Of course, as has already been noted, the elevation of the newer building relates significantly to that of the older landmark. But that is, like the mantelpiece in the Academy, another small thing. More significant than this now obvious comparison risked here is that the tall arched window of the Hynes you see clearly from Copley Square is one end of a great third-floor gallery there — a block-long, two-story-high vaulted room of great splendor, entirely comparable to any of the library's interiors. And that gallery takes

its place (churches and theaters aside) with perhaps five others as among the great rooms of Boston's nearly four centuries now. (Oh, well, *let's* ruffle some feathers: I judge the other five to be the Senate Reception Room in the Bulfinch State House, the Peabody-Essex Hall in Salem, Harvard's Memorial Hall Refectory and Lowell House Dining Hall, and, finally, the Sargent Gallery of the McKim Library.)

"Ancient secrets," murmurs Kallmann. "Consonance without replication," offers McKinnell.

The experience of history. It is, perhaps, the place to bring our own history here to an end, before it shades (in the next chapter) into criticism: the corner of Boylston and Dartmouth Streets at Copley Square — where McKim seems to foreshadow Kallmann and McKinnell, who profit greatly from the experience, and move on.

And who's that young man tearing across the slushy winter street from Copley subway station up Boylston?

Another I. M. Pei, perhaps, who we must all hope will find his Le Corbusier in the twenty-first century.

PART IV

MACHADO AND SILVETTI AND THE NEW MODERNS

14

FROM THE "VILLA TRANSFORMER" TO THE "ROMANTIC MACHINE"

THROUGHOUT THE 1980s, working somewhat below the threshold of fame, shall we say, there were a number of younger Boston architects (some of them students once of Sert, Boston's last Modernist master) conscious of Boston's role as the cradle of the Modern Movement in architecture in America, but jealous of how little vitality seemed left to that Modernist tradition. Often admiring, to be sure, of Kallmann and McKinnell, though more, perhaps, of that firm's practice of architecture than of its evolving aesthetic, some of these younger architects began in the 1980s to recognize a kind of like-mindedness among certain of themselves, a like-mindedness that might amount to something.

Although they have coalesced into no "Boston Six" or Eight or whatever, the fact of the existence of this group emerged very early in my research in 1998 and 1999 for this edition, coinciding with my conviction that rather than end *Built in Boston* with what might seem on the surface to be the dismal state of Boston architecture at century's end, it would be far more useful to project (and encourage) the promise discovered somewhat beneath the surface into the next century.

Those architects who might, meanwhile, see themselves as part of this group cooperated, doubtless interested to see, these forty-something and fifty-something architects, if an architectural historian of their own "boomer" generation would see any consonance or cohesion in their ideas — as well, I suppose, any future.

This was all the more true my being a historian specializing in American architecture and New England studies.

Who, then, are these architects? The roll, as I see it:

At somewhat of a distance, Gerhard Kallmann and Michael McKinnell, for so many decades Boston's presiding architects of power, have been in a kind of practical, exemplary sense the fulcrum of this group. It is a role fulfilled more immediately and more intimately, in what can only be called a more mystical sense, by Rodolfo Machado and Jorge Silvetti, who are very much the group's mentors and gurus, they having established themselves long before the days of their increasing fame (today they have arguably become Boston's great international architects) as visionary architectural theorists.

The fulcrum's lever? Schwartz/Silver, undoubtedly: they are Boston's boldest architectural adventurers, always in the vanguard. Ranged with these two firms at the group's heart are Leers, Weinzapfel, Peter Forbes, and Thompson and Rose, together with Woo and 30-something up-and-coming bright lights like the partners of Office dA, and Douglass Dolezal, Brian Healy and Kyo Sing Woo, and — at somewhat of a remove — Alex Krieger and William Rawn, these last two more for their role as civic thinkers and preachers (of architecture) than for their design.

What to call this very loose but very signal group? I will call them (with grateful acknowledgment to Charles Jencks, from whom I have lifted the term) the New Moderns.

The most immediate architectural community in which this gifted cohort stands out, Boston's, has become at the turn of the twenty-first century a notable one: only New York and Los Angeles, it would seem, are architectural centers in America that rival Boston, a city that has long had the repute of sheltering more architects per square foot than anything else except psychiatrists! (Certainly, of all the chapters nationwide of the American Institute of Architects, the Boston Society of Architects is the largest.)

By no means, however, is it a monolithic community: there are many mansions even just in Boston architecture — many universes of discourse, if you will — and though all are related each is also very distinct. For example, the New Moderns would all be called "design firms" in the professional jargon of the day, not "service firms," those makers of institutional background architecture, from corporate to religious, which range from small, specialized practices ("trophy homes" and so on) to global giants of corporate architecture like Bergmeyer and Tsoi/Kobus, two of many Boston firms with worldwide practices.

The design firms, of course, constitute the elite — whose role it is to push the envelope. Risk-takers who at one and the same time must be doctoral-level thinkers who advance the frontiers in their field and entrepreneurs who are able to set the design pace, these are the architectural offices historians and critics always focus on, easily identified through the years of this study. Indeed, the reader by now should certainly recognize those Boston-based design leaders in the last half of the twentieth century who have won either the Gold Medal (the highest award) of the American Institute of Architects (one Boston architect for each decade, really:

Gropius for the 1960s, Beluschi for the 1970s, Sert for the 1980s, Thompson for the 1990s) or the Institute's Firm of the Year Award (in the 1960s TAC and Stubbins; in the 1970s Sert and the Shepley office; in the 1980s Kallmann and McKinnell and Ben Thompson; in the 1990s Cambridge Seven).

This last firm, Cambridge Seven, is really, historically, in a class by itself, having been founded in 1962 to realize Boston's New England Aquarium, the design of which, by Peter Chermayeff and his partners, set a new world standard in a building type itself new enough and of rapidly increasing importance in an era of discovery of the natural environment. Most recently, Chermayeff — since becoming a partner in Chermayeff, Solluqub and Poole — designed the Lisbon Aquarium, the centerpiece of the 1998 World's Fair in the Portuguese capital.

Distinct from both the "design firms" and the "service firms," though linked especially closely to the former, is the Academy. This has become, of all the domains in Boston's architectural community, the one with the highest profile as New England's capital has evolved in the second half of the twentieth century into chiefly an international center of education, medicine, high technology, and financial services. Along with tourism, these four fields have become, according to the mayor of the core city, the economic generators of the entire metropolis in the present era, the engines, indeed, of its prosperity. And in that first and preeminent category are no less than five centers of architectural education — Harvard, M.I.T., Northeastern University, the Boston Architectural Center, and Wentworth Institute — the first two of world rank, and all of them key to staffing Boston's drafting rooms by day and by night.

It is the Academy, moreover, especially the elite departments of architecture at M.I.T. and Harvard, that also opens up for Boston's New Moderns the far wider and quite key context of national and international — what would be called today "global" — architecture, increasingly important in the post–World War II era, when most design leaders have not been Boston-based, or even necessarily American.

As a result, the stars of the global architectural firmament, however distant in one way, are always distinctly "presences" in Boston in a very immediate way, whether Boston-based (like Machado & Silvetti) or not. (Raffael Moneo, for example, though Madrid-based, was head of Harvard's architecture department before Silvetti.) One can never tell what it may mean that the likes of Tadao Ando and Rem Koolhaus pass through Logan International Airport week in and week out, to and from studio or podium or whatever at one school or another. (I recall a week in November of 1998 when Renzo Piano, Frank Gehry, and Richard Mier were all giving public lectures in Cambridge.)

And, of course, more than lectures and studios happen. Though not always! Zaha Hadid held the Kenzo Tange Chair at Harvard in 1994 but left no design work behind; any more than did Tange himself several decades earlier, when he taught at M.I.T. (Though there was a studio project for a Boston Harbor residential development that no less than Tafuri believes exerted "an incontrovertible international influence," it left no trace whatsoever in Boston!)

To be a regular stop on the international architectural circuit is important in other and perhaps deeper ways as well. As we have seen here more than once as this pattern of international practice has developed in this century — in the case of Le Corbusier, for instance, or Aalto — the visitations and rendezvous of these great luminaries often make for telling contributions to the regional as well as the wider culture.

In the first place there is the matter (even the need) of consciousness raising, impor-tant especially for Bostonians, who are apt to take things for granted, so satiated are they by cultural treasure, and, only too likely, like so many New Yorkers, to think in their parochial way that everything is in Boston (so amusing to see how annoying the *New York Times*'s architecture critic Herbert Muschamp found it to have to fly to Helsinki, God help us, to see the latest work of Holl, a New York architect). Thus it was a point worth making in aid of Boston's repute as well as of Le Corbusier's, when Charles Gwathmey allowed as how, in connection with his Werner Otto Hall of 1990 at Harvard (Figure 275), he "never wanted a job so badly," because, of course, Otto Hall adjoined Le Corbusier's only American work, itself perhaps the greatest architectural prize of Boston's Modernist legacy. Similarly, also in the 1990s, when one of the hottest of the great international star architects, Raffael Moneo, made his American debut in Boston, it did no harm to the now much-abused repute of Paul Rudolph, whose work in Boston's Government Center is constantly in danger from philistines, that Moneo should explain that in no small measure his interest in designing the Davis Museum at Wellesley College (Figure 276) was because it would adjoin Paul Rudolph's Jewett Art Center of three and more decades earlier, "one of the first modern buildings," Moneo remembered, "to strike my eye."

In the event, despite such nice touches as copper-clad clerestories sensitive to Rudolph's skylights and a Moneo-designed plaza that at last gives a worthy approach to the Jewett's splendid indoor-outdoor staircase (ascending which to the neo-Gothic quad behind is one of the great experiences of Boston architecture), and, indeed, despite the crisp elegance generally of the Davis's exterior, which I much admire, the work as a whole does not enhance Rudolph's landmark after all. Alas, the site was too crowded and the budget too meager.

FIGURE 275. Gwathmey Siegal: Otto Hall, Harvard, Cambridge, 1990; deft homage to Le Corbusier's adjoining Carpenter Center.

But like Sterling's museum at Harvard (is there a pattern here?) Moneo's at Wellesley, though not all it might have been on the outside, is wonderful within: the effect of ascending Moneo's own staircase inside (to a glorious, light-filled top-floor gallery) surpasses even the effect of climbing Rudolph's outside. Wrote Mildred Schmertz, "Because of the mastery with which the architect has arranged and scaled the interpenetrating spaces, the effect is uplifting, inspiring, even joyous" — not qualities often found, may I add, in architecture in any era.

Boston's Modernist legacy and its power to attract yet more gifts is, of course, as contributions go (to either the wider culture or to the architectural profession), a relatively uncomplicated one. As an example of a perhaps more edged

and penetrating contribution in Boston's orbit there is the work of Steven Holl, whose house of 1989 on Martha's Vineyard I greatly like — but have not quite entirely processed? Uncannily beautiful as it is, I am very much less clear about what it may mean that Holl, having explained himself as "trying to get back to the spirit of New England," forthwith produced a house so "skeleton like," in the words of one critic, as to seem (by almost universal consent; the image is not at all forced) "almost like a beached whale"!

Gwathmey in Cambridge, Holl on Nantucket, Moneo at Wellesley, are doing the work, all of them superbly, of classic "form-givers," to my mind (such an elitist I am in the era of — whatever) the highest art, as it is the most abused, of architecture.

It remains to be said that Moneo and

336

FIGURE 276. Rafaelo Moneo: Davis Museum, Wellesley College, Wellesley, 1989, the first American work of a contemporary master.

Holl particularly are very much admired by Boston's New Moderns, as I call them, on whom this chapter will focus — to all of whom the devastating critique of Andrea Leers and Alex Krieger (both themselves New Moderns) of Boston's drift into infill, contextualism, Po-Mo, and preservation seems quite alarming.

As NEW Moderns surfaced in Boston in the 1990s, so also there were their opposite numbers. What to call them? These are architects on whose work we must touch briefly here, if only by way of contrast, architects considerably less taken with Krieger and Leers's analysis, as one would expect of the progeny of unrepentant Post-Modernists and their close cousins, the contextualists. Witness the leading figure in Boston of the group — a

group I think we must, indeed, call the New Historicists — who emerged in the 1980s: Graham Gund.

An Ohio native drawn east first by his studies at the Rhode Island School of Design and then by Harvard's Design School, Gund trained thereafter with Gropius at TAC. Yet despite (or because of) these impeccable Modernist credentials, Gund's path has taken him far afield from any kind of Modernism. His present-day philosophy of architecture has been put succinctly enough by no less than Vincent Scully:

Graham Gund has to be valued as a convinced preservationist, and that role . . . is probably the most important that an architect can play at this moment in urban history. American cities were torn apart a generation ago by the automobile and the utopian horrors of International Style planning . . . and the most serious architects and planners of the past thirty years have been trying to put them back together again. Their efforts have been assisted and in good measure motivated and enforced by the only mass popular movement to have materially affected the course of architecture since World War II, the movement toward historic preservation. At present that powerful political force is being directed with increasing boldness by the National Trust for Historic Preservation, of which Graham Gund is a hardworking trustee.

Well! This from a scholar who has pronounced Kallmann and McKinnell's Boston City Hall an "uncouth monster" ought probably not to surprise. Scully, a great scholar of the past, is a very sorry critic of the present — evidence, perhaps, that people like me should not write afterwards like this ! But I digress — and persist.

Scully, in fact, is so much impressed with Gund's work that he repeatedly invokes the name of Boston's first great form-giver of the late eighteenth century and early nineteenth century, Charles Bulfinch. "The flavor of Bulfinch's high, thin, geometrically activated brick façade is present in one way or another in all Gund's work," Scully asserts (improbably to me), especially in "the very free treatment of façades"; though even Scully admits, "To be sure, the Boston Ballet [Building] does dance; one is not sure what the Harvard Inn does!" He is referring in the first instance to one of Gund's best designs, in the second to one of his worst.

Indeed, there is, so to speak, a really considerable point-spread in Gund's architecture. He has been capable of sparkling "Pop" elegance, as in the lobby of his Perkins School of 1980 in the South End, with its sinuous chrome appointments. He is also prone to work I find very vulgar: no other word will do for his 75 State Street lobby of 1989 or for the hallway parquetry of his Cohen Residence on Beacon Hill of three years earlier. At the same time his Northeastern University Boathouse of 1989 is nothing if not tasteful. And his Deutsch

House on Beacon Hill does have a welcome presence in that environment.

It is Gund's "best" work, however, that is in many ways the most problematic. The boathouse, for example, is so deft it could easily be mistaken for an antique. So could much of Gund's South Hadley Village Commons, a kind of Florida "Seaside" without Steven Holl. One is reminded of Henry James's complaint about Impressionism, for Gund's work also lacks emotional — or intellectual — complexity. Indeed, my favorite Gund design is distinctly a childish one: a gable of his 1989 addition to the town library in Lincoln, a gable that could stand up to Disneyland but at the same time would enliven any New England townscape with a kind of quirky elegance. All those discs on the gable's steps — speechless, I recline.

Another much less felicitous motif followed through Gund's work discloses more. It is that most conspicuous feature of the entry of 1 Bowdoin Square of 1989, "cut in the shape of a drawn curtain" (it is a feat, that, in granite). One sees this motif again — to my mind more fortuitously — in the profile of the principal gable of Gund's Boston Ballet Building in the South End. Then again — and here we round the circle, for the effect this time is to my eye vulgar in the extreme — this motif recurs in various of Gund's designs for fireplace mantles, designs which appear in those glossy home building magazines, much of which are dedicated to this or that example of the dreaded "trophy house" — usually by graduates of Gund's office! (Let us be fair: sometimes it's Robert Stern's office.)

Having so clearly tipped my (critical) hand here, I need doubtless to quickly affirm, lest I be misunderstood, that Modernism or nearly, no less than Historicism, has its villains the morning after Post-Modernism (for such it is at century's beginning in Boston as everywhere else).

Consider, for instance, the work of Moshe Safdie. To be sure, it is not always

338

crass any more than Gund's is, and sometimes it is even benign: Safdie's stone-arched and domed Jerusalem infill, not a whit different in concept from the red brick and white trim infill of his fellow contextualists in Boston, makes for good "plugs" in certain places. (Though even a plug can offend: for a lesson in how refined and lively pre–World War II Georgian Revival can be, and how deadly soulless and pasteboardish today's version usually is, study the new curving kitchen connector between Harvard's Eliot and Kirkland Houses.) But though Safdie's and Gund's vocabularies are very different, their architecture is only too similar in its stagecraft.

Safdie, who enjoys an international practice (and who was briefly an adjunct professor at Harvard), has taken more pains to distance himself from Post-Modernism than Gund. In "Private Jokes and Public Spaces," for instance, an article of 1981 in the *Atlantic*, Safdie depreciated "the tendency of Post-Modernists to build public buildings that incorporated obscure stylistic and historical references." But in his own way — Modernism or nearly, being now a historic "style" like any other at the designer's disposal — Safdie has done just that in his Boston work — not so much in his Esplanade Apartments of 1986 on the Charles River, a work reminiscent of his famous Habitat in Montreal; nor in his Rosovsky Hall of 1992 at Harvard, which has at least a certain skewed elegance; but in his Class of 1959 Chapel at Harvard Business School, erected in 1992.

The glaring corporate sheen and unrelenting glitz of this chapel, which extends even to the theatricality of a computer-driven manipulation of light (the walls are spotted with colors as the sun's rays are refracted through acrylic prisms in the chapel's skylights), finds its climax, in fact, in just such "obscure stylistic and historic references" as Safdie has protested. There is, first, the grossly shaped "lean-to" half-pyramid that seems almost to have grown like a lesion on the chapel's flank. Across the river from the original site of Pei's elegant Kennedy Library pyramid design now at the Louvre, Safdie's version is a very "obscure stylistic and historical reference" indeed. Only slightly less so, moreover, is the chapel's distinctive round shape, which upriver as Safdie's chapel is from Saarinen's famously round chapel at M.I.T., can hardly be understood as anything other than an "obscure stylistic and historic reference," and an unforgivable one, vulgarizing as it does Saarinen's wondrous landmark, a really grossly offensive thing to do. Safdie — and Harvard — should have known better.

As not all contextualism, so called, was beyond the pale (witness Koetter-Kim's St. Paul's Choir School, Cambridge), so also with Historicism, though, interestingly, the best by Boston's architects has been done overseas, as Margaret Henderson Floyd noticed. Writing of the Aga Kahn Medical College in Karachi, Pakistan, the work in 1988 of Payette Associates, Floyd described the "required interface of tradition and innovation . . . [that] has come to characterize work by Boston's finest architects; somehow they sense well the regional spirit of other cultures." Too bad Boston is less friendly to the other side of the equation, as we have seen in the cases of Zaha Hadid, who will make her American debut in Cincinnati, and Kenzo Tange himself, in whose name the chair she held at Harvard was established.

Furthermore, in the wake of so much of the work of Gund and Safdie alike, one senses Herbert Muschamp's frustration, for example, in a column of November 1998 in the *New York Times* when he writes of his hope that Frank Gehry's Bilboa Guggenheim has finally "banished the belief that the highest aspiration of our time should be the recycling of history's greatest hits." I wonder.

"Boston," architect Andrea Leers has written, "must not be afraid of the future."

FIGURE 277. Office dA (Nader Tehrani and Mónica Ponce de León): Northeastern University Multi-Faith Spiritual Center, the Fenway, 1998, the first built work of two of Boston's most gifted younger architects.

I T IS a world away and then some from the trophy houses of Gund and the unrelenting glitz of Safdie's Harvard chapel to the second-floor, windowless room in an undistinguished white brick building of Northeastern University, where the unsuspecting visitor is in for quite a surprise coming upon the first built interior of Nader Tehrani and Mónica Ponce de León of Office dA — the Northeastern Interfaith Spiritual Center (Figure 277). Office what? Northeastern what? But it is worth the (subway) pilgrimage to go and see.

Tehrani, the son of an Iranian diplomat, is a naturalized American who has pursued his education from Hotchkiss to the Rhode Island School of Design to Harvard's Design School, where he now teaches. Ponce de León, who is Venezuelan, holds degrees from the University of Miami and from Harvard, where she too is on the Design School faculty. Tehrani is the theorist, Ponce de León, more of a scholar. She was the organizer, for example, of an exhibition in 1998 on the Milanese Modernist architect, Gio Ponti. Both she and Tehrani struggle meanwhile to establish their architectural office, which, as one would expect, reflects strenuous ideals and is already the recipi-

ent (for unbuilt projects) of several prestigious awards. For their triumph at Northeastern there will assuredly be more.

The program could hardly have been more problematic: to create a worship space that would privilege no religious tradition but equally serve, indeed, uplift, them all — Jewish, Christian, and Muslim — and enhance equally the varied worship traditions of each; and to do this in a not overlarge, windowless room with HVAC ducts covering a ceiling only eleven feet high off a banal institutional corridor, halfway between the Coke machine, so to speak, and the broom closet. Joseph Giovannini is right on the mark to call it

a feat of architectural alchemy. . . . The results are other worldly. . . . Because they could not change the building's structure, the architects developed the idea of liners, or coverings, on the walls, floor and ceiling in order to transform the space. Office dA's originality resides in its investigations into the properties of materials. . . . Here [they] turned the walls into sheets of light . . . they inset back- and front-lit glass panels, lapped like cardboard. . . . Frosted glass and cove lighting create a mysterious glow and a sense of spatial indeterminacy.

(No idea is ever entirely new, of course. I was myself reminded, seeing the horizon-

340

tal "clapboards" of the side panels, of the way Ralph Adams Cram in 1900 converted a similarly hostile environment — a barn — to a church, seeking to control the light by installing simple square-headed rectangular windows of plain glass fitted with Venetian blinds.)

Office dA's design is even more dependent on light since it is the only "iconography" allowable in such an interfaith space, and while the framed glass wall panels play their part, it is in the three "domes" that Tehrani and Ponce de Leôn have surpassed themselves: inverted (because of the HVAC ducts they obscure), these domes are of perforated aluminum (through which comes the ventilation), but what catches the eye is how elegantly laid is the aluminum, in thin, overlapping sheets. Lit carefully, more by reflection than anything else, the effect of this minimalist design is to empty the mind in the way meditation requires in all religious tradition.

For their seating, Tehrani and Ponce de Leôn chose a chair design by Philippe Starck, raising an issue addressed by Herbert Muschamp:

Design has become a form of entertainment, fashion or play. Ettore Sottsass, Gaetano Pesce, Tibor Kalman, Philippe Starck, Shiro Kurainata: the most celebrated and influential designers of [the 1980 and nineties] have not sought to establish a set of rules for good design. Drawing on sources as diverse as Surrealism, pop culture, fairy tales and agitprop, they have developed highly personal vocabularies that resist being categorized.

Muschamp ascribes all this to "a reaction to the previous generation's idealization of cold, objective truth" in an era when the Bauhaus "laid down rules of taste." Yet Office dA's choice to annex Starck's aesthetic here to a very Bauhaus-positive overall aesthetic may say much. Perhaps the era of Mickey Mouse telephones is coming to an end after all. And that rebel-

lion over, in time-honored fashion Office dA may be looking past their parents' sensibility to that of their grandparents.

Who can know the future? Even Office dA's? But I think it will be brilliant enough.

Not all good architecture, nor all New Moderns, hang out in the heady intellectual world of Office dA. Brian Healy, for example. Though trained in architecture at Yale, and a sometime fellow of the American Academy in Rome who discourses easily on such early-twentieth-century Modernist masters as Schindler, whom he has studied closely, Healy is no more an Ivy League don than he is a corporate iconographer. No theorist he. Nor is Healy (who is new to Boston, a tough architectural community to break into) as well connected or well mentored as Office dA. But Healy is a gifted designer, and Bostonians alert to such things will likely more and more find the way to his door.

Office dA's drafting room is drop-dead chic — white, minimalist, and elegant after the fashion of Boston's South End, where it is located. Healy's is much more gritty — seven floors up on the top floor of a harborfront warehouse, the interior finish of which is mostly industrial concrete and linoleum. Healy's drafting room has its own drama, however: it is huge — a wonderful space, strangely freeing, hung with his own paintings, flooded by light from big, old-fashioned wood-sash windows.

The view, of course, is of other warehouses. But that's not just a matter of the rent; that's the aesthetic Healy responds to, whether in his design for the Dom Bosco School in Boston (aborted, alas, by that school's closing virtually on the eve of Healy's construction) or his plan for a proposed addition to the Fine Arts Building at Brandeis University. Both are eye-catching in form.

FIGURE 278. Brian Healy: proposed remodeling, Lincoln Street Garage, downtown, 1997, evidence in the era of the central artery's destruction of a revival of its gritty industrial aesthetic.

Most revealing of all Healy's projects, however, and most challenging, is one that discloses very well how architectural history, like everything else, accelerates ever more and more rapidly — his design for the remaking of the Lincoln Street Garage (Figure 278). In an era when Bostonians are at last tearing down their grimy old elevated central artery (never mind building Shingle Style houses by the sea), Healy's design for the remodeling of this garage, like so much of his work, celebrates exactly the 1950s industrial aesthetic of the disreputable and just-disappeared artery!

He is unrepentant, telling a critic: "The industrial age is something we should all look at with deference. I don't have a problem with being romantic about it."

Nor do I. A fact I first noticed when the old "El" came down — the elevated rapid transit line which "ruined" Roxbury and the South End, and which, the minute it was gone, I missed! An eyesore in many ways (yet it isn't in Chicago, where a similar El runs past a fashionable hotel), the El was a fascinating urban experience, one I delighted in as a boy, and by no means visually unrewarding, as Robert Campbell seemed to notice too in a rather poetic description of a photograph of the sun slanting through the old elevated structure: "The El was regarded as a blight,"

he wrote, "but [the photographer of a circa 1954 perspective being described] has made it look almost as elegant as a row of shade trees on a Parisian boulevard." So it seemed, I'm sure, to many, including author and historian Francis Russell, and an old friend, who more than once recounted in loving urban detail his rides to and from the original Roxbury Latin School on the old El — all of it right out of Edward Hopper.

Healy's romance with the industrial is not unusual either. Before we're done with the New Moderns we'll see how an old woebegone iron bridge of the same vintage as the El inspired a masterpiece of 1990s New Modernism.

In Healy's case, the Lincoln Street Garage will, I suspect, not be his masterwork. But what he has done with it is intriguing enough and more than one would think possible. A hybrid structure (ground-floor retail shops — built in 1956 and thus contemporaneous with the artery's erection — over which in 1959 were added four more levels — parking and commercial areas on the second level, parking alone on the third and fourth levels, and commercial space on the fifth — all in steel frame clad with aluminum), this garage would be pronounced by many, like the artery, as much an eyesore as the old El. But it will be High Grit when

342

Healy's face-lift is completed; for while his design never loses sight of the aesthetic of the surrounding warehouses of Boston's old leather district (a new parapet on the garage's north side will rise to just the height of those warehouses), Healy has so skillfully knit the garage's disparate structure together with deftly distributed exterior cladding of concrete panel and galvanized standing-seam metal that it looks in his renderings and models almost stylish.

In fact, Brian Healy has his stylish side: he is, for example, becoming well known for a building type not at all urban. He and a friend, Michael Ryan, a New Jersey architect, have designed a series of beach houses, of all things, that are quirky, colorful, altogether very cool and shapely in a way you just don't see all that often — so much so they've been published in *Abitare*. (An event, that, surely: a struggling young architect published in a fancy Italian design magazine so expensive that I suspect Healy, like most of us, goes to the library to read it.)

Housing of a more urban sort also interests Healy, and a design of his that stands out as characteristic of his architectural philosophy is his project for housing prototypes in East Cambridge and Atlantic City. These are inexpensive, wood-framed structures (plywood and cement-board sheathing on the outside; gypsum board on the inside) that Healy proposed to insert into empty sites on built-up streetscapes in inner-city neighborhoods, where such vacant lots depress already depressed areas. Entirely Healy's work, with Craig Scott as project architect, the design won a citation from *Architecture* magazine and some attention from critic David Eisen, who analyzed Healy's work insightfully:

Making a connection to history doesn't necessarily require houses with shutters and colonial trim. . . . [Healy's] houses have proportions that echo those of the surrounding buildings . . . they are not nostalgic reproductions . . . Windows that wrap around corners create an interesting alternative to the boring boxes most of us call "home." High bands of glass make the roofs appear to float and flood the interior with light.
So why don't we see houses like Healy's built? . . . Healy's sculptural forms can appear somewhat foreign. . . .
Innovative housing proposals can get bogged down in extended battles between zoning boards, neighbors and builders over density, image and the question of charge.

"Making a connection to history"? Of course. Healy's architecture is very different. So is his sense of history.

IT MAY seem too easy a contrast, not to say rashly irreverent, to hold up in such a critical way to the likes of Gund and Safdie (who if they are "lite" are famously so) much younger and radically different architects who have yet to make of themselves (according to any philosophy of architecture) the success Safdie and Gund have. The point of my doing so, however, is to make clear not just my own architectural ideals and tastes, but to underline the fact that New Historicists and New Moderns alike respond to history; the difference arises in how they respond.

Still, there is an even finer distinction to be made, evident in the work of another Boston architect, and one now well established and of wide repute: Ann Beha, who, though I count her here among the New Moderns, might reasonably be called the Great-Historicist-of-Them-All. But not, I think, a New Historicist. Beha is the old-fashioned kind. And to understand just what I mean by that it is timely to dwell for a moment on the philosophy of history and architecture of the legendary Boston architectural and cultural historian, Walter Muir Whitehill, the effect of whose influence we've already considered here in his lifetime, but whose thought ought hardly to matter less to his posterity, for like Eduard Sekler, Whitehill (who was a highly trained art historian as well as an important regional scholar) left Boston a priceless legacy of discourse on this subject.

In his 1968 addition to *Topographical History of Boston*, his major work, Whitehill argued strongly for historic preservation (of the Old City Hall, for example), citing the success of efforts (his, as we've seen) to save the Old Corner Bookstore and the waterfront warehouses. He despaired of how in the 1950s, the West End project had "brutally displaced people . . . and destroyed pleasing buildings," lamenting too the loss in the 1960s of the last waterfront buildings by Bulfinch on India Wharf, as well as the erection of the McCormack Building in the Government Center, as a result of which there occurred the "destr[uction of] a number of once handsome buildings" that might have been restored. Furthermore, he was merciless in his derision of the hideous Corbusian cityscape that replaced the West End, noting dryly of Charles River Parks', residential and retail architecture that the design had "the air of having wandered in from the suburbs of another city."

But at the same time, the loss of what Whitehill called "undistinguished neighbors" bothered him not at all (nor any supposed "un-Bostonian" grandeur) when the gain was the "imaginative and daring" plans of Pei's Christian Science Center with its "new tree-lined garden, with an 80-foot fountain and a 700-foot reflecting pool [and a] long lower building faced with 525 feet of columns." He rejoiced in all of it. Similarly, he liked Kallmann and McKinnell's Five-Cents Savings Bank (now a Borders Bookstore) almost as much as he had their splendid new City Hall. Especially important to him was the way the bank set off the Old South Church, and he praised Pei's idea for the placement of the 28 State Street tower (by Barnes) right on top of the Old State House because (as he quoted the architect saying) the tower's "plaza would provide a spacious and

attractive setting for the Old State House." Indeed, one of the reasons Whitehill liked Pei in the first place was that he found that Pei "wished not only to preserve the significant historic buildings in the area [of the Government Center], but to create spaces in which *immense new buildings might be placed in harmonious relation to their older neighbors* [emphasis added]."

One sees how wise and sophisticated were Whitehill's views. And how confident. In the way, say, of Carlo Scarpa, Whitehill knew the need of equipoise, that the old and the new alike need each other. What Whitehill commended to Boston was a proper balance between historical and modern, one each needed to enable and, indeed, enhance the other. And by *modern* Whitehill meant, moreover, *really modern*, not the "contextualism" of what he called "Madison Avenue Colonial." He wrote in 1968, "I hoped in 1958 that [Boston would] be spared both slavish antiquarianism and 'Madison Avenue Colonial' in new construction. . . . What I should not have dared to hope then was that so many first-rate contemporary architects [among the designers he cites by way of example are Aalto, Belluschi, Gropius, Le Corbusier, Pei, Rudolph, Saarinen, Sert, and Stubbins] would be adding distinguished contributions to the Boston scene." The Back Bay and Copley Square, of both of which it is not too much to say Whitehill "saved" from ruination by greedy developers, as we saw in Chapter 12, are a perfect example of his attitude in such things.

He argued in 1968 in *Topographical History* for preservation, and preservation of the most radical sort then (of Victorian buildings), and on a grand scale: the Back Bay, he insisted was

the handsomest and most consistent example of American architecture of the second half of the nineteenth century now existing in the United States. For the second half of that century it is every bit as typical as Beacon Hill is of the first.

344

[Wonderful echo here of the way Back Bay threatened Beacon Hill: Georgian silver to Victorian, as it were.] Although many Bostonians completely failed to realize this until very recently, the wind is changing. The Back Bay Neighborhood Association . . . has made valiant efforts to restore the residential quality of the region.

At the same time, and in the same book, Whitehill argued just as strongly for the most radically Modernist architecture in Copley Square, where what most concerned him then was the "gaping void," as he called it, at the southwest corner, between the library and the Copley Plaza, where because of the destruction of the S. S. Pierce Building in 1958 (ghastly year! — also the year of the destruction of the old Boston Opera House) the resulting void was such that Whitehill thought "the entire square look[ed] as if it were washing away into a vast hole in the ground."

But having protested the loss of Pierce's, Whitehill did not propose any parody to replace it. He argued instead that "the imaginative skill of an I. M. Pei or a Philip Johnson" be enlisted to solve the problem. Alas, Copley Place proved hardly any solution at all, for the corporate infill of late TAC is just a "Modern" version of Madison Avenue Colonial.

The admiring reference to Johnson is particularly significant, though remembering how much Whitehill liked the new City Hall it should not perhaps surprise that he was even more admiring of Johnson's Boston Public Library addition: it was "designed with the greatest respect for Charles F. McKim's masterpiece," Whitehill wrote, adding pointedly that "few great nineteenth-century buildings have received the loving care and consideration that Philip Johnson has lavished . . . on this addition."

Finally, to the consternation of the "traditionalists" and the knee-jerk preservationists, he argued fiercely for the new Hancock Tower. Both Pei and Cobb,

Whitehill wrote,

are intimately acquainted with and have a deep feeling for this section of the city. They have shown great imagination in attempting . . . a light and transparent building. . . . The nineteenth-century Back Bay skyline of 5-story houses, accented by church spires, is gone. The point of no return was reached in 1927 when the 12-story Ritz Carlton Hotel was, by exception, allowed. . . . One can no more justify "modest" violations of a height limit than to argue about the partial freshness of an egg or [of] pregnancy. . . . To me at least one slender 60-story tower clutters the skyline less than three 20-story buildings *or four of 15* [italics added].

Would that historians and preservationists (and activists of all kinds) saw the truth of that point of view today!

Some have: among architectural historians, Margaret Henderson Floyd, for instance. Of Pei's Christian Science Center she wrote, echoing Whitehill, "While one regrets the demolition of W. G. Preston's Mechanics Hall, one of the finest new urban spaces in America resulted." But wasn't it all there in her dedication of one of her books? "Dedicated to the Memory of Walter Muir Whitehill," Floyd wrote, "who knew that architects and historians must work together." Modernist architects.

Among architects, as opposed to architectural historians, few of this persuasion stand out. One is Ann Beha.

A New York native, yet another drawn to Boston by the academy — in her case Wellesley College and the M.I.T. School of Architecture — Beha, the protégé of Daniel Coolidge, heads a firm (along with her partner, Pamela Hawkes, a Columbia-trained architect) that now enjoys a national repute for historic restoration. In Boston alone the firm's restorations include such landmarks as Back Bay's Church of the Covenant, the Harvard Faculty Club (though someone has since compromised Beha's superb restoration by bringing in another firm to decorate her fine interiors), the Shaw Memorial on Boston Common, Austin Hall at Harvard Law School (as consultant to Goody, Clancy), the Gardner Museum, Jordan Hall at the New England Conservatory of Music, and the Clark Art Institute at Williams College.

It is the last work I find most interesting, not because it is better done or more important, but because Beha's work at Williams also included an addition — the firm at this point does a good deal of new as well as restoration work — and it was an addition to an older building that is itself a Modernist landmark, the work in 1973 of Belluschi and TAC. All of which points up the fact that Beha is as interested in preserving landmarks by Sert as by Bulfinch. Shades of Walter Muir Whitehill.

Now I have implied here before that there has been evident over the years an increasingly dark side in my view to historic preservation, dark in the sense that after those first heady years detailed in Chapter 11, of Sekler, Whitehill, Stahl, and company (when the most ardent Preservationists were the keenest Modernists), preservation came for many people to have much less to do with treasuring our history and more to do with pushing any alternative to Modernism in a world where they were more threatened than delighted by change. Today, alas, there is hardly any doubt in the matter. "Preservationists" regularly destroy early Modernist landmarks quite irrespective of whether they are or are not distinguished in design, but simply because they are "ugly" to those whose idea of "beautiful" is often very limited indeed — usually to something akin to columned plantation houses. (I remember once walking through Plymouth with Harvard professor Peter Gomes and despairing of the phony-baloney eighteenth-century shop signs that were proliferating; I hope Peter has followed through on his promise to protect the 1930s neon drugstore sign.) Recently in the Society of Architectural Historians newsletter Rodd L. Wheaton sounded the alarm. Arguing, he wrote, from a

preservation perspective, the assault on modern architecture, [and on] "modernism," has become epidemic. . . . Denver's Zeckendorf Plaza, which was one of I. M. Pei's early masterpieces, has been in part demolished, in part remodeled beyond recognition. . . . As historic preservationists, we need to dare to stand up and be counted. . . . Modernist structures are important to America's architectural history. . . . What we do not need is the demonstrated resistance to understanding the modernist style. . . . History is a continuum.

The battle cry, over and over, Wheaton reports, is "It's ugly!" Yet one wonders if such philistines have ever met a Modernist building they don't think ugly — or a Victorian one they don't think beautiful! Except, of course, their rather more snobby cousins, on "Colonial" Beacon Hill!

Beha, though she is one of the country's foremost preservation architects, will have none of this. In a 1998 speech, "Modernism and Renovation," she points out, with respect to Modernist buildings, that "'do we have to keep this?' [or] 'It doesn't work for us' . . . were [said] twenty years ago in regard to the nineteenth-century campus structures, even buildings then listed on the National Register."

As Victorian buildings needed defense then, so do Modernist buildings now. All of them? Of course not. Beha points out the obvious, but necessarily so, when she asserts: "Many Modernist buildings are inspired, unforgettable, moving, important. Many are not." It is, or should be, as is always the case with nearly anything in life, a matter of critical choice, not kneejerk bias. And Beha is just the one to lead people to make those choices.

"No, I don't think there's a signature, but there is handwriting," Beha once told a reporter; the signature, she thought, was the architectural equivalent to a sound bite.

It is the way an architect thinks. Beha is a preservationist because she is an architect, not the other way around. And she is no nostalgist.

Fascinatingly, it is in her restorations that one sees this most clearly (as is also the case with the New York architect Gerald Allen, always my choice for any church restoration work), and it is what one misses, for example, in restorations by Gund, on one of which, Bulfinch Square in Cambridge, Naomi Miller has written perceptively:

The renovation here is perhaps a bit too faithful to a late Victorian aesthetic, as seen in the court-room converted into a theatre, with its plaster ceiling décor, stenciled walls, ornamental balustrades, fanciful lighting appendages, and rich polychrome. Somehow, the verisimilitude of the restoration and the meticulous archival research on which it was based breathes the frozen culture of antiquarianism. Innovations are viewed in terms of precedents, creating a copy rather than a dialogue between the two principal defining cultures and all the intervening ones which have left their mark on the space.

History without such a dialogue — what is usually called Historicism — between one historical period and another and also with our own time, is inevitably stultifying, just as stultifying as the attempt to "begin again" — characteristic of early Modernism — without any reference at all to the past. Of course, to engage such a dialogue requires creativity of a very high order, as Daniel Coolidge showed, and Anne Beha shows today.

O F COURSE, it will be said, however gifted Beha is, restoration is not design. Nonsense. Recall Dan Coolidge's Bates Hall mirrors!

Moreover, Beha is not the only designer — New Modern or not — who has given

evidence of coming out of some closet or other as the oppressive grip of extreme "contextualism" and preservation under the aegis of Post-Modernism began to loosen even in Boston. After all, the old rule of politics holds true here too — as the politician's first duty is to get elected, so is the architect's to get a job, which means a client, and in the 1970s and eighties jobs in Boston went to contextualists. Even Kallmann and McKinnell, as we saw, barely survived that era, which William Rawn III calls "the hegemony of contextualism."

Rawn should know. His work from the beginning (he founded his firm in 1983) has verged on Historicism. But, as critic Witold Rybezynski has pointed out, with Rawn it has been a more complicated tale: "Some of the most interesting buildings today are the work of architects such as Alda Rossi in Europe, and Thomas Beeby and William Rawn in this country," Rybezynski has declared, impressed how keenly Rawn was "exploring the blurred edges between modernism and pre-modern architectural traditions." Significantly, Paul Goldberger has come to a similar conclusion, writing of how he sees in Rawn's work an affinity for "the strong, brooding, geometric forms of the architect Aldo Rossi." The Italian architect, of course, was just such a Modernist/Historicist.

Even now Rawn has been heard to say that "in Boston we are all prisoners of history." But today it is no longer the morose observation it might still sound like. For Rawn's Historicism may always have been closer conceptually to Beha's, for instance, than to Gund's, though Rawn's great popular success (his practice is now a national one; in 1998 it was Rawn's office that completed the Celebration School for the Walt Disney Company in Celebration, Florida) is such that it is more comparable to Gund's. This is all the more true because both men are highly public spirited. Rawn is very active in civic affairs, serving as a member, for example, of the Design

Review Board of the city (which has not been unfriendly to innovative design by any means), a job as demanding as it is thankless. Gund, a rich man in a city of great wealth but notable parsimony toward all the arts, is a considerable citizen-patron and benefactor to whom all Bostonians must be grateful.

But if they are similar in their civic-mindedness, they are very different in their aesthetics: to go from Gundland to Rawnland, though I would not want to dwell in either, is to be going distinctly in the right direction. Gund's world, it must be said, verges constantly on a theme park, putting one in mind of Ada Louise Huxtable's observations that on the one hand "Main Streets across America are dying, while everybody goes to Main Street in Disney World — a knockoff"; on the other hand, insofar as the real thing is concerned (writing of the architecture of downtown Boston specifically), "in the so-called postmodernist period, when architects were properly liberating themselves from the restrictions of modernism . . . they did not know enough about historical building, and built caricatures." What a choice: knockoffs or caricatures.

Rawn's work, both what I admire and what I do not, is neither. There is, in the first place, nothing at all of the stage set. Indeed, so strong are Rawn's forms sometimes, they seem almost "masculine" in just the way Louis Sullivan used the word to describe Richardson's work. All the more so because of Rawn's characteristic design concept, for his work is as serious socially as architecturally. Behold, the no-nonsense world of affordable housing, a subject I must admit has never gripped me. But in the late 1980s, when I was Senior Affiliate in the History of Architecture in Eliot House at Harvard, and the tutor in charge of the Architecture Table there, I was persuaded by one of my students, Carl Shannan, also one of Rawn's interns, to invite Rawn to speak to us

about it. Prepared at best to be edified, in fact I was charmed.

A latecomer to architecture at mid-life, who after Yale College and Harvard Law School and some years as a lawyer, bolted his life, so to speak, in middle age to study architecture at M.I.T., Rawn is a very attractive, articulate guy, albeit earnest to a fault, and very much a loner who holds the design initiative closely. He first came seriously to public attention for his uncanny success on the subject of his Eliot House talk. First in South Boston, later in Charlestown (at the Navy Yard), in Roxbury in his "Back of the Hill" project, Rawn pulled it off every time — even eventually in upper-middle-class, suburban Lincoln, where his mixed-income subsidized housing took the form of multifamily detached houses that I'm sure enhanced rather than depressed real estate values.

Always there were rave reviews, nothing else. Writing of the Charlestown Navy Yard project, Paul Goldberger in the *New York Times* thought Rawn's work characterized by both "gentleness and power." *Time's* critic declared: "Boston's 50-unit Charlestown Navy Yard Rowhouses designed by William Rawn are virtually miraculous: cheerful, dignified, altogether grand looking low-cost housing."

Unrepentant aesthete that I am, those qualities startled me. In my experience good intentions do not usually good architecture make. Yet as critics are drawn to the architecture as well as the cause in Rawn's case, so am I. Consider Rawn's Back of the Hill project of 1985 (Figure 279): Was ever so shapely an abstraction of historical form (the round bay town house, itself usually klunky enough) so robust and so stylish? Wonderful.

Perhaps because of the superior design of the Back of the Hill project I was not surprised that another and somewhat lighter sensibility began to emerge in a series of Rawn's works relating to the

FIGURE 279. William Rawn & Associates: "Back of the Hill," mixed-income housing, Roxbury, 1985. Good intentions do not good design make, but Rawn's thoughtful abstractions of Victorian townhouses are successful.

performing arts, and ranging from so small a job as an outdoor music pavilion in Lowell in 1987 to so major a commission as the Phillips Exeter Academy Music Building, completed in 1995. On the latter, a formal rectangular façade is linked with a more informal and gracefully curving façade, both of red brick cladding striped with cast-stone trim and lead-coated copper roof features — an altogether winning design.

Rawn's preeminent work in this vein is Ozawa Hall of 1989 for the Boston Symphony Orchestra at Tanglewood (Figure 280), a design widely published and much lauded, and for good reason. As a serious, even grave building, Ozawa Hall is also on a summer's night (when it is, of course, most used) beguilingly romantic. For all that, in the exposed timber framing of Ozawa's wonderful long porches, Rawn has used wood in as structurally crisp and stylish a way as ever any of the architects dealt with in this afterword have used steel and concrete with glass. For once his own best critic, Rawn has likened his BSO Hall to a Shaker meeting house and has spoken of a certain "elegant frugality" in its design. Exactly.

Also interesting, in a different way, is his response to another client's desire for a Gothic school chapel. What Rawn designed for Babson College in Waltham is a crisp cube of gray, cleft-faced Deer Island granite, one of two buildings completed in 1995 that are the beginning of something in his work I suspect will prove very rewarding to follow.

Inside, two of the walls (for their full two-story height) are all of glass, offering

FIGURE 280. William Rawn & Associates: Ozawa Hall, Berkshire Music Center, Tanglewood, 1994. Rawn has used timber here as finely as Peter Forbes uses steel.

woodland views. And the order that has been attempted is not uninteresting: two for the most part independent and free-standing white painted steel grids, about half of a foot apart, visually interpenetrate: the inner grid the heavy structural support of the building; the outer grid the steel tube framing of the floor-to-ceiling glass, the top ranges of which incorporate great swirling patterns in stained glass, the work of West Coast artist Peter McGrain, patterns whose shapes and palette reflect the trees and sky in rather a pale and — dare I say it? — Transcendental way. Certainly we are not far from Ralph Waldo Emerson here as we gaze past the altar into the trees. Although grossly detailed and nowhere near as fine as Ozawa's timber framing, the Babson Chapel shows Rawn reaching for something of Ozawa's structural aesthetic in steel and glass.

Equally at curvilinear odds with the overall cube of the chapel, as much at odds as the stained glass, is a huge wooden sculptural form, at once ominous and gracious, certainly other-worldly, a form suspended overhead and so large it virtually is the ceiling, a form that defies logic and eludes meaning, unless it is that the shape seems that of the outside of the hull of a great Norse ship. Know it or not, it is the Gothic of this chapel, this great suspended form of curving boards to pointed ends. The "nave," that portion of the traditional church plan lying between the porch and the chancel, is so called from the Latin word navis, "a ship," the ship of souls who would be saved. One thinks of Henry Adams looking up at the timber roof of a medieval landmark: "Serious and simple. . . . The quiet strength of those curved lines." Rawn solemnly assures he was just after some sort of shape that would give a "directionless" quality to his interior. Yet nothing is clearer to me than that this is the hull of a ship, unless it is that Rawn is an architect who has a Gothic strain in him that — at his best — has no need of Gothic

battlements or rose windows to express itself.

Rawn's Fire Station No. 6 is the second of his two works of 1995 that I find so interesting. Here is something else new in his work. Whence comes this joyful sweep of roof? Is this in elevation what one sees in plan in the graceful curve of the front façade of the wing of the Phillips Exeter building? And whence the almost lyrical clarity of form of this fire station so well suited to its highway location? Or how about the throwaway elegance of the fields of glass block, an elegance that sustains even the so very American signage, a bit vulgar, but (as can be seen at once by imagining the building without it) just what this curious, scintillant highway façade needed? Pressed, Rawn points out that just because the station is one of a famous series of works by modern architects (Fire Station No. 4 was by Venturi), there was no client to satisfy but himself; the only program (for once) his own. How telling this happens so far from home.

Still, Rawn's new Northeastern University residence hall (Figure 281) is a striking work, very much a curve ball thrown at one of Boston's most chaotic cityscapes. Already a landmark whose generative force is not to be denied, its strong form may yet persuade Northeastern, Wentworth, and the Museum of Fine Arts to cohere after all around a wonderful triangular greensward. There is much promise in Rawn's work.

Whatever it is Office dA and Brian Healy are pointing to, and among more established architects, Bill Rawn is feeling the pull of, history is clearly very much a part of it.

One thing above all, however, that Boston's New Moderns have in common is that the history in their work is rooted not at all in the immediate Post-Modernist legacy of the 1970s and eighties. Rather, like the Gothic Revivalists or Colonial Revivalists of old (for this is a hoary strate-

FIGURE 281. William Rawn's Northeastern University residence hall, 1997.

gy in the long history of Western architecture, as in art history generally; think neoclassicists or Pre-Raphaelites), the work of the New Moderns is rooted in a more distant and more ideal history. And although for nearly all these architects the precedents and ideals of post-Renaissance Italian classicism are precious, their "country of the mind" (the period with which they most intimately identify as working architects) more often than not is the first half of the twentieth century.

Granted, they are also spurred on by the audacities particularly of the school of designers led by Frank Gehry (perhaps our own generation's Gaudi, as Michael McKinnell suggests — or perhaps Gehry is much more of a prophet) on the other. But the aesthetic that seems for most of Boston New Moderns to start their most supple trains of thought is, in fact, that of the long-despised era of the Bauhaus — not, as it has seemed to many, the leftist ideology, nor the thought control of only this and nothing else, nor even necessarily the social reformist aspect, but the aesthetic, the style (the "look," one might say today), at once industrial and elegant.

Does a Bauhaus Revival portend? Even a Gropius Revival? Although Gropius's early work with Meyer, the Fagus Factory in Germany, is (like his later house in

Lincoln) one of the salient landmarks of the Bauhaus style whose influence is becoming stronger, and although there are those, including me, who find things to admire even in such late works by Gropius as the Harvard Graduate Center and the Kennedy Federal Building, it is likely any Gropius (even Bauhaus) revival will be called something else. Unlike Le Corbusier and Wright and Mies, those other great Modernist masters of twentieth-century architecture, Gropius's repute may have been too much eroded for rehabilitation.

Even his role as a teacher has been attacked. In 1983, for example, Columbia professor Klaus Herdeg, in his The Decorated Diagram: Harvard Architecture and the Failure of the Bauhaus Legacy, dedicated an entire book, so deep was his revulsion to that legacy, to a polemical attack that blamed Gropius for everything but the Cold War. As Herdeg explained in his introduction: "Some years ago, a well-known American critic, . . . asked me why there were so many ugly new buildings around. . . . In formulating a reply I realized that there appeared to exist a pattern of characteristics in most of the buildings cited in the course of our conversation, and that this pattern was related to the major constituents of the teaching ethos associated with Walter Gropius . . . in his years at Harvard University (1937–1953)."

Indeed, a generation later, in 1997, when Harvard's Graduate School of Design brought together many of Gropius's great galaxy of students (how many times have we called this role here: Pei, Johnson, Barnes, Rudolph, Cobb, Cossuta, to limit ourselves to just those whose work has figured in this book), the report of Elizabeth Padjen suggested rather a tepid affair: "A generation of architects committed to social reform who came of age in a time of economic devastation, the New Deal, and a world war . . . passionately asserted its activist pedigree before an audience of Boomers who remember their own, somewhat noisier, coming of age in the '60's, when the Gropius-era Modernists represented 'the establishment.'"

Yet consider how that report of the presentations of Gropius's students to their students spans three generations. Furthermore, at least one of Gropius's students sprang forcefully to his defense according to Padjen: Harry Cobb is quoted as insisting he had been as a student of Gropius very "excited to participate in a new vision of an architecture liberated from dead styles, and architecture in which art, technology and social purpose were joined for the benefit of humanity." And scholars too witnessed: Harvard professor Michael Hayes declaring in the 1990s "the period from the late 1930s to the early 1960s has captured the intense interest of scholars like never before." And there is evidence that even among today's international architects interest in Gropius's own design work persists. Andrea Leers told me when she asked Tadao Ando what he wanted most to see in Boston he answered at once: the Gropius House. Perhaps, too, it is significant that Alex Krieger, another Boston architect I include among the New Moderns, has chosen to locate his office, Chan/Krieger, in the old quarters of Gropius and TAC at Architects' Corner in Harvard Square.

CAMBRIDGE, Boston's Left Bank, has always attracted architects, and Architects' Corner is not Harvard Square's only architectural tradition. Others still being upheld there are the "Architect's Own House" (one of the latest, and most widely published, is that of Kyu Sung Woo, who teaches architecture at M.I.T.) and the "Star-Is-Born-Still-in-School" tradition (of precocious students like Philip Johnson). Consider Thompson and Rose. Now rapidly gaining national and even international repute for their Atlantic Center for the Arts, New Smyra Beach, Florida, Maryann Thompson and Charles Rose, two Princetonians who were by then married, were still students at Harvard's Graduate School of Design when, in 1987, they won their first commission (Figure 282) — a handsome barrel-vaulted Modernist investigation into the aesthetic of the New England barn (the Hartsbrook School in Hadley, Massachusetts).

Krieger, a tenured professor at the Design School, upholds perhaps the most important tradition of all, however, the long-standing Boston/Harvard tradition from which so much of the stature of each derive, a tradition that has flourished over the years in so many fields from medicine to electronics and not least in architecture, especially in the days of Gropius and Sert, each of whom, as we've seen, advised and mentored "the New Boston."

It is, of course, a tradition of which M.I.T. has long since become a part (witness Kevin Lynch's work, influential still today), as have to a lesser extent the area's other and newer universities (one thinks of the Boston College Seminars and the role today of the architecture program headed by George Thrush at Northeastern University). But Boston and Harvard go back a long way; that is the fundamental relationship, which in an age of international star faculty will probably never achieve again the intensity of the era of William James and Charles Eliot Norton,

FIGURE 282. Thompson and Rose, Hartsbrook School, Hadley, 1987. A brilliant Modernist essay on a theme of the New England barn.

but so long as figures like Krieger thrive will continue to be important.

Master of the master plan, the more controversial the better, Krieger is at the start of the twenty-first century at the center of every major issue of design and development Boston faces. Most valuable to my mind is the plan he has put forward to deal with the astonishing situation the metropolis will find itself in when early in the next century (after expending ten billion dollars to depress the central artery) there will appear in its downtown heartland a swath of twenty-seven acres of open space stretching for nearly eight miles. Arguing persuasively against the widespread but uncritical and very ill-considered view of too many that the area once occupied by the artery should become a sort of vast park, Krieger insists on asking, "Might open space be just as divisive as the Artery itself, perpetuating

the scar in a different form?" Bravo.

No question is more important to Boston's future. The nineteenth-century "emerald necklace" was fitting, indeed, an apt connector for the streetcar *suburbs*; to "suburbanize our city centers" in this way, however, Krieger is right to argue, is to misunderstand the nature of the urban experience. "Cities thrive," he insists, "on concentration, and the proximity of many activities in confined quarters." Thus he argues for the re-knitting together of the various quarters of the city the artery brutally cut through, taking advantage, however, of the opportunity offered to lay out a half dozen or so parklike city squares at appropriate points in each quarter.

A widely respected thinker, Krieger has been slower to establish himself as an architect. One of two founding principals of Chan/Krieger, established in 1984, in this department as well he has seemed, whether deliberately or not, to be following in famous footsteps and even to be revitalizing architectural tradition. Certainly two of his most high profile jobs have been extensive renovations of Sert's Holyoke Center at Harvard and of Gropius's 8 Story Street at Architects' Corner, where, as noted, his own office now is.

Much more important is Krieger's major work of late, including two Boston commissions of the late 1990s: the Shapiro Clinical Center at Beth Israel Deaconess in the Longwood Medical Area — a huge structure that yet has some flair as well as functionality — and, most important of all, the new gymnasium at Buckingham, Brown and Nichols, a structure of such plainspoken beauty it dazzles like a block of ice cut after a winter storm on a sunny day. Actually of concrete block, through which run ribbons of bright glazed yellow tile, it has a lofty glass clerestory above and glass block panels set into the façade and shielded by steely brise soleil; these giving the icy impression. Crisply gray and sharp-edged, with blocks of contrasting glazed color tiles, the design plays on themes of some of Gropius's earliest and best work, as well as those of 1920s Dutch designers.

More immediately, however, Krieger's gymnasium seems to me rather Kallmannesque: which is to raise an interesting question about the now-famous firm of Kallmann and McKinnell, still thriving. The third time around in this study, have Kallmann and McKinnell — first encountered here as rebellious Brutalists in the early 1960s, then again as the chief redeeming grace of the Post-Modernist 1970s and eighties — now become, in my meaning of the term, New Moderns?

I T MAY be, rather like Philip Johnson claiming to have been at the Boston Public Library the first Post-Modernist, that in some sense Kallmann and McKinnell have been all along New Moderns. Unless they attract the attention (God forbid) of medieval exegetes or French post-structualists, we will probably never know! But the question is a particularly relevant one in the beginning of the twenty-first century. Although the twentieth century's end found Gerhard Kallmann still at work every day with Michael McKinnell in their private studio off the firm's waiting room, his emeritus status and the bringing on board of several younger designers over the years (graduates all of McKinnell's Harvard GDS studio) have naturally had an effect on this celebrated office's evolution.

The comparison with Philip Johnson is, of course, a risky one: never mind that it is not often wise to compare a whore with a bishop. But, in fact, Kallmann and McKinnell are far more likely to have been in the Modernist vanguard than Johnson, who more than flirted with Po-Mo!

We are, of course, in danger again of tripping over words here, or, rather, labels. Charles Jencks includes among his New Moderns Charles Gwathmey, for instance, whom I numbered among the Post-Modernist "Whites" in the last chapter. Ada Louise Huxtable would surely agree. But in her and Jencks's reading of recent architectural history, Gwathmey would seem now less a Post-Modernist (of whatever color) and more of a late Modernist; between which New Modern is how much of a distinction? When Huxtable, who according to Jencks was his source for the term "New Modern," first used the term (as far back as in 1983), she left little doubt, in Jencks's words, that she meant it as a much needed "polemical counterpoint to Post Modernism." And in that sense KMW and company would certainly lift a glass to the New Moderns (McKinnell doubtless murmuring, "whatever that means"). Recent works, moreover, would indicate

FIGURE 283. Kallmann, McKinnell and Wood, New Chardon Street Courthouse, Government Center, 1995, evidence that this now legendary firm retains its vitality.

no flagging of vitality at KMW. Three in Boston stand out: the New Chardon Courthouse (Figure 283) in the Government Center, Hauser Hall at Harvard Law School, and the De Cordova Museum addition in Lincoln.

In the case of the courthouse, one is so grateful for the deference paid to Paul Rudolph's shamelessly neglected masterpiece that it takes a moment for the focus to shift to the newer building, the design of which is intriguing. It resonates equally, for one thing, with the early-nineteenth-century era of Boston's New World Greek Revival temple architecture (all that robustly rusticated and bright, becolumned limestone façade cladding) and the twenty-first-century era of the space station, the rims of which (do space stations have rims?) will never be more knife-edge sharp than the great space-age cornice that flares out from the top of this courthouse. All the while, moreover (KMW's work remains forever layered), the sheer surfaces so frequently and sharply punctured by the voids of the windows are a fine play on the 1900s work in Vienna of the pioneering Modernist master, Loos. Inside, the great central space, which, though private and inside, seems wonderfully public, surrounded as it is on all three sides by galleries off of which open the courtrooms. This central space rises to a surreal bluish cone of a "dome" of a magical, interplanetary hue, a cone that might just be Alfred Barr's Modern rocket bursting through history.

Also of interest is their Hauser Hall at Harvard. Wonder of wonders, the boldest stroke of this dark red brick and hardly much brighter red granite and cream limestone five-story monolith is that Hauser's back is shaped into a sweeping curve that "spoons" deferentially into the subtle arc of the Commons wing of Gropius's Harkness Graduate Center behind it. One is now doubly glad Derek Bok did not tear down Gropius's landmark!

Also worthy is KMW's addition of 1998 to the De Cordova Museum in Lincoln, wherein most notice the striking all-glass wall that lights the dramatic straight run of stairs that leads to the old museum. But a careful study of the entrance façade itself is to me most valuable, especially in light of our previous discussion of the exposed steel beams on the Hynes Center façades. Notice that the stone lintels atop the openings at the De Cordova are not toothed into the brick to either side. It is a subtle point but very much what one expects of KMW, who in this manner do not suggest the lintel is supported by the brickwork, but celebrate that it is suspended instead from the underlying steel frame, brackets of which also steady the brick wall itself. Rooted thus in the building's means of construction, the building's aesthetic is not misleading and does not trick the viewer. Nothing could be less Po-Mo, or more elegant, something project architect Bruce Wood was quick to point to when I raised the issue of how differently one might detail this sort of "veneer" brick wall from the old-fashioned fully structural kind: between Kallmann's point and Wood's are a host of issues thoughtful architects like KMW can be depended upon to work through on every job. That is why they are so good — whatever you call them.

ABOUT Peter Forbes there is no question at all what to call him — he is an arch Modernist! A story Forbes tells of himself is what happened once when he ran into one of his clients and another architect at the same party. Just how had Forbes landed the client, queried the other architect, with whom the same client had previously been in touch only to reply to the designer's question as to what was wanted by suggesting a Shingle Style house, which the other architect knew full well Forbes would never have on offer. However had Forbes pulled it off? It had never occurred to him to ask the client what he wanted, Forbes replied, without a moment's hesitation; he had just shown him some previous houses by Peter Forbes Associates, houses it turned out the client liked.

It is classic Peter Forbes. So was his Boston apartment, a wonderfully minimalist design centered on a curved blue green frosted glass screen, a screen "both reflective and luminescent," which, in the words of one critic, "gathers and distributes [light] to the rest of the apartment." Similarly, his harborfront is his drafting room, in the ground floor of the nearly 200-year-old granite building at the very end of Long Wharf. The austere gray granite interior — not at all cluttered in the traditional way of architects — overlooks the waters of Boston Harbor, and for most of New England's long winter water, sky, and drafting room shade beguilingly together from pewter to slate, the only accents a wall of books (real books, not hardware catalogues as in so many offices), and the constantly shifting, bright scrolling screens of computer consoles.

These are more important to Forbes than to most architects, for this graduate of the University of Michigan and the Yale School of Architecture virtually never draws; his exquisite Italian leather sketching book (he can draw) is hardly half full many years after its purchase. With an assistant at the computer manipulating either mouse or light pencil, Forbes designs on his feet, pacing back and forth, imagining, explaining, correcting, nowhere near a pencil. He is the most cerebral of architects, very committed, never giving an inch, his restless mind, I'm sure, never quite satisfied. Tough-minded. He is not looking for a fight; but I'm told others end up all but having them with him sometimes, such are Forbes's certitudes. "Peter could be a great architect," says a critic who prefers to remain anonymous, "but he is absolutely wedded to the pitch roof." Not so, Forbes protests (but all his houses do have pitch roofs). And there are only houses, by the way — another complaint. One striking design for a church in Maine was never realized, alas. So limiting, another critic remarks. Well, yes, but one could say the same of Chopin, whose work is not less superb a legacy for being only for the piano.

"To design is to explain" is an oft made observation of this architect, who knew and admired Mies and studied with Louis

FIGURE 284. The ocean front of a house designed in 1992 by Peter Forbes in Surry, Maine. Sturdy neo-Modernist evocations of a New England coastal and ship-building aesthetic, the architecture of Forbes utterly repudiates the values of design controls in historic old towns like Salem or Nantucket, which he feels have more to do with preserving real estate values than architectural values.

Kahn at Yale. Pilar Vilidas understands Forbes very well:

Set mostly along the rocky, forested coasts of Maine [Boston in the summer! My excuse for widening our net in Forbes's case] and Massachusetts, Forbes' houses are as spare and uncompromising as their surroundings, while they also capture the plain and elegant beauty of those settings.

New England looms large in Forbes' aesthetic. . . . An avid sailor, . . . [ship building] inform[s] his rigorous, yet sensual approach to architecture.

He prefers strong, clear, abstract forms. . . . His palette of materials is clearly Modernist — wood, steel, stone, glass, and concrete — but even as he balances them with a cool restraint, the effect is always warm.

A simple gabled box and massive stone chimney become Minimalist sculpture by the time Forbes gets done with them and they meet with a jeweler's precision.

It is an apt image, a jeweler's precision, for Forbes's house in Surry, Maine (Figures 284, 285), in which concrete piers carry a roof structure of steel angle rafters (infilled with wood panels) that allow all but independent glass walls to surround the house, is thus at once robustly tectonic in profile but almost ethereal in mass. It is a dazzling performance, all the more so for its chimney — an example of that "minimalist sculpture" Vilidas remarks upon. One could do a book of Forbes's boldly scaled chimneys — the best, perhaps, is in a house on Mount Desert Island in Maine (Figure 286). One could also do a companion book on Forbes's highly stylized fireplaces inside. How incredibly varied these are, and how very beautiful. A particularly fine example is illustrated in Figure 286.

Such works, as well as the austere shingled masses of his Marion House (Figure

FIGURE 285. Two parts of the Surry house meet with a minimalist intimacy that is also very plainspoken Bostonian. Forbes rails against "the Disneyfication [of] places like Seaside," Florida. "Those buildings cannot survive in that rigorous [oceanfront] environment," he asserts. "The materials will fail . . . we don't have wood of that quality anymore." Of such places, he insists, "the great hope is that the ocean will destroy quaint."

FIGURE 286. Forbes's aesthetic is at once stylish and constructional. In a house of 1991–93 on Mt. Desert Island in Maine, concrete and stone are beautifully ordered into a fireplace as bare bones as it is high style.

287), a design that must embarrass neo–Shingle-Style Historicist designers, disclose another historical vector in Forbes's work. His long, thin, only-one-room-deep houses recall some of Ralph Adams Cram's houses of the late 1880s and nineties, just as Forbes's breaking up of his long, thin masses into pavilions set diagonally to each other recalls somewhat William Ralph Emerson's diagonal plans of the late nineteenth century.

Forbes does both things, he is quick to say, because it gives more light and better views and often is more respectful of the terrain. Indeed, the slight reminiscence of the older work would be hardly worth focusing on, except that Forbes's very New England but very untraditional forms are just the contrast today with the conventional Shingle Style Revival houses of the New Historicists that Emerson's and Arthur Little's were with conventional Colonial Revival houses a hundred years ago. Just as the New England "colonial" tradition lived most vitally then in the brilliantly original work of Emerson and Little, so today that tradition's real heartbeat is in the work of Peter Forbes.

Though much admired for his work on the controversial Ward Commission on state contracts, this past president of the Boston Society of Architects, who has won award after award, will, after 2000, be based in Florence. Alas. But he will still summer in Maine — where Most Holy Trinity, Saco, may yet build Forbes's fine church (Figure 288).

I F THE most vital reflection today of the New England spirit in residential architecture is found in the work of Peter Forbes, in the realm of larger scale institutional architecture, the closest parallel is the work of Leers, Weinzapfel, a firm noted for a very hard-edged industrial aesthetic that is in their hands positively graceful.

This is only at first surprising. Remember Modernism and Puritanism. Mies always distanced himself from Chicago. ("No; living in Chicago has had no effect on me," he once observed, explaining, "I always take taxis. . . . I rarely see the city"; to which historian William Jordy could only add, "Of course he may have peeked!") Gropius, on the other hand, made it a point, as we've seen, to

FIGURE 287. Concrete columns, metal pipe railings, and abstracted shingled forms do not the Shingle Style make. But in one of his suburban Boston houses in Marion, Forbes achieved in 1985–87 a very thoughtful essay in the relationship of history and invention.

directly engage the New England culture in his work. Even Herdeg, in his diatribe against the Bauhaus master, found it necessary to recount how "in introducing [in his master's studio] an elementary school problem, Gropius call[ed] on Ralph Waldo Emerson . . . to bear witness to [Gropius's own] belief in the necessary recreation of the natural man." Similarly, Andrea Leers and Jane Weinzapfel, though neither natives nor any more wedded to Boston than Forbes, are rather proud that, historically, their firm is very Bostonian in its roots, both principals having originally met at Architects' Corner in the office of TAC alumnus Earl Flansborough in the glory days of Boston Modernism in the 1960s.

Leers received her liberal arts education at Wellesley College, taking her graduate degree in architecture at the University of Pennsylvania under Louis Kahn, teaching at Harvard after her apprenticeship with Flansborough. In 1970 she founded the firm of Andrea Leers Browning Associates in Boston, forever notable for pulling off perhaps the most unusual commission in the history of architecture in Boston: the Tobin Bridge Administration Building. A remodeling of a structure perched a hundred feet up in the air over a Boston Harbor container port (the only office building I know of actually slung like a hammock under a bridge deck and its toll booth) that Leers, in John Moris Dixon's words, "transformed into architecture," this odd structure is a measure of her considerable gifts as a designer.

Weinzapfel, who received her degree in architecture from the University of Arizona, had meanwhile achieved considerable expertise in transportation design. She taught at M.I.T. In 1982 the two old friends and colleagues threw in their lot together, forming the present firm.

Both are, independently, gifted, indeed, award-winning designers: the George Robert White Youth Development Center in Dorchester's Mattapan neighborhood (Figure 289), where Leers was the designing principal (given on that occasion for the first time in history to one or more women), won the J. Harleston Parker Gold Medal; the M.I.T. School of Architecture interior, where Weinzapfel took the design lead, earned an American Institute of Architects Honor Award. Each building is very different, reflecting the fact that

361

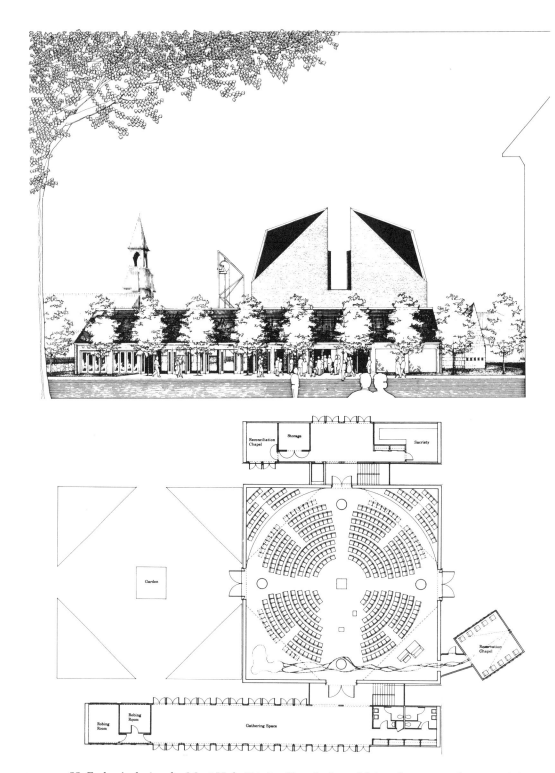

FIGURE 288. Forbes's design for Most Holy Trinity Church, Saco, Maine, focuses on the central altar of the modern liturgy. Similarly, the baptismal font at the west door is linked to the Blessed Sacrament Chapel by water-filled channels leading out to the pavement.

Weinzapfel and Leers do not keep company with each other at their boards in a private studio like Kallmann and McKinnell. As Weinzapfel puts it, "Andrea and I don't have the same eye, but we do see eye to eye." Nor should one imagine either like the solitary Rawn, sketching alone, or the restless Forbes circling his computer operator. "Neither Jane nor I sit in our offices and make sketches for other people to develop," Leers told a critic once. "Often a project will be started with an office-wide sketch program."

It is a custom that discloses how confident are both women, neither of whom is easily dissuaded of her design convictions, even by associates of long standing. Even between the two principals, there is a constant critical dialogue. It is perhaps easiest to imagine Leers as Weinzapfel's critic: one of the obvious differences in their buildings, for example, is that Leers tends toward a more colorful palette of materials and finishes, whereas Weinzapfel sees best I think in black and white. But if Weinzapfel is more a master of line, Leers must have an eye if not a proclivity for that, too, because she is an ardent student of the art of Japan, where she was, in fact, the first American architect to teach a design studio at the Tokyo Institute of Technology.

Characteristic of the firm's work is their huge, nearly 10,000-square-foot addition to the Worcester Federal Building (Figure 290), inserted into the lightwell of a Classical Revival landmark so as to be minimally disruptive and yet very refining of a rather pompous older building. Notice the beautiful detailing of the exterior.

The addition is also, conceptually and constructionally, very honest. Here, again, in Leers, Weinzapfel's work, one sees the same concern I find characteristic of New Moderns with architecture that does not mislead. At the White Center in South Boston the traditional pattern of the ground-face concrete block exterior proclaims an entirely structural, load-bearing wall. On the other hand, in their Newburyport District Courthouse the tight granite skin is "articulated to reveal that the masonry is veneered, not load-bearing," in Michael Crosbie's words, "and the thin metal-frame windows appear as though they are applied to the masonry surface."

The same non-load-bearing square block granite cladding, very svelte, is visible on the façades of Leers, Weinzapfel's masterwork, which is in downtown Boston: the operations control center (Figure 291) of Boston's subway and train and bus system, the Massachusetts Bay Transportation Authority (MBTA). This ten-story building, a considerable enlargement of a much smaller older building, of all the work of Boston's New Moderns, most exemplifies the way this group is continually influenced by what historian Leland Roth calls the "industrially inspired architecture of International Modernism," of which he cites the two classic examples of the AEG Factory of 1908 in Berlin by Peter Behrens, and the Fagus Factory, also in Germany, designed by Gropius in 1911, landmarks from which so many characteristic aspects of the work we are studying are derived.

Indeed, critic Vernon Mays has called Leers, Weinzapfel's MBTA Building "a romantic machine," which while most resonant historically of the thought of Le Corbusier ("The house," Corbu famously, and notoriously, insisted, "is a machine for living in"), aptly catches hold of what makes the MBTA Operations Center so exceptional: its bonding together of very basic vernacular, industrial components with such imagination and flair as to make a very high art indeed. The great steel struts of the cornice and the boldly over-scaled sixth-floor steel balcony are brilliant strokes considered just artistically, but the balcony, which Mays again hits upon just the right words to describe — "industrial sculpture" he calls it — is doubly interest-

FIGURE 289. Leers, Weinzapfel and Associates, White Center, Dorchester, 1996.

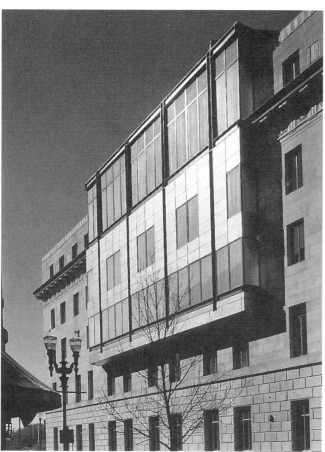

FIGURE 290. Leers, Weinzapfel and Associates, addition to Federal Building, Worcester, 1993. The exterior steel framing endows a rather pompous and florid building with a sparse neo-Modernist stylishness

FIGURE 291. Leers, Weinzapfel and Associates, M.B.T.A. Operations Control Center, downtown, 1993. The design brilliantly relates to South Station across the street and a nearby old iron bridge, achieving a contextualism all the more telling for its neo-Modernist aesthetic.

ing as being directly inspired by one of Boston's own grittiest landmarks, the nearby old steel-frame Northern Avenue drawbridge of 1908 that crosses Fort Point Channel in Boston Harbor.

But this is a tale we have heard before, this tale of a severely plain beauty: "The stripped-down aesthetic of Leers and Weinzapfel serves them well," Michael J. Crosbie has observed, "in a region where Puritan temperance has colored even the architecture." And though Leers does mention Alexander Paris, Puritanism and Modernism as we've seen well enough by now was a union consecrated by Gropius: good evidence of how New Moderns are picking up the strands of Boston's memorable Modernist legacy.

But architecture in Boston at the turn of the twenty-first century is about something else entirely. In what has become the post-Bilboa era, the era of Frank Gehry, who as we'll see is somewhat of an honorary Boston architect, we are now arrived at our finale in a far more complicated cohort than Puritans old or new. Instead we are called to keep company at the end of this long peregrination through Boston's architecture with four old friends and true; Bostonians all now, but not always — Warren Schwartz and Robert Silver, and, finally, Rodolfo Machado and Jorge Silvetti.

T HE four became friends as young men in 1977, when all of them participated in an architectural exhibition, "Imminent Domains." It was Schwartz, who was then at Hilgenhurst Associates (where he had designed with Silver and another Hilgenhurst architect, William D. Buckingham, the Parker-Award–winning addition to the East Cambridge Savings Bank), who organized the 1977 exhibition held at Boston's Harkness-Krakow Gallery on Newbury Street.

Machado and Silvetti participated independently, the latter scoring the show's

great success with his famous "Stair House." Schwartz and Silver collaborated on one entry, of which the author of the show's catalogue had many things to say, all pertinent:

Clues to an understanding of the only truly collaborative work shown in this exhibition can be found in the architects' training and practice. Schwartz as a student of Colin Rowe [at Cornell] and Silver while at Cambridge University learned to value the significance of the classical tradition. . . . Schwartz's prize-winning design for the New City Center of Perugia (with Francis McGuire), reveals his sensitivity to history and existing contexts. On the other hand, Silver's long-time interest in science and technology was given an imaginative expression in the New Science Center at Wellesley College [by the Perry office]. In their "Small villa" . . . Schwartz and Silver fuse the imagery of the past with the technology of the present.

When the two joined forces to form Schwartz/Silver in 1980 (some years later Robert Miklos became a third principal), the two founding partners, both Harvard graduates and by that time fast friends, became quickly known for their resolute idealism. Determined to sustain high design standards but in a studio setting with no thought police, they seemed by turns inspiring and pathetic in their determination to find something worthwhile in whatever job they could get their hands on, and in their propensity not to smooth over client conflict, but to encourage it as a means of intensifying dialogue so as to penetrate the design problem. Soon they came to be known, even admired, as much for their close calls as for their successes, as much for the risks they were always prepared to run as for the several triumphs they soon scored.

Their first major work to attract national and even international attention (it was published in Italy in both *L'Industria Delle Construzioni and Casa Vogue* in 1988) was Schwartz's own contribution to that long and fabled roll that we have traced here since Gropius of Architects'-Own-Houses by Boston Modernist form-givers: in this case (Figure 292) the Schwartz/Fiekowsky House (Sheila Fiekowsky, a violinist with the Boston Symphony Orchestra, is Schwartz's wife) nearby the BSO's summer music center at Tanglewood.

The house was inspired by the Villa Pisani at Lonigo, a notable work of one of Palladio's most gifted disciples, Vincenzo Scamozzi (whose work in St. Mark's Piaza in Venice makes so proud a contribution to that great square), and reflects as well the rapture of Schwartz and Fiekowsky's first visit to the villa Pisani on their honeymoon, when they fell in love with its great octagon lifting from the square podium on a grassy hillside.

As much we learn from critic Charles Gandee, who goes on to declare:

If Schwartz had slavishly copied Scamozzi . . . we would have simply averted our eyes from the surely Kitsch result. . . . But Schwartz prefers to leave pastiche to others, and draw inspiration, not façades, from history. True the Villa Schwartz/Fiekowsky owes much to the Villa Pisani, but the model has been so thoroughly reworked, so completely redrawn in Schwartz's own idiosyncratic hand, that we regard the house as original. . . .

Though Schwartz loads down his family getaway with a heavy referential package, the house shows no sign of strain. On the contrary, it exudes self-confidence. The key, of course, is control: knowing precisely — as Schwartz does — the point at which charming becomes cloying, serious becomes ponderous, clever becomes silly, proud becomes pompous, and playful becomes frivolous.

That said, it must also be said that the design of the UFO — ugh, sorry: house — reflects perfectly the slightly loopy genius for architecture of Warren Schwartz, who is equal parts Woody Allen, Seinfeld, and Bob Dylan, with screenplay by Monty Python productions. And this loopiness, while it does not entirely obscure either Schwartz's idealism or his shrewdness,

does disclose a key ground of his design gifts, the unusual way he seems to have preserved into a very mature adulthood a good deal of the imagination of a child.

To my inquiry, for example, about the design concept (not the sources) of the "Villa Transformer," as one wit has dubbed his house, Schwartz replied that he had wanted it to look on the one hand like it had always been there, but on the other, as if it had landed yesterday. And so it does; its elegant protruding aluminum scuppers, whose purpose is prosaic enough — to project rainwater away — in my mind's eye belch fire and smoke when the house takes off, which its design by no means seems to preclude.

Withal, there is in this house — widely published and much admired — the beginning of a remarkable architectural train of thought, one that may have reached its climax in another house nearby (across the Massachusetts border, in Copake, New York, in a valley overlooked by the Berkshires), the Lazarus House of 1989 (Figure 293). In both residences, Michael J. Crosbie has written, "The architect countered the country-house stereotype by inverting the typical house section. . . . Living spaces are placed on the top floor with bedrooms underneath. 'This arrangement allows the volumes and the roof forms of the living spaces to become more expressive, because there are no spaces above them,' Schwartz explains."

True enough. But that is an analysis for a critic, of course. For a historian, Schwartz produces an explication of the Lazarus House every bit as charming as the one for his earlier house nearby, and for both there are childhood stories. His own house, he thinks, came from a memory of climbing up into a howdah, one of those elaborate, domed, tabernacled seats used atop elephants. The Lazarus House, on the other hand, so notable for its beautifully arched profile, comes from thinking of the way a picnic blanket billows up when one throws

FIGURE 292. The Schwartz/Fiekowsky House, Lenox, 1988 (the "Villa Transformer," as one critic has called it), one of two houses in the neighborhood of the Boston Symphony Orchestra summer home in Tanglewood.

FIGURE 293. The Lazarus House, Copake, New York, is the second Tanglewood-area building by Schwartz/Silver in the 1990s. It is a work at once lyrical and masterful.

COLOR PLATE 9 Frank Gehry, design architect, with Schwartz/Silver: Tower Records Building, Back Bay, 1986. Until the forthcoming Stata Center at M.I.T., Gehry's only work in Boston, Tower is a landmark of the city's stylish Newbury Street area. The building's nighttime exterior illumination brings out the design's high-style industrial aesthetic in a wonderfully romantic way.

it into the air so as to float it down on to the ground — a thought for a vacation house.

The critic, again, sees something else entirely in the wonderfully serene gray, white, and yellow stucco Lazarus House:

Though the architect rendered the sculpted, abstract ensemble without a trace of rustic sentimentality, he arranged each element to sympathize with the landscape. The northeast side of the house nestles into a knoll; its small windows create a private face against the hills of the Taconic State Park, which are echoed in the curved profile of the roof. On the western elevation, a broad smile of windows along the living area offers expansive views of the Catskill Mountains to the east, and the corners of the sons' bedrooms are fitted in sliding glass doors to offer direct access to the surrounding open fields.

Pressed, the closest Schwartz comes to reconciling these polarities is to speak of what he calls "the slow arch" of the house's profile, which, in truth, is magical enough! Indeed, it already seems hardly possible to publish a book on American houses without illustrating this house, usually on the cover. Finally, the historian, I think, trumps critic and architect: the Lazarus House is a masterwork.

A more public strain appeared from the beginning of the firm's work. The "slow arch," in fact, made its first appearance in Schwartz/Silver's oeuvre in the very year of the design of the Tanglewood House in a much less well-known work, the Wellesley Fire Station. This more public dimension of the firm's work would achieve its own considerable repute, however, in Schwartz/Silver's design in 1988 of the Rotch Library of Architecture at M.I.T.

Before exploring that commission, however, yet another "visitor of power" needs to be folded into Boston's Modern architectural history, the architect in the years from 1987 to 1989 of Tower Records in the Back Bay, the design that may be said finally to have administered the coup de grâce to Post-Modernism in Boston.

Frank Gehry in Boston is a more complicated tale than is at once apparent.

In 1997, for example, when the Parker Gold Medal was given to Stanley Saitowitz's deeply moving Boston Holocaust Memorial, few realized that Gehry had chaired the jury that awarded the commission to Saitowitz, for whose design — six luminous sixty-eight-foot glass towers (etched with six million names) over grated pits that glow at night, all this on a black granite path that the visitor follows through the base of the towers — Gehry had gone to bat. Boston also in this connection owes much to Louis Kahn, whose never-realized Jewish Martyrs' Memorial (nine grouped massive glass blocks) was the inspiration for the Boston memorial. But Boston owes most to Gehry — who, in fact, owes much to Boston — whereby hangs a far older tale. For Gehry had his Boston/Harvard years as a young man. And as Thomas Hines, in his study of Gehry and his work, points out, Gehry's time in Boston was formative.

It was after taking his degree in architecture at the University of Southern California that in the fall of 1956 Gehry enrolled at Harvard. Notes Hines:

He quickly discovered that 'planning' at Harvard was too abstract for his tastes and was grounded too heavily in the statistical social sciences. He, therefore, abandoned the idea of a degree in planning and became a special student, auditing lectures throughout the university. He was particularly impressed by Arthur Schlesinger, Jr., John Kenneth Galbraith and Pitirim Sorokin. The intellectual riches at Harvard stimulated Gehry's penchant for reading and his lifelong pursuit of new ideas. He took courses with [the former dean of the School of Design] Joseph Hudnut and particularly enjoyed the philosophical walking tours with him through the old Boston neighborhoods. Through him, Gehry discovered the European modernists, particularly Le Corbusier. Yet he also shared Hudnut's enthusiasm for the rich historic architecture of America and Europe and slowly began to realize that the

Dean was actually struggling against the grip of the Bauhaus and its anti-historical influence on architectural education and design.

All of which is to tie up an important loose end: for the first time here, it is the legacy not of Gropius, but of Hudnut (as Gehry confirmed when I interviewed him in 1999 for this book).

Most forget it was Hudnut who actually transformed Harvard's schools of architecture, landscape architecture, and city planning in 1936 into the Graduate School of Design, of which he became the first dean. And that work, and then bringing Gropius to Harvard, was by no means Hudnut's only, or even first, Modernist credential.

Indeed, Hudnut had been in touch with Frank Lloyd Wright, with whom he corresponded throughout the 1930s, and Hudnut would be the author of the introduction to a small catalogue of the Wright Exhibition held in Boston at the Institute of Modern (later, of Contemporary) Art in 1940 in concert with the major Wright show at the Museum of Modern Art in New York. (Wright, indeed, was on more than one mind at Harvard that year. That was the year of the pioneering doctoral dissertation on Wright — written at Harvard by Grant Carpenter Manson).

Like Kenneth Conant, Cram's great friend, who, Alofsin notes, "included Wright's work in his survey of Modern architecture [at Harvard] at a time when there were no textbooks in English that dealt with the history of contemporary architecture," Hudnut, though a minor figure, was a minor figure of importance. Never mind that he and Conant, Modernists both in many ways, who argued passionately to retain architectural history at Harvard's Graduate School, lost out then to Gropius. Now, in the age of Gehry, Hudnut's life and work takes on new significance.

Sert and Sekler, of course, in the 1960s when Schwartz was Sert's student at the GSD, reversed direction and brought

architectural history back as a requirement. But in Gehry's day it was still very much Hudnut versus the Bauhaus. Indeed, in Boston in the 1950s was not Gehry reenacting Pei's discovery of Le Corbusier in the 1930s? The only difference is that the dean's name was different — not Emerson, but Hudnut — and what was being battled against in Gehry's case was not the Beaux Arts but the Bauhaus!

Nor was even that the extent of the influence on Gehry of his Boston year. Between 1957 and 1960, working for Victor Gruen in Los Angeles, Gehry felt more and more frustrated, according to Hines:

The discovery through Hudnot of architectural history had persuaded [Gehry] that he should live for a while in Europe and in 1961 he . . . moved to Paris. . . . He made pilgrimages to Le Corbusier's chapel at Ronchamp and his monastery at La Tourette and to the German baroque treasures of Balthasar Neumann. Most of all, he was drawn to the Romanesque buildings of France and Germany . . . and he felt angry that his modernist mentors at U.S.C. had failed to introduce him to these architectural miracles.

Though he would largely continue for the next decade to design within the prevailing modernist canon, he would slowly begin in the 1970's to explore more consciously the expressive possibilities of historical references and the relationship of architecture to painting and sculpture . . . [and] in such works as the Loyola Law School demonstrate that the legacies of "culture" and "history" need not be burdensome after all.

It was not only through Hudnut, furthermore, that Gehry discovered the joys of history, a discovery his biographer sees as influencing Gehry's work all through the 1970s and eighties. During 1956 and 1957, when he was not tramping around the city with Hudnut, Gehry's architectural apprenticeship in Boston, chiefly with Perry, Shaw and Hepburn, the architects of colonial Williamsburg, cannot but have reinforced his newfound interest in history, all the more because the Perry office has by no means over the years turned its back on Modernism.

Consider, for instance, three landmarks of the Perry office's design, many years apart, the aesthetics of which span half a century. Most recently, there is the South Postal Annex of 1980 near Dewey Square, wonderful in how its projecting exhaust ducts and streamlined, highly graphic aluminum façade suggest without mimicking the aesthetic of a pre–World War II ocean liner. Furthest back, there is the circa 1950 Jordan Marsh Building at Summer and Chauncy Streets (which I have long since repented of calling absurd), the latter's overall massing and dramatic cantilever both boldly Modernist, and in Gehry's day in the Perry office the firm's pride and joy. Third, there is what may be the firm's masterwork, the Wellesley College Science Center of 1972 (Figure 255).

A multistory concrete building, with exposed structure and ductwork on the exterior, all color coded for the future modification expected in a science building, this now obscure but extraordinary Boston building has been called by Nathan Silver the "unacknowledged sibling" of the Centre Pompidou in Paris, designed by Piano and Rogers with Ove Arup and Partners, a landmark that "scarcely had more than its primary steel up when Wellesley was finished."

Although it was only in the wake of the increasing fame of the Pompidou that the Wellesley Science Center received the attention it deserved (eventually winning the Parker Gold Medal years later), if there is a culminating building of the Boston Granite Style, William Curtis proposes it may well be this Wellesley center, so reminiscent in its concrete structure of the Boston Granite sensibility. Wrote Margaret Floyd, "The discipline of this design interfaces the new and the old to create yet another architecture that encompasses both. The small scale *articulation of this elevation translates the spirit of the Wellesley College campus into a present dimension* [my italics]." And just as the

Jordan Marsh Building had been in the 1950s the big deal of Gehry's time at Perry, so was the Wellesley Science Center in the 1970s when, such are the vagaries of history, it was Warren Schwartz and Robert Silver who were to be found in the Perry office. Silver, in fact, just out of architecture school, was the job captain for the science center.

Thus it was that when in the mid-1980s Portia Harcus (she of the Harcus Krakow Gallery that had sponsored *Imminent Domains* in 1977) brought Gehry, Schwartz, and Silver together for what became the Tower Record project on Newbury Street, it was something of a marriage of true minds; all three architects, when they discovered they were all graduates of the Perry firm, agreeing predictably (but not without reason) what an "incubator of architects," in Schwartz's words, that historic Boston architectural office was.

More than historical vectors enter in here, for real continuities can be shown to exist in the Perry office over these decades. Robert C. Dean, for instance, who taught design at M.I.T. in the 1930s (his students included both I. M. Pei and Gordon Bunshaft) and who had first worked as a draftsman in the Perry office in 1926, became a partner in 1940. Indeed, when Perry, Shaw and Hepburn became Aalto's executive architects in the design and erection of Baker House in 1948 to 1952, it was Dean, sympathetic to Modernism, who mostly carried the ball. Dean it was as well, it will be recalled, who Gropius attacked with reference to the Jordan Marsh design, and Dean, no admirer of the Bauhaus and a strong figure in the Perry office during Gehry's time there in the mid-1950s, would certainly have taken Hudnut's side in the argument between him and Gropius that Gehry was such a beneficiary of. Moreover, by Schwartz and Silver's time in the mid-1970s, Dean was a dominant figure in the Perry office. Dean's partner, Charles Rogers, the principal in charge of the Wellesley Science Center, had also been Schwartz's teacher at Cornell. And so it goes. Tower Records — begun in 1987 with Gehry as design architect and Schwartz/Silver as executive architects — for all the radical new dimensions it introduced into Boston's architectural history had more than a few Boston roots.

The architecture magazines, untroubled by history, as is so often the case, made much of the "juxtaposition of the past and the pop" in Tower's design, and of the problematic role of Gehry in Boston: "this apostle of impermanence in America's most permanent city." More pertinent, however, was the concern that "the Los Angeles architect did not have an easy time making his first Boston statement. . . . Gehry's firm found Boston 'one of the most restricted places in the world to build.'" (No hyperbole: Richard Bertman, then chair of the Back Bay Architectural Commission, reports that the Tower Records project was nearly not approved, requiring urgent last-minute appeals on his part to the City Council.) Yet Tower Records itself, doubtless to the surprise of many, was an immediate triumph.

"Gehry's metaphor," *Architecture* reported, was that of "two buildings, one wrapping up and over another." And then there was the "cornice," if that's what it was: "The most distinct and discussed element of the remake, the stiff angular brackets that support the roof of the new penthouse are far more heavy and brooding. A sculptural parody of a projecting cornice, they are paralleled and emphasized by a mock awning at the second floor. At once industrial in their metallic-gray cladding and unconventional in their thrusting forms, the treelike struts are pure Gehry." Not the usual architectural fantasy in tightly wrapped Post-Modernist Boston! But as Adele Freedman pointed out in *Progressive Architecture*, Tower Records was one of the projects that indicated that Gehry's hour had indeed come, and not just in Boston: "Gehry's projects have been growing in number and size, as well as confidence

and daring," Freeman reported. "The latest include the Yale Psychiatric Institute, 360 Newbury in Boston [Tower Records], and a huge mixed-use complex in Dallas waiting for the go-ahead. Gehry is going national."

So he was. And Freeman struggled to sort it out:

Gehry's conversation has a lot in common with his architecture. His words spill out in fragments, sometimes colliding, often jarring, always interconnected in mysterious ways. . . .
"I'm committed to the 20th century," he says with typical defiance. "It's an anti–Post-Modernist thing."
"You invent, you formulate ideas, they're slightly different. . . . It's not necessarily that new is better. It's just that we're tied to a roller coaster and can't get loose. I'm into this reality and I don't understand it."
With that, Gehry gets up and makes his way through a clearing in a forest of cardboard models. . . . Gehry designs in model, each project exhausting ten miniatures built on two scales. "It forces me to work from one to another and put myself in reality," he explains, "and then I do lots of little drawings which are in the notebooks. I never intend them to be seen by anyone. . . ."

Where history may be found on this roller coaster or in Tower's actual design may not at first glance seem clear. But Tower Records still lacks its most prominent ornamental highlight: the sculptor, Claus Oldenberg, Gehry's long-time friend and collaborator, was to have created a huge tea bag to serve that purpose. And while such a sculptural work might seem more bizarre than historical, it would actually have been in the great Boston tradition of, for example, the great gilded (and steaming) teapot of Scollay Square, still there (a few doors up from its original location) in Government Center today because of Walter Muir Whitehill and another controversial Modernist architect, I. M. Pei.

If the tea bag seems still too trivial, a far more deep-seated and Bostonian character

FIGURE 294. Schwartz/Silver, M.I.T. Architectural Library, Cambridge, a brilliant and award-winning design. The splayed steel beams accommodate truck access in and out of the facility.

FIGURE 295. Frank Gehry Associates, design architects, with Schwartz/Silver, executive architects: entrance wing to the Boston Children's Museum, waterfront, 1994. The apparent abandonment of this project is a very great loss.

is also discernible at Tower in the building's palette and changing patina. And here was, perhaps, where Gehry's executive architects mattered most. "Schwartz/Silver shared in the arduous procedure of design and redesign," as it was reported, an area in which Robert Silver took the lead. And he did so most conspicuously in convincing Gehry to abandon his first idea of using galvanized steel as the cladding or weathering surface of the façades and the structural steel struts of the cornice (structural steel can no longer be exposed, because of fire codes; unclad, it melts) and use lead-coated copper cladding instead — in the first place because in New England's climate galvanized steel rusts, but also to very great aesthetic effect. Silver observed that over time the lead-coated copper would "age to a deeper pewter tone, adding a Boston surface to Gehry's palette."

Finally, though, historian Naomi Miller sees much more in Tower:

The true power of the structure . . . is perhaps most apparent in the view from the southeast. It is a perfect Gehry site, for the building looms above the [Massachusetts] Turnpike. . . . We cannot but admire the articulation of the rectilinear fenestration, the fine balance between the

projecting struts and the indentations of the roof line, the force of the gray lead panels, all of which evoke historical elements in the most subtle manner. Tower Records succeeds as an extraordinary modern composition, being of our time, yet perpetuating the memory of older times.

Especially at night, when Tower is so beautifully illuminated, washed in warm pink with its topmost struts glowing a subtle green, I for one am sure one of the memories of older times invoked by Frank Gehry in Boston was of those long walks of thirty years earlier with Joe Hudnut.

IF ROBERT Silver worked more closely with Frank Gehry on Tower Records than Warren Schwartz did, that is because of the nature of Schwartz/Silver's by now well-established collaboration: "I can design anything," Schwartz is fond of saying, "and Robert can build anything." More than that, Silver has a very critical eye (one Miklos profits from now too); Schwartz has also been heard to liken himself to a pencil and Silver to an eraser. As it happened on Gehry's beat, there was more need of an eraser.

However, for Schwartz, meeting Gehry was formative, for the younger man found

FIGURE 296. Schwartz/Silver, design architects: projected complete design for additions to the New England Aquarium, waterfront, 1996. Always in the vanguard, these architects here achieved a remarkable work; certainly the part already built is not only powerfully energizing architecture but very rewarding in its underlying compositional coherency.

in Gehry the inspiration every good designer needs, especially the strongest (because they know they can stand up to it, gaining much and losing nothing). Schwartz saw in Gehry, he says, "a true original, not a knock-off," and Gehry's influence on Schwartz's design subsequently is not hard to see. That what Schwartz has made of Gehry's inspiration is very much his own, however, is evident in Schwartz/Silver's award-winning design of the Rotch Architectural Library at M.I.T.

Tower Records, the design process of which under Gehry began in the spring of 1986, was well under way by the time two years later that Schwartz began work on his own M.I.T. design (Figure 294) in the spring of 1988, and the Tower and M.I.T. jobs, at each end of intown Massachusetts Avenue and on either side of the river, make for an interesting comparison. Robert Campbell has described the result beautifully. The Rotch, he wrote, is

a building that is much like a bridge. It touches the ground at only six points, so as to leave

room for the trucks. From these six points, a powerful concrete frame rises to the roof, six stories up. Then, from huge concrete beam s at the roof, the whole interior of the library — six levels of it — *is suspended*.

The Rotch is simply a gem of a building. Crisp and logical, yet expressive and poetic, it is the ideal metaphor for its contents — that is to say, for the subject of architecture at an institute of technology. . . . Warren Schwartz and Robert Silver have found a way to symbolize this building's meaning through its architecture. . . .

The façade could not be more Miesian in style — it is virtually a geometer's glass cage — nor more monumental. And what is for me the greatest wonder is how through the two *A*-forms on the façade's ground story Schwartz contrived, not only the necessary structural bracing, but the equally necessary truck access (in/out), all the while it seems to me with the form of Gehry's diagonal struts at Tower in mind, but at the same time creating what is very much Schwartz's own and quite strikingly original form. This is wonderful architec-

375

ture, a worthy comparison to the Lazarus House.

Inside the M.I.T. Library, Gehry's influence is also evident. John Dixon has noted "intuitive, subtly playful, elements . . . occasional angular elements in the gridded field." And at various places, especially around the lobby reception desk, odd angles and such capture interest. But the truth is, it's a kind of "Boston Gehry," understated rather than tentative, and quite delightful.

More of the same, but in the more playful mode in which Schwartz excels, would doubtless have characterized any design of his for Boston's Children's Museum, which in 1994 decided instead to commission such a project from Gehry. By then, of course, Schwartz/Silver were the architects of perhaps the most widely published recent house in America (the Lazarus House), but the Children's Museum sought the prestige of an international architect, and Schwartz/Silver, by now well enough acquainted with Gehry to feel able to play Sert to Le Corbusier, as it were (as at the Carpenter Center), threw in their lot with Gehry for the second time as executive architects. (Another contribution of the younger firm to the office: one of Gehry's leading designers, Michael Maltzen, a Schwartz/Silver graduate.)

As it turned out, Gehry's design of Children's (Figure 295) began by all accounts a much wilder ride than Tower had. At one point, for example, it was presumably in that great forest of cardboard models of Gehry's already noted here that, driven almost to distraction according to Warren Schwartz by the admiring but demanding director of Children's, Gehry just went over to his model of the Bilboa Guggenheim, removed a good-sized part, and carried it over to the Boston model and attached it, a proceeding reported with neither pride nor shame. Nor any need of either in the face of the power of Gehry's final design.

Centered on a new lobby, which the architect describes as "a copper-clad, heavy-timber 'wave' form," the effect, judged in colored models, is breathtaking. One enters the "wave" through a woven, free-form, sheet metal canopy. Then, within the great "wave" of the lobby, a ramped gallery leads to a steel and glass bridge that in turn gives access to a new stainless-steel-clad water-related exhibition space in the form of a barge built on a pontoon over the waters of Fort Point Channel. Against the backdrop of the plain rectangular loft building of the museum, this entrance wing design is brilliant sculpture foiled by industrial weight.

It is a tragedy that due to a failure of nerve only too likely in Boston — though the Civic Design Board, to its great credit, did approve the controversial project — Gehry's design has been abandoned. One wonders if he retrieved the piece of the Bilboa Guggenheim and restored it to the model of what is now increasingly coming to be seen as the greatest piece of architecture of the second half of the twentieth century. One wonders too, remembering how beautifully Pei's Kennedy Library pyramid now adorns the Louvre, if there is a kind of a pattern here.

If there is such a pattern, at least one Boston institution, the New England Aquarium, has taken measures to counter it. In 1993 the aquarium proposed quite a historic rendezvous for a Boston board of directors, for Schwartz/Silver this time would be the lead designers of a vast new Boston Harbor aquarium (Figure 296).

For Schwartz, the aquarium posed not only a tremendous opportunity, but also a baffling problem: almost within sight of where Gehry's addition to Children's would be, Schwartz had to conceive of a considerable Boston Harbor landmark that would stand up to one of Gehry's strongest designs, for which Schwartz/Silver had just completed making the working drawings. To do that, Schwartz decided the new building would somehow have to engage Gehry's older building

376

(assured then to be on the verge of construction); his and Gehry's work would have to have, as he puts it, "some sort of conversation." Not what every architect would want, such a conversation with a now acknowledged master, but an opportunity the best kind of architect would kill for.

What could two such buildings have to say to each other? Perhaps if one were seen as posing a question, the other might attempt an answer. Such a dialogue to ruminate over. Such sleepless nights. Such dreams to have.

Certainly, it is not difficult to call to mind the architects whose characteristically free-wheeling forms would fill such dreams: Eero Saarinen, above all. Nor is the assigned reading hard to imagine: surely Venturi, for example, ruminating in his *Iconography* on the "tendency to modify and distort the order of architectural parts . . . found in the angles and curves of Alvar Aalto." Just thinking about the problem I began to think that, seen one way, Gehry's canopy at the Children's Museum is Aalto's Baker House "wave" laid flat as a roof. Gehry's restless genius by no means has come out of nowhere. Nor would Schwartz's design for Boston's aquarium.

All speculation, of course; though Schwartz will allow the influence of Aalto at least, and Gehry. Yet there is (as there always is with Schwartz) a story — in fact, a dream — in which he is sailing into Boston Harbor, past all of Gehry's compound curves and elegant volumes, but toward what seems to be a very different form, all straight and pointed edges and crystalline angles; like an iceberg, really. It is a story I especially like because though Schwartz, when pressed, will admit he never *has* sailed into Boston (nor I), it is a story, an experience, a vision, I somehow recognize, common perhaps to a Bostonian who thinks at all about his city's history. (I think of the conclusion of David McCord's *About Boston*.) I also like the story because it admits to the architect's anxiety *and*

ambition as well as to his imagination and bravura (how intuitively he differentiates his two landmarks), as well as to his ingrained practicality; compound curves à la Gehry are very expensive — already (in his dreams, no less) Schwartz is saving his client money.

David Eisen's critique of what has been built is perhaps the best:

Both wonderfully entertaining and a profound piece of architecture, a futuristic vision and a seemingly ancient geological formation. Its frenetic composition is different from anything Boston has ever seen. . . .

Clad in stainless-steel fish scales, the solid elements are penetrated by shards of glass that make their monolithic forms seem light and accessible. Wedges and wings project out to greet you, while the spaces between them pull you into the building. . . . Schwartz/Silver's brilliance lies in [the aquarium's] use of architectural forms and spaces to evoke memories of places and experiences associated with the sea. The craggy profiles of rocky coastlines . . . the hull of a boat or the back of a whale are associations that are overlapped like a dreamy seaside collage.

And, perhaps, the profile of an iceberg.

My own reaction to what has been built was, for all my study of the work, both very personal and rather startling. I was at once entranced by the building, around which I could scarcely stop myself moving from side to side, so varied were its forms and volumes and so magical the reflection of the changing light on the steel fish scales. A line from Kahn (a line I've since verified about the steel panels of his Yale Center for British Studies) kept running through my head: "On a gray day, it will look like a moth; on a sunny day, like a butterfly." Boston's aquarium looks like whatever the weather (very like New England, that) and changes all the time as you keep moving — which may be the point: losing one effect, one wants the other back, or something like that, and the result is to keep one moving, which is perhaps a part of why, more than anything else, I found Schwartz's design *energizing*.

Yet the seemingly wildly slanting planes and peaks (not a compound curve in sight) and the great volumes colliding do in the end cohere. Although Schwartz sketches compulsively (and quite fantastically), he designs in models, and it shows in just that underlying compositional coherence of the aquarium design and the way it satisfies the mind so roused by all this delight of scintillant chaos on Boston's old waterfront.

Aaccording to one's point of view, the second pair of the foursome I have cast here as a finale, Rodolfo Machado and Jorge Silvetti, are theorists of baffling and impenetrable vision, or, now, in the new century, Boston's hottest architects: masters already, in their discreet way, of what Lutyens famously called the "great game" of his mature classical mode.

These four old friends (who have made it a point to share Christmas dinner every year since the late 1970s) — Schwartz, Silver, Machado, and Silvetti — clearly somewhat pace each other. And thus far the significance to Boston's built fabric of the work of Schwartz/Silver has been far greater. But about Machado & Silvetti, in the way theory, teaching, and practice come together in their work, in the seriousness and gravity of their sensuality, in the nobility of aspiration of these thinkers, designers, and teachers — one part Palladio to another part rocker Patti Smith — there has always been a certain expectation.

I recall my surprise in reading (in the notable World of Art series of the British publisher, Thames and Hudson) Diane Ghirardo's *Architecture after Modernism* of 1996 and finding in the last chapter — wonder of wonders — a Boston architectural firm keeping company with Tadao Ando, Renzo Piano, Alvaro Siza, Norman Foster, all the other great international architects; it was Machado & Silvetti, of course, the "noble achievement" and

"understated grandeur" of one of whose works was actually the climax of Ghirardo's book. And then, two years later, Machado & Silvetti won the competition (in which, in fact, Siza was also invited to participate) to master plan the renovation and expansion of the John Paul Getty Villa at Malibu, in Los Angeles. Many who were pleased were not surprised.

Both men are Argentinean-born Americans who fled their homeland during years of oppression. First in architecture in university in Buenos Aires, then in Paris, where he went for further study in urban design, and finally in graduate work in architecture at Berkeley, Machado honed clearly prodigious gifts, expanded in his practice of architecture in San Francisco and in Pittsburgh. In 1978 he came to New England to the Rhode Island School of Design, where he headed the Department of Architecture until 1980, when he was appointed Professor of Architecture at Harvard.

Silvetti, his life partner as well as his professional partner, followed a similar course, from university in Buenos Aires to graduate study at Berkeley, and has written and taught widely since 1975 at Harvard, where he is now chair of the Department of Architecture. Both men have thus headed important architecture schools. And both remain influential teachers and theorists of international standing. Each has been extensively published and their work exhibited at the Museum of Modern Art in New York, at the Pompideau Center in Paris, and at the 1980 Venice Biennale.

Associated professionally since 1974, they founded Machado & Silvetti in 1985. Among many awards heaped upon them one stands out: the First Award in Architecture from the American Academy of Arts and Letters for two decades of "boldly conceived and brilliantly executed urban projects." No fewer than three books have been published on their work.

Much impenetrable discourse to my

mind obscures perhaps more than celebrates that work, but Machado and Silvetti themselves have no trouble finding words of power: "We are concerned . . . ," they declare, "with a manner of producing architecture that is personal . . . with an individual authorship . . . that is riskier than most in its desire to propose a world and a difference."

George Baird explains:

Forming their intellectual position in architecture in the wake of the startling events of 1968, Machado and Silvetti nevertheless sedulously avoided the literal politicizations of practice that became widespread among thoughtful young architects in the 1970s. Holding fast to a belief in the continuing efficacy of form, they declared themselves very early to be primarily concerned with the importance of making concrete proposals for buildings to be built. At the same time, they also resisted the more popular modalities of so-called "postmodernism" . . . especially its consumerist North American version.

Which is not to say these are ivory tower theorists. When a Texas firm, Sonic, a national drive-in fast-food chain, reached all the way up to Boston in 1995 to hire Machado & Silvetti and the corporate identity company Lippincott & Margulies to create a replacement prototype for their tired roadside image, the "involvement of such a highbrow architect in the conception of a fast-food outlet" startled Architecture magazine more than it did Machado, who retorted, "Corporate identity consultants and graphic designers . . . deal more directly than most architects with the cultural readings, allusions, and analogies possible with a specific visual language. We think that architectural invention results not from the development of a universal architectural language (like late Mies) but from the way a language is deployed (like Eero Saarinen)."

Expressive of this firm's philosophy of design and aspiration is their conversion of a nondescript 1920s Cambridgeport warehouse (Figure 297) into offices with a top-story residence and roof garden. By regularizing the fenestration and running a pair of top-floor windows together behind a new steel balcony, painting the exterior brick walls a steely gray with a pale yellow accent on the vertical plane of the balcony, and, finally, by adding a concrete stair, steel columns, and roof canopy with a glass vestibule behind, Machado & Silvetti have transformed this prosaic building into a work of such exquisite line and finesse that one can only call it Industrial High Style. It is a superb example of what Machado means when he declares:

Invention is extremely personal, and comes from wherever you can get it. For me it comes from movies and theater, fashion design, and especially the design of objects — industrial design. The key notion is transformation. There are forms that one puts together, transforms, and manipulates. It's tricky when you say there is nothing new, but the extreme transformation of known sources can yield a new product. In our case, the use of form is very conscious, rather than subconscious.

The Sydney Street building, so very reminiscent of Gropius and Meyer's early-twentieth-century industrial sensibility, is yet another indication of the strength of the revival of this aesthetic. But the work of Machado & Silvetti particularly can help us to understand that much more than a revival, in the conventional terms of architectural history, is involved in the work of all the New Moderns, for there is a key difference to take note of here between their work and their inspiration, even insofar as it is recognizably derived from the modes of International Style Modernism up through the 1960s. International Style Modernism argued for a fundamental change in the time-honored definition of architecture laid down by Vitruvius in ancient times, according to which the architect must strive, to use Leland Roth's words (which are clearest), for utility, firmness, and beauty. The Modernist argued that in a truly Modern architecture utility

FIGURE 297. Machado & Silvetti, Sydney Street Building, Cambridge, 1988. Only these architects could endow a remodeled warehouse with such elegance of line.

and firmness virtually equaled beauty. Period.

New Moderns would disagree. To be sure, they would say the plan yields the section, and both the elevation — in general. They are also open to the basic Modernist premise that, generally speaking, form ought to proceed from function (a proposition, after all, eclectics and gothicists of the 1900s like Ralph Adams Cram and Bertram Grosvenor Goodhue also asserted, Modernist polemics to the contrary). New Moderns are also respectful (again in a general way) of Modernist ideas of constructional honesty. But they would *not* argue that utility and firmness at all equal beauty. Not only have they observed, like everyone else, that the premise is faulty, but the architects I've called New Moderns here — Machado & Silvetti above all — would argue that in the twenty-first century, unlike in most previous eras and certainly in Vitruvius's, architects now have at hand a diverse and richly layered historical range of design languages, including that of the Modern Movement itself and its International Style. And being literate in that design history — which is to say, knowing when and how to bring this design history to bear in modern design — is vital. Indeed, they would argue that utility, firmness, and beauty are hardly possible any longer without literacy in all the historical design languages. (Machado and Silvetti, for example, cite three chief influences on their work: "the residential work of Le Corbusier, the thinking of Aldo Rossi, and especially the oeuvre of Palladio.")

This is, of course, where New Moderns part company from Post-Modernists and their heirs, the New Historicists and the like. From the point of view of the New Modern, Post-Modernism was the illiterate groping of architects ill trained in architectural history (poor Gropius gets it from all sides) who, perhaps, sensed a need, but a need they could not fill. Incited by corporate America's exaltation of commercialism, and not knowing how to bring to bear the wide range of historical design languages on new work, Po-Mo designers created instead a sort of cartoonish mimicry of "historic" form, at worst an illiterate pastiche, not to say kitsch. (Nor is any of this surprising. As Cram used to say of Modernists, the skill to tear down and liberate is different from the skill to revitalize and rebuild.) We owe a certain debt to Post-Modernists for liberating us from the International Style. But it will be the New Moderns who will rebuild.

Machado and Silvetti know this. As early as 1977 they declared that "the designer finds the whole past of architecture [Modern Movement included] as material to interpret, to reflect upon, to respond to and use." Especially was this called for, Machado thought, in the land of their adoption, given "the peculiarities of [American architecture's] history . . . [which] evolved as the product of constant transformation and reinterpretation of European models, which, when removed from their original contexts, acquired distinctly different meanings. . . . This process . . . ," he continues, "seems to be American architecture's main asset."

It was an extraordinary concession, after all from a Modernist — an olive branch to the much-maligned eclectics of the late nineteenth and early twentieth centuries. And it was a concession that pointed to the future he hoped for, a future mapped by Silvetti in 1980 in an essay entitled "Realism in Architecture":

Are we then to interpret the Modern Movement as a parenthesis in the history of architecture . . . with the aspiration of seeing a continuity with the various traditions, be they classical, local, vernacular, etc.? I simply believe we cannot. . . . The attempt to reinstate an orthodox verisimilitude [is] not the result of a restored "continuity." Indeed, [it is] the result, as Colin Rowe says, of "the lapse of consciousness" and "the end of innocence." In my view, this indicates a profound ideological mutation that is indeed new in the history of architecture. For the first

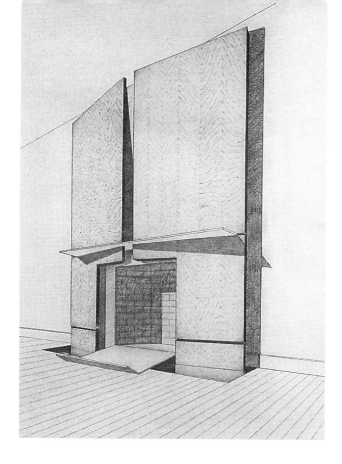

FIGURE 298. Machado & Silvetti, design for a Marlborough Street mantlepiece, Back Bay, 1988. Always there is strong form, ever so deftly tweaked.

time the architect chooses "history" as a whole, as an alternative. History, as the repository of forms has been separated from the continuum of time by that rebel, the Modern Movement, and as such it affords the designer a distance that never before existed. Before modern architecture, the use of history was not a problem to be discussed, it was the way architecture operated. . . . History had never been consciously "used," but naturally assumed. That detachment has been produced by modern architecture, and things will never be the same. . . . Architecture [has now] a consciousness of itself and of its cultural origins that did not exist before.

I am reminded of Cram's never widely understood view that "modern" Gothic could not but be very different — very detached, even — from medieval Gothic because, whether one liked it or not, the Renaissance had intervened.

This deep perspective, if I may call it so, empowers Machado and Silvetti's own architectural transformations, that and their determination that "technical veracity and proficient detailing should be present in the design in order to demonstrate that the dream that has been dreamt can be made tangible and 'true.'" Consider, for instance, their series of three Boston residential works: two remodelings in the Back Bay and an entirely new residence outside the city in Concord.

Both remodelings are on Marlborough Street. The first, Machado and Silvetti's own home of nearly twenty years, is one of a row of eight red-brick Victorian speculator-built town houses of robust design, erected in 1885. Attractive because of its spaciousness, the house as originally planned annoyed, however, because of the odd proportions of those spaces. Behold Machado and Silvetti's classical side. While the very sober interior finishes of the original house were nowhere enhanced the basic proportions of the rooms were attacked ruthlessly, for these two men are also designers of insistent conviction. As Oscar Riera Ojeda records, in order "to correct their predecessor's oversight[s] they extended the curve of the bay window on the top floor. . . . A small third floor bedroom was removed . . . [and on] the second floor the music room was reconfigured (made symmetrical), while at the entry level the library and the back terrace were also corrected."

This is not to say they invariably scant finish. Where that addresses the design problem they have created interiors that can only be described as gorgeous; one of which is a duplex condominium nearby their house on Marlborough Street (Figure 298), where they created a sumptuous yet disciplined series of interiors, Machado explains:

The design concentrated on materials, finishes, and details as a means to establish the character of the project, choosing a palette of materials with striking and unique natural qualities — strong, deep color and pattern in the wood paneling and stone; texture and opaqueness in the glass. The interventions were treated as veneers, panels or planes, which were applied to, or set within, the existing rooms. Visually stronger and richer materials were used on the vertical surfaces, such as the walls and cabinet faces (lacewood, satinwood, pomelle mahogany; gray/green travertine) and contrasted with more neutral materials (black granite and plain maple) on the horizontal surfaces, such as the floors, countertops, establishing a contrast between the two surfaces.

The new house, the third example, in Concord, was in 1992 their first completely realized purpose-built work in Boston. And it disclosed very well the nature of the distinctions Machado and Silvetti make between Classicism and Modernism and the methods of their fusion of them as well. Machado again:

The geometric underpinnings, the grids, the symmetries, the rhythms and hierarchies, the orthogonal precision and the regulated collisions are unmistakably of classical origin. This inherited compositional baggage we treasure, and find very practical. . . . On the other hand, for those knowing our work, it should be clear that a certain theatricality, the emphasis on the production of effects, shifting scales, . . . all that comes from the use of perspectival techniques, which are very useful for the generation of character.

At the Concord house this takes the form of "a carefully choreographed sequence of spaces that proceeds," in Karen Stein's words, "from outside to inside to outside, elongating and foreshortening views like a shifting camera lens," a wonderfully kinetic, very modern image.

The crisp, *L*-shaped volume of the house is for me most winningly presented on the court side (Figure 299), where, above a ground story of slate of three variations of gray and blue superbly patterned and laid up without visible mortar joints, there rises an upper story of red-cedar shingles, the whole façade nobly ordered, and with many subtle touches: it may be hard to see the four-inch flare of the courtyard façade at the roof line to conceal the gutters, but notice the way the plane of one panel of the ground-story slate wall to the left of the front door inclines inward toward it.

It is all very New England — the stone walls, the wood shingles, the double-hung windows — but it is also, as the designers would say, "unprecedented." (Their major book is entitled *Unprecedented Realism*.) There is, of course, a theory; there always is with these architects. They call it "'resemantization,' a process of giving old forms fresh meaning by placing them in new contexts." It is the technique, so to speak, of their transformations.

Similarly, the mass of the very classical house is engaged — indeed penetrated — by three quite picturesque, even gothic, ancillary volumes: a salon, itself a rectangle, but which penetrates the main volume diagonally (so as to command an exterior

383

FIGURE 299. Machado & Silvetti, house at Concord, 1992-94. The courtyard façades.

view), and a breakfast room and screened-in porch, both of which engage the main volume more conventionally, but are in each case trapezoidal. All three, of course, are examples of the theatrical "effects [and] shifting scales" in the architects' work just referred to.

Indeed, of just this house Machado has written:

Perspectival considerations determine the relationships between the . . . volumes. . . . From the entrance hall the salon is seen in a two-point *"theatrical perspective."* . . . From the kitchen, the breakfast room is seen in forced perspective, the elongation rhetorically emphasizing the view of the pond beyond. From the conservatory, the porch is seen in a compressed, foreshortened perspective, the compression of the space brings "into it" the grass meadow.

The staircase (Figure 300) is particularly notable: was ever a "trophy house" endowed with grander? Chaste, yet the-atrical; very simple; very sensuous (notice the graceful garlands of one balustrade, not repeated on the other).

The work of these men is always subtle, and worth second, third, and, indeed, repeated glances, always rewarding the viewer. A signal achievement for me, for example, is the way the architects invariably try to achieve their effects without misleading the eye. There is a difference between a liar and a fabulist, and a master may get away with much. But to mislead risks being at best condescending and perhaps even insulting. An architect, who expresses ideas visually, must be as rigorous as the writer who expresses them verbally; and the architect will be no more edifying if the various elements of his or her design are not what they seem to be, or do not do what they are made to look like they do, than will the writer whose words are obscure or don't mean what they seem to mean. Of course, writers like that are

FIGURE 300. Interior of the Concord house. Notice the design of the mantlepiece, the contrasting detailing of the staircase balustrades, and the way the salon as a whole engages the main volume of the house diagonally.

FIGURE 301. A veneer brick wall can be detailed so as not to dupe the beholder into thinking it structural and, indeed, to enhance the beholder's pleasure. Such is the message of this steel and brick arch over a window opening in a building designed by Machado & Silvetti.

hardly unknown; but not the best writers — nor the best architects.

Not everyone would agree with me. For example, in Wagner Park, at the southern tip of Battery Park City in Manhattan, overlooking the Statue of Liberty, two powerful viewing pavilions of Machado & Silvetti's design (open-air viewing decks above, interior restaurant and rest room facilities below) are of brick-clad poured concrete, topped with great free-form arches. These arches, which could hardly be built only of brick anyway, are of brick infill set into steel in a free-floating system that enables movement, and the brick cladding — lovely, dark red Roman brick — is shown to be infill by being framed by visible steel rims and divided into discernible panels within the arches by equally visible steel radials.

Yet Clifford Pearson has actually complained that "the thin metal frame around one of the brick arches gives the joke away . . . . After expending so much effort creating the illusion of mass, why undermine it with a sly architectural wink? Do we really want the magician to tell us how he does his tricks?" What "tricks"? What "illusion of mass" is that? How sad. The sort of attitude of mind that finds in architecture

jokes not to be given away or illusions not to be undermined, would, perhaps, in the literary realm, have a taste for "spinning," as political-speak is sometimes called, if not for outright propaganda.

How important this matter of constructional honesty can be becomes clear if one considers, for example, these terms of praise for Louis Kahn by Carter Wiseman: the architect "made a connection with the viewer, who instinctively relates to the process of construction. . . . Kahn showed a kinship with Mies, and even [Louis] Sullivan, both of whom had expanded their definitions of functionalism to include the appetite of the viewer for visual pleasure."

Pleasure, of course is the key. Moralistic preaching about anything, including constructional honesty (pace, Ruskinians) is perhaps even more harmful — certainly more boring — than constructional deception of any sort. That is why the best architects — remember Kallmann and McKinnell's "floating" lintels and Leers, Weizapfel's tight granite skin — are rigorous about the principle but not heavy-handed about its explication. Least of all are Machado & Silvetti, who are, in fact, never anxious about such things. Rather, they celebrate constructional honesty, usually hitting upon the most elegant way the nature of the building's materials and its structure can be most logically and beautifully expressed.

At Princeton, for instance, in one of their finest works, the Engineering Quadrangle Parking Structure of 1991, they set themselves the task of designing a building the appearance of which would disclose not only that it was a garage, but a garage in sympathy with historic Princeton. They extended an adjacent brick garden wall of 1911 by McKim, Mead and White so as to enclose and frame the lower level of their new garage. Then, wrapping the upper levels, they created a remarkable structure, which Diane Ghirardo well describes in her book, *Architecture after Modernism*:

Along the garden side a steel screen is to become an ivy-covered trellis, while along the other three sides the architects arranged a bronze double lattice screen . . . [which] curves at the top into a projecting cornice. With these three deceptively simple design solutions — lattice screen, masonry wall and trellis — the parking structure acquired an austere elegance in keeping with its context. At the same time it challenged recent additions to the campus that fail to match its understated grandeur.

Bronze, no less, on a garage. Yet in their own description of the work, Machado & Silvetti, while making it clear that "the inclusion of this noble material and the articulation of the [screen's] design — its cornice, its supports . . ." was, of course, quite deliberate, do not even mention (nor does Ghirardo) a more subtle but to me very telling aspect of the work that Philip Arcidi did notice: "At close range to the garage, you can see steel lintels and imposts, cues that the [brick] arches are not load bearing. The brick base [of the garage, the extension of the historic garden wall] is a cavity structure, a rhetorical counterpart to the 1911 wall."

The accompanying photograph (Figure 301) illustrates how beautifully this was done. The brick work flares upward above the opening as would a traditional load-bearing architectural in a structural brick wall. But that this is brick infill, entirely "rhetorical," is expressed by its being contained in and framed by a steel I-beam, the bottom flange of which arches up to support the brick arch at each flank. Where in a structural wall there would be impost blocks, Machado & Silvetti have left voids that frankly disclose the galvanized steel I-beam — and with what elegance: the shape of the voids being that of a traditional impost, the effect is at once structural and decorative–almost as if one were looking at a Mannerist (because it is recessed and manifestly "unstructural") impost block of galvanized steel. Meanwhile, the large grilled window opening itself discloses matter of factly the structural system of the garage behind the lower brick wall and the metal screens above it. The little business of the infill brick and the recessed steel "imposts" hardly calls attention to itself at all in the overall form of this great work. But the little business is truly a tour de force all the more telling for its reticence.

Machado & Silvetti's design — which in its initial conceptual stage is by the admission of both men very private and very contentious — is, however, at its core, always supremely about form, form so strong it easily accommodates a certain elegance. Their Allston Library, for example, with its butterfly roof: not everyone could sing so lyrical a song so boldly, nor fuse so deftly past and present (Figure 302).

In this Machado & Silvetti, though very cosmopolitan, even global, architects, show themselves to be truly Bostonian, any ill-considered generalizations about Boston notwithstanding. One of the few critics who has seen the truth of the matter is Paul Goldberger: "In Boston," he has noticed, unusually, "the impulse toward architectural innovation, which has always been strong, exists in a kind of balance with the moral presence of history — a balance more profound, surely, than in any other city in the United States."

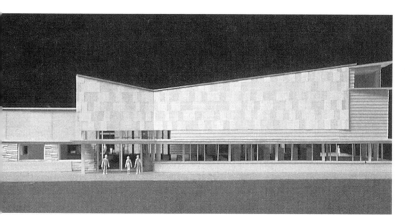

FIGURE 302. Machado & Silvetti's Allston branch of the Boston Public Library, one of two sparkling new designs for city branches under way in 2000.

FIGURE 303. Schwartz/Silver's Hyde Park Library addition in its clarity and elegance is comparable to Stahl's Park Street Church addition of 1974.

T WENTY years ago I ended *Built in Boston* rather confidently with Ada Louise Huxtable's observations about history and the uses of architectural preservation. In 2000 it is a very different message of hers — from her *Unreal America* of 1997 — that I find most arresting, a message this time about the *abuses* of history:

It would be nice to say that the airhead aesthetic that postmodernism encouraged has passed . . . its fate . . . to become the style of choice for shopping centers and for slip-covering skyscrapers. . . . [But] as the expression of a residential vernacular [it] seems here to stay, . . . equal parts of nostalgia, superficiality and calculated guile. [Yet] it is safe to say that [anyone] coming out of architectural school now is [doing work] firmly rooted in modernism; . . . a modernism carried further and significantly transformed. . . . An era of unrestricted exploration has followed modernism's rigid limits and post-modernism's partying with the past.

What these architects are doing, in a sense, is reinventing architecture. . . .

Not in Boston, however, if some of our old fogies — or young fogies — have anything to do with it. So wary, actually, are so many Bostonians of their architects and their works these days (incredible exceptions, actually commissioned and erected by the core city government, are the Allston branch library and the addition to the old Hyde Park branch libraries [Figures 302, 303]) that more than one designer whose work is discussed in this chapter has allowed that too often it is much more interesting to be a Boston architect at, say, Princeton, than in Boston (I have in mind design architects, not service architects), so stultifying have things become at home. Indeed, Elizabeth Padjen, a Boston architect, editor, and critic has actually complained in print about "an

388

FIGURE 304. Gary Edward Handel (Blake Middleton and David Nagahiro, designers): Boylston Place, 1999. As elegant and urbane a gesture as Boston has seen since the Hancock tower.

unnatural fixation with the past" in Boston's architecture today. I myself sometimes think the only hope of eradicating this pathology (which ranges from "Reproduction Gothic" to "Victorian Style town houses) is for all architects just simply to refuse to design anything in Boston in red brick for at least a decade.

A case in point: Boylston Place (Figure 304), the proposed millennium project at Massachusetts Avenue and Boylston Street in the Back Bay. George Thrush, head of architecture at Northeastern University, a gifted architect and town planner and above all, a lover of urban life dedicated to battling what he aptly calls the "creeping suburbanization" of core Boston by people who don't understand that cities *thrive* on congestion, has argued that the Boylston Place tower will "offer an excellent terminal view looking west on Boylston (from Copley Square) and mark a grand entry to

the city. This kind of judicious use of slender towers as markers for different districts in Boston," Thrush continues, "could serve as a model for future development in other parts of town." Yet how many share his vision (or have his eye)? Awesomely poised and adroitly proportioned, as elegantly urbane an architectural gesture as Boston has seen in years, the Boylston Place tower, the design of Blake Middleton and David Nagahiro of Gary Edward Handel of New York, is also highly contextual. But its contextualism is cheerfully cast in the language, not of historicism, but of modernism, so it is controversial.

Indeed, it brings to mind just those teachings, alluded to previously here, of Walter Muir Whitehill, the preeminent twentieth-century authority on the historic architecture of Boston: one carefully sited tall tower (Whitehill was referring to the Hancock tower), he always insisted, would

389

always be preferable to any number of squat thirty-story buildings. It is a truth too often ignored. Thus it is that the naysayers about Boylston Place, a likely aesthetic triumph, have otherwise been asleep while several other Back Bay towers have gone forward unopposed — towers short enough for those opposed to Boylston Place — but towers that are *disasters* for the Back Bay, not because of their density or height, but because of their ghastly design. Does not the most cursory glance at Copley Square document conclusively that whereas the (exceedingly tall) Hancock Tower is a splendid landmark worthy to keep company with the square's older masterpieces, it is the (very low rise) office buildings on the Boylston Street corners of Clarendon and Dartmouth Streets that have most despoiled the square over the years. Similarly, Trinity Place, the medium-rise condo-tower just now being built between Copley Place and the Boston Public Library as this book goes to press, trashes the library in a way the Hancock Tower never has Trinity Church.

Worst of all is the virulent schlock architecture projected for 111 Huntington Avenue at the Prudential Center, which will make it virtually impossible for any person of taste to enjoy the magnificent, austere serenities of the Christian Science Center unless walking *away* from Prudential. Of course not only architects are to blame. The developers (in the case of Trinity Place and 111 Huntington Avenue the Raymond Property Company and media mogul Mortimer Zuckerman's Boston Properties) deserve their share of the blame. Ditto Boston's design review board. But there were architects, after all, and their responsibility is primary: CBT/Childs, Bertman, Tseckares in both cases, a firm whose work has been praised here, but whose large-scale commercial projects are proving to be as harmful to Boston as their work in adaptive re-use was originally beneficial.

Nor is it a coincidence that CBT arrived

at their Po-Mo skyscraper mode for new work via what has become more and more a kind of "Preservation Style" arising out of adaptive re-use — preservation having become increasingly code for anti-Modernist, a fundamentally Po-Mo stance. Others (Goody, Clancy and Associates, for example) have done the opposite: from a starting point in the world of the Po-Mo skyscraper mode they have extrapolated its habits of mind into an adaptive re-use on smaller scale but with a very similar aesthetic. The results, whether a new building in "retro-tecture" by CBT or an old building "revivified" by Goody, Clancy are very similar in effect and deeply problematic. One sees this especially in McKim, Mead and White's Harvard Union, remodeled (skillfully, I admit) by Goody, Clancy, which stands across the street from the Inn at Harvard, a hotel designed by Graham Gund. To study the exteriors of the Union and the Inn (though it is perhaps unfair to compare Gund with McKim) is to see at a glance the difference between Georgian Revival blood and muscle in the hands of a master and what Ralph Adams Cram used to call the "scenic mimicry of historic form," for the Post-Modernist Inn is little more than a postcard of a building by comparison. But the more telling contrast for us here is that between the newly configured spaces made out of the Union's Great Hall with the Inn's interior atrium. Although the Union's new spaces are better done (Goody, Clancy had, of course, more to work with because of McKim's interiors) in both cases there is the sense that the only place the train to Boston ever stops in is Williamsburg of Disneyland!

Now preservation, both restoration and adaptive re-use, has a legitimate role in architecture. And recent triumphs abound in Boston's orbit. Witness Rockwell Kent's gorgeous ceiling mural of 1927–30 at the old Cape Cinema in Dennis, and the magnificent tower of Harvard's Memorial Hall, both of which have lately been gloriously restored; in the case of Memorial Hall, I must add, more typical than the Union fiasco of Harvard architecture in the era of President Neil Rudenstine, as well as a case of CBT's doing very well what it does best. Similarly, an example of successful adaptive re-use rather than pure restoration is the Reed Block nearby in Harvard Square. Unlike the case of the Union, the Reed block hardly warranted preservation in the first place — on any other ground, that is, than the highly suspect end-justifies-the-means one that a corporate client erecting a new building was unlikely to hire a good modern architect and more apt instead to force a red-brick "contextual" monster on Harvard Square of the sort that abounds in Brattle Square. And perhaps just because it was never any sort of masterpiece, the Reed Block was far more boldly handled by its adaptive re-use architects, Symmes, Maine and McKee, than the Harvard Union. Very neo-Modernist exposed steel framed entrances were added both to the block itself on John F. Kennedy Street and at its other access from Dunster Street. Yet though the original work at the Reed Block was not of high quality, as it was at the Union, the new work at the Reed Block is! Strikingly different stylistically from the old, it has the effect of enhancing that old work, not dumbing it down with mimicry, setting up sophisticated and thoughtful oppositions of form and material quite different from the ostensibly more respectful but really quite banal new work at the Union, which, though skillfully done, is still nowhere near as stimulating as the Reed Block work. The splendid hall of the Union is haunted not only by what it was, but also by what it could have been; the mediocre Reed Block exterior, on the other hand, is triumphantly more now than it ever was before.

The reason is not hard to find: the Cambridge Historical Commission, as directed by Charles Sullivan, is a very sophisticated operation, and for that reason I do not worry either about another

Harvard Square building surely soon to be remodeled —Longfellow Court —a rare example, I have concluded, of pre–World War I American Modernist architecture clearly related to the work of a contemporaneous avant-garde European master. Located at 1280 Massachusetts Avenue, Longfellow Court is felt most keenly where it backs onto Arrow Street opposite St. Paul's Church at Bow Street, endowing that picturesque intersection with a wonderfully urbane and astringent Old World character, a character that suggests strongly that whoever the architects of record (the Sanitary Engineering Construction Company) engaged in 1916 to design Longfellow Court was clearly aware of Adolf Loos's famous building of five years earlier in Vienna, the Looshaus of 1912. In its striking monolithic volume, utterly unornamented except for just the same sort of strongly jutting cornice of horizontal planes Loos used on the Vienna building, the Cambridge building shows exactly the geometrical purity for which Loos's work is so much esteemed, a purity that could hardly survive the Po-Mo/Preservation style treatment in whatever remodeling is necessary.

A harder test will come with Beacon Hill's Amory-Tichnor House opposite the State House on the corner of Beacon and Park Streets. Harder because the alterations of one hundred years or so ago to this Bulfinch-designed building of some two hundred years ago are now as valuable as the original design of the house. These alterations, high-style Queen Anne and Arts and Crafts ornamental bays, shop fronts, and ironwork, were, I suspect, designed by Arthur Little, and are perhaps related to the fact that in the nineteen hundreds the Society of Arts and Crafts operated a gallery at 9 Park Street. These charming alterations have endowed this Federal house with a layered, historical picturesqueness that is certainly unique — and just because these additions in their own era reflected very much the sort of

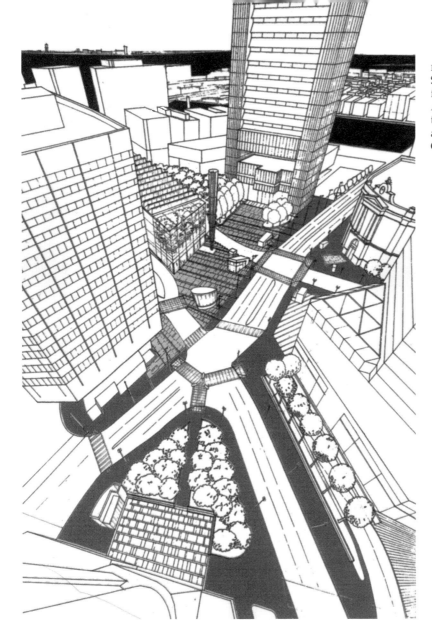

FIGURE 305. Machado &
Silvetti, proposed design
for Dewey Square, 1999.
A promising start on knit-
ting the city together
again over the suppressed
Central Artery.

adaptive re-use design concept, not of the
Harvard Union, but of the Reed Block,
which is to say high style contemporary
design, thoughtfully fused to the original
historic fabric.

And it is just that point of view that one
hopes will also imbue the design of the
blocks of entirely new buildings that must
knit downtown back together over the
soon-to-be-finally-suppressed Central
Artery through Boston's waterfront. All
that can be said now is that Machado &

Silvetti have given a superb lead in their
projected designs for Dewey Square
(Figure 305).

Many such challenges face Boston in the
twenty-first century insofar as entirely
new design is concerned. Consider the
new Seaport District. The new convention
center by Rafael Viñoly (Figure 306) is a
good sign. And Harry Cobb's Federal
Courthouse, though certainly not the
Sydney Opera House, will seem much less
of a monster as blocks are built up around

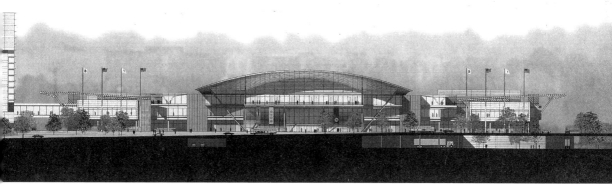

FIGURE 306. HNTB/Rafael Viñoly, Boston Convention and Exhibition Center, schematic design, 1999.

it. Yet where is the bright vision one might have hoped for here? The architect of the glowing translucent landmarks of the Kursaal Cultural Center overlooking the water at St. Sebastian in Spain, Rafael Moneo, was for a decade head of architecture at Harvard. Why is his striking waterfront ensemble not in Boston? One can only hope that Schwartz/Silver's scintillating design for a harborfront Institute of Contemporary Art will survive to give some vitality to the Seaport District. And that it is not, perhaps, too late to heed Michael McKinnell's warning in *Architecture/Boston*:

I think about the contribution that the architectural community could make [to the Seaport]. . . . And I can absolutely predict that were I or anybody else to produce such a vi-sionary plan, it would be completely nixed by all the people who want something rather homey and comfortable and picturesque. I think that's the real missed opportunity here. . . . The really important thing here is to produce a fantastic vision for the waterfront and let the rest follow — and the rest would follow if it was fantastic.

But, of course, it is *not* very likely.

For one thing, and it may be the most important thing, the Boston media makes nothing like the effort to educate the eye of Bostonians to its architecture and public art that it does to educate their ear to

music, for example. Although the newspaper of record no longer runs architectural reviews on the real estate page, it nonetheless completely ignores, for instance, the work of Machado & Silvetti, Boston's foremost architects today. Nor does the leading firm of younger architects, Thompson and Rose, fare any better. Only a few journalists — Martin Nolan is one — have much worthwhile to say on the subject of architecture. Mainstream media also invariably favor the more conservative corporate-oriented service firms (draftspeople still in white shirts and dark ties, if you can believe it) and pay scant attention to the cutting edge design firms (jeans there, of course). Nor do radio and television make any contribution at all, with the conspicuous and distinguished exception of "The Connection," Christopher Lydon's Emersonian talk show on NPR. The alternative press? I have to be careful here, being myself a refugee architecture critic from that realm, of which I once had high hopes only too recently dashed. But even the most arts-oriented of the alternative papers has forsworn independent architectural criticism for stories about proposed architecture in Boston which totally ignore historical and design issues and settle instead for the old formulaic business of pro and con: the former usually by way of Some Important Bureaucrat at City Hall, the latter courtesy of The Loudest Mouth to Be Found in some

FIGURE 307. Machado & Silvetti, graduate student housing, Harvard University, Allston, 2000. Schematic study from Charles River of court and tower façades.

FIGURE 308. Schematic study from within the court looking across the river to José luis Sert's towers on the Cambridge bank.

self-appointed neighborhood protest group. It's pretty much a hopeless vacuum in which dedicated architects and planners get very little worthwhile response. Is it any wonder so few aspects of the plans for the Seaport encourage? And that McKinnell's vision is so unlikely to be realized?

Yet Boston's New Moderns are, I believe, going to have more and more effect — if only because notable form-givers, wherever from, are now well poised at the start of the twenty-first century to make a difference in Boston and give a lead. Frank Gehry's Stata Center at M.I.T., Stephen Holl's work on the same campus, Sir (now Lord) Norman Foster's much anticipated additions to the Museum of Fine Arts — one or more or all will surely stimulate architecture in Boston as form-givers always do — and as once the Saarinens, Gropius, Sert, Aalto, Rudolph, Belluschi, and Kallmann and McKinnell did in the 1960's.

Best of all, I think, are the possibilities along the Charles River at Harvard, where that university has projected a most exciting architectural scenario to either side of the Western Avenue Bridge. For the Allston side graduate student housing by Machado & Silvetti has already reached the stage of completed conceptual studies (Figures 307, 308). Theirs is a formidable and wonderful design, bold, bravely and powerfully conceived, gracefully sited, a respectful but confident rejoinder to Sert's landmark towers of the sixties and the famous Coolidge courts of the riverfront ranges along the opposite Cambridge bank. Let us hope Renzo Piano's commission to design next to Sert's towers a new Harvard Museum of Modern Art will soon be realized—achieving at last for Boston the dream Lincoln Kirstien and his cohort could only accomplish in New York in the 1930s — Boston's conservatism again! If Piano's design goes forward (Figure 309) — was ever line so elegant? — it may be that it will fall to Piano and Machado & Silvetti — a stellar grouping — to make that first great leap of the imagination we are so ready for in the old Puritan capital in these first decades of the new millennium on the eve of Boston's fifth century.

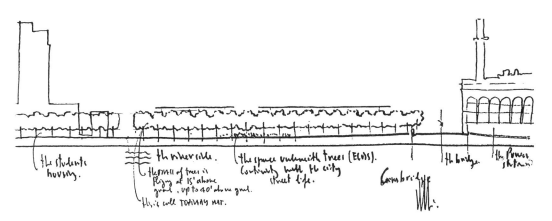

FIGURE 309. Renzo Piano, study sketch for proposed Harvard Museum of Modern Art on the banks of the Charles River, 1999.

ACKNOWLEDGMENTS, 2000

FIRST THANKS MUST go to Bruce Wilcox at the University of Massachusetts Press for the idea of this edition, which has proved to be quite a fructifying life experience. Second: Warren Schwartz, who pointed me in all the right directions — most notably toward Rodolfo Machado, Jorge Silvetti, Peter Forbes (through Paul Robertson), Gerhard Kallmann, an old acquaintance from Eliot House at Harvard with whom it was a great pleasure to become friendly again, Andrea Leers, Jane Weinzapfel, and William Rawn III, who like Warren (introduced to me years ago by William Buckingham) was yet another old acquaintance. Add Nader Tehrani and Mónica Ponce de Leôn, Michael McKinnell, Ann Beha, Alex Krieger, F. A. Stahl, Bruce Brooks Pfeiffer, Robert Silver, Mark Pasnik, Naomi Miller, Jean Paul Carlhian, Roger Webb, William Osgood, and Maryann Thompson, Brian Healy, and Robert Mikios and the heady company I've been keeping will be clear. None of these people has given me less than a very long interview, and most have given me far more.

Intellectual excitements do not suffice, however, and for the logistical support without which no book, I must thank, above all, the woman (anonymous by her wish), who does all my word processing, and Ella Kusnetz, the indefatigable editor at the University of Massachusetts Press. Then there is Susan Lewis of the Boston Architectural Center and Mary Daniels of Harvard's Loeb Library at the Design School, both of whom graciously make me free of both libraries, and Kimberly Shilland at the M.I.T. Museum, to whom I am also indebted for many kindnesses.

Other helpmates who stand out are George Dowd at the John Hancock Life Insurance Company, who came to our rescue in the matter of the cover illustration, Bridgit Carr at the Boston Symphony Orchestra Archives, Jane Thompson of the Thompson Design Group, Charles Daly at the Kennedy Library, Jacqueline Thomas at Phillips Exeter Academy, T. Kinney Frelinghuysen at the Frelinghuysen-Morris Foundation, Nick DeBrule of Schwartz/Silver, and the archival staffs at Hugh Stubbins Associates, Pei, Cobb, Freed and Partners, the Davis Museum at Wellesley, and Charles Gwathmey Associates.

I am in particularly indebted to Christopher Lydon for arranging for me to have a quiet hour with Frank Gehry in Cambridge before his Harvard lecture, to Harvard's President Neil Rudenstine for sharing with me his vision of Harvard's architecture in the future, and to H. A. Crosby Forbes for setting up the first of two very useful lunches with James Cuno, director of Harvard's museums.

Acknowledgments that must be carried over from the first edition are Theresa Cederholm, Richard Cheek, Ronald Havern, Robert Bell Rettig, Cynthia Zaitzevsky, Margaret Henderson Floyd, and Wheaton Holden.

Of Geraldine Groves Tucci and F. W. Atherton I have written elsewhere.

D.S—T., 1999

Acknowledgments, 1978

S EVERAL FRIENDS and colleagues have helped in the preparation of this book in a variety of ways: particularly Wheaton Holden, with whom I talked about both the Shingle Style and the Chicago School; Robert Bell Rettig, who has continued to encourage my interest in multifamily housing; Cynthia Zaitzevsky, whose tour of those parts of Jamaica Plain she judged comparable to Dorchester proved of great benefit; and Leland Roth, who discussed with me his work on Charles Follen McKim and first prompted my reflection that McKim and Ralph Adams Cram were two sides of the same coin. The late Walter Muir Whitehill acted as my reader.

I am also indebted to a number of people for a wide miscellany of kindnesses: Mr. and Mrs. Laurence Etter; William N. McCarthy; Lawrence G. Driscoll; William Smith; Mrs. Nicholas Hume; Walter Carney; Frederic Detweiller; John T. Doran; Eugene Kennedy; and John B. Carney. Florence Connolly, Curator of Fine Arts of the Boston Public Library, and Theresa Cederholm of the same department both helped in a multitude of ways, as did Thomas Parker, Director of the Bostonian Society, Rodney Armstrong, Director of the Boston Athenaeum, Heath Aldridge of the Brookline Planning Department, Victoria L. DiStefano of the Cambridge Historical Commission, Deborah A. Gribbon of the Gardner Museum, and Donald Tirabassi of the Colonial Theatre. So also did my typists, Doris Haskell and Mary Nadler.

The staffs of many institutions were also helpful, including those of the Boston Athenaeum; the Bostonian Society; the President's Office at Boston University; the State Street Bank and Trust Company; St. John's Seminary; the Library of the Society for the Preservation of New England Antiquities; the *Boston Herald-American;* and the Boston Building Department and those of Brookline and Newton particularly.

Many of the photographs and drawings were prepared especially for this book. Ron Havern and Leslie Larson, two good friends who are also excellent photographers have greatly enlivened it visually. The value of John Tankard's drawings and Ann Lampton Curtis's maps is self-evident. Jonathan Goell's photographs are, as always, distinguished. I am also grateful to Richard Cheek, whose work I have long admired, for allowing me to reproduce several of his photographs.

Finally, there are those people without whom there would have been either no book or at least a much poorer book — the staff of the New York Graphic Society and Little, Brown and Company. My editor, Robin Bledsoe, whose idea this book was, has been more than painstaking; she has been unfailingly stimulating throughout its preparation. I am also grateful to Tim Hill, Editor-in-Chief of New York Graphic Society, and to Betsy Pitha of Little, Brown's copyediting department for her always careful perusal of both manuscript and galleys. The designer, Barbara Bell Pitnof, has endowed the book with a considerable distinction.

All these good people have made the writing of this book a positive pleasure. My only comparable debt is to my mother, Geraldine Groves Tucci, who typed and proofread the first handwritten drafts, which no one else could have understood.

BIBLIOGRAPHY
FOR PARTS I AND II

THIS BIBLIOGRAPHY consists primarily of sources consulted and quoted from in the preparation of this study. It has been broken down into the following several sections so as to make it easier for the reader to find the principal sources for particular areas, buildings, building types, or architects discussed in the text.

A. Boston: Metropolitan, City, and Boston Proper
B. Cities and Towns of Metropolitan Boston (including those annexed)
C. Sections of Boston Proper
D. Individual Buildings throughout Metropolitan Boston
E. Building Types
F. Architects Who Worked in Boston
G. Boston Artists and Craftsmen and Architectural Art
H. General Sources and Suggested Further Reading

The following abbreviations and short titles are used in the bibliography and picture credits:

AABN	*American Architect and Building News* (so titled from 1876 to 1908; thereafter, until it ceased publication in 1938, known under various titles: 1909–1921, *American Architect*; 1921–1924, *American Architect and Architectural Review*; 1925–1936, *The American Architect*; 1936–1938, *American Architect and Architecture*)
A.I.A.	American Institute of Architects
Arch. Forum	*Architectural Forum*
Arch. Record	*Architectural Record*
Arch. Review	*Architectural Review*
Inland Architect	*Inland Architect and News Record*
JSAH	*Journal of the Society of Architectural Historians*
OTNE	*Old-Time New England*
Proc. Bost. Soc.	*Proceedings of the Bostonian Society*
SPNEA	Society for the Preservation of New England Antiquities

(Note: city of publication is listed in references only when it is other than Boston.)

A. BOSTON: METROPOLITAN, CITY, AND BOSTON PROPER

The area each source deals with is indicated by the words Metropolitan, City, or Boston Proper. For the definitions of these areas see caption to Map 1, page iv.

1 Bacon, Edwin M., ed. *Bacon's Dictionary of Boston.* 1883. *City*
   An invaluable source. Includes brief but highly informative articles not only on such general subjects as "Architecture and Architects" and "Painters and Sculptors" but also on the different neighborhoods of the city (except for Hyde Park, not yet annexed) and on specific buildings and monuments, which are often described in great detail. Articles pertinent to this study are listed separately.

2 ———. *Boston: A Guide Book.* 1903. *Metropolitan*
   The only extensive and dependable guidebook ever issued for Greater Boston; covers Boston Proper and 45 suburban communities.

3 Beale, Joseph H. "Metropolitan Boston." In no. *13*, pp. 116–127. *Metropolitan*

4 Boston Architectural Club. *Year Books:* 1907, 1911, 1913, 1918, 1923, 1924, 1925, 1928, 1929. *Metropolitan*
   The 1929 volume deals entirely with Art Deco and contemporary work of that period, much of it in and around Boston.

5 Boston Board of Commissioners of the Department of Parks. *Annual Reports* and *Special Reports.* 1876–1937. *City*

6 Boston [*Street*] *Directories.* 1850–1940. *City*
   These list the occupations and business addresses (and residential addresses if they lived in the city) of all persons in business in the city of Boston. Used in conjunction with real estate atlases and such directories as *Clark's Boston Blue Book* (no. *736*), the street directories are the chief aids in reconstructing the social character of residential areas.

7 Boston Elevated Railway Company. *Fifty Years of Unified Transportation in Metropolitan Boston.* 1938. *Metropolitan*

8 Boston Public Library. Boston Architecture Reference File. Fine Arts Department (Research). *Metropolitan*
   This card index is divided into three sections: architects (more than 250), buildings by building type, and buildings by name (if any) and/or address.

9 ———. Boston Pictorial Archive, Print Department. *Metropolitan*

10 ———. "Boston Views: An Index Recording Views of Boston in the Library's Collections . . ." Typescript. 1963. *Metropolitan*

11 Boston Society of Architects. *Boston Architecture.* Intro. by John Coolidge. Cambridge, 1970. *Boston Proper*

12 Boston Street Commissioners. *Record of Streets, Alleys, Places, etc., in the City of Boston.* 1910. 2d ed. *City*
   Authoritatively traces the history of every street in the city.

13 Boston Tercentenary Committee. *Fifty Years of Boston,* ed. Elizabeth Herlihy. 1930. *City*
   Anthology of authoritative articles on all aspects of life in the city from 1880 to 1930; intended as a continuation of no. *65.* Articles pertinent to this study are listed separately.

14 Bromley, George W. and Walter S. *Atlas of the City of Boston.* 7 vols. Philadelphia, 1883–1928, with periodic revisions. *City*
   This source and no. *34* are invaluable in reconstructing the history of the city and all the annexed cities and towns. Each volume documents the location and size of every parcel of land on every street; its owner; and the size, outline, and materials of any building thereon. Although absolutely dependable in these respects, any additional information (such as dates of erection) given under major landmarks must be treated very carefully, since errors are frequent.

15 Bureau for Research in Municipal Government, Harvard Graduate School of Public Administration. *Metropolis in Maps: Graphic References for the Boston Area.* Cambridge, 1946. *Metropolitan*

16 Bushee, Frederick A. "Ethnic Factors in the Population of Boston." *Publications of the American Economic Association,* 3d series. New York, 1903. *City*

17 Bynner, Edwin L., and Edwin Stanwood. "Topography [and Landmarks]." In no. *65,* 1:521–556; 2:491–532; 4:25–63. *Boston Proper*

18 *Church Militant.* 1898–1940. *Metropolitan*
   This journal is an authoritative source for dates and attributions of all Episcopal churches and institutions in Greater Boston. An index by parish exists at the Diocesan Library, 1 Joy Street, Boston.

19 City of Boston Building Department. Records. *City*
   A most important source for this study. Photocopies of building permits and other records relating to buildings discussed have been given to the Fine Arts Department (Research) of the Boston Public Library. Eventually such data will be added to the Boston Architecture Reference File (no. *8*).

20 Cram, Ralph Adams. "Architecture." In no. *13,* pp. 340–346. *City*

21 Cummings, Charles A. "Architecture." In no. *65,* 4:465–489. *Boston Proper*

22 Damrell, Charles S. *A Half Century of Boston Building.* 1895. *City*
   A generally dependable work that discusses in detail all major buildings and many minor buildings, particularly those erected between 1875 and 1895. Articles pertinent to this study are listed separately.

23 Eldredge, Joseph. *Architecture, Boston.* 1976. *Boston Proper*
   Includes three sections beyond Boston Proper: Charlestown, Roxbury, and Cambridge.

24 Eliot, Charles W., II. "The Boston Park System." In no. *13,* pp. 657–671. *City*

25 Engelhardt, George W. *Boston Illustrated.* 1897. *Metropolitan*
   Invaluable illustrations of office interiors and of private homes in city and suburbs.

26 Estabrook, Harold K. *Some Slums of Boston.* 1898. *City*

27 Fay, Frederick H. "The Planning of a City." In no. *13,* pp. 41–61. *City*

28 Federal Writers' Project. *Massachusetts: A Guide to Its Places and People.* 1937. *Metropolitan and beyond*
   A part of the American Guide Series, this dependable source includes a surprising amount of architectural material as well as a general history of architecture in Massachusetts.

29 Firey, Walter. *Land Use in Central Boston.* Cambridge, 1947. *Boston Proper*

30 Forbes, Allan. *Towns of New England and Old England, Part I.* 1920. *Metropolitan and beyond*

31 Goody, Joan E. *New Architecture in Boston*. Cambridge, 1965. *Metropolitan*
32 Herndon, Richard. *Boston of Today*. 1892. *City*
    In addition to articles on Boston proper and on all the annexed cities and towns, there are short biographical notices of many prominent Bostonians, including a great many architects, for which see Section F.
33 Hitchcock, Henry Russell. *A Guide to Boston Architecture, 1637–1954*. New York, 1954. *Metropolitan*
    The only architectural survey of Metropolitan Boston; informative but occasionally unreliable, it also reflects the strong bias of its period against late Victorian and early twentieth-century architecture.
34 Hopkins, G. Morgan. *Atlas of the County of Suffolk, Massachusetts*. 7 vols. Philadelphia, 1873–1874. *City* (See also no. 14.)
35 Howe, M. A. De Wolfe. *Boston: The Place and the People*. 1903. *Boston Proper*
36 Hubbard, Henry V. "Landscape Architecture." In no. 13, pp. 347–352. *Metropolitan*
37 Keach, Leon. "Recent Architecture in Boston." *Pencil Points* 18 (1937): 277–284. *Metropolitan*
38 Kilham, Walter. *Boston after Bulfinch . . . 1800–1900*. Cambridge, 1946. *Metropolitan*
    An invaluable source but sometimes misleading.
39 King, Moses. *King's Handbook of Boston*. Cambridge, 1883, 1885. *Metropolitan*
    Reliable and detailed articles on all aspects of Boston in the late nineteenth century, including many lengthy descriptions of major buildings. Articles pertinent to this study are listed separately.
40 Langtry, Albert P. *Metropolitan Boston: A Modern History*. 4 vols. New York, 1929. *Metropolitan*
41 Lankevich, George J., ed. *Boston: A Chronological and Documentary History, 1602–1970*. Dobbs Ferry, N.Y., 1974. *Boston Proper*
42 Lord, Robert, et al. *A History of the Archdiocese of Boston*. 3 vols. 1929. *Metropolitan*
    While maddeningly silent on architects and artists, this work nonetheless records the construction dates of all Roman Catholic churches and institutions in and beyond Greater Boston. It is also excellent background material for the whole period of this study.
43 McCord, David. *About Boston*. 1948. *Metropolitan*
44 McNamara, Katherine. *The Boston Metropolitan District*. Cambridge, 1946. *Metropolitan*
    A bibliography of pamphlet literature on this subject.
45 "Metropolitan Boston." *AABN* 134 (1928): 632–716. *Metropolitan*
46 *Official Chronicle and Tribute Book*. 1930. *Metropolitan*
    An anthology of articles on Massachusetts and particularly on Greater Boston, issued for the 1930 Tercentenary of the state's settlement.
47 Rettig, Robert Bell, ed. *The Architecture of H. H. Richardson and His Contemporaries in Boston and Vicinity*. 1972. *Metropolitan*
    An excellent compendium of the latest scholarship on Victorian Boston architecture. Articles pertinent to this study are listed separately.
48 Rodwin, Lloyd. "Middle Income Housing Problems in Boston." Ph.D. diss., Harvard, 1949. *City*
49 Seaburg, Carl. *Boston Observed*. 1971. *Metropolitan*
    Sections pertinent to this study are listed separately.
50 Selig, J. Daniel. "The History of the Harleston Parker Medal." In no. 725, pp. 133–140. *Metropolitan*
51 ———. "Traditional Architecture." In no. 714, pp. 84–97. *Boston Proper*
52 Shackleton, Robert. *The Book of Boston*. Philadelphia, 1916. *Metropolitan*
    Interesting chiefly for the comparisons of Richardsonian and Classical architecture, reflecting the taste of its period.
53 Shaw, Charles. *A Topographical and Historical Description of Boston*. 1817. *Boston Proper*
54 Smith, Margaret Supplee. "Italianate Architecture in Mid-Nineteenth Century Boston." *JSAH* 34 (1975): 312–313. *Boston Proper*
55 Stanley, E. O. *Boston and Its Suburbs*. 1888. *Metropolitan*
    An excellent guide and one of the earliest to define Boston in larger terms than the city.
56 Stanwood, Edward. *Boston Illustrated*. 1872. *Metropolitan*
    Valuable for descriptive articles on the suburbs.
57 State Street Trust Co. *Boston's Growth*. 1910. *Boston Proper*
58 "Suburbs of Boston." In no. 1, pp. 389–391. *Metropolitan*
59 Suffolk County Registry of Deeds, County Courthouse, Boston. *City*
    Boston's deeds are indexed from 1630 to the present and often include subdivision plans that can be studied in conjunction with street atlases.
60 Thwing, Annie Haven. *The Crooked and Narrow Streets of the Town of Boston, 1630–1822*. 1920. *Boston Proper*
61 Tucci, Douglass Shand. *Church Building in Boston*. 1974. *Metropolitan*
    The photographic archive deals with Boston Proper and 20 suburbs. The checklist of selected late nineteenth- and early twentieth-century church work includes all of Greater Boston.
62 Whitehill, Walter Muir. *Boston: A Topographical History*. 2d ed. Cambridge, 1968. *Boston Proper*
    The definitive study; touches also on most major Boston buildings.
63 ———. *Boston: Distinguished Buildings and Sites within the City and Its Orbit . . .* 1975. *Metropolitan*
64 ———. "Boston Society of Architects, 1867–1967: A Centennial Sketch." In no. 725, pp. 15–70. *Metropolitan*
65 Winsor, Justin, ed. *Memorial History of Boston*. 4 vols. 1881–1883. *City*
    The standard and authoritative history of Boston to 1880. Articles pertinent to this study are listed separately.
66 Zaitzevsky, Cynthia. "Boston Park System." In no. 47, p. 22. *City*

B. CITIES AND TOWNS OF METROPOLITAN BOSTON

Only sources that cover, at least in part, the 1850–1940 period are included. An asterisk (*) indicates that the city or town was subsequently annexed to the town or city of Boston.

In this section and the next, the entry following each city, town, or area indicates the pages on which its history and architecture are discussed in nine works of reference that cover metropolitan Boston. These sources range in date of publication from 1883 to 1972, and if read in chronological sequence will yield some sense of the area's relative importance throughout the period during which it became a suburb of Boston in the modern sense. The works are short-titled as follows, in order of publication.

Bacon's Dict.   Edwin M. Bacon, ed. *Bacon's Dictionary of Boston.* 1883. (No. *1*)
Stanley   E. O. Stanley. *Boston and Its Suburbs.* 1888. (No. *55*)
Bacon   Edwin M. Bacon. *Boston: A Guide Book.* 1903. (No. *2*)
Forbes   Allan Forbes. *Towns of New England and Old England, Part I.* 1920. (No. *30*)
OCTB   *Official Chronicle and Tribute Book.* 1930. (No. *46*)
Mass.   Federal Writers' Project. *Massachusetts: A Guide to Its Places and People.* 1937. (No. *28*)
Hitchcock   Henry-Russell Hitchcock. *A Guide to Boston Architecture, 1637–1954.* 1954. (No. *33*)
Seaburg   Carl Seaburg. *Boston Observed.* 1971. (No. *49*)
Rettig   Robert Bell Rettig, ed. *The Architecture of H. H. Richardson and His Contemporaries in Boston and Vicinity.* 1972. (No. *47*)

ABINGTON. Mass., 626–627.
  67 Hobart, Benjamin. *History of the Town of Abington.* 1866.
*ALLSTON. See BRIGHTON/ALLSTON.
ARLINGTON. Stanley, 127–128; Bacon, 152–153; Mass., 130–135; Seaburg, 302–303.
  68 Cutter, Benjamin and William. *History of the Town of Arlington.* 1880.
AVON. Mass., 588–589.
BEDFORD. Mass., 434.
  69 Brown, Abram E. *History of the Town of Bedford.* 1891.
BELMONT. Mass., 444–445; Hitchcock, 36; Rettig, 36–37.
  70 Baldwin, Francis B. *The Story of Belmont.* Belmont, 1953.
BEVERLY. Bacon, 161; Forbes, 62–67; Mass., 421–422; Hitchcock, 55; Rettig, 45–46.
*BOSTON HIGHLANDS. See ROXBURY.
BRAINTREE. Stanley, 139; Bacon, 2; Mass., 587; Seaburg, 304–305.
BRIDGEWATER. Mass., 589.
*BRIGHTON/ALLSTON. Annexed 1874. Bacon's Dict., 70–71; Bacon, 97.
  71 Drake, Francis S. "Brighton." In no. *65*, 1:439–444, 2:369–374, 3:601–610.
BROCKTON. Stanley, 105–106; Mass., 176–178.
  72 Kingman, Bradford. *History of Brockton, 1656–1894.* Syracuse, N.Y., 1895.
BROOKLINE. Stanley, 103–105; Bacon, 109–115; Mass., 179–183; Hitchcock, 33–34; Seaburg, 305.
  73 Bolton, Charles K. *Brookline: The History of a Favored Town.* Brookline, 1897.
  74 Brookline Historical Commission. *Brookline Village Walking Tours.* Brookline, 1977.
  75 Chandler, Alfred D. *Annexation of Brookline to Boston.* Brookline, 1880.
  76 Curtis, J. G. *History of the Town of Brookline.* 1933.
  77 Wardwell, Anne. " 'Longwood' and 'Cottage Farm' in Brookline." In no. *807*, pp. 57–69.
  78 Woods, H. F. *Historical Sketches of Brookline.* 1874.
BURLINGTON. Mass., 465–466; Seaburg, 305.
CAMBRIDGE. Stanley, 112–120; Bacon, 98–109; Forbes, 74–81; OCTB, 386; Hitchcock, 24–33; Seaburg, 306; Rettig, 32–35.
  79 Batchelder, Samuel F. *Bits of Cambridge History.* Cambridge, 1930.
  80 Cambridge Historical Commission. Survey files.
  81 ———. *A Survey of Architectural History in Cambridge.* 5 vols. Cambridge, 1965–1977. Vol. 1 [no author], *East Cambridge*; vol. 2, Antoinette F. Downing, Elizabeth MacDougall, and Eleanor Pearson, *Mid Cambridge*; vol. 3 [no author], *Cambridgeport*; vol. 4, Bainbridge Bunting and Robert H. Nylander, *Old Cambridge*; vol. 5, Arthur J. Krim, *Northwest Cambridge and Survey Index.*
  82 Davies, Walter G., ed. *Cambridge: Fifty Years a City.* Cambridge, 1897.
  83 Eliot, Samuel. *A History of Cambridge, Massachusetts.* Cambridge, 1913.
  84 Rettig, Robert Bell. *Guide to Cambridge Architecture: Ten Walking Tours.* Cambridge, 1969.
CANTON. Stanley, 149–150; Mass., 614–615; Seaburg, 306.
*CHARLESTOWN. Annexed 1874. Bacon's Dict., 91, 263; Stanley, 97–100; Bacon, 65–68; Mass., 173–174, 270–271; Hitchcock, 23.
  85 Bartlett, Joseph. *Historical Sketch of Charlestown.* 1813.
  86 *Considerations Respectfully Submitted to the Citizens of Boston and Charlestown on the Proposed Annexation of the Two Cities.* 1854.
  87 Edes, Henry H. "Charlestown." In no. *65*, 1:383–401, 2:311–330, 3:547–570.
  88 Frothingham, Richard. *History of Charlestown.* 1845.
  89 Hunnewell, James F. *A Century of Town Life: A History of Charlestown, . . . 1775–1887,* 1888.
CHELSEA. Stanley, 100–101; Bacon, 142–143; Mass., 205–208; Seaburg, 307.
  90 Chamberlain, Mellen. "Chelsea, Revere and Winthrop . . ." In no. *65*, 3:611–617. See also Chamberlain's *A Documentary History of Chelsea.* 2 vols. 1908.
COHASSET. Stanley, 137, 141; Bacon, 167; Mass., 623; Hitchcock, 37; Seaburg, 307.
  91 Howe, Oliver H. "A Brief History of Cohasset . . ." *OTNE* 32 (1941): 43–51.
CONCORD. Bacon, 156–159; OCTB, 379; Mass., 25, 210–217; Hitchcock, 37–38; Seaburg, 308.
DANVERS. Bacon, 161; Hitchcock, 38; Mass., 430–431.
DEDHAM. Stanley, 145, 149; Bacon 137–139; Forbes, 104–110; Mass., 217–222; Hitchcock, 38; Rettig, 27; Seaburg, 308.
*DORCHESTER. Annexed 1870. Bacon's Dict., 131–134; Stanley, 122–124; Bacon, 97, 134; Forbes, 111–123; OCTB, 364; Mass., 217–222; Hitchcock, 34.
  92 *American Series of Biographies, Massachusetts Volume.* Micah Dyer, biographical notice. 1901.
  93 Bellows, Samuel F. "Dorchester." In no. *65*, 1:423–438, 2:357–368, 3:589–600.

94 Clapp, David. *The Ancient Proprietors of Jones's Hill.* 1883.

95 Coffin, Nathaniel W. *A Few Reasons in Favor of the Annexation of a Part of the Town of Dorchester to the City of Boston.* 1867.

96 *Dorchester Blue Books.* Vols. 1885–86, 1898, 1902, 1908. Dorchester is also included in nos. 724 and 736 below.

97 Dorchester Tercentenary Committee. *Dorchester . . . 1630–1930.* Dorchester, 1930.

98 Orcutt, William Dana. *Good Old Dorchester: A Narrative History . . . 1630–1893.* Cambridge, 1893.

99 Tucci, Douglass Shand. *The Gothic Churches of Dorchester.* 2 vols. Ann Arbor, Mich., 1974. 2d ed.

100 ———. *The Second Settlement: A Case Study in the Development of Victorian Boston.* 1974.

101 Warner, Sam B., Jr. "The Residential Development of Roxbury, West Roxbury and Dorchester . . . 1870–1900." Ph.D. diss., Harvard, 1959.

102 ———. *Streetcar Suburbs: The Process of Growth in Boston, 1870–1900.* Cambridge, 1962.

   This work, the foundation of all studies of Boston's streetcar suburbs, derives from no. 101.

DOVER. Mass., 440–441; Seaburg, 308.

*EAST BOSTON. Annexed 1635–1637. Bacon's Dict., 138–139; Stanley, 101–102; Bacon, 94; *OCTB*, 366; Mass., 175; Hitchcock, 23.

103 Boston City Planning Board. *East Boston: A Survey and a Comprehensive Plan.* 1916.

104 Summer, William H. *A History of East Boston.* 1858.

105 Woods, Robert, and Albert J. Kennedy. *The Zone of Emergence.* Ed. Sam B. Warner, Jr. Cambridge, 1962. 2d ed. 1969.

EAST BRIDGEWATER. Mass., 628–629.

EASTON. Mass., 616.

EVERETT. Mass., 227–229, 270; Seaburg, 308.

FOXBOROUGH. Mass., 612.

FRAMINGHAM. Stanley, 151; Mass., 435–436; Hitchcock, 39.

GLOUCESTER. Stanley, 165–166; Bacon, 161; *OCTB*, 130–143; Mass., 435–436; Hitchcock, 39; Seaburg, 309.

106 O'Gorman, James F. *This Other Gloucester.* 1976.

HANOVER. Mass., 619.

HINGHAM. Stanley, 137–138; Bacon, 167; Forbes, 162–169; Mass., 622; Hitchcock, 40–41; Seaburg, 309.

107 Town of Hingham. *History of the Town of Hingham.* 3 vols. Hingham, 1893.

HOLBROOK. Stanley, 139; Mass., 588; Seaburg, 310.

HULL. Stanley, 135–136; Bacon, 171; Mass., 623; Seaburg, 310.

*HYDE PARK. Annexed 1912. Stanley, 145.

108 Knight, Joseph, et al. *Memorial Sketch of Hyde Park . . .* 1888.

*JAMAICA PLAIN. See WEST ROXBURY/JAMAICA PLAIN/ROSLINDALE.

LEXINGTON. Bacon, 152–156; *OCTB*, 380; Mass., 255–260; Hitchcock, 43; Seaburg, 310.

LINCOLN. Stanley, 159; Mass., 445; Hitchcock, 43–44; Seaburg, 310.

LYNN. Stanley, 163–164; Bacon, 159; Mass., 266–270, 424; Seaburg, 311; Rettig, 44.

LYNNFIELD. Mass., 412; Seaburg, 312.

MALDEN. Bacon, 143; *OCTB*, 384; Mass., 270–273; Hitchcock, 46; Seaburg, 312.

MANCHESTER-BY-THE-SEA. Stanley, 165; Hitchcock, 55; Mass., 422; Rettig, 46–49.

MANSFIELD. Mass., 616.

MARBLEHEAD. Stanley, 164–165; Bacon, 160; Mass., 273–279; Hitchcock, 45.

109 Cord, Priscilla S., and Virginia C. Gamage. *Marblehead.* Philadelphia, 1972.

MEDFIELD. Mass., 441.

110 Tilden, William S. *History of the Town of Medfield, 1650–1886.* 1887.

MEDFORD. Stanley, 129, 154–155; Bacon, 144–145; *OCTB*, 371; Mass., 279–284; Seaburg, 312.

111 Brooks, Charles. *The History of the Town of Medford.* Rev. ed., 1886. Reprint, 1975.

MELROSE. Forbes, 170–174; Mass., 489–490; Hitchcock, 55; Seaburg, 313.

112 Goss, Eldridge H. *The History of Melrose.* Melrose, 1880.

113 Kemp, Edwin C. *Melrose, Massachusetts, 1900–1950.* Melrose, 1950.

MILTON. Stanley, 124–125; Bacon, 130–134; Mass., 586–587; Hitchcock, 46; Seaburg, 313; Rettig, 31.

114 Hamilton, Edward P. *A History of Milton.* Milton, 1957.

115 Teele, A. K. *A History of Milton.* 1887.

NAHANT. Stanley, 164; Bacon, 159, 171; Mass., 424; Seaburg, 314.

NATICK. Stanley, 150–151; Bacon, 123; Mass., 23, 25, 519; Hitchcock, 59; Seaburg, 315.

NEEDHAM. Bacon, 123–124; Mass., 518–519; Seaburg, 315.

NEWTON. Stanley, 106; Bacon, 116–120; *OCTB*, 368–369; Mass., 295–301; Hitchcock, 48–49; Rettig, 42–43.

116 King, Moses. *King's Handbook of Newton.* 1889.

117 [City of] *Newton Centennial, 1873–1973.* Newton, 1973.

118 Town of Newton. *Tercentenary of Newton, 1630–1930.* Newton, 1930.

NORWELL. Mass., 618–619.

NORWOOD. Stanley, 146; Mass., 426–427; Seaburg, 316.

PEABODY. Bacon, 161; Mass., 119, 422–423.

QUINCY. Stanley, 125–126; Bacon, 134–136; *OCTB*, 365; Mass., 335–340; Hitchcock, 51–52; Seaburg, 316–317.

RANDOLPH. Stanley, 142; Mass., 588; Seaburg, 317.

READING. Mass., 490; Seaburg, 317.

REVERE. Bacon, 141–142; Mass., 341–343; Seaburg, 317–318.

119 Chamberlain, Mellen. "Chelsea, Revere and Winthrop . . ." In no. 65, 3:611–617.

120 Shurtleff, Benjamin. *The History of the Town of Revere.* 1937.

ROCKLAND. Mass., 627.

ROCKPORT. Stanley, 166; Bacon, 161; Mass., 235–244.

*ROSLINDALE. See WEST ROXBURY/JAMAICA PLAIN/ROSLINDALE.

*ROXBURY. Annexed 1868. Bacon's Dict., 351–353; Stanley, 121–122; Bacon, 95–96; Mass., 172–173; Hitchcock, 34. See also nos. 101, 102.

121 Boston City Council and Roxbury City Council. *Reports in Relation to the Annexation of Roxbury . . .* Roxbury City Doc., no. 3, 1967.

122 Clifford, John H. *Argument on the Question of the Annexation of Roxbury to Boston before the Legislative Committee, Thursday, February 23, 1865.* 1867.

123 Committee in Favor of the Union of Boston and Roxbury. *Report.* 1851.

124 Drake, Francis S. "Roxbury." In no. 65, 3:571–588.

125 ———. *The Town of Roxbury.* Roxbury, 1878.

126 Quincy, Josiah. *Annexation of Roxbury and Boston: Remonstrance of Bostonians against the Measure.* 1865.

127 Roxbury Committee Opposed to the Annexation to Boston. *A Word for Old Roxbury.* Roxbury, 1851.

SALEM. Stanley, 165; Bacon, 160–166; *OCTB*, 374; Mass., 32, 343–352; Hitchcock, 52–55.

SAUGUS. Bacon, 159–160; Mass., 413; Seaburg, 318.

SCITUATE. Stanley, 140; Bacon, 167; Mass., 624; Hitchcock, 51.

SHARON. Stanley, 150; Mass., 615.

SOMERVILLE. Stanley, 154; Bacon, 143–144; *OCTB*, 378; Mass., 353–356; Seaburg, 318–319.

*SOUTH BOSTON. Annexed 1804. Bacon's Dict., 373; Stanley, 93–96; Bacon, 95; *OCTB*, 387; Mass., 167–169.

128 Gillespie, Charles B. *Illustrated History of South Boston.* 1900.

129 Severy, Robert B. "South Boston." In no. 807, pp. 27–40.

130 Simmonds, Thomas C. *History of South Boston . . .* 1857.

131 Toomey, John J., and Edward P. P. Rankin. *History of South Boston . . .* 1901.

STONEHAM. Stanley, 155; Mass., 489–490; Seaburg, 319.

STOUGHTON. Stanley, 142; Mass., 615; Rettig, 27.

SUDBURY. Mass., 470–471.

SWAMPSCOTT. Stanley, 164; Mass., 423–424; Hitchcock, 55; Seaburg, 319–320.

WAKEFIELD. Stanley, 162; Mass., 490; Seaburg, 320.

WALPOLE. Stanley, 162; Mass., 490.

WALTHAM. Stanley, 159; Bacon, 126–128; Mass., 370–373; Hitchcock, 56–58; Seaburg, 320; Rettig, 37–38.

WATERTOWN. Stanley, 159; Bacon, 126, 128–129; *OCTB*, 370; Mass., 374–378; Hitchcock, 48; Seaburg, 321.

WAYLAND. Stanley, 157; Mass., 435, 469–470; Hitchcock, 62; Seaburg, 321.

WELLESLEY. Bacon, 120–122; Mass., 379–382; Hitchcock, 58–59; Seaburg, 322; Rettig, 38–41.

132 Fiske, Joseph E. *History of the Town of Wellesley.* 1917.

133 *Town of Wellesley, 1881–1931.* Wellesley, 1931.

WEST BRIDGEWATER. Mass., 589.

WESTON. Stanley, 159; Bacon, 117; Mass., 469; Seaburg, 322; Rettig, 38.

*WEST ROXBURY/JAMAICA PLAIN/ROSLINDALE. Annexed 1874. Bacon's Dict., 219, 436; Stanley, 107–111; Bacon, 96–97; Hitchcock, 34. See also nos. 101, 102.

134 Austin, Arthur, W. *Address at the Dedication of the Town House at Jamaica Plain, . . .* 1860.

135 *West Roxbury Magazine.* Hudson, Mass., 1900.

136 Whitcomb, Harriet M. *Annals and Reminiscences of Jamaica Plain.* Cambridge, 1897.

137 Zaitzevsky, Cynthia. "Victorian Jamaica Plain." In no. 807, pp. 71–86.

WESTWOOD. Mass., 440–441; Seaburg, 322.

WEYMOUTH. Stanley, 140; Mass., 31, 382–385; Seaburg, 322–323.

WINCHESTER. Stanley, 128–129; Bacon, 145; Mass., 465; Seaburg, 323.

138 Chapman, Henry S. *History of Winchester, Massachusetts.* Winchester, 1936.

WINTHROP. Bacon, 139–141; Mass., 425; Seaburg, 323.

139 Chamberlain, Mellen. "Chelsea, Revere and Winthrop . . ." In no. 65, 3:611–617.

WILMINGTON. Mass., 433.

WOBURN. Stanley, 155; Mass., 389–392; Hitchcock, 63; Seaburg, 325.

140 Sewall, Samuel. *The History of Woburn.* 1868.

C. SECTIONS OF BOSTON PROPER

BACK BAY/FENWAY. Bacon's Dict., 31–32, 90, 119; Stanley, 3–34; Bacon, 74–92; Hitchcock, 15–22; Rettig, 16–21.

141 Baxter, Sylvester. "Boston's Fenway . . ." Undentified magazine, ca. 1908, pp. 894–908. Author's collection.

142 Bruce, James L. "Filling In of the Back Bay and the Charles River Development." *Proc. Bost. Soc.* (1940), pp. 25–38.

143 Bunting, Bainbridge. *Houses of Boston's Back Bay . . . 1840–1917.* Cambridge, 1967.

144 Eliot, Christopher R. "The Boston Public Garden." *Proc. Bost. Soc.* (1939), pp. 27–45.

145 Floyd, Margaret Henderson. "Copley Square and Dartmouth Street: A Showcase for Architectural Terra Cotta, Sculpture and Mural Painting." In no. 807, pp. 40–55.

146 Forbes, Allan. *Copley Square.* 1941.

147 Mumford, Lewis. "The Significance of Back Bay Boston." In no. 148, pp. 18–35.

148 Museum of Fine Arts, Boston. *Back Bay Boston: The City as a Work of Art.* 1969.

149 Whitehill, Walter Muir. "Back Bay Churches and Public Buildings." *Proc. Bost. Soc.* (1967), n.p.

BEACON HILL. Bacon's Dict., 38–39; Stanley, 61–72, 75; Bacon, 37–47, 68–73; Hitchcock, 6–10. See also no. 169.

150 Boston Historic Conservation Committee. *Beacon Hill: The North Slope.* 1963.

151 Chamberlain, Allen. *Beacon Hill: Its Ancient Pastures and Early Mansions.* 1955.

152 Lawrence, Robert M. *Old Park Street and Its Vicinity.* 1922.

153 McIntyre, A. McVoy. *Beacon Hill: A Walking Tour.* 1975.

154 Warren, William M. "Beacon Hill and Boston University." *Bostonia* 4 (1930): 3–21.

155 Weinhardt, Carl, Jr. "The Domestic Architecture of Beacon Hill, 1800–1850." *Proc. Bost. Soc.* (1958), pp. 11–32.

156 Whitehill, Walter Muir. "A Corner of Louisburg Square . . ." In no. 63, pp. 14–17.

DOWNTOWN COMMERCIAL DISTRICT. Stanley, 35–60, 74, 83–86; Bacon, 4–36, 48–54; Hitchcock, 3–4, 10–14. See also no. 517.

157 Boston Redevelopment Authority. *Broad Street.* 1974.

158 "The Boston Theatre District." *Drumlin* 3 (Jan. 1978). Entire issue.
159 McKay, Robert. "Downtown Boston: The Waterfront and Commercial Districts." In no. *807*, pp. 1–11.
160 "Some Noteworthy Buildings." In no. 32, pp. 27–54.
161 *Washington Street, Old and New.* 1913.
162 Whitehill, Walter Muir. "The Metamorphoses of Scollay and Bowdoin Squares." *Proc. Bost. Soc.* (1972), n.p.
163 ———. *The Neighborhood of the Tavern Club.* 1971.
HARBOR AND WATERFRONT. See also no. *159*.
164 King, Moses. *King's Handbook of Boston Harbor.* Cambridge, 1882.
165 Payson, Gilbert R. "Long Wharf and the Old Waterfront." *Proc. Bost. Soc.* (1926), pp. 23–40.
166 Snow, Edward Rowe. *The Romance of Boston Bay.* 1944.
NORTH AND WEST ENDS. Bacon's Dict., 275, 435–436; Stanley, 72, 78–83; Bacon, 54–65, 73–74; Hitchcock, 2–3, 4–5.
167 Cummings, Abbott Lowell. "Charles Bulfinch and Boston's Vanishing West End." *OTNE* 52 (1961): 46–47.
168 Flower, Benjamin O. *Civilization's Inferno, or Studies in the Social Cellar.* 1893.
169 "North and Old West Ends." In no. 32, pp. 81–85.
170 Woods, Robert A., ed. *Americans in Process: A Settlement House Study.* 1903.
171 Wieder, Arnold A. *The Early Jewish Community of Boston's North End.* Waltham, 1962.
SOUTH END. Bacon's Dict., 374–375; Stanley, 87–93; Bacon, 92–94; Hitchcock, 14.
172 Smith, Margaret Supplee. "Boston's South End: Mid-Century Urban Planning and Architecture." In no. *807*, pp. 13–26.
173 "The South End." In no. 32, pp. 73–80.
174 Van Meter, Mary. *Bay Village, or the Church Street District.* 1970.
175 Whitehill, Walter Muir. "Worcester Square . . ." In no. *63*, pp. 50–53.
176 Wolfe, Albert B. *The Lodging House Problem in Boston.* Cambridge, 1913.
177 Woods, Robert A., ed. *The City Wilderness: A Settlement House Study.* 1899.

D. INDIVIDUAL BUILDINGS THROUGHOUT METROPOLITAN BOSTON

Books or articles devoted entirely to one building are rare, and a number of significant buildings that are worthy of such attention are as yet untreated except in general works. For such major buildings not listed here, see under their architects (Section F); under the city, town, or area in which they are located (Section B); or under the appropriate building type (Section E). Institutional histories have been included here only when the institution's building is discussed. Only in the case of a few major works has any attempt been made to list illustrations published without accompanying text. Collegiate buildings will be found under their respective colleges or universities. Except for theaters, buildings are listed by present-day name; for example, for the Museum of Natural History in the Back Bay, see Bonwit Teller. Note also that descriptions cited in *AABN* are often untitled.

ADVENT, CHURCH OF THE (BEACON HILL). See also nos. *259, 444, 643, 664, 665*.
178 Goodrich, Wallace. *The Parish of the Advent in the City of Boston.* 1944.
179 Tucci, Douglass Shand. "Liturgical Art at the Church of the Advent in Boston, 1850–1950." Typescript. Fine Arts Dept. (Research), Boston Public Library. 1973.
180 Wright, John. "The High Altar Reredos of the Church of the Advent." In no. *682*, pp. 310–311.
181 Wuonola, Mark. *Church of the Advent, Boston: A Guidebook.* 1975.
ALL SAINTS' CHURCH (ASHMONT). See also nos. *436, 542, 547, 552, 661, 703, 767, 768*.
182 Brown, Robert. "All Saints' Church . . ." *Arch. Record* 7 (1900): 101–104.
183 Cram, Ralph Adams. "All Saints' Church . . ." *Churchman* 79 (1899): 559–564.
184 ———. "Architecture." In *The New Parish Church of All Saints.* 1892.
185 Floyd, A. P. *The History of the Parish of All Saints . . .* 1945.
186 Tucci, Douglass Shand. *All Saints', Ashmont: A Centennial History.* 1974.
187 ———. *All Saints' Church, Boston: An Introduction to the Architecture of Ralph Adams Cram.* Ann Arbor, Mich., 1975. (vol. 2 of no. *99*).
188 ———. "Articles, Exhibition Reviews and Published Plates in American and British Books and Periodicals on the Architectural Art of the Chancel and Lady Chapel of All Saints', Ashmont: A Checklist, 1897–1920." Typescript. Cram Collection, Print Dept., Boston Public Library.
189 Wright, John. "The High Altar Reredos of All Saints' Church, Boston." In no. *682*, pp. 313–314.
ALL SAINTS' CHURCH (BROOKLINE). See also nos. *436, 547, 686*.
190 *A Tour of All Saints' Church.* 1954.
AMES BUILDING (DOWNTOWN; WASHINGTON STREET). See also nos. *493, 616, 747*.
191 *AABN* 26 (1889): 18.
AMES ESTATE STORE (demolished; Harrison Avenue). See nos. *605, 611*.
AMES-WEBSTER HOUSE (BACK BAY). See also no. *143*.
192 Floyd, Margaret Henderson. "Another French Connection for American Mural Painting: *The Justinian Cycle* by Benjamin Constant for a Back Bay Queen Anne Palace." *JSAH* 34 (1975): 312.
ARLINGTON STREET CHURCH (BACK BAY). See also no. *684*.
193 Gilman, Arthur. "A Return to Solid and Classical Principles . . ." (1859). *JSAH* 20 (1961): 191–193.
ATWOOD HOUSE (DORCHESTER)
194 Tucci, Douglass Shand. "The Most Curious House in Dorchester." *Dorchester Argus-Citizen,* 1 June 1972, p. 3.
AYER HOUSE (BACK BAY)
195 *AABN* 74 (1901): 94.
BATTERYMARCH BUILDING (DOWNTOWN; formerly Public Services Building)
196 Kellogg, Harold F. "The Use of Color — The Part It Plays in the Design of the Public Services Building, Boston." *AABN* 134 (1928): 211–216.

BONWIT TELLER (BAY BAY; originally Museum of Natural History). See also no. *39*.
197 "Exit Taxidermist . . ." *Interiors* 107 (1947): 82–87.
BOSTON ATHENAEUM (BEACON HILL). See also nos. *38, 54*.
198 *Change and Continuity: A Pictorial History of the Boston Athenaeum.* 1976.
199 Whitehill, Walter Muir. "Portrait Busts in . . . the Boston Athenaeum." *Antiques* 103 (1973): 1141–1156.
BOSTON CITY HALL, OLD (DOWNTOWN). See also no. *38*.
200 "Uses of the Past . . ." *Arch. Forum* 137 (1972): 24–33.
201 Wren, George L. "The Boston City Hall, Bryant and Gilman, Architects, 1862–1865." *JSAH* 21 (1962): 188–192.
BOSTON CITY HALL ANNEX (DOWNTOWN)
202 *Architecture and Building* 47 (1915): 265–267.
BOSTON CITY HOSPITAL (SOUTH END; partially demolished). See also no. *1*.
203 *Documents of the City of Boston*, doc. 34, 11:31.
BOSTON COLLEGE (NEWTON). See also nos. *42, 592, 686*.
204 "Boston College." In no. *712*, pp. 70–71.
205 *Boston College Library: History and Description.* 1933.
206 Cram, Ralph Adams. "The New Boston College." *AABN* 119 (1921): 615–618.
207 Dunigan, David R. *A History of Boston College.* Milwaukee, 1947.
BOSTON EVENING CLINIC (BACK BAY; originally Burrage House). See also no. *143*.
208 *AABN* 74 (1901): 56.
BOSTON LYING-IN HOSPITAL (THE FENWAY). See also nos. *37, 50, 461*.
209 "Boston Lying-In Hospital." In no. *712*, pp. 64–65.
BOSTON NAVAL SHIPYARD BUILDINGS (CHARLESTOWN)
210 Norton, Bettina A. "The Boston Naval Shipyard." *Proc. Bost. Soc.* (1974), n.p.
BOSTON OPERA HOUSE (demolished). See also nos. *510, 741*.
211 Jackson, Frank H. *Monograph of the Boston Opera House . . .* 1909.
BOSTON PARK PLAZA HOTEL (BACK BAY; originally Statler Hotel)
212 *AABN* 132 (1927): 14–16.
BOSTON PUBLIC LIBRARY (BACK BAY). See also nos. *696, 697, 704, 763, 767, 768*.
213 "Boston Public Library." *Brickbuilder* 19 (1910): 32–37.
214 Burke, Doreen Bolger. "*Astarte*: Sargent's Study for *The Pagan Gods* Mural in the Boston Public Library." *Fenway Court* (1977), pp. 9–20.
215 *Edwin Austin Abbey, 1852–1911.* Intros. by Kathleen A. Foster and Michael Quick. New Haven, 1973.
216 Fenollosa, Ernest F. *Mural Painting in the Boston Public Library.* New York, 1896.
217 *Handbook of the New Public Library of the City of Boston.* 1895.
218 Jordy, William H. "The Beaux-Arts Renaissance: Charles McKim's Boston Public Library." In no. *765*, pp. 314–375, 392–396.
219 Kingsbury, Martha. "Sargent's Murals in the Boston Public Library." *Winterthur Portfolio* 11 (1976): 153–172.
220 Moloney, Francis. *Tour of the Boston Public Library, Copley Square.* 1966.
221 Moore, Charles. "The Boston Public Library: A Manifestation of Civic Consciousness" and "Charles McKim Summons Saint-Gaudens . . . and Other Artists." In no. *586*, pp. 62–95.
222 *Thirty-Seventh Annual Report of the Trustees* (of the Boston Public Library). 1888.
223 Whitehill, Walter Muir. *Boston Public Library: A Centennial History.* Cambridge, 1956.
224 ———. "The Making of an Architectural Masterpiece: The Boston Public Library." *American Art Journal* 11 (1970): 13–35.
225 ———. "The Vicissitudes of *Bacchante* in Boston." *New England Quarterly* 27 (1954): 435–454.
BOSTON PUBLIC LIBRARY, OLD (demolished). See nos. *39, 163*.
BOSTON THEATRE, FIRST (demolished). See also nos. *516, 530*.
226 Brown, Frank C. "The First Boston Theatre . . ." *OTNE* 36 (1945): 1–7.
BOSTON THEATRE, SECOND (demolished). See also no. *516*.
227 Kavanaugh, Joseph. "Three American Opera Houses." M.A. thesis, University of Delaware. 1967.
228 Tompkins, Eugene. *The History of the Boston Theatre, 1854–1901.* 1908.
BOSTON SUB-TREASURY AND POST OFFICE (demolished). See nos. *38, 39*.
BRAZER BUILDING (DOWNTOWN). See also no. *38*.
229 *AABN* 56 (1897): 64.
CARTER BUILDING. See WINTHROP BUILDING
CHADWICK HOUSE (DORCHESTER). See also no. *100*.
230 Tucci, Douglass Shand. "A Discovery . . . of the Plans of 20 Cushing Avenue . . ." *Dorchester Day Magazine, Dorchester Argus-Citizen*, June 1972, pp. 12–13.
CHARLESGATE, THE (BACK BAY). See also no. *22*.
231 *AABN* 32 (1891): 14.
CHARLES PLAYHOUSE (DOWNTOWN; originally Fifth Universalist Church). See also no. *38*.
232 Van Meter, Mary. "A New Asher Benjamin Building in Boston." *Drumlin* 3 (Jan. 1978): 1–2.
CHARLES STREET MEETING HOUSE (BEACON HILL)
233 Greene, Joseph G. "The Charles Street Meeting House." *OTNE* 30 (1946): 87–93.
234 Whitehill, Walter Muir. "A View of the Charles Street Church . . ." In no. *63*, pp. 22–25.
CHRIST CHURCH (NORTH END)
235 Bolton, Charles K. *Christ Church.* 1912.
236 Foley, Suzanne. "Christ Church, Boston." *OTNE* 51 (1961): 67–85.
CLUNY, HOTEL (demolished)
237 *AABN* 4 (1878): 40.
COLONNADE ROW (demolished). See also no. *470*.
238 Brent, Samuel A. "Colonnade Row." *Bostonian Society Publications* 40 (1914): 11–13.
239 Kirker, Harold. 'The Colonnade, Boston." In no. *530*, pp. 258–260.
COLONIAL THEATRE (DOWNTOWN)
240 Blackall, C. H. "The Colonial Theatre and Building." *AABN* 72 (1901): 11–12, 27–28, 44–45, 51–52, 67–69.

CONGREGATIONAL HOUSE (BEACON HILL)
241   *AABN* 64 (1899): 16.
CONVERSE MEMORIAL LIBRARY (MALDEN). See nos. *611, 614, 659.*
COVENANT, CHURCH OF THE (BACK BAY; originally Central Church). See also nos. *446, 630, 684.*
242   Koch, Robert. *The Tiffany Windows and Lantern at the Church of the Covenant.* 1966.
COWLEY FATHERS MONASTERY (CAMBRIDGE). See nos. *81, 703.*
CRANE MEMORIAL LIBRARY (QUINCY). See nos. *659, 662.*
CUSHING-ENDICOTT HOUSE (BACK BAY). See also no. *143.*
243   Laing, Diana Whitehill. "Cushing Endicott House, 463 Marlborough Street." *Proc. Bost. Soc.* (1960), pp. 15–52.
CUSTOM HOUSE (DOWNTOWN). See also no. *752.*
244   Smith, Margaret S. "The Custom House Controversy." *19th Century* 3 (1977): 99–105.
DAVENPORT HOUSE (MALDEN). See no. *659.*
DEWEY HOUSE (THE FENWAY). See no. *411.*
ELLINGWOOD MEMORIAL CHAPEL (NAHANT). See no. *353.*
EMMANUEL CHURCH (BACK BAY). See no. *682.* See also under LINDSEY MEMORIAL CHAPEL.
EXCHANGE BUILDING (DOWNTOWN). See no. *22.*
EXETER STREET THEATRE (BACK BAY; originally First Spiritualist Temple). See no. *567.*
FAIRBANKS HOUSE (DEDHAM). See no. *793.*
FANEUIL HALL (DOWNTOWN). See also no. *530.*
245   Whitehill, Walter Muir. "A View of Faneuil Hall." In no. *63,* pp. 6–9.
FANEUIL HALL MARKETS (DOWNTOWN). See also no. *787.*
246   Brown, Abram E. *Faneuil Hall and the Faneuil Hall Market.* 1901.
247   Monkhouse, Christopher P. "Consideration of Faneuil Hall Market and the Architect, Alexander Parris." *JSAH* 28 (1969): 212.
248   SPNEA and Architectural Heritage, Inc. *Faneuil Hall Markets: Historical Study.* 1958.
249   Webb, Roger S. "The History and Restoration of Boston's Faneuil Hall Markets." *JSAH* 28 (1969): 225.
250   Whitehill, Walter Muir. "Historical Continuity versus Synthetic Reconstruction." *Athenaeum Items* 67 (Jan. 1958): 1–3.
FEDERAL BUILDING (DOWNTOWN). See also nos. *542, 716.*
251   Loring, Charles G. "The Boston Federal Building." *AABN* 143 (1933): 15–19.
FENWAY COURT (ISABELLA STEWART GARDNER MUSEUM; THE FENWAY)
252   Baxter, Sylvester. *An American Palace of Art, Fenway Court . . .* 1904.
253   Carter, Morris. *Isabella Stewart Gardner and Fenway Court.* 1925.
254   *Guide to the Collection: Gardner Museum.* 1976.
255   O'Haggan, Anne. "The Treasures of Fenway Court." *Munsey's Magazine* 34 (1906): 655–678.
256   Saarinen, Aline B. *The Proud Possessors.* New York, 1958.
257   Stout, George L. *Treasures from the Isabella Stewart Gardner Museum.* New York, 1969.
258   Tharp, Louise Hall. *Mrs. Jack.* 1965.
259   Tucci, Douglass Shand. "Ralph Adams Cram and Mrs. Gardner: The Movement toward a Liturgical Art." *Fenway Court* (1975), pp. 27–34.
FILENE BOSTON STORE (DOWNTOWN). See also no. *534.*
260   "The New Filene Store." *Brickbuilder* 21 (1912): 247–250.
FIRST BAPTIST CHURCH (BACK BAY; formerly Brattle Square Church). See nos. *47, 611, 614.*
FIRST CHURCH OF BOSTON (BACK BAY; partially demolished). See also nos. *47, 149, 446.*
261   Ellis, Arthur E. *History of the First Church . . .* 1881.
FIRST CHURCH OF CHRIST, SCIENTIST, EXTENSION (BACK BAY)
262   Armstrong, Joseph. *The Mother Church.* 1911 and later eds.
263   Williamson, Margaret. *The Mother Church Extension.* 1939.
FISKE BUILDING (demolished). See no. *22.*
FORT INDEPENDENCE (CASTLE ISLAND; SOUTH BOSTON)
264   Whitehill, Walter Muir. "A View of Fort Independence." In no. *63,* pp. 62–65.
GALLERY ON THE MOORS AND ATWOOD HOUSE (GLOUCESTER). See also no. *320.*
265   O'Gorman, James F. "Parnassus on Ledge Road." In no. *106,* pp. 77–96.
GARDNER MUSEUM. See FENWAY COURT
GATE OF HEAVEN CHURCH (SOUTH BOSTON). See also nos. *42, 686.*
266   *AABN* 55 (1897): 15.
GORE PLACE (WALTHAM). See also no. *63.*
267   Wick, Peter A. "Gore Place: . . ." *Antiques* 110 (1976): 1250–1261.
GRAIN AND FLOUR EXCHANGE (DOWNTOWN; originally Chamber of Commerce Building). See no. *22.*
GROPIUS HOUSE (LINCOLN). See also nos. *31, 33, 774.*
268   Huxtable, Ada Louise. "Gropius House . . ." *The New York Times,* 18 May 1975, p. 36.
269   "Tomorrow's Antiquity Today . . ." *Architecture: New England* 1 (1975): 16–19.
HADDON HALL (BACK BAY)
270   *AABN* 49 (1895): 42.
HAMILTON, HOTEL (demolished)
271   *AABN* 1 (1876): 373.
HAMMOND CASTLE (GLOUCESTER)
272   Witham, Corinne B. *The Hammond Museum Guide Book.* Gloucester, 1966.
HANCOCK HOUSE (demolished)
273   Millar, Donald. "Notes on the Hancock House, Boston." *OTNE* 17 (1927): 121–124.
274   Watkins, Walter K. "The Hancock House and Its Builder." *OTNE* 17 (1926): 3–19.
HARRIS WOOD CRESCENT (ROXBURY). For a discussion of Townsend Street see nos. *101–102.*
275   *AABN* 29 (1890): 74.
HARVARD UNIVERSITY BUILDINGS (CAMBRIDGE; THE FENWAY; BRIGHTON). See also nos. *47, 141, 616, 686, 782.*
276   Barton, George E. "Harvard University." *AABN* 112 (1917): 31.

277 Bunting, Bainbridge, and Robert H. Nylander. "Harvard University Architecture." In no. *81*, 2:149–203.

278 "Fogg Art Museum." *Arch. Record* 61 (1927): 465–477.

279 *Harvard College Yearbook, 1932.* Cambridge, 1932. The first yearbook to treat in some detail all the new Houses, which are lavishly illustrated.

280 "Harvard University Business School Competition." *Architecture* 51 (1925): 131 et seq.

281 *Harvard University: Education, Bricks and Mortar.* Cambridge, 1949.

282 Moore, Charles. "Puritan Liberalism and Pagan Austerity in New England Architecture." In no. *586*, pp. 95–112. This chapter deals almost entirely with McKim, Mead and White's Georgian Revival work at Harvard.

283 Parsons, David McI., and Douglass Shand Tucci. "The Idea of the House." Typescript. Harvard University Archives, Harvard College Library. 1971.

284 "Recent Collegiate Architecture as Exemplified by the Work of Messrs. Shepley, Rutan and Coolidge at Harvard . . ." *Brickbuilder* 23 (1914): 259–273.

285 Reiff, Daniel D. "[Memorial Hall:] Splendor beneath the Dust." *Harvard Bulletin* 74 (1972): 28–42.

286 Schuyler, Montgomery. "Harvard University." *Arch. Record* 26 (1909): 243–269.

287 Ticknor and Company. "Austin Hall." Monographs on American Architecture, no. 1 (*Arch. Record*, 1886).

288 Whitehill, Walter Muir, "Noble, Neglected Memorial Hall Turns 100." *Harvard Bulletin* 74 (1972): 22–27.

289 ———. "A View of Gore Hall . . ." In no. *63*, pp. 70–73, 74–77.

290 Yeomans, Henry. *Abbott Lawrence Lowell.* Cambridge, 1948. The chapters on the freshman dormitories and the Houses contain all the pertinent background material from Lowell's Annual Reports after the announcement of these projects.

HOLY CROSS, CATHEDRAL OF THE (SOUTH END). See also nos. *39, 446, 571.*

291 Murphy, Francis. *Centennial of Holy Cross Cathedral.* 1975.

HORTICULTURAL HALL (BACK BAY)

292 *AABN* 74 (1901): 71.

293 Benson, Albert E. *History of the Massachusetts Horticultural Society.* 1929.

HOWARD ANTHENAEUM (demolished). See nos. *1, 516.*

HUNNEWELL ESTATES (WELLESLEY). See no. *47.*

IMMACULATE CONCEPTION, CHURCH AND CONVENT OF (MALDEN). See nos. *37, 50.*

IMMACULATE CONCEPTION, CHURCH OF THE (SOUTH END). See also nos. *39, 446, 571.*

294 "Dedication of the Church of the Immaculate Conception." *Boston Journal,* 10 March 1861.

295 Murray, Thomas, and Douglass Shand Tucci. "The South End's Neglected Treasures . . ." *Drumlin* 1 (Sept. 1976): 45.

296 Santayana, George. "The Church of the Immaculate Conception." In *Persons and Places,* pp. 163–177. New York, 1944.

INTERNATIONAL TRUST BUILDING (DOWNTOWN). See also no. *22.*

297 *AABN* 39 (1893): 14.

JESUIT NOVITIATE (WESTON). See also no. *703.*

298 "Jesuit Novitiate." In no. *434,* pp. 37–38.

KEITH MEMORIAL THEATRE, B. F. (DOWNTOWN; now Savoy Theatre). See also no. *517.*

299 *The B. F. Keith Memorial Theatre. Boston Sunday Herald,* 28 Oct. 1928. Special rotogravure section.

KEITH'S THEATRE, B. F. (DOWNTOWN; partially demolished)

300 Birkmire, William. "The Gaiety Theatre." In no. *508.* For some reason this chapter on Keith's Theatre is mistitled.

KENNEDY HOUSE (BROOKLINE)

301 Cameron, Gail. *Rose: A Biography of Rose Kennedy.* New York, 1971.

KINGMAN HOUSE (BROCKTON).

302 Floyd, Margaret Henderson. *309 Main Street . . .* Brockton, 1973.

KING'S CHAPEL (DOWNTOWN). See also no. *566.*

303 Metcalf, Priscilla. "Boston before Bulfinch: Harrison's King's Chapel." *JSAH* 13 (1954): 11–14.

KOCH HOUSE (CAMBRIDGE). See nos. *81, 618.*

KRAGSYDE (MANCHESTER-BY-THE-SEA). See nos. *604, 605, 793.*

LINDSEY MEMORIAL CHAPEL OF EMMANUEL CHURCH (BACK BAY). See also no. *37.*

304 *The Leslie Lindsey Chapel.* 1966.

305 "The Lindsey Chapel." *Architecture* 50 (1924): 393–398.

LONGWOOD TOWERS (BROOKLINE)

306 "Alden Park Manor [Longwood Towers]." In no. *712,* pp. 210–211.

MAJESTIC THEATRE (DOWNTOWN; now Saxon Theatre). See also no. *509.*

307 *AABN* 80 (1903): 24 et seq.

308 "The Majestic." *Boston Sunday Globe,* 15 Feb. 1903, p. 44.

MASONIC TEMPLE (DOWNTOWN; 1867 building). See nos. *39, 628.*

MASSACHUSETTS HISTORICAL SOCIETY BUILDING (THE FENWAY)

309 *Handbook of the Massachusetts Historical Society.* 1949.

MASSACHUSETTS INSTITUTE OF TECHNOLOGY BUILDING, OLD (demolished). See no. *1.*

MASSACHUSETTS INSTITUTE OF TECHNOLOGY (CAMBRIDGE). See also nos. *31, 81, 448.*

310 Kebbon, H. E. "Building the 'New Technology.'" *Arch. Review* 4 (1916): 85–92.

MERCANTILE WHARF (WATERFRONT). See also no. *730.*

311 Huxtable, Ada Louise. "Progressive Architecture in America." *Progressive Architecture* 39 (1958): 117–118.

METROPOLITAN THEATRE (DOWNTOWN; originally Music Hall). See also nos. *510, 515, 708.*

312 Boston Redevelopment Authority. *The Metropolitan Theatre.* 1975.

313 "Metropolitan Theatre." In no. *712,* pp. 136–137.

314 "The Metropolitan Theatre." Scrapbook of newspaper clippings of the theater's history. Fine Arts Dept. (Research), Boston Public Library.

MOTOR MART GARAGE (BACK BAY). See nos. *37, 50.*

MUSEUM OF FINE ARTS (FIRST BUILDING; demolished). See also nos. *321, 480.*

315 Floyd, Margaret Henderson. "A Terra-Cotta Cornerstone for Copley Square: Museum of Fine Arts, Boston, 1870–1876, by Sturgis and Brigham." *JSAH* 32 (1973): 83–103.

410

MUSEUM OF FINE ARTS (SECOND BUILDING; BACK BAY)
316 Addison, Julia de Wolf. *The Boston Museum of Fine Arts.* 1910.
317 Blackall, C. H. "The Sargent Decorations . . ." *American Architecture* 121 (1922): 241–244.
318 Brown, Frank Chouteau. "The Boston Museum's New Wing." *Architecture* 58 (1928): 315–320.
319 Coburn, F. W. "The New Art Museum . . ." *International Studio* 33 (1907–1908): 57–62.
320 Tucci, Douglass Shand. "Three New England Art Galleries by Ralph Adams Cram: The Japanese Department of the Museum of Fine Arts, Boston; the Currier Gallery in Manchester, N.H., and the Gallery on the Moors in Gloucester, Massachusetts." *Currier Gallery Bulletin*, forthcoming issue.
321 Whitehill, Walter Muir. *Museum of Fine Arts, Boston: A Centennial History.* 2 vols. Cambridge, 1970.
MUTUAL LIFE INSURANCE BUILDING (demolished). See also no. 22.
322 *AABN* 3 (1878): 84.
NEW ENGLAND CONSERVATORY OF MUSIC (BACK BAY)
323 *The Conservatory Building.* 1928.
NEW ENGLAND MUTUAL BUILDING (demolished). See no. 22.
NEW ENGLAND MUTUAL BUILDING (BACK BAY). See no. 770.
NEW OLD SOUTH CHURCH (BACK BAY). See also nos. 22, 64, 145, 446.
324 Hill, A. Hamilton. *History of The Old South Church (Third Church), 1869–1884.* 1890.
NEWTON CITY HALL (NEWTON). See also nos. 37, 50.
325 *The Official Dedication Program of the Newton City Hall . . .* Newton, 1932.
OLD SOUTH CHURCH (DOWNTOWN). See no. 1.
OLD STATE HOUSE (DOWNTOWN)
326 Bruce, James L. *The Old State House.* 1965.
327 Whitehill, Walter Muir. "A View of the Old State House . . ." In no. 63, pp. 2–5.
OLD WEST CHURCH (BEACON HILL)
328 Voye, Nancy S. "Asher Benjamin's West Church: A Model for Change." *OTNE* 67 (1976): 7–15.
329 Whitehill, Walter Muir. "A View of the Old West Church." In no. 63, pp. 10–13.
OTIS, HARRISON GRAY, FIRST HOUSE (WEST END). See also nos. 530, 779.
330 Cummings, Abbott Lowell. "The First Harrison Gray Otis House in Boston: A Study in Pictorial Evidence." *OTNE* 60 (1970): 105–108.
331 Nylander, Richard. *The First Harrison Gray Otis House.* 1975.
OTIS, HARRISON GRAY, SECOND HOUSE (BEACON HILL). See also nos. 530, 787.
332 Parsons, Susan, and Wendell D. Garrett. "The Second Harrison Gray Otis House." *Antiques* 92 (1967): 536–541.
OTIS, HARRISON GRAY, THIRD HOUSE (BEACON HILL). See nos. 530, 787.
OUR SAVIOUR, CHURCH OF (BROOKLINE). See also no. 686.
333 Fletcher, Herbert H. *The Church of Our Saviour.* Brookline, 1936.
PAINE HOUSE (WALTHAM). See nos. 47, 611, 793.
PARK STREET CHURCH (DOWNTOWN)
334 Whitehill, Walter Muir. "A View of the Granary Burying Ground . . . and Park Street Church." In no. 63, pp. 30–33.
PARKER HOUSE (DOWNTOWN)
335 "Parker House." In no. 712, pp. 126–127.
336 Spring, James W. *Boston and the Parker House.* 1927.
PARSHLEY HOUSES (DORCHESTER). See also no. 100.
337 Tucci, Douglass Shand. *The Master Builders.* Parts V–VIII of this series appeared in *Dorchester Argus-Citizen,* 15 June–6 July 1972, pp. 3 et seq.
PEABODY, THE (DORCHESTER). See also no. 186.
338 *AABN* 58 (1897): 43.
339 *Brickbuilder* 9 (1900): Plate 72.
PERKINS SCHOOL FOR THE BLIND (WATERTOWN, originally Perkins Institution for the Blind)
340 Perkins Institute. *Eighty-first Annual Report of the Trustees.* 1913. Includes Sturgis's plans.
341 "The Perkins Institute . . ." *Brickbuilder* 22 (1913): 154–156.
PERPETUAL HELP, BASILICA OF OUR LADY OF (MISSION CHURCH; ROXBURY). See also no 42.
342 *AABN* 12 (1877): 240.
343 Byrne, John. *The Glories of Mary in Boston.* 1921.
344 Currier, Charles W. "History of the Church of Our Lady of Perpetual Succor in Boston." *American Catholic Historical Society Report* 2 (1886–1888): 206–224.
PIERCE, S. S., STORE (BROOKLINE)
345 *AABN* 62 (1898): 92.
PINEBANK (JAMAICA PLAIN)
346 Floyd, Margaret Henderson. "Pinebank: Another Conservation Challenge for Boston." *Drumlin* 1 (July 1976): 4–5.
RADCLIFFE COLLEGE. See HARVARD UNIVERSITY BUILDINGS
REDEEMER, CHURCH OF THE (CHESTNUT HILL). See no. 632.
347 Morgan, William D., and Douglass Shand Tucci. "A Guide to the Church of the Redeemer." Typescript. Church of the Redeemer. 1974.
REVERE, PAUL, HOUSE (NORTH END)
348 *Handbook of the Paul Revere Memorial Association.* 1950.
349 "Restoration of the Paul Revere House." *Arch. Record* 36 (1914): 80.
RICHMOND COURT (BROOKLINE). See also no. 542.
350 Cram, Ralph Adams. *Richmond Court Apartments.* 1899. The only known extant copy of this booklet is in the Boston Athenaeum. Plans and exterior photographs were also published in *Brickbuilder* 9 (1900), Plates 40 et seq.
RITZ-CARLTON HOTEL (BACK BAY)
351 "Mural Decorations for the Ritz Carlton Hotel in Boston." *Arch. Record* 63 (1926): 178–179.
352 "Ritz-Carlton Hotel." In no. 712, pp. 134–135.
ROXBURY LATIN SCHOOL (WEST ROXBURY). See no. 37.
ST. ANNE'S CONVENT CHAPEL (ARLINGTON)

353 Cram, Ralph Adams. "Three Small Chapels." *Architecture* 46 (1922): 363–369.
ST. CATHERINE OF GENOA (SOMERVILLE). See nos. *42, 592.*
ST. CATHERINE OF SIENA (NORWOOD). See nos. *42, 686.*
ST. CLEMENT'S CHURCH (CHURCH OF THE REDEEMER; BACK BAY). See also no. *42.*
354 "Church of the Redeemer." In no. *434,* pp. 16–50.
ST. CLEMENT'S CHURCH (SOMERVILLE). See also nos. *42, 50.*
355 "St. Clement's Church, . . ." *Liturgical Arts* 12 (1943): 15–16, 17–20.
ST. ELIZABETH'S CHAPEL (SUDBURY). See no. *353.*
ST. JAMES CHURCH (SOUTH END). See nos. *42, 446.*
ST. JOHN THE EVANGELIST, CHURCH OF (BEACON HILL; originally Beecher Congregational Church). See also nos. *446, 542.*
356 Smith, Robert C. *The Shrine on Bowdoin Street.* 1958.
ST. JOHN'S SEMINARY (BRIGHTON). See also no. *42.*
357 Sexton, John E., and Arthur J. Riley. *History of Saint John's Seminary.* 1945.
ST. LUKE'S CHURCH (CHELSEA)
358 Bourne, Frank. "The Possibilities of Concrete in Building Churches." *Church Militant* (March 1907), p. 6.
ST. PAUL'S CHURCH (BROOKLINE; partially demolished). See also nos. *74, 154, 442, 630.*
359 Bigelow, Robert Payne. "Movements and Men in the Early History of St. Paul's Church . . ." Manuscript in parish archives, 1951.
ST. PAUL'S CHURCH (DEDHAM)
360 Worthington, Arthur M. *History of St. Paul's Episcopal Church . . . 1758–1958.* Dedham, 1958.
ST. PAUL'S CHURCH (DORCHESTER). See nos. *37, 42.*
ST. PETER'S CHURCH (DORCHESTER). See also no. *42.*
361 Marnell, William, and Douglass Shand Tucci. *Saint Peter's Centennial.* 1974.
ST. STEPHEN'S CHURCH (NORTH END). See also nos. *42, 530.*
362 *Saint Stephen's Church, Boston, Massachusetts.* 1966.
363 Whitehill, Walter Muir. "Saint Stephen's Church . . ." In no. *63,* pp. 38–41.
ST. THERESA'S CHURCH (WEST ROXBURY). See nos. *37, 42.*
SALADA TEA BUILDING (BACK BAY). See also no. *707.*
364 Cowell, Mark S. "Echoes of the Tea Trade." *Boston Globe Magazine,* 3 Nov. 1974, pp. 28–32.
365 "Salada Building." In no. *712,* pp. 180–181.
366 Société des Artistes Français. *Salon de 1927.* Paris, 1927.
SECOND CHURCH IN NEWTON (CONGREGATIONAL). See also no. *686.*
367 *Our Church.* Newton, 1926.
SECOND UNIVERSALIST CHURCH (SOUTH END). See no. *446.*
SOMERSET CLUB (BEACON HILL; originally Sears House). See also no. *752.*
368 Whitney, Hugh, and Walter Muir Whitehill. "The Somerset Club." In *The Somerset Club, 1851–1951,* pp. 18–20. 1951.
STATE HOUSE, NEW (BEACON HILL). See also no. *787.*
369 Burrill, Ellen M. *The State House.* 1914.
370 Hitchings, Sinclair, and Caroline H. Farlow. *The Massachusetts State House.* 1964.
371 Kirker, Harold. "The Massachusetts State House." In no. *530,* pp. 101–114.
372 —— and James Kirker. "Bulfinch's Design for the Massachusetts State House." *OTNE* 55 (1964): 43–45.
373 Pickens, Buford. "Wyatt's Pantheon, the State House in Boston and a New View of Bulfinch." *JSAH* 29 (1970): 124–131.
374 Thwing, Leroy. "The Bulfinch State House." *OTNE* 43 (1952): 63–67.
STOUGHTON HOUSE (CAMBRIDGE). See nos. *475, 611, 793.*
SUFFOLK COUNTY COURT HOUSE (1886 BUILDING; BEACON HILL). See no. *22.*
SUFFOLK COUNTY JAIL (WEST END). See No. *1.*
"SUNFLOWER CASTLE" (BEACON HILL)
375 *AABN* 4 (1878): 85.
SYMPHONY HALL (BACK BAY). See also no. *586.*
376 Johnson, H. Earle. *Symphony Hall, Boston,* 1950.
TEMPLE ISRAEL (BACK BAY)
377 Blackall, C. H. "The Symbolism of Temple Israel." In no. *379,* pp. 28–31.
378 Mann, Arthur. *Growth and Achievement: Temple Israel, 1854–1954.* Cambridge, 1953.
379 Obst, S. D. *The Story of Adath Israel.* 1917.
TEMPLE OHABEI SHALOM (BROOKLINE)
380 *American Architecture* 134 (1928): 707–711.
TONTINE CRESCENT (demolished). See also nos. *470, 530.*
381 Waite, Emma F. "The Tontine Crescent and Its Architecture." *OTNE* 43 (1953): 74–77.
TORREY HOUSE (demolished)
382 *AABN* 7 (1880): 141.
TOURAINE HOTEL (DOWNTOWN)
383 *AABN* 58 (1897): 35.
TREMONT HOUSE (demolished). See also nos. *467, 739, 752.*
384 Eliot, William Howard. *Description of the Tremont House . . .* 1830?
385 Lee, Henry. "Boston's Greatest Hotel." *OTNE* 55 (1965): 97–106.
TREMONT TEMPLE (DOWNTOWN)
386 Blackall, C. H. "Tremont Temple." In *Tremont Temple Sketch Book,* pp. 45–64. 1896.
TRINITY CHURCH (BACK BAY). See also nos. *47, 64, 145, 611, 684, 768.*
387 "A Boston Basilica." *Architect* 18 (1877): 274.
388 Chester, Arthur H. *Trinity Church.* Cambridge, 1888.
389 Graff, Myrtle S. *Guidebook to Trinity Church . . .* 1924.
390 Richardson, Henry Hobson. *A Description of Trinity Church.* 1877.

391 Romig, Edgar D. *The Story of Trinity Church* . . . 1952.

392 Sergeant, Perry T. "Colour Decoration in America." *Architect* 18 (1877): 210–211.

393 Stebbins, Theodore E., Jr. "Richardson and Trinity Church . . ." *JSAH* 27 (1968): 181–198.

394 Ticknor and Co. "Trinity Church." Monographs on American Architecture, no. 5 (*Arch. Record,* 1888).

395 Weinberg, Helene B. "John La Farge and the Decoration of Trinity Church, Boston." *JSAH* 33 (1974): 323–353.

TRINITY CHURCH RECTORY (BACK BAY). See nos. *143, 611.*

UNITED SHOE MACHINERY CORPORATION BUILDING (DOWNTOWN). See also no. *489.*

396 *AABN* 134 (1928): 270.

UNION CONGREGATIONAL CHURCH (SOUTH END). See no. *446.*

UNION STATION (demolished). See no. *22.*

VENDOME HOTEL (BACK BAY). See also no. *1.*

397 "Uses of the Past . . ." *Arch. Forum* 137 (1972): 24–33.

VINAL HOUSE (DORCHESTER)

398 Tucci, Douglass Shand. "Dorchester Sinecure at City Hall." *Dorchester Argus-Citizen,* 25 May 1972, p. 2.

WARREN, THE (demolished)

399 *AABN* 20 (1886): 231.

WELLESLEY COLLEGE (WELLESLEY). See also nos. *449, 615, 686.*

400 Clements, Lee Ann. "A New Light on College Hall." *Wellesley Alumnae Magazine* 62 (Spring 1978): 4–7.

401 Poindexter, Jean, and Louise Sander. *The New Wellesley.* 1931.

402 Schuyler, Montgomery. "Three Women's Colleges . . ." *Arch. Record* 31 (1912): 513–537.

WELLESLEY TOWN HALL. See no. *47.*

WESTMINSTER CHAMBERS HOTEL (demolished)

403 *AABN* 71 (1901): 40.

WILBUR THEATRE (DOWNTOWN)

404 "Georgian Architecture in Business." *Boston Evening Transcript,* 2 May 1914, p. 3.

WINN MEMORIAL LIBRARY (WOBURN). See nos. *611, 613, 614.*

WINTHROP (CARTER) BUILDING (DOWNTOWN). See also nos. *38, 486, 542.*

405 Damrell, Charles. "The Carter Building." In no. *22,* pp. 70–71.

406 "The Carter Building." *Inland Architect* 22 (1893): 31.

WOMEN'S CITY CLUB (BEACON HILL; originally Appleton and Parker houses). See no. *752.*

WORTHINGTON BUILDING (DOWNTOWN)

407 "The Worthington Building . . ." *Brickbuilder* 3 (1895): 33–34.

E. BUILDING TYPES

APARTMENT HOUSES AND APARTMENT HOTELS

408 Apartment House Number. *AABN* 110 (29 Nov. 1916): 332–350.

409 Apartment House Number. *Arch. Forum* 43 (1925): 121–184.

410 Bacon, Edwin M. "Apartment Houses and Family Hotels." In no. *1,* pp. 16–17.

411 "Boston Flats." *Brickbuilder* 14 (1905): 119–123.

412 Boston Redevelopment Authority, and the Boston Urban Observatory. *Three Decker Housing in the City of Boston: A Reconnaissance.* 1974.

413 Boston *Transcript.* Real Estate pages, 1870–1925.

414 Brown, Frank Chouteau. "Some Recent Apartment Buildings." *Arch. Record* 63 (1928): 193–278.

415 Comstock, William T. *Two Family and Twin Houses.* New York, 1908.

416 Edgell, G. H. Section on apartment houses in no. *744,* pp. 144–150.

417 Hall, Prescott F. "The Menace of the Three-Decker," and discussion by Edwin H. Marble. In no. *760* (1917), pp. 133–152, 321–327.

418 Hill, George. "Apartment House" and "Tenement House." In no. *802,* cols. 82–89, 777–781.

419 Kilham, Walter H. "The Planning of Apartment Houses." *Brickbuilder* 13 (1904): 2–8.

420 Krim, Arthur J. "The Three Decker as Urban Architecture in New England." *The Monadnock* 44 (1970): 45–55.

421 Logue, Charles. "How It Strikes a Bostonian." In no. *760* (1919), pp. 342–348.

422 May, Charles C. "The Group House — Its Advantages and Possibilities." In no. *760* (1919), pp. 308–311.

423 Newman, Bernard J. "Shall We Encourage or Discourage the Apartment House," and discussion by James H. Hurley, et al. In no. *760* (1917), pp. 153–166, 328–348.

424 Peters, Andrew J. "The City's Obligation in Housing." In no. *760* (1919), pp. 329–335.

425 Sexton, R. W. *American Apartment Houses of Today.* New York, 1926.

BANKS

426 Bank Number. *Arch. Forum* 38 (1923): 253–312.

427 Edgell, G. H. Section on banks in no. *744,* pp. 345–348.

BRIDGES. See also no. *613.*

428 Schweinfurth, Julius. "Some Bridges of Boston's Park System." *AABN* 116 (1919): 329–333.

CHURCHES AND SYNAGOGUES. For a complete checklist of Boston area churches, see no. *61.* See also nos. *18, 42, 99, 149.*

429 Anson, Peter. *Fashions in Church Furnishings, 1840–1940.* London, 1960.

430 Blackall, C. H. "Boston Sketches — Churches." *Inland Architect* 12 (1888): 77–78.

431 Brandeis University, Rose Art Museum. *Two Hundred Years of Synagogue Architecture.* Waltham, Mass., 1976.

432 Coolidge, John P. "Gothic Revival Churches in New England and New York." B.A. thesis, Harvard, 1935.

433 Cram, Ralph Adams. *American Church Architecture of Today.* New York, 1929.

434 ———. *American Churches.* 2 vols. New York, 1915.

435 ———. *The Catholic Church and Art.* New York, 1930.

436 ———. *Church Building.* 1899.

437 ———. "The Philosophy of the Gothic Restoration" and "The Artist and the World." In no. *544*, pp. 19–63, 105–139.

438 Edgell, G. H. Section on churches and synagogues in no. *744*, pp. 197–226.

439 Kervick, Francis. *Architects in America of Catholic Tradition*. Rutland, Vt., 1962.

440 Maginnis, Charles. "Catholic Church Architecture." *Brickbuilder* 15 (1906): 25–28, 46–52.

441 ———. "The Movement for a Vital Christian Architecture and the Obstacles — The Roman Catholic View." *Christian Art* 1 (1917): 22–26.

442 Shinn, George W. *King's Handbook of Notable Episcopal Churches in the United States*. 1889.

443 Short, Ernest H. *A History of Religious Architecture*. New York, 1936.

444 Stanton, Phoebe B. *The Gothic Revival and American Church Architecture*. Baltimore, 1968.

445 Taylor, Walter. "Protestant Churches." In *Forms and Functions of Twentieth-Century Architecture*, ed. Talbot Hamlin, 3:335–336. 3 vols. New York, 1952.

446 Willard, A. R. "Recent Church Architecture in Boston," *New England Magazine* (Feb. 1890), pp. 641–662.

COLLEGIATE AND SCHOOL DESIGN. See also no. *141*.

447 Cram, Ralph Adams. "American University Architecture." In no. *544*, pp. 169–211.

448 Edgell, G. H. Section on academic architecture in no. *744*, pp. 156–163.

449 Klauder, Charles Z., and Herbert C. Wise. *College Architecture in America*. New York, 1929.

450 Schuyler, Montgomery. "Architecture of American Colleges." *Arch. Record* 26 (1909): 243–269.

451 Tolles, Bryant Franklin, Jr. "College Architecture in New England before 1860 . . ." *Antiques* 103 (1973): 502–509.

452 Wheelwright, Edmund M. "The School House." In no. *802*, cols. 422–434. A series by Wheelwright on the same subject appeared in *Brickbuilder* throughout 1897, beginning in 6 (1897): 244–247.

GARAGES AND SERVICE STATIONS. See also no. *81*.

453 Automotive Buildings Number. *Arch. Forum* 46 (1927): 201–312.

454 Blanchard, Harold. "Ramp Design in Public Garages." *Arch. Forum* 35 (1921): 169–175.

455 Guth, Alexander G. "The Automobile Service Station." *Arch. Forum* 45 (1926): 33–56.
    Several early Boston service stations are discussed and illustrated, including a no longer extant duplicate in Dorchester of the South End service station shown in Figure 194.

GOVERNMENT BUILDINGS. See also LIBRARIES AND MUSEUMS; NO. *149*.

456 Edgell, G. H. Section on civic architecture in no. *744*, pp. 226–241.

457 Loring, Charles G. "The Small Town Hall: Plattsburgh, N. Y.; Arlington, Mass.; Tewksbury, Mass.; Weston, Mass., etc. . . ." *Arch. Forum* 47 (1927): 193–204.

458 Sexton, R. W. *American Public Buildings of Today*. New York, 1928.

459 Wheelwright, Edmund M. *Annual Reports of City of Boston Architect Department*. 1891–1894.

460 ———. *Municipal Architecture in Boston*. 1898.

HOSPITALS

461 Edgell, G. H. Section on hospitals in no. *744*, pp. 314–322.

462 Hospital Number. *Arch. Forum* 37 (1922): 245–314.

463 Stevens, Edward F. *The American Hospital of the 20th Century*. New York, 1921. Rev. ed.

HOTELS

464 Edgell, G. H. Section on hotels in no. *744*, pp. 334–345.

465 Hardenburgh, H. J. "Hotel." In no. *802*, cols. 400–414.

466 Hotel Number. *Arch. Forum* 39 (1923): 195–274.

467 Williamson, Jefferson. *The American Hotel*. New York, 1930.

HOUSES (SINGLE-FAMILY). For a checklist of Back Bay town houses, see no. *143*. For a checklist of representative streetcar-suburb houses, see no. *100*. See also nos. *81, 150–156, 167, 172, 174*.

468 Blackall, C. H. "Boston Sketches — Suburban Work." *Inland Architect* 13 (1889): 40–41, 53–54.

469 Brown, Frank Chouteau. "Boston Suburban Architecture." *Arch. Record* 21 (1907): 245–280.

470 ———. "The First Residential 'Row Houses' in Boston." *OTNE* 37 (1947): 60–69.

471 Edgell, G. H. Section on domestic architecture in no. *744*, pp. 87–144, 149–154.

472 Kocher, A. Lawrence. "The American Country House." *Arch. Record* 58 (1925): 401–512.

473 Lancaster, Clay. "The American Bungalow." *Art Bulletin* 40 (1958): 239–253.

474 Seale, William. *The Tasteful Interlude*. New York, 1975.

475 Sheldon, George. *Artistic Country Seats . . .* New York, 1886.

476 "The Narrowness of City House Fronts and the Abuses That Have Arisen in Their Treatment." *AABN* 4 (1878): 51.

477 Wharton, Edith, and Ogden Codman, Jr. *The Decoration of Houses*. New York, 1897.

INDUSTRIAL BUILDINGS. See also no. *81*.

478 Edgell, G. H. Section on factories in no. *744*, pp. 289–294.

479 Industrial Building Number. *Arch. Forum* 39 (1923): 83–151.

LIBRARIES AND MUSEUMS

480 Burt, Nathaniel. *Palaces for the People*. 1977.

481 Edgell, G. H. Section on libraries and museums in no. *744*, pp. 241–271.

482 Harris, Neil. "The Gilded Age Revisited: Boston and the Museum Movement." *American Quarterly* 14 (1962): 545–566.

483 Library and Museum Number. *Arch. Forum* 47 (1927): 497–608.

OFFICE BUILDINGS. See also nos. *27, 32, 157–162, 534, 611, 623–629*.

484 Birkmire, William H. *The Planning and Construction of High Office Buildings*. New York, 1898.

485 Blackall, Clarence H. "Boston Sketches — Business Buildings." *Inland Architect* 12 (1889): 94–96.

486 ———. "The Legitimate Design of the Architectural Casing for Steel Skeleton Structures." *AABN* 66 (1899): 78–80.

487 Corbett, Harvey. "High Buildings on Narrow Streets." *AABN* 119 (1921): 603–608, 617.

488 Edgell, G. H. Section on commercial architecture in no. *744*, pp. 350–375.

489 Fay, Frederick. Section on heights in "The Planning of a City." In no. *13*, pp. 41–61.

490 Jordy, William H. "Masonry Block and Metal Skeleton . . ." and "Functionalism as Fact and Symbol . . ." In no. *765*, pp. 1–180.

491 Nimmons, George C. "Skyscrapers in America." *A.I.A. Journal* 11 (1923): 370–372.

414

492 Office Building Number. *Arch. Forum* 41 (1924): 89–160.
493 Ripley, Hubert G. "Office Buildings of the '90s." *Architecture* 59, 60 (1926): 583–585, 275–278.
494 Sexton, R. W. *American Commercial Buildings of Today.* New York, 1928.
495 "Skyscrapers: Prophecy in Steel: Houston, Philadelphia, Miami, Cleveland, Hollywood, New York, Chicago, Detroit, Boston, Minneapolis." *Fortune* 2 (1930): 84–88.
496 Sullivan, Louis. "The Tall Building, Artistically Considered." *Lippincott's Magazine* 57 (1896): 403–409.
497 Weisman, Winston. "New York and the Problem of the First Skyscraper." *JSAH* 12 (1953): 13–21. Weisman later reorganized and somewhat modified his views in his "A New View of Skyscraper History" in Edgar Kaufmann, Jr., ed., *The Rise of an American Architecture*, New York, 1970, pp. 113–160.

STORES AND SHOPS
498 Edgell, G. H. Section on stores and shops in no. 744, pp. 306–314.
499 French, Leigh, Jr. "Show Windows and Shop Fronts." *Arch. Forum* 46 (1927): 177–192.
500 "Innovations in Small Store Design . . . Three Candy Stores in Boston." *Arch. Forum* 34 (1921): 135–138.
501 Marnell, William. *Once Upon a Store: A Biography of the World's First Supermarket.* New York, 1971.
502 Shop and Store Number. *Arch. Forum* 40 (1924): 233–287.
503 Soames, Dana. "Recent Shop Fronts in New England." *Arch. Forum* 40 (1924): 249–257.

SUBWAY AND ELEVATED SYSTEM
504 "The Boston Subway . . ." *Brickbuilder* 7 (1898): 133–134.
505 Cudahy, Brian J. *Change at Park Street Under . . . Boston's Subways.* Brattleboro, Vt., 1972.
506 "Enameled Brick Treatment of Subway Construction." *Brickbuilder* 9 (1900): 262. The still-extant kiosks of Park Street Station were illustrated in *AABN* 56 (1897): 47.
507 Smith, H. McKelden, III. "The 'El': Boston's Elevated Railroad Stations." In no. 807, pp. 133–139.

THEATERS AND HALLS. For a complete checklist of Boston theaters, see no. 517. See also nos. 158, 162.
508 Birkmire, William. *The Planning and Construction of American Theatres.* New York, 1896.
509 Blackall, Clarence H. "The American Theatre." *Brickbuilder* 17 (1908): 2–8 et seq.
510 Edgell, G. H. Section on theaters and halls in no. 744, pp. 322–333.
511 Hall, B. M. *The Best Remaining Seats.* New York, 1961.
512 Mullin, Donald C. *The Development of the Playhouse: A Survey of Theatre Architecture from the Renaissance to the Present.* Berkeley, Calif., 1970.
513 Motion Picture [Theater] Number. *Arch. Forum* 42 (1925): 361–432.
514 Pichel, Irving. *Modern Theatres.* New York, 1925.
515 Sexton, R. W. *American Theatres of Today.* New York, 1930.
516 Stoddard, Richard. "The Architecture and Technology of Boston Theatres, 1794–1854." Ph.D. diss., Yale, 1971.
517 Tucci, Douglass Shand. *The Boston Rialto: Playhouses, Concert Halls and Movie Palaces.* 1977.
518 Young, William C. *Famous American Playhouses.* Chicago, 1973.

F. ARCHITECTS WHO WORKED IN BOSTON

Architects who practiced chiefly elsewhere are included if they worked also in Boston, as are one or two who briefly lived in the Boston area. For specific buildings by the architects below, see Section D.

ARCHITECTS COLLABORATIVE, THE. See GROPIUS, WALTER.
ATWOOD, HARRISON. See no. 32, pp. 130–131; no. 811, p. 32.
BACON, WILLARD M. See no. 32, p. 401.
BANNER, PETER. See also no. 38.
519 Keith, Elmer D., and William L. Warren. "Peter Banner, Architect, . . ." *OTNE* 57 (1967): 57–76.
BATEMAN, CHARLES J. See no. 32, p. 139.
BEAL, J. WILLIAMS. See no. 811, pp. 61–62.
BENJAMIN, ASHER
520 Benjamin, Asher. *The Works of . . .* 7 vols. 1806–1853. Reprint, New York, 1973.
521 Howe, Florence T. "More about Asher Benjamin." *JSAH* 13 (1954): 16–19.
BESARICK, JOHN H. See no. 32, p. 144.
BLACKALL, CLARENCE H. See also nos. 32, 64, 810.
522 Blackall, C. H. "American Architecture Since the War." *AABN* 133 (1928): 1–11.
523 ——. "Fifty Years Ago." *AABN* 129 (1926): 7–9.
524 ——. "Looking Back on Fifty Years of Architecture." *AABN* 132 (1930): 38–41, 86, 88, 90.
525 ——. "Notes on Travel — Chicago." *AABN* 23 (1888): 90–94.
526 ——. "Notes on Travel — [Adler and Sullivan's] McVickers Theatre [in Chicago]." *AABN* 22 (1887): 299–300, 313–315.
BRADLEE, N. J. See no. 64.
BRIGHAM, CHARLES W. See no. 32, pp. 156–157. See also no. 47.
BROWN, FRANK C. See no. 811, pp. 113–114.
BROWN, J. MERRILL. See no. 32, p. 160.
BRYANT, GRIDLEY J. FOX. See also no. 38.
527 Bailey, Henry T. "An Architect of the Old School." *New England Magazine* 25 (1901): 326–349.
BULFINCH, CHARLES. See also nos. 150–156, 167.
528 Bulfinch, Ellen Susan. *The Life and Letters of Charles Bulfinch.* 1896.
529 Hudnut, Joseph. "The Romantic Architecture of Boston." In no. 725, pp. 6–11.
530 Kirker, Harold. *The Architecture of Charles Bulfinch.* Cambridge, 1969.
531 Kirker, Harold and James. *Bulfinch's Boston 1787–1817.* New York, 1964.
532 Place, Charles A. *Charles Bulfinch, Architect and Citizen.* 1925.

533 Stanley, William H., ed. *Mr. Bulfinch's Boston*. 1963.
BURNHAM, DANIEL H. See also no. *497*.
534 Hines, Thomas S. *Burnham of Chicago*. New York, 1974.
535 Moore, Charles. *Daniel H. Burnham, Architect, Planner of Cities*. 2 vols. 1921. Reprint, New York, 1968.
536 Schuyler, Montgomery. "D. H. Burnham and Co." Great American Architects Series, no. 2 (*Arch. Record*, 1896), pp. 49–71.
CABOT, EDWARD. See no. *38*, pp. 53–54, no. *64*, pp. 17–18.
CARRÈRE AND HASTINGS
537 "The Work of Carrère and Hastings." *Arch. Record* 27 (1910): 1–120.
538 Gray, David. *Thomas Hastings, Architect*. 1933.
CLOUGH, GEORGE A. See no. *32*, p. 186.
COOLIDGE, CHARLES A. See SHEPLEY FIRM
COOLIDGE, CORNELIUS
539 Bernstein, Allen. "Cornelius Coolidge, Architect of Beacon Hill Row Houses, 1810–1840." *OTNE* 39 (1948): 45–46.
CRAM, RALPH ADAMS. For a complete bibliography of Cram's writings, which run into the hundreds, see no. *554*.
540 Allen, George H. "Yankee Medievalist." *Arch. Forum* 55 (1931): 79–80.
541 Cram, Ralph Adams. *Impressions of Japanese Architecture and the Allied Arts*. New York, 1906. Reprint, New York, 1916–1917.
542 ———. *My Life in Architecture*. 1936.
543 ———. "The Architecture of Japan" and "The Architecture of China." In no. *802*, cols. 541–547.
544 ———. *The Ministry of Art*. 1914.
545 ———. *The Substance of Gothic*. 1917.
546 The Cram Collection of Drawings and Memorabilia in the Boston Public Library.
547 Daniel, Ann Miner. "The Early Architecture of Ralph Adams Cram, 1889–1902." Ph.D. diss., University of North Carolina. Chapel Hill, 1978.
548 Hamlin, A. D. F. *A Study of the Designs for the Cathedral of St. John the Divine*. New York, 1925.
549 Muccigrosso, Robert. "American Gothic: Ralph Adams Cram." *Thought* 47 (1972): 102–118.
550 North, Arthur T. *Ralph Adams Cram*. New York, 1931.
551 Porter, Kingsley. Letter of 22 June 1926 to Dr. Cram printed in no. *554*.
552 Schuyler, Montgomery. "The Work of Cram, Goodhue and Ferguson." *Arch. Record* 29 (1911): 4–112.
553 *Times Literary Supplement*, 30 March 1916, p. 141.
554 Tucci, Douglass Shand. *Ralph Adams Cram, American Medievalist*. 1974.
555 ———. "Ralph Adams Cram: America's Foremost Gothic Scholar-Architect." *American Art Review* 111 (1976): 125–136.
556 ———. "Ralph Adams Cram and the Boston Gothicists: A Reappraisal." *JSAH* 34 (1975): 311–312.
557 *The Work of Cram and Ferguson, including Cram, Goodhue and Ferguson*. New York, 1929.
DOANE, RALPH HARRINGTON. See no. *811*, p. 233.
EMERSON, WILLIAM RALPH. See also no. *793*.
558 Zaitzevsky, Cynthia. *The Architecture of William Ralph Emerson, 1837–1917*. Cambridge, 1969.
FOX, JOHN A. See no. *32*, p. 230.
GILBERT, CASS
559 Gilbert, Julia, ed. *Cass Gilbert: Reminiscences and Addresses*. New York, 1935.
GILMAN, ARTHUR. See also nos. *444, 497, 793*.
560 Gilman, Arthur. "Architecture in the U.S." *National Review* 58 (1844): 436–480.
561 ———. *The Story of Boston*. New York, 1889.
GOODHUE, BERTRAM. See also under CRAM, RALPH ADAMS
562 Whitaker, Charles H., ed. *Bertram Grosvenor Goodhue: Architect and Master of Many Arts*. New York, 1925.
GRECO, CHARLES R. See no. *811*, p. 335.
GROPIUS, WALTER (THE ARCHITECTS COLLABORATIVE)
563 Giedion, Sigfried. *Walter Gropius: Work and Teamwork*. New York, 1954.
564 Gropius, Walter. *The New Architecture and the Bauhaus*. New York, 1937.
565 ———, ed. *The Architects Collaborative, 1945–1965*. New York, 1966.
HARRISON, PETER
566 Bridenbaugh, Carl. *Peter Harrison: First American Architect*. Chapel Hill, N.C., 1949.
HARTWELL, HENRY W.
567 Vogel, Susan Maycock. "Hartwell and Richardson: An Introduction to Their Work." *JSAH* 32 (1973): 132–146.
HASTY, JOHN. See no. *32*, p. 255. See also no. *81*.
HOWARD, JOHN GALEN
568 Hays, William C. "Some Architectural Work of John Galen Howard." *Architect and Engineer* 40 (Jan. 1915): 47–92.
HUNT, RICHARD MORRIS
569 Gass, John B. "American Architects . . . Richard Morris Hunt and Henry Hobson Richardson." *Journal of the Royal Institute of British Architects* 3 (1896): 229–232.
570 Schuyler, Montgomery. "A Review of the Works of the Late Richard M. Hunt." *Arch. Record* 5 (1895): 97–108.
KEELEY, PATRICK C.
571 Kervick, Francis. *Patrick Charles Keeley*. South Bend, Ind. 1953.
572 Tucci, Douglass Shand. "The *Other* Gothic Revival: The Work of P. C. Keeley and Maginnis and Walsh." *Drumlin* 1 (March 1976): 4–5.
KILHAM, WALTER. See also no. *38*.
573 Croly, Herbert. "The Work of Kilham and Hopkins." *Arch. Record* 31 (1912): 97–128.
LEMOULNIER, JEAN
574 Kirker, Harold, and David Van Zanten. "Jean Lemoulnier in Boston." *JSAH* 31 (1972): 204–208.
LEWIS, EDWIN J., JR. See no. *32*, p. 290; no. *810*, p. 1408.
LEWIS, W. WHITNEY. See no. *32*, p. 291.
LITTLE, ARTHUR. See also no. *32*.

575 Little, Arthur. *Early New England Interiors.* 1878.
576 Sturges, Walter Knight. "Arthur Little and the Colonial Revival." *JSAH* 32 (1973): 147–163.
LONGFELLOW, ALEXANDER W. See no. 32, p. 295; no. 810, p. 1441.
LORING, GEORGE F. See no. 32, p. 296.
LOWELL, GUY
577 "The Works of Guy Lowell." *Arch. Record* 13 (1906): 13–40.
MCINTIRE, SAMUEL
578 Cousins, Frank, and P. M. Ripley. *The Woodcarver of Salem.* 1916.
579 Kimball, Fiske. *Mr. Samuel McIntire, Carver: The Architect of Salem.* Salem, Mass. 1940.
MCKAY, HENRY S. See no. 32, p. 307.
MCKIM, CHARLES FOLLEN
580 Bacon, Henry. "Charles Follen McKim . . ." *Brickbuilder* 19 (1910): 38–47.
581 Cortissoz, Royal. "Some Critical Reflections on the Architectural Genius of Charles Follen McKim." *Brickbuilder* 19 (1910): 23–37.
582 Desmond, Henry W. "The Work of McKim, Mead and White." *Arch. Record* 20 (1906): 153–268.
583 Granger, Alfred H. *Charles Follen McKim.* 1913.
584 Hudnut, Joseph. "The Romantic Architecture of Boston." In no. 725, pp. 11–13.
585 *Monograph of the Work of McKim, Mead and White, 1879–1915.* New York, 1915. Rev. ed., New York, 1973. Intro. by Leland Roth.
586 Moore, Charles. *The Life and Times of Charles Follen McKim.* 1929. Reprint, New York, 1969.
587 Moses, Lionel. "McKim, Mead and White . . ." *AABN* 121 (1922): 413–424.
588 Peabody, Robert S. "A Tribute." *Brickbuilder* 19 (1910): 55–56.
589 Ramsey, Stanley. "The Work of McKim, Mead and White." *Journal of the Royal Institute of British Architects* 25 (1917): 25–29.
590 Reilly, C. H. *McKim, Mead and White.* London, 1924.
591 Sturgis, Russell. "McKim, Mead and White." Great American Architects Series, no. 1 (*Arch. Record*, 1895): 1–111.
MAGINNIS, CHARLES DONAGH. See also nos. 434, 436.
592 Baxter, Sylvester. "The Works of Maginnis and Walsh." *Arch. Record* 53 (1923): 93–115.
593 Dooley, William Germain. "Charles Donagh Maginnis." In no. 725, pp. 83–84.
594 Maginnis, Charles. Introduction to no. 557.
595 Maginnis and Walsh Collection of Drawings in the Boston Public Library.
596 Walsh, Robert, and Andrew W. Roberts, eds. *Charles Donagh Maginnis: A Selection of His Essays and Addresses.* New Haven, Conn., 1956.
MOSELEY, HERBERT. See no. 32, p. 319.
NEWCOMB, E. A. P. See no. 32, p. 323.
OLMSTED, FREDERICK LAW. See also no. 613.
597 Broadus, Mitchell. *Frederick Law Olmsted.* Baltimore, 1924.
598 Olmsted, Frederick L., Jr., and Theodora Kimball. *Frederick Law Olmsted.* New York, 1922.
599 Roper, Laura Wood. *FLO.* Baltimore, 1973.
600 Zaitzevsky, Cynthia. "Frederick Law Olmstead and the Boston Park System." In *Boston's Uncommon Parks.* 1976.
PARKER, THOMAS AND RICE
601 "Notes on the Work of Parker, Thomas and Rice of Boston and Baltimore." *Arch. Record* 34 (1913): 97–184.
PARRIS, ALEXANDER. See also no. 752.
602 "Parris' Perusal." *OTNE* 58 (1967): 51–59.
PEABODY, ROBERT SWAIN. See also nos. 64, 793.
603 Dooley, William Germain. "Robert Swain Peabody." In no. 725, pp. 72–74.
604 Holden, Wheaton. "Robert Swain Peabody of Peabody and Stearns in Boston — The Early Years (1870–1886)." Ph.D. diss., Boston University, 1969.
605 ———. "The Peabody Touch: Peabody and Stearns of Boston, 1870–1917." *JSAH* 32 (1973): 114–131.
606 Peabody, Robert S. "Georgian Houses of New England." *AABN* 2 (1877): 338–339; 3 (1878): 54–55.
607 The Peabody and Stearns Collection of Drawings in the Boston Public Library.
608 Sturgis, Russell. "The Work of Peabody and Stearns." Great American Architects Series, no. 6 (*Arch. Record*, 1896), pp. 53–97.
PERRY, SHAW AND HEPBURN. See no. 811, pp. 376, 608. See also no. 37.
PRESTON, WILLIAM G. See also no. 32.
609 The William Preston Collection of Drawings in the Boston Public Library.
PUTNAM, J. PICKERING. See no. 32, p. 363.
RICHARDSON, HENRY HOBSON. See also nos. 783, 793.
610 Bosworth, Welles. "I Knew Richardson." *Journal of the A.I.A.* 16 (1951): 115–127.
611 Hitchcock, Henry-Russell. *The Architecture of H. H. Richardson and His Times.* New York, 1936, Rev. ed., Cambridge, 1961.
612 Langton, W. A. "The Method of H. H. Richardson." *Architect and Contract Reporter* 63 (1900): 156–158.
613 O'Gorman, James F. "Henry Hobson Richardson and Frank Lloyd Wright." *Art Quarterly* 32 (1969): 308–311.
614 Van Rensselaer, M. Griswold. *Henry Hobson Richardson and His Works.* New York, 1969.
RINN, J. PHILIP. See no. 32, p. 371.
ROGERS, ISAIAH. See no. 752, pp. 111–117.
ROTCH AND TILDEN. See no. 32, pp. 375, 423. See also no. 542.
SCHWEINFURTH, JULIUS
615 Neitz, Stephen J. *Julius A. Schweinfurth: Master Designer, 1858–1931.* Ed. Wheaton Holden. 1975.
SEARS, WILLARD. See no. 810, p. 2091.
SHEPLEY FIRM. See also nos. 32, 810, 811.
616 Forbes, J. D. "Shepley, Bulfinch, Richardson and Abbott, . . ." *JSAH* 17 (1958): 19–31.
617 Sturgis, Russell. "The Work of Shepley, Rutan and Coolidge." Great American Architects Series, no. 3 (*Arch. Record*, 1896), pp. 1–51.

417

SPOFFORD, JOHN C. See no. 32, p. 401.

STONE, EDWARD DURELL

618 Stone, Edward Durell. *The Evolution of An Architect*. New York, 1962.

STRICKLAND, BLODGET AND LAW. See no. 618, p. 21.

STURGIS, JOHN HUBBARD. See also no. 143.

619 Floyd, Margaret Henderson. "Sturgis and Brigham." In no. 47, pp. 8–10.

STURGIS, R. CLIPSTON. See also nos. 32, 810.

620 Dooley, William Germain. "R. Clipston Sturgis." In no. 725, pp. 79–80.

621 Sturgis, R. Clipston. "Architecture in England." In no. 802, cols. 886–914.

622 ———. Collection of Notebooks at the Boston Athenaeum.

SULLIVAN, LOUIS. See also nos. 47, 490, 497, 534.

623 Bush-Brown, Albert. *Louis Sullivan*. New York, 1960.

624 Connely, Willard. *Louis Sullivan As He Lived*. New York, 1960.

625 Hoffman, Donald. "The Set-back City of 1891: An Unknown Essay by Louis H. Sullivan." *JSAH* 29 (1970): 181–187.

626 Morrison, Hugh. *Louis Sullivan: Prophet of Modern Architecture*. New York, 1935.

627 Schuyler, Montgomery. "Adler and Sullivan." Great American Architects Series, no. 2 (*Arch. Record*, 1896), pp. 3–48.

628 Sullivan, Louis. *Autobiography of an Idea*. New York, 1924. Reprint, New York, 1956.

629 Weisman, Winston. "Philadelphia Functionalism and Sullivan." *JSAH* 20 (1961): 3–19.

THAYER, S. J. F. See no. 32, p. 421.

UPJOHN, RICHARD. See also no. 444.

630 Upjohn, Everard. *Richard Upjohn: Architect and Churchman*. New York, 1939. Reprint, New York, 1968.

VAN BRUNT, HENRY

631 Coles, William A., ed. *Architecture and Society: Essays of Henry van Brunt*. Cambridge, 1969.

VAUGHAN, HENRY. See also nos. 436, 554.

632 Morgan, William. *The Architecture of Henry Vaughan*. Ann Arbor, Mich., 1972.

WALKER, C. HOWARD. See no. 32, p. 431.

WARE, WILLIAM R. See also no. 38.

633 Bunting, Bainbridge. "Ware and Van Brunt." In no. 47, pp. 6–7.

634 Ware, William R. "Eclecticism." In no. 802, cols. 846–848.

WARREN, H. LANGFORD. See no. 32, p. 437.

WETHERELL, GEORGE H. See no. 32, p. 444; no. 810, p. 2462.

WHEELWRIGHT, EDMUND M.

635 Dooley, William Germain. "Edmund M. Wheelwright." In no. 725, pp. 75–78.

WILLARD, SOLOMON. See also nos. 38, 752.

636 Wheildon, William W. *Memoir of Solomon Willard . . .* Ca. 1865.

WILLS, ROYAL BARRY. See also no. 811.

637 Wills, Royal Barry. *Houses for Homemakers*. New York, 1945.

WRIGHT, FRANK LLOYD. See also nos. 585, 768, 793.

638 Hitchcock, Henry-Russell. "Frank Lloyd Wright and the 'Academic Tradition.' " *Journal of the Warburg and Courtauld Institutes* 7 (1944): 46–53.

YOUNG, AMMI B. See also no. 752.

639 Woodhouse, Lawrence. "Ammi Burnham Young, 1798–1874." *JSAH* 25 (1966): 268–280.

640 ———. "Architectural Projects in the Greek Revival Style by Ammi B. Young." *OTNE* 60 (1970): 73–85.

G. BOSTON ARTISTS AND CRAFTSMEN
AND ARCHITECTURAL ART

GENERAL

641 American Federation of Arts. *Art in Our Country*. Washington, D.C., 1923.

642 Boston Society of Arts and Crafts. *Annual Reports*. 1901, 1908, 1909, 1912, 1914, 1917, 1918, 1919, 1920.

643 Cleveland, Frank. "The Arts and Crafts." *Christian Art* 2 (1907): 72–80.

644 Code, Grant H. "The Decorative Arts." In no. 13, pp. 379–390.

645 Cram, Ralph Adams. "The Artist Crafts." In no. 436, pp. 217–238.

646 ———. "The Craftsman and the Architect." In no. 544, pp. 143–166.

647 Dexter, Arthur. "The Fine Arts in Boston." In no. 65, 4:383–444.

648 Downes, William H. "General Progress in the Fine Arts." In no. 13, pp. 335–339.

649 Gordon, Jean. *The Fine Arts in Boston*. Ann Arbor, Mich., 1965.

650 Fielding, Mantle. *Dictionary of American Painters, Sculptors and Engravers*. New York, 1926. Reprint, 1965.
      Lists many of the artists and craftsmen mentioned in the text. No. 655, however, often contains fuller entries.

651 Marlat, Earl. "Transfiguration." In no. 686.

652 Ritter, Richard H. *The Arts of the Church*. 1947.

653 Society of Arts and Crafts, Boston and New York. *Annual Reports*, 1925, 1927.

654 Whitehill, Walter Muir. "Boston Artists and Craftsmen at the Opening of the Twentieth Century." Unpublished paper given in 1976 to the Art-Workers' Guild, London.

655 "Who's Who in Art." *American Art Annual* 24 (1927): 465–802.

ARCHITECTURAL SCULPTURE (WOOD) INCLUDING CARVING AND JOINERY. See also nos. 181, 186.

656 Blake, Channing. "Architects as Furniture Designers." *Antiques* (1976): 1042–1047.

657 Coburn, Frank W. "Wood Carving and Architecture." *The Studio* 41 (1910): lxiv.

658 Cram, Ralph Adams. "John Kirchmayer, Master Craftsman." *Architecture* 63 (1931): 87–92.

659 Farnam, Anne. "A. H. Davenport and Company, Boston Furniture Makers." *Antiques* 109 (1976): 1048–1055.

660 Gibson, Katharine. "A Wood-Carver of Today: I. Kirchmayer." In *The Goldsmith of Florence*, pp. 171–186. New York, 1929.

661 Karnagahn, A. W. "Ecclesiastical Wood Carving in America." *International Studio* 85 (1926): 50–53.

662 Museum of Fine Arts, Boston. *The Furniture of H. H. Richardson*. 1962.

663 O'Gorman, James F. "Decorative Arts." In no. 613, pp. 203–210.

664 Sturgis, R. Clipston. "On Certain Carvings of I. Kirchmayer." *Christian Art* 4 (1908): 131–144.

665 Tower, L. Leslie. "The Wood Carvings of I. Kirchmayer." Reprint, ca. 1910, from unidentified journal. Cram Collection, Boston Public Library.

ARCHITECTURAL SCULPTURE (STONE AND CUT-STONE DETAIL). See also nos. *145, 181, 186*.

666 Adams, Adeline. *Daniel Chester French: Sculptor*. 1932.

667 Cresson, Margaret. *Journey into Fame: The Life of Daniel Chester French*. Cambridge, 1947.

668 Forbes, Allan. *Some Statues of Boston*. 1946.

669 ———. *Other Statues of Boston*. 1947.

670 Gardner, Albert TenEyck. *American Sculpture*. New York, 1965.

671 Geranio, Silvio. "Domingo Mora." *Revisto de la Sociedad Amigos de la Argueologia* (Montevideo, 1924), pp. 247–268.

672 John Evans Collection. Print Dept., Boston Public Library.

673 Laroche, Ernest. "Domingo Mora." In *Alqunos: Pintores y Escultorres*, pp. 151–156. Montevideo, 1939.

674 Maginnis, Charles D. "Sculpture." In no. 13, pp. 365–378.

675 Metropolitan Museum of Art. *American Sculpture*. New York, 1965.

676 Saint-Gaudens, Augustus. *Reminiscences . . .* 2 vols. New York, 1913.

677 Taft, Lorado. *The History of American Sculpture*. New York, 1903.

678 Tharp, Louise Hall. *Saint-Gaudens and the Gilded Era*. 1970.

679 *The Sculpture of Joseph Coletti*. Intro. by Allan Priest. New York, 1968.

680 Whitney Museum of American Art. *200 Years of American Sculpture*. 1976.

681 Whitehill, Walter Muir. *Boston Statues*. Barre, Mass., 1970.

682 Wright, John. *Some Notable Altars in the Church of England and in the American Episcopal Church*. New York, 1908.

STAINED GLASS AND MURAL DECORATION. See also nos. *145, 186, 215, 216, 219, 242, 392, 395*.

683 "Belligerent Gothicist, Patron of Glass — Cram." *Fortune* 2 (1930): 77.

684 Berkon, Susan F. "Stained Glass in Back Bay Churches." In no. *807*, pp. 121–131.

685 Brown, R. Walter. "Singer in Light — Charles J. Connick." Reprint, ca. 1940, from unidentified journal. Cram Collection, Boston Public Library.

686 Connick, Charles J. *Adventures in Light and Colour*. New York, 1937.
    The appendices include a discussion of Boston glassmen and a list, for the most part accurate, of stained glass by well-known studios in the Boston area.

687 ———. "Boston Stained Glass Craftsmen." *Stained Glass* 28 (1933): 84–93.

688 ———. "Stained Glass Windows: The Craft." *Technology Monthly and Harvard Engineering Journal* 3 (1916): 3–7.

689 "Connick, Charles J." *Cowley* 19 (1946): 25–28.

690 Charles Connick Collection. Print Dept., Boston Public Library.

691 Cortissoz, Royal. *John La Farge: A Memoir and a Study*. 1911.

692 Cram, Ralph Adams. "Stained Glass and Decoration." In no. *436*, pp. 127–150.

693 Goodhue, Harry Eldridge. "Church Windows in America." *Arch. Review* 12 (1905): 196–199.

694 Harrison, Martin. "Victorian Stained Glass." *Connoisseur* 182 (1973): 251–254.
    The author discusses only English glass, but by several makers (Westlake; Clayton and Bell) whose work is extant in Boston and is not generally well documented.

695 Koch, Robert. *Louis C. Tiffany: Rebel in Glass*. New York, 1966.

696 Lucas, E. V. *Edwin Austin Abbey: Royal Academician*. 1921.

697 McKibbin, David. *Sargent's Boston*. 1965.

698 Mount, Charles. *John Singer Sargent: A Biography*. New York, 1955.

699 Museum of Fine Arts, Boston. "Augustus Saint-Gaudens," "John La Farge," and "John Singer Sargent." In no. *148*, pp. 122–133.

700 Purtell, Joseph. *The Tiffany Touch*. New York, 1971.

701 Skinner, Orin. "Stained Glass Tours: Boston." *Stained Glass* 60 (1965): 7–17.

702 Tiffany, Louis C. "American Art Supreme in Colored Glass." *The Forum* 15 (1893): 621–628.

703 Tucci, Douglass Shand. "Yankee Stained Glass: Windows as Architecture in Four Boston Churches." *American Art Review*, forthcoming issue.

704 Wattenmaker, Richard J. *Puvis de Chavannes and the Modern Tradition*. Toronto, 1975.

705 Weinberg, Helene. "The Early Stained Glass Work of John LaFarge (1835–1910)." *Stained Glass* 77 (Summer 1972): 4–16.

706 ———. "A Note on the Chronology of LaFarge's Early Windows." *Stained Glass* 77 (Winter 1972–1973): 13–15.

METALWORK

707 Cram, Ralph Adams. "The Work of Henry Wilson." *Christian Art* 2 (1907–1908): 261–273.

708 Geerlings, Gerald K. *Metal Crafts in Architecture*. New York, 1929. Reprint, 1957.

709 ———. *Wrought Iron in Architecture*. New York, 1929.

710 Gibson, Katharine. "Master Smith: Frank Koralewsky." In *The Goldsmith of Florence*, pp. 187–206. New York, 1929.

711 Glendenning, Herman W. "Arthur J. Stone, Master Craftsman." *Silver* (Sept. 1973), pp. 27–28.

H. GENERAL SOURCES AND SUGGESTED FURTHER READING

This is a highly selective bibliography. See also "Suggested Reading" in no. *63*, pp. 195–200.

712 *Achievements of New England Architects*. 1923.
    A collection of plates, with text, of then-prominent buildings erected throughout New England.

713 Adams, Adeline. *Childe Hassam*. New York, 1938.
714 American Federation of Arts and Institute of Contemporary Art. *The Cultural Resources of Boston*. New York, 1965.
715 *American Victorian Architecture*. Intro. by Arnold Lewis. New York, 1975. Republication of *L'Architecture Américaine*. Paris, 1886.
716 Appleton, Jane. "Theatrical Art Deco Swayed Bulfinch Boston." *Boston Sunday Globe Magazine*, 30 Nov. 1975, pp. 15–62.
717 Austin, William D. "A History of the Boston Society of Architects in the Nineteenth Century." 3 vols. 1942. Typescript. Boston Athenaeum.
718 *Avery Index to Architectural Periodicals*. 1973. 2d ed.
719 *Avery Obituary Index of Architects and Artists*. 1963.
720 Bacon, Edwin M. *The Book of Boston*. 1916.
721 Bannister, Turpin C. "Bogardus Revisited . . . The Iron Fronts." *JSAH* 15 (1956): 12–22.
722 Berenson, Bernard. *Sunset and Twilight*. New York, 1963.
723 Blake, Peter. *Form Follows Fiasco: Why Modern Architecture Hasn't Worked*. 1977.
724 *Boston Blue Book*. 1931. See no. *736*.
725 *Boston Society of Architects: The First Hundred Years, 1867–1967*. Ed. Marvin E. Goody and Robert P. Walsh. 1967.
726 Boston Transcript. *Index to Obituaries*. 5 vols. 1875–1930.
   A chief source here for the biographical profiles of Cushing Avenue residents; a number of Boston architects are also included.
727 Bragdon, Claude. "The Gothic Spirit." *Christian Art* 2 (1908): 165–172.
728 Brooks, Van Wyck. *The Flowering of New England*. New York, 1936.
729 ———. *New England Indian Summer: 1865–1915*. New York, 1940.
730 Bryan, John. *Boston's Granite Architecture, c. 1810–60*. Ann Arbor, Mich., 1972.
731 Burchard, John, and Albert Bush-Brown. *The Architecture of America*. 1961.
732 Bush-Brown, Harold. *Beaux-Arts to Bauhaus and Beyond*. New York, 1976
733 Carrott, Richard C. "The Neo-Egyptian Style in American Architecture." *Antiques* 90 (1966): 482–488.
734 Chapman, John Jay. *Memories and Milestones*. New York, 1915.
735 Clark, Kenneth. *Civilisation*. New York, 1969.
736 *Clark's Boston Blue Book, 1913: The Elite Private Address and Club Directory and Ladies Visiting List*.
   Includes listings of upper and upper-middle-class residential streets in all parts of the city of Boston and in suburban Brookline and Cambridge; listed alphabetically by residents' name and also by street number, and including the residents of the principal apartment houses and hotels and the membership of the important social clubs. The 1931 volume (no. *724*) includes also Milton and Chestnut Hill.
737 Conant, Kenneth John. "The New Boston Architecture in an Historical Setting." In no. *725*, pp. 89–98.
738 Cook, Clarence. "Architecture in America." *North American Review* 135 (1882): 247–249.
739 Dickens, Charles. *American Notes*. London, 1855.
740 Downing, Andrew J. *The Architecture of Country Houses. . . .* New York, 1850.
741 Eaton, Quaintance. *The Boston Opera Company*. New York, 1965.
742 Economy Concrete Company. *Many Examples of The Use of Decorative Concrete Stone*. New Haven, 1915.
743 Edgell, George H. "The Development of American Architecture." In no. *744*, pp. 3–84.
744 ———. *American Architecture of Today*. New York, 1928. Sections pertinent to this study are listed separately.
745 Eliot, Charles W. *The Book of American Interiors*. 1876.
746 Emerson, Ralph Waldo. "The American Scholar: An Oration . . . 1837." In *Emerson's Essays*, pp. 113–154. New York, 1900.
747 Fergusson, James. *History of the Modern Styles of Architecture*. 3d ed. revised by Robert Kerr. London, 1891.
748 Girouard, Mark. *Sweetness and Light: The 'Queen Anne' Movement, 1860–1900*. London, 1978.
749 Green, Martin. *The Problem of Boston*. New York, 1966.
750 Hale, Edward Everett. *A New England Boyhood*. 1893.
751 Hamlin, A. D. F. "Twenty-five Years of American Architecture." *Arch. Record* 40 (1916): 1–4.
752 Hamlin, Talbot. "The Greek Revival in Boston." In *Greek Revival Architecture in America*. New York, 1944, pp. 90–118.
753 ———. *The American Spirit in Architecture*. New Haven, 1926.
754 Handlin, Oscar. *Boston's Immigrants*. Cambridge, 1959. Rev. ed.
755 "Highlights of American Architecture, 1776–1976." *A.I.A. Journal* 65 (1976): 88–158.
   The source of the survey of significant U.S. buildings discussed in the Introduction.
756 Historic American Buildings Survey. *Massachusetts Catalogue*. 1964.
757 Hitchcock, Henry-Russell. *Architecture; Nineteenth and Twentieth Centuries*. Baltimore, 1958.
758 ———, and Philip Johnson. *The International Style . . .* New York, 1932. 2d ed., New York, 1966.
759 Hobson, Barbara, and Paul M. Wright. *Boston, A State of Mind: An Exhibition Record*. 1977.
760 *Housing Problems in America*. New York, 1914–1920.
   A series of volumes issued every year. Articles pertinent to this study are listed separately throughout this bibliography with the year of the volume in parentheses after the identifying numbers.
761 Howe, Helen. *The Gentle Americans, 1864–1960*. New York, 1965.
762 Howells, John Mead. *Lost Examples of Colonial Architecture*. New York, 1931. Reprint, New York, 1963.
763 James, Henry. *The American Scene*. New York, 1907.
764 Jones, Howard Mumford and Bessie Zaban. *The Many Voices of Boston . . .* 1975.
   Includes selections from such classics as *The Late George Apley*, *The Last Hurrah*, etc.
765 Jordy, William H. *American Buildings and Their Architects: Progressive and Academic Ideals at the Turn of the Twentieth Century*. New York, 1976.
766 Kidney, Walter. *The Architecture of Choice: Eclecticism in America, 1880–1930*. New York, 1974.
767 Kimball, Fiske, and G. H. Edgell. *A History of Architecture*. New York, 1918.
768 Kimball, Fiske. "Eclecticism and Functionalism." *Arch. Forum* 29 (1918): 21–25.
769 Lancaster, Osbert. *Pillar to Post*. London, 1938.
770 LeMessurier, William J. "Architecture and Engineering in Boston." In no. *725*, pp. 119–120.

771 Logue, Charles. "How It Strikes a Bostonian." In no. *760* (1918): 342–348.
772 Loth, Calder, and Julius Trousdale Sadler, Jr. *The Only Proper Style: Gothic Architecture in America.* 1975.
773 Maass, John. *The Gingerbread Age.* New York, 1957.
774 McAndrew, John. "Massachusetts." In *Guide to Modern Architecture: Northeast States.* New York, 1940.
775 Madsen, Stephen Tschudi. *Art Nouveau.* New York, 1967.
776 Major, Howard. *The Domestic Architecture of the Early American Republic: The Greek Revival.* Philadelphia, 1926.
777 Mann, Arthur. *Yankee Reformers in an Urban Age.* Chicago, 1974.
778 Metropolitan Boston Number. *AABN* 134 (1928): 632–716.
779 Morison, Samuel Eliot. *The Life and Letters of Harrison Gray Otis . . .* 1913.
780 ———. *The Maritime History of Massachusetts, 1783–1860.* 1921.
781 ———. *One Boy's Boston.* Garden City, N.Y., 1948.
782 ———. *Three Centuries of Harvard, 1636–1936.* Cambridge, 1936.
783 Mumford, Lewis. *The Brown Decades.* New York, 1931.
784 ———. *Sticks and Stones.* New York, 1924. Reprint, with new preface, Cambridge, 1955.
785 Myerson, Martin, and Edward C. Banfield. *Boston: The Job Ahead.* Cambridge, 1966.
786 Norton, Charles Eliot, ed. *The Letters of John Ruskin to Charles Eliot Norton.* 2 vols. 1904.
787 Pierson, William H., Jr. *American Buildings and Their Architects: The Colonial and Neo-Classical Styles.* New York, 1976.
788 *Rand McNally Guide to Boston.* 1911.
789 Ruskin, John. *The Seven Lamps of Architecture.* London, 1849. Reprint, New York, 1966.
790 Santayana, George. *The Letters of . . .* New York, 1955.
791 ———. *People and Places.* New York, 1944.
792 Schuyler, Montgomery. "The Romanesque Revival in America." *Arch. Record* 1 (1891): 151–198.
793 Scully, Vincent. *The Shingle Style . . .* New Haven, Conn., 1955.
794 Seale, William. *The Tasteful Interlude: American Interiors through the Camera's Eye, 1860–1917.* New York, 1975.
795 Selz, Peter. *Art Nouveau.* New York, 1959.
776 Shannon, Martha A. S. *Boston Days of William Morris Hunt.* 1923.
797 Smith, Norris Kelly. Review of nos. *534, 585,* and *766. JSAH* 34 (1975): 324–326.
798 Solomon, Barbara. *Ancestors and Immigrants: A Changing New England Tradition.* Chicago, 1956.
799 Stein, Roger. *John Ruskin and Aesthetic Thought in America, 1840–1900.* Cambridge, 1969.
800 Story, Grace Haskell. *Edward Howard Haskell: A Memoir.* Cambridge, 1927.
801 Sturges, Walter Knight. "The Long Shadow of Norman Shaw." *JSAH* 9 (1950): 15–20.
802 Sturgis, Russell, ed. *A Dictionary of Architecture and Building . . .* 3 vols. New York, 1901–1902.
     Articles pertinent to this study are listed separately.
803 Tallmadge, Thomas E. *The Story of Architecture in America.* New York, 1927.
804 Torre, Susana, ed. *Women in American Architecture: A Historical and Contemporary Perspective.* New York, 1977.
805 Tyron, W. S. *Parnassus Corner: A Life of James T. Fields, Publisher to the Victorians.* 1963.
806 Upjohn, Everard, et al. *History of World Art.* New York, 1949.
807 Victorian Society of America, New England Chapter. *Victorian Boston Today: Ten Walking Tours.* Ed. Pauline Chase Harrell and Margaret Supplee Smith. 1975.
808 Weston, George F., Jr. *Boston Ways: High, By, and Folk.* 1957 and later eds.
     Interesting enough to be worth reading despite a number of misleading statements and inaccuracies.
809 Whitehill, Walter Muir. *Boston in the Age of John Fitzgerald Kennedy.* Norman, Okla., 1966.
810 *Who's Who in America 1914–1915.* Vol. 8. Chicago, 1914.
811 *Who's Who in Massachusetts 1940–1941.* 1940.
812 [Wines, E. C.] *A Trip to Boston in a Series of Letters to the Editor of the Boston Gazette.* 1838.
813 Withey, Henry F. and Elsie. *Dictionary of American Architects, Deceased.* Los Angeles, 1957.

Bibliography
for Parts iii and iv

THIS BIBLIOGRAPHY is restricted to sources significant for the new sections of *Built in Boston,* or that offer further data or a range of critical opinion of which the reader ought to be mindful. Like the bibliography of the original two parts, this one has been broken down into several sections on the model designed by the late Betsy Pitha, former head of Little, Brown's copyediting department, whose gift it was to know how to organize such things. Besides the sources listed here, the many artists and architects who contributed their knowledge and expertise to the project were an invaluable resource. Interviews and conversations with the following individuals are referred to throughout the text and are gratefully acknowledged: Ann Beha; Jean Paul Carlhian; James Cuno; Peter Forbes; H. A. Crosby Forbes; T. Kinney Frelinghuysen; Frank Gehry; Brian Healy; Gerhard Kallmann; Alex Krieger; Andrea Lears; Rodolpho Machado; Robert Mack; Michael McKinnell; Tim O'Donnell; William Osgood; Bruce Brooks Pfeiffer; Mónica Ponce de Leôn; William Rawn; Neil Rudenstine; Robert Rettig; Warren Schwartz; Robert Silver; Jorge Silvetti; F. A. Stahl; Nader Tehrani; Jane Thompson; Roger Webb; Jane Weinzapfel; Bruce Wood.

Six sections follow:

I.   Boston and Modernism
J.   Boston Generally
K. Modernism, Post-Modernism, and Preservation
L.   Individual Buildings 1950–2000
M. Architects Who Worked in Boston 1950–2000
N. Artists and Craftspeople Who Worked in Boston 1950–2000

The following abbreviations and short titles are used regularly:

Arch.	*Architecture*
Arch. Boston	*Architecture Boston*
Arch. Forum	*Architectural Forum*
Arch. Record	*Architectural Record*

Arch. Review	*Architectural Review*
B&T	*Banker and Tradesman*
Boston	*Boston Tradesman*
Globe	*Boston Globe*
Harvard	*Harvard Magazine*
Herald	*Boston Herald*
Int. Des.	*Interior Design*
JAIA	*Journal of the American Institute of Architects*
JSAH	*Journal of the Society of Architectural Historians*
NEQ	*New England Quarterly*
NYT	*New York Times*
NYTBR	*New York Times Book Review*
NYTM	*New York Times Magazine*
PA	*Progressive Architecture*
Phoenix	*Boston Phoenix*

I. BOSTON AND MODERNISM

814   Anderson, Lawrence. "Architectural Education at M.I.T.: The 1930's and After." In *Architectural Education and Boston,* M. H. Floyd, ed. Boston Architectural Center, 1989, pp. 87–90.

815   Blake, Peter. *Form Follows Fiasco.* Boston: Houghton Mifflin, 1977.

816   Campbell, Robert. *Cityscapes of Boston.* Boston: Houghton, 1992.

817   Capitman, Barbara. *Rediscovering Art Deco USA.* New York: Viking, 1994, pp. 48–53.

818   Clausen, Meredith L. "Modernism in the 1950's." In *Pietro Belluschi: Modern American Architect.* Cambridge: MIT Press, 1994, pp. 207–214.

819   Coolidge, John. "Harvard's Teaching . . . 1928–1985." In *Architectural Education and Boston*, pp. 59–63.

820   Curtis, William J. R. *Boston: Forty Years of Modern Architecture.* Boston: ICA, 1980.

821   Floyd, M. H. "Ralph Rapson: Modernism at M. I. T." In *Architectural Education and Boston*, pp. 90–96.

822   Gaddis, Eugene R., ed. *Avery Memorial, Wadsworth Atheneum: The First Modern Museum.* Hartford, Conn: The Athenaeum, 1984.

823   Goldberger, Paul. Prologue to *Boston Architecture, 1950–1975*, by Naomi Miller and Keith Morgan, Munich: Prestel, 1975, pp. 13–16.

824   Goody, Marvin E., and Robert P. Walsh. *Boston Society of Architects: The First Hundred Years, 1867–1967.* Boston Society of Architects, 1967, pp. 89–98.

825   Hudnut, Joseph. "The Romantic Architecture of Boston." In Goody and Walsh, *Boston Society of Architects*, pp. 3–14.

826   Huxtable, Ada Louise. "The Shot Heard 'Round the World." *NYT*, 28 Sept. 1980.

827   ———. "The Skyscraper Style." In *Kicked a Building Lately?* New York: Quadrangle, 1978, pp. 213–217.

828   Jencks, Charles. *Modern Movements in Architecture.* [1973]. London: Penguin, 1987.

829   ———. *The New Moderns.* London: Academy, 1999, pp. 86, 89, 148.

830   Jones, Caroline A., and John Coolidge. *Modern Art at Harvard.* New York: Abbeville Press, 1985.

831   Kennedy, Lawrence W. *Planning the City upon a Hill.* Amherst: University of Massachusetts Press, 1992.

832   Kirstein, Lincoln. *Mosaic: Memoirs.* New York: Farrar, Straus & Giroux, 1994.

833   Krieger, Alex, and Andrea Leers. "Extending and Redefining Traditions: Recent Boston Architecture." *A&U/Japan* (July 1988).

834   Leers, Andrea P. "Boston Looks at Tokyo." *Build Boston Magazine* (Nov. 1988): 22–23.

835   Lyndon, Donlyn. *Boston: The City Observed.* New York: Vintage, 1982.

836   Maybank, Joseph. "Harvard and M.I.T." In *Architectural Education and Boston*, pp. 125–129.

837   Miller, Naomi, and Keith Morgan. *Boston Architecture, 1950–1975.* Munich: Prestel, 1975.

838   Moore, Honor. *The White Blackbird.* New York: Viking, 1996.

839   O'Connell, Shaun. *Imagining Boston.* Boston: Beacon, 1990.

840   Rifkind, Carole. *A Field Guide to Contemporary Architecture.* New York: Dutton, 1998.

841   Ross, David A. Introduction to *Dissent: The Issue of Modern Art in Boston,* by Elizabeth Sussman. Boston: Institute of Contemporary Art, 1985.

842   Sturgis, Robert. "Urban Planning." In *Architectural Education and Boston*, pp. 109–118.

843   Venturi, Robert, Denise Scott-Brown, and Steven Izenover. *Learning from Las Vegas.* Cambridge: MIT Press, 1979.

844   Weber, Nicholas Fox. "The Harvardites" and "Hartford, Connecticut." In *Patron Saints.* New York: Knopf, 1992, pp. 1–176.

845   Whitehill, Walter Muir. "Decade of Renewal." In *Topographical History of Boston.* Boston: Harvard University Press, 1975, pp. 200–240.

J. BOSTON GENERALLY

846   Apple, R. W., Jr. "In Boston, a Boom . . . ." *NYT*, 29 Jan. 1999, B31.
847   Banerjee, T., and M. Southworth, eds. *City Sense and City Design: Writings and Projects of Kevin Lynch.* Cambridge: MIT Press, 1996.
848   Carter, Holland. "In Boston All Roads . . . ." *NYT*, 7 Aug. 1998, B31–B33.
849   Krieger, Alex. *Past Futures: Two Centuries of Imagining Boston.* Cambridge: Harvard University Press, 1985, pp. 46–53.
850   Lynch, Kevin. *The Image of the City.* Cambridge: MIT Press, 1960.
851   Southworth, Susan and Michael. *A.I.A. Guide to Boston.* Guilford, Conn.: Globe-Pequot Press, 1992.

K. MODERNISM, POST-MODERNISM, AND PRESERVATION

852   Anderson, Michael. Review of Shelby Steele's *A Dream Deferred. NYTBR*, 22 Nov. 1998.
853   Brown, Patricia Leigh. "Ingredient: Where Do You Hang the 747?" *NYT*, 13 Dec. 1998, pp. 110–114.
854   Campbell, Robert. "Echoes of the Prairie Style." *Arch.* (Oct. 1985).
855   ———. "Nutty, Delightful Children's Museum." *Arch.* (Oct. 1988): 64–69.
856   Carlhian, Jean Paul. "Guides, Guideposts and Guidelines." *Old and New Architecture.* Washington, D. C.: Preservation Press, 1980, pp. 49–68.
857   Faush, Deborah. "Modernism and History." *JSAH* (Dec. 1998): 483.
858   Freeman, Suzanne. "This Old Hassle." *Historic Preservation* (May/June 1996): 54–59.
859   Holleran, Michael. *Boston's Changeful Times.* Baltimore: Johns Hopkins University Press, 1998.
860   Huxtable, Ada Louise. "[Marblehead:] Spirit of '76." In *Kicked a Building Lately?* New York: Quadrangle, 1978, pp. 175–178.
861   ———. "New York." In *Kicked a Building Lately?*
862   ———. "The New Architecture." In *The Unreal American.* New York: The New Press, 1997, pp. 126–173.
863   Jacobs, Jane. *Death & Life of Great American Cities.* New York: Random House, 1963.
864   Jencks, Charles. *The Language of Post-Modern Architecture.* New York: Rizzoli, 1995.
865   Koch, John. "Ada Louise Huxtable." *Globe*, 17 Aug. 1997, p. 10.
866   Krieger, Alex. "Between the Crusaders' Jerusalem and Piranesi' Rome." In *Form, Modernism and History.* Cambridge: Harvard University Press, 1996, pp. 151–164.
867   Lindgren, James M. "A Constant Incentive." *NEQ* (Dec. 1991).
868   McCormick, Kathleen. "Coming into Their Own." *Historic Preservation* (May/June 1996): 108–115.
869   McDaniels, Andrea. "Save Brasilia?" *Christian Science Monitor*, 20 Oct. 1998, p. 3.
870   McKinnell, Michael, et al. "The Architecture of the Seaport District." *Arch. Boston* (Winter 1999): 10–17
871   McNeely, James. "The Williamsburg Principle." *Beacon Hill Paper*, 17 Feb. 1998, p. 16.
872   Padjen, Elizabeth S. Editor's forward. *Arch. Boston* (Winter, 1999): 1
873   Rybczynski, Witold. "Keeping the Modern Modern." *Atlantic Monthly* (Oct. 1997): 108–112.
874   Scully, Vincent. *The Shingle Style Today.* New York: Brazilier, 1944.
875   Tempko, Alan. *No Way to Build a Ballpark.* San Francisco: Chronicle Books, 1993.
876   Wheaton, Rodd L. "Modernism Under Siege." *SAH Newsletter* (Aug. 1998): 6–7.
877   Wiseman, Carter. "The Power of Preservation." In *Shaping a Nation.* New York: Norton, 1998, pp. 219–245.

L. INDIVIDUAL BUILDINGS 1950–2000

In this section and the two that follow, the alphabetized short-titled entries listed immediately after each subheading (building or architect) provide page numbers for the following frequently referenced publications:

BERDINI.   Berdini, Paolo. *Walter Gropius.* Bologna: Gustavo Gili, 1983.
BUNTING/FLOYD.   Bunting, Bainbridge, and M. H. Floyd. *Harvard: An Architectural History.* Cambridge: Harvard University Press, 1985.
BUNTING/NYLANDER.   Bunting, Bainbridge, and Robert Nylander. *Report 4: Old Cambridge.* Cambridge: Cambridge Historical Commission, 1973.
CARLOCK.   Carlock, Marty. *A Guide to Public Art in Greater Boston: From Newburyport to Plymouth.* Harvard, Mass.: Harvard Common Press, 1993.
CURTIS.   Curtis, William J. R. *Boston: Forty Years of Modern Architecture.* Boston: Institute of Contemporary Art, 1980.
DAL CO/TARFURI.   Dal Co, Francesco, and Manfredo Tarfuri. *Modern Architecture/2.* New York: Electa/Rizzoli, 1976.
GIEDION.   Giedion, Sigfried. *Space, Time and Architecture.* Cambridge: Harvard University Press, 1966.
GOODY.   Goody, Joan. *Modern Architecture in Boston.* Cambridge: MIT Press, 1965.
ISAACS.   Isaacs, Reginald. *Gropius.* Boston: Little, Brown, 1983.
LYNDON.   Lyndon, Donlyn. *Boston: The City Observed.* New York: Vintage, 1982.
MILLER/MORGAN.   Miller, Naomi, and Keith Morgan. *Boston Architecture, 1979–1990.* Munich: Prestel, 1990.
PETER.   Peter, John. *The Oral History of Modern Architecture.* New York: Abrams, 1994.
RETTIG.   Rettig, Robert Bell. *Guide to Cambridge Architecture: 10 Walking Tours.* Cambridge: MIT Press 1969.
RIFKIND.   Rifkind, Carole. *A Field Guide to Contemporary Architecture.* New York: Dutton, 1998.
WISEMAN.   Wiseman, Carter. *Shaping a Nation.* New York: Norton, 1998.

ALEWIFE STATION, CAMBRIDGE. Miller/Morgan, 240.
ALTO-DESIGNED INTERIOR, LAMONT LIBRARY, CAMBRIDGE. Bunting/Floyd, 217.
AMERICAN ACADEMY OF ARTS AND SCIENCES, CAMBRIDGE.
878   E. C. "The American Academy." *Int. Des.* (Dec. 1981).

879   Schmertz, Mildred F. "A New 'House.'" *Arch. Record* (Nov. 1981): 79–87.

880   Silver, Robert. "American Academy." *Arch. Review* 1016 (1981): 215–221.

ANDOVER HARVARD LIBRARY, CAMBRIDGE. Bunting/Floyd, 244–245.

ARCHITECTS' CORNER, CAMBRIDGE. Isaacs, 304–305.

881   Coolidge, John. "Harvard's Teaching." In *Architectural Education and Boston*, ed. M. H. Floyd. Boston Architectural Center, 1989, p. 64.

882   Southworth, Susan and Michael. *A.I.A. Guide to Boston*. Guilford, Conn.: Globe-Pequot Press, 1992, pp. 413-414.

ATTLEBOROUGH (THATCHER) HIGH SCHOOL, ATTLEBOROUGH. Berdini, 199–200.

BACK BAY CENTER, BACK BAY. Berdini, 216–217; Giedion, 513, 869; Lyndon, 196–197.

883   Clausen, Meredith L. *Pietro Belluschi: Modern American Architect*. Cambridge: MIT Press, 1994, pp. 251–254.

BACK BAY STATION, BACK BAY

884   Campbell, Robert. "Architecture along a Transportation Spine." *Arch.* (Dec. 1988).

885   ———. "From the People . . . ." *Globe*, 3 May 1988.

886   Carter, Brian. "Back Bay Arches."*Arch. Review* (Dec. 1989).

BACK OF THE HILL HOUSING, ROXBURY. Rifkind, 94.

BAIRD HOUSE

887   Levine, Neil. *Frank Lloyd Wright*. Princeton: Princeton University Press, 1996, p. vii.

888   Pfeiffer, Bruce Brooks. *Frank Lloyd Wright*. Vol. 6, 1937–1941. Tokyo: ADA Edition, 1984–1988.

889   Storrer, William A. *The Architecture of Frank Lloyd Wright*. Cambridge: MIT Press, 1992, p. 227.

890   ———. *The Frank Lloyd Wright Companion*. Chicago: University of Chicago Press, 1993, s277a, s277b.

BAKER HOUSE, M.I.T., CAMBRIDGE. Curtis, 4, 24; Dal Co/Tarfuri, 336, 338; Giedion, 636–640; Peter, 107.

891   Curtis, William J. R. *Modern Architecture since 1900*. London: Phaidon, 1987, pp. 454–455, 537, 591.

892   Gössel, Peter, and Gabriele Leuthäuser. *Architecture in the Twentieth Century*. Cologne: Taschen, 1991, pp. 239, 240.

893   Koshalek, Richard, and Elizabeth A. T. Smith. *At the End of the Century*. Los Angeles and New York: Abrams, 1998, pp. 183, 184.

894   Richards, J. M. *An Introduction to Modern Architecture*. Harmondsworth, U.K.: Penguin, 1940, p. 111.

895   Roth, Leland. *Understanding Architecture*. Boulder, Colo.: Westview, 1993.

896   Turner, Paul Venable. *Campus*. New York: Architectural History Foundation, 1984, pp. 260–261.

897   Watkin, David. *A History of Western Architecture*. London: Lawrence King, 1996, p. 568.

BANK OF BOSTON TOWER, FINANCIAL DISTRICT. Lyndon, 260.

BLUE CROSS/BLUE SHIELD BUILDING, FINANCIAL DISTRICT. Goody, 68–69; Lyndon, 259–260; Peter, 37.

BOGNER HOUSE, CAMBRIDGE. Bunting/Nylander, 130.

BOSTON ARCHITECTURAL CENTER, BACK BAY. Curtis, 12, 34; Lyndon, 179–180.

898   Myer. "The New Building." In *Architectural Education and Boston*, pp. 129–135.

BOSTON BALLET BUILDING, SOUTH END.

899   *Graham Gund Architects*. Washington, D.C.: A.I.A. Press, 1993, pp. 154–161.

BOSTON CITY HALL AND PLAZA, DOWNTOWN. Curtis, 10, 30–31; Dal Co/Tarfuri, 281, 349; Lyndon, 35–36; Rifkind, 124, 126.

900   Carr, Stephen, et al. "City Hall Plaza." *Public Space*. Cambridge: Cambridge University Press, 1992, pp. 88–91.

901   "Chandigarah on Scollay Square." *PA* (July 1962): 65.

902   Curtis, William J. R. *Modern Architecture since 1900*, pp. 515–16, 550.

903   Fitch, J. M. "City Hall." *Arch. Review* 880 (1970): 398–411.

904   Jencks, Charles. *The New Moderns*. London: Academy, 1990, p. 73.

905   Schmertz, Mildred. "The New Boston City Hall." *Arch. Review* (Feb 1969): 133–144.

BOSTON COMPANY BUILDING, FINANCIAL DISTRICT. Rifkind, 284.

906   Clausen, Meredith L. *Pietro Belluschi*, pp. 318–321.

BOSTON FIVE CENTS SAVINGS BANK, DOWNTOWN. Lyndon, 12–20.

BOSTON PUBLIC LIBRARY (JOHNSON). Curtis, 13, 15, 40; Lyndon, 170–171.

907   Carlhian, Jean Paul. "Guides, Guideposts and Guidelines." *Old And New Architecture*. Washington, D. C..: Preservation Press, 1980, p. 65.

908   Huxtable, Ada Louise. "Boston: A Sensitive Succession." In *Kicked a Building Lately?* New York: Quadrangle, 1978, pp. 242–245.

909   Jencks, Charles. *The New Moderns*, pp. 148–149.

910   Lewis, Hilary, and John O'Connor. *Philip Johnson*. New York: Rizzoli, 1994, pp. 12, 84, 93, 160, 163.

911   Miller, Ivory. *Johnson/Burgee Architects*. New York: Random House, 1979, pp. 34–37.

BOSTON PUBLIC LIBRARY (MCKIM/RESTORATION)

912   Shand-Tucci, Douglass. "Paradise Lost." *Phoenix*, 12 Feb. 1999, p. 12.

BOSTON UNIVERSITY LAW TOWER, WEST BACK BAY. Goody, 60–61.

913   Jencks, Charles. *Modern Movements in Architecture*. [1973]. London: Penguin, 1987, pp. 224–226.

914   Salzman, Nancy L. *Buildings and Builders*. Boston: Boston University, 1985, pp. 13, 80, 99–105.

BOYLSTON PLACE, BACK BAY.

915   Shand-Tucci, Douglass. "Whitehills Law." *Phoenix*, 14 May 1999, pp. 16–17.

BRADLEY BUNGALOW, WOODS HOLE. Wiseman, 109, 111.

916   Brooks, H. Allen. *The Prairie School*. New York: Norton, 1972, pp. 132, 145, 206–210, 223.

BRANDEIS UNIVERSITY CHAPELS, WALTHAM

917   Turner, Paul Venable. *Campus: An American Planning Tradition*. New York: Architectural History Foundation, 1984, p. 264.

BREUER HOUSE, LINCOLN. Berdini, 168–169; Curtis, 2, 20; Goody, 94–95.

918   Ford, James, and Katherine Ford. *Classic Modern Houses of the Thirties*. New York: Dover, 1989 (originally published 1940 as *The Modern House in America*), pp. 46–48.

BROWN HOUSE, FISHERS ISLAND, NEW YORK

919   Ford, James, and Katherine Ford. *Classic Modern Houses of the Thirties*, pp. 88–89.

920   Hines, Thomas. "John Nicholas Brown House." In William H. Jordy, *Building on Paper*. Providence: Brown University Press, 1982, pp. 130–132.

921   ——. *Richard Neutra.* Berkeley: University of California Press, 1982, pp. 151–159, 251.

BULFINCH SQUARE, CAMBRIDGE. Miller/Morgan, 214–215.

922   *Graham Gund Architects*, pp. 56–63.

BURR HALL, CAMBRIDGE. Bunting/Floyd, 225–228; Bunting/Nylander, 190.

CAMBRIDGESIDE GALLERIA, CAMBRIDGE. Miller/Morgan, 204; Rifkind, 339, 351.

CARLTON HOUSE, BACK BAY. Miller/Morgan, 139.

CARPENTER CENTER, HARVARD, CAMBRIDGE. Bunting/Floyd, 234–235; Bunting/Nylander, 190–191; Curtis, 7–8, 26–27; Giedion, 556–563; Peter, 108.

923   Bunting, Bainbridge, and M. H. Floyd. "Visual Arts Center, Cambridge." In *Le Corbusier, 1957–1965.* Zurich: Les Editions d'Architecture, 1995, pp. 54–67.

924   Campbell, Robert. "Evaluation: Corbu's Only U.S. Building." *Arch.* (Oct. 1987): 36–43.

925   Curtis, William J. R. *Le Corbusier: Ideas and Forms.* London: Phaidon, 1986, pp. 215–221.

926   Le Messuier, William, and Daniel L. Schodek. "The Inside Story of the Carpenter Center." In *Form, Modernism and History.* Cambridge: Harvard University Press, 1996, pp. 99–108.

927   Sekler, Eduard F., and William Curtis. *Le Corbusier at Work: The Genesis of the Carpenter Center for the Visual Arts* Cambridge.: Harvard University Press, 1978.

CENTER PLAZA, GOVERNMENT CENTER

928   Clausen, Meredith L. *Pietro Belluschi*, pp. 279–280.

CHAMBERLAIN HOUSE, WAYLAND. Berdini, 174; Giedion, 505; Peter, 176.

929   Jencks, Charles. *Modern Movements in Architecture*, pp. 118–119.

CHARLESTOWN NAVY YARD HOUSING, CHARLESTOWN. Miller/Morgan, 189; Rifkind, 93, 97.

930   Campbell, Robert. "Low Income Housing Made High Architecture." *Arch.* (July 1989): 54–57.

CHILDREN'S MUSEUM ADDITION, WATERFRONT

931   "Boston's Children's Museum." *PA* (Jan. 1995): 84–85.

932   Campbell, Robert. "Children's Museum." *Globe*, 22 Apr. 1992.

CHILMARK, MARTHA'S VINEYARD

933   Campbell, Robert. "Shingle Style Reinvented." In Donald Canty, et al., *American Architecture of the 1980's.* Washington, D. C.: AIA Press, 1990, pp. 174–177.

CHRISTIAN SCIENCE WORLD HEADQUARTERS, BACK BAY. Lyndon, 198–202.

934   Jencks, Charles. *The Language of Post-Modern Architecture.* New York: Rizzoli, 1977, p. 18.

935   ——. *The New Moderns*, p. 89.

936   Sims, Melanie. *Sasaki Associates.* Washington D. C.: Spacemaker, 1997, pp. 158–159.

CHURCH COURT, BACK BAY. Miller/Morgan, 142–143.

937   *Graham Gund Architects*, pp. 42–51.

CHURCH PARK, BACK BAY. Lyndon, 202–203.

CLARK UNIVERSITY LIBRARY, WORCESTER

938   Jencks, Charles. *Modern Movements in Architecture*, pp. 204–205.

CLOVERLEAF, PITTSFIELD

939   Pfeiffer, Bruce Brooks. *Frank Lloyd Wright.* Vol. 8, 1951–1959. See also vol. 7, 1942–1950.

COHEN RESIDENCE, BEACON HILL

940   *Graham Gund Architects*, pp. 80–89.

CONANTUM DEVELOPMENT, CONCORD. Goody, 90–91.

COPLEY PLACE, BACK BAY. Miller/Morgan, 144–145.

COPLEY SQUARE, BACK BAY (VENTURI PROJECT). Miller/Morgan, 164–165.

941   von Moos, Stanislaus. *Venturi, Rauch and Scott-Brown: Buildings and Projects.* New York: Rizzoli, 1987, pp. 48, 88–89, 116.

DAVIS MUSEUM, WELLESLEY COLLEGE, WELLESLEY

942   Ghirardo, Diane. *Architecture after Modernism.* London: Thames and Hudson, 1996, pp. 75–76.

943   Newhouse, Victoria. *Towards a New Museum.* New York: Monacelli, 1998.

944   Schmertz, Mildred F. "The Davis Museum." *Arch.* (Jan. 1994): 78–81.

945   Walters, David. "Teamwork . . . Campus Clients." *Christian Science Monitor*, 10 Oct. 1993, pp. 10–11.

DE CORDOVA MUSEUM ADDITION, LINCOLN

946   Hale, Jonathan. "De Cordova's Artful Addition." *B&T*, 20 Apr. 1998.

DESIGN RESEARCH BUILDING, CAMBRIDGE. Curtis, 12, 33.

947   Floyd, M. H., ed. *Architectural Education and Boston.* Boston Architectural Center, 1989, p. 64.

948   Muschamp, H. "The Shock of the Familiar." *NYT*, 13 Dec. 1998, pp. 65–66.

DEUTSCH HOUSE, BEACON HILL. Miller/Morgan, 167.

949   *Graham Gund Architects*, pp. 38–41.

EASTGATE APARTMENTS, CAMBRIDGE. Goody, 30–31; Peter, 41–42.

950   Floyd, M. H. "Ralph Rapson: Modernism at M. I. T." In *Architectural Education and Boston*, p. 92.

855 BOYLSTON STREET, BACK BAY. Miller/Morgan, 148.

ELEVATED RAILROAD (TRANSIT), INTOWN, ROXBURY, CHARLESTOWN

951   Campbell, Robert. "Washington Street." *Globe Magazine*, 20 Dec. 1998, p. 14.

ESPLANADE APARTMENTS, CAMBRIDGE. Miller/Morgan, 86–87.

952   Kohn, Wendy, ed. *Moshe Safdie.* London: Academy, 1996, pp. 148–149.

EXCHANGE PLACE, FINANCIAL DISTRICT. Miller/Morgan, 86–87.

EXETER LIBRARY, EXETER, N.H.. Wiseman, 205n, 210, 213n, 214.

953   Brownlee, David, and David DeLong. *Louis I. Kahn.: In the Realm of Architecture.* Los Angeles: Museum of Modern Art, 1991, pp. 10, 137, 202, 205–207, 241.

954   Huxtable, Ada Louise. *Kicked a Building Lately?* pp. 95–101.

FANEUIL HALL MARKETPLACE, DOWNTOWN. Lyndon, 48–50; Miller/Morgan, 68–69.

955   Carr, Stephen, et al. *Public Space.* Cambridge: Cambridge University Press, 1992, pp. 218–221.

956   "Faneuilization." *PA* (July 1981).

957   "James W. Rouse." *Globe,* 10 Apr. 1976, p. 31.
958   Stahl, Frederick. "Educational Highlights." In *Architectural Education and Boston*, pp. 118–124.
FEDERAL COURTHOUSE, SEAPORT DISTRICT
959   Rawn, William. "The Boston Federal Courthouse: The Role of the Civic Design Commission." In *Federal Buildings in Context: The Role of Design Review*, ed. J. Carter Brown. Washington, D.C.: The National Gallery, 1995, pp. 95–104.
FEDERAL RESERVE TOWER, DOWNTOWN. Curtis, xx-xxx; Lyndon, 256–257; Miller/Morgan, 78–79; Rifkind, 289, 293.
960   Floyd, M. H. "Stubbins." In *Architectural Education and Boston*, pp. 96–101.
961   Ludman, Dianne M. *Hugh Stubbins and His Associates.* Cambridge, Mass.: Hugh Stubbins Associates, 1986, 95–101
ARTHUR FIEDLER BRIDGE, BACK BAY. Goody, 66–67.
FIRST AND SECOND CHURCH OF BOSTON, BACK BAY. Lyndon, 125–127.
FIRST LUTHERAN CHURCH, BACK BAY. Lyndon, 127; Goody, 64–65.
500 BOYLSTON STREET, BACKBAY. Miller/Morgan, 152–153.
962   Knight, Carlton III. Introduction to *Phillip Johnson/John Burgee 1979–1985.* New York: Rizzoli, 1985, pp. 148–151.
963   Lewis, Hilary, and John O'Connor. *Phillip Johnson.* New York: Rizzoli, 1994, pp.170–173, 187.
FORBES APARTMENT, WATERFRONT
964   "Apartment Interior." *International Architecture.* New York: McGraw Hill, 1998, pp. 266, 267.
FORBES-DESIGNED HOUSE, MARION
965   Boissiere, Olivier, ed. *Houses by the Sea.* Paris: Telleri, 1998, pp. 143–147.
966   Ojeda, Oscar R., ed. *Ten Houses: Peter Forbes and Associates.* Rockport: Rockport Press, 1995, pp. 50–57.
FORBES-DESIGNED HOUSE, SURRY, MAINE
967   Ojeda, Oscar R. "House in Surry." In *The New American House/2.* New York, 1997, pp. 160–167.
FORD HOUSE, LINCOLN. Berdini, 168–169; Isaacs, 240.
968   Ford, James, and Katherine Ford. *Classic Modern Houses of the Thirties* pp. 49–51.
FORREST HILLS STATION. Miller/Morgan, 239.
GOVERNMENT CENTER (SEE ALSO INDIVIDUAL BUILDINGS). Dal Co/Tarfuri, 281, 307; Peter, 267.
969   Barnes, Rebecca. Interview with Edward Logue. *Arch. Boston* 2 (1990): 30–34.
970   Clausen, Meredith L. *Pietro Belluschi*, pp. 278–279, 321–322, 342.
971   Sturgis, Robert. "Urban Planning." In *Architectural Education and Boston*, pp. 109–118.
GREEN BUILDING, M.I.T., CAMBRIDGE. Goody, 32–33.
GRIECO HOUSE, ANDOVER
972   Pfeiffer, Bruce Brooks. *Frank Lloyd Wright.* Vol. 7, 1942–1950.
GROPIUS HOUSE, LINCOLN (see also Parts 1 and 2, checklist under Gropius). Berdini, 163–165; Curtis, 2–3, 19; Dal Co/Tarfuri, 306; Giedion, 502; Isaacs, 232–236; Peter, 177; Rifkind, 17.
973   Corimer, Leslie H. "Walter Gropius House." In *International Dictionary of Architects and Architecture*, vol. 2, ed. Randall Van Vynckt. Detroit: St. James Press, 1993, pp. 947–948.
974   Ford, James, and Katherine Ford. *Classic Modern Houses of the Thirties*, p. 43.
975   Huxtable, Ada Louise. "The Future Grows Old." In *Kicked a Building Lately?* pp. 224–227.
976   Jordy, William H. *American Buildings and Their Architects: The Impact of European Modernism in the Mid-Twentieth Century.* New York: Anchor/Doubleday, 1976, pp. 177n, 180, 181.
977   Cantacuzino, Sherban. *Modern Houses.* New York: Dutton, 1964.
GUND HALL, HARVARD, CAMBRIDGE. Bunting/Nylander, 192; Bunting/Floyd, 235–340.
HAGERTY HOUSE, COHASSET
978   Ford, James, and Katherine Ford. *Classic Modern Houses of the Thirties*, pp. 44–45.
HANCOCK TOWER, BACK BAY. Curtis, 13, 14, 38–39; Dal Co/Tarfuri, 283, 339, 366; Lyndon, 193–195; Miller/Morgan, 134–135; Rifkind, 297, 360–361; Wiseman, 299, 385.
979   Campbell, Robert. "Learning from the Hancock." *Arch.* (Mar. 1988): 68–94.
980   Carlhian, Jean Paul. "Guides, Guideposts and Guidelines," p. 54.
981   Curtis, William J. R. *Modern Architecture since 1900.* London: Phaidon, 1987, p. 558.
982   Jencks, Charles. *The New Moderns*, p. 86.
983   Wiseman, Carter. *I. M. Pei.* New York: Abrams, 1990, pp. 138–153.
HARBOR TOWERS, WATERFRONT. Lyndon, 53.
HARKNESS CENTER, HARVARD, CAMBRIDGE. Berdini, 205–207; Bunting/Floyd, 59–63, 221–223, 229; Curtis, 4–5, 2–23; Giedion, 504–510; Isaacs, 264–266; Rifkind, 231; Wiseman, 170, 171, 174, 213.
984   Coolidge, John. "Harvard's Teaching . . . 1928–1985." In *Architectural Education and Boston*, pp. 59–63.
985   Richards, J. M. *An Introduction to Modern Architecture.* Harmondsworth, U.K.: Penguin, 1940, p. 111.
HAUSER HALL, HARVARD, CAMBRIDGE
986   Bierman, M. L. "Campus Justice." *Arch.* (Feb. 1995).
987   Campbell, Robert. "Harvard Law." *Globe,* 20 May 1994, p. 57.
HEALTH, WELFARE AND EDUCATION SERVICE CENTER, GOVERNMENT CENTER. Curtis, 10, 32; Dal Co/Tarfuri, 281, 307; Lyndon, 84–85.
988   Rudolph, Paul. "Boston Government Center." In *The Architecture of Paul Rudolph.* New York: Prager, 1970, pp. 94–101.
989   ———. *Paul Rudolph.* New York: Architectural Book Publishing Co., 1981, pp. 126–136.
HILLEL HOUSE, BOSTON UNIVERSITY
990   Salzman, Nancy L. *Buildings and Builders*, pp. 120–123.
HOLL-DESIGNED HOUSE, MARTHA'S VINEYARD. Rifkind, 18, 25.
HOLOCAUST MEMORIAL, DOWNTOWN
991   Salzman, Nancy L. *PA* (Feb. 1993): 78.
HOLYOKE CENTER, CAMBRIDGE. Bunting/Floyd, 235; Bunting/Nylander, 191–192; Goody, 8–9; Peter, 256.
992   Jencks, Charles. *Modern Movements in Architecture*, pp. 225–226.
HOOD MUSEUM, DARTMOUTH
993   Campbell, Robert. "An Architecture of Verve." In Donald Canty, et al. *American Architecture of the 1980's*, pp. 238–245.
HYNES AUDITORIUM, BACK BAY
994   Campbell, Robert. "Boston's Best Piece of Public Architecture." *Arch.* (May 1989).

995   ———."Civil Center," *PA* (May 1989).

INN AT HARVARD, CAMBRIDGE

996   *Graham Gund Architects*, pp. 148–153.

INSTITUTE OF CONTEMPORARY ART, BACK BAY, . Miller/Morgan, 98–99, 136.

INTERNATIONAL PLACE, DOWNTOWN.

997   Lewis, Hilary, and John O'Connor. *Philip Johnson.* New York: Rizzoli, 1994, pp.170, 187.

998   Knight, Carleton III. Introduction to "International Place. . . ." In *PJ/John Burgee 1979–1985.* New York: Rizzoli, 1985, pp. 146–147.

WILLIAM JAMES HALL, CAMBRIDGE. Bunting/Nylander, 193; Bunting/Floyd, 239.

JEWETT ART CENTER, WELLESLEY. Goody, 86–87; Peter, 75.

999   Carlhian, Jean Paul. "Guides, Guideposts and Guidelines," pp. 62–64.

1000   Rudolph, Paul. "Mary Cooper Jewett Art Center." In *The Architecture of Paul Rudolph*, 50–55.

1001   ———. *Paul Rudolph*, pp. 90–93.

1002   Turner, Paul Venable. *Campus.* New York: Architectural History Foundations, 1984, pp. 294, 295.

JOHNSON HOUSE, CAMBRIDGE. Goody, 18–19.

1003   Lewis, Hilary, and John O'Connor. *Philip Johnson*, pp.18–27.

JOSIAH QUINCY SCHOOL, SOUTH END. Lyndon, 228–229, 230, 231; Rifkind, 239–243.

KALIL HOUSE, MANCHESTER, N.H.

1004   Storrer, William A. *The Frank Lloyd Wright Companion.* Chicago: University of Chicago Press, 1993, pp. 2, 387.

KENNEDY FEDERAL BUILDING, GOVERNMENT CENTER. Lyndon, 40–41; Isaacs, 302–303.

1005   Brown, J. Carter, ed. *Federal Buildings in Context: The Role of Design Review.* Washington, D.C.: The National Gallery, 1995, pp. 39–43.

KENNEDY LIBRARY, DORCHESTER. Miller/Morgan, 194–195; Peter, 268.

1006   Abercrombie, Stanley. "Complicated Shapes." *AIA Journal* (May 1980).

1007   Cannell, Michael. *I. M. Pei.* New York: Carol Southern Books, 1995, pp. 163–196.

1008   Marlin, William. "Lighthouse of an Era." *Arch. Record* (Feb. 1980).

1009   Watkin, David. *A History of Western Architecture.* London: Lawrence King, 1996, pp. 570, 571.

1010   Wiseman, Carter. *I. M. Pei*, pp. 92–119.

KENNEDY SCHOOL, CAMBRIDGE. Bunting/Floyd, 274–276.

KEYSTONE BUILDING, DOWNTOWN. Lyndon, 255, 257.

1011   Clausen, Meredith L. *Pietro Belluschi*, pp. 322–323.

KOCH HOUSE, CAMBRIDGE. Bunting/Nylander, 129–130; Rettig, D43.

KRESGE AUDITORIUM, M.I.T., CAMBRIDGE. Peter, 194, 196, 209, 281; Dal Co/Tarfuri, 352.

1012   Clausen, Meredith L., *Pietro Belluschi*, p. 205.

1013   Christ-Janer, Albert. *Eliel Saarinen.* Chicago: University of Chicago Press, 1948.

1014   Jencks, Charles. *Modern Movements in Architecture*, p. 325.

1015   Sanderson, George A. "New M.I.T. Buildings Open." *PA* (July 1955): 74–75.

1016   Turner, Paul Venable. *Campus*, p. 260.

LAZARUS HOUSE, COPAKE, N.Y.

1017   Crosbie, Michael J. "Sculptural Retreat." *Arch.* (Apr. 1992): 52–59.

1018   Dyer-Szabo, Brenda. "Colore natura." *Ville Giardine* (Feb. 1994): 10–15.

1019   Giovannini, Joseph. "Home to Rest." *Elle Décor* (Oct. 1993): 161–167.

1020   Ojeda, Oscar R. *The New American House/1.* New York: 1995, pp. 228–235.

1021   Pröhl, Undine. "Addizione geometric." *Abitare* (July 1994): 80–83.

1022   Rasch, Horst. "Five Individualists." *Häuser* (Spring 1993): 112–116.

1023   Vercelloni, Matteo. *New American Houses.* Milan: Edizioni L' Archivolto, 1997, pp. 172–181.

LEWIS WHARF, WATERFRONT. Lyndon, 66–67.

LINCOLN LIBRARY, LINCOLN

1024   *Graham Gund Architects*, pp. 102–107.

LOEB DRAMA CENTER, HARVARD, CAMBRIDGE. Bunting/Floyd, 252; Goody, 12–13; Rifkind, 240, 245.

1025   Ludman, Dianne M., *Hugh Stubbins*, pp. 47–48.

LONG WHARF MARRIOT HOTEL. Miller/Morgan, 88–89.

1026   Campbell, Robert. "A Strong Contextual Gesture Gone Astray." *Arch.* (July 1983): 42–47.

LYMAN HOUSE, DOVER. Rifkind, 41, 45.

MACHADO & SILVETTI-DESIGNED CONDOMINIUM, BACK BAY

1027   Levinson, Nancy. "Against the Grain." *Arch. Record* (Sept 1992): 107–113.

1028   Ojeda, Oscar R. "Back Bay Residence." In *The New American Apartment.* New York: Whitney, Waton-Guptill, 1997, pp. 6, 7, 80–87.

MACHADO & SILVETTI-DESIGNED HOUSE, CONCORD

1029   Hays, Michael K. *Unprecedented Realism: The Architecture of Machado & Silvetti.* Princeton: Princeton Architectural Press, 1995, pp. 236–241.

1030   Ojeda, Oscar R. "House in Concord." *The New American House/1.* New York, 1995, pp. 176–187.

1031   ———, comp. *Rodolfo Machado and Jorge Silvetti.* Asppan: Kliczkowski, 1995, pp. 8–19.

1032   Stein, Karen B. "New House on the Block." *Arch. Record* (Apr. 1994): 107.

MASON MUSIC BUILDING, CAMBRIDGE. Bunting/Floyd, 248–249.

M.B.T.A. TRANSPORTATION CONTROL CENTER, DOWNTOWN

1033   "Transportation Control Center." *PA* (Jan. 1993).

MEIER-DESIGNED HOUSE, CONCORD

1034   ———. "Suburban Prototype House in Concord." In Philip Tedidio, *Richard Meier.* Cölgne: Taschen, 1995.

M.I.T. ARCHITECTURAL LIBRARY, CAMBRIDGE

1035   Campbell, Robert. "A Gem of a Building." *Globe*, 30 Apr. 1991.

1036   ———. "M.I.T.'s Rotch Library." *Globe*, 22 July 1994.

1037   Dixon, John Morris. "Bookcage," *PA* (May 1991).
1038   Tattellman, Ira. "In a Glass Cage." *Bay Windows*, 9 Apr. 1993, p. 3B.
M.I.T. CHAPEL, CAMBRIDGE. Peter, 81, 194, 196, 209; Rifkind, 212, 214.
1039   Roth, Leland. *Understanding Architecture*. Boulder, Colo.: Westview, 1993.
1040   Saarinen, Aline, ed. "M.I.T. Auditorium and Chapel." In *Eero Saarinen and His Work*. New Haven: Yale University Press, 1962, pp. 34–39.
1041   Sanderson, George A. "New M.I.T. Buildings Open." *PA* (July 1955): 74–75.
M.I.T. SCHOOL OF ARCHITECTURE, CAMBRIDGE
1042   Dillon, David. "Artful Cohesion." *Arch.* (Aug 1996).
M.I.T. STUDENT CENTER, CAMBRIDGE. Goody, 38–39.
MORRIS STUDIO, LENOX (NOW FRELINGHUYSEN-MORRIS HOUSE AND STUDIO)
1043   Berman, Avis. "The Frelinghuysen-Morris House and Studio." *Architectural Digest* (Mar. 1999): 48–58.
1044   "Modern Estate." *Berkshire Eagle*, 17 Sept. 1949.
1045   Morris, George L. K. "Correction." *Berkshire Eagle*, 21 Sept. 1949.
MUSEUM OF FINE ARTS, PEI WING, FENWAY. Miller, 224–225.
1046   Campbell, Robert. "Pei: Our Architect du Roi." *Globe*, 16 Oct. 1987.
1047   Huxtable, Ada Louise. "Pei's Elegant Addition." *NYT*, 12 July 1987.
1048   Suner, Bruno. *Pei*. Paris: Hazan, 1988, pp. 107–108.
NEW CHARDON STREET COURTHOUSE, GOVERNMENT CENTER
1049   Campbell, Robert. "Court Appeal." *Globe*, 27 Nov. 1998.
1050   Eisen, David. "Justice Is Served." *Herald*, 1 Nov. 1998.
1051   Hale, Jonathan. "Out of the Weeds." *B&T*, 21 Sept. 1998.
NEW ENGLAND AQUARIUM, SCHWARTZ/SILVER ADDITION, WATERFRONT
1052   Campbell, Robert. "Waterwing." *Globe*, 10 Jan. 1998.
1053   Eisen, David. "Aquarium Wing." *Herald*, 1 Feb. 1998.
1054   Hale, Jonathan. "New England Aquarium." *B&T*, 16 Feb. 1998.
NEW ENGLAND AQUARIUM, WATERFRONT (ORIGINAL BUILDING). Curtis, 12, 35; Lyndon, 56–57.
NEW ENGLAND TELEPHONE BUILDING, FINANCIAL DISTRICT. Lyndon, 262.
NEWTON PUBLIC LIBRARY, NEWTON
1055   Campbell, Robert. "Newton Rewrites the Book." *Globe*, 22 Nov. 1991.
1056   McManus, Otile. "Newton Scores a Coup." *Globe*, 16 Sept. 1991.
NINETY SUMMER STREET, FINANCIAL DISTRICT. Rifkind, 305, 310.
NORTHEASTERN UNIVERSITY BOATHOUSE, RIVERFRONT
1057   *Graham Gund Architects*, pp. 134–139.
NORTHEASTERN UNIVERSITY MULTIFAITH SPIRITUAL CENTER, THE FENWAY
1058   Giovannini, Joseph. "A Luminous Interfaith Chapel." *Arch.* (Sept. 1998): 132.
1059   Shand-Tucci, Douglass. "Believe Less is More." *Phoenix*, 29 Jan. 1999, p. 10.
OLIVETTI BRANCH OFFICE PROTOTYPE, BOSTON
1060   Jodidio, Philip. *Richard Meier*.
ONE BOWDOIN SQUARE, DOWNTOWN. Miller/Morgan, 45.
1061   *Graham Gund Architects*, pp. 108–111.
OTTO HALL, HARVARD, CAMBRIDGE
1062   Collins, B. and D. Kasprowiz. *Gwathmey Siegel . . . 1982–1992*. New York: Rizzoli, 1993, pp. 106–119.
1063   Crosbie, M. J. "Modern Mediator." *Arch.* (Nov. 1991): 52–57.
OZAWA HALL, TANGLEWOOD, LENOX
1064   "Decorated Shed." *Arch.* (Dec. 1994).
PAINE WEBER BUILDING, FINANCIAL DISTRICT. Miller/Morgan, 92–93.
PEABODY-ESSEX MUSEUM, EAST ASIAN WING, SALEM
1065   Campbell, Robert. "Asian Export Wing." *Globe*, 16 Aug. 1988.
PEABODY STUDIO, DOVER
1066   Cole, Doris. *Eleanor Raymond*. Philadelphia: Art Alliance, 1981, pp. 133–137.
PEABODY TERRACE, HARVARD, CAMBRIDGE. Bunting/Nylander, 199; Curtis, 7–8, 26–27; Giedion, 865, 868; Goody, 4–5; Peter, 257.
1067   Campbell, Robert. "Court Appeal."
1068   Curtis, Robert. *Modern Architecture since 1900*, pp. 448–449, 557.
1069   Turner, Paul Venable. *Campus*, pp. 271, 273.
POINT WEST PLACE, FRAMINGHAM
1070   Stern, Robert A. M. *Architectural Monograph #17*. New York: St. Martins, 1991, pp. 46–49.
POST OFFICE SQUARE, FINANCIAL DISTRICT (ELLENZWEIG). Miller, 130–131.
PRUDENTIAL CENTER: (SEE ALSO BACK BAY CENTER)
1071   Carlhian, Jean Paul. "Guides, Guideposts and Guidelines," p. 54.
PURA-WILLIAMS HOUSE, MANCHESTER-BY-THE SEA.
1072   Nichols, Karen, ed. *Michael Graves . . . 1990–1994*. New York: Rizzoli 1995.
PUSEY LIBRARY, HARVARD, CAMBRIDGE. Bunting/Floyd, 271–273.
1073   Floyd, M. H. "Stubbins." In *Architectural Education and Boston*, pp. 98–99.
1074   Ludman, Dianne M., *Hugh Stubbins*, p. 64.
QUINCY HOUSE, HARVARD, CAMBRIDGE. Bunting/Floyd, 262–265; Bunting/Nylander, 197–198; Goody, 6–7.
RAYMOND HOUSE, BELMONT
1075   Cole, Doris. *Eleanor Raymond*. Philadelphia: Art Alliance, 1981, pp. 40–41, 129–132.
ROEWS WHARF, WATERFRONT. Miller/Morgan, 108–109.
ROSOVSKY HALL, HARVARD, CAMBRIDGE
1076   Kohn, Wendy, ed. *Moshe Safdie*. London: Academy, 1996, pp. 252–255.
RUDOLF-DESIGNED HOUSE, CAMBRIDGE. Goody, 20–21; Rettig, F36.

1113   Carr, Stephen, et al. *Public Space*. Cambridge: Cambridge University Press, 1992, pp. 191–192.
1114   Simo, Melanie. *Sasaki Associates*. Washington, D.C.: Spacemaker, 1997, pp. 168–171.
WELLESLEY COLLEGE SCIENCE CENTER, WELLESLEY
1115   Floyd, M. H. "Robert C. Dean. . . ." In *Architectural Education and Boston*, p. 72, Plate 8.
1116   Silver, Nathan. *The Making of Beaubourg*. Cambridge: MIT Press, 1994, p. 186.
WELLESLEY FIRE STATION, WELLESLEY
1117   ———. *Architecture and Urbanism* (March 1989): 76–79.
1118   Campbell, Robert. "Wellesley's Fire House." *Globe*, 9 May 1989.
1119   Smith, Herbert. "Civic Overture." *Arch. Record* (Mar. 1988).
WELLESLEY OFFICE PARK, WELLESLEY
1120   Clausen, Meredith L. *Pietro Belluschi*, pp. 284–286.
WHITE CENTERS, SOUTH BOSTON AND MATTAPAN
1121   Linn, Charles. "South Boston Super Club." *Arch. Record* (June 1995).
1122   Stein, Karen. "Youth Oriented." *Arch. Record* (June 1996).
WIESNER BUILDING, M.I.T., CAMBRIDGE
1123   Campbell, Robert. "Pei in Harmony." *Arch.* (Feb. 1986).
1124   Suner, Bruno. *Pei*, pp. 134–136.
ZIMMERMAN HOUSE, MANCHESTER, N.H.
1125   Pfeiffer, Bruce Brooks, *Frank Lloyd Wright*. Vol. 7, 1942–1950.
1126   Storrer, William A. *The Frank Lloyd Wright Companion*, p. 333.

M. ARCHITECTS WHO WORKED IN BOSTON 1950–2000

ABRAMOVITZ, MAX
1127   Emanuel, Muriel, ed. *Contemporary Architects*. New York: St. Martin's, 1980, pp. 10–12.
ANDREWS, JOHN
1128   Lum, B. P. "John Andrews." In *International Dictionary of Architects and Architecture*, vol. 2, ed. Randall Van Vynckt. Detroit: St. James Press, 1993, pp. 27–29.
THE ARCHITECTS COLLABORATIVE. Berdini, 194–255; Dal Co/Tarfuri, 342, Goody, 7, 8, 9, 14, 48, 50, 80, 86, 98, 100.
1129   Christ-Janer, Albert, and Mary Mix Foley. *Modern Church Architecture*. New York: McGraw Hill, 1962.
1130   Alofsin, Anthony. "TAC." In *Macmillan Encyclopedia of Architects*. 4 vols. Adolf K. Placzek, ed. New York: Free Press, 1982, pp. 201–202.
1131   Burns, Carol. Interview with Norman Fletcher. "Master Piece." *Arch. Boston* 1 (1998): 27, 33.
1132   Crowell, S. Fiske, Jr. "TAC." In *Contemporary Architects*, pp. 807–810.
ARCHITECTURAL RESOURCES CAMBRIDGE
1133   Campbell, Robert. "Something Old, Something New." *Globe*, 15 Oct. 1978.
BARNES, EDWARD LARRABEE
1134   Koerble, Barbara. "Edward Larrabee Barnes." In *International Dictionary of Architects and Architecture*, vol. 2, pp. 54–55.
BEHA, ANN
1135   Dean, Andrea Oppenheimer. "Affirmative Actions." *Historic Preservation* (Mar./Apr. 1992).
1136   Howard, Margo. "Lunch on the Left Bank." *Boston* (Mar. 1995): 168–169.
1137   Kahn, Eve M. "Transmuting History." *Traditional Building* (Sept./Oct. 1993): 5–7.
1138   McManus, Otile. "Architects' Best Work. . . ." *Globe*, 6 Dec. 1991.
BELLUSCHI, PIETRO. Wiseman, 179, 236.
1139   Arms, Meredith. "Pietro Belluschi." In *International Dictionary of Architects and Architecture*, pp. 69–70.
1140   Christ-Janer, Albert, and Mary Mix Foley. *Modern Church Architecture*, pp. 37–39, 137–145, 154–161, 171–183, 207–214.
1141   Clausen, Meredith L. *Pietro Belluschi*. Cambridge: MIT Press, 1994.
1142   Jordy, William H. *American Buildings and Their Architects: The Impact of European Modernism in the Mid-Twentieth Century*. New York: Anchor/Doubleday, 1976, p. 233.
1143   Kay, J. H. "Architect Pietro Belluschi: Broker Between Budgets and Beauty." *Globe*, 14 May 1972.
1144   Ross, M. D. "The 'Attainment and Restraint' of Pietro Belluschi." *A.I.A. Journal* 58 (1972): 17–24.
1145   ——————. "Belluschi, Pietro." In *Macmillan Encyclopedia of Architects*, pp. 172–174.
BOGNER, WALTER
1146   Ford, James, and Katherine Ford. *Classic Modern Houses of the Thirties*. New York: Dover, 1989.
BREUER, MARCEL
1147   Cantacuzino, Sherban. *Modern Houses*. New York: Dutton, 1964.
1148   Huxtable, Ada Louise. "The Work of Marcel Breuer." In *Kicked a Building Lately?* New York: Quadrangle, 1978, pp. 90–92.
1149   Jordy, William H. *American Buildings and Their Architects*, pp. 169–219.
1150   Seidler, Harry. "Breuer, Marcel." In *Contemporary Architects*, pp. 117–119.
BREWSTER, GEORGE W.
1151   Ford, James, and Katherine Ford. *Classic Modern Houses of the Thirties*.
CAMBRIDGE SEVEN
1152   Czarnecki, John E. "Taking Our Leisure." *Arch. Record* (Aug. 1998): 105–110.
1153   Schmertz, Mildred. "Cambridge Seven." In *Contemporary Architects*, pp. 133–135.
1154   Shaw, Jonathan. "Ocean. . . ." *Harvard* (Jan./Feb. 1999): 81–82.
CARLU, JACQUES
1155   Donhauser, Peter L. "Carlo, Jacques." In *Macmillan Encyclopedia of Architects*, p. 384.
1156   Floyd, M. H. *Architectural Education and Boston*. Boston: Boston Architectural Center, 1989, Plate 5, pp. 55, 58, 66, 68, 69, 72, 87, 97, 145, 198, 164, 165.

432

CHAN, KRIEGER

1157 Chan, Krieger, Levi, Architects. *Urban Design Studies for the Central Artery Corridor*. Boston: Chan, Kreiger, Levi, Architects, 1990.

1158 Mackin, Anne, and Alex Krieger. *A Design Primer for Cities and Towns*. Boston: Massachusetts Council on the Arts and Humanities, 1989.

EISENMAN, PETER. Wiseman, pp. 270–271, 346–348, 350–353.

1159 Frank, Suzanne S. "Peter Eisenman." In *International Dictionary of Achitects and Architecture*, vol. 2, pp. 233–236.

FORBES, PETER

1160 Boissiere, Olivier, ed. *Houses by the Sea*. Paris: Telleri, 1998, pp. 34–35.

1161 Campbell, Robert. "Triad." In Canty, et. al., *Architecture of the 1980's*, pp. 226–231.

1162 Forbes, Peter, and George Warner. "A House by the Sea." *Arch. Boston* (Spring 1999): 36–39.

1163 Ojeda, Oscar R., ed. *Ten Houses: Peter Forbes Associates*. Rockport: Rockport Press, 1995.

GEHRY, FRANK. Wiseman, 340–345.

1164 Dal Co, Francesco, and Kurt W. Foster. *Frank Gehry: The Complete Works*. New York: Monacelli, 1998.

1165 Hines, Thomas S. "Heavy Metal: The Education of F. O. G." In *The Architecture of Frank Gehry*. New York: Rizzoli, 1986, pp. 10–21.

GRAVES, MICHAEL. Wiseman, 271–278, 285–291.

GROPIUS, WALTER. Giedion, 499–517; Isaacs, 253–263; Peter, 176–191; Wiseman,151–153, 167–170.

1166 Hale, Jonathan. "The Failure and Success of Walter Gropius." *PA* (Jan. 1992): 108–110.

1167 Herdig, Klaus. *The Decorated Diagram*. Cambridge: MIT Press, 1983.

1168 Jordy, William H. *American Buildings and Their Architects*, p. 181.

1169 Kallmann, Gerhard. *Four Great Makers of Modern Architecture: Gropius, Le Corbusier, Mies van der Rohe, Wright*. New York: Columbia School of Architecture, 1963.

1170 Padjen, Elizabeth. "Walter Gropius: A Legacy Reconsidered." *Art New England* (Aug./Sept. 1997): 18–19.

GUND, GRAHAM. Curtis, 17, 44–45.

1171 *Graham Gund Architects*. Washington, D. C.: AIA Press, 1993.

GWATHMEY, SIEGEL. Curtis, 15, 46–47.

HEALY, BRIAN

1172 Eisen, David. "Cambridge Plan Homes." *Herald*, 6 Apr. 1997.

JOHNSON, PHILIP. Wiseman, 303–316.

1173 Muschamp, H. "Regent and King." *NYT*, 29 Nov. 1998.

1174 Schulze, Franz. *Philip Johnson*. New York: Knopf, 1994.

KALLMANN AND MCKINNELL

1175 Beddal, Thomas G. "Kallmann and McKinnell." In *Macmillan Encyclopedia of Architects*, p. 549.

1176 Campbell, Robert. "Kallmann, McKinnell & Wood: Architects of the Metaphorical, the Narrative and the Evocative." In *The Architecture of Kallmann, McKinnell and Wood*, ed. Alex Kreiger. Boston: Harvard Graduate School of Design, 1988, pp. 101–102.

1177 ——. "Designing Men." *Globe Magazine*, 21 June 1992.

1178 ——. "Kallmann, McKinnell and Wood: AIA Firm of the Year." *Arch.* (Mar. 1984).

1179 ——. "Kallmann, McKinnell and Wood Receive AIA Firm Award." *JAIA* (Mar. 1984).

1180 ——. "Tradition Triumphs." *Arch. Record* (Mar. 1995).

1181 Eisenman, Peter. "Two Teachers." In *Kallmann, McKinnell and Wood*, pp. 95–97.

1182 Kallmann, Gerhard. "The Action Architecture of a New Generation." *Arch. Forum* 4 (1959): 132–137.

1183 ——. "Movement Systems as Generators of Built Form." *Arch. Record* 7 (1975): 105–116.

1184 Kay, Jane Holtz. "The Saving Grace." *Arch. Forum* (Mar. 1973): 52–57.

1185 Krieger, Alex. "The Studied Imperfections of Kallmann, McKinnell and Wood." In *The Architecture of Kallmann, McKinnell and Wood*, 11–20.

1186 Schmertz, Mildred. "Kallmann, Gerhard" and "McKinnell, N. M." In *Contemporary Architects*, pp. 412–413, 535.

1187 Sekler, Eduard. "Gerald Kallmann and Michael McKinnell as Educators." In *The Architecture of Kallmann, McKinnell and Wood*, pp. 90–100.

KOCH, CARL. Goody, 22–23, 52–53, 84–85; Rifkind, 11, 22.

1188 Ford, James, and Katherine Ford. *Classic Modern Houses of the Thirties*.

1189 Hamilton, Stephen P. "Carl Koch." In *Contemporary Architects*, pp. 433–434.

KOETTER-KIM

1190 Plattus, Alan T. *Koetter-Kim and Associates*. New York: Rizzoli, 1997.

LE CORBUSIER

1191 Benton, T. Quoted in M. Raeburn and V. Wilson, eds., *Le Corbusier: Architect of the Century*. London: Tate Gallery, 1987.

1192 Curtis, William J. R. *Le Corbusier: Ideas and Forms*. London: Phaidon, 1986.

1193 Le Corbusier. "A Businessman's Dinner in Boston." In *When the Cathedrals Were White*. New York: Reyhal and Hitchcock, 1947, pp. 105–106.

1194 Papadaki, Stamo, ed. *Le Corbusier*. New York: Macmillan, 1948.

LEERS, WEINZAPFEL (PREVIOUSLY ANDREA LEERS BROWNING)

1195 Campbell, Robert. "Welcome to the Club." *Globe*, 14 Feb. 1997.

1196 Crosbie, Michael J. "Yankee Duet." *Arch.* (Oct. 1991).

1197 Landecker, Heidi. "Urban Heart." *Arch.* (Nov. 1995).

MACHADO & SILVETTI

1198 Arcidi, Philip. "Scrim-side Parking." *PA* (Dec. 1992): 68–69.

1299 Dixon, John M. "View Point." *PA* (Aug. 1995): 90–96.

1200 Doublet, Susan, and D. Boles. *American House Now*. New York: Universe, 1997, p. 160.

1201 Ghirardo, Diane. *Architecture after Modernism*. London: Thames and Hudson, 1996.

433

1202   Goldberger, Paul. "A Small Park." *NYT*, 24 Nov. 1996.
1203   Hays, Michael K., ed. *Architecture Theory Since 1968*. Cambridge: MIT Press, 1998.
1204   ———. *Unprecedented Realism: The Architecture of Machado & Silvetti*. Princeton: Princeton Architectural Press, 1995.
1205   Machado, Rodolfo, and Rodolphe el-Khoury. *Monolithic Architecture*. Munich: Prestel, 1995.
1206   Ojeda, Oscar R. *Rodolpho Machado and Jorge Silvetti*. Asppan: Kliczkowski, 1995.
1207   Ouroussoff, Nicolai. "A Classic Conflict." *Los Angeles Times*, 1 Nov. 1998.
1208   Pearson, Clifford A. "Wagner Park." *Arch. Record* (Feb. 1997): 65–69.
1209   Peter, Serenyi. Introduction to *Imminent Domains*. Boston: Harcus Krakow Gallery, 1977.
1210   Silvetti, Jorge. "The Beauty of Shadows." In Hays, *Unprecedented Realism*. Princeton: Princeton University Press, 1955: pp. 22–25, 365–389.
1211   Shand-Tucci, Douglass. "Allston and Beyond." *Phoenix* (26 Feb. 1999).
MEIER, RICHARD. Wiseman, 273–277.
1212   Jodidio, Philip. *Richard Meier*. Cologne: Taschen, 1995.
MONEO, RAFAEL
1213   Capitel, Anton. "José Rafael Moneo." In *Contemporary Architects*, pp. 551–552.
1214   Machado, Rodolfo, and Rodolphe el-Khoury. "Rafael Moneo." In *Monolithic Architecture*.
MOORE, CHARLES. Wiseman, 278–284.
1215   Keim, Kevin P. *An Architectural Life*. New York: Little, Brown, 1996.
OFFICE DA
1216   Office dA. *Fabrications*. Barcelona: Museum of Contemporary Art, 1998, pp. 94–95.
PEI, I. M.
1217   Cannell, Michael. *I.M. Pei*. New York: Carol Southern Books, 1995.
1218   Clausen, Meredith L. *Pietro Belluschi*. Cambridge: MIT Press, 1994, pp. 201–203.
1219   Huxtable, Ada Louise. "The National Gallery." In *Kicked a Building Lately?* pp. 84–87.
PERKINS, G. HOLMES
1220   Ford, James, and Katherine Ford. *Classic Modern Houses of the Thirties*.
PURCELL AND ELMSLIE
1221   Gebhard, David. "Purcell and Elmslie." In *Macmillan Encyclopedia of Architects*, pp. 500–503.
RAPSON, RALPH
1222   Hibbard, Don J. "Ralph Rapson." In *Contemporary Architects*, pp. 655–657.
RAWN, WILLIAM
1223   Kidder, Tracy. *House*. New York: Avon, 1985.
1224   Levinson, Nancy. "Fitting Harmony." *Arch. Record* (May 1996).
RAYMOND, ELEANOR
1225   Cole, Doris. *Eleanor Raymond*. Philadelphia: Art Alliance, 1981.
RUDOLPH, PAUL. Wiseman, 202–204, 256–258.
1226   Becherer, Richard. "Rudolph, Paul M." In *Macmillan Encyclopedia of Architects*, pp. 618–619.
1227   Lorance, Loreth. "Paul Rudolph." In *International Dictionary of Architects and Architecture*, pp. 757–759.
1228   Schmertz, Mildred. "Paul Rudolph." In *Contemporary Architects*, pp. 691–693.
1229   Stahl, Frederick A. "Educational Highlights." In *Architectural Education and Boston*, pp. 118, 124.
SAARINEN, ELIEL AND EERO. Peter, 192–209; Wiseman, 198–201, 247–248.
1230   Christ-Janer, Albert. *Eliel Saarinen*. Chicago: University of Chicago Press, 1948.
1231   Miller, R. Craig. "Saarinen, Eliel and Eero." In *Macmillan Encyclopedia of Architects*, pp. 628–633.
1232   Saarinen, Aline B., ed. *Eero Saarinen on His Work*. New Haven: Yale University Press, 1962.
1233   Tempko, Allan Tempko. *Eero Saarinen*. New York: Brazilier, 1982.
SAFDIE, MOSHE
1234   Kohn, Wendy, ed. *Moshe Safdie*. London: Academy, 1996.
SASAKI ASSOCIATES
1235   Clausen, Meredith L. *Pietro Belluschi*, pp. 281–283.
1236   Eckbo, Garrett. "Hideo Sasaki." In *Contemporary Architects*, pp. 709–710.
1237   Simo, Melanie. *Sasaki Associates*. Washington, D.C.: Spacemaker, 1997.
SERT, JOSÉ LLUIS. Peter, 192–209.
1238   Dean, Andrea. "The Urbane and Varied Buildings of Sert." *JAIA* (May 1977): 50–58.
1239   Isaacs, Reginald R. "Sert, José Lluis." In *Macmillan Encyclopedia of Architects*, pp. 40–41.
1240   Schmertz, Mildred. "José Lluis Sert." In *Contemporary Architects*, pp. 740–742.
SKIDMORE, OWINGS AND MERRILL
1241   Winter, John. "Skidmore, Owings & Merrill." In *Macmillan Encyclopedia of Architects*.
STAHL, FREDERICK A.
1242   Stahl, F. A. "Educational Highlights." In *Architectural Education and Boston*, pp. 118–124.
STERN, ROBERT. Wiseman, 291–294.
1243   Dixon, Peter M. *Robert A. M. Stern*. New York: Monacelli, 1998.
1244   Macrae-Gibson, Gavin. *The Secret Life of Buildings*. Cambridge: MIT Press, 1985, pp. 98–117.
1245   Stern, Robert A. M. *Pride of Place*. Boston: Houghton, 1986.
STIRLING, JAMES
1246   Kultermann, Udo. "James Stirling." In *Contemporary Architects*, pp. 777–779.
STUBBINS, HUGH
1247   Curtis, *Modern Architecture since 1900*. London: Phaidon, 1987.
1248   Floyd, M. H. "Royal Barry Wills." In *Architectural Education and Boston*, pp. 72–77.
1249   Ford, James, and Katherine Ford. *Classic Modern Houses of the Thirties*.
1250   Hayes, Bartlett. *Hugh Stubbins: Tradition Becomes Innovation*. New York: Pilgrim Press, 1983.
1251   Hunt, William D., Jr. "Hugh Stubbins." In *Contemporary Architects*, pp. 782–785.
1252   Rose, Charles. Interview with Hugh Stubbins. *Arch. Boston* 3 (1998): 33–37.

434

1253   Strauss, Susan. "Stubbins, Hugh Asher, Jr." In *Macmillan Encyclopedia of Architects*, pp. 146–147.

TANGE, KENZO. Dal Co/Tafuri, 349, 358, 360, 363.

THOMPSON, BENJAMIN

1254   Balfour, Alan. "Benjamin Thompson." In *Contemporary Architects*, pp. 814–816.

1255   Stoddard, Whitney S. "Thompson, Benjamin." In *Macmillan Encyclopedia of Architects*.

THOMPSON AND ROSE

1256   Jodidio, Philip. *Contemporary American Architecture*. Cologne: Taschen, pp. 178–185, 189.

1257   Padjen, Elizabeth. "Thompson and Rose." *Art New England* (June/July 1997): 26–27.

VENTURI, ROBERT. Wiseman, 256–267.

1258   Steele, James. "Robert Venturi." In *International Dictionary of Architects and Architecture*, pp. 944–946.

1259   Venturi, Robert. *Complexity and Contradiction in Architecture*. New York: Museum of Modern Art, 1966.

WRIGHT, FRANK LLOYD

1260   Alofsin, Anthony. Review of Neil Levine's *The Architecture of Frank Lloyd Wright*. *Harvard Design Magazine* (Summer 1998): 76–77.

1261   Cram, Ralph Adams. "Promise of American House Building." In Richardson Wright, ed. *Low Cost Suburban Homes*. New York: McBride & Co., 1916, pp. 31–39.

1262   Gill, Brendan. *Many Masks*. New York: Ballantine, 1987.

1263   Hitchcock, Henry-Russell. *In The Nature of Materials: The Buildings of Frank Lloyd Wright 1887–1941*. New York: Duell, Sloan and Pearce, 1942.

1264   Hudnut, Joseph, ed. *Supplement to the Loan Exhibition . . . ICA*. Boston: 1940.

1265   Mason, Grant Carpenter. *Frank Lloyd Wright to 1910*. [1940]. New York: Van Nostrand, 1958.

1266   Wright, Frank Lloyd. *An Autobiography*. New York: Duell, Sloan & Pearce, 1943.

1267   Wright, Frank Lloyd. *A Testament*. New York: Horizon, 1957.

YAMASAKI, MINORU

1268   Winter, John. "Minoru Yamasaki." In *International Dictionary of Architects and Architecture*, pp. 1006–1008.

N. ARTISTS AND CRAFTSPEOPLE WHO WORKED IN BOSTON 1950–2000

AMORY, ROBERT. *Helion* (100 Summer Street). Carlock, 63, 130.

ARP, HANS. Harkness Center Dining Room mural. Carlock, 114.

BERTOIA, HARRY. Exterior sculpture at M.I.T. Chapel. Carlock, 98; Peter, 98.

CALDER, ALEXANDER. *The Big Sail* (Green Building, M.I.T.). Carlock, 100, 101. *Onion* (Pusey Library). Carlock, 110.

DUCA, ALFRED M. *Computersphere* (Government Center Post Office). Carlock, 24.

HAAS, RICHARD. Boston Architectural Center mural. Carlock, 46–47. Milk Street murals (Milk near Broad Streets). Carlock, 59.

1269   Myer, "The New Building." In *Architectural Education and Boston*, pp. 125–129.

HADZI, DIMITRI. *Primavera* (Pine Manor College, Brookline). Carlock, 129.

1270   Heaney, Seamus, et al. *Dimitri Hadzi*. New York: Hudson Hills, 1996.
           Thermopylae (Kennedy Building, Government Center), pp. 38–41.
           Omphalos (Harvard Square), pp. 66–73.
           Fountain (Copley Place), p. 152.

HARRIES, MAGS. *Asaroton* (originally Hanover and Haymarket Streets, North End). Carlock, 13.

KEPES, GYORGY. Harvard Square Station stained-glass wall. Carlock, 81.

1271   Brown, Robert F. "New England." *Archive of American Art Journal* 32 (1992): 37.

1272   Erikson, Erik H., et al. *Gyorgy Kepes: Works in Review*. Boston: Museum of Science, 1973.

1273   McIntyre, A. McVoy. *Beacon Hill*. Boston: Little, Brown, 1975.

1274   "New Art Form" *Globe*, 2 Oct. 1964, p. 6.
           Entrance, St. Johns, Bowdoin Street, Government Center, with Alfred Duca.

LEOPOLD, RICHARD. Harkness Center exterior sculpture. Carlock, 114.

LILLIE, LLOYD. *Red Auerback* (Quincy Market) and *James Michael Curley* (Congress and North Streets, Government Center). Carlock, 18, 20.

MIRO, JOAN. Harkness Center mural. Carlock, 114.

MOORE, HENRY. *Three Piece Reclining Figure, Draped* (Killian Court, main building). Carlock, 99. *Reclining Figure* (Wiesner Building, M.I.T.). Carlock, 102. *Large Four-Piece Reclining Figure* (Lamont Library). Carlock, 110.

MOTHERWELL, ROBERT. Kennedy Building, Government Center. Carlock, 21.

NEVELSON, LOUISE. *Transparent Horizon* (Landau Building, M.I.T.). Carlock, 101.

PEABODY, AMELIA. *Mother and Child* (Mugar Building, Northeastern). Carlock 51.

1275   Driscoll, Edgar J., Jr. "Amelia Peabody." *Globe*, 31 May 1984, p. 64.

PICASSO, PABLO. *Figure Découpée* (Wadsworth and Amherst Streets, M.I.T.). Carlock, 103.

ROZAK, THEODORE. Interior sculpture at M.I.T. Chapel. Carlock, 98; Peter, 80.

STUBBINS, HUGH. Murals in the Federal Reserve Bank lobby. Carlock, 64.

TERMINI, MARIA. Josiah Quincy School mural. Carlock, 40.

WALKER, PETER AND JOAN BRIGHAM. Tanner Fountain (Science Center, Harvard). Carlock, 110.

PICTURE CREDITS

437

Figure 14 is reproduced from *Charles Bulfinch: Architect and Citizen* by Charles A. Place. Copyright 1925 and renewed 1953. Reprinted by permission of the publisher, Houghton Mifflin Company. Figures 15 and 20 are reproduced from *The Domestic Architecture of the Early American Republic: The Greek Revival* by Howard Major. Copyright 1926 by J. B. Lippincott Company. Reproduced by permission of J. B. Lippincott Company. Figure 64 is reproduced from the second edition of *The Architecture of H. H. Richardson and His Times* by Henry-Russell Hitchcock. Copyright 1961 The Shoe String Press, Inc.

For the 2000 edition, I wish to express my thanks to those photographers who have agreed in the customary way for scholarly books (where authors are responsible for permissions) to waive their usual fees. These are Paul Warchol, Chuck Choi, Antoine Grassi, Eduard Heubner, Peter Aaron, Bob Frichetts, Norman Liebenthal, Matt Wargo, Mick Hales, Flint Born, Richard Cheek, and Steve Rosenthal. The work of Nick Wheeler appears through the courtesy of Peter Forbes.

Andrea Leers, Bill Rawn, Bruce Wood, Jacqueline Thomas, and Nicholas DeBrule made much appreciated efforts on my behalf and their various employers'. The color plate by David Hewitt was virtually commissioned by Schwartz/Silver, and its reproduction here was arranged by Nicholas DeBrule.

439

INDEX

Specific buildings and streets appear under their own names and not under their locales; location is given for all buildings and streets except in the case of Boston Proper. Harvard buildings not listed separately are under Harvard University. For further information on individual suburbs, the reader is referred to Section B of the Bibliography. Page numbers in italics indicate illustrations.

445

About the Author

Douglass Shand-Tucci is a historian of American art and architecture and New England studies. He has been senior affiliate in the history of architecture at Eliot House, Harvard University, and has also taught American architectural history at M.I.T. His most recent book, *The Art of Scandal: The Life and Times of Isabella Stewart Gardner* was featured on the cover of the *New York Times Book Review* and as an editor's choice on the *Times*'s best seller page, while his *Boston Bohemia* was a finalist in 1995 for the PEN/ Winship Prize for best book of the year by a New England author. The biographer of Ralph Adams Cram (the second volume of which, *Gothic Modernist*, is forthcoming in fall 2000), Shand-Tucci in 1999 became architecture critic of the *Boston Phoenix*. He is currently at work on an architectural guide to Harvard University.